iAPX 86, 88, 186 and 188 User's Manual
Programmer's Reference

1985

PREFACE

This manual describes the iAPX 86,88, and iAPX 186,188 family of microprocessor systems. It is divided into two volumes.

Volume 1 is a general introduction and contains an overview of the CPUs along with some design information. In addition, Volume 1 includes a general description of the 8087 numeric processor extension (NPX), the 8089 I/O processor (IOP), and the 80130 operating system firmware (OSF).

Volume 2 is a reference source, containing detailed hardware information on the major components making up the systems, the various configurations available and implementation data. Volume 2 also includes the Device Specifications and several Application Notes.

Volume 1 is divided as follows:

Chapter 1 introduces microcomputer concepts and associated terminology.

Chapter 2 is an overview of the iAPX 86,88 and the iAPX 186,188 CPU family with its key features. It covers the CPU Architecture, Memory, Interrupts, the 80186,188 extensions, and a short overview of the 8087, 8089, and 80130 processors.

Chapter 3 provides a detailed discussion of the programmer's architecture including the EU and BIU, Register Structure, Memory structure, I/O Port Organization, Addressing Modes, the Instruction Set and Programming Examples.

Chapter 4 contains general information, on the block diagram level, needed by the hardware designer to incorporate the basic 8086 and 8088 microprocessors into microcomputer systems. Included is a discussion of the Bus Structures, Multiprocessing and Processor Control.

Chapter 5 contains general information needed by the hardware designer to incorporate the 80186 and 80188 microprocessors into microcomputer systems. Included is a discussion of 8086,88 and 80186,188 Bus Differences, Multiprocessing, Processor Control and the integrated peripherals of the 80186 and 80188 processors, such as Clock Generator, Chip Select/Ready Logic, DMA Channels, Timers and the Interrupt Controller.

Chapter 6 describes the 8087 Numeric Processor Extension (NPX). Included is an overview of the processor, the Architecture, Computational Fundamentals, the Instruction Set, and Programming Examples.

Chapter 7 describes the 8089 Input/Output Processor (IOP). It covers the Processor Overview, Architecture, I/O, the Instruction Set, Addressing Modes, and Programming Examples.

Chapter 8 describes the 80130 Operating System Firmware (OSF) component. The chapter covers the Architecture, Multitasking, Multiprogramming, Intertask Coordination, Dynamic Memory Relocation, Extendability, the Primitives, and Programming Examples.

RELATED DOCUMENTATION

- The iAPX 88 Book
  Describes the Intel iAPX 88 (8088) microprocessor in detail.

- The Peripheral Design Handbook
  Contains data sheets and application notes featuring Intel peripheral devices.

- The Intel Component Data Catalog
  Contains data sheets for all Intel semiconductor components, including memories and peripherals.

- ASM86 Language Reference Manual
  Describes the assembly language for the 8086/8088 and the 8087.

- ASM86 Language Reference Manual
  Describes the assembly language for the 8086, 88/80186, 188 and the 8087.

- iOSP 86 Support Package Reference Manual

These books, and other documentation, are available from
Literature Department
Intel Corporation
3065 Bowers Avenue
Santa Clara, California 95051

THE INTEL MICROSYSTEM 80 NOMENCLATURE

As Intel's product line has evolved, its component-based product numbering system has become inappropriate for all the possible VLSI computer solutions offered. While the components retain their names, Intel has moved to a new system-based naming scheme to accommodate these new VLSI systems.

The following prefixes have been adopted for Intel's product lines, all of them under the general heading of Microsystem 80:

iAPX	— Processor Series
iRMX	— Operating Systems
iSBC	— Single Board Computers
iSBX	— MULTIMODULE Boards

In the iAPX Series, the following processor lines are currently defined:

iAPX 86	— 8086 CPU-based system
iAPX 88	— 8088 CPU-based system
iAPX 186	— 80186 CPU-based system
iAPX 188	— 80188 CPU-based system
iAPX 286	— 80286 CPU-based system

Configuration options within each iAPX system are identified by adding a numerical suffix, for example:

iAPX 186/10	— CPU alone (80186)
iAPX 186/11	— CPU + IOP (80186 + 8089)
iAPX 186/20	— CPU with Math Extension (80186 + 8087)
iAPX 186/21	— CPU with Math Extension + IOP (80186, 8087 + 8089)
iAPX 186/30	— CPU with Operating System Processor (80186 + 80130)
iAPX 186/40	— CPU with Math Extension + OSP (80186, 8087 + 80130)

This improved numbering system provides a more meaningful view of the capabilities of Intel's evolving Microsystem 80.

Table of Contents

TABLE OF CONTENTS

TABLE OF CONTENTS

Introduction to
Microcomputers

1

CHAPTER 1
INTRODUCTION TO MICROCOMPUTERS

1.1 WHAT IS A MICROCOMPUTER?

A microcomputer is a system of one or more integrated circuit devices, using semiconductor technology and digital logic to implement large computer functions on a smaller scale.

The Intel iAPX 86,88 and iAPX 186,188 family of microprocessors, along with other closely related Intel processors described in this manual, are essential functional blocks of such microcomputers.

There are three main elements in a microcomputer. These elements and their functions parallel those found in all computers. Each has a special role to play in the overall operation of the computer system. The block diagram in Figure 1-1 shows these three elements. They are the *central processing unit* (CPU), the *memory*, and the *input/output* (I/O) devices or ports.

1.2 THE CPU

The heart of the microcomputer system is the CPU. It performs the numerical processing (additions, subtractions, etc.), logical operations, and timing functions.

CPU operations are controlled by a set of *instructions*, called a *program*. Programs are stored in the memory. Data is also kept in the memory and processed according to programmed instructions. The CPU reads in data and control signals (instructions) through the input ports, executes one instruction at a time, and sends data and control signals to the outside world through the output ports.

A typical CPU consists of the following three functional units: the *registers*, the *arithmetic/logic unit* (ALU), and the *control circuitry*. Each is briefly described below.

Registers provide temporary storage within the CPU for memory addresses, status codes, and other information useful during program execution. Different microprocessors have different numbers and sizes of registers. The Intel iAPX 86,88 and the iAPX 186,188 family of microprocessors have 16-bit registers.

All CPUs contain an *arithmetic/logic unit* or *ALU*. The ALU contains an adder to perform binary arithmetic operations on the data obtained from memory, the registers or other inputs. Some ALUs perform more complex operations such as multiplication and division. ALUs provide other functions as well, including Boolean logic and data shifting.

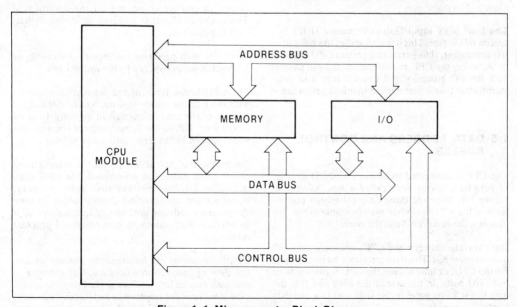

Figure 1-1 Microcomputer Block Diagram

The ALU also contains flag bits that signal the results of arithmetic and logical manipulations such as sign, zero, carry, and parity information.

The *control circuitry* coordinates all microprocessor activity. Using clock inputs, the control circuitry maintains the proper sequence of events required for any processing task. The control circuitry decodes the instruction bits and issues control signals to units both internal and external to the CPU to perform the proper processing action.

1.3 MEMORY

Microcomputers generally use semiconductor devices to store programs and data. Two examples of these are the RAM - Random Access Memory, and the ROM - Read Only Memory. To expand memory space, microcomputer systems often use some kind of mass storage device such as floppy-disks or magnetic tape.

1.4 INPUT/OUTPUT OR I/O DEVICES

I/O devices, also called *peripherals*, are the means by which the CPU communicates with the outside world. In a typical microcomputer system with a CRT terminal, the input ports (or channels) are connected to the keyboard, while the output ports are connected to hardware that generates the characters displayed on the screen.

The Intel 8089 Input/Output Processor (IOP) is a special I/O device. This device handles the burden of I/O processing, thus permitting greater CPU efficiency. Allowing the CPU to perform its tasks in parallel with the I/O processor is a concept typical of large mainframes that is here applied to microcomputers.

1.5 DATA, ADDRESS AND CONTROL BUSSES

The CPU is connected to memory and I/O by a set of parallel wires or lines called a *bus*. As seen in Figure 1-1, there are three different busses that interface the CPU to other system components: the *data bus*, the *address bus* and the *control bus*.

Data travels between the CPU, memory, and I/O over the *data bus*. This data can either be instructions for the CPU, or information the CPU is passing to or from I/O ports. In the case of the 8088 and 188, the data bus is 8-bits wide; in the 8086 and 186, the data bus is 16-bits wide.

The CPU uses the *address bus* to select the desired memory or I/O device by providing a unique address that corresponds to one of the memory or I/O elements of the system.

The *control* bus carries control signals to the memory and I/O devices, specifying whether data is to go into or out of the CPU, and exactly when the data is being transferred.

1.6 BUS CYCLES

As the microcomputer program executes, data is transferred to and from memory and I/O devices. Each instance of data transfer from one part of the system to another is called a *bus cycle* (or *machine cycle*). The timing of these cycles is done by the CPU clock signal. Operations like instruction fetch, memory read, memory write, read from an input port, or write to an output port are operations taking place in one or more bus cycles.

The length of bus cycles is determined relative to the frequency of a clock signal. Typical clock rates at which microcomputers operate are 5, 8 and 10 MHz. The 8 MHz versions of the Intel iAPX 86 and 186 have clock cycles of 125 nanoseconds (or .125 microseconds).

At the beginning of a bus cycle, the CPU issues a code to the address bus to identify the memory location or I/O device to be accessed. Next, the CPU issues an activity command on the control bus. Third, the CPU either receives or transmits data over the data bus.

The CPU then performs the logical, arithmetic, or I/O operations as required by the instructions.

The CPU keeps track of the instruction sequence with the *program counter* register, which contains the address of the next instruction in memory. In more recent Intel CPUs, the term 'program counter' has been replaced by the term 'instruction pointer'.

Normally, the instruction pointer is incremented after a given instruction is executed. The CPU automatically fetches instructions from memory, decodes them, and executes them in sequence until the program ends, or until special instructions tell it to execute instructions in other parts of program memory.

Certain situations can interrupt the normal sequential flow of instruction execution. For example, a *wait state* may be imposed in a given bus cycle to provide more time for memory or an I/O device to communicate with the CPU. Wait states are needed when the rate of data transfer from memory is slower than the rate at which the CPU requests it. In such cases, the memory must request a wait state when it receives the CPU signal that a memory read or write operation has commenced. After the memory responds, it signals the CPU to leave the wait state and continue processing.

1.7 INTERRUPTS

Another situation that alters sequential instruction execution is an *interrupt*. For example, consider a computer which is processing a large volume of data, portions of which are to be output to a printer. The CPU can send to the printer a given amount of data in a single bus cycle, but the printer may take several bus cycles to print the characters specified by that data. Thus, the CPU must remain idle until the printer can accept the next data. The interrupt capability permits the CPU to output to the printer and then return to other data processing.

When the printer is ready to accept the next data byte, it signals the CPU via a special interrupt control line. When the CPU receives the interrupt signal, it suspends the main program execution and automatically switches to the instructions that output to the printer, after which the CPU continues with the main program execution where processing was suspended.

Often several interrupting devices share the same CPU. In order to service all of them, interrupts can be prioritized. When two or more interrupts occur simultaneously, the one with the higher priority will be serviced first.

1.8 DIRECT MEMORY ACCESS

Another feature that improves microprocessor efficiency is *direct memory access*, also called DMA.

In ordinary input/output operations, the CPU supervises the entire data transfer as it executes I/O instructions to transfer data from the input device to the CPU, and then from the CPU to a specified memory location. Similarly, data going from memory to an output device goes by way of the CPU.

Some peripheral devices transfer information to and from memory faster than the CPU can accomplish the transfer under program control. By using DMA, the CPU allows the peripheral device to hold and control the bus, transferring the data directly to and from memory without involving the CPU itself. When the DMA transfer is done, the peripheral releases the hold request signal. The CPU then resumes processing instructions where it left off.

1.9 ADDRESSING MODES

The address that the CPU provides on the address bus selects one specific memory or I/O device from all those available. This address can be generated in different ways depending on the operation being performed. The ways of generating these addresses are called *addressing modes.*

In the simplest addressing mode, the desired data item is contained within the instruction being executed. In a more complex addressing mode, the instruction contains the memory address of the data. Or, the instruction may reference a CPU register that contains the memory address of the data.

Finally, within some microprocessors, the instruction may tell the control circuitry to generate a complex address that is the sum of several address components, such as multiple registers plus data contained in the instruction itself.

Generally, the most powerful microprocessors are the ones with the widest variety of addressing modes available.

1.10 INTEL MICROCOMPUTER COMPONENTS

Intel manufactures a complete line of microcomputer components. These components constitute building blocks, which can be tailored to fit the performance needs of a particular application precisely. This manual describes the following components: the iAPX 86 (8086) CPU, the iAPX 88 (8088) CPU, the iAPX 186 (80186) CPU, the iAPX 188 (80188) CPU, the 8087 Numeric Processor Extension (NPX), the 8089 I/O Processor (IOP), and the 80130 Operating System Firmware (OSF).

The iAPX 86,88,186,188 Family Overview

2

CHAPTER 2
THE iAPX 86,88, 186,188 FAMILY OVERVIEW

2.1 INTRODUCTION

The iAPX 86,88 and iAPX 186,188 family consists of advanced, high-performance microprocessors. The family includes general data processors (8086, 8088, 80186 and 80188), specialized coprocessors such as the 8087 numeric processor extension (NPX) and the 8089 I/O processor (IOP), as well as the 80130 operating system firmware (OSF).

Four key architectural concepts shaped the microprocessor designs. All four reflect the family's role as vehicles for modular, high-level language programming (in addition to assembly language programming).

The concepts are:

- Memory segmentation,
- Operand addressing structure,
- Operation register set, and
- Instruction encoding scheme.

The iAPX 86,88/186,188 memory segmentation scheme is optimized for the reference needs of computer programs, and is separate from the operand addressing structure.

The structure for addressing operands within segments directly supports the various data types found in high level programming languages.

An operation register set is provided to support general computation requirements. It also provides for optimized operation register sets to do specialized data processing functions with its inherent multiprocessor and coprocessor support.

The family uses optimized instruction encoding for high performance and memory efficiency.

High-level languages using modular programming have become the norm on large software development projects in the last decade. The iAPX 86,88/186,188 microprocessor family with its memory segmentation scheme is designed for modular programs. It supports the static and dynamic memory requirements of program modules, as well as their communication needs. The register scheme employs specialized registers and implicit register usage.

These CPUs are substantially more powerful than microprocessors previously offered by Intel. High

performance is realized by combining a 16-bit internal data path with a pipelined architecture that allows instructions to be prefetched during spare bus cycles. A compact instruction format that enables more instructions to be fetched in a given amount of time also contributes to the performance.

Software need not be written in assembly language. These CPUs are designed to provide direct hardware support for programs written in high-level languages such as Pascal-86 and Intel's PL/M-86. However, routines with critical performance requirements that cannot be met with a high-level language may be written in ASM-86 (the 8086/80186 assembly language) and linked with Pascal-86 or PL/M-86 code.

While these CPUs are totally new designs, they make the most of the user's existing investments in systems designed around the 8080/8085 microprocessors. Many of the standard Intel memory, peripheral control, and communication chips are compatible with the 8086,88 and the 80186,188.

Other important features of the family are, in the case of the 8086 and 8088 CPUs, dual operating modes (minimum and maximum) and built-in multiprocessing capability. The 80186 and 80188 CPUs, on the other hand, integrate many key functions including a programmable interrupt controller, chip select logic, two high speed DMA channels, timers, and a clock generator.

These characteristics, as well as others to be described in following chapters, make the iAPX 86,88, 186,188 family suitable for a wide spectrum of microcomputer applications. Systems can range from the uniprocessor, minimal-memory designs implemented with a handful of chips (Figure 2-1) to multiprocessor systems with up to a megabyte of memory (Figure 2-2).

2.2 THE CPU ARCHITECTURE

The following sections of this chapter describe the mainstays of the microprocessor family: the central processing units. The internal operation of the CPU and the interaction of the processors with other devices are discussed in functional terms. Electrical characteristics, timing, and other hardware related information may be found in Volume 2 of this set.

210911

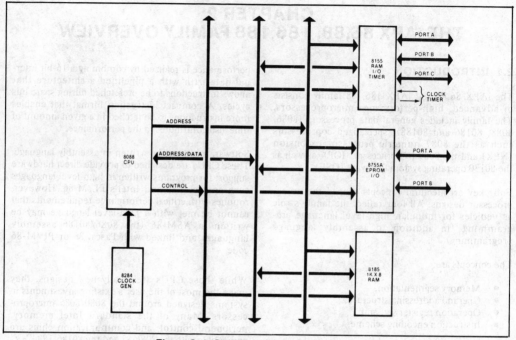

Figure 2-1 Small 8088-Based System

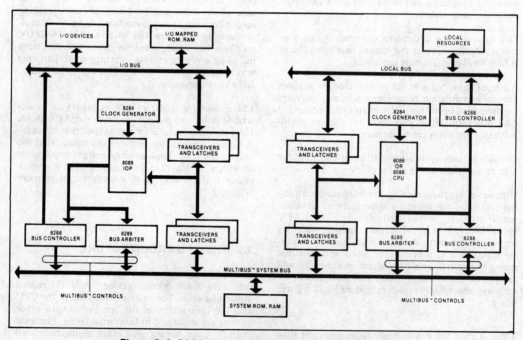

Figure 2-2 8086/8088/8089 Multiprocessing System

Functional Units

Standard microprocessors execute a program by repeatedly cycling through the steps shown in Figure 2-3. First, the microprocessor must fetch the instruction to be performed, then it executes the instruction. Only after the execution is complete is the CPU ready to fetch the next instruction, execute that instruction, etc.

The CPU hardware that executes instructions must obviously wait until the instruction is fetched and decoded before execution begins. Therefore, in standard microprocessors, the execution hardware (primarily the control circuitry and the arithmetic and logic unit) spends a lot of time waiting for instructions to be fetched. The 8086,88 and 80186,188 microprocessors eliminate this wasted time by dividing the internal CPU into two independent functional units (see Figure 2-4).

The BIU and EU — Pipelined Architecture

The CPUs have a separate bus interface unit (BIU), whose only job is to fetch instructions from memory and pass data to and from the execution hardware and the outside world. Since the execution unit and the bus interface unit are independent, the bus interface unit fetches additional instructions while the execution unit (sometimes called the EU) executes a previously fetched instruction. This is made possible by the instruction pipeline (or queue) between the bus interface unit and the execution unit. The BIU fills this pipeline with instructions awaiting execution. Thus, whenever the execution unit finishes executing a given instruction, the next instruction is usually ready for immediate execution without delays caused by instruction fetching. Figure 2-5 shows parallel fetching and executing in these CPUs.

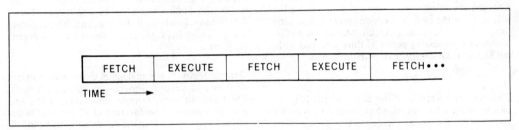

Figure 2-3 Program Execution in Standard Microprocessor

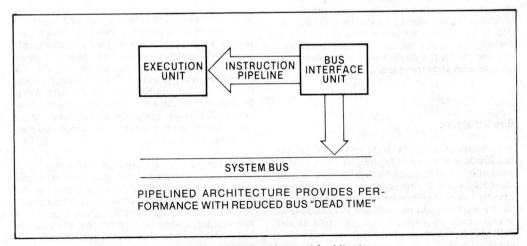

Figure 2-4 Pipelined Internal Architecture

210911

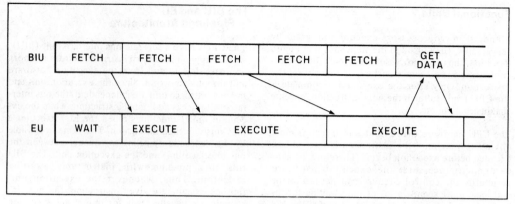

Figure 2-5 Parallel Operation In CPU

Because the BIU is usually busy fetching instructions for the pipeline, the bus is more fully utilized. Another benefit of this parallel operation is that since the execution unit seldom needs to wait for the BIU to fetch the next instruction, there is less need for the BIU to fetch data quickly. Maximum performance and processing power is thus achieved without high speed memory devices in the system.

This parallel operation of the BIU and EU is transparent to the user, except when program execution transfers to a new, non-sequential address. When this happens, the bus interface unit is given the new address by the execution unit; it then begins fetching instructions sequentially from the new address. The execution unit must wait for the next instruction to be fetched the way most CPUs wait for every instruction to be fetched. After the first instruction is fetched from the new location, the bus interface unit continues to fill the pipeline with instructions, and fetch-time becomes transparent.

Bus Structure

A summary of the iAPX 86,88 and iAPX 186,188 bus structure is shown in Figure 2-6. There are two types of buses: system and local. Both buses may be shared by multiple processors, i.e., both are multimaster buses. Microprocessors are always connected to a local bus, and memory and I/O components usually reside on a system bus. The 8086,88 and 80186,188 bus interface components link a local bus to a system bus.

Register Resources

Figure 2-7 gives an overview of the registers available in the 8086,88 and 80186,188 CPUs. These CPUs have fourteen 16-bit registers. The registers are grouped into general, control and segment registers.

General registers are analogous to the accumulators of first and second generation microprocessors. They are, in turn, grouped into data, index and pointer registers. The function of all registers is described in more detail in the following paragraphs.

Data Registers

The data registers are unique in that their upper and lower halves are separately addressable. This means that each data register can be used interchangeably as a 16-bit register, or as two 8-bit registers. In their 16-bit form, the data registers are the AX, BX, CX and DX registers (Figure 2-8). For 8-bit operations, they are divided into high byte and low byte. AH is the high byte of the AX register, AL is the low byte of the AX register, and so on. As mentioned, these registers have general usage for arithmetic and logical operations.

Some registers have additional special functions, which are performed in the execution of certain instructions. For example, the CX register is frequently used to contain a count value during repetitive instructions, and the BX register is used as a base register in some of the more powerful addressing modes. This implicit use of registers allows a very compact instruction encoding.

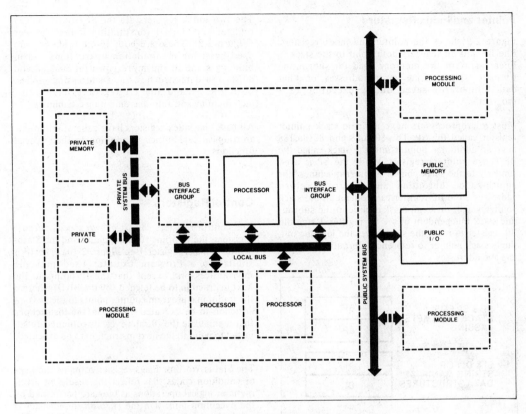

Figure 2-6 Generalized iAPX 86/186 Bus Structure

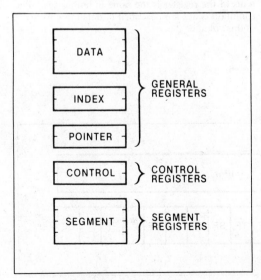

Figure 2-7 CPU Register Set

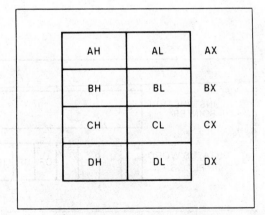

Figure 2-8 Data Group Registers

210911

Pointer and Index Registers

Figure 2-9 shows the pointer and index registers. The BP and SP registers both point to the stack, a linear array in the memory used for subroutine parameters, subroutine return addresses, or other data temporarily saved during execution of a program.

Most microprocessors have a single stack pointer register called the SP. The 8086,88 and 80186,188 have an additional pointer into the stack called the BP (base pointer) register. While the SP is used similarly to the stack pointer in other machines (for pointing to subroutine and interrupt return addresses), the BP register can contain an old stack pointer value, or it can mark a place in the subroutine stack independent of the SP register. Using the BP register to mark the stack saves the juggling of a single stack pointer to reference subroutine parameters and addresses.

The two index registers are the SI (source index) register and the DI (destination index) register (Figure 2-9). These are both 16-bits wide and are used by string manipulation instructions and in building some of the more powerful 8086,88 and 80186,188 data structures and addressing modes. Both the SI and the DI registers have auto-incrementing and auto-decrementing capabilities.

All base and index registers have general arithmetic and logical capabilities in addition to their special functions.

Control Registers

The control registers consist of two special purpose registers, the IP or instruction pointer and the Status Word or Flags register (see Figure 2-10). The IP is similar to a Program Counter used in some microprocessors, except that the IP points to the next instruction to be fetched (by the BIU), whereas the traditional program counter points to the next instruction to be executed. For 8086/186 instructions that manipulate the IP, however, its contents are adjusted to point to the next instruction to be executed.

The Status Word or Flags register contains the flags or condition codes that reflect the results of arithmetic or logical operations as they are performed by the execution unit. (On the 8086/88 this register is referred to as the Flags register; on the 80186/188 it is referred to as the Status Word register. The contents of the register is the same in both cases.) The condition codes are described in detail in Chapter 3 of this volume.

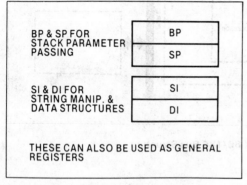

Figure 2-9 Base and Index Registers

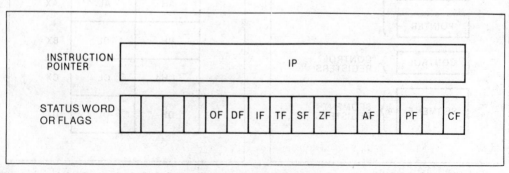

Figure 2-10 Control Registers

Segment Registers

Four 16-bit special purpose registers, called segment registers, are provided in a segment register file. They are the code segment (CS), stack segment (SS), data segment (DS) and extra segment (ES). Segment registers are used by the 8086,88 and 80186,188 in the formulation of memory addresses. Their usage is described in the following section on memory addressing.

2.3 MEMORY ADDRESSING

Memory is organized in sets of segments. Each segment consists of a linear sequence of up to 64K bytes. These bytes are stored sequentially from byte 00000 to byte FFFFF hex. The memory is addressed using a two-component address (a pointer) that consists of a 16-bit segment base (specifying the beginning address of the segment in memory) and a 16-bit offset (specifying the address relative to the beginning of the segment). The base values are contained in one of the four internal segment registers (CS, DS, SS, ES). A 20-bit physical memory address is calculated by shifting the base value in the appropriate segment register left by four bits and adding the 16-bit offset value to it (Figure 2-11). This form of addressing allows access to one million bytes of memory.

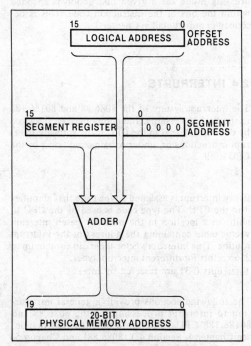

Figure 2-11 Memory Addressing

Every 20-bit memory address points either to program code, data, or stack area in memory (Figure 2-12). Each of the four different memory spaces is pointed to by one of the segment base registers (Figure 2-13). The code segment register points to the base of the program currently executing, the stack segment register points to the base of the stack, the data segment register points to the base of one data area, and the extra segment register points to the base of another area where data may be stored.

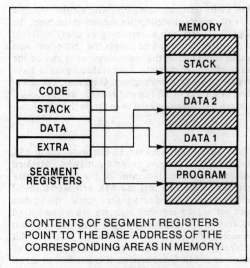

CONTENTS OF SEGMENT REGISTERS POINT TO THE BASE ADDRESS OF THE CORRESPONDING AREAS IN MEMORY.

Figure 2-12 Segment Registers

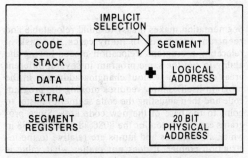

Figure 2-13 How an Address Is Built

Generating Addresses

Each time the CPU needs to generate a memory address, one of the segment registers is automatically chosen and its contents added to a logical address.

For an instruction fetch, the code segment register is automatically added to the logical address (in this case, the contents of the instruction pointer) to compute the value of the instruction address.

For an instruction referencing the stack, the stack segment register is automatically added to the logical address (the SP or BP register contents) to compute the value of the stack address.

For a data reference operation, where either the data or extra segment register are chosen as the base, the logical address can be made up of many different types of values: it can be simply the immediate data value contained in the instruction, or it can be the sum of an immediate data value, plus a base register, plus an index register. Generally, the selection of the DS or ES register is made automatically, though provisions do exist to override this selection.

Since logical addresses are 16-bits wide, up to 64K (65,536) bytes in a given segment may be addressed without changing the value of the segment base register. In systems that use 64K or fewer bytes of memory for each memory area (code, stack, data and extra), the segment registers can be initialized to zero at the beginning of the program and then ignored, since zero plus a 16-bit offset yields a 16-bit address. In a system where the total amount of memory is 64K bytes or less, it is possible to set all segment registers equal and have fully overlapping segments.

Segment registers are also very useful for large programming tasks, which require isolation of program code from the data area, or isolation of module data from the stack information, etc.

Segmentation makes it easy to build relocatable and reentrant programs. In many cases, the task of relocating a program (relocation means having the ability to run the same program in several different areas of memory without changing addresses in the program itself) simply requires moving the program code and then adjusting the code segment register to point to the base of the new code area. Since programs can be written for the 8086,88 or 80186,188 in which all branches and jumps are relative to the instruction pointer, it does not matter what value is kept in the code segment register.

Figure 2-14 shows how an entire process, consisting of code, stack and data areas, can be relocated. Likewise, in a reentrant program, a single program uses multiple data areas. Before the reentrant code is entered the second time, the data segment register value is changed so that a different data area is made available to the program.

Addressing Modes

The 8086,88 and 80186,188 provide 24 different addressing modes. Various logical address combinations are shown in Figure 2-15, from the simplest immediate data mode to the register addressing mode, where a selected register contains the data being used by the instruction. In the direct addressing mode, the instruction itself contains the address of the data. In the register indirect mode, the instruction points to a register containing the memory address of the desired data. There are both indexed and based addressing modes where the contents of an index or base register is added to an immediate data value contained in the instruction to form the memory address.

Exactly how the 8086,88 and 80186,188 select an addressing mode for a given instruction is encoded within the bits of the instruction code. This is described in more detail in Chapter 3.

2.4 INTERRUPTS

The interrupt system of the 8086,88 and 80186,188 is simple but versatile. Interrupts may be triggered by devices external to the CPU or by software interrupt instructions or, under certain conditions, by the CPU itself.

Every interrupt is assigned a type code that identifies it to the CPU. The type code is used by the CPU to point to a location in the memory based interrupt vector table containing the address of the interrupt routine. This interrupt vector table can contain up to 256 vectors for different interrupt types. Interrupts 0-31 are reserved by Intel.

The following sections provide a general introduction to interrupt processing for the 8086,88 and 80186,188 CPUs. For more detailed information, see Chapter 4, Section 4.3 (8086,88) and Chapter 5, Section 5.4 (80186,188).

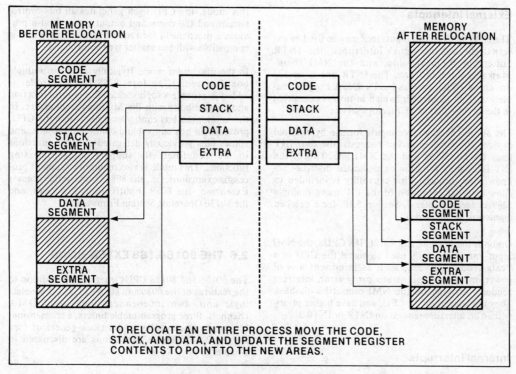

TO RELOCATE AN ENTIRE PROCESS MOVE THE CODE,
STACK, AND DATA, AND UPDATE THE SEGMENT REGISTER
CONTENTS TO POINT TO THE NEW AREAS.

Figure 2-14 Process Relocation

MODE	LOCATION OF DATA
IMMEDIATE	WITHIN INSTRUCTION
REGISTER	IN REGISTER
DIRECT	AT MEMORY LOCATION POINTED TO BY ADDRESS CONTAINED IN INSTRUCTION.
REGISTER INDIRECT	AT MEMORY LOCATION POINTED TO BY ADDRESS CONTAINED IN REGISTER.
INDEXED OR BASED	AT MEMORY LOCATION POINTED TO BY SUM OF INDEX REGISTER OR BASE REGISTER CONTENTS AND IMMEDIATE DATA CONTAINED IN INSTRUCTION.
BASED AND INDEXED WITH DISPLACEMENT	MEMORY ADDRESS IS SUM OF BASE REGISTER CONTENTS AND INDEX REGISTER CONTENTS AND IMMEDIATE DATA.

THE LOCATION OF DATA IS REALLY THE LOGICAL ADDRESS, WHICH IS ADDED TO THE SEGMENT
REGISTER VALUE TO FORM THE PHYSICAL MEMORY ADDRESS.

Figure 2-15 iAPX 88 Addressing Modes

210911

External Interrupts

The 8086,88 have two inputs that may be used by external devices to signal interrupts, the INTR (Interrupt Request) line, and the NMI (Non-Maskable Interrupt) line. The INTR line is usually driven by a PIC, such as Intel's 8259A Programmable Interrupt Controller, which in turn is connected to the devices that need interrupt service.

The 80186,188 have five inputs for use by external devices to signal interrupt requests: the four INT lines (INT0-INT3) and the NMI line. Two of the INT lines may function as dedicated interrupt acknowledge outputs. This capability is included to allow external expansion of the PIC using multiple 8259As (see Chapter 5, Section 5.10, for a detailed discussion of this facility).

On both the 8086,88 and 80186,188 CPUs, the NMI input line is generally used to signal the CPU of a "catastrophic" event, such as imminent loss of power, memory error, or bus parity error. Interrupt requests arriving on the NMI cannot be disabled. They are latched by the CPU, and have higher priority than an interrupt request on INTR or INT0-3.

Internal Interrupts

Internal interrupts are generated by two instructions (INT and INTO), by conditions resulting from the execution of two instructions (DIV, IDIV), and by most instructions when the Single Step flag in the Flags or Status Word register is set. In addition to all these, the 80186,188 provide interrupts generated by the integrated peripherals (see Section 2.6), by two instructions (ESC and BOUND) and by the occurrence of undefined opcodes.

A detailed discussion of interrupts is included in Chapters 4 and 5, which deal with the 8086,88 and the 80186,188 respectively, as well as in Volume 2 of this set, which covers the hardware details of interrupts for both CPUs.

2.5 MINIMUM AND MAXIMUM MODES (8086,88 ONLY)

A unique feature of the 8086,88 CPUs is the ability of a user to define a subset of the CPU's control signal outputs to tailor it to its intended system environment.

In the minimum mode, the CPU supports small, single-processor systems (usually single board) that consist of a few devices, and that use a local bus rather than support the Multibus architecture. In this mode, the CPU itself generates all bus control signals and the command output signal. It also provides a mechanism for requesting bus access that is compatible with bus master type controllers.

In the maximum mode (typically used for multiple board systems), an Intel 8288 Bus Controller is added to provide a sophisticated bus control function and compatibility with the Multibus architecture. In this mode, the bus controller, rather than the CPU, provides all bus control and command outputs, and allows pins previously delegated to these functions to be redefined to support multiprocessing functions. This mode is also required to support processor extensions, i.e., the 8087 Numerical Processor Extension, the 8089 Input/Output Processor, and the 80130 Operating System Firmware.

2.6 THE 80186,188 EXTENSIONS

The 80186 and 80188 CPUs integrate, in addition to the features of the 8086 and 8088 CPUs, a chip-select logic unit, two independent high-speed DMA channels, three programmable timers, a programmable interrupt controller and a clock generator (see Figure 2-16). These extensions are discussed in Chapter 5.

The register set of the 80186,188 is identical to that of the 8086,88 with the minor exception that the 8086,88 Flags register is referred to as the Status Word register in the 80186,188; the contents of the two registers is the same. The 80186,188 is object code compatible with the 8086,88 and adds ten additional instruction types to the existing 8086,88 instruction set.

Integrated Peripherals

All the 80186,188 CPU integrated peripherals are controlled by 16-bit registers contained in a 256-byte control block, which may be mapped into either the memory or I/O space. A 16-bit relocation register within this control block contains the base addresses. The integrated peripherals operate semi-autonomously from the CPU.

The 80186,188 Chip-Select Logic

The chip-select logic provides programmable chip-select generation for both memories and peripherals.

Six memory chip-select outputs are provided for 3 address areas: upper memory, lower memory, and midrange memory. The range of each chip-select is

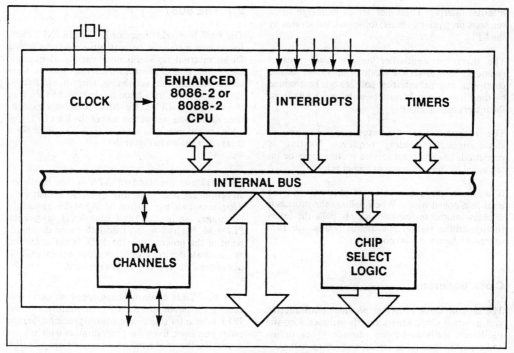

Figure 2-16 iAPX 186,188 Block Diagram

user programmable. The 80186,188 can also generate chip-selects for up to seven peripheral devices.

In addition, the chip-select logic can be programmed to provide READY (or WAIT state) generation.

DMA Channels

The 80186,188 DMA controller provides two independent high-speed DMA channels. This controller can transfer data between memory and I/O, between memory and memory, or between I/O and I/O. Data can be transferred in bytes or in words (bytes only in the case of the 188) and may be transferred to or from even or odd addresses. The channels maintain both a 20-bit source and destination pointer which can be optionally incremented or decremented after each data transfer.

Each DMA channel has six registers in the control block defining the channels specific operation. The channels may be programmed to always give priority to one channel over the other, or they may be programmed to alternate cycles when both have DMA requests pending.

Timers

The 80186,188 include three internal 16-bit programmable timers. Two of these are highly flexible and are connected to external pins. They can be used to count external events, time external events, generate nonrepetitive waveforms, etc. The third timer is not connected to external pins, and is useful for real-time coding and time delays.

The timers are controlled by eleven 16-bit registers in the internal peripheral control block. A timer mode/control register within this block allows the user to program the specific mode of operation or check the current programmed status for any of the timers.

Each timer has a 16-bit count register, the current contents of which may be read or written to by the CPU at any time.

Interrupt Controller

The 80186,188 can receive interrupts from a number of sources, both internal and external. The

210911

internal interrupt controller serves to merge these requests on a priority basis, for individual service by the CPU.

The interrupt controller has its own control registers, used to set the mode of operation for the controller. Internal interrupt sources can be disabled by their own control registers or by mask bits from the interrupt controller.

The interrupt controller resolves priority among simultaneously pending requests. Nesting is permitted, i.e., interrupt service routines may be interrupted by those of equal or higher priority.

If interrupts are undesirable, the controller may be used in a polled mode. When polling, the processor disables interrupts and then simply polls the interrupt controller (rather than the individual interrupt sources) whenever it is convenient.

Clock Generator

The on-chip clock generator provides both internal and external clock generation. It includes a crystal oscillator, a divide-by-two counter, synchronous and asynchronous ready inputs, and reset circuitry.

The oscillator circuit is designed to operate with a parallel resonant fundamental mode crystal. The crystal frequency is double the CPU clock frequency. An external oscillator may be used instead of the crystal, which may be connected directly to the X1 input in lieu of a crystal, with X2 left open.

2.7 THE 8087

The 8087 Numeric Processor Extension (NPX) performs arithmetic and comparison operations (using 80-bit internal registers) on a variety of numeric data types. It also executes numerous built-in transcendental functions such as log, tangent, etc. In conjunction with the maximum mode 8086,88 CPUs, or the 80186,188 CPUs, the NPX effectively extends the register and instruction sets of the host CPU and adds several new data types as well. The 8087 block diagram is shown in Figure 2-17.

The 8087 uses the standard iAPX 86/186 family instruction set plus over fifty numeric instructions. Programs can be written in ASM-86 assembly language, or in the Intel high-level languages PL/M-86, Fortran-86 and Pascal-86. From the standpoint of the programmer the NPX is not perceived as a separate device; instead, the computational abilities of the CPU appear greatly expanded.

The 8087 adds extensive high-speed numeric processing capabilities to the CPU. It conforms to the IEEE format for single- and double-precision floating point numbers. Even for programmers who are not expert in the problems of numerical analysis (for instance, the accumulation of rounding errors which may result from a long chain of floating point calculations), the 8087 will provide correct results, and is straightforward and easy to program. Chapter 6 of this volume describes the software aspects of the 8087; Chapter 3 of Volume 2 covers the hardware.

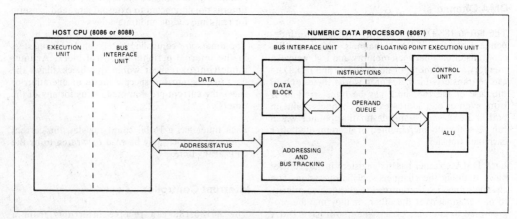

Figure 2-17 Numeric Data Processor Block Diagram

2.8 THE 8089 I/O PROCESSOR (IOP)

The 8089 Input/Output Processor is a high-performance, general purpose I/O system on a chip (see Figure 2-18). It is an independent microprocessor that optimizes input/output operations. It is designed to remove all I/O details from applications software. Responding to the CPU direction, but executing its own instruction stream in parallel with other processors, it can transfer 16-bit data at rates up to 1.25 megabytes per second.

In conjunction with the 8086,88, the 8089 combines the attributes of both a CPU and a DMA controller to provide a powerful I/O subsystem. I/O subsystem changes or upgrades can be made without impact to application software.

The CPU communicates with the IOP in two modes: initialization and command. The IOP has two independent channels, each with its own register set, channel attention, interrupt request and DMA control signals.

Programs are written in ASM-89, the 8089 assembly language. About 50 basic instructions are available, including general purpose instructions similar to those found in CPUs as well as instructions specifically tailored for I/O operations.

In the case of the 80186,188 and 8089 combination, the 8089 is used in the remote mode only. This is described in Chapter 7 of this manual; hardware considerations are in Volume 2, Chapter 4.

2.9 THE 80130 OPERATING SYSTEM FIRMWARE (OSF)

The 80130 firmware (software in silicon) is, in conjunction with the 8086,88 or 80186,188 CPUs, the nucleus of a real-time, high-performance multitasking operating system. The 80130 adds task management, interrupt management, message passing, synchronization and memory allocation capabilities to the CPU. A block diagram of the OSF is shown in Figure 2-19.

The 80130 OSF has five operating system data types: jobs, tasks, segments, mailboxes and regions. To create, manipulate and delete these data types, the 80130 uses 35 operating-system instructions or primitives. Programs using the 80130 primitives may be written in ASM-86, PL/M-86, Fortran-86 or Pascal-86.

The OSF contains a 16-bit operating-system, a programmable interrupt controller, delay timers, and a variable baud-rate generator, thus replacing about 10 LSI ICs in a system. It is connected directly to the multiplexed address/data bus of the 8086,88 or 80186,188 CPUs.

Scheduling of tasks is based on priority. Each task is given a priority and interrupt level relative to other tasks when created, but priorities may be altered dynamically. The design approach used in the 80130 OSF is one common to mini and mainframe computers.

The 80130 OSF is described in detail in Chapter 8; hardware considerations are found in Chapter 5, Volume 2.

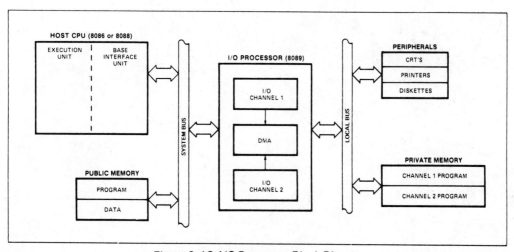

Figure 2-18 I/O Processor Block Diagram

210911

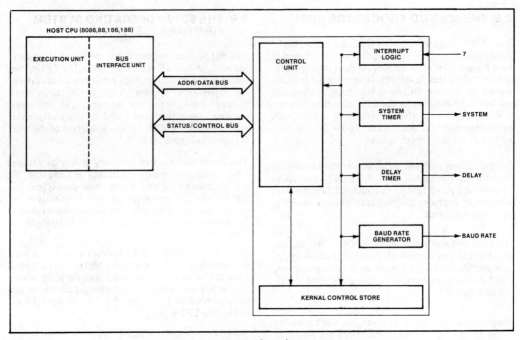

Figure 2-19 80130 (OSP) Block Diagram

The iAPX 86, 88 and iAPX 186,188 Architecture and Instructions

3

CHAPTER 3
THE iAPX 86,88 and iAPX 186,188
ARCHITECTURE AND INSTRUCTIONS

3.1 INTRODUCTION

This chapter describes the programmer's architecture of the iAPX 86,88 and iAPX 186,188 CPUs. It is divided into the following sections:

- CPU Architecture
- Register Structure
- Memory Structure
- I/O Port Organization
- Addressing Modes
- Instruction Set
- Programming Examples

3.2 CPU ARCHITECTURE

The two independently operating functional units of the CPU, the BIU and EU, are able, under most circumstances, to extensively overlap instruction fetch with execution. The result is that, in most cases, the time normally required to fetch instructions "disappears" because the EU executes instructions that have already been fetched by the BIU. Figure 3-1 illustrates this overlap and compares it with traditional microprocessor operation. In the example, overlapping reduces the elapsed time required to execute three instructions, and allows two additional instructions to be prefetched as well.

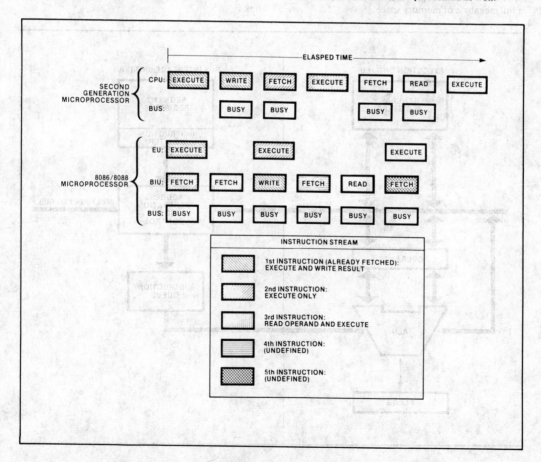

Figure 3-1 Overlapped Instruction Fetch and Execution

210911

Execution Unit

In the execution unit, a 16-bit ALU maintains the CPU status and control flags, and manipulates the general registers and instruction operands. All registers and data paths within the EU are 16 bits wide (Figure 3-2).

The EU has no connection to the system bus, the "outside world." It obtains instructions from a queue maintained by the BIU. Likewise, when an instruction requires access to memory or to a peripheral device, the EU requests the BIU to fetch or store the data. All addresses manipulated by the EU are 16 bits wide. However, the address relocation facility provided by the BIU provides the EU with access to a full megabyte of memory space.

Bus Interface Unit

The BIUs of the 8088/80188 and the 8086/80186 are functionally identical, but are implemented differently to match the data path size of their buses, which are 8 bits and 16 bits respectively.

The BIU performs all bus operations for the EU. Data is transferred between the CPU and memory or I/O devices upon demand from the EU.

In addition, during periods when the EU is busy executing instructions, the BIU "looks ahead" and fetches more instructions from memory. The instructions are stored in an internal RAM array called the instruction stream queue. The 8088/80188 instruction queue holds up to four bytes of the instruction stream, while the 8086/80186 queue can store up to six instruction bytes. These queue sizes keep the EU supplied with prefetched instructions under most conditions without monopolizing the system bus.

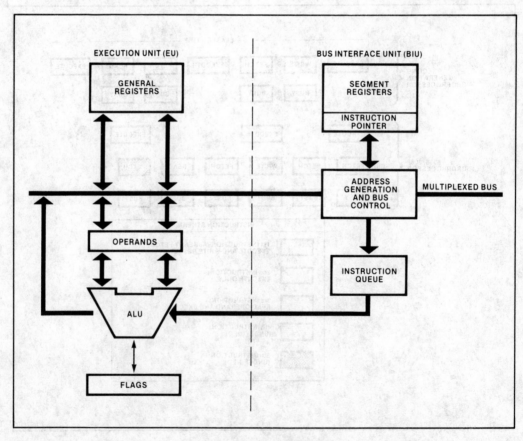

Figure 3-2 Execution and Bus Interface Units (EU and BIU)

210911

The 8088/80188 BIU fetches another instruction byte whenever there is one empty byte in its queue, and there is no active request for bus access from the EU. The 8086/80186 BIU operates similarly except that it does not normally initiate a fetch until there are two empty bytes in its queue.

The 8086/80186 BIU will generally obtain two instruction bytes per fetch; if a program transfer forces fetching from an odd address, the BIU automatically reads one byte from the odd address and then resumes fetching two-byte words from the subsequent even address.

Under most circumstances, the queue contains at least one byte of the instruction stream, and the EU does not have to wait for instructions to be fetched. The instructions in the queue are those stored in the memory locations immediately adjacent to and higher than the instruction currently being executed. That is, they are the next logical instructions so long as execution proceeds serially. If the EU executes an instruction that transfers control to another location, the BIU fetches the instruction from the new address, passes it immediately to the EU, and then begins refilling the queue from the new location (no flushing of the previous contents is necessary). In addition, the BIU suspends instruction fetching whenever the EU requests a memory or I/O read or write (except that a fetch already in progress is completed before executing the EU's bus request).

3.3 REGISTER STRUCTURE

The 8086,88 and 80186,188 contain the same basic set of fourteen registers as shown in Figure 3-3. These registers are grouped into the following categories: general registers, segment registers, and status and control registers.

General Registers

The CPUs have eight 16-bit general registers. They are divided into two files of four registers each: the data register file and the pointer and index register file.

The upper and lower halves of the data registers are separately addressable. This means that each data register can be used interchangeably as a 16-bit register, or as two 8-bit registers.

The 16-bit data registers are named AX, BX, CX, and DX; the 8-bit registers are named AL, AH, BL, BH, CL, CH, DL, and DH (the H or L suffix designates high-order or low-order byte of the 16-bit register). The other registers are always accessed as 16-bit units only.

The data registers can be used in most arithmetic and logic operations. Some instructions (e.g. string instructions), however, require certain general registers for specific uses (see Table 3-1). This implicit register use allows a more compact instruction encoding.

Table 3-1 Implicit Use of General Register

REGISTER	OPERATIONS
AX	Word Multiply, Word Divide, Word I/O
AL	Byte Multiply, Byte Divide, Byte I/O, Translate, Decimal Arithmetic
AH	Byte Multiply, Byte Divide
BP	Enter, Leave (186, 188 only)
BX	Translate
CX	String Operations
CL	Variable Shift and Rotate
DX	Word Multiply, Word Divide, Indirect I/O
SP	Stack Operations
SI	String Operations
DI	String Operations

The pointer and index registers consist of the 16-bit registers SP, BP, SI, and DI as shown in Figure 3-3. They can also be used in most arithmetic and logic operations. These registers usually contain offset addresses for addressing within a segment. They reduce program size by eliminating the need for each instruction to specify frequently used addresses. These registers serve another function; they provide for dynamic logical address computation as described in the section on operand addressing. The pointer and index registers are also used implicitly in some instructions (Table 3-1).

As shown in Figure 3-3, this register file is divided into the pointer subfile (SP and BP) and the index subfile (SI and DI). The pointer registers provide convenient access to the current stack segment (as opposed to the data segment). Unless otherwise specified in the instruction, pointer registers refer to the current stack segment while index registers refer to the current data segment. In certain instances, specific uses of these four registers are indicated by the mnemonic phrases "stack pointer," "base pointer," "source index," and "destination index."

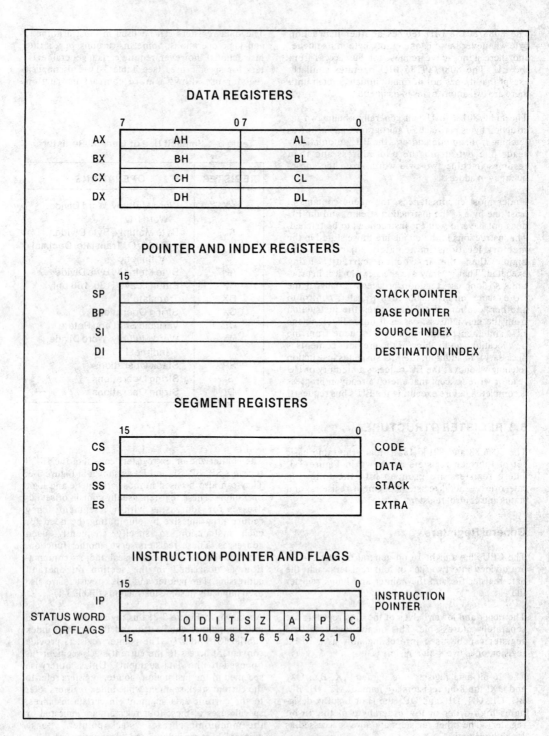

Figure 3-3 Register Structure

Segment Registers

The segment registers are also 16-bit registers. These registers specify the four currently addressable memory segments: CS (code segment), DS (data segment), SS (stack segment), and ES (extra segment). All instructions are fetched from the current code segment, offset by the instruction pointer (IP) register. Operand fetches are usually made from the current data segment (DS) or the current stack segment (SS), depending on whether the offset address was calculated from the contents of a pointer register. For the exceptional cases where operand references are required outside the default segment, a segment override prefix may be added to the instruction to designate the required segment.

Status and Control Registers

The status and control registers consist of the instruction pointer and the status word or flags.

The 16-bit instruction pointer (IP) is analogous to the program counter (PC) in earlier CPUs and points to the next instruction. The instruction pointer is updated by the BIU so that it contains the offset (distance in bytes) of the next instruction from the beginning of the current code segment. During normal execution, the IP contains the offset of the next instruction to be fetched by the BIU. However, for all instructions that manipulate the IP, the contents of IP are adjusted to point to the next instruction to be executed, for example, when the IP is pushed on the stack or is used to calculate the address of a relative jump.

The status word or flags is a 16-bit register consisting of three control flags and six status flags (see Figure 3-4). The status flags record specific characteristics of the result of logical and arithmetic instructions (bits 0, 2, 4, 6, 7, and 11); the control flags control the operation of the CPU within a given operating mode (bits 8, 9, and 10).

The status flags provide status information that the EU posts to reflect certain properties of the result of an arithmetic or logic operation. A group of instructions is available that allows a program to alter its execution depending on the contents of the status flags, that is, on the result of a prior operation. Table 3-2 summarizes the status word or flag bit functions.

Different instructions affect the status flags differently; in general, however, the flags reflect the following conditions:

1) If AF (the auxiliary flag) is set, there has been a carry out of the low nibble (the low order 4-bits of a byte) into the high nibble or a borrow from the high nibble into the low nibble of an 8-bit quantity (low-order byte of a 16-bit quantity). This flag is used by decimal arithmetic instructions.

2) If CF (carry flag) is set, there has been a carry out of, or a borrow into, the high-order bit of the result (8- or 16-bit). The flag is used by instructions that add and subtract multibyte numbers. Rotate instructions can also isolate a bit in memory or a register by placing it in the carry flag.

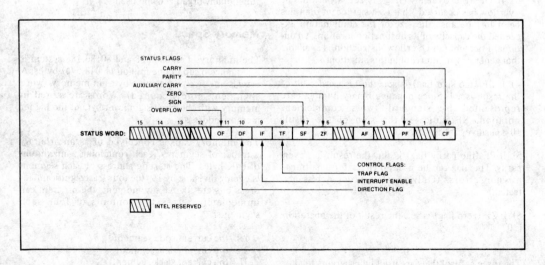

Figure 3-4 Status Word or Flags Format

210911

**Table 3-2 Status Word or Flags
Bit Functions**

Bit Position	Name	Function
0	CF	Carry Flag—Set on high-order bit carry or borrow; cleared otherwise
2	PF	Parity Flag—Set if low-order 8 bits of result contain an even number of 1-bits; cleared otherwise
4	AF	Set on carry from or borrow to the low order four bits of AL; cleared otherwise
6	ZF	Zero Flag–Set if result is zero; cleared otherwise
7	SF	Sign Flag—Set equal to high-order bit of result (0 if positive, 1 if negative)
8	TF	Single Step Flag—Once set, a single step interrupt occurs after the next instruction executes. TF is cleared by the single step interrupt.
9	IF	Interrupt-enable Flag—When set, maskable interrupts will cause the CPU to transfer control to an interrupt vector specified location.
10	DF	Direction Flag—Causes string instructions to auto decrement the appropriate index register when set. Clearing DF causes auto increment.
11	OF	Overflow Flag—Set if the signed result cannot be expressed within the number of bits in the destination operand; cleared otherwise

3) If OF (the overflow flag) is set, an arithmetic overflow has occurred; that is, a significant digit has been lost because the size of the computation exceeded the capacity of its destination location. An optional Interrupt On Overflow instruction is available that generates an interrupt in this situation.

4) If SF (the sign flag) is set, the high-order bit of the result is a 1. Since negative binary numbers are represented by standard two's complement notation, SF indicates the sign of the result (0=positive, 1=negative).

5) If PF (the parity flag) is set, the result has even parity. This flag can be used to check for data transmission errors. (Only the low-order 8 bits are tested.)

6) If ZF (zero flag) is set, the result of the operation is 0.

The three control flags are used by programs to alter processor operations in specified ways. The direction flag controls the direction of the string manipulations, the interrupt flag enables or disables external interrupts, and the trap flag puts the processor into a single-step mode for debugging.

The control flags are set and cleared as follows:

1) Setting DF (the direction flag) causes string instructions to auto-decrement, that is, to process strings from high addresses to low addresses, or from right to left. Clearing DF causes string instructions to auto-increment, or to process strings from left to right.

2) Setting IF (the interrupt-enable flag) allows the CPU to recognize maskable, external interrupt requests (including interrupts from 80186,188 integrated peripherals). Clearing IF disables these interrupts. IF has no effect on either nonmaskable external or internally generated interrupts.

3) Setting TF (the trap flag) puts the processor into single-step mode for debugging. In this mode, the CPU automatically generates an internal interrupt after each instruction, allowing a program to be inspected as it executes, instruction by instruction.

3.4 MEMORY STRUCTURE

The memory and input/output space of the 8086,88 and 80186,188 are treated in parallel and are collectively referred to as the memory structure. Code and data reside in the memory space, while (non-memory-mapped) peripheral devices reside in the I/O space. This section describes how memory is functionally organized and used.

Memory Space

The memory in an 8086,88 and 80186,188 system is a sequence of up to one million (1,048,576) bytes. A *word* is any two consecutive bytes in memory (word alignment is not required). Words are stored in memory with the most significant byte at the higher memory address.

The memory can be conceived of as an arbitrary number of segments, each containing a maximum of 64K bytes. The starting address of each segment is evenly divisible by 16 (the four least significant address bits are 0). At any moment, the program can immediately access the contents of four such segments:

1) the current code segment
2) the current data segment
3) the current stack segment
4) the current extra segment

Each of these segments can be identified by placing the 16 most significant bits of the segment's starting address into one of the four 16-bit segment registers. Instructions can refer to bytes or words within a segment by using a 16-bit offset address. The processor constructs the 20-bit byte or word address automatically by adding the 16-bit offset address (also called the logical address) to the contents of a 16-bit segment register, with four low-order zeros appended (see Figure 3-5).

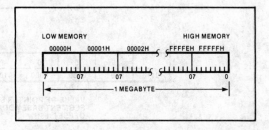

Figure 3-6 Storage Organization

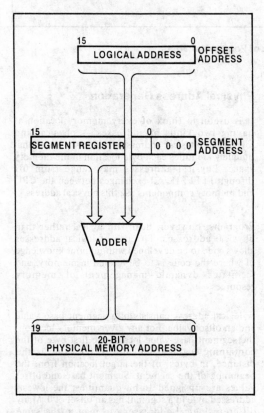

Figure 3-5 How to Address One Million Bytes

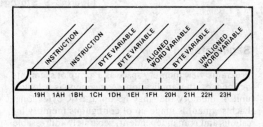

Figure 3-7 Instruction and Variable Storage

Word data is always stored with the most-significant byte in the higher memory location (Figure 3-8). Most of the time this storage convention is transparent to the programmer, except when monitoring the system bus or reading memory dumps.

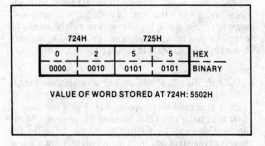

Figure 3-8 Storage of Word Variables

Storage Organization

From the storage point of view, memory spaces are organized as arrays of 8-bit bytes (Figure 3-6). Instructions, byte data and word data may be freely stored at any byte address without regard for alignment, thereby saving memory space by allowing code to be densely packed in memory (Figure 3-7).

Pointers addressing data and code that are outside the currently-addressable segments are stored as doublewords. The lower-addressed word of a pointer contains an offset value; the higher-addressed word contains a segment base address. By convention, each word is stored with the higher-addressed byte holding the most-significant eight bits of the word (Figure 3-9).

210911

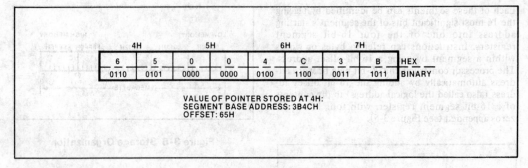

	4H		5H		6H		7H	
6	5	0	0	4	C	3	B	HEX
0110	0101	0000	0000	0100	1100	0011	1011	BINARY

VALUE OF POINTER STORED AT 4H:
SEGMENT BASE ADDRESS: 3B4CH
OFFSET: 65H

Figure 3-9 Storage of Pointer Variables

Segmentation

Programs view memory space as a group of segments defined by the application. A segment is a logical unit of memory that may be up to 64K bytes long. Each segment is made up of contiguous memory locations and is an independent, separately addressable unit. Every segment is assigned (by software) a base address, which is its starting location in the memory space. All segments start on 16-byte memory boundaries. There are no other restrictions on segment locations. Segments may be adjacent, disjoint, partially overlapped, or fully overlapped (Figure 3-10). A physical memory location may be mapped into (contained in) one or more logical segments.

The segment registers point to (contain the base address values of) the four immediately addressable segments (Figure 3-11). Programs obtain access to code and data in other segments by changing the segment registers to point to the desired segments.

Every application will define and use segments differently. The currently addressable segments provide a generous work space: 64K bytes for code, a 64K byte stack and 128K bytes of data storage. Many applications can be written to simply initialize the segment registers and then forget them. Larger applications should be designed with careful consideration given to segment definition. This segmented structure of the memory space supports modular software design by discouraging very large, monolithic programs. Segments can also be used to advantage in many programming situations. An example is the case of an editor for several on-line terminals. A 64K byte text buffer (say, an extra segment) could be assigned to each terminal. A single program could maintain all the buffers by simply changing register ES to point to the buffer of the terminal requiring service.

Physical Address Generation

It is useful to think of every memory location as having two kinds of addresses — physical and logical. A physical address is the 20-bit value that uniquely identifies each byte location in the memory space. Physical addresses may range from 0H through FFFFFH. All exchanges between the CPU and memory components use this physical address.

Programs, however, deal with logical rather than physical addresses. The use of logical addresses allows code to be developed without prior knowledge of where the code is to be located in memory, and facilitates dynamic management of memory resources.

A logical address consists of a segment base value and an offset value. For any given memory location, the segment base value locates the first byte of the containing segment and the offset value is the distance, in bytes, of the target location from the beginning of the segment. Segment base and offset values are unsigned 16-bit quantities; the lowest-addressed byte in a segment has an offset of 0. Many different logical addresses can map to the same physical location as shown in Figure 3-12.

Whenever the BIU accesses memory—to fetch an instruction or to obtain or store a variable—it generates a physical address from a logical address. This is done by shifting the segment base value four bit positions and adding the offset as illustrated in Figure 3-13. This addition process provides for modulo 64K addressing (addresses wrap around from the end of a segment to the beginning of the same segment).

The BIU obtains the logical address of a memory location from different sources depending on the type of reference that is being made (see Table 3-3).

210911

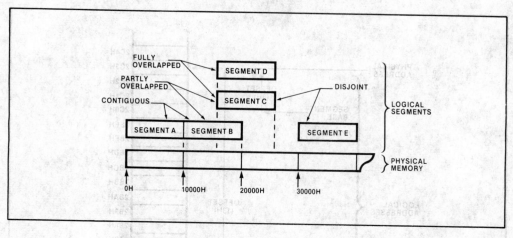

Figure 3-10 Segment Locations in Physical Memory

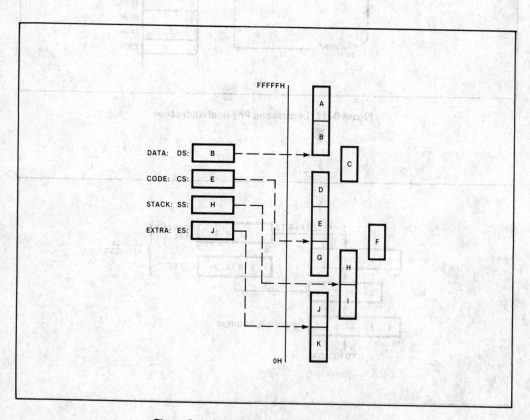

Figure 3-11 Currently Addressable Segments

210911

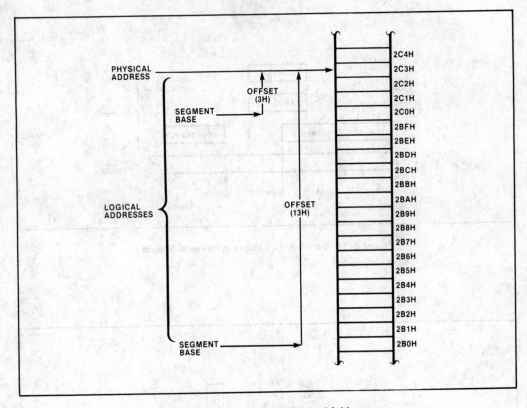

Figure 3-12 Logical and Physical Addresses

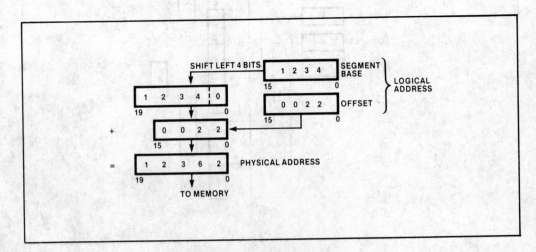

Figure 3-13 Physical Address Generation

210911

Table 3-3 Logical Address Sources

TYPE OF MEMORY REFERENCE	DEFAULT SEGMENT BASE	ALTERNATE SEGMENT BASE	OFFSET
Instruction Fetch	CS	NONE	IP
Stack Operation	SS	NONE	SP
Variable (exectp following)	DS	CS, ES, SS	Effective Address
String Souce	DS	CS, ES, SS	SI
String Destination	ES	NONE	DI
BP Used AS Base Register	SS	CS, DS, ES	Effective Address
BX Used As Base Register	DS	CS, ES, SS	Effective Address

Instructions are always fetched from the current code segment. The instruction pointer (IP) contains the offset of the target instruction from the beginning of the segment.

Stack instructions always operate on the current stack segment. The stack pointer (SP) contains the offset of the top of the stack. Most variables (memory operands) are assumed to reside in the current data segment, although a program can instruct the BIU to access a variable in one of the other currently addressable segments. The offset of a memory variable is calculated by the EU. This calculation is based on the addressing mode specified in the instruction; the result of the calculation is called the operand's effective address (EA). Section 3.6 covers addressing modes and effective address calculation in detail.

Strings are addressed differently from other variables. The source operand of a string instruction is assumed to lie in the current data segment, but another currently addressable segment may be specified. Its offset is taken from register SI, the source index register. The destination operand of a string instruction always resides in the current extra segment (ES). Its offset is taken from the DI, the destination index register. The string instructions automatically adjust SI and DI as they process the strings one byte or word at a time.

When register BP, the base pointer register, is designated as a base register in an instruction, the variable is assumed to reside in the current stack segment. Register BP thus provides a convenient way to address data on the stack. BP can be used, however, to access data in any of the other currently addressable segments.

In most cases, the BIU's segment assumptions are a convenience to the programmer, since they are based on the most frequent typical usage. It is possible, however, to explicitly direct the BIU to access a variable in any of the currently addressable segments (the only exception is the destination operand of a string instruction which must be in the extra segment). This is done by preceding an instruction with a segment override prefix. This one-byte machine instruction tells the BIU which segment register to use to access a variable referenced in the following instruction.

Dynamically Relocatable Code

The segmented memory structure of the 8086,88 and 80186,188 makes it possible to write programs that are position-independent, or dynamically relocatable. Dynamic relocation allows a multiprogramming or multitasking system to make particularly effective use of the available memory. Inactive programs can be written to disk, and the space they occupied allocated to other programs. If a disk-resident program is needed later, it can be read back into any available memory location and restarted. Similarly, if a program needs a large contiguous block of storage, and the total amount is available only in nonadjacent fragments, other program segments can be compacted to free up a continuous space. This process is shown graphically in Figure 3-14.

In order to be dynamically relocatable, a program must not load or alter its segment registers and must not transfer directly to a location outside the current code segment. In other words, all offsets in the program must be relative to fixed values contained in the segment registers. This allows the program to be moved anywhere in memory as long as the segment registers are updated to point to the new base addresses.

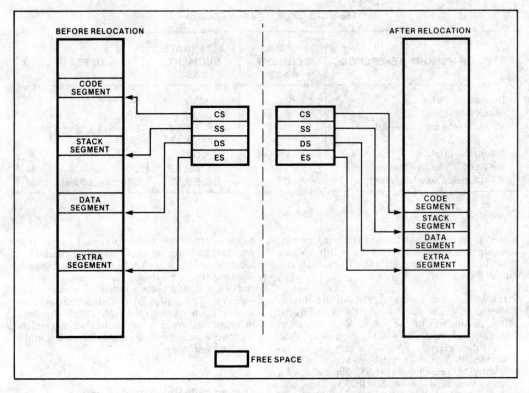

Figure 3-14 Dynamic Code Relocation

Stack Implementation

Stacks are located in memory and are accessed by the stack segment register (SS) and the stack pointer register (SP). A system may have an unlimited number of stacks, and a stack may be up to 64K bytes long, the maximum length of a segment. (An attempt to expand a stack beyond 64K bytes overwrites the beginning of the stack.) One stack is directly addressable at a time, the current stack, generally referred to simply as the stack. SS contains the base address of this stack and SP points to the top of the stack (TOS). In other words, SP contains the offset of the top of the stack from the stack segment's base address. The stack's base address (contained in SS), however, is not the bottom of the stack.

Stacks are 16-bits wide; thus, instructions that operate on stacks add and remove stack items one word at a time. A word is pushed onto the stack by *decrementing* SP by 2 and writing the item at the new TOS (see Figure 3-15). A word is popped off the stack by copying it from TOS and then *incrementing* SP by 2.

In other words, the stack grows *down* in memory towards its base address. Stack operations never move items on the stack, nor do they erase them. The top of the stack changes only as a result of updating the stack pointer.

Dedicated and Reserved Memory Locations

Two areas in extreme low and high memory are dedicated to specific processor functions or are reserved by Intel Corporation for use by Intel hardware and software products. As shown in Figure 3-16, the locations are: 0H through 7FH (128 bytes) and FFFF0H through FFFFFH (16 bytes). These areas are used for interrupt and system reset processing. Application systems should not use these areas for any other purpose. Doing so may make these systems incompatible with future Intel products.

As Figure 3-16 indicates, the 8086,88 and the 80186,188 processors differ in the proportion of dedicated to reserved locations.

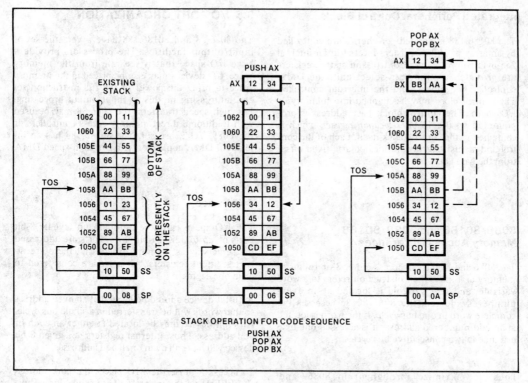

Figure 3-15 Stack Operation

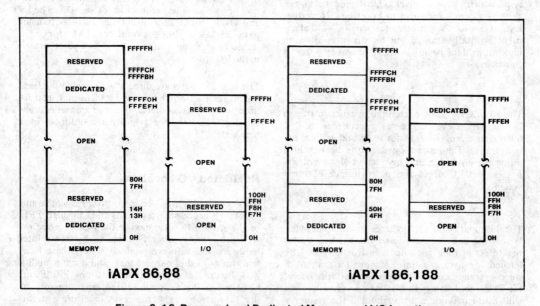

Figure 3-16 Reserved and Dedicated Memory and I/O Locations

Integrated Peripheral Control Block

The 80186,188 integrated peripherals are controlled by an array of 16-bit registers located in an internal 256-byte control block. Control and status registers are provided for the chip select unit, the DMA controller, the timers, and the interrupt controller. The control block may be mapped into memory or I/O space. The control block base address is programmed by the 16-bit *relocation register*, which is contained in the control block itself. Each of the control and status registers are located at a fixed offset from the base address.

8086/80186 and 8088/80188 Memory Access Differences

The 8086 and 80186 can access either 8 or 16 bits of memory at a time. If an instruction refers to a word variable, and that variable is located at an even-numbered address, the 8086/80186 accesses the complete word in one bus cycle. If the word is located at an odd-numbered address, it is accessed one byte at a time in two consecutive bus cycles.

Thus, to maximize throughput in 8086- and 80186-based systems, 16-bit data should be stored at even addresses (i.e., it should be word aligned). This is particularly true of stacks. Unaligned stacks can slow a system's response to interrupts. Nevertheless, except for the performance penalty, word alignment is totally transparent to software, allowing maximum data packing where memory space is constrained.

The 8086/80186 always fetch the instruction stream in words from even addresses, except that the first fetch after a program transfer to an odd address obtains a byte. The instruction stream is disassembled inside the processor, and instruction alignment will not materially affect the performance of most systems.

The 8088 and 80188 always access memory in bytes. Word operands are accessed in two bus cycles regardless of their alignment. Instructions are also fetched one byte at a time. Although alignment of word operands does not affect the performance of the 8088/188, locating 16-bit data on even addresses will insure maximum throughput if the system is ever transferred to an 8086 or 80186.

3.5 I/O PORT ORGANIZATION

The 8086,88 and 80186,188 have a versatile set of input/output facilities. The processors provide a large I/O space that is separate from the memory space. I/O devices may also be placed in the memory space to bring the power of the full instruction set and addressing modes to input/output processing. For high speed transfers, the 8086,88 may be used with traditional direct memory access controllers or the 8089 I/O Processor. The 80186,188 has an integrated DMA controller with two high-speed DMA channels.

I/O Space

The I/O space can accommodate up to 64K 8-bit ports or up to 32K 16-bit ports. Ports are addressed the same way as memory except that there are no port segment registers. All ports are considered to be in one segment.

A 16-bit device should be located at an even address so that words will be transferred in a single bus cycle. An 8-bit device may be located at either an even or odd address. Thus, internal registers in a given 8-bit device will have all even or all odd addresses.

To access a port, the BIU places the port address (0-FFFFH) on the lower 16 lines of the address bus. Different forms of the I/O instructions allow the address to be specified as a fixed value in the instruction or as a variable taken from register DX. The IN and OUT (input and output) instructions transfer data between the accumulator (AL for byte transfers, AX for word transfers) and ports located in the I/O space.

The first 256 ports are directly addressable (address in the instruction) by some input/output instructions; other instructions let the programmer address the total of 64K ports indirectly (address in a register).

Restricted I/O Locations

As shown in Figure 3-16, on both the 8086,88 and 80186,188 processors, locations F8H through FFH (eight of the 64K locations) in the I/O space are reserved by Intel Corporation for use by future Intel hardware and software products. Using these locations for any other purpose may inhibit compatibility with future Intel products. Locations FFFE and FFFF are dedicated, on the 80186,188 processors, to the relocation register's reset location. On the 8086,88 these locations are reserved.

210911

Memory-Mapped I/O

I/O devices may also be placed in the memory space. This memory-mapped I/O provides additional programming flexibility. Any instruction that references memory may be used to access an I/O port located in the memory space. A group of terminals, for example, could be treated as an array in memory, with an index register selecting one of the terminals in the array.

Memory reference instructions take longer to execute, however, and are less compact than the simpler IN and OUT instructions.

3.6 ADDRESSING MODES

The 8086,88 and 80186,188 provide many different ways of addressing operands. Operands may be contained in registers, within the instruction itself, in memory or in I/O ports. In addition, the addresses of memory and I/O port operands can be calculated in several different ways. These addressing modes greatly extend the flexibility and convenience of the instruction set.

Register and Immediate Operands

Instructions that specify only register operands are generally the most compact and fastest executing. This is because the register addresses are encoded in instructions in just a few bits, and because these operations are performed entirely within the CPU (no bus cycles are run). Registers may serve as source operands, destination operands, or both.

Immediate operands are constant data contained in an instruction. The data may be either 8 or 16 bits long. Immediate operands can be accessed quickly because they are available directly from the instruction queue; (as in the case of register operands, no bus cycles need to be run to obtain an immediate operand). The limitations of immediate operands are that they may only serve as source operands and that they are constant values.

Memory Addressing Modes

Unlike register and immediate operands, which are directly accessible to the EU, memory operands must be transferred to and from the CPU over the bus. When the EU needs to read or write a memory operand, it must pass an offset value to the BIU. The BIU adds the offset to the (shifted) contents of a segment register, producing a 20-bit physical address, and then executes the bus cycle(s) needed to access the operand.

The Effective Address

The offset that the EU calculates for a memory operand is called the operand's effective address or EA. It is an unsigned 16-bit number that expresses the operand's distance in bytes from the beginning of the segment in which it resides. The EU can calculate the effective address in several different ways. Information encoded in the second byte of the instruction tells the EU how to calculate the effective address of each memory operand. A compiler or assembler derives this information from the statement or instruction written by the programmer. Assembly language programmers have access to all addressing modes.

As shown in Figure 3-17, the EU calculates the EA by summing a displacement, the contents of a base register, and the contents of an index register. The fact that any combination of these three components may be present in a given instruction results in the great variety of memory addressing modes provided by the 8086,88 and 80186,188.

The displacement element is an 8- or 16-bit number that is contained in the instruction. The displacement generally is derived from the position of the operand name (a variable or label) in the program. The programmer can also modify this value or specify the displacement explicitly.

A programmer may specify that either BX or BP is to serve as a base register whose contents are to be used in the EA computation. Similarly, either SI or DI may be specified as an index register. Whereas the displacement value is a constant, the contents of the base and index registers may change during the execution. This makes it possible for one instruction to access different memory locations as determined by the current value in the base and/or index registers.

Effective address calculations with the BP are made, by default, using the SS register, though either the DS or the ES registers may be specified instead.

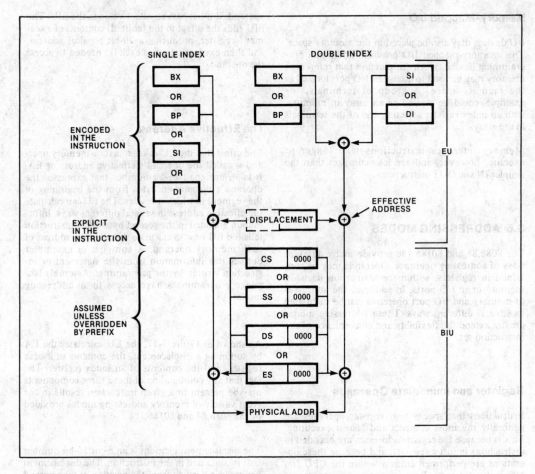

Figure 3-17 Memory Address Computation

Direct Addressing

Direct addressing (see Figure 3-18) is the simplest memory addressing mode. No registers are involved; the EA is taken directly from the displacement field of the instruction. Direct addressing typically is used to access simple variables (scalars).

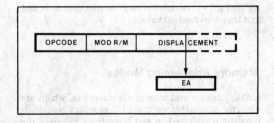

Figure 3-18 Direct Addressing

210911

Register Indirect Addressing

The EA of a memory operand may be taken directly from the BP, BX, SI or DI register (see Figure 3-19). One instruction can operate on many different memory locations if the value in the pointer or index register is updated appropriately. The load effective address (LEA) and arithmetic instructions might be used to change the register value.

Note that with the JMP and CALL instructions, any 16-bit general register may be used for register indirect addressing.

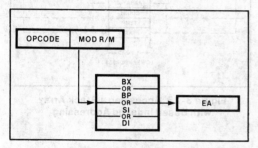

Figure 3-19 Register Indirect Addressing

Base Addressing

In base addressing (Figure 3-20), the effective address is the sum of a displacement value and the contents of register BX or register BP. Specifying BP as a base register directs the BIU to obtain the operand from the current stack segment (unless a segment override prefix is present). This makes base addressing with BP a very convenient way to access stack data.

When BX is used as the base register, the operand by default resides in the current Data Segment, and the DS register is used to compute the operand's EA.

Base addressing provides a straightforward way to address structures which may be located at different places in memory (see Figure 3-21). A base register can be set to point to the base of the structure, and elements of the structure can then be addressed by their displacement from the base. Different copies of the same structure can be accessed by simply changing the base register.

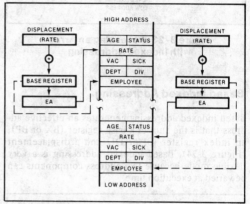

Figure 3-21 Accessing a Structure with Based Addressing

Indexed Addressing

In indexed addressing, the EA is calculated from the sum of a displacement and the contents of an index register, SI or DI, as shown in Figure 3-22. Indexed addressing is often used to access elements in an array (Figure 3-23). The displacement locates the beginning of the array, and the value of the index register selects one element (the first element is selected if the index register contains 0). Since all array elements are the same length, simple arithmetic on the index register will select any element.

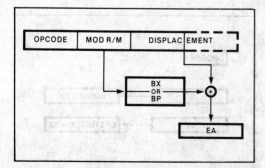

Figure 3-20 Based Addressing

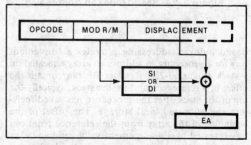

Figure 3-22 Indexed Addressing

210911

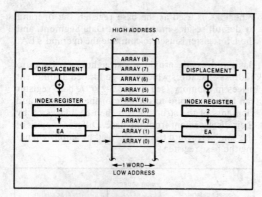

Figure 3-23 Accessing an Array with Indexed Addressing

Based Indexed Addressing

Based indexed addressing generates an effective address that is the sum of a base register (BX or BP), an index register (SI or DI) and a displacement (Figure 3-24). Based indexed addressing is a very flexible mode because two address components can be varied at execution time.

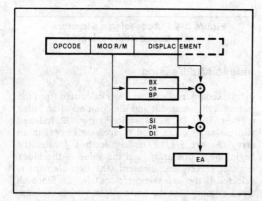

Figure 3-24 Based Indexed Addressing

Based indexed addressing provides a convenient way for a procedure to address an array allocated on a stack (Figure 3-25). Register BP can contain the offset of a reference point on the stack, typically the top of the stack after the procedure has saved registers and allocated local storage. The offset of the beginning of the array from the reference point can be expressed by a displacement value, and an index register can be used to access individual array elements.

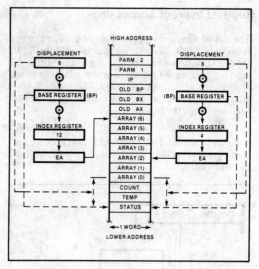

Figure 3-25 Accessing a Stack Array with Based Indexed Addressing

Arrays contained in structures and matrices (two-dimensional arrays) can also be accessed with based indexed addressing.

String Addressing

String instructions do not use the normal memory addressing modes to access their operands. Instead, the index registers are used implicitly as shown in Figure 3-26. When a string instruction is executed, SI is assumed to point to the first byte or word of the source string, and DI is assumed to point to the first byte or word of the destination string. In a repeated string operation, the CPU automatically adjusts SI and DI to obtain subsequent bytes or words.

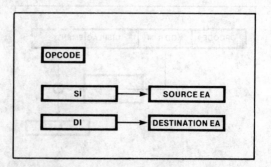

Figure 3-26 String Operand Addressing

210911

I/O Port Addressing

If an I/O port is memory mapped, any of the memory operand addressing modes may be used to access the port (for example, a group of terminals can be accessed as an array). String instructions can also be used to transfer data to memory-mapped ports with an appropriate hardware interface.

To access ports located in the I/O space, the two different addressing modes illustrated in Figure 3-27 can be used. In direct port addressing, the port number is an 8-bit immediate operand. This allows fixed access to ports numbered 0 to 255. Indirect port addressing is similar to register indirect addressing of memory operands. The port number is taken from register DX and can range from 0 to 65,535 (providing access to any port in the I/O space). A group of adjacent ports can be accessed using a simple software loop that adjusts the value in DX.

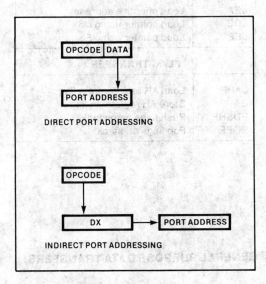

DIRECT PORT ADDRESSING

INDIRECT PORT ADDRESSING

Figure 3-27 I/O Port Addressing

3.7 THE INSTRUCTION SET

The 8086,88 and 80186,188 instructions include equivalents to the instructions typically found in such CPUs as the 8080 and 8085. Significant new instructions added by the 8086 are:

- multiplication and division of signed and unsigned binary numbers as well as unpacked decimal numbers,

- move, scan and compare operations for strings up to 64K bytes in length,

- non-destructive bit testing,

- byte translation from one code to another,

- additional software-generated interrupts, and

- a group of instructions that can help coordinate the activities of multiprocessor systems.

In addition to these instructions, the 80186,188 provides ten new instruction types that serve to streamline existing code or produce optimum iAPX 186 code.

All instructions treat different types of operands uniformly. Nearly every instruction can operate on either byte or word data. Register, memory and immediate operands may be specified interchangeably in most instructions. The exception is that immediate values may only serve as source and not destination operands. In particular, memory variables can be added to, subtracted from, shifted, compared, and so on, in place, without moving them in and out of registers. This saves instructions, registers, and execution time in assembly language programs. In high-level languages, where most variables are memory-based, compilers, such as PL/M-86, can produce faster and shorter object programs.

The instruction set can be viewed as existing at two levels: the assembly level and the machine level. To the assembly language programmer the 8086 and 80186 appear to have about 100 instructions. One MOV (move) instruction, for example, transfers a byte or a word from a register or a memory location or an immediate value to either a register or a memory location. The CPUs, however, recognize 28 different MOV machine instructions (move byte register to memory, move word immediate to register, etc.). The ASM-86 assembler translates the assembly-level instructions written by a programmer into the machine-level instructions that are actually executed by the CPU. Compilers such as the PL/M-86 translate high-level language statements directly into machine-level instructions.

The two levels of the instruction set address two different requirements: efficiency and simplicity. The numerous—about 300 in all—forms of machine-level instructions allow these instructions to make very efficient use of storage. For example, the machine instruction that increments a memory operand is three or four bytes long because the address of the operand must be encoded in the instruction. To

210911

increment a register, however, does not require as much information, so the instruction can be shorter. In fact, the 8086,88 and 80186,188 have eight different machine-level instructions that increment a different 16-bit register; these instructions are only one byte long.

This section presents the instruction set from two perspectives. First, the assembly-level instructions are described in functional terms. They are then presented in a reference table format that specifies all permissible operand combinations, provides execution times and machine instruction length, and shows the effect that the instruction has on the CPU flags.

The details of the syntax of the instruction set are described fully in Intel's "ASM86 Language Reference Manual," #121703. A shorter treatment of the assembly language can be found in Intel's "An Introduction to ASM 86" manual, #121689.

Instruction Set Organization

The instructions are divided into the following functional groups:

- Data transfer
- Arithmetic
- Bit manipulation
- String manipulation
- Control transfer
- High-level (186,188 only)
- Processor control

Data Transfer Instructions

The data transfer instructions (Table 3-4) move single bytes, words, and doublewords between memory and registers, as well as between register AL or AX and I/O ports. The stack manipulation instructions are included in this group, as are instructions for transferring flag contents and for loading segment registers.

Sub-groups of the data transfer instructions are the general purpose data transfer, I/O, address object, and flag transfer instructions.

Table 3-4 Data Transfer Instructions

GENERAL PURPOSE	
MOV	Move byte or word
PUSH	Push word onto stack
POP	Pop word off stack
PUSHA	Push all registers on stack
POPA	Pop all registers from stack
XCHG	Exchange byte or word
XLAT	Translate byte

INPUT/OUTPUT	
IN	Input byte or word
OUT	Output byte or word

ADDRESS OBJECT	
LEA	Load effective address
LDS	Load pointer using DS
LES	Load pointer using ES

FLAG TRANSFER	
LAHF	Load AH register from flags
SAHF	Store AH register in flags
PUSHF	Push flags onto stack
POPF	Pop flags off stack

GENERAL PURPOSE DATA TRANSFERS:

MOV destination, source

MOV transfers a byte or a word from the source operand to the destination operand.

PUSH source

PUSH decrements SP (the stack pointer) by two and then transfers a word from the source operand to the top of the stack now pointed to by SP. PUSH is often used to place parameters on the stack before calling a procedure; more generally, it is the basic means of storing temporary data on the stack.

PUSH immediate (186,188 only)

The PUSH (push immediate) instruction allows immediate data to be pushed onto the stack. The data can be either immediate byte or immediate word. Byte data will be sign extended to word size before it is pushed onto the stack (since all stack operations are done on word data).

POP destination

POP transfers the word at the current top of stack (pointed to by SP) to the destination operand, and then increments SP by two to point to the new top of the stack. POP can be used to move temporary variables from the stack to registers or memory.

PUSHA/POPA (186,188 only)

These instructions (push all, pop all) allow all CPU general purpose registers to be stored and restored. The PUSHA instruction pushes all CPU registers onto the stack, and the POPA instruction pops all CPU registers from the stack. The order in which the registers are saved is: AX, CX, DX, BX, SP, BP, SI and DI. The SP value pushed is the SP value before the first register (AX) is pushed. When the POPA instruction is executed, the SP value is popped, but the value is discarded.

Note that this instruction does not save any of the segment registers (CS, DS, SS, ES), the instruction pointer (IP), the flag register, or any of the integrated peripheral registers.

XCHG destination, source

XCHG (exchange) switches the contents of the source and destination (byte or word) operands. When used in conjunction with the LOCK prefix, XCHG can test and set a semaphore that controls access to a resource shared by multiple processors.

XLAT translate-table

XLAT (translate) replaces a byte in the AL register with a byte from a 256-byte, user-coded translation table. Register BX is assumed to point to the beginning of the table. The byte in AL is used as an index into the table and is replaced by the byte at the offset in the table corresponding to AL's binary value. The first byte in the table has an offset of 0. For example, if AL contains 5H, and the sixth element of the translation table contains 33H, then AL will contain 33H following the instruction. XLAT is useful for translating characters from one code to another, such as ASCII to EBCDIC or the reverse.

INPUT/OUTPUT:

IN accumulator, port

IN transfers a byte or a word from an input port to the AL register or the AX register respectively. The port number may be specified either with an immediate byte constant, allowing access to ports numbered 0 through 255, or with a number previously placed in the DX register, allowing variable access (by changing the value in DX) to ports numbered from 0 through 65,535.

OUT port, accumulator

OUT transfers a byte or a word from the AL register or the AX register, respectively, to an output port. The port number may be specified either with an immediate byte constant, allowing access to ports numbered 0 through 255, or with a number previously placed in register DX, allowing variable access (by changing the value in DX) to ports numbered from 0 through 65,535.

ADDRESS OBJECT TRANSFERS:

These instructions manipulate the addresses of variables rather than the contents or values of variables. They are most useful for list processing, based variables, and string operations.

LEA destination, source

LEA (load effective address) transfers the offset of the source operand (rather than its value) to the destination operand. The source operand must be a memory operand, and the destination operand must be a 16-bit general register. LEA does not affect any flags. The XLAT and string instructions assume that certain registers point to operands. LEA can be used to load these registers (e.g., loading BX with the address of the translate table used by the XLAT instruction).

LDS *destination, source*

LDS (load pointer using DS) transfers a 32-bit pointer variable from the source operand, which must be a memory operand, to the destination operand and register DS. The offset word of the pointer is transferred to the destination operand, which may be any 16-bit general register. The segment word of the pointer is transferred to register DS. Specifying SI as the destination operand is a convenient way to prepare to process a source string that is not in the current data segment (string instructions assume that the source string is located in the current data segment and that SI contains the offset of the string).

LES *destination, source*

LES (load pointer using ES) transfers a 32-bit pointer variable from the source operand, which must be a memory operand, to the destination operand and register ES. The offset word of the pointer is transferred to the destination operand, which may be any 16-bit register. The segment word of the pointer is transferred to register ES. Specifying DI as the destination operand is a convenient way to prepare to process a destination string that is not in the current extra segment. (The destination string must be located in the extra segment, and DI must contain the offset of the string.)

FLAG TRANSFERS:

LAFH

LAHF (load register AH from flags) copies SF, ZF, AF, PF and CF (the 8080/8085 flags) into bits 7, 6, 4, 2 and 0 respectively, of register AH (see Figure 3-28). The contents of bits 5, 3 and 1 is undefined; the flags themselves are not affected. LAHF is provided primarily for converting 8080/8085 assembly language programs to run on 8086 and 80186 CPUs.

SAHF

SAHF (store register AH into flags) transfers bits 7, 6, 4, 2 and 0 from register AH into SF, ZF, AF, PF and CF respectively, replacing whatever values these flags previously had. OF, DF, IF and TF are not affected. This instruction is provided for 8080/8085 compatibility.

PUSHF

PUSHF decrements SP (the stack pointer) by two and then transfers all flags to the word at the top of stack pointed to by SP (see Figure 3-28). The flags themselves are not affected.

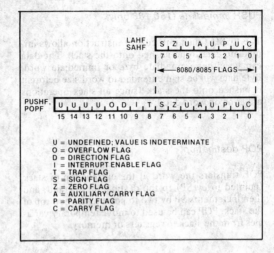

Figure 3-28 Flag Storage Formats

POPF

POPF transfers specific bits from the word at the current top of stack (pointed to by register SP) into flags, replacing whatever values the flags previously contained (see Figure 3-28). SP is then incremented by two to point to the new top of stack. PUSHF and POPF allow a procedure to save and restore a calling program's flags.

Arithmetic Instructions

Arithmetic operations (Table 3-5) may be performed on four types of numbers: unsigned binary, signed binary (integers), unsigned packed decimal and unsigned unpacked decimal (see Table 3-6). Binary numbers may be 8 or 16 bits long. Decimal numbers are stored in bytes, two digits per byte for packed decimal and one digit per byte for unpacked decimal. The processor always assumes that the operands specified in arithmetic instructions contain data that represents valid numbers for the type of instruction being performed. Invalid data may produce unpredictable results.

Unsigned binary numbers may be either 8 or 16 bits long; all bits are considered in determining a number's magnitude. The value range of an 8-bit unsigned binary number is 0-255. Values from 0 to 65,535 can be represented by 16 bits. Addition, subtraction, multiplication and division operations are available for unsigned binary numbers.

210911

Table 3-5 Arithmetic Instructions

ADDITION	
ADD	Add byte or word
ADC	Add byte or word with carry
INC	Increment byte or word by 1
AAA	ASCII adjust for addition
DAA	Decimal adjust for addition
SUBTRACTION	
SUB	Subtract byte or word
SBB	Subtract byte or word with borrow
DEC	Decrement byte or word by 1
NEG	Negate byte or word
CMP	Compare byte or word
AAS	ASCII adjust for subtraction
DAS	Decimal adjust for subtraction
MULTIPLICATION	
MUL	Multiply byte or word unsigned
IMUL	Integer multiply byte or word
AAM	ASCII adjust for multiply
DIVISION	
DIV	Divide byte or word unsigned
IDIV	Integer divide byte or word
AAD	ASCII adjust for division
CBW	Convert byte to word
CWD	Convert word to doubleword

Signed binary numbers (integers) may be 8 or 16 bits long. The high-order (leftmost) bit is interpreted as the number's sign: 0 = positive and 1 = negative. Negative numbers are represented in standard two's complement notation. Since the high-order bit is used as a sign, the range of an 8-bit integer is -128 through $+127$; 16-bit integers may range from $-32,768$ through $+32,767$. The value of zero has a positive sign. Multiplication and division operations are provided for signed binary numbers. Addition and subtraction are performed with the unsigned binary instructions. Conditional jump instructions, as well as an "interrupt on overflow" instruction, can be used following an unsigned operation on an integer to detect overflow into the sign bit.

Packed decimal numbers are stored as unsigned byte quantities. The byte is treated as having one decimal digit in each half-byte (nibble); the digit in the high-order half-byte is the most significant. Hexadecimal values 0-9 are valid in each half-byte, and the range of a packed decimal number is 0-99. Addition and subtraction are performed in two steps. First an unsigned binary instruction is used to produce an intermediate result in register AL. Then an adjustment operation is performed which changes the intermediate value in AL to a final correct packed decimal result. Multiplication and division adjustment are not available for packed decimal numbers.

Unpacked decimal numbers are stored as unsigned byte quantities. The magnitude of the number is determined from the low-order half-byte. Hexadecimal values 0-9 are valid and are interpreted as decimal numbers. The high-order half-byte must be zero for multiplication and division; it may contain any value for addition and subtraction. Arithmetic operations on unpacked decimal numbers are performed in two steps. The unsigned binary addition, subtraction and multiplication operations are used to produce an intermediate result in register AL. An adjustment instruction then changes the value in AL to a final correct unpacked decimal number. Division is performed similarly, except that the adjustment is carried out on the numerator operand in register AL first, and then a following unsigned binary division instruction produces a correct result.

Table 3-6 Arithmetic Interpretation of 8-Bit Numbers

HEX	BIT PATTERN	UNSIGNED BINARY	SIGNED BINARY	UNPACKED DECIMAL	PACKED DECIMAL
07	00000111	7	+7	7	7
89	10001001	137	−119	invalid	89
C5	11000101	197	−59	invalid	invalid

210911

Unpacked decimal numbers are similar to the ASCII character representations of the digits 0-9. Note, however, that the high-order half-byte of an ASCII numeral is always 3H. Unpacked decimal arithmetic may be performed on ASCII numeric characters under the following conditions:

- the high-order half-byte of an ASCII numeral must be set to 0H prior to multiplication or division.

- unpacked decimal arithmetic leaves the high-order half-byte set to 0H; it must be set to 3H to produce a valid ASCII numeral.

ARITHMETIC INSTRUCTIONS AND FLAGS

Arithmetic instructions post certain characteristics of the result of the operation to six flags. Most of these flags can be tested by following the arithmetic instruction with a conditional jump instruction, and the INTO (interrupt on overflow) instruction may also be used. The various instructions affect the flags differently, as explained in the instruction descriptions. However, they follow these general rules:

- **CF (carry flag):** If an addition results in a carry out of the high-order bit of the result, then CF is set; otherwise CF is cleared. If a subtraction results in a borrow into the high-order bit of the result, then CF is set; otherwise CF is cleared. Note that a signed carry is indicated by CF = OF (overflow flag). CF can be used to detect an unsigned overflow. Two instructions, ADC (add with carry) and SBB (subtract with borrow), incorporate the carry flag in their operations and can be used to perform multibyte (e.g., 32-bit, 64-bit) addition and subtraction.

- **AF (auxiliary carry flag):** If an addition results in a carry out of the low-order half-byte of the result, then AF is set; otherwise AF is cleared. If a subtraction results in a borrow into the low-order half-byte of the result, then AF is set; otherwise AF is cleared. The auxiliary carry flag is provided for the decimal adjust instructions and ordinarily is not used for any other purpose.

- **SF (sign flag):** Arithmetic and logical instructions set the sign flag equal to the high-order bit (bit 7 or 15) of the result. For signed binary numbers, the sign flag will be 0 for positive results and 1 for negative results (so long as overflow does not occur). A conditional jump instruction can be used following addition or subtraction to alter the flow of the program depending on the sign of the result. Programs performing unsigned operations typically ignore SF since the high-order bit of the result is interpreted as a digit rather than a sign.

- **ZF (zero flag):** If the result of an arithmetic or logical operation is zero, then ZF is set; otherwise ZF is cleared. A conditional jump instruction can be used to alter the flow of the program if the result is or is not zero.

- **PF (parity flag):** If the low-order eight bits of an arithmetic or logical result contain an even number of 1- bits, then the parity flag is set; otherwise it is cleared. PF is provided for 8080/8085 compatibility. It can also be used to check ASCII characters for correct parity.

- **OF (overflow flag):** If the result of an operation is too large a positive number, or too small a negative number to fit in the destination operand (excluding the sign bit), then OF is set; otherwise OF is cleared. OF thus indicates signed arithmetic overflow. It can be tested with a conditional jump or the INTO (interrupt on overflow) instruction. OF may be ignored when performing unsigned arithmetic. OF is set if the operation results in a carry into the high-order bit of the result but not a carry out of the high-order bit, or vice versa; otherwise OF is cleared.

ADDITION

ADD *destination, source*

The sum of two operands, which may be bytes or words, replaces the destination operand. Both operands may be signed or unsigned binary numbers (see AAA and DAA). ADD updates AF, CF, OF, PF, SF and ZF.

ADC *destination, source*

ADC (add with carry) sums the operands, which may be bytes or words, adds one if CF is set and replaces the destination operand with the result. Both operands may be signed or unsigned binary numbers (see AAA and DAA). ADC updates AF, CF, OF, PF, SF and ZF. Since ADC incorporates a carry from a previous operation, it can be used to write routines to add numbers longer than 16 bits.

INC *destination*

INC (increment) adds one to the destination operand. The operand may be a byte or a word and is treated as an unsigned binary number (see AAA and DAA). INC updates AF, OF, PF, SF and ZF; it does not effect CF.

AAA

AAA (ASCII adjust for addition) changes the contents of register AL to a valid unpacked decimal number; the high-order half-byte is zeroed. AAA updates AF and CF; the contents of OF, PF, SF and ZF is undefined following execution of AAA.

DAA

DAA (decimal adjust for addition) corrects the result of previously adding two valid packed decimal operands (the destination operand must have been register AL). DAA changes the contents of AL to a pair of valid packed decimal digits. It updates AF, CF, PF, SF and ZF; the contents of OF is undefined following execution of DAA.

SUBTRACTION

SUB *destination, source*

The source operand is subtracted from the destination operand, and the result replaces the destination operand. The operands may be signed or unsigned binary numbers (see AAS and DAS). SUB updates AF, CF, OF, PF, SF and ZF.

SBB *destination, source*

SBB (subtract with borrow) subtracts the source from the destination, subtracts one if CF is set, and returns the result to the destination operand. Both operands may be bytes or words. Both operands may be signed or unsigned binary numbers (see AAS and DAS). SBB updates AF, CF, OF, PF, SF and ZF. Since it incorporates a borrow from a previous operation, SBB may be used to write routines that subtract numbers longer than 16 bits.

DEC *destination*

DEC (decrement) subtracts one from the destination, which may be a byte or a word. DEC updates AF, OF, PF, SF and ZF; it does not affect CF.

NEG *destination*

NEG (negate) subtracts the destination operand, which may be a byte or a word, from 0 and returns the result to the destination. This forms the two's complement of the number, effectively reversing the sign of an integer. If the operand is zero, its sign is not changed. Attempting to negate a byte containing -128 or a word containing $-32,768$ causes no change to the operand and sets OF. NEG updates AF, CF, OF, PF, SF and ZF. CF is always set except when the operand is zero, in which case it is cleared.

CMP *destination, source*

CMP (compare) subtracts the source from the destination, which may be bytes or words, but does not return the result. The operands are unchanged, but the flags are updated and can be tested by a subsequent conditional jump instruction. CMP updates AF, CF, OF, PF, SF and ZF. The comparison reflected in the flags is that of the destination to the source. If a CMP instruction is followed by a JG (jump if greater) instruction, for example, the jump is taken if the destination operand is greater than the source operand.

AAS

AAS (ASCII adjust for subtraction) corrects the result of a previous subtraction of two valid unpacked decimal operands (the destination operand must have been specified as register AL). AAS changes the contents of AL to a valid unpacked decimal number; the high-order half-byte is zeroed. AAS updates AF and CF; the contents of OF, PF, SF and ZF is undefined following execution of AAS.

DAS

DAS (decimal adjust for subtraction) corrects the results of a previous subtraction of two valid packed decimal operands (the destination operand must have been specified as register AL). DAS changes the contents of AL to a pair of valid packed decimal digits. DAS updates AF, CF, PF, SF and ZF; the contents of OF is undefined following execution of DAS.

MULTIPLICATION

MUL *source*

MUL (multiply) performs an unsigned multiplication of the source operand and the accumulator. If the source is a byte, then it is multiplied by register

AL, and the double-length result is returned in AH and AL. If the source operand is a word, then it is multiplied by register AX, and the double-length result is returned in registers DX and AX. The operands are treated as unsigned binary numbers (see AAM). If the upper half of the results (AH for byte source, DX for word source) is nonzero, CF and OF are set; otherwise they are cleared. When CF and OF are set, they indicate that AH or DX contains significant digits of the result. The contents of AF, PF, SF and ZF is undefined following execution of MUL.

IMUL source

IMUL (integer multiply) performs a signed multiplication of the source operand and the accumulator. If the source is a byte, then it is multiplied by register AL, and the double-length result is returned in register AH and AL. If the source is a word, then it is multiplied by register AX, and the double-length result is returned in registers DX and AX. If the upper half of the result (AH for byte source, DX for word source) is not the sign extension of the lower half of the result, CF and OF are set; otherwise they are cleared. When CF and OF are set, they indicate that AH or DX contains significant digits of the result. The content of AF, PF, SF and ZF is undefined following execution of IMUL.

IMUL destination-register, source, immediate (186,188 only)

The IMUL (integer immediate multiply, signed) instruction allows a value to be multiplied by an immediate value. This value may be a byte or word; if it is a byte, it will be sign extended to 16 bits. When this instruction is used, only the lower 16 bits of the result will be saved. The result must always be placed in one of the general purpose registers. The two operands are the immediate value, and the data at an effective address (which may be the same register in which the result will be placed, another register, or a memory location). This instruction requires three arguments: the immediate value, the effective address of the second operand, and the register in which the result is to be placed.

AAM

AAM (ASCII adjust for multiply) corrects the result of a previous multiplication of two valid unpacked decimal operands. A valid 2-digit unpacked decimal number is derived from the content of AH and AL and is returned to AH and AL. The high-order half-bytes of the multiplied operands must have been 0H for AAM to produce a correct result. AAM updates PF, SF and ZF; the content of AF, CF and OF is undefined following execution of AAM.

DIVISION

DIV source

DIV (divide) performs an unsigned division of the accumulator (and its extension) by the source operand. If the source operand is a byte, it is divided into the double-length dividend assumed to be in register AH and AL. The single-length quotient is returned in AL, and the single-length remainder in AH. If the source operand is a word, it is divided into the double-length dividend in registers DX and AX. The single-length quotient is returned in AX, and the single-length remainder is returned in DX. If the quotient exceeds the capacity of its destination register (FFH for byte source, 0FFFFH for word source), as when division by zero is attempted, a type 0 interrupt is generated, and the quotient and the remainder are undefined. Nonintegral quotients are truncated to integers. The content of AF, CF, OF, PF, SF and ZF is undefined following execution of DIV.

IDIV source

IDIV (integer divide) performs a signed division of the accumulator (and its extension) by the source operand. If the source operand is a byte, it is divided into the double-length dividend assumed to be in registers AH and AL. The single-length quotient is returned in AL, and the single-length remainder is returned in AH. For byte integer division, the maximum positive quotient is +127 (7FH) and the minimum negative quotient is −127 (81H). If the source operand is a word, it is divided into the double-length dividend in registers DX and AX (the high-order 16 bits are in DX and the low-order 16 bits in AX). The single-length quotient is returned in AX, and the the single-length remainder is returned in DX. For word integer division, the maximum positive quotient is +32,767 (7FFFH) and the minimum negative quotient is −32,767 (8001H). If the quotient is positive and exceeds the maximum, or is negative and is less then the minimum, the quotient and the remainder are undefined, and a type 0 interrupt is generated. In particular, this occurs if division by 0 is attempted. Nonintegral quotients are truncated (toward 0) to integers, and the remainder has the same sign as the dividend. The content of AF, CF, OF, PF, SF and ZF is undefined following execution of IDIV.

AAD

AAD (ASCII adjust for division) modifies the numerator in AL before dividing two valid unpacked decimal operands so that the quotient produced by the division will be a valid unpacked decimal number. AH must be zero for the subsequent DIV to produce the correct result. The quotient is returned in AL, and the remainder is returned in AH; both high-order half-bytes are zeroed. AAD updates PF, SF and ZF; the content of AF, CF and OF is undefined following execution of AAD.

CBW

CBW (convert byte to word) extends the sign of the byte in register AL throughout register AH. CBW does not affect any flags. CBW can be used to produce a double-length (word) dividend from a byte prior to performing byte division.

CWD

CWD (convert word to doubleword) extends the sign of the word in register AX throughout register DX. CWD does not affect any flags. CWD can be used to produce a double-length (doubleword) dividend from a word prior to performing word division.

Bit Manipulation Instructions

Three groups of instructions (Table 3-7) are available for manipulating bits within both bytes and words: logical, shift and rotates.

Table 3-7 Bit Manipulation Instructions

LOGICALS	
NOT	"Not" byte or word
AND	"And" byte or word
OR	"Inclusive or" byte or word
XOR	"Exclusive or" byte or word
TEST	"Test" byte or word
SHIFTS	
SHL/SAL	Shift logical/arithmetic left byte or word
SHR	Shift logical right byte or word
SAR	Shift arithmetic right byte or word
ROTATES	
ROL	Rotate left byte or word
ROR	Rotate right byte or word
RCL	Rotate through carry left byte or word
RCR	Rotate through carry right byte or word

LOGICAL

The logical instructions include the boolean operators "not," "and,". "inclusive or," and "exclusive or," plus a TEST instruction that sets the flags, but does not alter either of its operands.

AND, OR, XOR and TEST affect the flags as follows:

The overflow (OF) and carry (CF) flags are always cleared by logical instructions, and the contents of the auxiliary carry (AF) flag is always undefined following execution of a logical instruction.

The sign (SF), zero (ZF) and parity (PF) flags are always posted to reflect the result of the operation and can be tested by conditional jump instructions. The interpretation of these flags is the same as for arithmetic instructions. SF is set if the result is negative (high-order bit is 1), and is cleared if the result is positive (high-order bit is 0). ZF is set if the result is zero, cleared otherwise. PF is set if the lower 8-bits of the result contains an even number of 1-bits (has even parity) and is cleared if the number of 1-bits is odd (the result has odd parity).

Note that NOT has no effect on the flags.

NOT *destination*

NOT inverts the bits (forms the one's complement) of the byte or word operand.

AND *destination, source*

AND performs the logical "and" of the two operands (byte or word) and returns the result to the destination operand. A bit in the result is set if both corresponding bits of the original operands are set; otherwise the bit is cleared.

OR *destination, source*

OR performs the logical "inclusive or" of the two operands (byte or word) and returns the result to the destination operand. A bit in the result is set if either or both corresponding bits in the original operands are set; otherwise the result bit is cleared.

XOR *destination, source*

XOR (exclusive or) performs the logical "exclusive or" of the two operands and returns the result to the destination operand. A bit in the result is set if the corresponding bits of the original operands contain opposite values (one is set, the other is cleared); otherwise the result bit is cleared.

TEST *destination, source*

TEST performs the logical "and" of the two operands (byte or word), updates the flags, but does not return the result, i.e., neither operand is changed. If a TEST instruction is followed by a JNZ (jump if not zero) instruction, the jump will be taken if there are any corresponding 1-bits in both operands.

SHIFTS

The bits in bytes and words may be shifted arithmetically or logically. On the 8086,88 up to 255 shifts may be performed, according to the value of the count operand coded in the instruction. The count may be specified as the constant 1, or as register CL, allowing the shift count to be a variable supplied at execution time. In addition, the 80186,188 allow the number of shifts to be specified as an immediate value in the instruction. This eliminates the need for a MOV immediate to the CL register if the number of shifts required is known at assembly time. Before the 80186,188 perform a shift (or rotate) they AND the value to be shifted with 1FH, thus limiting the number of shifts occurring to 32 bits.

Arithmetic shifts may be used to multiply and divide binary numbers by powers of two (see note in description of SAR). Logical shifts can be used to isolate bits in bytes or words.

Shift instructions affect the flags as follows:

AF is always undefined following a shift operation. PF, SF and ZF are updated normally, as in the logical instructions. CF always contains the value of the last bit shifted out of the destination operand. The contents of OF is always undefined following a multibit shift. In a single-bit shift, OF is set if the value of the high-order (sign) bit was changed by the operation; if the sign bit retains its original value, OF is cleared.

SHL/SAL *destination, count*

SHL and SAL (shift logical left and shift arithmetic left) perform the same operation and are physically the same instruction. The destination byte or word is shifted left by the number of bits specified in the count operand. Zeroes are shifted in on the right. If the sign bit retains its original value, then OF is cleared.

SHR *destination, source*

SHR (shift logical right) shifts the bits in the destination operand (byte or word) to the right by the number of bits specified in the count operand. Zeros are shifted in on the left. If the sign bit retains its original value, then OF is cleared.

SAR *destination, count*

SAR (shift arithmetic right) shifts the bits in the destination operand (byte or word) to the right by the number of bits specified in the count operand. Bits equal to the original high-order (sign) bit are shifted in on the left, preserving the sign of the original value. Note that SAR does not produce the same result as the dividend of an "equivalent" IDIV instruction if the destination operand is negative and 1-bits are shifted out. For example, shifting -5 right by one bit yields -3, while integer division of -5 by 2 yields -2. The difference in the instructions is that IDIV truncates all numbers toward zero, while SAR truncates positive numbers toward zero and negative numbers toward negative infinity.

ROTATES

Bits in bytes and words may also be rotated. Bits rotated out of an operand are not lost as in a shift, but are "circled" back into the other "end" of the operand. As in the shift instructions, the number of bits to be rotated is taken from the count operand, which may specify either a constant 1, or the CL register. The carry flag may act as an extension of the operand in two of the rotate instructions, allowing a bit to be isolated in CF and then tested by a JC (jump if carry) or JNC (jump if not carry) instruction.

Rotates affect only the carry and overflow flags. CF always contains the value of the last bit rotated out. On multibit rotates, the value of OF is Always undefined. In single-bit rotates, OF is set if the operation changes the high-order (sign) bit of the destination operand. If the sign bit retains its original value, OF is cleared.

ROL *destination, count*

ROL (rotate left) rotates the destination byte or word by the number of bits specified in the count operand.

ROR *destination, count*

ROR (rotate right) operates similar to ROL except that the bits in the destination byte or word are rotated right instead of left.

RCL *destination, count*

RCL (rotate through carry left) rotates the bits in the byte or word destination operand to the left by the number of bits specified in the count operand.

The carry flag (CF) is treated as "part of" the destination operand; that is, its value is rotated into the low-order bit of the destination, and itself is replaced by the high-order bit of the destination.

RCR destination, count

RCR (rotate through carry right) operates exactly like RCL except that the bits are rotated right instead of left.

Immediate Shifts/Rotates

All the shift/rotate instructions of the 80186,188 allow the number of bits shifted to be specified by an immediate value. These instructions require two operands: the operand to be shifted (which may be a register or a memory location specified by any of the addressing modes) and the number of bits to be shifted.

String Instructions

The basic string instructions, also called primitives, operate on strings of bytes or words, one element (byte or word) at a time. Strings of up to 128K bytes may be manipulated with these instructions. Instructions are available to move, compare and scan for a value, as well as for moving string elements to and from the accumulator, and, in the case of the 80186,188, to and from I/O ports (see Table 3-8). These basic operations may be preceded by a special one-byte prefix that causes the instruction to be repeated by the hardware, processing long strings much faster than would be possible with a software loop. The repetitions can be terminated by a variety of conditions, and a repeated operation may be interrupted and resumed.

The string instructions operate similarly in many respects; the common characteristics are covered here and in Table 3-9 and in Figure 3-29, rather than in the descriptions of the individual instructions. A string instruction may have a source operand, a destination operand, or both. The hardware assumes that a source string resides in the current data segment; a segment prefix byte may be used to override this assumption. A destination string must be in the current extra segment. The assembler checks the attributes of the operands to determine if the elements of the strings are bytes or words. The assembler does not, however, use the operand names to address the strings. Rather, the contents of register

Table 3-8 String Instructions

REP	Repeat
REPE/REPZ	Repeat while equal/zero
REPNE/REPNZ	Repeat while not equal/not zero
MOVS	Move byte or word string
MOVSB/MOVSW	Move byte or word string
CMPS	Compare byte or word string
INS	Move byte or word string from I/O port
OUTS	Move byte or word string to I/O port
SCAS	Scan byte or word string
LODS	Load byte or word string
STOS	Store byte or word string

SI (source index) is used as an offset to address the current element of the source string, and the contents of register DI (destination index) is taken as the offset of the current destination string element. These registers must be initialized to point to the source/destination strings before executing the string instruction; the LDS, LES and LEA instructions are useful in this regard.

Table 3-9 String Instruction Register and Flag Use

SI	Index (offset) for source string
DI	Index (offset) for destination string
DX	Port Address
CX	Repetition counter
AL/AX	Scan value Destination for LODS Source for STOS
DF	0 = auto-increment SI, DI 1 = auto-decrement SI, DI
ZF	Scan/compare terminator

210911

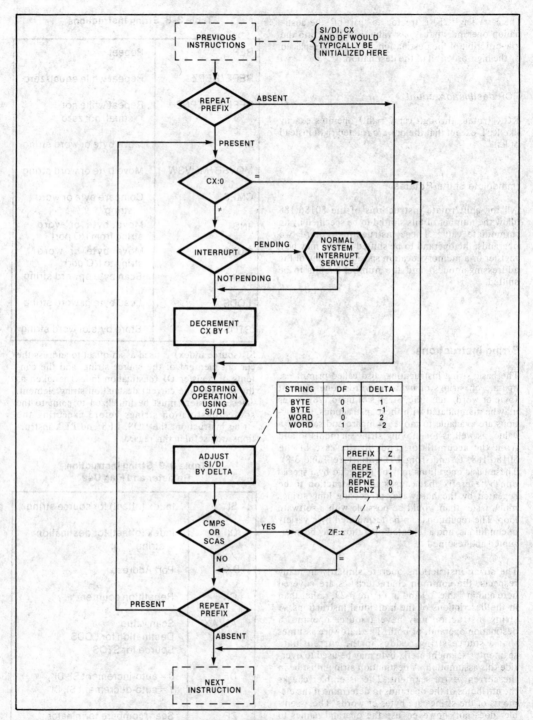

Figure 3-29 String Operation Flow

The string instructions automatically update SI and/or DI in anticipation of processing the next string element. The setting of DF (direction flag) determines whether the index registers are auto-incremented (DF=0) or auto-decremented (DF=1). If byte strings are being processed, SI and/or DI is adjusted by 1. The adjustment is 2 for word strings.

If a repeat prefix has been coded, then register CX (count register) is decremented by 1 after each repetition of the string instruction. CX must be initialized to the number of repetitions desired before the string instruction is executed. If CX is 0, the string instruction is not executed, and control goes to the following instruction.

Section 3.8 contains examples illustrating the use of string instructions.

REP/REPE/REPZ/REPNE/REPNZ

Repeat, Repeat While Equal, Repeat While Zero, Repeat While Not Equal, and Repeat While Not Zero are five mnemonics for three forms of the prefix byte that controls repetition of a subsequent string instruction. The different mnemonics are provided to improve program clarity. The repeat prefixes do not affect the flags.

REP is used in conjunction with the MOVS (move string), the STOS (store string), the INS (in string) and OUTS (out string) instructions and is interpreted as "repeat while not end-of-string" (CX not 0). REPE and REPZ operate identically and are physically the same prefix byte as REP. These instructions are used with the CMPS (compare string) and SCAS (scan string) instructions and require ZF (posted by these instructions) to be set before initiating the next repetition. REPNE and REPNZ are two mnemonics for the same prefix byte. These instructions function the same as REPE and REPZ except that the zero flag must be cleared or the repetition is terminated. Note that ZF does not need to be initialized before executing the repeated string instruction.

Repeated string sequences are interruptable; the processor recognizes the interrupt before processing the next string element. System interrupt processing is not affected in any way. Upon return from the interrupt, the repeated operation is resumed from the point of interruption. Note, however, that on the 8086,88 execution does not resume properly if a second or third prefix (i.e., segment override or LOCK) has been specified in addition to any of the repeat prefixes. The processor "remembers" only one prefix in effect at the time of the interrupt, i.e., the prefix that immediately precedes the string instruction; after returning from the interrupt, processing resumes at this point, but any additional prefixes specified are not in effect. On the 80186,188, however, interrupt string instructions resume executing from the first prefix of the repeated instruction; thus, interrupted string move instructions with multiple prefixes will resume execution properly.

If more than one prefix must be used with a string instruction executing on the 8086,88, interrupts may be disabled for the duration of the repeated execution. However, this will not prevent a non-maskable interrupt from being recognized. Also, the time that the system is unable to respond to interrupts may be unacceptable if long strings are being processed.

Repeated string instructions (MOVS, INS, OUTS) operate at full bus bandwidth on the 80186,188, allowing very high speed memory-to-memory and memory-to-I/O transfers by the CPU.

MOVS destination-string, source-string

MOVS (move string) transfers a byte or a word from the source string (addressed by SI) to the destination string (addressed by DI) and updates SI and DI to point to the next string element. When used in conjunction with REP, MOVS performs a memory-to-memory block transfer.

MOVSB/MOVSW

These are alternate mnemonics for the move string instruction. These mnemonics are coded without operands. They tell the assembler explicitly that a byte string (MOVSB) or a word string MOVWS) is to be moved (when MOVS is coded, the assembler determines the string type from the attribute of the operands). These mnemonics are useful when the assembler cannot determine the attributes of a string, e.g., when a section of code is being moved.

CMPS destination-string, source-string

CMPS (compare string) subtracts the destination byte or word (addressed by DI) from the source byte or word (addressed by SI). CMPS affects the flags but does not alter either operand, updates SI and DI to point to the next string element and updates AF, CF, OF, PF, SF and ZF to reflect the relationship of the destination element to the source element. For example, if a JG (jump if greater) instruction follows CMPS, the jump is taken if the destination element is greater than the source element. If the CMPS is prefixed with REPE or REPZ, the operation is interpreted as "compare while not end-of-string (CX not zero) and strings are equal (ZF=1)." If CMPS is preceded by REPNE or REPNZ, the operation is interpreted as "compare while not end-of-string (CX not zero) and strings are not equal (ZF=0)." Thus, CMPS can be used to find matching or differing string elements.

SCAS destination-string

SCAS (scan string) subtracts the destination string element (byte or word) addressed by DI from the contents of AL (byte string) or AX (word string) and updates the flags, but does not alter the destination string or the accumulator. SCAS also updates DI to point to the next string element and AF, CF, OF, PF, SF and ZF to reflect the relationship of the scan value in AL/AX to the string element. If SCAS is prefixed with REPE or REPZ, the operation is interpreted as "scan while not end-of string (CX not 0) and string-element = scan-value (ZF=1)." This form may be used to scan for departure from a given value. If SCAS is prefixed with REPNE or REPNZ, the operation is interpreted as "scan while not end-of-string (CX not 0) and string-element is not equal to scan-value (ZF=0)." This may be used to locate a value in a string.

LODS source-string

LODS (load string) transfers the byte or word string element addressed by SI to register AL or AX, and updates SI to point to the next element in the string. This instruction is not ordinarily repeated since the accumulator would be overwritten by each repetition, and only the last element would be retained. However, LODS is very useful in software loops as part of a more complex string function built up from string primitives and other instructions.

STOS destination-string

STOS (store string) transfers a byte or word from register AL or AX to the string element addressed by DI and updates DI to point to the next location in the string. As a repeated operation, STOS provides a convenient way to initialize a string to a constant value (e.g., to blank out a print line).

INS source-string, port (186,88 only)
OUTS port, destination-string

INS and OUTS (in string, out string) instructions perform block input/output. Their operation is similar to the string move instructions. In both the INS and OUTS instructions, the port address is placed in the DX register. For INS, the memory address is placed in the DI register; for OUTS, the memory address is placed in the SI register. In the case of INS, the segment register used is the ES register, and this may not be overridden. In the case of OUTS, the segment register used is the DS register; this may be overridden with a segment override instruction. In both cases, after the transfer has taken place (in two subsequent bus cycles), the pointer register is incremented or decremented (depending on the state of the DF flag) by an appropriate amount (1 for byte, 2 for word transfers).

Control Transfer Instructions

The sequence of instructions executing in an 8086,88 or 80186,188 program is determined by the contents of the code segment register (CS) and the instruction pointer (IP). The CS register contains the base address of the current code segment, the 64K portion of memory from which instructions are presently being fetched. The IP is used as an offset from the beginning of the code segment; the combination of CS and IP points to the memory location from which the next instruction is to be fetched. (Under most operating conditions, the next instruction to be executed has already been fetched from memory and is waiting in the CPU instruction queue.) The program transfer instructions operate on the instruction pointer and on the CS register; changing the contents of these causes normal sequential execution to be altered. When a program transfer occurs, the queue no longer contains the correct instruction, and the BIU obtains the next instruction from memory using the new IP and CS values, passes the instruction directly to the EU, and then begins refilling the queue from the new location.

Four groups of program transfers are available (see Table 3-10): unconditional transfers, conditional transfers, iteration control instructions and interrupt-related instructions. Only the interrupt-related instructions affect any CPU flags. However, the execution of many of the program transfer instructions is affected by the states of the flags.

UNCONDITIONAL TRANSFERS

The unconditional transfer instructions may transfer control to a target instruction within the current code segment (intrasegment transfer) or to a different code segment (intersegment transfer). (The ASM-86 assembler terms an intrasegment target NEAR and an intersegment target FAR.) The transfer is made unconditionally any time the instruction is executed.

Table 3-10 Program Transfer Instructions

UNCONDITIONAL TRANSFERS	
CALL	Call procedure
RET	Return from procedure
JMP	Jump

CONDITIONAL TRANSFERS	
JA/JNBE	Jump if above/not below nor equal
JAE/JNB	Jump if above or equal/not below
JB/JNAE	Jump if below/not above nor equal
JBE/JNA	Jump if below or equal/not above
JC	Jump if carry
JE/JZ	Jump if equal/zero
JG/JNLE	Jump if greater/not less nor equal
JGE/JNL	Jump if greater or equal/not less
JL/JNGE	Jump if less/not greater nor equal
JLE/JNG	Jump if less or equal/not greater
JNC	Jump if not carry
JNE/JNZ	Jump if not equal/not zero
JNO	Jump if not overflow
JNP/JPO	Jump if not parity/parity odd
JNS	Jump if not sign
JO	Jump if overflow
JP/JPE	Jump if parity/parity even
JS	Jump if sign

ITERATION CONTROLS	
LOOP	Loop
LOOPE/LOOPZ	Loop if equal/zero
LOOPNE/LOOPNZ	Loop if not equal/not zero
JCXZ	Jump if register CX = 0

INTERRUPTS	
INT	Interrupt
INTO	Interrupt if overflow
IRET	Interrupt return

CALL *procedure-name*

CALL activates an out-of-line procedure, saving information on the stack to permit a RET (return) instruction in the procedure to transfer control back to the instruction following the CALL. The assembler generates a different type of CALL instruction depending on whether the programmer has defined the procedure name as NEAR or FAR. For control to return properly, the type of CALL instruction must match the type of RET instruction that exits from the procedure. (The potential for mismatch exists if the procedure and the CALL are contained in separately assembled programs.) Different forms of the CALL instruction allow the address of the target procedure to be obtained from the instruction itself (direct CALL) or from a memory location or register referenced by the instruction (indirect CALL).

In the following descriptions, bear in mind that the processor automatically adjusts IP to point to the next instruction to be executed before saving it on the stack.

For an intrasegment *direct* CALL, SP is decremented by two and IP is pushed onto the stack. The relative displacement (up to plus or minus 32K) of the target procedure from the CALL instruction is then added to the instruction pointer. This form of the CALL instruction is "self-relative" and is appropriate for position-independent (dynamically relocatable) routines in which the CALL and its target are in the same segment and are moved together.

An intrasegment *indirect* CALL may be made through memory or through a register. SP is decremented by two and IP is pushed onto the stack. The offset of the target procedure is obtained from the memory word or 16-bit general register referenced in the instruction and replaces IP.

For an intersegment *direct* CALL, SP is decremented by two, and CS is pushed onto the stack. CS is replaced by the segment word contained in the instruction. SP again is decremented by two. IP is pushed onto the stack and is replaced by the offset word contained in the instruction.

For an intersegment *indirect* CALL (which may only be made through memory), SP is decremented by two, and CS is pushed onto the stack. CS is then replaced by the contents of the second word of the doubleword memory pointer referenced by the instruction. SP again is decremented by two, and IP is pushed onto the stack and is replaced by the contents of the first word of the doubleword pointer referenced by the instruction.

RET optional-pop-value

RET (return) transfers control from a procedure back to the instruction following the CALL that activated the procedure. The assembler generates an intrasegment RET if the programmer has defined the procedure NEAR, or an intersegment RET if the procedure has been defined as FAR. RET pops the word at the top of the stack (pointed to by register SP) into the instruction pointer and increments SP by two. If RET is intersegment, the word at the new top of stack is popped into the CS register, and SP is again incremented by two. If an optional pop value has been specified, RET adds that value to SP. This feature may be used to discard parameters pushed onto the stack before the execution of the CALL instruction.

JMP target

JMP unconditionally transfers control to the target location. Unlike a CALL instruction, JMP does not save any information on the stack, and no return to the instruction following the JMP is expected. Like CALL, the address of the target operand may be obtained from the instruction itself (direct JMP) or from memory or a register referenced by the instruction (indirect JMP).

An intrasegment direct JMP changes the instruction pointer by adding the relative displacement of the target from the JMP instruction. If the assembler can determine that the target is within 127 bytes of the JMP, it automatically generates a two-byte form of this instruction called a SHORT JMP; otherwise, it generates a NEAR JMP that can address a target within plus or minus 32K. Intrasegment direct JUMPs are self-relative and are appropriate in position-independent (dynamically relocatable) routines in which the JMP and its target are in the same segment and are moved together.

An intrasegment indirect JMP may be made either through memory or through a 16-bit general register. In the first case, the contents of the word referenced by the instruction replaces the instruction pointer. In the second case, the new IP value is taken from the register named in the instruction.

An intersegment direct JMP replaces IP and CS with values contained in the instruction.

An intersegment indirect JMP may be made only through memory. The first word of the doubleword pointer referenced by the instruction replaces IP, and the second word replaces CS.

CONDITIONAL TRANSFERS

The conditional transfer instructions are jumps that may or may not transfer control depending on the state of the CPU flags at the time the instruction is executed. These instructions (see Table 3-11) each test a different combination of flags for a condition. If the condition is "true," then control is transferred to the target specified in the instruction. If the condition is "false," then control passes to the instruction that follows the conditional jump. All conditional jumps are SHORT, that is, the target must be in the current code segment and within −128 to +127 bytes of the first byte of the next instruction (JMP 00H jumps to the first byte of the next instruction). Since the jump is made by adding the relative displacement of the target to the instruction pointer, all conditional jumps are self-relative and are appropriate for position-independent routines.

ITERATION CONTROL

The iteration control instructions can be used to regulate the repetition of software loops. These instructions use the CX register as a counter. Like the conditional transfers, the iteration control instructions are self-relative and may only transfer to targets that are within −128 to +127 bytes of themselves, i.e., they are SHORT transfers.

LOOP short-label

LOOP decrements CX by 1 and transfers control to the target operand if CX is not 0; otherwise the instruction following LOOP is executed.

LOOP/LOOPNZ short-label

LOOPE and LOOPZ (loop while equal and loop while zero) are different mnemonics for the same instruction (similar to the REPE and REPZ repeat prefixes). CX is decremented by 1, and control is transferred to the target operand if CX is not 0 and if ZF is set; otherwise the instruction following LOOPE/LOOPZ is executed.

LOOPNE/LOOPNZ short-label

LOOPNE/LOOPNZ (loop while not equal and loop while not zero) are also synonyms for the same instruction. CX is decremented by 1, and control is transferred to the target operand if CX is not 0 and if ZF is clear; otherwise the next sequential instruction is executed.

210911

Table 3-11 Interpretation of Conditional Transfers

MNEMONIC	CONDITION TESTED	"JUMP IF ..."
JA/JNBE	(CF OR ZF)=0	above/not below nor equal
JAE/JNB	CF=0	above or equal/not below
JB/JNAE	CF=1	below/not above nor equal
JBE/JNA	(CF OR ZF)=1	below or equal/not above
JC	CF=1	carry
JE/JZ	ZF=1	equal/zero
JG/JNLE	((SF XOR OF) OR ZF)=0	greater/not less nor equal
JGE/JNL	(SF XOR OF)=0	greater or equal/not less
JL/JNGE	(SF XOR OF)=1	less/not greater nor equal
JLE/JNG	((SF XOR OF) OR ZF)=1	less or equal/not greater
JNC	CF=0	not carry
JNE/JNZ	ZF=0	not equal/not zero
JNO	OF=0	not overflow
JNP/JPO	PF=0	not parity/parity odd
JNS	SF=0	not sign
JO	OF=1	overflow
JP/JPE	PF=1	parity/parity equal
JS	SF=1	sign

Note: "above" and "below" refer to the relationship of two unsigned values;
"greater" and "less" refer to the relationship of two signed values.

JCXZ short-label

JCXZ (jump if CX zero) transfers control to the target operand if CX is 0. This instruction is useful at the beginning of a loop to bypass the loop if CX has a zero value, i.e., to execute the loop zero times.

INTERRUPT INSTRUCTIONS

The interrupt instructions allow interrupt service routines to be activated by programs as well as by external hardware devices. The effect of software interrupts is similar to hardware-initiated interrupts. However, the processor does not execute an interrupt acknowledge bus cycle if the interrupt originates in software or with an NMI (non-maskable interrupt). The effect of the interrupt instructions on the flags is covered in the description of each instruction.

INT interrupt-type

INT (interrupt) activates the interrupt procedure specified by the interrupt-type operand. INT decrements the stack pointer by two, pushes the flags onto the stack, and clears the trap (TF) and interrupt-enable (IF) flags to disable single-step and maskable interrupts. The flags are stored in the same format used by the PUSHF instruction. SP is decremented again by two, and the CS register is pushed onto the stack. The address of the interrupt pointer is calculated by multiplying interrupt-type by four; the second word of the interrupt pointer replaces CS. SP again is decremented by two, and IP is pushed onto the stack and is replaced by the first word of the interrupt pointer. If interrupt-type = 3, the assembler generates a short (1 byte) form of the instruction, known as the breakpoint interrupt.

Software interrupts can be used as "supervisor calls," i.e., requests for service that the operating system could supply for an application program. A different interrupt-type can be used for each type of service that the operating system could supply for an application program. Software interrupts also may be used to check out interrupt service procedures written for hardware-initiated interrupts.

INTO

INTO (interrupt on overflow) generates a software interrupt if the overflow flag (OF) is set; otherwise control proceeds to the following instruction without activating an interrupt procedure. INTO addresses the target interrupt procedure (its type is 4) through the interrupt pointer at location 10H; it clears the TF and IF flags and otherwise operates like INT. INTO may be written following an arithmetic or logical operation to activate an interrupt procedure if overflow occurs.

210911

IRET

IRET (interrupt return) transfers control back to the point of interruption by popping IP, CS and the flags from the stack. IRET thus affects all flags by restoring them to previously saved values. IRET is used to exit any interrupt procedure, whether activated by hardware or software.

High-level Instructions

ENTER

The ENTER (enter procedure) instruction executes the calling sequence for a high-level language. It provides for saving the current stack frame pointer (which is in the BP register), copying down stack frame pointers from procedures below the current call (to allow access to local variables in these procedures), and allocating space on the stack for the local variables of the current procedure invocation. This instruction requires two arguments: the size of the local variables (the displacement), and the level of the procedure (which may be as great as 255).

The algorithm for this instruction is:

```
PUSH BP          /* save the previous frame pointer */
if level = 0 then
    BP := SP;
else       templ := SP; /* save current frame pointer*/
    temp2 := level − 1;
    do while temp2 > 0      /* copy down previous level
    frame */
        BP := BP − 2;    /* pointers */
        PUSH [BP];
    BP := templ;
PUSH BP;           /* put current level frame pointer */
                   /* in the save area */
SP := SP − disp;   /*create space on the stack for */
                   /* local variables */
```

Figure 3-30 shows the layout of the stack after this operation.

LEAVE

The LEAVE (leave procedure) instruction is the opposite of the ENTER instruction. This instruction "cleans up" the procedure's stack to prepare for returning from the procedure. It deallocates all local or automatic variables, and returns the stack registers (SP and BP) to the same values they were immediately after the procedure invocation. As can be seen from the layout of the stack left by the ENTER instruction (see Figure 3-30), this involves moving the contents of the BP register to the SP register, and popping the old BP value off of the stack.

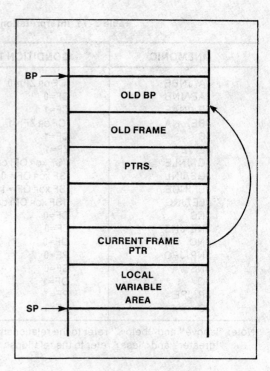

**Figure 3-30 Stack Layout
After ENTER Instruction**

Note that neither the ENTER nor the LEAVE instructions save any of the 80186,188 general purpose registers. If they must be saved, this must be done in addition to the ENTER and LEAVE. Also, the LEAVE instruction does not perform a return from subroutine. If this is desired, the LEAVE instruction must be explicitly followed by the RET instruction.

BOUND

The BOUND (detect value out of range) instruction allows for array bounds checking in hardware. The calculated array index is placed in one of the general purpose registers, and the upper and lower bounds of the array are placed in two consecutive memory locations. The instruction compares the contents of the specified register against the memory location values, and if the register value is less than the first memory location or greater than the second memory location, a trap type 5 is generated. The comparisons performed are signed comparisons. A register value equal to either the upper or lower bound will not cause a trap. Following a trap, the IP (which has been pushed on the stack) will point to the instruction following the BOUND instruction.

The instruction requires two arguments: the register in which the calculated array index is placed, and the effective address of the memory location containing the lower bound of the array (which can be specified by any of the 80186,188 memory addressing modes). The memory location containing the upper bound of the array must follow immediately the memory location containing the lower bound of the array, i.e., the address of the memory location containing the upper bound of the array is the address of the lower bound location plus 2.

Processor Control Instructions

These instructions (see Table 3-12) allow programs to control various CPU functions. One group of instructions updates flags, and another group is used primarily for synchronizing the processor with external events. A final instruction causes the CPU to do nothing. Except for the flag operations, none of the processor instructions affect the flags.

Table 3-12 Processor Control Instructions

FLAG OPERATIONS	
STC	Set carry flag
CLC	Clear carry flag
CMC	Complement carry flag
STD	Set direction flag
CLD	Clear direction flag
STI	Set interrupt enable flag
CLI	Clear interrupt enable flag

EXTERNAL SYNCHRONIZATION	
HLT	Halt until interrupt or reset
WAIT	Wait for TEST pin active
ESC	Escape to external processor
LOCK	Lock bus during next instruction

NO OPERATION	
NOP	No operation

FLAG OPERATIONS

CLC

CLC (clear carry flag) zeroes the carry flag (CF) and affects no other flags. It (and CMC and STC) is useful in conjunction with the RCL and RCR instructions.

CMC

CMC (complement carry flag) "toggles" CF to its opposite state and affects no other flags.

STC

STC (set carry flag) sets CF to 1 and affects no other flags.

CLD

CLD (clear direction flag) zeroes DF causing the string instructions to auto-increment the SI and /or DI index registers. CLD does not affect any other flags.

STD

STD (set direction flag) sets DF to 1 causing the string instructions to auto-decrement the SI and/or DI index registers. STD does not affect any other flags.

CLI

CLI (clear interrupt-enable flag) zeroes IF. When the interrupt-enable flag is cleared, the processor does not recognize an external interrupt request that appears on the INTR line; in other words maskable interrupts are disabled. A non-maskable interrupt appearing on the NMI line, however, is honored, as is a software interrupt. CLI does not affect any other flags.

STI

STI (set interrupt-enable flag) sets IF to 1, enabling processor recognition of maskable interrupt requests appearing on the INTR line. Note, however, that a pending interrupt will not actually be recognized until the instruction following STI has executed. STI does not affect any other flags.

EXTERNAL SYNCHRONIZATION

HLT

HLT (halt) causes the processor to enter the halt state. The processor leaves the halt state upon activation of the RESET line, upon receipt of a non-maskable interrupt request on NMI, or, if interrupts are enabled, upon receipt of a maskable interrupt request on INTR. HLT does not affect any flags. It may be used as an alternative to an endless software loop in situations where a program must wait for an interrupt.

WAIT

WAIT causes the CPU to enter the wait state while its TEST line is not active. WAIT does not affect any flags.

ESC external-opcode, source

ESC (escape) provides a means for an external processor to obtain an opcode and possibly a memory operand from the 8086 or 80186. The external opcode is a 6-bit immediate constant that the assembler encodes in the machine instruction it builds. An external processor may monitor the system bus and capture this opcode when the ESC is fetched. Then, using the second byte of the opcode, the CPU performs an operand access. If the source operand is a register, the processor does nothing. If the source operand is a memory variable, the processor obtains the operand from memory and discards it. An external processor may capture the memory operand and the memory operand's 20-bit address when the processor reads it from memory.

LOCK

LOCK is a one-byte prefix that causes the processors to assert their bus LOCK signals while the following instructions execute. LOCK does not affect any flags.

NO OPERATION

NOP

NOP (no operation) causes the CPU to do nothing. NOP does not affect any flags.

Instruction Operation Differences, 8086,88 – 80186,188

There are a few instruction operation differences between the 8086,88 and 80186,188, most of which have been previously discussed in this chapter and in Chapter 2. The following is a summary of these differences:

UNDEFINED OPCODES

When the opcodes 63H, 64H, 65H, 66H, 67H, F1H, FEH XX111XXXB and FFH XX111XXXB are executed, the 80186,188 will execute an illegal instruction exception (interrupt type 6). The 8086,88 will ignore these opcodes.

0FH OPCODE

When the opcode 0FH is encountered, the 8086,88 will execute a POP CS; the 80186,188 will execute an illegal instruction exception.

WORD WRITE AT OFFSET FFFFH

When a word write is performed at offset FFFFH in a segment, the 8086,88 will write one byte at offset FFFFH, and the other at offset 0; the 80186,188 will write one byte at offset FFFFH, and the other at offset 10000H (one byte beyond the end of the segment). One byte segment underflow will also occur on the 80186,188 if a stack PUSH is executed and the Stack Pointer contains the value 1.

SHIFT/ROTATE BY VALUE GREATER THAN 31

Before the 80186,188 performs a shift or rotate by a value (either in the CL register, or by an immediate value) it ANDs the value with 1FH, limiting the number of bits rotated to less than 32. The 8086,88 does not do this.

LOCK PREFIX

The 8086,88 activates its LOCK signal immediately after executing the LOCK prefix. The 80186,188 does not activate the LOCK signal until the processor is ready to begin the data cycles associated with the LOCKed instruction.

INTERRUPTED STRING MOVE INSTRUCTIONS

If an 8086,88 is interrupted during the execution of a repeated string move instruction, the return value pushed on the stack will point to the last prefix instruction before the string move instruction. If the instruction had more than one prefix (e.g., a segment override prefix in addition to the repeat prefix), the prefix will not be re-executed upon returning from the interrupt. The 80186,188, on the other hand, pushes the value of the *first* prefix to the repeated instruction. Thus, so long as prefixes are not themselves repeated, string instructions will properly resume execution.

CONDITIONS CAUSING DIVIDE ERROR WITH AN INTEGER DIVIDE

The 8086,88 will cause a divide error whenever the absolute value of the quotient is greater then 7FFFH (for word operations) or if the absolute value of the quotient is greater than 7FH (for byte operations). The 80186,188 has expanded the range of negative numbers allowed as a quotient by 1 to include 8000H and 80H. These numbers represent the most negative numbers representable using two's complement arithmetic (equal to −32768 and −128 in decimal, respectively).

ESC OPCODE

The 80186,188 may be programmed to cause an interrupt type 7 whenever an ESCape instruction (used for co-processors like the the 8087) is executed. The 8086,88 has no such provision.

Instruction Set Reference

The instruction set summary which follows provides detailed operational information for the iAPX 86/186 (8086, 8088, 80186, and 80186) instruction set. The information is presented from the point of view of utility to the assembly language programmer.

Instruction timings are represented as the number of clock periods required to execute a particular form (register-to-register, immediate-to-memory, etc.) of instruction. At 5MHz clock, the clock period is 200 ns; at 8MHz, the clock period is 125 ns. For 8086,88 instruction timings which use memory operands, "+EA" denotes the number of additional clock periods needed to calculate the operand's effective address. (On the 80186,188 this computation is performed in hardware.)

For control transfer instructions, the timings given include any additional clocks required to reinitialize the instruction queue as well as the time required to fetch the target instruction. For the 8086, four clocks should be added for each instruction reference to a word operand located at an odd memory address to reflect any additional operand bus cycles required. The required number of data references is listed in the instruction set summary for each instruction to aid in this calculation.

All of the instruction times given are of the form "n(m)," where n is the number of clocks required for the 8086 to execute the given instruction, and m is the time required by the 80186 for the same instruction. The number of clocks required for the 8088 will be n for 8-bit operations and n + (4 * transfers) for 16-bit operations. For the 80188, the number of clocks will be m for 8-bit operations and m + (4 * transfers) for 16-bit operations.

For instructions which repeat a specified number of times, the values m and n each consist of two parts in the relation "x + y/rep," where x is the initial number of clocks required to start the instruction, and y is the number of clocks corresponding to the number of iterations specified. For 16-bit repeated instructions on the 8088 and 80188, when the expression "(4 * transfers)" has to be added to m or n, it should be added to the y part of the expression before it is multiplied by the number of repetitions.

Several additional factors can increase actual execution time over the figures shown in Table 3-13. The time provided assumes that the instruction has already been prefetched and that it is waiting in the instruction queue, an assumption that is valid under most, but not all, operating conditions. A series of fast executing (fewer than two clocks per opcode byte) instructions can drain the queue and increase execution time. Execution time also is slightly impacted by interaction of the EU and BIU when memory operands must be read or written. If the EU needs access to memory, it may have to wait for up to one clock if the BIU has already started an instruction fetch bus cycle. (The EU can detect the need for a memory operand and post a bus request far enough in advance of its need for this operand to avoid waiting a full 4-clock bus cycle.) Of course the EU does not have to wait when the queue is full, because the BIU is idle. (This assumes that the BIU can obtain the bus on demand, i.e., no other processors are competing for the bus.)

With typical instruction mixes, the time actually required to execute a sequence of instructions will typically be within 5-10% of the sum of the individual timings given in the instruction set summary. Cases can be constructed, however, in which execution time may be much higher than the sum of the figures provided in the table. The execution time for a given sequence of instructions, however, is always repeatable, assuming comparable external conditions (interrupts, coprocessor activity, etc.). If the execution time for a given series of instructions must be determined exactly, the instructions should be run on an execution vehicle such as the iSBC 88/25[TM] or the 86/30 board.

REF

REFERENCES FOR INSTRUCTION SET

REF

Key to following Instruction Set Reference Pages

IDENTIFIER	USED IN	EXPLANATION
destination	data transfer, bit manipulation	A register or memory location that may contain data operated on by the instruction, and which receives (is replaced by) the result of the operation.
source	data transfer, arithmetic, bit manipulation	A register, memory location or immediate value that is used in the operation, but is not altered by the instruction.
source-table	XLAT	Name of memory translation table addressed by register BX.
target	JMP, CALL	A label to which control is to be transferred directly, or a register or memory location whose *content* is the address of the location to which control is to be transferred indirectly.
short-label	cond. transfer, iteration control	A label to which control is to be conditionally transferred; must lie within −128 to +127 bytes of the first byte of the next instruction.
accumulator	IN, OUT	Register AX for word transfers, AL for bytes.
port	IN, OUT	An I/O port number; specified as an immediate value of 0-255, or register DX (which contains port number in range 0-64k).
source-string	string ops.	Name of a string in memory that is addressed by register SI; used only to identify string as byte or word and specify segment override, if any. This string is used in the operation, but is not altered.
dest-string	string ops.	Name of string in memory that is addressed by register DI; used only to identify string as byte or word. This string receives (is replaced by) the result of the operation.
count	shifts, rotates	Specifies number of bits to shift or rotate; written as immediate value 1 or register CL (which contains the count in the range 0-255).
interrupt-type	INT	Immediate value of 0-255 identifying interrupt pointer number.
optional-pop-value	RET	Number of bytes (0-64k, ordinarily an even number) to discard from stack.
external-opcode	ESC	Immediate value (0-63) that is encoded in the instruction for use by an external processor.
above-below	conditional jumps	Above and below refer to the relationship of two unsigned values.
greater-less	conditional jumps	Greater and less refer to the relationship of two signed values.

REF REFERENCES FOR INSTRUCTION SET REF

Key to Operand Types

IDENTIFIER	EXPLANATION
(no operands)	No operands are written
register	An 8- or 16-bit general register
reg 16	An 16-bit general register
seg-reg	A segment register
accumulator	Register AX or AL
immediate	A constant in the range 0-FFFFH
immed8	A constant in the range 0-FFH
memory	An 8- or 16-bit memory location[1]
mem8	An 8-bit memory location[1]
mem16	A 16-bit memory location[1]
source-table	Name of 256-byte translate table
source-string	Name of string addressed by register SI
dest-string	Name of string, addressed by register DI
DX	Register DX
short-label	A label within −128 to +127 bytes of the end of the instruction
near-label	A label in current code segment
far-label	A label in another code segment
near-proc	A procedure in current code segment
far-proc	A procedure in another code segment
memptr16	A word containing the offset of the location in the current code segment to which control is to be transferred[1]
memptr32	A doubleword containing the offset and the segment base address of the location in another code segment to which control is to be transferred[1]
regptr16	A 16-bit general register containing the offset of the location in the current code segment to which control is to be transferred
repeat	A string instruction repeat prefix

[1] Any addressing mode — direct, register indirect, based, indexed, or based indexed — may be used (see Section 3.6).

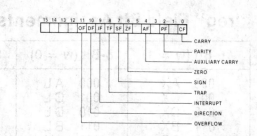

Effective Address Calculation Time (8086,88 ONLY)

EA COMPONENTS		CLOCKS*
Displacement Only		6
Base or Index Only (BX,BP,SI,DI)		5
Displacement + Base or Index (BX,BP,SI,DI)		9
Base + Index	BP + DI, BX + SI	7
	BP + SI, BX + DI	8
Displacement + Base + Index	BP + DI + DISP BX + SI + DISP	11
	BP + SI + DISP BX + DI + DISP	12

*Add 2 clocks for segment override

NOTE: Effective Address Calculation for the 186/188 is done in hardware. The time to execute the calculation is included in the time given for each instruction.

Notation Key

+	Addition
−	Subtraction
*	Multiplication
/	Division
%	Modulo
:	Concatenation
&	And
←	Assignment

REF   REFERENCES FOR INSTRUCTION SET   REF

"reg" Field Bit Assignments:

16-Bit (w = 1)	8-Bit (w = 0)	Segment
000 AX	000 A L	00 ES
001 CX	001 C L	01 CS
010 DX	010 D L	10 SS
011 BX	011 B L	11 DS
100 S P	100 AH	
101 BP	101 CH	
110 S I	110 DH	
111 D I	111 BH	

"mod" Field Bit Assignments:

mod xxx r/m

mod	Displacement
00	DISP = 0*, disp-low and disp-high are absent
01	DISP = disp-low sign-extended to 16-bits, disp-high is absent
10	DISP = disp-high: disp-low
11	r/m is treated as a "reg" field

"r/m" Field Bit Assignments:

r/m	Operand Address
000	(BX) + (SI) + DISP
001	(BX) + (DI) + DISP
010	(BP) + (SI) + DISP
011	(BP) + (DI) + DISP
100	(SI) + DISP
101	(DI) + DISP
110	(BP) + DISP
111	(BX) + DISP

DISP follows 2nd byte of instruction (before data if required).

*except if mod = 00 and r/m = 110 then EA = disp-high: disp-low.

210911

AAA

ASCII ADJUST FOR ADDITION

AAA

Operation:

if ((AL) & 0FH) >9 or (AF) = 1 then
   (AL) ← (AL) + 6
   (AH) ← (AH) + 1
   (AF) ← 1
(CF) ← (AF)
(AL) ← (AL) & 0FH

Flags Affected:

AF, CF.
OF, PF, XF, ZF undefined

Description:

AAA (ASCII Adjust for Addition) changes the contents of register AL to a valid unpacked decimal number; the high-order half-byte is zeroed. AAA updates AF and CF; the content of OF, PF, SF and ZF is undefined following execution of AAA.

Encoding:

```
00110111
```

AAA Operands	Clocks	Transfers	Bytes	AAA Coding Example
(no operands)	8(8)	-	1	AAA

AAD

ASCII ADJUST
FOR DIVISION

AAD

Operation:

$(AL) \leftarrow (AH) * 0AH + (AL)$
$(AH) \leftarrow 0$

Flags Affected:

PF, SF, ZF.
AF, CF, OF undefined

Description:

AAD (ASCII Adjust for Division) modifies the numerator in AL *before* dividing two valid unpacked decimal operands so that the quotient produced by the division will be a valid unpacked decimal number. AH must be zero for the subsequent DIV to produce the correct result. The quotient is returned in AL, and the remainder is returned in AH; both high-order half-bytes are zeroed. AAD updates PF, SF and ZF; the content of AF, CF and OF is undefined following execution of AAD.

Encoding:

11010101	00001010

AAD Operands	Clocks	Transfers	Bytes	AAD Coding Example
(no operands)	60(15)	-	2	AAD

210911

AAM   ASCII ADJUST FOR MULTIPLY   AAM

Operation:

(AH) ← (AL) / 0AH
(AL) ← (AL) % 0AH

Flags Affected:

PF, SF, ZF.
AF, CF, OF undefined

Description:

AAM (ASCII Adjust for Multiply) corrects the result of a previous multiplication of two valid unpacked decimal operands. A valid 2-digit unpacked decimal number is derived from the content of AH and AL and is returned to AH and AL. The high-order half-bytes of the multiplied operands must have been 0H for AAM to produce a correct result. AAM updates PF, SF and ZF; the content of AF, CF and OF is undefined following execution of AAM.

Encoding:

| 11010100 | 00001010 |

AAM Operands	Clocks	Transfers	Bytes	AAM Coding Example
(no operands)	83(19)	-	2	AAM

AAS   ASCII ADJUST FOR SUBTRACTION   AAS

Operation:

if ((AL) & 0FH) >9 or (AF) = 1 then
   (AL) ← (AL) - 6
   (AH) ← (AH) - 1
   (AF) ← 1
(CF) ← (AF)
(AL) ← (AL) & 0FH

Flags Affected:

AF, CF.
0F, PF, SF, ZF undefined

Description:

AAS (ASCII Adjust for Subtraction) corrects the result of a previous subtraction of two valid unpacked decimal operands (the destination operand must have been specified as register AL). AAS changes the content of AL to a valid unpacked decimal number; the high-order half-byte is zeroed. AAS updates AF and CF; the content of OF, PF, SF and ZF is undefined following execution of AAS.

Encoding:

```
00111111
```

AAS Operands	Clocks	Transfers	Bytes	AAS Coding Example
(no operands)	8(7)	-	1	AAS

ADC ADD WITH CARRY ADC

Operation:

if (CF) = 1 then (DEST) ← (LSRC)
+ (RSRC) + 1
else (DEST) ← (LSRC) + (RSRC)

Flags Affected:

AF, CF, OF, PF, SF, ZF

Description:

ADC *destination,source*

ADC (Add with Carry) sums the operands, which may be bytes or words, adds one if CF is set and replaces the destination operand with the result. Both operands may be signed or unsigned binary numbers (see AAA and DAA). ADC updates AF, CF, OF, PF, SF and ZF. Since ADC incorporates a carry from a previous operation, it can be used to write routines to add numbers longer than 16 bits.

210911

ADC ADD WITH CARRY ADC

Encoding:

Memory or Register Operand with Register Operand:

0 0 0 1 0 0 d w	mod reg r/m

if d = 1 then LSRC = REG, RSRC = EA, DEST = REG
else LSRC = EA, RSRC = REG, DEST = EA

Immediate Operand to Memory or Register Operand:

1 0 0 0 0 0 s w	mod 0 1 0 r/m	data	data if s:w=01

LSRC = EA, RSRC = data, DEST = EA

Immediate Operand to Accumulator:

0 0 0 1 0 1 0 w	data	data if w=1

if w = 0 then LSRC = AL, RSRC = data, DEST = AL
else LSRC = AX, RSRC = data, DEST = AX

ADC Operands	Clocks	Transfers	Bytes	ADC Coding Example
register, register	3(3)	-	2	ADC AX, SI
register, memory	9(10)+EA	1	2-4	ADD DX, BETA [SI]
memory, register	16(10)+EA	2	2-4	ADC ALPHA [BX][SI],DI
register, immediate	4(4)	-	3-4	ADC BX, 256
memory, immediate	17(16)+EA	2	3-6	ADC GAMMA, 30H
accumulator, immediate	4(3-4)	-	2-3	ADC AL, 5

210911

ADD ADDITION ADD

Operation:

(DEST) ← (LSRC) + (RSRC)

Flags Affected:

AF, CF, OF, PF, SF, ZF

Description:

ADD *destination,source*

The sum of the two operands, which may be
bytes or words, replaces the destination
operand. Both operands may be signed or
unsigned binary numbers (see AAA and
DAA). ADD updates AF, CF, OF, PF, SF and
ZF.

210911

ADD ADDITION ADD

Encoding:

Memory or Register Operand with Register Operand:

0 0 0 0 0 0 d w	mod reg r/m

if d = 1 then LSRC = REG, RSRC = EA, DEST = REG
else LSRC = EA, RSRC = REG, DEST = EA

Immediate Operand to Memory or Register Operand:

1 0 0 0 0 0 s w	mod 0 0 0 r/m	data	data if s:w=01

LSRC = EA, RSRC = data, DEST = EA

Immediate Operand to Accumulator:

0 0 0 0 0 1 0 w	data	data if w=1

if w = 0 then LSRC = AL, RSRC = data, DEST = AL
else LSRC = AX, RSRC = data, DEST = AX

ADD Operands	Clocks	Transfers	Bytes	ADD Coding Example
register, register	3(3)	-	2	ADD CX, DX
register, memory	9(10)+EA	1	2-4	ADD DI, [BX].ALPHA
memory, register	16(10)+EA	2	2-4	ADD TEMP, CL
register, immediate	4(4)	-	3-4	ADD CL, 2
memory, immediate	17(16)+EA	2	3-6	ADD ALPHA, 2
accumulator, immediate	4(3-4)	-	2-3	ADD AX, 200

210911

AND   AND LOGICAL   AND

Operation:

(DEST) ← (LSRC) & (RSRC)
(CF) ← 0
(OF) ← 0

Flags Affected:

CF, OF, PF, SF, ZF.
AF undefined

Description:

AND *destination,source*

AND performs the logical "and" of the two
operands (byte or word) and returns the result
to the destination operand. A bit in the result
is set if both corresponding bits of the original
operands are set; otherwise the bit is cleared.

210911

AND   AND LOGICAL   AND

Encoding:

Memory or Register Operand with Register Operand:

0 0 1 0 0 0 d w	mod reg r/m

if d = 1 then LSRC = REG, RSRC = EA, DEST = REG
else LSRC = EA, RSRC = REG, DEST = EA

Immediate Operand to Memory or Register Operand:

1 0 0 0 0 0 0 w	mod 1 0 0 r/m	data	data if w=1

LSRC = EA, RSRC = data, DEST = EA

Immediate Operand to Accumulator:

0 0 1 0 0 1 0 w	data	data if w=1

if w = 0 then LSRC = AL, RSRC = data, DEST = AL
else LSRC = AX, RSRC = data, DEST = AX

AND Operands	Clocks	Transfers	Bytes	AND Coding Example
register, register	3(3)	-	2	AND AL, BL
register, memory	9(10)+EA	1	2-4	AND CX, FLAG_WORD
memory, register	16(10)+EA	2	2-4	AND ASCII [DI],AL
register, immediate	4(4)	-	3-4	AND CX, 0F0H
memory, immediate	17(16)+EA	2	3-6	AND BETA, 01H
accumulator, immediate	4(3-4)	-	2-3	AND AX, 01010000B

BOUND DETECT VALUE OUT OF RANGE (iAPX 186/188 ONLY) BOUND

Operation:

Flags Affected:

None

If ((LSRC) < (RSRC) OR (LSRC) > ((RSRC) + 2) then
    (SP) ← (SP) - 2
    ((SP) + 1: (SP)) ←FLAGS
    (IF) ← 0
    (TF) ← 0
    (SP) ← (SP) - 2
    ((SP) + 1: (SP)) ← (CS)
    (CS) ← (1EH)
    (SP) ← (SP) - 2
    ((SP) + 1: (SP)) ← (IP)
    (IP) ← (1CH)

Description:

BOUND *destination, source*

BOUND provides array bounds checking in hardware. The calculated array index is placed in one of the general purpose registers, and the upper and lower bounds of the array are placed in two consecutive memory locations. The contents of the register are compared with the memory location values, and if the register value is less than the first location or greater than the second memory location, a trap type 5 is generated.

BOUND

DETECT VALUE
OUT OF RANGE
(iAPX 186/188 ONLY)

BOUND

Encoding:

01100010	mod req r/m

BOUND Operands	Clocks	Transfers	Bytes	BOUND Coding Example
register, memory	(35)	2	2	BOUND AX, ALPHA

210911

CALL CALL PROCEDURE CALL

Operation:

if Inter-Segment then
  $(SP) \leftarrow (SP) - 2$
  $((SP) + 1:(SP)) \leftarrow (CS)$
  $(CS) \leftarrow SEG$
$(SP) \leftarrow (SP) - 2$
$((SP) + 1:(SP)) \leftarrow (IP)$
$(IP) \leftarrow DEST$

Flags Affected:

None

Description:

CALL *procedure-name*

CALL activates an out-of-line procedure, saving information on the stack to permit a RET (return) instruction in the procedure to transfer control back to the instruction following the CALL. The assembler generates a different type of CALL instruction depending on whether the programmer has defined the procedure name as NEAR or FAR. For control to return properly, the type of CALL instruction must match the type of RET instruction that exits from the procedure. (The potential for a mismatch exists if the procedure and the CALL are contained in separately assembled programs.) Different forms of the CALL instruction allow the address of the target procedure to be obtained from the instruction itself (direct CALL) or from a memory location or register referenced by the instruction (indirect CALL). In the following descriptions, bear in mind that the processor automatically adjusts IP to point to the next instruction to be *executed* before saving it on the stack.

For an intrasegment direct CALL, SP (the stack pointer) is decremented by two and IP is pushed onto the stack. The target procedure's relative displacement (up to ±32k) from the CALL instruction is then added to the instruction pointer. This CALL instruction form is "self-relative" and appropriate for position-independent (dynamically relocatable) routines in which the CALL and its target are moved together in the same segment.

An intrasegment indirect CALL may be made through memory or a register. SP is decremented by two; IP is pushed onto the stack. The target procedure offset is obtained from the memory word or 16-bit general register referenced in the instruction and replaces IP.

For an intersegment direct CALL, SP is decremented by two, and CS is pushed onto the stack. CS is replaced by the segment word contained in the instruction. SP again is decremented by two. IP is pushed onto the stack and replaced by the offset word in the instruction.

For an intersegment indirect CALL (which only may be made through memory), SP is decremented by two, and CS is pushed onto the stack. CS is then replaced by the content of the second word of the doubleword memory pointer referenced by the instruction. SP again is decremented by two, and IP is pushed onto the stack and replaced by the content of the first word of the doubleword pointer referenced by the instruction.

210911

CALL   CALL PROCEDURE   CALL

Encoding:

Intra-segment direct:

| 1 1 1 0 1 0 0 0 | disp-low | disp-high |

DEST   (EA)

Intra-Segment Indirect:

| 1 1 1 1 1 1 1 1 | mod 0 1 0 r/m |

DEST = (IP) + disp

Inter-Segment Direct:

| 1 0 0 1 1 0 1 0 | offset-low | offset-high |
| seg-low | seg-high |

DEST = offset, SEG = seg

Inter-Segment Indirect:

| 1 1 1 1 1 1 1 1 | mod 0 1 1 r/m |

DEST = (EA), SEG = (EA + 2)

CALL Operands	Clocks	Transfers	Bytes	CALL Coding Examples
near-proc	19(15)	1	3	CALL NEAR_PROC
far-proc	28(23)	2	5	CALL FAR_PROC
memptr16	21(19)+EA	2	2-4	CALL PROC_TABLE [SI]
regptr16	16(13)	1	2	CALL AX
memptr32	37(38)+EA	4	2-4	CALL [BX].TASK [SI]

CBW   CONVERT BYTE TO WORD   CBW

Operation:

if (AL) < 80H then (AH) ← 0 else (AH) ← FFH

Flags Affected:

None

Description:

CBW (Convert Byte to Word) extends the sign of the byte in register AL throughout register AH. CBW does not affect any flags. CBW can be used to produce a double-length (word) dividend from a byte prior to performing byte division.

Encoding:

```
10011000
```

CBW Operands	Clocks	Transfers	Bytes	CBW Coding Example
(no operands)	2(2)	-	1	CBW

CLC   CLEAR CARRY   CLC

Operation:

(CF) ← 0

Flags Affected:

CF

Description:

CLC (Clear Carry flag) zeroes the carry flag (CF) and affects no other flags. It (and CMC and STC) is useful in conjunction with the RCL and RCR instructions.

Encoding:

| 1 1 1 1 1 0 0 0 |

CLC Operands	Clocks	Transfers	Bytes	CLC Coding Example
(no operands)	2(2)	-	1	CLC

210911

CLD   CLEAR DIRECTION FLAG   CLD

Operation:

(DF) ← 0

Flags Affected:

DF

Description:

CLD (Clear Direction flag) zeroes DF causing the string instructions to auto-increment the SI and/or DI index registers. CLD does not affect any other flags.

Encoding:

| 1 1 1 1 1 1 0 0 |

CLD Operands	Clocks	Transfers	Bytes	CLD Coding Example
(no operands)	2(2)	-	1	CLD

210911

CLI CLEAR INTERRUPT-ENABLE FLAG CLI

Operation:

(IF)← 0

Flags Affected:

IF

Description:

CLI (Clear Interrupt-enable flag) zeroes IF. When the interrupt-enable flag is cleared, the 8086 and 8088 do not recognize an external interrupt request that appears on the INTR line; in other words maskable interrupts are disabled. A non-maskable interrupt appearing on the NMI line, however, is honored, as is a software interrupt. CLI does not affect any other flags.

Encoding:

```
11111010
```

CLI Operands	Clocks	Transfers	Bytes	CLI Coding Example
(no operands)	2(2)	-	1	CLI

210911

CMC COMPLEMENT CARRY FLAG CMC

Operation:

if (CF) = 0 then (CF) ← 1 else (CF) ← 0

Flags Affected:

CF

Description:

CMC (Complement Carry flag) "toggles" CF
to its opposite state and affects no other flags.

Encoding:

| 11110101 |

CMC Operands	Clocks	Transfers	Bytes	CMC Coding Example
(no operands)	2(2)	-	1	CMC

CMP COMPARE CMP

Operation:

(LSRC) - (RSRC)

Flags Affected:

AF, CF, OF, PF, SF, ZF

Description:

CMP *destination,source*

CMP (Compare) subtracts the source from the destination, which may be bytes or words, but does not return the result. The operands are unchanged, but the flags are updated and can be tested by a subsequent conditional jump instruction. CMP updates AF, CF, OF, PF, SF and ZF. The comparison reflected in the flags is that of the destination to the source. If a CMP instruction is followed by a JG (jump if greater) instruction, for example, the jump is taken if the destination operand is greater than the source operand.

210911

CMP COMPARE CMP

Encoding:

Memory or Register Operand with Register Operand:

0 0 1 1 1 0 d w	mod reg r/m

if d = 1 then LSRC = REG, RSRC = EA
else LSRC = EA, RSRC = REG

Immediate Operand with Memory or Register Operand:

1 0 0 0 0 0 s w	mod 1 1 1 r/m	data	data if s:w=01

LSRC = EA, RSRC = data

Immediate Operand with Accumulator:

0 0 1 1 1 1 0 w	data	data if w=1

if w = 0 then LSRC = AL, RSRC = data
else LSRC = AX, RSRC = data

CMP Operands	Clocks	Transfers	Bytes	CMP Coding Examples
register, register	3(3)	-	2	CMP BX, CX
register, memory	9(10)+EA	1	2-4	CMP DH, ALPHA
memory, register	9(10)+EA	1	2-4	CMP [BP+2],SI
register, immediate	4(3)	-	3-4	CMP BL, 02H
memory, immediate	10(10)+EA	1	3-6	CMP [BX].RADAR [DI],3420H
accumulator, immediate	4(3-4)	-	2-3	CMP AL, 00010000B

210911

CMPS COMPARE STRING (BYTE OR WORD) CMPS

Operation:

(LSRC) - (RSRC)
if (DF) = 0 then
  (SI) ← (SI) + DELTA
  (DI) ← (DI) + DELTA
else
  (SI) ← (SI) - DELTA
  (DI) ← (DI) - DELTA

Flags Affected:

AF, CF, OF, PF, SF, ZF

Description:

CMPS *destination-string,source-string*

CMPS (Compare String) subtracts the destination byte or word (addressed by DI) from the source byte or word (addressed by SI). CMPS affects the flags but does not alter either operand, updates SI and DI to point to the next string element and updates, AF, CF, OF, PF, SF and ZF to reflect the relationship of the destination element to the source element. For example, if a JG (Jump if Greater) instruction follows CMPS, the jump is taken if the destination element is greater than the source element. If CMPS is prefixed with REPE or REPZ, the operation is interrupted as "compare while not end-of-string (CX not zero) and strings are equal (ZF = 1)." If CMPS is preceded by REPNE or REPNZ, the operation is interrupted as "compare while not end-of-string (CX not zero) and strings are not equal (ZF = 0)." Thus, CMPS can be used to find matching or differing string elements.

Encoding:

```
1010011w
```

if w = 0 then LSRC = (SI), RSRC = (DI), DELTA = 1
else LSRC = (SI) + 1:(SI), RSRC = (DI) + 1:(DI), DELTA = 2

CMPS Operands	Clocks	Transfers	Bytes	CMPS Coding Examples
dest-string, source-string	22(22)	2	1	CMPS BUFF1, BUFF2
(repeat)dest-string, source-string	9+22 (5+22/rep)	2/rep	1	REP COMPS ID, KEY

210911

CWD

CONVERT WORD TO DOUBLEWORD

CWD

Operation:

if (AX) < 8000H then (DX) ← 0
else (DX) ← FFFFH

Flags Affected:

None

Description:

CWD (Convert Word to Doubleword) extends the sign of the word in register AX throughout register DX. CWD does not affect any flags. CWD can be used to produce a double-length (doubleword) dividend from a word prior to performing word division.

Encoding:

```
10011001
```

CWD Operands	Clocks	Transfers	Bytes	CWD Coding Example
(no operands)	5(4)	-	1	CWD

210911

DAA DECIMAL ADJUST FOR ADDITION DAA

Operation:

if ((AL) & 0FH) > 9 or (AF) = 1 then
   (AL) ← (AL) + 6
   (AF) ← 1
if (AL) > 9FH or (CF) = 1 then
   (AL) ← (AL) + 60H
   (CF) ← 1

Flags Affected:

AF, CF, PF, SF, ZF
OF undefined

Description:

DAA (Decimal Adjust for Addition) corrects the result of previously adding two valid packed decimal operands (the destination operand must have been register AL). DAA changes the content of AL to a pair of valid packed decimal digits. It updates AF, CF, PF, SF and ZF; the content of OF is undefined following execution of DAA.

Encoding:

```
00100111
```

DAA Operands	Clocks	Transfers	Bytes	DAA Coding Example
(no operands)	4(4)	-	1	DAA

DAS DECIMAL ADJUST FOR SUBTRACTION DAS

Operation:

if ((AL) & 0FH) >9 or (AF) = 1 then
   (AL) ← (AL) - 6
   (AF) ← 1
if (AL) > 9FH or (CF) = 1 then
   (AL) ← (AL) - 60H
   (CF) ← 1

Flags Affected:

AF, CF, PF, SF, ZF.
0F undefined

Description:

DAS (Decimal Adjust for Subtraction) corrects the result of a previous subtraction of
two valid packed decimal operands (the destination operand must have been specified as
register AL). DAS changes the content of AL
to a pair of valid packed decimal digits. DAS
updates AF, CF, PF, SF and ZF; the content
of OF is undefined following execution of
DAS.

Encoding:

```
00101111
```

DAS Operands	Clocks	Transfers	Bytes	DAS Coding Example
(no operands)	4(4)	-	1	DAS

DEC   DECREMENT   DEC

Operation:

(DEST) ← (DEST) - 1

Flags Affected:

AF, OF, PF, SF, ZF

Description:

DEC (Decrement) subtracts one from the destination operand. The operand may be a byte or a word and is treated as an unsigned binary number (see AAA and DAA). DEC updates AF, OF, PF, SF and ZF; it does not affect CF.

Encoding:

Memory or Register Operand:

1111111w	mod 001 r/m

DEST = EA

16-Bit Register Operand:

01001 reg

DEST = REG

DEC Operands	Clocks	Transfers	Bytes	DEC Coding Example
reg16	3(3)	-	1	DEC AX
reg8	3(3)	-	2	DEC AL
memory	15(15)+EA	2	2-4	DEC ARRAY [SI]

DIV   DIVIDE   DIV

Operation:

(temp) ← (NUMR)
if (temp) / (DIVR) > MAX then the
   following, in sequence
(QUO), (REM) undefined
(SP) ← (SP) - 2
((SP) + 1:(SP)) ← FLAGS
(IF) ← 0
(TF) ← 0
(SP) ← (SP) - 2
((SP) + 1:(SP)) ← (CS)
(CS) ← (2) i.e., the contents of
    memory locations 2 and 3
(SP) ← (SP) - 2
((SP) + 1:(SP)) ← (IP)
(IP) ← (0) i.e., the contents of
    locations 0 and 1
else
   (QUO) ← (temp) / (DIVR), where
    / is unsigned division
   (REM) ← (temp) % (DIVR) where
    % is unsigned modulo

Flags Affected:

AF, CF, OF, PF, SF, ZF undefined

Description:

DIV *source*

DIV (divide) performs an unsigned division of the accumulator (and its extension) by the source operand. If the source operand is a byte, it is divided into the two-byte dividend assumed to be in registers AL and AH. The byte quotient is returned in AL, and the byte remainder is returned in AH. If the source operand is a word, it is divided into the two-word dividend in registers AX and DX. The word quotient is returned in AX, and the word remainder is returned in DX. If the quotient exceeds the capacity of its destination register (FFH for byte source, FFFFH for word source), as when division by zero is attempted, a type 0 interrupt is generated, and the quotient and remainder are undefined. Nonintegral quotients are truncated to integers. The content of AF, CF, OF, PF, SF and ZF is undefined following execution of DIV.

DIV DIVIDE DIV

Encoding:

| 1 1 1 1 0 1 1 w | mod 1 1 0 r/m |

if w = 0 then NUMR = AX, DIVR = EA, QUO = AL, REM = AH, MAX = FFH
else NUMR = DX:AX, DIVR = EA, QUO = AX, REM = DX, MAX = FFFFH

DIV Operands	Clocks	Transfers	Bytes	DIV Coding Example
reg8	80-90(29)	-	2	DIV CL
reg16	144-162(38)	-	2	DIV BX
mem8	86-96 +EA(35)	1	2-4	DIV ALPHA
mem16	154-172 +EA(44)	1	2-4	DIV TABLE [SI]

210911

ENTER PROCEDURE ENTRY (iAPX 186/188 ONLY) ENTER

Operation:

Flags Affected:

None

```
(SP) ← (SP) - 2
((SP+1: (SP)) ← (BP)
(FP) ← (SP)
IF LEVEL > 0 then
    Repeat (Level - 1) times
        (BP) ← (BP) - 2
        (SP) ← (SP) - 2
        ((SP) +1: (SP)) ← ((BP))
    End Repeat
    (SP) ← (SP) - 2
    ((SP) +1: (SP)) ← (FP)
End if
(BP) ← (FP)
(SP) ← (SP) - (LSRC)
```

Description:

ENTER executes the calling sequence for a high-level language. It saves the current frame pointer (in BP), copies frame pointers from procedures below the current call (to allow access to local variables in these procedures) and allocates space on the stack for the local variables of the current procedure invocation.

210911

ENTER PROCEDURE ENTRY (iAPX 186/188 ONLY) ENTER

Encoding:

1 1 0 0 1 0 0 0	data low	data high

ENTER Operands	Clocks	Transfers	Bytes	ENTER Coding Example
Locals, level	L=0(15) L=1(25) L>1(22+16 (n-1))	-	4	ENTER 28,3

210911

ESC   ESCAPE   ESC

Operation:

if mod ≠ 11 then data bus ← (EA)

Flags Affected:

None

Description:

The ESC (Escape) instruction provides a mechanism by which other processors (coprocessors) may receive their instructions from the 8086 or 8088 instruction stream and make use of the 8086 or 8088 addressing modes. The CPU (8086 or 8088) does a no operation (NOP) for the ESC instruction other than to access a memory operand and place it on the bus. On the 80186,188, if bit 15 in the relocation register is set, a trap type 7 will be generated; if this bit is set to 0, the 80186,188 will respond to the ESC opcode in the same way as the 8086,88.

Encoding:

11011 x	mod x r/m

ESC Operands	Clocks	Transfers	Bytes	ESC Coding Example
immediate, memory	8(6)+EA	1	2-4	ESC 6, ARRAY [SI]
immediate, register	2(2)	-	2	ESC 20, AL

HLT HALT HLT

Operation:

None

Flags Affected:

None

Description:

HLT (Halt) causes the CPU to enter the halt state. The processor leaves the halt state upon activation of the RESET line, upon receipt of a non-maskable interrupt request on NMI, or, if interrupts are enabled, upon receipt of a mask-able interrupt request on INTR. HLT does not affect any flags. It may be used as an alternative to an endless software loop in situations where a program must wait for an interrupt.

Encoding:

| 11110100 |

HLT Operands	Clocks	Transfers	Bytes	HLT Coding Example
(no operands)	2(2)	-	1	HLT

210911

IDIV   INTEGER DIVIDE   IDIV

Operation:

(temp) ← (NUMR)
if (temp) / (DIVR) > 0 and (temp)
    / (DIVR) > MAX
or (temp) / (DIVR) < 0 and (temp)
    / (DIVR) < 0 - MAX - 1 then
    (QUO), (REM) undefined
    (SP) ← (SP) - 2
    ((SP) + 1:(SP)) ← FLAGS
    (IF) ← 0
    (TF) ← 0
    (SP) ← (SP) - 2
    ((SP) + 1:(SP)) ← (CS)
    (CS) ← (2)
    (SP) ← (SP) - 2
    ((SP) + 1:(SP)) ← (IP)
    (IP) ← (0)
else
    (QUO) ← (temp) / (DIVR), where
      / is signed division
    (REM) ← (temp) % (DIVR) where
      % is signed modulo

Flags Affected:

AF, CF, OF, PF, SF, ZF undefined

Description:

IDIV *source*

IDIV (Integer Divide) performs a signed division of the accumulator (and its extension) by the source operand. If the source operand is a byte, it is divided into the double-length dividend assumed to be in registers AL and AH; the single-length quotient is returned in AL, and the single-length remainder is returned in AH. For byte integer division, the maximum positive quotient is +127 (7FH) and the minimum negative quotient is −127 (81H). If the source operand is a word, it is divided into the double-length dividend in registers AX and DX; the single-length quotient is returned in AX, and the single-length remainder is returned in DX. For word integer division, the maximum positive quotient is +32,767 (7FFFH) and the minimum negative quotient is −32,767 (8001H). If the quotient is positive and exceeds the maximum, or is negative and is less than the minimum, the quotient and remainder are undefined, and a type 0 interrupt is generated. In particular, this occurs if division by 0 is attempted. Nonintegral quotients are truncated (toward 0) to integers, and the remainder has the same sign as the dividend. The content of AF, CF, OF, PF, SF and ZF is undefined following IDIV.

IDIV   INTEGER DIVIDE   IDIV

Encoding:

| 1 1 1 1 0 1 1 w | mod 1 1 1 r/m |

if w = 0 then NUMR = AX, DIVR = EA, QUO = AL, REM = AH, MAX = 7FH
else NUMR = DX:AX, DIVR = EA, QUO = AX, REM = DX, MAX = 7FFFH

IDIV Operands	Clocks	Transfers	Bytes	IDIV Coding Example
reg8	101-112 (44-52)	-	2	IDIV BL
reg16	165-184 (53-61)	-	2	IDIV CX
mem8	107-118 +EA(50-58)	1	2-4	IDIV DIVISOR_BYTE[SI]
mem16	171-190 +EA(59-67)	1	2-4	IDIV [BX].DIVISOR_WORD

IMUL   INTEGER MULTIPLY   IMUL

Operation:

(DEST) ← (LSRC) * (RSRC) where
  * is signed multiply
if (ext) = sign-extension of (LOW)
  then (CF) ← 0
else (CF) ← 1;
(OF) ← (CF)

Flags Affected:

CF, OF
AF, PF, SF, ZF undefined

Description:

IMUL *source*

IMUL (Integer Multiply) performs a signed multiplication of the source operand and the accumulator. If the source is a byte, then it is multiplied by register AL, and the double-length result is returned in AH and AL. If the source is a word, then it is multiplied by register AX, and the double-length result is returned in registers DX and AX. If the upper half of the result (AH for byte source, DX for word source) is not the sign extension of the lower half of the result, CF and OF are set; otherwise they are cleared. When CF and OF are set, they indicate that AH or DX contains significant digits of the result. The content of AF, PF, SF and ZF is undefined following execution of IMUL.

Encoding:

```
1111011w  mod101r/m
```

if w = 0 then LSRC = AL, RSRC = EA, DEST = AH, EXT = AH, LOW = AL
else LSRC = AX, RSRC = EA, DEST = DX:AX, EXT = DX, LOW = AX

IMUL Operands	Clocks	Transfers	Bytes	IMUL Coding Example
reg8	80-98(25-28)	-	2	IMUL CL
reg16	128-154 (34-37)	-	2	IMUL BX
mem8	86-104 +EA(31-34)	1	2-4	IMUL RATE_BYTE
mem16	134-160 +EA(40-43)	1	2-4	IMUL RATE_WORD[BP][DI]

210911

IMUL INTEGER MULTIPLY IMMEDIATE (iAPX 186/188 ONLY) IMUL

Operation:

(DEST) ← (SRC) * IMMEDIATE
  where
  * is signed multiply
if product fits in destination
register then CF ← OF ← O;
else CF ← OF ← 1

Flags Affected:

CF, OF
AF, DF, SF, ZF undefined

Description:

IMUL *destination-register, source, immediate*

The IMUL (integer immediate multiply, signed) instruction allows a value to be multiplied by an immediate value. This value may be a byte or word; if it is a byte, it will be sign extended to 16 bits. When this instruction is used, only the lower 16 bits of the result will be saved. The result must always be placed in one of the general purpose registers. The two operands are the immediate value, and the data at an effective address (which may be the same register in which the result will be placed, another register, or a memory location). This instruction requires three arguments: the immediate value, the effective address of the second operand, and the register in which the result is to be placed. If the product fits in the 16 bit destination register, the CF and OF are cleared. If the product is larger than the 16 bit register, CF and OF are set.

Encoding:

| 0 1 1 0 1 0 s 1 | mod reg r/m | data | data if s = 0 |

IMUL Operands	Clocks	Tranfers	Bytes	IMUL Coding Example
immediate8	(22-25)	-	3	IMUL Bx, SI, 5
immediate8	(22-25)	-	3	IMUL BX, 5 ;product→BX
immediate8	(22-25)	-	3	IMUL BX, WORDSMTHING, 5
immediate16	(29-32)	-	4	IMUL BX, SI, 400H
immediate16	(29-32)	-	4	IMUL BX, 400H ; product →BX
immediate16	(29-32)	-	4	IMUL BX, WORDSMTHING, 5

210911

IN   INPUT BYTE OR WORD   IN

Operation:

(DEST) ← (SRC)

Flags Affected:

None

Description:

IN *accumulator,port*

IN transfers a byte or a word from an input port to the AL register or the AX register, respectively. The port number may be specified either with an immediate byte constant, allowing access to ports numbered 0 through 255, or with a number previously placed in the DX register, allowing variable access (by changing the value in DX) to ports numbered from 0 through 65,535.

Encoding:

Fixed Port:

1110010 w	port

if w = 0 then SRC = port, DEST = AL
else SRC = port + 1:port, DEST = AX

Variable Port:

1110110 w

if w = 0 then SRC = (DX), DEST = AL
else SRC = (DX) + 1:(DX), DEST = AX

IN Operands	Clocks	Transfers	Bytes	IN Coding Example
accumulator, immed8	10(10)	1	2	IN AL, OEAH
accumulator,DX	8(8)	1	1	IN AX, DX

INC INCREMENT INC

Operation:

(DEST) ← (DEST) + 1

Flags Affected:

AF, OF, PF, SF, ZF

Description:

INC *destination*

INC (Increment) adds one to the destination operand. The operand may be a byte or a word and is treated as an unsigned binary number (see AAA and DAA). INC updates AF, OF, PF, SF and ZF; it does not affect CF.

Encoding:

Memory or Register Operand:

| 1 1 1 1 1 1 1 w | mod 0 0 0 r/m |

DEST = EA

16-Bit Register Operand:

| 0 1 0 0 0 reg |

DEST = REG

INC Operands	Clocks	Transfers	Bytes	INC Coding Example
reg16	3(3)	-	1	INC CX
reg8	3(3)	-	2	INC BL
memory	15(15)+EA	2	2-4	INC ALPHA [DI][BX]

210911

INS
INPUT STRING
(iAPX 186/188 ONLY)
INS

Operation:

(DEST) ← (SRC)

Flags Affected:

None

Description:

INS *source-string, port*

INS (Input String) transfers a byte or a word from an I/O port (addressed by DX) to a memory address (pointed to by DI) and updates DX to point to the next string element. When used in conjunction with REP, INS performs block transfers at full bus bandwidth.

Encoding:

```
0 1 1 0 1 1 0 W
```

INS Operands	Clocks	Transfers	Bytes	INS Coding Example
dest-string,port	(14)	2	1	INS BUFF1, USART D
(repeat)dest-string, port	(8+8/rep)	2/rep	1	REP INS BUFF1, USART D

210911

INT   INTERRUPT   INT

Operation:

$(SP) \leftarrow (SP) - 2$
$((SP) + 1{:}(SP)) \leftarrow FLAGS$
$(IF) \leftarrow 0$
$(TF) \leftarrow 0$
$(SP) \leftarrow (SP) - 2$
$((SP) + 1{:}(SP)) \leftarrow (CS)$
$(CS) \leftarrow (TYPE * 4 + 2)$
$(SP) \leftarrow (SP) - 2$
$((SP) + 1{:}(SP)) \leftarrow (IP)$
$(IP) \leftarrow (TYPE * 4)$

Flags Affected:

IF, TF

Description:

INT *interrupt-type*

INT (Interrupt) activates the interrupt procedure specified by the interupt-type operand. INT decrements the stack pointer by two, pushes the flags onto the stack, and clears the trap (TF) and interrupt-enable (IF) flags to disable single-step and maskable interrupts. The flags are stored in the format used by the PUSHF instruction. SP is decremented again by two, and the CS register is pushed onto the stack. The address of the interrupt pointer is calculated by multiplying interrupt-type by four; the second word of the interrupt pointer replaces CS. SP again is decremented by two, and IP is pushed onto the stack and is replaced by the first word of the interrupt pointer. If interrupt-type = 3, the assembler generates a short (1 byte) form of the instruction, known as the breakpoint interrupt.

Software interrupts can be used as "supervisor calls," i.e., requests for service from an operating system. A different interrupt-type can be used for each type of service that the operating system could supply for an application program. Software interrupts also may be used to check out interrupt service procedures written for hardware-initiated interrupts.

INT INTERRUPT INT

Encoding:

| 1100110 v | type if v = 1 |

if v = 0 then TYPE = 3
else TYPE = type

INT Operands	Clocks	Transfers	Bytes	INT Coding Example
immed8(type=3)	52(45)	5	1	INT 3
immed8(type≠3)	51(47)	5	2	INT 67

210911

INTO INTERRUPT ON OVERFLOW INTO

Operation:

if (OF) = 1 then
  (SP) ← (SP) - 2
  ((SP) + 1:(SP)) ← FLAGS
  (IF) ← 0
  (TF) ← 0
  (SP) ← (SP) - 2
  ((SP) + 1:(SP)) ← (CS)
  (CS) ← (12H)
  (SP) ← (SP) - 2
  ((SP) + 1:(SP)) ← (IP)
  (IP) ← (10H)

Flags Affected:

None

Description:

INTO (Interrupt on Overflow) generates a software interrupt if the overflow flag (OF) is set; otherwise control proceeds to the following instruction without activating an interrupt procedure. INTO addresses the target interrupt procedure (its type is 4) through the interrupt pointer at location 10H; it clears the TF and IF flags and otherwise operates like INT. INTO may be written following an arithmetic or logical operation to activate an interrupt procedure if overflow occurs.

Encoding:

```
11001110
```

INTO Operands	Clocks	Transfers	Bytes	INTO Coding Example
(no operands)	53 or 4 (48 or 4)	5	1	INTO

IRET INTERRUPT RETURN IRET

Operation:

$(IP) \leftarrow ((SP)+1:(SP))$
$(SP) \leftarrow (SP) + 2$
$(CS) \leftarrow ((SP)+1:(SP))$
$(SP) \leftarrow (SP) + 2$
$FLAGS \leftarrow ((SP) + 1:(SP))$
$(SP) \leftarrow (SP) + 2$

Flags Affected:

All

Description:

IRET (Interrupt Return) transfers control back to the point of interruption by popping IP, CS and the flags from the stack. IRET thus affects all flags by restoring them to previously saved values. IRET is used to exit any interrupt procedure, whether activated by hardware or software.

Encoding:

| 11001111 |

IRET Operands	Clocks	Transfers	Bytes	IRET Coding Example
(no operands)	32(28)	3	1	IRET

JA   JUMP ON ABOVE   JA

JNBE   JUMP ON NOT BELOW OR EQUAL   JNBE

Operation:

if (CF) & (ZF) = 0 then
  (IP) ← (IP) + disp (sign-extended
    to 16-bits)

Flags Affected:

None

Description:

Jump on Above (JA)/Jump on Not Below or
Equal (JNBE) transfers control to the target
operand (IP + displacement) if CF and ZF = 0.

Encoding:

01110111	disp

JA/JNBE Operands	Clocks	Transfers	Bytes	JA Coding Example
short-label	16 or 4 (13 or 4)	-	2	JA ABOVE
				JNBE Coding Example
				JNBE ABOVE

210911

JAE JNB

JUMP ON ABOVE OR EQUAL

JUMP ON NOT BELOW

JAE JNB

Operation:

if (CF) = 0 then
   (IP) ← (IP) + disp (sign-extended
     to 16-bits)

Flags Affected:

None

Description:

JAE (Jump on Above or Equal)/JNB (Jump on Not Below) transfers control to the target operand (IP + displacement) if CF = 0.

Encoding:

01110011	disp

JAE/JNB Operands	Clocks	Transfers	Bytes	JAE Coding Example
short-label	16 or 4 (13 or 4)	-	2	JAE ABOVE_EQUAL

210911

JB   JUMP ON BELOW   JB

JNAE   JUMP ON NOT ABOVE OR EQUAL   JNAE

Operation:

if (CF) = 1 then
   (IP) ← (IP) + disp (sign-extended
    to 16-bits)

Flags Affected:

None

Description:

JB (Jump on Below)/JNAE (Jump on Not Above or Equal) transfers control to the target operand (IP + displacement) if CF = 1.

Encoding:

01110010	disp

JB/JNAE Operands	Clocks	Transfers	Bytes	JB Coding Example
short-label	16 or 4 (13 or 4)	-	2	JB BELOW

JBE

JUMP ON BELOW OR EQUAL

JBE

JNA

JUMP ON NOT ABOVE

JNA

Operation:

IF (CF) or (ZF) = 1 then
  (IP) ← (IP) + disp (sign-extended
    to 16-bits)

Flags Affected:

None

Description:

JBE (Jump on Below or Equal)/JNA (Jump on Not Above) transfers control to the target operand (IP + displacement) if CF or ZF = 1.

Encoding:

01110110	disp

JBE/JNA Operands	Clocks	Transfers	Bytes	JNA Coding Example
short-label	16 or 4 (13 or 4)	-	2	JNA NOT_ABOVE

210911

JC   JUMP ON CARRY   JC

Operation:

if (CF) = 1 then
   (IP) ← (IP) + disp (sign-extended
     to 16-bits)

Flags Affected:

None

Description:

JC (Jump on Carry) transfers control to the
target operand (IP + displacement) on the condition CF = 1.

Encoding:

01110010	disp

JC Operands	Clocks	Transfers	Bytes	JC Coding Example
short-label	16 or 4 (13 or 4)	-	2	JC CARRY_SET

     210911

JCXZ   JUMP IF CX REGISTER ZERO   JCXZ

Operation:

if (CX) = 0 then
  (IP) ← (IP) + disp (sign-extended
    to 16-bits)

Flags Affected:

None

Description:

JCXZ *short-label*

JCXZ (Jump if CX Zero) transfers control to
the target operand if CX is 0. This instruction
is useful at the beginning of a loop to bypass
the loop if CX has a zero value, i.e., to execute
the loop zero times.

Encoding:

11100011	disp

JCXZ Operands	Clocks	Transfers	Bytes	JCXZ Coding Example
short-label	18 or 6 (16 or 5)	-	2	JCXZ COUNT_DONE

210911

JE   JUMP ON EQUAL   JE
JZ   JUMP ON ZERO   JZ

Operation:

if (ZF) = 1 then
(IP) ← (IP) + disp (sign-extended
to 16-bits)

Flags Affected:

None

Description:

JE (Jump on Equal)/JZ (Jump on Zero)
transfers control to the target operand (IP +
displacement) if ZF = 1.

Encoding:

01110100	disp

JE/JZ Operands	Clocks	Transfers	Bytes	JZ Coding Example
short-label	16 or 4(13 or 4)	-	2	JZ ZERO

JG   JUMP ON GREATER   JG
JNLE   JUMP ON NOT LESS OR EQUAL   JNLE

Operation:

if ((SF) = (OF)) or (ZF) = 0 then
  (IP) ← (IP) + disp (sign-extended
   to 16-bits)

Flags Affected:

None

Description:

JG (Jump on Greater Than)/JNLE (Jump on
Not Less Than or Equal) transfers control to
the target operand (IP + displacement) if the
conditions ((SF XOR OF) or ZF = 0) are
greater than/not less than or equal to the
tested value.

Encoding:

01111111	disp

JG/JNLE Operands	Clocks	Transfers	Bytes	JG Coding Example
short-label	16 or 4 (13 or 4)	-	2	JG GREATER

JGE   JUMP ON GREATER OR EQUAL   JGE

JNL   JUMP ON NOT LESS   JNL

Operation:

if (SF) = (OF) then
  (IP) ← (IP) + disp (sign-extended
    to 16-bits)

Flags Affected:

None

Description:

JGE (Jump on Greater Than or Equal)/JNL (Jump on Not Less Than) transfers control to the target operand (IP + displacement) if the condition (SF XOR OF = 0) is greater than or equal/not less than the tested value.

Encoding:

01111101	disp

JGE/JNL Operands	Clocks	Transfers	Bytes	JGE Coding Example
short-label	16 or 4 (13 or 4)	-	2	JGE GREATER_EQUAL

210911

JL   JUMP ON LESS   JL

JNGE   JUMP ON NOT GREATER OR EQUAL   JNGE

Operation:

if (SF) ≠ (OF) then
    (IP) ← (IP) + disp (sign-extended
        to 16-bits)

Flags Affected:

None

Description:

JL (Jump on Less Than)/JNGE (Jump on Not Greater Than or Equal), transfers control to the target operand if the condition (SF XOR OF = 1) is less than/not greater than or equal to the tested value.

Encoding:

01111100	disp

JL/JNGE Operands	Clocks	Transfers	Bytes	JL Coding Example
short-label	16 or 4 (13 or 4)	-	2	JL LESS

JLE JNG

JUMP ON LESS OR EQUAL
JUMP ON NOT GREATER

JLE JNG

Operation:

if ((SF) ≠ (OF)) or ((ZF) = 1) then
(IP) ← (IP) + disp (sign-extended
to 16-bits)

Flags Affected:

None

Description:

JLE (Jump on Less Than or Equal to)/JNG (Jump on Not Greater Than) transfers control to the target operand (IP + displacement) if the conditions tested ((SF XOR OF) or ZF = 1) are less than or equal to/not greater than the tested value.

Encoding:

01111110	disp

JLE/JNG Operands	Clocks	Transfers	Bytes	JNG Coding Example
short-label	16 or 4 (13 or 4)	-	2	JNG NOT_GREATER

210911

JMP JUMP UNCONDITIONALLY JMP

Operation:

if Inter-Segment then (CS) ← SEG
(IP) ← DEST

Flags Affected:

None

Description:

JMP *target*

JMP unconditionally transfers control to the target location. Unlike a CALL instruction, JMP does not save any information on the stack; no return to the instruction following the JMP is expected. Like CALL, the address of the target operand may be obtained from the instruction itself (direct JMP), or from memory or a register referenced by the instruction (indirect JMP).

An intrasegment direct JMP changes the instruction pointer by adding the relative displacement of the target from the JMP instruction. If the assembler can determine that the target is within 127 bytes of the JMP, it automatically generates a two-byte instruction form called a SHORT JMP; otherwise, it generates a NEAR JMP that can address a target within ±32k. Intrasegment direct JMPS are self-relative and appropriate in position-independent (dynamically relocatable) routines in which the JMP and its target are moved together in the same segment.

An intrasegment indirect JMP may be made either through memory or a 16-bit general register. In the first case, the word content referenced by the instruction replaces the instruction pointer. In the second case, the new IP value is taken from the register named in the instruction.

An intersegment direct JMP replaces IP and CS with values contained in the instruction.

An intersegment indirect JMP may be made only through memory. The first word of the doubleword pointer referenced by the instruction replaces IP and the second word replaces CS.

210911

JMP JUMP UNCONDITIONALLY JMP

Encoding:

Intra-Segment Direct:

11101001	disp-low	disp-high

DEST = (IP) + disp

Intra-Segment Direct Short:

11101011	disp

DEST = (IP) + disp sign extended to 16-bits

Intra-Segment Indirect:

11111111	mod 1 0 0 r/m

DEST = (EA)

Inter-Segment Direct:

11101010	offset-low	offset-high
	seg-low	seg-high

DEST = offset, SEG = seg

Inter-Segment Indirect:

11111111	mod 1 0 1 r/m

DEST = (EA), SEG = (EA + 2)

JMP Operands	Clocks	Transfers	Bytes	JMP Coding Example
short-label	15(14)	-	2	JMP SHORT
near-label	15(14)	-	3	JMP WITHIN_SEGMENT
far-label	15(14)	-	5	JMP FAR_LABEL
memptr16	18(17)+EA	-	2-4	JMP [BX].TARGET
regptr16	11(11)	-	2	JMP CX
memptr32	24(26)+EA	-	2-4	JMP OTHER.SEG[SI]

JNC JUMP ON NOT CARRY JNC

Operation:

if (CF) = 0 THEN
   (IP) ← (IP) + disp (sign-extended
      to 16-bits)

Flags Affected:

None

Description:

JNC (Jump on Not Carry) transfers control to
the target operand (IP + displacement) on the
condition CF = 0.

Encoding:

01110011	disp

JNC Operands	Clocks	Transfers	Bytes	JNC Coding Example
short-label	16 or 4 (13 or 4)	-	2	JNC NO_CARRY

JNE   JUMP ON NOT EQUAL   JNE

JNZ   JUMP ON NOT ZERO   JNZ

Operation:

if (ZF) = 0 then
  (IP) ← (IP) + disp (sign-extended
    to 16-bits)

Flags Affected:

None

Description:

JNE (Jump on Not Equal to)/ JNZ (Jump on Not Zero) transfers control to the target operand (IP + displacement) if the condition tested (ZF = 0) is true.

Encoding:

01110101	disp

JNE/JNZ Operands	Clocks	Transfers	Bytes	JNE Coding Example
short-label	16 or 4 (13 or 4)	-	2	JNE NOT_EQUAL

JNO　　JUMP ON NOT OVERFLOW　　JNO

Operation:

if (OF) = 0 then
   (IP) ← (IP) + disp (sign-extended
    to 16-bits)

Flags Affected:

None

Description:

JNO (Jump on Not Overflow) transfers control to the target operand (IP + displacement)
if the condition tested (OF = 0) is true.

Encoding:

01110001	disp

JNO Operands	Clocks	Transfers	Bytes	JNO Coding Example
short-label	16 or 4 (13 or 4)	-	2	JNO NO_OVERFLOW

210911

JNS   JUMP ON NOT SIGN   JNS

Operation:

if (SF) = 0 then
(IP) ← (IP) + disp (sign-extended
to 16-bits)

Flags Affected:

None

Description:

JNS (Jump on Not Sign) transfers control to
the target operand (IP + displacement) when
the tested condition (SF = 0) is true.

Encoding:

01111001	disp

JNS Operands	Clocks	Transfers	Bytes	JNS Coding Example
short-label	16 or 4 (13 or 4)	-	2	JNS POSITIVE

210911

JNP   JUMP ON NOT PARITY   JNP

JPO   JUMP ON PARITY ODD   JPO

Operation:

if (PF) = 0 then
  (IP) ← (IP) + disp (sign-extended
    to 16-bits)

Flags Affected:

None

Description:

JNP (Jump on Not Parity)/JPO (Jump on Parity Odd) transfers control to the target operand if the condition tested (PF = 0) is true.

Encoding:

01111011	disp

JNP/JPO Operands	Clocks	Transfers	Bytes	JPO Coding Example
short-label	16 or 4 (13 or 4)	-	2	JPO ODD_PARITY

210911

JO   JUMP ON OVERFLOW   JO

Operation:

if (OF) = 1 then
  (IP) ← (IP) + disp (sign-extended
    to 16-bits)

Flags Affected:

None

Description:

JO (Jump on Overflow) transfers control to
the target operand (IP + displacement) if the
tested condition (OF = 1) is true.

Encoding:

01110000	disp

JO Operands	Clocks	Transfers	Bytes	JO Coding Example
short-label	16 or 4 (13 or 4)	-	2	JO SIGNED_OVERFLOW

210911

JP JUMP ON PARITY JP

JPE JUMP ON PARITY EQUAL JPE

Operation:

if (PF) = 1 then
   (IP) ← (IP) + disp (sign-extended
     to 16-bits)

Flags Affected:

None

Description:

JP (Jump on Parity)/JPE (Jump on Parity Equal) transfers control to the target operand (IP + displacement) if the condition tested (PF = 1) is true.

Encoding:

01111010	disp

JP/JPE Operands	Clocks	Transfers	Bytes	JPE Coding Example
short-label	16 or 4 (13 or 4)	-	2	JPE EVEN_PARITY

JS JUMP ON SIGN JS

Operation:

if (SF) = 1 then
 (IP) ← (IP) + disp (sign-extended
  to 16-bits)

Flags Affected:

None

Description:

JS (Jump on Sign) transfers control to the target operand (IP + displacement) if the tested condition (SF = 1) is true.

Encoding:

01111000	disp

JS Operands	Clocks	Transfers	Bytes	JS Coding Example
short-label	16 or 4 (13 or 4)	-	2	JS NEGATIVE

LAHF LOAD REGISTER AH FROM FLAGS LAHF

Operation:

(AH) ← (SF):(ZF):X:(AF):X:(PF):X:(CF)

Flags Affected:

None

Description:

LAHF (load register AH from flags) copies
SF, ZF, AF, PF and CF (the 8080/8085 flags)
into bits 7, 6, 4, 2 and 0, respectively, of
register AH. The content of bits 5, 3 and 1 is
undefined; the flags themselves are not
affected. LAHF is provided primarily for converting 8080/8085 assembly language programs to run on an 8086 or 8088.

Encoding:

```
10011111
```

LAHF Operands	Clocks	Transfers	Bytes	LAHF Coding Example
(no operands)	4(2)	-	1	LAHF

LDS LOAD POINTER USING DS LDS

Operation:

(REG) ← (EA)
(DS) ← (EA + 2)

Flags Affected:

None

Description:

LDS *destination,source*

LDS (load pointer using DS) transfers a 32-bit pointer variable from the source operand, which must be a memory operand, to the destination operand and register DS. The offset word of the pointer is transferred to the destination operand, which may be any 16-bit general register. The segment word of the pointer is transferred to register DS. Specifying SI as the destination operand is a convenient way to prepare to process a source string that is not in the current data segment (string instructions assume that the source string is located in the current data segment and that SI contains the offset of the string).

Encoding:

11000101	mod reg r/m

if mod = 11 then undefined operation

LDS Operands	Clocks	Transfers	Bytes	LDS Coding Example
reg16, mem32	16(18)+EA	2	2-4	LDS SI, DATA.SEG[DI]

LEA   LOAD EFFECTIVE ADDRESS   LEA

Operation:

(REG) ← EA

Flags Affected:

None

Description:

LEA *destination,source*

LEA (load effective address) transfers the off-set of the source operand (rather than its value) to the destination operand. The source operand must be a memory operand, and the destination operand must be a 16-bit general register. LEA does not affect any flags. The XLAT and string instructions assume that certain registers point to operands; LEA can be used to load these registers (e.g., loading BX with the address of the translate table used by the XLAT instruction).

Encoding:

10001101	mod reg r/m

if mod = 11 then undefined operation

LEA Operands	Clocks	Transfers	Bytes	LEA Coding Example
reg16, mem16	2(6)+EA	-	2-4	LEA BX,[BP][DI]

    210911

LEAVE

RESTORE STACK FOR PROCEDURE EXIT (iAPX 186/188 ONLY)

LEAVE

Operation:

$(SP) \leftarrow (BP)$
$(BP) \leftarrow ((SP) + 1 : (SP))$
$(SP) \leftarrow (SP) + 2$

Flags Affected:

None

Description:

LEAVE executes a procedure return for a high level language. It deallocates all local variables and restores the SP and BP registers to their values immediately after the procedure's invocation.

Encoding:

1 1 0 0 1 0 0 1

LEAVE Operands	Clocks	Transfers	Bytes	LEAVE Coding Example
(no operands)	(8)	1	1	LEAVE

LES   LOAD POINTER USING ES   LES

Operation:

(REG) ← (EA)
(ES) ← (EA + 2)

Flags Affected:

None

Description:

LES *destination,source*

LES (load pointer using ES) transfers a 32-bit pointer variable from the source operand, which must be a memory operand, to the destination operand and register ES. The offset word of the pointer is transferred to the destination operand, which may be any 16-bit general register. The segment word of the pointer is transferred to register ES. Specifying DI as the destination operand is a convenient way to prepare to process a destination string that is not in the current extra segment. (The destination string must be located in the extra segment, and DI must contain the offset of the string.)

Encoding:

```
11000100 | mod reg r/m
```

if mod = 11 then undefined operation

LES Operands	Clocks	Transfers	Bytes	LES Coding Example
reg16, mem32	16(18)+EA	2	2-4	LES DI,[BX].TEXT_BUFF

LOCK   LOCK THE BUS   LOCK

Operation:

None

Flags Affected:

None

Description:

LOCK is a one-byte prefix that causes the 8088 (configured in maximum mode) to assert its bus LOCK signal while the following instruction executes. LOCK does not affect any flags.

The instruction most useful in this context is an exchange register with memory. A simple software lock may be implemented with the following code sequence:

```
Check:        MOV     AL,1        ;set AL to 1 (implies locked)
    LOCK      XCHG    Sema,AL     ;test and set lock
              TEST    AL,AL       ;set flags based on AL
              JNZ     Check       ;retry if lock already set

              MOV     Sema,0      ;clear the lock when done
```

The LOCK prefix may be combined with the segment override and/or REP prefixes.

Encoding:

    11110000

LOCK Operands	Clocks	Transfers	Bytes	LOCK Coding Example
(no operands)	2(2)	-	1	LOCK XCHG FLAG, AL

LODS LOAD STRING LODS
(BYTE OR WORD)

Operation:

(DEST) ← (SRC)
if (DF) = 0 then (SI) ← (SI) + DELTA
else (SI) ← (SI) - DELTA

Flags Affected:

None

Description:

LODS *source-string*

LODS (Load String) transfers the byte or word string element addressed by SI to register AL or AX, and updates SI to point to the next element in the string. This instruction is not ordinarily repeated since the accumulator would be overwritten by each repetition, and only the last element would be retained. However, LODS is very useful in software loops as part of a more complex string function built up from string primitives and other instructions.

Encoding:

```
1010110 w
```

if w = 0 then SRC = (SI), DEST = AL, DELTA = 1
else SRC = (SI) + 1:(SI), DEST = AX, DELTA = 2

LODS Operands	Clocks	Transfers	Bytes	LODS Coding Example
source-string	12(10)	1	1	LODS CUSTOMER_NAME
(repeat)	9+13			
source-string	(6+11/rep)	1/rep	1	REP LODS NAME

210911

LOOP   LOOP   LOOP

Operation:

(CX) ← (CX) - 1
if (CX) ≠ 0 then
  (IP) ← (IP) + disp (sign-extended
    to 16-bits)

Flags Affected:

None

Description:

LOOP *short-label*

LOOP decrements CX by 1 and transfers control to the target operand if CX is not 0; otherwise the instruction following LOOP is executed.

Encoding:

11100010	disp

LOOP Operands	Clocks	Transfers	Bytes	LOOP Coding Example
short-label	17 or 5 (15 or 5)	-	2	LOOP AGAIN

210911

LOOPE LOOP WHILE EQUAL LOOPE

LOOPZ LOOP WHILE ZERO LOOPZ

Operation:

(CX) ← (CX) - 1
if (ZF) = 1 and (CX) ≠ 0 then
   (IP) ← (IP) + disp (sign-extended
    to 16-bits)

Flags Affected:

None

Description:

LOOPE/LOOPZ *short-label*

LOOPE and LOOPZ (Loop While Equal and Loop While Zero) are different mnemonics for the same instruction (similar to the REPE and REPZ repeat prefixes). CX is decremented by 1, and control is transferred to the target operand if CX is not 0 and if ZF is set; otherwise the instruction following LOOPE/LOOPZ is executed.

Encoding:

11100001	disp

LOOPE/LOOPZ Operands	Clocks	Transfers	Bytes	LOOPE Coding Example
short-label	18 or 6 (16 or 6)	-	2	LOOPE AGAIN

LOOPNZ LOOP WHILE NOT ZERO LOOPNZ

LOOPNE LOOP WHILE NOT EQUAL LOOPNE

Operation:

(CX) ← (CX) - 1
if (ZF) = 0 and (CX) ≠ 0 then
  (IP) ← (IP) + disp (sign-extended
    to 16-bits)

Flags Affected:

None

Description:

LOOPNE/LOOPNZ *short-label*

LOOPNE and LOOPNZ (Loop While Not Equal and Loop While Not Zero) are also synonyms for the same instruction. CX is decremented by 1, and control is transferred to the target operand if CX is not 0 and if ZF is clear; otherwise the next sequential instruction is executed.

Encoding:

11100000	disp

LOOPNE/LOOPNZ Operands	Clocks	Transfers	Bytes	LOOPNE Coding Example
short-label	19 or 5 (16 or 5)	-	2	LOOPNE AGAIN

MOV MOVE (BYTE OR WORD) MOV

Operation:

(DEST) ← (SRC)

Flags Affected:

None

Description:

MOV destination,source

MOVE transfers a byte or a word from the
source operand to the destination operand.

Encoding:

Memory or Register Operand to/from Register Operand:

100010 d w	mod reg r/m

if d = 1 then SRC = EA, DEST = REG
else SRC = REG, DEST = EA

Immediate Operand to Memory or Register Operand:

1100011 w	mod 000 r/m	data	data if w=1

SRC = data, DEST = EA

Immediate Operand to Register:

1011 w reg	data	data if w=1

SRC = data, DEST = REG

MOV MOVE (BYTE OR WORD) MOV

Encoding:

Memory Operand to Accumulator:

| 1 0 1 0 0 0 0 w | addr-low | addr-high |

if w = 0 then SRC = addr, DEST = AL
else SRC = addr + 1:addr, DEST = AX

Accumulator to Memory Operand:

| 1 0 1 0 0 0 1 w | addr-low | addr-high |

if w = 0 then SRC = AL, DEST = addr
else SRC = AX, DEST = addr + 1:addr

Memory or Register Operand to Segment Register:

| 1 0 0 0 1 1 1 0 | mod 0 reg r/m |

if reg ≠ 01 then SRC = EA, DEST = REG
else undefined operation

Segment Register to Memory or Register Operand:

| 1 0 0 0 1 1 0 0 | mod 0 reg r/m |

SRC = REG, DEST = EA

MOV Operands	Clocks	Transfers	Bytes	MOV Coding Example
memory, accumulator	10(9)	1	3	MOV ARRAY AL
accumulator, memory	10(8)	1	3	MOV AX, TEMP_RESULT
register, register	2(2)	-	2	MOV AX, CX
register, memory	8(12) + EA	1	2-4	MOV BP, STACK_TOP
memory, register	9(9) + EA	1	2-4	MOV COUNT [DI], CX
register, immediate	4(3-4)	-	2-3	MOV CL, 2
memory, immediate	10(12-13) + EA	1	3-6	MOV MASK[BX][SI], 2CH
seg-reg, reg16	2(2)	-	2	MOV ES, CX
seg-reg, mem16	8(9) + EA	1	2-4	MOV DS, SEGMENT_BASE
reg16, seg-reg	2(2)	-	2	MOV BP, SS
memory, seg-reg	9(11) + EA	1	2-4	MOV[BX]SEG_SAVE, CS

210911

MOVS   MOVE STRING   MOVS

Operation:

(DEST) ← (SRC)

Flags Affected:

None

Description:

MOVS *destination-string,source-string*

MOVS (Move String) transfers a byte or a word from the source string (addressed by SI) to the destination string (addressed by DI) and updates SI and DI to point to the next string element. When used in conjunction with REP, MOVS performs a memory-to-memory block transfer.

Encoding:

| 1 0 1 0 0 1 0 w |

if w = 0 then SRC = (SI), DEST = AL, DELTA = 1
else SRC = (SI) + 1:(SI), DEST = AX, DELTA = 2

MOVS Operands	Clocks	Transfers	Bytes	MOVS Coding Example
dest-string, source-string	18(9)	2	1	MOVS LINE_EDIT_DATA
(repeat) dest-string, source-string	9+17/rep (8+8/rep)	2/rep	1	REP MOVS SCREEN, BUFFER

MUL   MULTIPLY   MUL

Operation:

(DES) ← (LSRC) * (RSRC), where *
  is unsigned multiply
if (EXT) = 0 then (CF) ← 0
else (CF) ← 1;
(OF) ← (CF)

Flags Affected:

CF, OF.
AF, PF, SF, ZF undefined

Description:

MUL *source*

MUL (Multiply) performs an unsigned multiplication of the source operand and the accumulator. If the source is a byte, then it is multiplied by register AL, and the double-length result is returned in AH and AL. If the source operand is a word, then it is multiplied by register AX, and the double-length result is returned in registers DX and AX. The operands are treated as unsigned binary numbers (see AAM). If the upper half of the result (AH for byte source, DX for word source) is non-zero, CF and OF are set; otherwise they are cleared. When CF and OF are set, they indicate that AH or DX contains significant digits of the result. The content of AF, PF, SF and ZF is undefined following execution of MUL.

Encoding:

| 1 1 1 1 0 1 1 w | mod 1 0 0 r/m |

if w = 0 then LSRC = AL, RSRC = EA, DEST = AX, EXT = AH
else LSRC = AX, RSRC = EA, DEST = DX:AX, EXT = DX

MUL Operands	Clocks	Transfers	Bytes	MUL Coding Example
reg8	70-77 (26-28)	-	2	MUL BL
reg16	118-113 (35-37)	-	2	MUL CX
mem8	76-83 + EA(32-34)	1	2-4	MUL MONTH [SI]
mem16	124-139 +EA(41-43)	1	2-4	MUL BAUD_RATE

210911

NEG NEGATE NEG

Operation:

(EA) ← SRC - (EA)
(EA) ← (EA) + 1 (affecting flags)

Flags Affected:

AF, CF, OF, PF, SF, ZF

Description:

NEG destination

NEG (Negate) subtracts the destination operand, which may be a byte or a word, from 0 and returns the result to the destination. This forms the two's complement of the number, effectively reversing the sign of an integer. If the operand is zero, its sign is not changed.

Attempting to negate a byte containing −128 or a word containing −32,768 causes no change to the operand and sets OF. NEG updates AF, CF, OF, PF, SF and ZF. CF is always set except when the operand is zero, in which case it is cleared.

Encoding:

1111011w	mod 011 r/m

if w = 0 then SRC = FFH
else SRC = FFFFH

NEG Operands	Clocks	Transfers	Bytes	NEG Coding Example
register	3(3)	-	2	NEG AL
memory	16(3)+EA	2	2-4	NEG MULTIPLIER

210911

NOP NO OPERATION NOP

Operation:

None

Flags Affected:

None

Description:

NOP

NOP (No Operation) causes the CPU to do
nothing. NOP does not affect any flags.

Encoding:

```
10010000
```

NOP Operands	Clocks	Transfers	Bytes	NOP Coding Example
(no operands)	3(3)	-	1	NOP

210911

NOT   LOGICAL NOT   NOT

Operation:

(EA) ← SRC - (EA)

Flags Affected:

None

Description:

NOT *destination*

NOT inverts the bits (forms the one's complement) of the byte or word operand.

Encoding:

| 1 1 1 1 0 1 1 w | mod 0 1 0 r/m |

if w = 0 then SRC = FFH
else SRC = FFFFH

NOT Operands	Clocks	Transfers	Bytes	NOT Coding Example
register	3(3)	-	-	NOT AX
memory	16(3) + EA	2	-	NOT CHARACTER

210911

OR LOGICAL OR OR

Operation:

(DEST) ← (LSRC) OR (RSRC)
(CF) ← 0
(OF) ← 0

Flags Affected:

CF, OF, PF, SF, ZF.
AF undefined

Description:

OR destination,source

OR performs the logical "inclusive or" of the
two operands (byte or word) and returns the
result to the destination operand. A bit in the
result is set if either or both corresponding bits
in the original operands are set; otherwise the
result bit is cleared.

210911

OR LOGICAL OR OR

Encoding:

Memory or Register Operand with Register Operand:

0 0 0 0 1 0 d w	mod reg r/m

if d = 1 then LSRC = REG, RSRC = EA, DEST = REG
else LSRC = EA, RSRC = REG, DEST = EA

Immediate Operand to Memory or Register Operand:

1 0 0 0 0 0 0 w	mod 0 0 1 r/m	data	data if w=1

LSRC = EA, RSRC = data, DEST = EA

Immediate Operand to Accumulator:

0 0 0 0 1 1 0 w	data	data if w=1

if w = 0 then LSRC = AL, RSRC = data, DEST = AL
else LSRC = AX, RSRC = data, DEST = AX

OR Operands	Clocks	Transfers	Bytes	OR Coding Example
register,register	3(3)	-	2	OR AL, BL
register, memory	9(10)+EA	1	2-4	OR DX,PORT_ID[DI]
memory,register	16(10)+EA	2	2-4	OR FLAG_BYTE, CL
accumulator, immediate	4(3-4)	-	2-3	OR AL, 01101100B
register, immediate	4(4)	-	3-4	OR CX, 01H
memory, immediate	17(16)+EA	2	3-6	OR[BX].CMD_WORD,0CFH

210911

OUT

OUTPUT

OUT

Operation:

(DEST) ← (SRC)

Flags Affected:

None

Description:

OUT port,accumulator

OUT transfers a byte or a word from the AL register or the AX register, respectively, to an output port. The port number may be specified either with an immediate byte constant, allowing access to ports numbered 0 through 255, or with a number previously placed in register DX, allowing variable access (by changing the value in DX) to ports numbered from 0 through 65,535.

Encoding:

Fixed Port:

1 1 1 0 0 1 1 w	port

if w = 0 then SRC = AL, DEST = port
else SRC = AX, DEST = port + 1:port

Variable Port:

1 1 1 0 1 1 1 w

if w = 0 then SRC = AL, DEST = (DX)
else SRC = AX, DEST = (DX) + 1:(DX)

OUT Operands	Clocks*	Transfers	Bytes	OUT Coding Example
immed8,accumulator	10(9)	1	2	OUT 44, AX
DX, accumulator	8(7)	1	1	OUT DX, AL

OUTS   OUTPUT STRING   OUTS
(iAPX 186/188 ONLY)

Operation:

(DST) ← (SRC)

Flags Affected:

None

Description:

OUTS *port, destination string*

OUTS transfers a byte or word from a destination string (addressed by SI) to an output port (addressed by DX). After the transfer, SI is updated to point to the next string element. When used with REP, the block transfer takes place at full bus bandwidth.

Encoding:

0 1 1 0 1 1 1 W

OUTS Operands	Clocks	Transfers	Bytes	OUTS Coding Example
port,source-string	(14)	2	1	OUTS PORT2, BUFF2
(repeat) port, source-string	(8+8/rep)	2/rep	1	REP OUTS PORT4, BUFF2

210911

POP POP POP

Operation:

(DEST) ← ((SP) + 1:(SP))
(SP) ← (SP) + 2

Flags Affected:

None

Description:

POP *destination*

POP transfers the word at the current top of stack (pointed to by SP) to the destination operand, and then increments SP by two to point to the new top of stack. POP can be used to move temporary variables from the stack to registers or memory.

POP　　　POP　　　POP

Encoding:

Memory or Register Operand:

| 1 0 0 0 1 1 1 1 | mod 0 0 0 r/m |

DEST = EA

Register Operand:

| 0 1 0 1 1 reg |

DEST = REG

Segment Register:

| 0 0 0 reg 1 1 1 |

if reg ≠ 01 then DEST = REG
else undefined operation

POP Operands	Clocks	Transfers	Bytes	POP Coding Example
register	8(10)	1	1	POP DX
seg-reg(CS illegal)	8(8)	1	1	POP DS
memory	17(20)+EA	2	2-4	POP PARAMETER

210911

POPA POP ALL REGISTERS (iAPX 186/188 ONLY) POPA

Operation:

$(DI) \leftarrow ((SP) + 1: (SP))$
$(SP) \leftarrow (SP) + 2$
$(SI) \leftarrow ((SP) + 1: (SP))$
$(SP) \leftarrow (SP) + 2$
$(BP) \leftarrow ((SP) + 1: (SP))$
$(SP) \leftarrow (SP) + 2$
$(BX) \leftarrow ((SP) + 1: (SP))$
$(SP) \leftarrow (SP) + 2$
$(DX) \leftarrow ((SP) + 1: (SP))$
$(SP) \leftarrow (SP) + 2$
$(CX) \leftarrow ((SP) + 1: (SP))$
$(SP) \leftarrow (SP) + 2$
$(AX) \leftarrow ((SP + 1: (SP))$
$(SP) \leftarrow (SP) + 2$

Flags Affected:

None

210911

POPA   POP ALL REGISTERS   POPA
(iAPX 186/188 ONLY)

Description:

POPA pops all data, pointer and index registers
off of the stack. The SP value popped is discarded.

Encoding:

```
01100001
```

POPA Operands	Clocks	Transfers	Bytes	POPA Coding Example
(no operands)	(51)	8	1	POPA

210911

POPF   POP FLAGS   POPF

Operation:

Flags ← ((SP) + 1:(SP))
(SP) ← (SP) + 2

Flags Affected:

All

Description:

POPF

POPF transfers specific bits from the word at the current top of stack (pointed to by register SP) into the 8086/8088 flags, replacing whatever values the flags previously contained (see figure 2-32). SP is then incremented by two to point to the new top of stack. PUSHF and POPF allow a procedure to save and restore a calling program's flags. They also allow a program to change the setting of TF (there is no instruction for updating this flag directly). The change is accomplished by pushing the flags, altering bit 8 of the memory-image and then popping the flags.

Encoding:

| 1 0 0 1 1 1 0 1 |

POPF Operands	Clocks	Transfers	Bytes	POPF Coding Example
(no operands)	8(8)	1	1	POPF

PUSH   PUSH   PUSH

Operation:

(SP) ← (SP) - 2
((SP) + 1:(SP)) ← (SRC)

Flags Affected:

None

Description:

PUSH *source*

PUSH decrements SP (the stack pointer) by two and then tranfers a word from the source operand to the top of stack now pointed to by SP. PUSH often is used to place parameters on the stack before calling a procedure; more generally, it is the basic means of storing temporary data on the stack.

210911

PUSH   PUSH   PUSH

Encoding:

Memory or Register Operand:

| 1 1 1 1 1 1 1 1 | mod 1 1 0 r/m |

SRC = EA

Register Operand:

| 0 1 0 1 0 reg |

SRC = REG

Segment Register:

| 0 0 0 reg 1 1 0 |

SRC = REG

PUSH Operands	Clocks	Transfers	Bytes	PUSH Coding Example
register	11(10)	1	1	PUSH SI
seg-reg(CS legal)	10(9)	1	1	PUSH ES
memory	16(16)+EA	2	2-4	PUSH RETURN_CODE[SI]

PUSH PUSH IMMEDIATE (iAPX 186/188 ONLY) PUSH

Operation:

$(SP) \leftarrow (SP) - 2$
$((SP) + 1 : (SP)) \leftarrow$ immediate

Flags Affected:

None

Description:

PUSH *immediate*

The PUSH (push immediate) instruction allows immediate data to be pushed onto the stack. The data can be either immediate byte or immediate word. Byte data will be sign extended to word size before it is pushed onto the stack (since all stack operations are done on word data).

Encoding:

0 1 1 0 1 0 s 0	data	data if s = 0

PUSH Operands	Clocks	Tranfers	Bytes	PUSH Coding Example
immediate8	10	1	2	PUSH 5
immediate8	10	1	3	PUSH 400H

210911

PUSHA PUSH ALL REGISTERS (iAPX 186/188 ONLY) PUSHA

Operation:

temp ← (SP)
(SP) ← (SP) - 2
((SP) + 1: (SP)) ← (AX)
(SP) ← (SP) - 2
((SP) + 1: (SP)) ← (CX)
(SP) ← (SP) - 2
((SP) + 1: (SP)) ← (DX)
(SP) ← (SP) - 2
((SP) + 1: (SP)) ← (BX)
(SP) ← (SP) - 2
((SP) + 1: (SP)) ← (temp)
(SP) ← (SP) - 2
((SP) + 1: (SP)) ← (BP)
(SP) ← (SP) - 2
((SP) + 1: (SP)) ← (SI)
(SP) ← (SP) - 2
((SP) + 1: (SP)) ← (DI)

Flags Affected:

None

210911

PUSHA PUSH ALL REGISTERS PUSHA (iAPX 186/188 ONLY)

Description:

PUSHA pushes all data, pointer and index registers onto the stack. The order in which the registers are saved is: AX, CX, DX, BX, SP, BP, SI and DI. The SP value pushed is the SP value before the first register (AX) is pushed.

Encoding:

0 1 1 0 0 0 0 0

PUSHA Operands	Clocks	Transfers	Bytes	PUSHA Coding Example
(no operands)	(36)	8	1	PUSHA

210911

PUSHF   PUSH FLAGS   PUSHF

Operation:

(SP) ← (SP) - 2
((SP) + 1:(SP)) ← Flags

Flags Affected:

None

Description:

PUSHF

PUSHF decrements SP (the stack pointer) by two and then transfers all flags to the word at the top of stack pointed to by SP. The flags themselves are not affected.

Encoding:

| 1 0 0 1 1 1 0 0 |

PUSHF Operands	Clocks	Transfers	Bytes	PUSHF Coding Example
(no operands)	10(9)	1	1	PUSHF

210911

RCL ROTATE THROUGH CARRY LEFT RCL

Operation:

(temp) ← COUNT
do while (temp) ≠ 0
  (tmpcf) ← (CF)
  (CF) ← high-order bit of (EA)
  (EA) ← (EA) * 2 + (tmpcf)
  (temp) ← (temp) - 1
if COUNT = 1 then
  if high-order bit of (EA) ≠ (CF)
    then (OF) ← 1
  else (OF) ← 0
else (OF) undefined

Flags Affected:

CF, OF

Description:

RCL *destination,count*

RCL (Rotate through Carry Left) rotates the bits in the byte or word destination operand to the left by the number of bits specified in the count operand. The carry flag (CF) is treated as "part of" the destination operand; that is, its value is rotated into the low-order bit of the destination, and itself is replaced by the high-order bit of the destination.

210911

RCL ROTATE THROUGH CARRY LEFT RCL

Encoding:

Rotate by 1 or CL:

1 1 0 1 0 0 v w

if v = 0 then COUNT = 1
else COUNT = (CL)

Rotate by Immed8:
(iAPX 186/188 only)

1 1 0 0 0 0 0 w	mod 0 1 0 r/m		count

RCL Operands	Clocks	Transfers	Bytes	RCL Coding Example
register, n	(5+1/bit)	-	3	RCL CX, 5
memory, n	(17+1/bit)	2	3-5	RCL ALPHA, 5
register 1,	2(2)	-	2	RCL CX, 1
register, CL	8+4/bit			
	(5+1/bit)	-	2	RCL AL, CL
memory, 1	15(15)+EA	2	2-4	RCL ALPHA, 1
memory, CL	20+4/bit			
	(17+1/bit)+EA	2	2-4	RCL[BP].PARAM, CL

210911

RCR ROTATE THROUGH CARRY RIGHT RCR

Operation:

(temp) ← COUNT
do while (temp) ≠ 0
  (tmpcf) ← (CF)
  (CF) ← low-order bit of (EA)
  (EA) ← (EA) / 2
  high-order bit of (EA) ← (tmpcf)
  (temp) ← (temp) - 1
if COUNT = 1 then
  if high-order bit of (EA) ≠ next-
    to-high-order bit of (EA)
    then (OF) ← 1
  else (OF) ← 0
else (OF) undefined

Flags Affected:

CF, OF

Description:

RCR *destination,count*

RCR (Rotate through Carry Right) operates exactly like RCL except that the bits are rotated right instead of left.

Encoding:

Rotate by 1 or CL:

1 1 0 1 0 0 v w	mod 0 1 1 r/m

if v = 0 then COUNT = 1
else COUNT = (CL)

Rotate by Immed8:
(iAPX 186/188 only)

1 1 0 0 0 0 0 w	mod 0 1 1 r/m		count

RCR Operands	Clocks	Transfers	Bytes	RCR Coding Example
register, n	(5 + 1/bit)	-	3	RCR BX, 5
memory, n	(17 + 1/bit)	2	3-5	RCR [BX].STATUS, 5
register, 1	2(2)	-	2	RCR BX, 1
register, CL	8 + 4/bit			
	(5 + 1/bit)	-	2	RCR BL, CL
memory, 1	15(15) + EA	2	2-4	RCR [BX].STATUS, 1
memory, CL	20 + 4/bit			
	(17 + 1/bit) + EA	2	2-4	RCR ARRAY[DI], CL

210911

REP   REPEAT   REP

REPE/REPZ   REPE/REPZ
REPEAT WHILE EQUAL/
REPEAT WHILE ZERO

REPNE/REPNZ REPNE/REPNZ
REPEAT WHILE NOT EQUAL/
REPEAT WHILE NOT ZERO

Operation:

do while (CX) ≠ 0
   service pending interrupt (if
  any) execute primitive string
   operation in succeeding byte
$(CX) \leftarrow (CX) - 1$
if primitive operation is CMPB,
  CMPW, SCAB, or SCAW and
  (ZF) ≠ z then exit from
  while loop

Flags Affected:

None

210911

REP REPEAT REP

REPE/REPZ REPE/REPZ
REPEAT WHILE EQUAL/
REPEAT WHILE ZERO

REPNE/REPNZ REPNE/REPNZ
REPEAT WHILE NOT EQUAL/
REPEAT WHILE NOT ZERO

Description:

REP/REPE/REPZ/REPNE/REPNZ

Repeat, Repeat While Equal, Repeat While Zero, Repeat While Not Equal and Repeat While Not Zero are mnemonics for two forms of the prefix byte that controls subsequent string instruction repetition. The different mnemonics are provided to improve program clarity. The repeat prefixes do not affect the flags.

REP is used in conjunction with the MOVS (Move String) and STOS (Store String) instructions and is interpreted as "repeat while not end-of-string" (CX not 0). REPE and REPZ operate identically and are physically the same prefix byte as REP. These instructions are used with the CMPS (Compare String) and SCAS (Scan String) instructions and require ZF (posted by these instructions) to be set before initiating the next repetition. REPNE and REPNZ are mnemonics for the same prefix byte. These instructions function the same as REPE and REPZ except that the zero flag must be cleared or the repetition is terminated. ZF does not need to be initialized before executing the repeated string instruction.

Repeated string sequences are interruptable; the processor will recognize the interrupt before processing the next string element. System interrupt processing is not affected in any way. Upon return from the interrupt, the repeated operation is resumed from the point of interruption. However, execution does *not* resume properly if a second or third prefix (i.e., segment override or LOCK) has been specified in addition to any of the repeat prefixes. At interrupt time, the processor "remembers" only the prefix that immediately precedes the string instruction. After returning from the interrupt, processing resumes, but any additional prefixes specified are not in effect. If more than one prefix must be used with a string instruction, interrupts may be disabled for the duration of the repeated execution. However, this will not prevent a nonmaskable interrupt from being recognized. Also, the time that the system is unable to respond to interrupts may be unacceptable if long strings are being processed.

210911

REP — REPEAT — REP

REPE/REPZ — REPE/REPZ
REPEAT WHILE EQUAL/ REPEAT WHILE ZERO

REPNE/REPNZ REPNE/REPNZ
REPEAT WHILE NOT EQUAL/ REPEAT WHILE NOT ZERO

Encoding:

```
1111001z
```

REP Operands	Clocks	Transfers	Bytes	REP Coding Example
(no operands)	2(2)	—	1	REP MOVS DEST, SRCE
REPE/REPZ Operands	**Clocks**	**Transfers**	**Bytes**	**REPE Coding Example**
(no operands)	2(2)	—	1	REPE CMPS DATA, KEY
REPNE/REPNZ Operands	**Clocks**	**Transfers**	**Bytes**	**REPNE Coding Example**
(no operands)	2(2)	—	1	REPNE SCAS INPUT__LINE

RET   RETURN   RET

Operation:

$(IP) \leftarrow ((SP)=1:(SP))$
$(SP) \leftarrow (SP) + 2$
if Inter-Segment then
   $(CS) \leftarrow ((SP)+1:(SP))$
   $(SP) \leftarrow (SP) + 2$
if Add Immediate to Stack Pointer
   then $(SP) \leftarrow (SP) + data$

Flags Affected:

None

Description:

RET *optional-pop-value*

RET (Return transfers control from a procedure back to the instruction following the CALL that activated the procedure. The assembler generates an intrasegment RET if the programmer has defined the procedure NEAR, or an intersegment RET if the procedure has been defined as FAR. RET pops the word at the top of the stack (pointed to by register SP) into the instruction pointer and increments SP by two. If RET is intersegment, the word at the new top of stack is popped into the CS register, and SP is again incremented by two. If an optional pop value has been specified, RET adds that value to SP. This feature may be used to discard parameters pushed onto the stack before the execution of the CALL instruction.

210911

RET   RETURN   RET

Encoding:

Intra-Segment:

11000011

Intra-Segment and Add Immediate to Stack Pointer:

11000010	data-low	data-high

Inter-Segment:

11001011

Inter-Segment and Add Immediate to Stack Pointer:

11001010	data-low	data-high

RET Operands	Clocks	Transfers	Bytes	RET Coding Example
(intra-segment, no pop)	16(16)	1	1	RET
(intra-segment,pop)	20(18)	1	3	RET 4
(inter-segment, no pop)	26(22)	2	1	RET
(inter-segment,pop)	25(25)	2	3	RET 2

ROL   ROTATE LEFT   ROL

Operation:

(temp) ← COUNT
do while (temp) ≠ 0
  (CF) ← high-order bit of (EA)
  (EA) ← (EA) * 2 + (CF)
  (temp) ← (temp) - 1
if COUNT = 1 then
  if high-order bit of (EA) ≠ (CF)
    then (OF) ← 1
  else (OF) ← 0
else (OF) undefined

Flags Affected:

CF, OF

Description:

ROL destination,count

ROL (Rotate Left) rotates the destination byte
or word left by the number of bits specified in
the count operand.

Encoding:

Rotate by 1 or CL:

| 1 1 0 1 0 0 v w | mod 0 0 0 r/m |

if v = 0 then COUNT = 1
else COUNT = (CL)

Rotate by Immed8:
  (iAPX 186/188 only)

| 1 1 0 1 0 0 0 w | mod 0 0 0 r/m | | count |

ROL Operands	Clocks	Transfers	Bytes	ROL Coding Example
register, n	(5 + 1/bit)	-	3	ROL BX,5
memory, n	(17 + 1/bit)	2	3-5	ROL FLAG_BYTE[DI],5
register, 1	2(2)	-	2	ROL BX, 1
register, CL	8 + 4/bit			ROL DI, CL
	(5 + 1/bit)	-	2	
memory, 1	15(15) + EA	2	2-4	ROL FLAG_BYTE[DI],1
memory, CL	20 + 4/bit			ROL ALPHA, CL
	(17 + 1/bit) + EA	2	2-4	

210911

ROR   ROTATE RIGHT   ROR

Operation:

(temp) ← COUNT
do while (temp) ≠ 0
  (CF) ← low-order bit of (EA)
  (EA) ← (EA) / 2
  high-order bit of (EA) ← (CF)
  (temp) ← (temp) - 1
if COUNT = 1 then
  if high-order bit of (EA) ≠ next-
to-high-order bit of (EA)
then (OF) ← 1
  else (OF) ← 0
else (OF) undefined

Flags Affected:

CF, OF

Description:

ROR *destination,count*

ROR (Rotate Right) operates similar to ROL
except that the bits in the destination byte or
word are rotated right instead of left.

Encoding:

Rotate by 1 or CL:

| 1 1 0 1 0 0 v w | mod 0 0 1 r/m |

if v = 0 then COUNT = 1
else COUNT = (CL)

Rotate by Immed8:
  (iAPX 186/188 only)

| 1 1 0 1 0 0 0 w | mod 0 0 1 r/m | : | count |

ROR Operands	Clocks	Transfers	Bytes	ROR Coding Example
register, n	(5+1/bit)	-	3	ROR AL, 5
memory, n	(17+1/bit)	2	3-5	ROR PORT_STATUS, 5
register, 1	2(2)	-	2	ROR AL, 1
register, CL	8+4/bit			
	(5+1/bit)	-	2	ROR BX, CL
memory, 1	15(15)+EA	2	2-4	ROR PORT_STATUS, 1
memory, CL	20+4/bit			
	(17+1/bit)+EA	2	2-4	ROR CMD_WORD, CL

210911

SAHF STORE REGISTER AH INTO FLAGS SAHF

Operation:

(SF):(ZF):X:(AF):X:(PF):X:(CF) ← (AH)

Flags Affected:

AF, CF, PF, SF, ZF

Description:

SAHF

SAHF (store register AH into flags) transfers bits 7, 6, 4, 2 and 0 from register AH into SF, ZF, AF, PF and CF, respectively, replacing whatever values these flags previously had. OF, DF, IF and TF are not affected. This instruction is provided for 8080/8085 compatibility.

Encoding:

```
10011110
```

SAHF Operands	Clocks	Transfers	Bytes	SAHF Coding Example
(no operands)	4(3)	-	1	SAHF

SAL   SHIFT ARITHMETIC LEFT   SAL
SHL   SHIFT LOGICAL LEFT   SHL

Operation:

    (temp) ← COUNT
    do while (temp) ≠ 0
       (CF) ← high-order bit of (EA)
       (EA) ← (EA) * 2
       (temp) ← (temp) - 1
    if COUNT = 1 then
       if high-order bit of (EA) ≠ (CE)
          then (OF) ← 1
       else (OF) ← 0
    else (OF) undefined

Flags Affected:

CF, OF, PF, SF, ZF.
AF undefined

Description:

SHL/SAL *destination,count*

SHL and SAL (Shift Logical Left and Shift Arithmetic Left) perform the same operation and are physically the same instruction. The destination byte or word is shifted left by the number of bits specified in the count operand. Zeros are shifted in on the right. If the sign bit retains its original value, then OF is cleared.

210911

SAL SHIFT ARITHMETIC LEFT SAL
SHL SHIFT LOGICAL LEFT SHL

Encoding:

Shift by 1 or CL:

| 1 1 0 1 0 0 v w | mod 1 0 0 r/m |

if v = 0 then COUNT = 1
else COUNT = (CL)

Shift by Immed8:
  (iAPX 186/188 only)

| 1 1 0 1 0 0 0 w | mod 1 0 0 r/m | | count |

SAL/SHL Operands	Clocks	Transfers	Bytes	SAL/SHL Coding Example
register, n	(5+1/bit)	-	3	SAL AH, 5
memory, n	(17+1/bit)	2	3-5	SAL[BX].OVERDRAW, 5
register, 1	2(2)	-	2	SAL AH, 1
register, CL	8+4/bit			
	(5+1/bit)	-	2	SHL DI, CL
memory, 1	15(15)+EA	2	2-4	SHL[BX].OVERDRAW, 1
memory, CL	20+4/bit			
	(17+1/bit)+EA	2	2-4	SAL STORE_COUNT, CL

SAR SHIFT ARITHMETIC RIGHT SAR

Operation:

(temp) ← COUNT
do while (temp) ≠ 0
  (CF) ← low-order bit of (EA)
  (EA) ← (EA) / 2, where / is
    equivalent to signed division,
    rounding down
  (temp) ← (temp) - 1
if COUNT = 1 then
  if high-order bit of (EA) ≠ next-
    to-high-order bit of (EA)
    then (OF) ← 1
  else (OF) ← 0
else (OF) ← 0

Flags Affected:

CF, OF, PF, SF, ZF.
AF undefined

Description:

SAR destination,count

SAR (Shift Arithmetic Right) shifts the bits in the destination operand (byte or word) to the right by the number of bits specified in the count operand. Bits equal to the original high-order (sign) bit are shifted in on the left, preserving the sign of the original value. Note that SAR does not produce the same result as the dividend of an "equivalent" IDIV instruction if the destination operand is negative and 1-bits are shifted out. For example, shifting −5 right by one bit yields −3, while integer division −5 by 2 yields −2. The difference in the instructions is that IDIV truncates all numbers toward zero, while SAR truncates positive numbers toward zero and negative numbers toward negative infinity.

SAR SHIFT ARITHMETIC RIGHT SAR

Encoding:

Shift by 1 or CL:

| 1 1 0 1 0 0 v w | mod 1 1 1 r/m |

if v = 0 then COUNT = 1
else COUNT = (CL)

Shift by Immed8:
(iAPX 186/188 only)

| 1 1 0 1 0 0 0 w | mod 1 1 1 r/m | | count |

SAR Operands	Clocks	Transfers	Bytes	SAR Coding Example
register, n	(5 + 1/bit)	-	3	SAR DX, 5
memory, n	(17 + 1/bit)	2	3-5	SAR N_BLOCKS, 5
register, 1	2(2)	-	2	SAR DX, 1
register, CL	8 + 4/bit			
	(5 + 1/bit)	-	2	SAR DI, CL
memory, 1	15(15) + EA	2	2-4	SAR N_BLOCKS, 1
memory, CL	20 + 4/bit			
	(17 + 1/bit) + EA	2	2-4	SAR N_BLOCKS, CL

210911

SBB SUBTRACT WITH BORROW SBB

Operation:

if (CF) = 1 then (DEST) = (LSRC) -
(RSRC) - 1
else (DEST) ← (LSRC) - (RSRC)

Flags Affected:

AF, CF, OF, PF, SF, ZF

Description:

SBB *destination,source*

SBB (Subtract with Borrow) subtracts the source from the destination, subtracts one if CF is set, and returns the result to the destination operand. Both operands may be bytes or words. Both operands may be signed or unsigned binary numbers (see AAS and DAS). SBB updates AF, CF, OF, PF, SF, and ZF. Since it incorporates a borrow from a previous operation, SBB may be used to write routines that subtract numbers longer than 16 bits.

210911

SBB   SUBTRACT WITH BORROW   SBB

Encoding:

Memory or Register Operand and Register Operand:

0 0 0 1 1 0 d w	mod reg r/m

if d = 1 then LSRC = REG, RSRC = EA, DEST = REG
else LSRC = EA, RSRC = REG, DEST = EA

Immediate Operand from Memory or Register Operand:

1 0 0 0 0 0 s w	mod 0 1 1 r/m	data	data if s:w=01

LSRC = EA, RSRC = data, DEST = EA

Immediate Operand from Accumulator:

0 0 0 1 1 1 0 w	data	data if w=1

if w = 0 then LSRC = AL, RSRC = data, DEST = AL
else LSRC = AX, RSRC = data, DEST = AX

SBB Operands	Clocks	Transfers	Bytes	SBB Coding Example
register, register	3(3)	-	2	SBB BX, CX
register, memory	9(10)+EA	1	2-4	SBB DI,[BX].PAYMENT
memory, register	16(10)+EA	2	2-4	SBB BALANCE, AX
accumulator, immediate	4(3-4)	-	2-3	SBB AX, 2
register, immediate	4(4)	-	3-4	SBB CL, 1
memory, immediate	17(16)+EA	2	3-6	SBB COUNT [SI], 10

SCAS SCAN (BYTE OR WORD) STRING SCAS

Operation:

(LSRC) - RSRC)
if (DF) = 0 then (DI) ← (DI) + DELTA
else (DI) ← (DI) - DELTA

Flags Affected:

AF, CF, OF, PF, SF, ZF

Description:

SCAS *destination-string*

SCAS (Scan String) subtracts the destination string element (byte or word) addressed by DI from the content of AL (byte string) or AX (word string) and updates the flags, but does not alter the destination string or the accumulator. SCAS also updates DI to point to the next string element and AF, CF, OF, PF, SF and ZF to reflect the relationship of the scan value in AL/AX to the string element. If

SCAS is prefixed with REPE or REPZ, the operation is interpreted as "scan while not end-of-string (CX not 0) and string-element = scan-value (ZF = 1)." This form may be used to scan for departure from a given value. If SCAS is prefixed with REPNE or REPNZ, the operation is interpreted as "scan while not end-of-string (CX not 0) and string-element is not equal to scan-value (ZF = 0)." This form may be used to locate a value in a string.

Encoding:

```
1 0 1 0 1 1 1 w
```

if w = 0 then LSRC = AL, RSRC = (DI), DELTA = 1
else LSRC = AX, RSRC = (DI) + 1:(DI), DELTA = 2

SCAS Operands	Clocks	Transfers	Bytes	SCAS Coding Example
dest-string	15(15)	1	1	SCAS INPUT_LINE
(repeat)dest-string	9+15 (5+15/rep)	1/rep	1	REPNE SCAS BUFFER

210911

SHR SHIFT LOGICAL RIGHT SHR

Operation:

(temp) ← COUNT
do while (temp) ≠ 0
   CF) ← low-order bit of (EA
   (EA) ← (EA) / 2, where / is
     equivalent to unsigned
     division
   (temp) ← (temp) - 1
if COUNT = 1 then
   if high-order bit of (EA) ≠ next-
     to-high-order bit of (EA)
     then (OF) ← 1
   else (OF) ← 0
else (OF) undefined

Flags Affected:

CF, OF, PF, SF, ZF.
AF undefined

Description:

SHR *destination,source*

SHR (Shift Logical Right) shifts the bits in the destination operand (byte or word) to the right by the number of bits specified in the count operand. Zeros are shifted in on the left. If the sign bit retains its original value, then OF is cleared.

SHR   SHIFT LOGICAL RIGHT   SHR

Encoding:

Shift by 1 or CL:

1 1 0 1 0 0 v w	mod 1 0 1 r/m

if v = 0 then COUNT = 1
else COUNT = (CL)

Shift by Immed8:
  (iAPX 186/188 only)

1 1 0 1 0 0 0 w	mod 1 0 1 r/m	count

SHR Operands	Clocks	Transfers	Bytes	SHR Coding Example
register, n	(5+1/bit)	-	3	SHR SI, 5
memory, n	(17+1/bit)	2	3-5	SHR ID_BYTE[SI][BX], 5
register, 1	2(2)	-	2	SHR SI, 1
register, CL	8+4/bit			
	(5+1/bit)	-	2	SHR SI, CL
memory, 1	15(15)+EA	2	2-4	SHR ID_BYTE[SI][BX], 1
memory, CL	20+4/bit			
	(17+1/bit)+EA	2	2-4	SHR INPUT_WORD, CL

210911

STC   SET CARRY   STC

Operation:

(CF) ← 1

Flags Affected:

CF

Description:

STC

STC (Set Carry flag) sets CF to 1 and affects no other flags.

Encoding:

1 1 1 1 1 0 0 1

STC Operands	Clocks	Transfers	Bytes	STC Coding Example
(no operands)	2(2)	-	1	STC

210911

STD   SET DIRECTION FLAG   STD

Operation:

(DF) ← 1

Flags Affected:

DF

Description:

STD

STD (Set Direction flag) sets DF to 1 causing the string instructions to auto-decrement the SI and/or DI index registers. STD does not affect any other flags.

Encoding:

| 11111101 |

Timing: 2 clocks

STD Operands	Clocks	Transfers	Bytes	STD Coding Example
(no operands)	2(2)	-	1	STD

210911

STI SET INTERRUPT-ENABLE FLAG STI

Operation:

$(IF) \leftarrow 1$

Flags Affected:

IF

Description:

STI (Set Interrupt-enable flag) sets IF to 1, enabling processor recognition of maskable interrupt requests appearing on the INTR line. Note however, that a pending interrupt will not actually be recognized until the instruction following STI has executed. STI does not affect any other flags.

Encoding:

11111011

STI Operands	Clocks	Transfers	Bytes	STI Coding Example
(no operands)	2(2)	-	1	STI

210911

STOS STORE (BYTE/OR/ STOS
WORD) STRING

Operation:

(DEST) ← (SRC)
if (DF) = 0 then (DI) ← (DI) + DELTA
else (DI) ← (DI) - DELTA

Flags Affected:

None

Description:

STOS *destination-string*

STOS (Store String) transfers a byte or word from register AL or AX to the string element addressed by DI and updates DI to point to the next location in the string. As a repeated operation, STOS provides a convenient way to initialize a string to a constant value (e.g., to blank out a print line).

Encoding:

```
1010101w
```

if w = 0 then SRC = AL, DEST = (DI), DELTA = 1
else SRC = AX, DEST = (DI) + 1:(DI), DELTA = 2

STOS Operands	Clocks	Transfers	Bytes	STOS Coding Example
dest-string	11(10)	1	1	STOP PRINT_LINE
(repeat)dest-string	9+10/rep			
	(6+9/rep)	1/rep	1	REP STOS DISPLAY

210911

SUB SUBTRACT SUB

Operation:

(DEST) ← (LSRC) - (RSRC)

Flags Affected:

AF, CF, OF, PF, SF, ZF

Description:

SUB *destination,source*

The source operand is subtracted from the destination operand, and the result replaces the destination operand. The operands may be bytes or words. Both operands may be signed or unsigned binary numbers (see AAS and DAS). SUB updates AF, CF, OF, PF, SF and ZF.

210911

SUB   SUBTRACT   SUB

Encoding:

Memory or Register Operand and Register Operand:

0 0 1 0 1 0 d w	mod reg r/m

if d = 1 then LSRC = REG, RSRC = EA, DEST = REG
else LSRC = EA, RSRC = REG, DEST = EA

Immediate Operand from Memory or Register Operand:

1 0 0 0 0 0 s w	mod 1 0 1 r/m	data	data if s:w=01

LSRC = EA, RSRC = data, DEST = EA

Immediate Operand from Accumulator:

0 0 1 0 1 1 0 w	data	data if w=1

if w = 0 then LSRC = AL, RSRC = data, DEST = AL
else LSRC = AX, RSRC = data, DEST = AX

SUB Operands	Clocks	Transfers	Bytes	SUB Coding Example
register, register	3(3)	-	2	SUB CX, BX
register, memory	9(10)+EA	1	2-4	SUB DX,MATH_TOTAL[SI]
memory, register	16(10)+EA	2	2-4	SUB[BP + 2], C̄L
accumulator, immediate	4(3-4)	-	2-3	SUB AL, 10
register, immediate	4(4)	-	3-4	SUB SI, 5280
memory, immediate	17(16)+EA	2	3-6	SUB[BP].BALANCE, 1000

210911

TEST   TEST   TEST

Operation:

(LSRC) & (RSRC)
(CF) ← 0
(OF) ← 0

Flags Affected:

CF, OF, PF, SF, ZF.
AF undefined

Description:

TEST *destination,source*

TEST performs the logical "and" of the two operands (byte or word), updates the flags, but does not return the result, i.e., neither operand is changed. If a TEST instruction is followed by a JNZ (jump if not zero) instruction, the jump will be taken if there are any corresponding 1-bits in both operands.

210911

TEST   TEST   TEST

Encoding:

Memory or Register Operand with Register Operand:

1 0 0 0 0 1 0 w	mod reg r/m

LSRC = REG, RSRC = EA

Immediate Operand with Memory or Register Operand:

1 1 1 1 0 1 1 w	mod 0 0 0 r/m	data	data if w=1

LSRC = EA, RSRC = data

Immediate Operand with Accumulator:

1 0 1 0 1 0 0 w	data	data if w=1

if w = 0 then LSRC = AL, RSRC = data
else LSRC = AX, RSRC = data

TEST Operands	Clocks	Transfers	Bytes	TEST Coding Example
register, register	3(3)	-	2	TEST SI, DI
register, memory	9(10)+EA	1	2-4	TEST SI, END_COUNT
accumulator, immediate	4(3-4)	-	2-3	TEST AL, 00100000B
register, immediate	5(4)	-	3-4	TEST BX, 0CC4H
memory, immediate	11(10)+EA	-	3-6	TEST RETURN_CODE,01H

WAIT   WAIT   WAIT

Operation:

None

Flags Affected:

None

Description:

WAIT causes the CPU to enter the wait state while its TEST line is not active. WAIT does not affect any flags.

Encoding:

```
10011011
```

WAIT Operands	Clocks	Transfers	Bytes	WAIT Coding Example
(no operands)	4 + 5n(6)	-	1	WAIT

210911

XCHG EXCHANGE XCHG

Operation:

(temp) ← (DEST)
(DEST) ← (SRC)
(SRC) ← (temp)

Flags Affected:

None

Description:

XCHG *destination,source*

XCHG (exchange) switches the contents of the source and destination (byte or word) operands. When used in conjunction with the LOCK prefix, XCHG can test and set a semaphore that controls access to a resource shared by multiple processors (see section 2.5).

210911

XCHG   EXCHANGE   XCHG

Encoding:

Memory or Register Operand with Register Operand:

| 1 0 0 0 0 1 1 w | mod reg r/m |

SRC = EA, DEST = REG

Register Operand with Accumulator:

| 1 0 0 1 0 reg |

SRC = REG, DEST = AX

XCHG Operands	Clocks	Transfers	Bytes	XCHG Coding Example
accumulator,reg16	3(3)	-	1	XCHG AX, BX
memory, register	17(17) + EA	2	2-4	XCHG SEMAPHORE, AX
register, register	4(4)	-	2	XCHG AL, BL

XLAT TRANSLATE XLAT

Operation:

AL ← ((BX) + (AL))

Flags Affected:

None

Description:

XLAT *translate-table*

XLAT (translate) replaces a byte in the AL register with a byte from a 256-byte, user-coded translation table. Register BX is assumed to point to the beginning of the table. The byte in AL is used as an index into the table and is replaced by the byte at the offset in the table corresponding to AL's binary value.

The first byte in the table has an offset of 0. For example, if AL contains 5H, and the sixth element of the translation table contains 33H, then AL will contain 33H following the instruction. XLAT is useful for translating characters from one code to another, the classic example being ASCII to EBCDIC or the reverse.

Encoding:

| 1 1 0 1 0 1 1 1 |

XLAT Operands	Clocks	Transfers	Bytes	XLAT Coding Example
source-table	11(11)	1	1	XLAT ASCII_TAB

XOR   EXCLUSIVE OR   XOR

Operation:

(DEST) ← (LSRC) XOR (RSRC)
(CF) ← 0
(OF) ← 0

Flags Affected:

CF, OF, PF, SF, ZF.
AF undefined

Description:

XOR *destination,source*

XOR (Exclusive Or) performs the logical "exclusive or" of the two operands and returns the result to the destination operand. A bit in the result is set if the corresponding bits of the original operands contain opposite values (one is set, the other is cleared); otherwise the result bit is cleared.

210911

XOR   EXCLUSIVE OR   XOR

Encoding:

Memory or Register Operand with Register Operand:

0 0 1 1 0 0 d w	mod reg r/m

if d = 1 then LSRC = REG, RSRC = EA, DEST = REG
else LSRC = EA, RSRC = REG, DEST = EA

Immediate Operand to Memory or Register Operand:

1 0 0 0 0 0 0 w	mod 1 1 0 r/m	data	data if w=1

LSRC = EA, RSRC = data, DEST = EA

Immediate Operand to Accumulator:

0 0 1 1 0 1 0 w	data	data if w=1

if w = 0 then LSRC = AL, RSRC = data, DEST = AL
else LSRC = AX, RSRC = data, DEST = AX

XOR Operands	Clocks	Transfers	Bytes	XOR Coding Example
register, register	3(3)	-	2	XOR CX, BX
register, memory	9(10)+EA	1	2-4	XOR CL, MASK_BYTE
memory, register	16(10)+EA	2	2-4	XOR ALPHA[SI],DX
accumulator, immediate	4(3-4)	-	2-3	XOR AL, 01000010B
register, immediate	4(4)	-	3-4	XOR SI, 00C2H
memory, immediate	17(16)+EA	2	3-6	XOR RETURN_CODE,0D2H

210911

3.8 8086,88 PROGRAMMING EXAMPLES

In this section and the section following, specific programming examples are provided which illustrate how the instruction set and addressing modes may be used in various, commonly encountered programming situations.

The programs are primarily written in ASM-86. ASM-86 is the 8086/80186 assembly language. It provides the programmer who is familiar with the CPU architecture, access to all processor features. For critical code segments within programs that make sophisticated use of the hardware, have extremely demanding performance or memory constraints, ASM-86 is the best choice. For detailed information about Intel's 8086/80186 assembly language see: ASM86 Language Reference Manual, 121703.

Programs can also be written in high-level languages such as PL/M-86. PL/M-86 is a high-level language suitable for most microprocessor applications. It is easy to use, even by programmers who have little experience with microprocessors. Because it reduces software development time, PL/M-86 is ideal for most of the programming in any application, especially applications that must get to market quickly.

The languages are completely compatible, and a judicious combination of the two often makes good sense. Prototype software can be developed rapidly with a high-level language. When the system is operating correctly, it can then be analyzed to see which sections can best profit from being written in ASM-86. Since the logic of these sections has already been debugged, selective rewriting can be done quickly and with low risk.

The programming examples in this section address the following topics:

- Procedures

- JMP and CALL (jump, call)

- Bit manipulation

- Dynamic code relocation

- Memory mapped I/O

- Breakpoints

- Interrupt handling

- String operations

The examples are intended to show one way to use the instruction set and addressing modes. They do not demonstrate the "best" way to solve a particular problem. The flexibility of the 8086 and 80186 application differences plus variations in programming style usually add up to a number of ways to implement a programming solution.

Procedures (parameters, reentrancy)

The code in Figure 3-31 illustrates several techniques that are typically used in writing ASM-86 procedures. In this example a calling program invokes a procedure (called EXAMPLE) twice, passing it a different byte array each time. Two parameters are passed on the stack; the first contains the number of elements in the array, and the second contains the address (offset in DATA2SEG) of the first array element. This same technique can be used to pass a variable-length parameter list to a procedure (the "array" could be any series of parameters or parameter addresses). Thus, although the procedure always receives two parameters, these can be used to indirectly access any number of variables in memory.

Any results returned by a procedure should be placed in registers or in memory, but not on the stack. AX or AL is often used to hold a single word or byte result. Alternatively, the calling program can pass the address (or addresses) of a result area to the procedure as a parameter. It is good practice for ASM-86 programs to follow the calling conventions used by PL/M-86.

EXAMPLE is defined as a FAR procedure, meaning it is in a different segment than the calling program. The calling program must use an intersegment CALL to activate the procedure. Note that this type of CALL saves CS and IP on the stack. If EXAMPLE were defined as NEAR (in the same segment as the caller) then an intrasegment CALL would be used, and only IP would be saved on the stack. It is the responsibility of the calling program to know how the procedure is defined and to issue the correct type of CALL.

Figure 3-32 shows the stack before the caller pushes the parameters onto it. Figure 3-33 shows the stack as the procedure receives it after the CALL has been executed.

EXAMPLE is divided into four sections. The "prolog" sets up register BP so it can be used to address data on the stack (specifying BP as a base register in an instruction automatically refers to the stack segment unless a segment override prefix is coded). The next step in the prolog is to save the "state of the machine" as it existed when the procedure was activated. This is done by pushing any registers used by the procedure (only CX and BP in this case) onto the stack. If the procedure changes the flags, and the caller expects the flags to be unchanged following execution of the procedure, they also may be saved on the stack. The last instruction in the prolog allocates three words on the stack for the procedure to use as local temporary storage. Figure 3-34 shows the stack at the end of the prolog. Note that PL/M procedures assume that all registers except SP and BP can be used without saving and restoring.

```
        STACK__SEG      SEGMENT
                        DW          20 DUP (?)    ; ALLOCATE 20-WORD STACK

        STACK__TOP      LABEL       WORD          ; LABEL INITIAL TOS
        STACK__SEG      ENDS

        DATA__SEG       SEGMENT
        ARRAY__1        DB          10 DUP (?)    ; 10-ELEMENT BYTE ARRAY

        ARRAY__2        DB          5 DUP (?)     ; 5-ELEMENT BYTE ARRAY

        DATA__SEG       ENDS

        PROC__SEG       SEGMENT
        ASSUME  CS:PROC__SEG,DS:DATA__SEG,SS:STACK__SEG,ES:NOTHING

        EXAMPLE         PROC        FAR           ; MUST BE ACTIVATED BY
                                                  ;     INTERSEGMENT CALL

        ; PROCEDURE PROLOG
                        PUSH        BP            ; SAVE BP
                        MOV         BP, SP        ; ESTABLISH BASE POINTER
                        PUSH        CX            ; SAVE CALLER'S
                        PUSH        BX            ;     REGISTERS
                        PUSHF                     ;     AND FLAGS
                        SUB         SP, 6         ; ALLOCATE 3 WORDS LOCAL STORAGE
                        ; END OF PROLOG
        ; PROCEDURE BODY
                        MOV         CX, [BP+8]    ; GET ELEMENT COUNT
                        MOV         BX, [BP+6]    ; GET OFFSET OF 1ST ELEMENT
                        ; PROCEDURE CODE GOES HERE
                        ; FIRST PARAMETER CAN BE ADDRESSED:
                        ;    [BX]
                        ; LOCAL STORAGE CAN BE ADDRESSED:
                        ;    [BP-8], [BP-10], [BP-12]
                        ; END OF PROCEDURE BODY
```

Figure 3-31 Procedure Example 1

```
; PROCEDURE EPILOG
                ADD       SP, 6        ; DE-ALLOCATE LOCAL STORAGE
                POPF                   ; RESTORE CALLER'S
                POP       BX           ;    REGISTERS
                POP       CX           ;    AND
                POP       BP           ;    FLAGS
                ; END OF EPILOG
; PROCEDURE RETURN
                RET       4            ; DISCARD 2 PARAMETERS

EXAMPLE         ENDP                   ; END OF PROCEDURE "EXAMPLE"

PROC__SEG       ENDS
CALLER__SEG     SEGMENT
; GIVE ASSEMBLER SEGMENT/REGISTER CORRESPONDENCE
ASSUME          CS:CALLER__SEG,
&               DS:DATA__SEG,
&               SS:STACK__SEG,
&               ES:NOTHING             ; NO EXTRA SEGMENT IN THIS PROGRAM

; INITIALIZE SEGMENT REGISTERS
START:          MOV       AX,DATA__SEG
                MOV       DS,AX
                MOV       AX,STACK__SEG
                MOV       SS,AX
                MOV       SP,OFFSET STACK__TOP  ; POINT SP TO TOS

; ASSUME ARRAY__1 IS INITIALIZED
;
; CALL "EXAMPLE", PASSING ARRAY__1, THAT IS, THE NUMBER OF ELEMENTS
;   IN THE ARRAY, AND THE LOCATION OF THE FIRST ELEMENT.
                MOV       AX,SIZE ARRAY__1
                PUSH      AX
                MOV       AX,OFFSET ARRAY__1
                PUSH      AX
                CALL      EXAMPLE

; ASSUME ARRAY__2 IS INITIALIZED
;
; CALL "EXAMPLE" AGAIN WITH DIFFERENT SIZE ARRAY.
                MOV       AX,SIZE ARRAY__2
                PUSH      AX
                MOV       AX,OFFSET ARRAY__2
                PUSH      AX
                CALL      EXAMPLE
CALLER__SEG     ENDS

                END       START
```

Figure 3-31 Procedure Example 1 (continued)

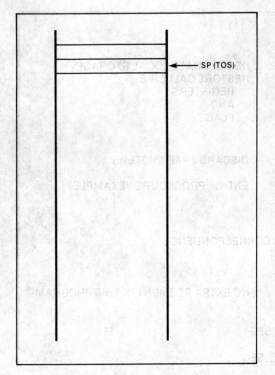

Figure 3-32 Stack Before Pushing Parameters

Figure 3-33 Stack at Procedure Entry

The procedure "body" does the actual processing (none in the example). The parameters on the stack are addressed relative to BP. Note that if EXAMPLE were a NEAR procedure, CS would not be on the stack and the parameters would be two bytes "closer" to BP. BP also is used to address the local variables on the stack. Local constants are best stored in a data or extra segment.

The procedure "epilog" reverses the activities of the prolog, leaving the stack as it was when the procedure was entered (see Figure 3-35).

The procedure "return" restores CS and IP from the stack and discards the parameters. As Figure 3-36 shows, when the calling program is resumed, the stack is in the same state as it was before any parameters were pushed onto it.

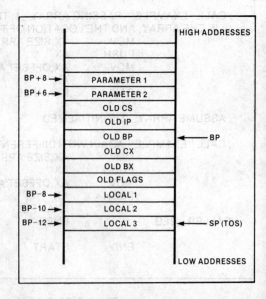

Figure 3-34 Stack Following Procedure Prolog

210911

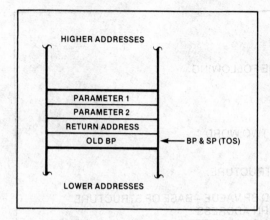

Figure 3-35 Stack Following Procedure Epilog

Figure 3-37 shows a simple procedure that uses an ASM-86 structure to address the stack. Register BP points to the base of the structure, which is the top of the stack since the stack grows toward lower addresses (see Figure 3-38). Any structure element can then be addressed by specifying BP as a base register:

    [BP].structure_element

Figure 3-39 shows a different approach to using as ASM-86 structure to define the stack layout. As shown in Figure 3-40, register BP is pointed at the middle of the structure (at OLD_BP) rather than at the base of the structure. Parameters and the return address are thus located at positive displacements (high addresses) from BP, while local variables are at negative displacements (lower addresses) from BP. This means that the local variables will be "closer" to the beginning of the stack segment and increase the likelihood that the assembler will be able to produce shorter instructions to access these variables, i.e., their offset from SS may be 255 bytes or less and can be expressed as a 1-byte value rather than a 2-byte value. Exit from the subroutine also is slightly faster because a MOV instruction can be used to deallocate the local storage instead of an ADD (compare Figure 3-31).

It is possible for a procedure to be activated a second time before it has returned from its first activation. For example, procedure A may call procedure B, and an interrupt may occur while procedure B is executing. If the interrupt service procedure calls B, then procedure B is reentered and must be written to handle this situation correctly, i.e., the procedure must be made reentrant.

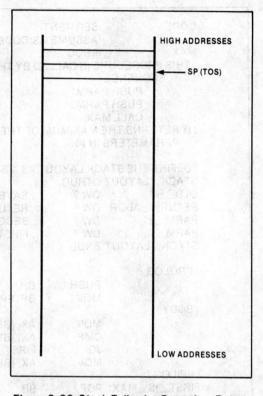

Figure 3-36 Stack Following Procedure Return

In PL/M-86 this can be done by simply writing:

    B:PROCEDURE(PARM1, PARM2)REENTRANT;

An ASM-86 procedure will be reentrant if it uses the stack for storing all local variables. When the procedure is reentered, a new "generation" of variables will be located on the stack. The stack will grow, but the sets of variables (and the parameters and return addresses as well) will automatically be kept straight. The stack must be large enough to accommodate the maximum "depth" of procedure activation that can occur under actual running conditions. In addition, any procedure called by a reentrant procedure must itself be reentrant.

A related situation that also requires reentrant procedures is recursion:

- A calls A (direct recursion),

- A calls B, B calls A (indirect recursion),

- A calls B, B calls C, C calls A (indirect recursion).

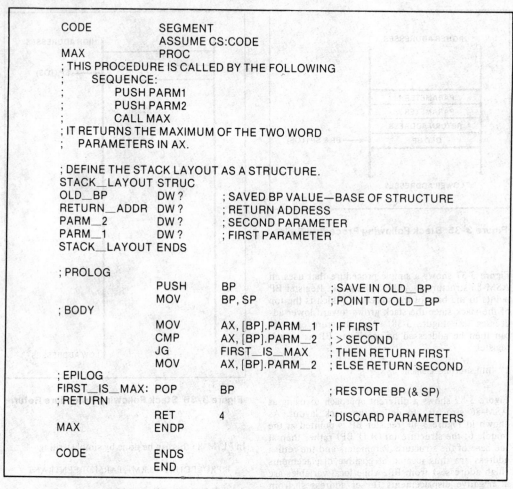

```
CODE            SEGMENT
                ASSUME CS:CODE
MAX             PROC
; THIS PROCEDURE IS CALLED BY THE FOLLOWING
;       SEQUENCE:
;           PUSH PARM1
;           PUSH PARM2
;           CALL MAX
; IT RETURNS THE MAXIMUM OF THE TWO WORD
;   PARAMETERS IN AX.

; DEFINE THE STACK LAYOUT AS A STRUCTURE.
STACK__LAYOUT   STRUC
OLD__BP         DW ?        ; SAVED BP VALUE—BASE OF STRUCTURE
RETURN__ADDR    DW ?        ; RETURN ADDRESS
PARM__2         DW ?        ; SECOND PARAMETER
PARM__1         DW ?        ; FIRST PARAMETER
STACK__LAYOUT   ENDS

; PROLOG
                PUSH    BP              ; SAVE IN OLD__BP
                MOV     BP, SP          ; POINT TO OLD__BP
; BODY
                MOV     AX, [BP].PARM__1    ; IF FIRST
                CMP     AX, [BP].PARM__2    ; > SECOND
                JG      FIRST__IS__MAX      ; THEN RETURN FIRST
                MOV     AX, [BP].PARM__2    ; ELSE RETURN SECOND
; EPILOG
FIRST__IS__MAX: POP     BP              ; RESTORE BP (& SP)
; RETURN
                RET     4               ; DISCARD PARAMETERS
MAX             ENDP

CODE            ENDS
                END
```

Figure 3-37 Procedure Example 2 The Stack as a Structure

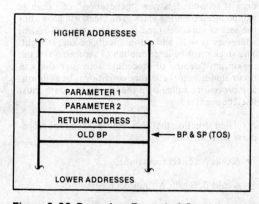

HIGHER ADDRESSES

PARAMETER 1
PARAMETER 2
RETURN ADDRESS
OLD BP   ← BP & SP (TOS)

LOWER ADDRESSES

Figure 3-38 Procedure Example 2 Stack Layout

Jumps and Calls

The instruction set contains many different types of JMP and CALL instructions (e.g., direct, indirect, through register, indirect through memory, etc.). These varying types of transfer provide efficient use of space and execution time in different programming situations. Figure 3-41 illustrates typical use of the different forms of these instructions. Note that the ASM-86 assembler uses the terms "NEAR" and "FAR" to denote intrasegment and intersegment transfers, respectively.

```
EXTRA           SEGMENT
; CONTAINS STRUCTURE TEMPLATE THAT "NEARPROC"
;      USES TO ADDRESS AN ARRAY PASSED BY ADDRESS.
DUMMY           STRUC
PARM__ARRAY     DB          256 DUP ?
DUMMY           ENDS
EXTRA           ENDS

CODE            SEGMENT
                ASSUME CS:CODE,ES:EXTRA
NEARPROC        PROC
; LAY OUT THE STACK (THE DYNAMIC STORAGE AREA OR DSA).
DSASTRUC        STRUC
I               DW          ?                   ; LOCAL VARIABLES FIRST
LOC__ARRAY      DW          10 DUP (?)          ;
OLD__BP         DW          ?                   ; ORIGINAL BP VALUE
RETADDR         DW          ?                   ; RETURN ADDRESS
POINTER         DD          ?                   ; 2ND PARM—POINTER TO "PARM__ARRAY".
COUNT           DB          ?                   ; 1ST PARM—A BYTE OCCUPIES
                DB          ?                   ;      A WORD ON THE STACK
DSASTRUC        ENDS

; USE AN EQU TO DEFINE THE BASE ADDRESS OF THE
;     DSA. CANNOT SIMPLY USE BP BECAUSE IT WILL
;     BE POINTING TO "OLD__BP" IN THE MIDDLE OF
;     THE DSA.
DSA             EQU         [BP – OFFSET OLD__BP]

; PROCEDURE ENTRY
                PUSH        BP                  ; SAVE BP
                MOV         BP, SP              ; POINT BP AT OLD__BP
                SUB         SP, OFFSET OLD__BP  ; ALLOCATE LOC__ARRAY & I

; PROCEDURE BODY
                ; ACCESS LOCAL VARIABLE I
                MOV         AX,DSA.I

                ; ACCESS LOCAL ARRAY (3) I.E., 4TH ELEMENT
                MOV         SI,6                ; WORD ARRAY-INDEX IS 3*2
                MOV         AX,DSA.LOC__ARRAY [SI]

                ; LOAD POINTER TO ARRAY PASSED BY ADDRESS
                LES         BX,DSA.POINTER

                ; ES:BX NOW POINTS TO PARM__ARRAY (0)
                ; ACCESS SI'TH ELEMENT OF PARM__ARRAY
                MOV         AL,ES:[BX].PARM__ARRAY [SI]

                ; ACCESS THE BYTE PARAMETER
                MOV         AL,DSA.COUNT
```

Figure 3-39 Procedure Example 3

210911

```
; PROCEDURE EXIT
            MOV      SP,BP              ; DE-ALLOCATE LOCALS
            POP      BP                 ; RESTORE BP
            ; STACK NOW AS RECEIVED FROM CALLER
            RET      6                  ; DISCARD PARAMETERS

NEARPROC    ENDP
CODE        ENDS
            END
```

Figure 3-39 Procedure Example 3 (continued)

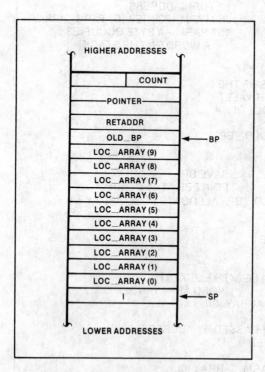

**Figure 3-40 Procedure Example 3
Stack Layout**

The procedure in Figure 3-41 illustrates how a PL/M-86 DO CASE construction may be implemented in ASM-86. It also shows:

- an indirect CALL through memory to a procedure located in another segment,

- a direct JMP to a label in another segment,

- an indirect JMP through memory to a label in the same segment,

- an indirect JMP through a register to a label in the same segment,

- a direct CALL to a procedure in another segment,

- a direct CALL to a procedure in the same segment,

- direct JMPs to labels in the same segment, within −128 to +127 bytes ("SHORT") and farther than −128 to +127 bytes ("NEAR").

Bit Manipulation w/RECORD

Figure 3-42 shows the ASM-86 RECORD facility may be used to manipulate bit data. The example shows how to:

- right-justify a bit field,

- test for a value,

- assign a constant known at assembly time,

- assign a variable,

- set or clear a bit field.

```
DATA            SEGMENT
; DEFINE THE CASE TABLE (JUMP TABLE) USED BY PROCEDURE
;       "DO_CASE." THE OFFSET OF EACH LABEL WILL
;       BE PLACED IN THE TABLE BY THE ASSEMBLER.
CASE_TABLE      DW              ACTION0, ACTION1, ACTION2,
&                               ACTION3, ACTION4, ACTION5
DATA            ENDS

; DEFINE TWO EXTERNAL (NOT PRESENT IN THIS
;       ASSEMBLY BUT SUPPLIED BY R & L FACILITY)
;       PROCEDURES. ONE IS IN THIS CODE SEGMENT
;       (NEAR) AND ONE IS IN ANOTHER SEGMENT (FAR).
                EXTRN           NEAR_PROC: NEAR, FAR_PROC: FAR

; DEFINE AN EXTERNAL LABEL (JUMP TARGET) THAT
;       IS IN ANOTHER SEGMENT.
                EXTRN           ERR_EXIT: FAR

CODE            SEGMENT
                ASSUME    CS: CODE, DS: DATA
; ASSUME DS HAS BEEN SET UP
;       BY CALLER TO POINT TO "DATA" SEGMENT.

DO_CASE         PROC            NEAR
; THIS EXAMPLE PROCEDURE RECEIVES TWO
;       PARAMETERS ON THE STACK. THE FIRST
;       PARAMETER IS THE "CASE NUMBER" OF
;       A ROUTINE TO BE EXECUTED (0-5). THE SECOND
;       PARAMETER IS A POINTER TO AN ERROR
;       PROCEDURE THAT IS EXECUTED IF AN INVALID
;       CASE NUMBER (>5) IS RECEIVED.

; LAY OUT THE STACK.
STACK_LAYOUT STRUC
OLD_BP          DW      ?
RETADDR         DW      ?
ERR_PROC_ADDR   DD      ?
CASE_NO         DB      ?
                DB      ?
STACK_LAYOUT ENDS

; SET UP PARAMETER ADDRESSING
                PUSH            BP
                MOV             BP, SP

; CODE TO SAVE CALLER'S REGISTERS COULD GO HERE.

; CHECK THE CASE NUMBER
                MOV             BH, 0
                MOV             BL, [BP].CASE_NO
                CMP             BX, LENGTH CASE_TABLE
                JLE             OK              ; ALL CONDITIONAL JUMPS
                                                ; ARE SHORT DIRECT
```

Figure 3-41 JMP and Call Examples

210911

```
        ; CALL THE ERROR ROUTINE WITH A FAR
        ;    INDIRECT CALL. A FAR INDIRECT CALL
        ;    IS INDICATED SINCE THE OPERAND HAS
        ;    TYPE "DOUBLEWORD."
                      CALL        [BP].ERR__PROC__ADDR

        ; JUMP DIRECTLY TO A LABEL IN ANOTHER SEGMENT.
        ;    A FAR DIRECT JUMP IS INDICATED SINCE
        ;    THE OPERAND HAS TYPE "FAR."
                      JMP         ERR__EXIT

OK:
        ; MULTIPLY CASE NUMBER BY 2 TO GET OFFSET
        ;    INTO CASE__TABLE (EACH ENTRY IS 2 BYTES).
                      SHL         BX, 1
        ; NEAR INDIRECT JUMP THROUGH SELECTED
        ;    ELEMENT OF CASE__TABLE. A NEAR
        ;    INDIRECT JUMP IS INDICATED SINCE THE
        ;    OPERAND HAS TYPE "WORD."
                      JMP         CASE__TABLE [BX]

ACTION0:          ; EXECUTED IF CASE__NO = 0
        ; CODE TO PROCESS THE ZERO CASE GOES HERE.
        ; FOR ILLUSTRATION PURPOSES, USE A
        ;    NEAR INDIRECT JUMP THROUGH A
        ;    REGISTER TO BRANCH TO THE POINT
        ;    WHERE ALL CASES CONVERGE.
        ;    A DIRECT JUMP (JMP ENDCASE) IS
        ;    ACTUALLY MORE APPROPRIATE HERE.
                      MOV         AX, OFFSET ENDCASE
                      JMP         AX

ACTION1:          ; EXECUTED IF CASE__NO = 1
        ; CALL A FAR EXTERNAL PROCEDURE. A FAR
        ;    DIRECT CALL IS INDICATED SINCE OPERAND
        ;    HAS TYPE "FAR."
                      CALL        FAR__PROC
        ; CALL A NEAR EXTERNAL PROCEDURE.
                      CALL        NEAR__PROC
        ; BRANCH TO CONVERGENCE POINT USING NEAR
        ;    DIRECT JUMP. NOTE THAT "ENDCASE"
        ;    IS MORE THAN 127 BYTES AWAY
        ;    SO A NEAR DIRECT JUMP WILL BE USED.
                      JMP         ENDCASE

ACTION2:          ; EXECUTED IF CASE__NO = 2
        ; CODE GOES HERE
                      JMP         ENDCASE        ; NEAR DIRECT JUMP
```

Figure 3-41 JMP and CALL Examples (continued)

```
ACTION3:          ; EXECUTED IF CASE__NO = 3
     ; CODE GOES HERE
                JMP        ENDCASE      ; NEAR DIRECT JMP

; ARTIFICIALLY FORCE "ENDCASE" FURTHER AWAY
;    SO THAT ABOVE JUMPS CANNOT BE "SHORT."
                ORG        500

ACTION4:          ; EXECUTED IF CASE__NO = 4
     ; CODE GOES HERE
                JMP        ENDCASE      ; NEAR DIRECT JUMP

ACTION5:          ; EXECUTED IF CASE__NO = 5
     ; CODE GOES HERE.
     ; BRANCH TO CONVERGENCE POINT USING
     ;     SHORT DIRECT JUMP SINCE TARGET IS
     ;     WITHIN 127 BYTES. MACHINE INSTRUCTION
     ;     HAS 1-BYTE DISPLACEMENT RATHER THAN
     ;     2-BYTE DISPLACEMENT REQUIRED FOR
     ;     NEAR DIRECT JUMPS. "SHORT" IS
     ;     WRITTEN BECAUSE "ENDCASE" IS A FORWARD
     ;     REFERENCE, WHICH ASSEMBLER ASSUMES IS
     ;     "NEAR." IF "ENDCASE" APPEARED PRIOR
     ;     TO THE JUMP, THE ASSEMBLER WOULD
     ;     AUTOMATICALLY DETERMINE IF IT WERE REACHABLE
     ;     WITH A SHORT JUMP.
                JMP        SHORT ENDCASE

ENDCASE:          ; ALL CASES CONVERGE HERE.

     ; POP CALLER'S REGISTERS HERE.
     ; RESTORE BP & SP, DISCARD PARAMETERS
     ;    AND RETURN TO CALLER.
                MOV        SP, BP
                POP        BP
                RET        6

DO__CASE        ENDP
CODE            ENDS
                END        ; OF ASSEMBLY
```

Figured 3-41 JMP and CALL Examples (continued)

```
DATA              SEGMENT
; DEFINE A WORD ARRAY
XREF              DW 3000 DUP (?)
; EACH ELEMENT OF XREF CONSISTS OF 3 FIELDS:
;         A 2-BIT TYPE CODE,
;         A 1-BIT FLAG,
;         A 13-BIT NUMBER.
; DEFINE A RECORD TO LAY OUT THIS ORGANIZATION.
LINE__REC         RECORD    LINE__TYPE: 2,
&                           VISIBLE: 1,
&                           LINE__NUM: 13
DATA              ENDS

CODE              SEGMENT
                  ASSUME CS: CODE,   DS: DATA
; ASSUME SEGMENT REGISTERS ARE SET UP PROPERLY
;       AND THAT SI INDEXES AN ELEMENT OF XREF.

; A RECORD FIELD-NAME USED BY ITSELF RETURNS
;     THE SHIFT COUNT REQUIRED TO RIGHT-JUSTIFY
;     THE FIELD. ISOLATE "LINE__TYPE" IN THIS
;     MANNER.
                  MOV       AL, XREF [SI]
                  MOV       CL, LINE__TYPE
                  SHR       AX, CL

; THE "MASK" OPERATOR APPLIED TO A RECORD
;     FIELD-NAME RETURNS THE BIT MASK
;     REQUIRED TO ISOLATE THE FIELD WITHIN
;     THE RECORD. CLEAR ALL BITS EXCEPT
;     "LINE__NUM."
                  MOV       DX, XREF[SI]
                  AND       DX, MASK LINE__NUM

; DETERMINE THE VALUE OF THE "VISIBLE" FIELD
                  TEST      XREF[SI], MASK VISIBLE
                  JZ        NOT__VISIBLE
; NO JUMP IF VISIBLE = 1
NOT__VISIBLE:     ; JUMP HERE IF VISIBLE = 0

; ASSIGN A CONSTANT KNOWN AT ASSEMBLY-TIME
;     TO A FIELD, BY FIRST CLEARING THE BITS
;     AND THEN OR'ING IN THE VALUE. IN
;     THIS CASE "LINE__TYPE" IS SET TO 2 (10B).
                  AND       XREF[SI], NOT MASK LINE__TYPE
                  OR        XREF[SI],2 SHL LINE__TYPE
; THE ASSEMBLER DOES THE MASKING AND SHIFTING.
; THE RESULT IS THE SAME AS:
                  AND       XREF[SI], 3FFFH
                  OR        XREF[SI], 8000H
;     BUT IS MORE READABLE AND LESS SUBJECT
;     TO CLERICAL ERROR.
```

Figure 3-42 RECORD Example

210911

```
; ASSIGN A VARIABLE (THE CONTENT OF AX)
;      TO LINE__TYPE.
              MOV      CL, LINE__TYPE   ; SHIFT COUNT
              SHL      AX, CL   ; SHIFT TO "LINE UP" BITS
              AND      XREF[SI], NOT MASK LINE__TYPE   ; CLEAR BITS
              OR       XREF[SI], AX   ; OR IN NEW VALUE

; NO SHIFT IS REQUIRED TO ASSIGN TO THE
;    RIGHT-MOST FIELD. ASSUMING AX CONTAINS
;    A VALID NUMBER (HIGH 3 BITS ARE 0),
;    ASSIGN AX TO "LINE__NUM."
              AND      XREF[SI], NOT MASK LINE__NUM
              OR       XREF[SI], AX

; A FIELD MAY BE SET OR CLEARED WITH
;    ONE INSTRUCTION. CLEAR THE "VISIBLE"
;    FLAG AND THEN SET IT.
              AND      XREF[SI], NOT MASK VISIBLE
              OR       XREF[SI], MASK VISIBLE

CODE          ENDS
              END      ; OF ASSEMBLY
```

Figure 3-42 RECORD Example (continued)

Position-Independent Code

The following considerations apply to position-independent code sequences:

- A label that is referenced by a direct FAR (intersegment) transfer is not moveable.

- A label that is referenced by an indirect transfer (either NEAR or FAR) is moveable so long as the register or memory pointer to the label contains the label's current address.

- A label that is referenced by a SHORT (e.g., conditional jump) or a direct NEAR (intrasegment) transfer is moveable so long as the referencing instruction is moved with the label as a unit. These transfers are self-relative; that is, they require only that the label maintain the same distance from the referencing instruction, and actual addresses are immaterial.

- Data is segment-independent, but not offset-independent. That is, a data item may be moved to a different segment, but it must maintain the same offset from the beginning of the segment. Placing constants in a unit of code also effectively makes the code offset-dependent, and therefore is not recommended.

- A procedure should not be moved while it is active or while any procedure it has called is active.

- A section of code that has been interrupted should not be moved.

The segment that is receiving a section of code must have "room" for the code. If the MOVS (or MOVSB or MOVSW) instruction attempts to auto-increment DI past 64K, it wraps around to 0 and causes the beginning of the segment to be overwritten. If a segment override is needed for the source operand, code similar to the following can be used to properly resume the instruction if it is interrupted:

```
RESUME: REP MOVS            DESTINATION,ES:SOURCE
;IF CX NOT = 0 THEN INTERRUPT HAS OCCURRED
        AND CX,CX           ;CX = 0?
        JNZ RESUME          ;NO,FINISH EXECUTION
;CONTROL COMES HERE WHEN STRING HAS BEEN MOVED.
```

On the 8086,88, if the MOVS is interrupted, the CPU "remembers" the segment override but "forgets" the presence of the REP prefix when execution resumes. Testing CX indicates whether the instruction is completed or not. Jumping back to the instruction resumes it where it left off. Note that a segment override cannot be specified with MOVSB or MOVSW.

Dynamic Code Relocation

Figure 3-43 illustrates one approach to moving programs in memory at execution time. A "supervisor" program (which is not moved) keeps a pointer variable that contains the current location (offset and segment base) of a position-independent procedure. The supervisor always calls the procedure through this pointer. The supervisor also has access to the procedure's length in bytes. The procedure is moved with the MOVSB instruction. After the procedure is moved, its pointer is updated with the new location. The ASM-86 WORD PTR operator is written to inform the assembler that one word of the double-word pointer is being updated at a time.

```
MAIN__DATA      SEGMENT
; SET UP POINTERS TO POSITION-INDEPENDENT PROCEDURE
;     AND FREE SPACE.
PIP__PTR        DD        EXAMPLE
FREE__PTR       DD        TARGET__SEG
; SET UP SIZE OF PROCEDURE IN BYTES
PIP__SIZE       DW        EXAMPLE__LEN
MAIN__DATA      ENDS

STACK           SEGMENT
                DW        20 DUP (?)           ; 20 WORDS FOR STACK

STACK__TOP      LABEL     WORD                 ; TOS BEGINS HERE
STACK           ENDS

SOURCE__SEG     SEGMENT
; THE POSITION-INDEPENDENT PROCEDURE IS INITIALLY IN THIS SEGMENT.
; OTHER CODE MAY PRECEDE IT, I.E., ITS OFFSET NEED NOT BE ZERO.
ASSUME          CS:SOURCE__SEG
EXAMPLE         PROC      FAR
    ; THIS PROCEDURE READS AN 8-BIT PORT UNTIL
    ; BIT 3 OF THE VALUE READ IS FOUND SET. IT
    ; THEN READS ANOTHER PORT. IF THE VALUE READ
    ; IS GREATER THAN 10H IT WRITES THE VALUE TO
    ; A THIRD PORT AND RETURNS; OTHERWISE IT STARTS
    ; OVER.
STATUS__PORT    EQU       0D0H
PORT__READY     EQU       008H
INPUT__PORT     EQU       0D2H
THRESHOLD       EQU       010H
OUTPUT__PORT    EQU       0D4H
```

Figure 3-43 Dynamic Code Relocation Example

210911

```
CHECK__AGAIN: IN          AL,STATUS__PORT    ; GET STATUS
              TEST        AL,PORT__READY     ; DATA READY?
              JNE         CHECK__AGAIN       ; NO, TRY AGAIN
              IN          AL,INPUT__PORT     ; YES, GET DATA
              CMP         AL,THRESHOLD       ; > 10H?
              JLE         CHECK__AGAIN       ; NO, TRY AGAIN
              OUT         OUTPUT__PORT,AL    ; YES, WRITE IT

              RET                            ; RETURN TO CALLER
; GET PROCEDURE LENGTH
EXAMPLE__LEN  EQU         (OFFSET THIS BYTE)—(OFFSET CHECK__AGAIN)
              ENDP        EXAMPLE   ENDP
SOURCE__SEG   ENDS

TARGET__SEG   SEGMENT
; THE POSITION-INDEPENDENT PROCEDURE
;    IS MOVED TO THIS SEGMENT, WHICH IS
;    INITIALLY "EMPTY."
; IN TYPICAL SYSTEMS, A "FREE SPACE MANAGER" WOULD
;    MAINTAIN A POOL OF AVAILABLE MEMORY SPACE
; FOR ILLUSTRATION PURPOSES, ALLOCATE ENOUGH
;    SPACE TO HOLD IT
              DB          EXAMPLE__LEN DUP (?)

TARGET__SEG   ENDS

MAIN__CODE    SEGMENT
; THIS ROUTINE CALLS THE EXAMPLE PROCEDURE
; AT ITS INITIAL LOCATION, MOVES IT, AND
; CALLS IT AGAIN AT THE NEW LOCATION.

              ASSUME      CS:MAIN__CODE,SS:STACK,
              &           DS:MAIN__DATA,ES:NOTHING

; INITIALIZE SEGMENT REGISTERS & STACK POINTER.
START:        MOV         AX,MAIN__DATA
              MOV         DS,AX
              MOV         AX,STACK
              MOV         SS,AX
              MOV         SP,OFFSET STACK__TOP

; CALL EXAMPLE AT INITIAL LOCATION.
              CALL        PIP__PTR

; SET UP CX WITH COUNT OF BYTES TO MOV
              MOV         CX,PIP__SIZE
```

Figure 3-43 Dynamic Code Relocation Example (continued)

```
        ; SAVE DS, SET UP DS/SI AND ES/DI TO
        ;    POINT TO THE SOURCE AND DESTINATION
        ;    ADDRESSES.
                        PUSH        DS
                        LES         DI,FREE__PTR
                        LDS         SI,PIP__PTR
        ; MOVE THE PROCEDURE.
                        CLD                                  ; AUTO INCREMENT
                        REP MOVSB

        ; RESTORE OLD ADDRESSABILITY.
                        MOV         AX,DS                    ; HOLD TEMPORARILY
                        POP         DS
        ; UPDATE POINTER TO POSITION-INDEPENDENT PROCEDURE
                        MOV         WORD PTR PIP__PTR+2,ES
                        SUB         DI,PIP__SIZE             ; PRODUCES OFFSET
                        MOV         WORD PTR PIP__PTR,DI

        ; UPDATE POINTER TO FREE SPACE
                        MOV         WORD PTR FREE__PTR+2,AX
                        SUB         SI,PIP__SIZE             ; PRODUCES OFFSET
                        MOV         WORD PTR FREE__PTR,SI

        ; CALL POSITION-INDEPENDENT PROCEDURE AT
        ;    NEW LOCATION AND STOP
                        CALL        PIP__PTR
        MAIN__CODE      ENDS
                        END         START
```

Figure 3-43 Dynamic Code Relocation Example (continued)

Memory Mapped I/O

Figure 3-44 shows how memory-mapped I/O can be used to address a group of communication lines as an "array." In the example, indexed addressing is used to poll the array of status ports, one port at a time. Any of the other memory addressing modes may be used in conjunction with memory-mapped I/O devices as well.

In Figure 3-45 a MOVS instruction is used to perform a high-speed transfer to a memory-mapped line printer. Using this technique requires the hardware to be set up as follows. Since the MOVS instruction transfers characters to successive memory addresses, the decoding logic must select the line printer if any of these locations is written. One way of accomplishing this is to have the chip select logic decode only the upper 12 lines of the address bus (A19-A8), ignoring the contents of the lower eight lines (A7-A0). When data is written to any address in this 256-byte block, the upper 12 lines will not change, so the printer will be selected.

Breakpoints

Figure 3-46 illustrates how a program may set a breakpoint. In the example, the breakpoint routine puts the processor into single-step mode, but the same general approach could be used for other purposes as well. A program passes the address where the break is to occur to a procedure that saves the byte located at that address and replaces it with an INT 3 (breakpoint) instruction. When the CPU encounters the breakpoint instruction, it calls the type 3 interrupt procedure. In the example, this procedure places the processor into single-step mode starting with the instruction where the breakpoint was placed.

Interrupt Handling

Figure 3-47 is a block diagram of a hypothetical 8086,88 system that is used to illustrate three different examples of interrupt handling: an external (maskable) interrupt, an external non-maskable interrupt and a software interrupt.

```
COM_LINES      SEGMENT   AT 800H
; THE FOLLOWING IS A MEMORY MAPPED "ARRAY"
;      OF EIGHT 8-BIT COMMUNICATIONS CONTROLLERS
;      (E.G., 8251 USARTS). PORTS HAVE ALL-ODD
;      OR ALL-EVEN ADDRESSES (EVERY OTHER BYTE
;      IS SKIPPED) FOR 8086-COMPATIBILITY.

COM_DATA       DB     ?
               DB     ?                     ; SKIP THIS ADDRESS
COM_STATUS     DB     ?
               DB     ?                     ; SKIP THIS ADDRESS
               DB     28   DUP (?)          ; REST OF "ARRAY"
COM_LINES      ENDS

CODE           SEGMENT
; ASSUME STACK IS SET UP, AS ARE SEGMENT
;      REGISTERS (DS POINTING TO COM_LINES).
;      FOLLOWING CODE POLLS THE LINES.

CHAR_RDY       EQU    00000010B       ; CHARACTER PRESENT
START_POLL:    MOV    CX, 8           ; POLL 8 LINES ZERO
               SUB    SI, SI          ; ARRAY INDEX

POLL_NEXT:     TEST   COM_STATUS [SI], CHAR_RDY
               JE     READ_CHAR ; READ IF PRESENT
               ADD    SI, 4           ; ELSE BUMP TO NEXT LINE
               LOOP   POLL_NEXT ; CONTINUE POLLING UNTIL
                                ;     ALL 8 HAVE BEEN CHECKED
               JMP    START_POLL; START OVER

READ_CHAR:     MOV    AL,COM_DATA [SI]   ;GET THE DATA
; ETC.
CODE           ENDS
               END
```

Figure 3-44 Memory Mapped I/O "Array"

In this hypothetical system, an 8253 Programmable Interval Timer is used to generate a time base. One of the three timers on the 8253 is programmed to repeatedly generate interrupt requests at 50 millisecond intervals. The output from this timer is tied to one of the eight interrupt request lines of an 8259A Programmable Interrupt Controller. The 8259A, in turn, is connected to the INTR line of an 8086.

A power-down circuit is used in the system to illustrate one application of the NMI (non-maskable interrupt) line. If the ac line voltage drops below a certain threshold, the power supply activates ACLO.

The power-down circuit then sends a power-fail interrupt (PFI) pulse to the CPU's NMI input. After 5 milliseconds, the power-down circuit activates MPRO (memory protect) to disable reading from and writing to the system's battery-powered RAM. This protects the RAM from fluctuations that may occur when power is actually lost 7.5 milliseconds after the power failure is detected. The system software must save all vital information in the battery-powered RAM segment within 5 milliseconds of the activation of NMI.

When power returns, the power-down circuit activates the system RESET line. Pressing the "cold start" switch also produces a system RESET. The

```
PRINTER          SEGMENT
; THIS SEGMENT CONTAINS A "STRING" THAT
;    IS ACTUALLY A MEMORY-MAPPED LINE PRINTER.
;    THE SEGMENT (PRINTER) MUST BE ASSIGNED (LOCATED)
;    TO A BLOCK OF THE ADDRESS SPACE SUCH
;    THAT WRITING TO ANY ADDRESS IN THE
;    BLOCK SELECTS THE PRINTER.

PRINT_SELECT     DB 133    DUP (?)                 ; "STRING" REPRESENTING PRINTER
                 DB 123    DUP (?)                 ; REST OF 256-BYTE BLOCK
PRINTER          ENDS

DATA             SEGMENT
PRINT_BUF        DB 133    DUP (?)                 ; LINE TO BE PRINTED
PRINT_COUNT      DB 1      ?                       ; LINE LENGTH
; OTHER PROGRAM DATA
DATA             ENDS

CODE             SEGMENT
; ASSUME STACK AND SEGMENT REGISTERS HAVE
;     BEEN SET UP (DS POINTS TO DATA SEGMENT).
;     FOLLOWING CODE TRANSFERS A LINE TO
;     THE PRINTER.

                 ASSUME    ES: PRINTER
                 MOV       AX, PRINTER             ; PREVENT SEGMENT OVERRIDE
                 MOV       ES, AX
                 SUB       DI, DI                  ; CLEAR SOURCE AND
                 SUB       SI, SI                  ;     DESTINATION POINTERS
                 MOV       CX, PRINT_COUNT
                 CLD       ; AUTO-INCREMENT
        REP      MOVS      PRINT_SELECT, PRINT_BUF
                 ; ETC.
CODE             ENDS
                 END
```

Figure 3-45 Memory Mapped Block Transfer Example

PFS (power fail status) line, which is connected to the low-order bit of port E0, identifies the source of the RESET. If the bit is set, the software executes a "warm start" to restore the information saved by the power-fail routine. If the PFS bit is cleared, the software executes a "cold start" from the beginning of the program. In either case, the software writes a "one" to the low-order bit of port E2. This line is connected to the power-down circuit's PFSR (power failure status reset) signal and is used to enable the battery-powered RAM segment.

A software interrupt is used to update a simple real-time clock. This procedure is written in PL/M-86, while the rest of the system is written in ASM-86 to demonstrate the interrupt handling capability of both languages. The system's main program simply initializes the system following receipt of a RESET and then waits for an interrupt. An example of this interrupt procedure is given in Figure 3-48.

In the case of the 80186,188, the equivalent function of the two blocks designated as the 8259A Interrupt Controller and the 8253 Counter Timer chip are integrated on the chip. Thus, the example in Figure 3-48 remains essentially the same except for the initialization code (INIT) which will need to be changed to reflect the presence of the integrated Interrupt Controller and Counter Timer.

```
INT__PTR__TAB    SEGMENT
; INTERRUPT POINTER TABLE-LOCATE AT 0H
TYPE__0          DD          ?                    ; NOT DEFINED IN EXAMPLE
TYPE__1          DD          SINGLE__STEP
TYPE__2          DD          ?                    ; NOT DEFINED IN EXAMPLE
TYPE__3          DD          BREAKPOINT
INT__PTR__TAB    ENDS

SAVE__SEG        SEGMENT
SAVE__INSTR      DB 1        DUP (?)              ; INSTRUCTION REPLACED
                                                  ; BY BREAKPOINT
SAVE__SEG        ENDS

MAIN__CODE       SEGMENT
; ASSUME STACK AND SEGMENT REGISTERS ARE SET UP.

; ENABLE SINGLE-STEPPING WITH INSTRUCTION AT
;     LABEL "NEXT" BY PASSING SEGMENT AND
;     OFFSET OF "NEXT" TO "SET__BREAK" PROCEDURE
                 PUSH        CS
                 LEA         AX, CS: NEXT
                 PUSH        AX
                 CALL        FAR SET__BREAK
; ETC.

NEXT:            IN          AL, 0FFFH            ; BREAKPOINT SET HERE
                 ; ETC.

MAIN__CODE       ENDS

BREAK            SEGMENT
SET__BREAK       PROC        FAR
; THIS PROCEDURE SAVES AN INSTRUCTION BYTE (WHOSE
;     ADDRESS IS PASSED BY THE CALLER) AND WRITES
;     AN INT 3 (BREAKPOINT) MACHINE INSTRUCTION
;     AT THE TARGET ADDRESS.

TARGET           EQU         DWORD PTR [BP + 6]

; SET UP BP FOR PARM ADDRESSING & SAVE REGISTERS
                 PUSH        BP
                 MOV         BP, SP
                 PUSH        DS
                 PUSH        ES
                 PUSH        AX
                 PUSH        BX
; POINT DS / BX TO THE TARGET INSTRUCTION
                 LDS         BX, TARGET
```

Figure 3-46 Breakpoint Example

```
                ; POINT ES TO THE SAVE AREA
                        MOV        AX, SAVE__SEG
                        MOV        ES, AX
                ; SWAP THE TARGET INSTRUCTION FOR INT 3 (0CCH)
                        MOV        AL, 0CCH
                        XCHG       AL, DS: [BX]
                ; SAVE THE TARGET INSTRUCTION
                        MOV        ES: SAVE__INSTR, AL
                ; RESTORE AND RETURN
                        POP        BX
                        POP        AX
                        POP        ES
                        POP        DS
                        POP        BP
                        RET        4
                SET__BREAK  ENDP

                BREAKPOINT    PROC    FAR
                ; THE CPU WILL ACTIVATE THIS PROCEDURE WHEN IT
                ;   EXECUTES THE INT 3 INSTRUCTION SET BY THE
                ;   SET__BREAK PROCEDURE. THIS PROCEDURE
                ;   RESTORES THE SAVED INSTRUCTION BYTE TO ITS
                ;   ORIGINAL LOCATION AND BACKS UP THE
                ;   INSTRUCTION POINTER IMAGE ON THE STACK
                ;   SO THAT EXECUTION WILL RESUME WITH
                ;   THE RESTORED INSTRUCTION. IT THEN SETS
                ;   TF (THE TRAP FLAG) IN THE FLAG-IMAGE
                ;   ON THE STACK. THIS PUTS THE PROCESSOR
                ;   IN SINGLE-STEP MODE WHEN EXECUTION
                ;   RESUMES.

                FLAG__IMAGE    EQU      WORD PTR [BP + 6]
                IP__IMAGE      EQU      WORD PTR [BP + 2]
                NEXT_INSTR     EQU      DWORD PTR [BP + 2]
                ; SET UP BP TO ADDRESS STACK AND SAVE REGISTERS
                        PUSH       BP
                        MOV        BP, SP
                        PUSH       DS
                        PUSH       ES
                        PUSH       AX
                        PUSH       BX
                ; POINT ES AT THE SAVE AREA
                        MOV        AX, SAVE  SEG
                        MOV        ES, AX
                ; GET THE SAVED BYTE
                        MOV        AL, ES: SAVE  INSTR

                ; GET THE ADDRESS OF THE TARGET + 1
                ;    (INSTRUCTION FOLLOWING THE BREAKPOINT)
                        LDS        BX, NEXT__INSTR
```

Figure 3-46 Breakpoint Example (continued)

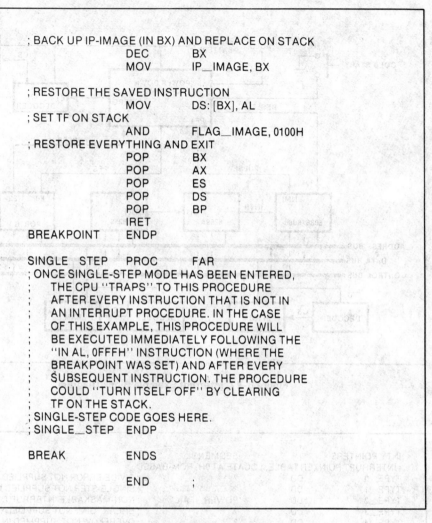

```
                ; BACK UP IP-IMAGE (IN BX) AND REPLACE ON STACK
                            DEC         BX
                            MOV         IP__IMAGE, BX

                ; RESTORE THE SAVED INSTRUCTION
                            MOV         DS: [BX], AL
                ; SET TF ON STACK
                            AND         FLAG__IMAGE, 0100H
                ; RESTORE EVERYTHING AND EXIT
                            POP         BX
                            POP         AX
                            POP         ES
                            POP         DS
                            POP         BP
                            IRET
                BREAKPOINT  ENDP

                SINGLE   STEP   PROC    FAR
                ; ONCE SINGLE-STEP MODE HAS BEEN ENTERED,
                ;     THE CPU "TRAPS" TO THIS PROCEDURE
                ;     AFTER EVERY INSTRUCTION THAT IS NOT IN
                ;     AN INTERRUPT PROCEDURE. IN THE CASE
                ;     OF THIS EXAMPLE, THIS PROCEDURE WILL
                ;     BE EXECUTED IMMEDIATELY FOLLOWING THE
                ;     "IN AL, 0FFFH" INSTRUCTION (WHERE THE
                ;     BREAKPOINT WAS SET) AND AFTER EVERY
                ;     SUBSEQUENT INSTRUCTION. THE PROCEDURE
                ;     COULD "TURN ITSELF OFF" BY CLEARING
                ;     TF ON THE STACK.
                ; SINGLE-STEP CODE GOES HERE.
                ; SINGLE__STEP   ENDP

                BREAK       ENDS

                            END         ;
```

Figure 3-46 Breakpoint Example (continued)

String Operations

Figure 3-49 illustrates typical use of string instructions and repeat prefixes. The XLAT instruction also is demonstrated. The first example simply moves 80 words of a string, as might be done in a sort. Next a string is scanned from right to left (the index register is auto-decremented) to find the last period (".") in the string. Finally a byte string of EBCDIC characters is translated to ASCII. The translation is stopped at the end of the string or when a carriage return character is encountered, whichever occurs first. This is an example of using the string primitives in combination with other instructions to build up more complex string processing operations.

3.9 80186,188 Programming Examples

Figures 3-50 through 3-53 provide code examples for DMA, timer, interrupt controller and system initialization.

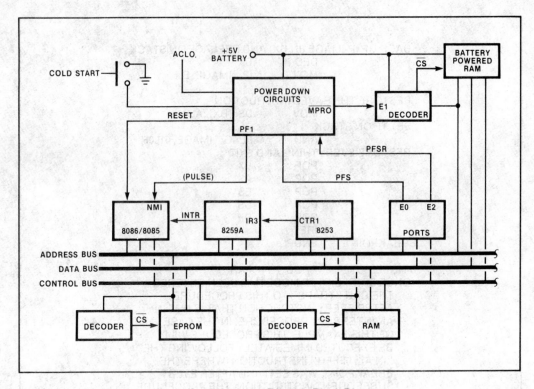

Figure 3-47 Interrupt Example Block Diagram

```
INT_POINTERS                        SEGMENT
; INTERRUPT POINTER TABLE, LOCATE AT 0H, ROM-BASED
TYPE_0          DD          ?              ; DIVIDE-ERROR NOT SUPPLIED IN EXAMPLE.
TYPE_1          DD          ?              ; SINGLE-STEP NOT SUPPLIED IN EXAMPLE.
TYPE_2          DD          POWER_FAIL     ; NON-MASKABLE INTERRUPT
TYPE_3          DD          ?              ; BREAKPOINT NOT SUPPLIED IN EXAMPLE.
TYPE_4          DD          ?              ; OVERFLOW NOT SUPPLIED IN EXAMPLE.
; SKIP RESERVED PART OF EXAMPLE
                ORG         32*4
TYPE_32         DD          ?              ; 8259A IR0 - AVAILABLE
TYPE_33         DD          ?              ; 8259A IR1 - AVAILABLE
TYPE_34         DD          ?              ; 8259A IR2 - AVAILABLE
TYPE_35         DD          TIMER_PULSE    ; 8259A IR3
TYPE_36         DD          ?              ; 8259A IR4 - AVAILABLE
TYPE_37         DD          ?              ; 8259A IR5 - AVAILABLE
TYPE_38         DD          ?              ; 8259A IR6 - AVAILABLE
TYPE_39         DD          ?              ; 8259A IR7 - AVAILABLE
;
; POINTER FOR TYPE 40 SUPPLIED BY PL/M-86 COMPILER
;
INT_POINTERS                        ENDS
```

Figure 3-48 8086,88 Interrupt Procedures Example

```
BATTERY                        SEGMENT
; THIS RAM SEGMENT IS BATTERY-POWERED. IT CONTAINS VITAL DATA
;    THAT MUST BE MAINTAINED DURING POWER OUTAGES.
STACK_PTR        DW            ?               ; SP SAVE AREA
STACK_SEG        DW            ?               ; SS SAVE AREA
; SPACE FOR OTHER VARIABLES COULD BE DEFINED HERE.
BATTERY                        ENDS


DATA                           SEGMENT
; RAM SEGMENT THAT IS NOT BACKED UP BY BATTERY
N_PULSES         DB            1 DUP (0)       ; # TIMER PULSES

; ETC.
DATA                           ENDS


STACK                          SEGMENT
; LOCATED IN BATTERY-POWERED RAM
                 DW            100 DUP (?)     ; THIS IS AN ARBITRARY STACKSIZE

STACK_TOP        LABEL         WORD            ; LABEL THE INITIAL TOS
STACK                          ENDS


INTERRUPT_HANDLERS       SEGMENT
; INTERRUPT PROCEDURES EXCEPT TYPE 40 (PL/M-86)


                 ASSUME:       CS:INTERRUPT_HANDLERS,DS:DATA,SS:STACK,ES:BATTERY


POWER_FAIL                     PROC            ; TYPE 2 INTERRUPT
; POWER FAIL DETECT CIRCUIT ACTIVATES NMI LINE ON CPU IF POWER IS
;    ABOUT TO BE LOST. THIS PROCEDURE SAVES THE PROCESSOR STATE IN
;    RAM (ASSUMED TO BE POWERED BY AN AUXILIARY SOURCE) SO THAT IT
;    CAN BE RESTORED BY A WARM START ROUTINE IF POWER RETURNS


; IP, CS, AND FLAGS ARE ALREADY ON THE STACK.
;    SAVE THE OTHER REGISTERS.
                 PUSH          AX
                 PUSH          BX
                 PUSH          CX
                 PUSH          DX
                 PUSH          SI
                 PUSH          DI
                 PUSH          BP
                 PUSH          DS
                 PUSH          ES

; CRITICAL MEMORY VARIABLES COULD ALSO BE SAVED ON THE STACK AT THIS
;    POINT. ALTERNATIVELY, THEY COULD BE DEFINED IN THE "BATTERY"
;    SEGMENT, WHERE THEY WILL AUTOMATICALLY BE PROTECTED IF MAIN POWER
;    IS LOST.

; SAVE SP AND SS IN FIXED LOCATIONS THAT ARE KNOWN BY WARM START ROUTINE.
                 MOV           AX,BATTERY
                 MOV           ES,AX
                 MOV           ES:STACK_PTR,SP
                 MOV           ES:STACK_SEG,SS

; STOP GRACEFULLY
                 HLT
POWER_FAIL                     ENDP
```

Figure 3-48 8086,88 Interrupt Procedures Example (continued)

```
TIMER_PULSE                    PROC                    ; TYPE 35 INTERRUPT
; THIS PROCEDURE HANDLES THE 50MS INTERRUPTS GENERATED BY THE 8253.
;    IT COUNTS THE INTERRUPTS AND ACTIVATES THE TYPE 40 INTERRUPT
;    PROCEDURE ONCE PER SECOND.
;
; DS IS ASSUMED TO BE POINTING TO THE DATA SEGMENT
;
; THE 8253 IS RUNNING FREE, AND AUTOMATICALLY LOWERS ITS INTERRUPT
;    REQUEST. IF A DEVICE REQUIRED ACKNOWLEDGEMENT, THE CODE MIGHT GO HERE.
;
; NOW PERFORM PROCESSING THAT MUST NOT BE INTERRUPTED (EXCEPT FOR NMI).
                    INC        N_PULSES
; ENABLE HIGHER-PRIORITY INTERRUPTS AND DO LESS CRITICAL PROCESSING
                    STI
                    CMP        N_PULSES,200            ; 1 SECOND PASSED?
                    JBE        DONE                    ; NO, GO ON.
                    MOV        N_PULSES,0              ; YES, RESET COUNT.
                    INT        40                      ; UPDATE CLOCK
; SEND NON-SPECIFIC END-OF-INTERRUPT COMMAND TO 8259A, ENABLING EQUAL
;    OR LOWER PRIORITY INTERRUPTS.
DONE:               MOV        AL,020H                 ; EOI COMMAND
                    OUT        0C0H,AL                 ; 8259A PORT
                    IRET
TIMER_PULSE                    ENDP

INTERRUPT_HANDLERS             ENDS


CODE                SEGMENT
; THIS SEGMENT WOULD NORMALLY RESIDE IN ROM.

                    ASSUME     CS:CODE,DS:DATA,SS:STACK,ES:NOTHING

INIT                PROC       NEAR
; THIS PROCEDURE IS CALLED FOR BOTH WARM AND COLD STARTS TO INITIALIZE
;    THE 8253 AND THE 8259A. THIS ROUTINE DOES NOT USE STACK, DATA, OR
;    EXTRA SEGMENTS, AS THEY ARE NOT SET PREDICTABLY DURING A WARM START.
;    INTERRUPTS ARE DISABLED BY VIRTUE OF THE SYSTEM RESET.

; INITIALIZE 8253 COUNTER 1 - OTHER COUNTERS NOT USED.
; CLK INPUT TO COUNTER IS ASSUMED TO BE 1.23 MHZ.

LO50MS              EQU        000H                    ; COUNT VALUE IS
HI50MS              EQU        0F0H                    ;    61440 DECIMAL.
CONTROL             EQU        0D6H                    ; CONTROL PORT ADDRESS
COUNT_1             EQU        0D2H                    ; COUNTER 1 ADDRESS
MODE2               EQU        01110100B               ; MODE 2, BINARY

                    MOV        DX,CONTROL              ; LOAD CONTROL BYTE
                    MOV        AL,MODE2
                    OUT        DX,AL
                    MOV        DX,COUNT_1              ; LOAD 50MS DOWNCOUNT
                    MOV        AL,LO50MS
                    OUT        DX,AL
                    MOV        AL,HI50MS
                    OUT        DX,AL
                    ; COUNTER NOW RUNNING, INTERRUPTS STILL DISABLED.
```

Figure 3-48 8086,88 Interrupt Procedures Example (continued)

```
; INITIALIZE 8259A TO: SINGLE INTERRUPT CONTROLLER, EDGE-TRIGGERED,
;    INTERRUPT TYPES 32-40 (DECIMAL) TO BE SENT TO CPU FOR INTERRUPT
;    REQUESTS 0-7 RESPECTIVELY, 8086 MODE, NON-AUTOMATIC END-OF-INTERRUPT.
;    MASK OFF UNUSED INTERRUPT REQUEST LINES.

ICW1          EQU      00010011B      ; EDGE-TRIGGERED, SINGLE 8259A, ICW4 REQUIRED.
ICW2          EQU      00100000B      ; TYPE 20H, 32 - 40D
ICW4          EQU      00000001B      ; 8086 MODE, NORMAL EOI
OCW1          EQU      11110111B      ; MASK ALL BUT IR3
PORT__A       EQU      0C0H           ; ICW1 WRITTEN HERE
PORT__B       EQU      0C2H           ; OTHER ICW'S WRITTEN HERE

              MOV      DX,PORT__A     ; WRITE 1ST ICW
              MOV      AL,ICW1
              OUT      DX,AL
              MOV      DX,PORT__B     ; WRITE 2ND ICW
              MOV      AL,ICW2
              OUT      DX,AL
              MOV      AL,ICW4        ; WRITE 4TH ICW
              OUT      DX,AL
              MOV      AL,0CW1        ; MASK UNUSED IR'S
              OUT      DX,AL
; INITIALIZATION COMPLETE, INTERRUPTS STILL DISABLED
              RET
INIT          ENDP


USER__PGM:
; "REAL" CODE WOULD GO HERE. THE EXAMPLE EXECUTES AN ENDLESS LOOP
;     UNTIL AN INTERRUPT OCCURS.
              JMP      USER__PGM


; EXECUTION STARTS HERE WHEN CPU IS RESET.
POWER__FAIL__STATUS        EQU   0E0H      ; PORT ADDRESS
ENABLE__RAM                EQU   0E2H      ; PORT ADDRESS

; ENABLE BATTERY-POWERED RAM SEGMENT
START:        MOV      AL,001H
              OUT      ENABLE__RAM,AL

; DETERMINE WARM OR COLD START
              IN       AL,POWER__FAIL__STATUS
              RCR      AL,1           ; ISOLATE LOW BIT
              JC       WARM__START

COLD__START:
; INITIALIZE SEGMENT REGISTERS AND STACK POINTER
              ASSUME   CS:CODE,DS:DATA,SS:STACK,ES:NOTHING
              ; RESET TAKES CARE OF CS AND IP.
              MOV      AX,DATA
              MOV      DS,AX
              MOV      AX,STACK
              MOV      SS,AX
              MOV      SP,OFFSET STACK__TOP

; INITIALIZE 8253 AND 8259A.
              CALL     INIT

; ENABLE INTERRUPTS
              STI
```

Figure 3-48 8086,88 Interrupt Procedures Example (continued)

210911

```
; START MAIN PROCESSING
                JMP           USER_PGM
WARM_START:
; INITIALIZE 8253 AND 8259A.
                CALL          INIT

; RESTORE SYSTEM TO STATE AT THE TIME POWER FAILED
                ; MAKE BATTERY SEGMENT ADDRESSABLE
                    MOV       AX,BATTERY
                    MOV       DX,AX
                ; VARIABLES SAVED IN THE "BATTERY" SEGMENT WOULD BE MOVED
                ;   BACK TO UNPROTECTED RAM NOW. SEGMENT REGISTERS AND
                ;   "ASSUME" DIRECTIVES WOULD HAVE TO BE WRITTEN TO GAIN
                ;   ADDRESSABILITY.

                ; RESTORE THE OLD STACK
                    MOV       SS,DS:STACK_SEG
                    MOV       SP,DS:STACK_PTR
                ; RESTORE THE OTHER REGISTERS
                    POP       ES
                    POP       DS
                    POP       BP
                    POP       DI
                    POP       SI
                    POP       DX
                    POP       CX
                    POP       BX
                    POP       AX
                ; RESUME THE ROUTINE THAT WAS EXECUTING WHEN NMI WAS ACTIVATED.
                ;   I.E., POP CS, IP, & FLAGS, EFFECTIVELY "RETURNING" FROM THE
                ;   NMI PROCEDURE.
                    IRET
CODE            ENDS

                ; TERMINATE ASSEMBLY AND MARK BEGINNING OF THE PROGRAM.
                              END           START
            TYPE$40:  DO;
                DECLARE (HOUR, MIN, SEC) BYTE PUBLIC;
                UPDATE$TOD: PROCEDURE INTERRUPT 40;
                    /*THE PROCESSOR ACTIVATES THIS PROCEDURE
                     *TO HANDLE THE SOFTWARE INTERRUPT
                     *GENERATED EVERY SECOND BY THE TYPE 35
                     *EXTERNAL INTERRUPT PROCEDURE. THIS
                     *PROCEDURE UPDATES A REAL-TIME CLOCK.
                     *IT DOES NOT PRETEND TO BE "REALISTIC"
                     *AS THERE IS NO WAY TO SET THE CLOCK.*/

                SEC = SEC + 1;
                IF SEC = 60 THEN DO;
                  SEC = 0;
                  MIN = MIN + 1;
                  IF MIN = 60 THEN DO;
                    MIN = 0;
                    HOUR = HOUR + 1;
                    IF HOUR = 24 THEN DO;
                      HOUR = 0;
                      END;
                    END;
                  END;
                END UPDATE$TOD;
            END;
```

Figure 3-48 8086,88 Interrupt Procedures Example (continued)

```
ALPHA           SEGMENT
; THIS IS THE DATA THE STRING INSTRUCTIONS WILL USE
OUTPUT          DW 100    DUP (?)
INPUT           DW 100    DUP (?)
NAME__1         DB 'JONES, JONA'
NAME__2         DB 'JONES, JOHN'
SENTENCE        DB 80     DUP (?)
EBCDIC__CHARS   DB 80     DUP (?)
ASCII__CHARS    DB 80     DUP (?)
CONV_TAB        DB 64     DUP(0H)              ; EBCDIC TO ASCII

        ; ASCII NULLS ARE SUBSTITUTED FOR "UNPRINTABLE" CHARS
                DB 1      20H
                DB 9      DUP (0H)
                DB 7      '¢', '.', '<', '(', '+', 0H, '&'
                DB 9      DUP (0H)
                DB 8      '!', '$', '*', ')', ';', ' ', '–', '/'
                DB 8      DUP (0H)
                DB 6      ' ', ',', '%', '_', '>', '?'
                DB 9      DUP (0H)
                DB 17     ' ', ':', '#', '@', ' ' ', '=', ' " ',
                          0H, 'a', 'b', 'c', 'd', 'e', 'f', 'g', 'h', 'i'
                DB 7      DUP (0H)
                DB 9      'j', 'k', 'l', 'm', 'n', 'o', 'p', 'q', 'r'
                DB 7      DUP (0H)
                DB 9      '≃', 's', 't', 'u', 'v', 'w', 'x', 'y', 'z'
                DB 22     DUP (0H)
                DB 10     ' ', 'A', 'B', 'C', 'D', 'E', 'F', 'G', 'H', 'I'
                DB 6      DUP (0H)
                DB 10     ' ', 'J', 'K', 'L', 'M', 'N', 'O', 'P', 'Q', 'R'
                DB 6      DUP (0H)
                DB 10     ' ', 0H, 'S', 'T', 'U', 'V', 'W', 'X', 'Y', 'Z'
                DB 6      DUP (0H)
                DB 10     '0', '1', '2', '3', '4', '5', '6', '7', '8', '9'
                DB 6      DUP (0H)

ALPHA           ENDS

STACK           SEGMENT
                DW 100    DUP (?)              ; THIS IS AN ARBITRARY STACK SIZE
                                               ; FOR ILLUSTRATION ONLY.
STACK__BASE     LABEL     WORD                 ; INITIAL TOS
STACK           ENDS

CODE            SEGMENT
BEGIN:          ; SET UP SEGMENT REGISTERS. NOTICE THAT
                ; ES & DS POINT TO THE SAME SEGMENT, MEANING
                ; THAT THE CURRENT EXTRA & DATA
                ; SEGMENTS FULLY OVERLAP. THIS ALLOWS
                ; ANY STRING IN "ALPHA" TO BE USED
                ; AS A SOURCE OR A DESTINATION.
```

Figure 3-49 String Examples

```
                    ASSUME CS: CODE, SS: STACK,
&                       DS: ALPHA, ES: ALPHA
          MOV       AX, STACK
          MOV       SS, AX
          MOV       SP, OFFSET STACK__BASE ; INITIAL TOS
          MOV       AX, ALPHA
          MOV       DS, AX
          MOV       ES, AX
; MOVE THE FIRST 80 WORDS OF "INPUT" TO
;    THE LAST 80 WORDS OF "OUTPUT".
          LEA       SI, INPUT             ; INITIALIZE
          LEA       DI, OUTPUT + 20       ; INDEX REGISTERS
          MOV       CX, 80                ; REPETITION COUNT
          CLD                             ; AUTO-INCREMENT
     REP  MOVS      OUTPUT, INPUT

; FIND THE ALPHABETICALLY LOWER OF 2 NAMES.
          MOV       SI, OFFSET NAME__1    ; ALTERNATIVE
          MOV       DI, OFFSET NAME__2    ; TO LEA
          MOV       CX, SIZE NAME__2      ; CHAR. COUNT
          CLD                             ; AUTO-INCREMENT
     REPE CMPS      NAME__2, NAME__1      "WHILE EQUAL"
          JB        NAME__2__LOW
NAME__1__LOW:       ; NOT IN THIS EXAMPLE
NAME__2__LOW:       ; CONTROL COMES HERE IN THIS EXAMPLE.
                    ; DI POINTS TO BYTE ('H') THAT
                    ; COMPARED UNEQUAL.

; FIND THE LAST PERIOD ('.') IN A TEXT STRING.
          MOV       DI, OFFSET SENTENCE +
&                       LENGTH SENTENCE   ; START AT END
          MOV       CX, SIZE SENTENCE
          STD                             ; AUTO-DECREMENT
          MOV       AL, '.'               ; SEARCH ARGUMENT
    REPNE SCAS      SENTENCE              ; "WHILE NOT ="
          JCXZ      NO__PERIOD            ; IF CX=0, NO PERIOD FOUND
PERIOD:            ; IF CONTROL COMES HERE THEN
                   ;   DI POINTS TO LAST PERIOD IN SENTENCE.
NO__PERIOD:        ; ETC.

; TRANSLATE A STRING OF EBCDIC CHARACTERS
;    TO ASCII, STOPPING IF A CARRIAGE RETURN
;    (0DH ASCII) IS ENCOUNTERED.
          MOV       BX, OFFSET CONV__TAB   ; POINT TO TRANSLATE TABLE
          MOV       SI, OFFSET EBCDIC__CHARS  ; INITIALIZE
          MOV       DI, OFFSET ASCII__CHARS   ;    INDEX REGISTERS
          MOV       CX, SIZE ASCII__CHARS     ;    AND COUNTER
          CLD                             ; AUTO-INCREMENT
NEXT:     LODS      EBCDIC__CHARS         ; NEXT EBCDIC CHAR IN AL
          XLAT      CONV__TAB             ; TRANSLATE TO ASCII
          STOS      ASCII__CHARS          ; STORE FROM AL
          TEST      AL, 0DH               ; IS IT CARRIAGE RETURN?
          LOOPNE    NEXT                  ; NO, CONTINUE WHILE CX NOT 0
```

Figure 3-49 String Examples (continued)

```
            JE        CR_FOUND              ; YES, JUMP
      ; CONTROL COMES HERE IF ALL CHARACTERS
      ;      HAVE BEEN TRANSLATED BUT NO
      ;      CARRIAGE RETURN IS PRESENT.
      ; ETC.

CR_FOUND:
            ; DI-1 POINTS TO THE CARRIAGE RETURN
            ;   IN ASCII_CHARS.

CODE            ENDS
                END
```

Figure 3-49 String Examples (continued)

```
$mod186
name                    assembly_example_80186_DMA_support

;
;    This file contains an example procedure which initializes the 80186 DMA controller to perform the DMA
;           transfers between the 80186 system and the 8272 Floppy Disk Controller (FDC). It assumes that
;           the 80186 peripheral control block has not been moved from its reset location.
;
arg1                        equ     word ptr [BP + 4]
arg2                        equ     word ptr [BP + 6]
arg3                        equ     word ptr [BP + 8]
DMA_FROM_LOWER              equ     0FFC0h                  ; DMA register locations
DMA_FROM_UPPER              equ     0FFC2h
DMA_TO_LOWER                equ     0FFC4h
DMA_TO_UPPER                equ     0FFC6h
DMA_COUNT                   equ     0FFC8h
DMA_CONTROL                 equ     0FFCAh
DMA_TO_DISK_CONTROL         equ     01486h                  ; destination synchronization
                                                            ; source to memory, incremented
                                                            ; destination to I/O
                                                            ; no terminal count
                                                            ; byte transfers
DMA_FROM_DISK_CONTROL       equ     0A046h                  ; source synchronization
                                                            ; source to I/O
                                                            ; destination to memory, incr
                                                            ; no terminal count
                                                            ; byte transfers
FDC_DMA                     equ     6B8h                    ; FDC DMA address
FDC_DATA                    equ     688h                    ; FDC data register
FDC_STATUS                  equ     680h                    ; FDC status register

cgroup                      group   code
code                        segment                         public 'code'
                            public set_dma_
                            assume cs:cgroup
```

Figure 3-50 80186 DMA Initialization Example

```
;
;   set_dma (offset, to) programs the DMA channel to point one side to the disk DMA address, and the other
;       to memory pointed to by ds:offset. If 'to' = 0 then will be a transfer from disk to memory; if 'to' = 1
;       then will be a transfer from memory to disk. The parameters to the routine are passed on the stack.
;
set_dma_            proc    near
                    enter   0, 0                        ; set stack addressability

                    push    AX                          ; save registers used
                    push    BX
                    push    DX

                    test    arg2,1                      ; check to see direction of
                                                        ; transfer
                    jz      from_disk
;
;   performing a transfer from memory to the disk controller
;
                    mov     AX,DS                       ; get the segment value
                    rol     AX,4                        ; gen the upper 4 bits of the
                                                        ; physical address in the lower 4
                                                        ; bits of the register
                    mov     BX, AX                      ; save the result...
                    mov     DX,DMA_FROM_UPPER           ; prgm the upper 4 bits of the
                    out     DX,AX                       ; DMA source register
                    and     AX,0FFF0h                   ; form the lower 16 bits of the
                                                        ; physical address
                    add     AX,argl                     ; add the offset
                    mov     DX,DMA_FROM_LOWER           ; prgm the lower 16 bits of the
                    out     DX,AX                       ; DMA source register
                    jnc     no_carry_from               ; check for carry out of addition
                    inc     BX                          ; if carry out, then need to adj
                    mov     AX,BX                       ; the upper 4 bits of the pointer
                    mov     DX,DMA_FROM_UPPER
                    out     DX,AX

no_carry_from:
                    mov     AX,FDC_DMA                  ; prgm the lower 16 bits of the DMA
                    mov     DX,DMA_TO_LOWER             ; destination register
                    out     DX,AX
                    xor     AX,AX                       ; zero the upper 4 bits of the DMA
                    mov     DX,DMA_TO_UPPER             ; destination register
                    out     DX,AX
                    mov     AX,DMA_TO_DISK_CONTROL      ; prgm the DMA ctl reg
                    mov     DX,DMA_CONTROL              ; note: DMA may begin immediately
                    out     DX,AX                       ; after this word is output
                    pop     DX
                    pop     BX
                    pop     AX
                    leave
                    ret
from_disk:
;
;   performing a transfer from the disk to memory
;
                    mov     AX,DS
                    rol     AX,4
                    mov     DX,DMA_TO_UPPER
                    out     DX,AX
                    mov     BX,AX
                    and     AX,0FFF0h
                    add     AX,argl
                    mov     DX,DMA_TO_LOWER
```

Figure 3-50 80186 DMA Initialization Example (continued)

```
                      out       DX,AX
                      jnc       no_carry_to
                      inc       BX
                      mov       AX,BX
                      mov       DX,DMA_TO_UPPER
                      out       DX,AX
no_carry_to:
                      mov       AX,FDC_DMA
                      mov       DX,DMA_FROM_LOWER
                      out       DX,AX
                      xor       AX,AX
                      mov       DX,DMA_FROM_UPPER
                      out       DX,AX
                      mov       AX,DMA_FROM_DISK_CONTROL
                      mov       DX,DMA_CONTROL
                      out       DX,AX
                      pop       DX
                      pop       BX
                      pop       AX
                      leave
                      ret
set_dma_              endp

code                  ends
                      end
```

Figure 3-50 80186 DMA Initialization Example (continued)

```
$mod186
name                              example_80186_timer_code

;    This file contains example 80186 timer routines. The first routine sets up the timer and interrupt
;         controller to cause the timer to generate an interrupt every 10 milliseconds, and to service the
;         interrupt to implement a real time clock. Timer 2 is used in this example because no input or
;         output signals are required. The code example assumes that the peripheral control block has not
;         been moved from its reset location (FF00-FFFF in I/O space).
;
arg1                  equ       word ptr [BP + 4]
arg2                  equ       word ptr [BP + 6]
arg3                  equ       word ptr [BP + 8]
timer2_int            equ       19                              ; timer 2 has vector type 19
timer 2_control       equ       0FF66h
timer 2_max_ctl       equ       0FF62h
timer_int_ctl         equ       0FF32h                          ; interrupt controller regs
eoi_register          equ       0FF22h
interrupt_stat        equ       0FF30h

data                  segment                                   public 'data'
                      public hour_,minute_,second_,msec_
msec_                 db        ?
hour_                 db        ?
minute_               db        ?
second_               db        ?
data                  ends

cgroup                group     code
dgroup                group     data
```

Figure 3-51 80186 Timer Interface Code Example

```
code                        segment                        public 'code'
                            public set_time_
                            assume cs:code,ds:dgroup
;
;    set_time (hour, minute, second) sets the time variables, initializes the 80186 timer2 to provide interrupts
;            every 10 milliseconds, and programs the interrupt vector for  timer2
;
set_time_                   proc    near
                            enter   0,0                     ; set stack addressability
                            push    AX                      ; save registers used
                            push    DX
                            push    SI
                            push    DS

                            xor     AX,AX                   ; set the interrupt vector
                                                            ; the timers have unique
                                                            ; interrupt
                                                            ; vectors even though they share
                                                            ; the same control register
                            mov     DS,AX
                            mov     SI,4 * timer2_int
                            mov     DS:[SI],offset timer2_interrupt_routine
                            inc     SI
                            inc     SI
                            mov     DS:[SI],CS
                            pop     DS
                            mov     AX,arg1                 ; set the time values
                            mov     hour_,AL
                            mov     AX,arg2
                            mov     minute_,AL
                            mov     AX,arg3
                            mov     second_,AL
                            mov     msec_,0

                            mov     DX,timer2_max_ctl       ; set the max count value
                            mov     AX,20000                ; 10 ms / 500 ns (timer 2 counts
                                                            ; at ¼ the CPU clock rate)
                            out     DX,AX
                            mov     DX,timer2_control       ; set the control word
                            mov     AX,1110000000000001b    ; enable counting
                                                            ; generate interrupts on TC
                                                            ; continuous counting
                            out     DX,AX

                            mov     DX,timer_int_ctl        ; set up the interrupt
controller
                            mov     AX,0000b                ; unmask interrupts
                                                            ; highest priority interrupt
                            out     DX,AX
                            sti                             ; enable processor interrupts

                            pop     SI
                            pop     DX
                            pop     AX
                            leave
                            ret
set_time_                   endp

timer2_interrupt_routine            proc                   far
                            push    AX
                            push    DX
```

Figure 3-51 Timer Interface Code Example (continued)

```
                         cmp     msec_,99                    ; see if one second has passed
                         jae     bump_second                 ; if above or equal. . .
                         inc     msec_
                         jmp     reset_int_ctl
bump_second:
                         mov     msec_,0                     ; reset millisecond
                         cmp     second_,59                  ; see if one minute has passed
                         jae     bump_minute
                         inc     second_
                         jmp     reset_int_ctl
bump_minute:
                         mov     second_,0
                         cmp     minute_,59                  ; see if one hour has passed
                                                             ; single max count register
set_baud_                proc    near
                         push    AX                          ; save registers used
                         push    DX

                         mov     DX,timer1_max_cnt           ; set the max count value
                         mov     AX,13                       ; 500ns * 13 = 6.5 usec
                         out     DX,AX
                         mov     DX,timer1_control           ; set the control word
                         mov     AX,1100000000000001b        ; enable counting
                                                             ; no interrupt on TC
                                                             ; continuous counting
                         jae     bump_hour
                         inc     minute
                         jmp     reset_int_ctl
bump_hour:
                         mov     minute_,0
                         cmp     hour_,12                    ; see if 12 hours have passed
                         jae     reset_hour
                         inc     hour_
                         jmp     reset_int_ctl
reset_hour:
                         mov     hour_,1
reset_int_ctl:
                         mov     DX,eoi_register
                         mov     AX,8000h                    ; non-specific end of interrupt
                         out     DX,AX

                         pop     DX
                         pop     AX
                         iret
timer2_interrupt_routine         endp
code                     ends
                         end
$mod186
name                            example_80186_baud_code
;
;   This file contains example 80186 timer routines. The second routine sets up the timer as a baud rate
;       generator. In this mode, Timer 1 is used to continually output pulses with a period of 6.5 usec for
;       use with a serial controller at 9600 baud programmed in divide by 16 mode (the actual period
;       required for 9600 baud is 6.51 usec). This assumes that the 80186 is running at 8MHz. The code
;       example also assumes that the peripheral control block has not been moved from its reset location
;       (FF00-FFFF in I/O space).
;
timer1_control           equ     0FF5Eh
timer1_max_cnt           equ     0FF5Ah

code                     segment                             public 'code'
                         assume  cs:code
```

Figure 3-51 80186 Timer Interface Code Example (continued)

```
;
;    set_baud () initializes the 80186 timer1 as a baud rate generator for a serial port running at 9600 baud.
;
                             out     DX,AX

                             pop     DX
                             pop     AX
                             ret
set_baud_                    endp
code                         ends
                             end
$mod186
name                                   example_80186_count_code
;    This file contains example 80186 timer routines. The third routine sets up the timer as an external event
;         counter. In this mode, Timer1 is used to count transitions on its input pin. After the timer has been
;         set up by the routine, the number of events counted can be directly read from the timer count
;         register at location FF58H in I/O space. The timer will count a maximum of 65535 timer events
;         before wrapping around to zero. This code example also assumes that the peripheral control block
;         has not been moved from its reset location (FF00-FFFF in I/O space).
;
timer1_control               equ     0FF5Eh
timer1_max_cnt               equ     0FF5Ah
timer1_cnt_reg               equ     0FF58H

code                         segment                         public 'code'
                             assume  cs:code
;
;    set_count () initializes the 80186 timer1 as an event counter
;
set_count_                   proc    near
                             push    AX                      ; save registers used
                             push    DX

                             mov     DX,timer1_max_cnt       ; set the max count value
                             mov     AX,0                    ; allows the timer to count
                                                             ; all the way to FFFFH
                             out     DX,AX
                             mov     DX,timer1_control       ; set the control word
                             mov     AX,1100000000000101b    ; enable counting
                                                             ; no interrupt on TC
                                                             ; continuous counting
                                                             ; single max count register
                                                             ; external clocking
                             out     DX,AX

                             xor     AX,AX                   ; zero AX
                             mov     DX,timer1_cnt_reg       ; and zero the count in the
timer
                             out     DX,AX                   ; count register

                             pop     DX
                             pop     AX
                             ret
set_count_                   endp
code                         ends
                             end
```

Figure 3-51 Timer Interface Code Example (continued)

```
$mod186
name                            example_80186_interrupt_code
;
;   This routine configures the 80186 interrupt controller to provide two cascaded interrupt inputs (through an
;          external 8259A interrupt controller on pins INT0/INT2) and two direct interrupt inputs (on pins INT1
;          and INT3). The default priority levels are used. Because of this, the priority level programmed into the
;          control register is set the 111, the level all interrupts are programmed to at reset.
;
int0_control            equ     0FF38H
int_mask                equ     0FF28H
;
code                    segment                         public 'code'
                        assume CS:code
set_int_                proc    near
                        push    DX
                        push    AX

                        mov     AX,0100111B             ; cascade mode
                                                        ; interrupt unmasked
                        mov     DX,int0_control
                        out     DX,AX

                        mov     AX,01001101B            ; now unmask the other external
                                                        ; interrupts
                        mov     DX,int_mask
                        out     DX,AX
                        pop     AX
                        pop     DX
                        ret
set_int_                endp
code                    ends
                        end
$mod186
name                            example_80186_interrupt_code
;
;   This routine configures the 80186 interrupt controller into iRMX 86 mode. This code does not initialize
;          any of the 80186 integrated peripheral control registers, nor does it initialize the external 8259A
;          or 80130 interrupt controller.
;
relocation_reg          equ     0FFFEH
;
code                    segment                         public 'code'
                        assume CS:code
set_rmx_                proc    near
                        push    DX
                        push    AX

                        mov     DX,relocation_reg
                        in      AX,DX                   ; read old contents of register
                        or      AX,0100000000000000B    ; set the RMX mode bit

                        pop     AX
                        pop     DX
                        ret
set_rmx_                endp
code                    ends
                        end
```

Figure 3-52 80186 Interrupt Controller Interface Code Example

```
name                          example_80186_system_init
;
;    This file contains a system initialization routine for the 8086 or the 80186. The code determines whether
;        it is running on an 80186 or an 8086, and if it is running on an 80186, it initializ⌐ the integrated
;        chip select registers.
;
restart                       segment                         at 0FFFFh
;
;    This is the processor reset address at 0FFFF0H
;
                              org       0
                              jmp       far ptr initialize
restart                       ends
;
                              extrn     monitor:far
init_hw                       segment                         at 0FFF0h
                              assume CS:init_hw
;
;    This segment initializes the chip selects. It must be located in the top 1K to insure that the ROM remains
;        selected in the 80186 system until the proper size of the select area can be programmed.
;
UMCS_reg                      equ       0FFA0H                ; chip select register locations
LMCS_reg                      equ       0FFA2H
PACS_reg                      equ       0FFA4H
MPCS_reg                      equ       0FFA8H
UMCS_value                    equ       0F800H                ; 64K, no wait states
LMCS_value                    equ       07F8H                 ; 32K, no wait states
PACS_value                    equ       72H                   ; peripheral base at 400H, 2 ws
MPCS_value                    equ       0BAH                  ; PCS5 and 6 supplies,
                                                              ; peripherals in I/O space
initialize                    proc      far
                              mov       AX,2                  ; determine if this is an
                              mov       CL,33                 ; 8086 or an 80186 (checks
                              shr       AX,CL                 ; to see if the multiple bit
                              test      AX,1                  ; shift value was ANDed)
                              jz        not_80186

                              mov       DX,UMCS_reg           ; program the UMCS register
                              mov       AX,UMCS_value
                              out       DX,AX

                              mov       DX,LMCS_reg           ; program the LMCS register
                              mov       AX,LMCS_value
                              out       DX,AX

                              mov       DX,PACS_reg           ; set up the peripheral chip
                                                              ; selects (note the mid-range
                                                              ; memory chip selects are not
                                                              ; needed in this system, and
                                                              ; are thus not initialized
                              mov       AX,PACS_value
                              out       DX,AX

                              mov       DX,MPCS_reg
                              mov       AX,MPCS_value
                              out       DX,AX
;
;    Now that the chip selects are all set up, the main program of the computer may be executed.
;
not_80186:
                              jmp       far ptr monitor
initialize                    endp
init_hw                       ends
                              end
```

Figure 3-53 80186/8086 System Initialization Code Example

210911

iAPX 86,88 Hardware Design Overview

CHAPTER 4
iAPX 86,88 HARDWARE DESIGN OVERVIEW

4.1 INTRODUCTION

This chapter is a discussion of the hardware design of the iAPX 86,88 (8086, 8088) on the functional level. Electrical characteristics and other hardware references are discussed in Volume 2 of this set. Application Notes AP-67, "8086 System Design," and AP-51, "Designing 8086, 8088, 8089 Multiprocessing Systems with the 8289 Bus Arbiter," also in Volume 2, contain additional design information.

This chapter includes the following topics:

- Multiprocessing Features
- Bus Organization
- Processor Control
- Interfacing with Processor Extensions

4.2 MULTIPROCESSING FEATURES

The 8086 and 8088 are designed for the multiprocessing environment. Multiprocessing means using two or more coordinated processors in a system. These CPUs have built-in features that help solve the coordination problems that have made the development of multiprocessing systems difficult in the past.

Multiprocessing has become increasingly attractive as microprocessor prices have declined. Performance can be substantially improved by distributing system tasks among separate, concurrently executing processors. In addition, multiprocessing encourages a modular approach to design, usually resulting in systems that are more easily maintained and enhanced.

The example in Figure 4-1 shows a multiprocessor system in which I/O activities have been delegated to an 8089 IOP. (The 8089 IOP is described in Chapter 7 of this volume.) Should an I/O device in the system be changed (e.g., a hard disk substituted for a floppy), the impact of the modification is confined to the I/O subsystem and is transparent to the CPU and to the application software.

In general, using multiple processors offers several significant advantages over the centralized approach that relies on a single CPU and extremely fast memory:

1) System tasks may be allocated to special-purpose processors whose designs are optimized to perform specific (or classes of) tasks simply and efficiently;

2) Very high levels of performance can be attained when processors can execute simultaneously (parallel/distributed processing);

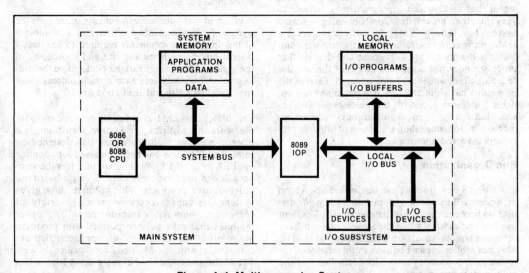

Figure 4-1 Multiprocessing System

3) Partitioning of the system promotes parallel development of subsystems, breaks the application into smaller, more manageable tasks, and helps isolate the effects of system modifications.

The 8086,88 architecture supports two types of processors: independent processors and processor extensions. An independent processor executes its own instruction stream. The 8086, the 8088 and the 8089 IOP are examples of independent processors. The 8086,88 typically execute a program in response to an interrupt. The IOP starts its channels in response to an interrupt-like signal called a channel attention; this signal is usually issued by a CPU.

The CPUs also support a second type of processor, called a processor extension, such as the 8087 NPX. (The 8087 NPX is described in Chapter 6 of this volume.) Processor extension "hooks" have been designed into the 8086,88 to allow this type of processor to be accommodated. The processor extension adds additional register, data type, and instruction resources directly to the system. A processor extension, in effect, extends the instruction set (and architecture) of its host processor.

This solves two classic multiprocessing coordination problems: bus arbitration and mutual exclusion. Bus arbitration may be performed by the bus request/grant logic contained in each of the processors (local bus arbitration), by 8289 bus arbiters (system bus arbitration), or by a combination of the two when processors have access to multiple shared buses. In all cases, the arbitration mechanism operates invisibly to software.

For mutual exclusion, each processor has a $\overline{\text{LOCK}}$ signal (bus lock) which a program may activate to prevent other processors from obtaining a shared system bus. The IOP may lock the bus during a DMA transfer to ensure both that the transfer completes in the shortest possible time and that another processor does not access the target of the transfer (e.g., a buffer) while it is being updated. Each of the processors has an instruction that examines and updates a memory byte with the bus locked. This instruction can be used to implement a semaphore mechanism for controlling the access of multiple processors to shared resources.

Bus Organization

The 8086,88 bus structure can be divided into a local or Resident Bus, and a system bus. The major distinction between the two is that the local or Resident Bus has one master, while the system bus can have several masters (multi-master system bus). The 8289 bus arbiter (described later in this chapter), interfaces the processors to the Resident Bus and the multi-master system bus.

LOCAL OR RESIDENT BUS

The local bus is optimized for use by the 8086,88 CPUs. Since standard memory and I/O components are not attached to the local bus, information can be multiplexed and encoded to make efficient use of processor pins. This allows several pins to be dedicated to coordinating the activity of multiple processors sharing the local bus. Both independent processors and processor extensions may share a local bus; on-chip arbitration logic determines which processor drives the bus. Because the processors on the local bus share the same bus interface components, the local configuration of multiple processors provides a compact and inexpensive multiprocessing system.

SYSTEM BUS

A system bus carries several signals designed to meet the needs of memory and I/O devices:

- Address bus

- Data bus

- Control lines

- Interrupt lines

- Arbitration lines

The system bus design is modular and subsets may be implemented according to the needs of the application. For example, the arbitration lines are not needed in single-processor systems or in multiple-processor systems that perform arbitration at the local-bus level.

A group of bus interface components transforms the signals of a local bus into a system bus. The number of bus interface components required to generate a system bus depends on the size and complexity of the system. Three main variables determine the configuration of a bus interface group: address space size, data bus width and arbitration needs.

The 8086,88 system bus can easily be made compatible with the Multibus™ system. Multibus is a general-purpose multiprocessing bus designed by Intel. The Multibus has been proposed for adoption by IEEE as the IEEE 796 standard bus. It is the standard design used in Intel's iSBC™ single-board microcomputer products. This compatibility gives system designers access to a wide variety of computer, memory, communication and other modules that may be incorporated into products. Many other manufacturers offer products that are compatible with the Multibus architecture as well. The Multibus is described in more detail later in this chapter.

Bus Lock

When configured in maximum mode, the 8086 and 8088 provide the $\overline{\text{LOCK}}$ (bus lock) signal. The BIU activates $\overline{\text{LOCK}}$ when the EU executes the one-byte LOCK prefix instruction. The $\overline{\text{LOCK}}$ signal remains active throughout execution of the instruction that follows the LOCK prefix. Interrupts are *not* affected by the LOCK prefix. If another processor requests use of the bus (via the request/grant lines, which are discussed later in this chapter), the CPU records the request, but does not honor it until execution of the locked instruction has been completed.

Note that the $\overline{\text{LOCK}}$ signal remains active for the duration of a *single* instruction. If two consecutive instructions are each preceded by a LOCK prefix, there will still be an unlocked period between these instructions. In the case of a locked repeated string instruction, $\overline{\text{LOCK}}$ does remain active for the duration of the block operation.

When the 8086 or 8088 is configured in minimum mode, the $\overline{\text{LOCK}}$ signal is not available. The LOCK prefix can be used, however, to delay the generation of an HOLDA response to a HOLD request until execution of the locked instruction is completed.

The $\overline{\text{LOCK}}$ signal provides information only. It is the responsibility of the other processors on the shared bus not to attempt to obtain the bus while $\overline{\text{LOCK}}$ is active. If the system uses 8289 Bus Arbiters to control access to the shared bus, the 8289s accept $\overline{\text{LOCK}}$ as an input and do not relinquish the bus while this signal is active.

$\overline{\text{LOCK}}$ may be used in multiprocessing systems to coordinate access to a common resource, such as a buffer or a pointer. If access to the resources is not controlled, one processor can read an erroneous value from the resource when another processor is updating it (see Figure 4-2).

BUS CYCLE	SHARED POINTER IN MEMORY		PROCESSOR ACTIVITIES
0	05 22	4C 1B	
1	C2 59	4C 1B	"A" UPDATES 1 WORD
2	C2 59	4C 1B	"B" READS PARTIALLY UPDATED VALUE
3	C2 59	31 05	"A" COMPLETES UPDATE

Figure 4-2 Uncontrolled Access to Shared Resource

Access can be controlled (see Figure 4-3) by using the LOCK prefix in conjunction with the XCHG (exchange register with memory) instruction. The basis for controlling access to a given resource is a semaphore, a software-settable flag or switch that indicates whether the resource is "available" (semaphore=0) or "busy" (semaphore=1). Procesors that share the bus agree by convention not to

BUS CYCLE	SEMAPHORE	SHARED POINTER IN MEMORY		PROCESSOR ACTIVITIES
0	0	05 22	4C 1B	
1	1	05 22	4C 1B	"A" OBTAINS EXCLUSIVE USE
2	1	C2 59	4C 1B	"A" UPDATES 1 WORD
3	1	C2 59	4C 1B	"B" TESTS SEMAPHORE AND WAITS
4	1	C2 59	31 05	"A" COMPLETES UPDATE
5	1	C2 59	31 05	"B" TESTS SEMAPHORE AND WAITS
6	0	C2 59	31 05	"A" RELEASES RESOURCE
7	1	C2 59	31 05	"B" OBTAINS EXCLUSIVE USE
8	1	C2 59	31 05	"B" READS UPDATED VALUE
9	0	C2 59	31 05	"B" RELEASES RESOURCE

Figure 4-3 Controlled Access to Shared Resource

210911

use the resource unless the semaphore indicates that it is available. They likewise agree to set the semaphore when they are using the resource and to clear it when they are finished.

The XCHG instruction can obtain the current value of the semaphore and set it to "busy" in a single instruction. The instruction, however, requires two bus cycles to swap 8-bit values. It is possible for another processor to obtain the bus between these two cycles and to gain access to the partially-updated semaphore. This can be prevented by preceding the XCHG instruction with a LOCK prefix, as illustrated in Figure 4-4. The bus lock establishes control over access to the semaphore and thus to the shared resource.

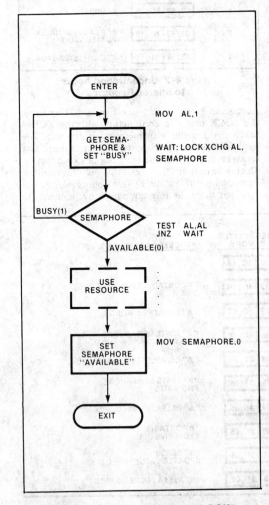

Figure 4-4 Using XCHG and LOCK

WAIT and $\overline{\text{TEST}}$

The 8086 and 8088 (in either maximum or minimum mode) can be synchronized to an external event with the WAIT (wait for TEST) instruction and the TEST input signal. When the EU executes a WAIT instruction, the result depends on the state of the $\overline{\text{TEST}}$ input line. If $\overline{\text{TEST}}$ is inactive, the processor enters an idle state and repeatedly retests the $\overline{\text{TEST}}$ line at five-clock intervals. If $\overline{\text{TEST}}$ is active, execution continues with the instruction following the WAIT.

Escape

The ESC (escape) instruction provides a way for another processor to obtain an instruction and/or a memory operand from an 8086,88 program. When used in conjunction with WAIT and TEST, ESC can initiate a "subroutine" that executes concurrently in another processor (see Figure 4-5). An example of the use of the WAIT, TEST and ESC instructions is the application of an 8087 NPX processor extension.

Six bits in the ESC instruction may be specified by the programmer when the instruction is written. By monitoring the bus and control lines, another processor (e.g., an 8087 NPX) can capture the ESC instruction when it is fetched by the BIU. The six bits may then direct the external processor to perform some predefined activity.

If an 8086 or 8088 is configured in maximum mode, the external processor, having determined that an ESC has been fetched, can monitor QS0 and QS1 (the queue status lines) and determine when the ESC instruction is executed. If the instruction references memory the external processor can then monitor the bus and capture the operand's physical address and/or operand itself.

Note that fetching an ESC instruction is not tantamount to executing it. The ESC may be preceded by a jump that causes the queue to be reinitialized. This event also can be determined from the queue status lines.

Request/Grant Lines

When the 8086 or 8088 is configured in maximum mode, the HOLD and HLDA lines evolve into two more sophisticated signals called $\overline{\text{RQ(/)GT0}}$ and $\overline{\text{RQ(/)GT1}}$. These are bidirectional lines that can be used to share a local bus between an 8086 or 8088 and two other processors via a handshake sequence.

210911

The request/grant sequence is a three-phase cycle: request, grant and release. First, the processor desiring the bus pulses a request/grant line. The CPU returns a pulse on the same line indicating that it is entering the "hold acknowledge" state and is relinquishing the bus. The BIU is logically disconnected from the bus during this period. The EU, however, will continue to execute instructions until an instruction requires bus access or the queue is emptied, whichever occurs first. When the other processor has finished with the bus, it sends a final pulse to the 8086,88 indicating that the request has ended and that the CPU may reclaim the bus.

$\overline{RQ(/)GT0}$ has higher priority than $\overline{RQ(/)GT1}$. If requests arrive simultaneously on both lines, the grant goes to the processor on $\overline{RQ(/)GT0}$ and $\overline{RQ(/)GT1}$ is acknowledged after the bus has been returned to the CPU. If, however, a request arrives on $\overline{RQ(/)GT0}$ while the CPU is processing a prior request on $\overline{RQ(/)GT1}$, the second request is not honored until the processor on $\overline{RQ(/)GT1}$ releases the bus.

Multibus Architecture

When the 8086 or 8088 is configured in maximum mode, the 8288 Bus Controller outputs signals that are electrically compatible with the Multibus protocol. Designers of multiprocessing systems may want to consider using the Multibus architecture in the design of their products to reduce development cost and time, and to obtain compatibility with the wide variety of boards available in the iSBC product line.

Multibus architecture provides a versatile communications channel that can be used to coordinate a wide variety of computing modules (see Figure 4-6). Modules in a Multibus system are designated as masters or slaves. Masters may obtain use of the bus and initiate data transfers on it. Slaves are the objects of data transfers only.

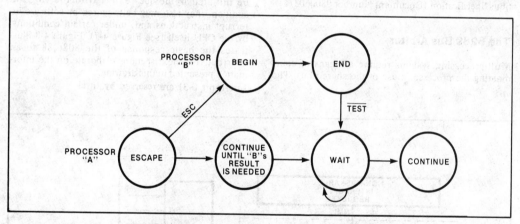

Figure 4-5 Using ESC with WAIT and TEST

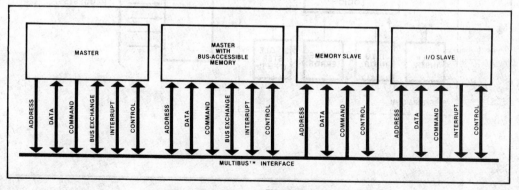

Figure 4-6 Multibus™-Based System

Both 8- and 16-bit masters can be intermixed in such a system. In addition to 16 data lines, the bus design has 20 address lines, eight multilevel interrupt lines, and control and arbitration lines. An auxiliary power bus also is provided to route standby power to memories if the normal supply fails.

The Multibus architecture maintains its own clock, independent of the clocks of the modules it links together. This allows different speed masters to share the bus and allows masters to operate asynchronously with respect to each other. The arbitration logic of the bus permits slow-speed masters to compete equitably for use of the bus. Once a module has obtained the bus, however, transfer speeds are dependent only on the capabilities of the transmitting and receiving modules. Finally, the Multibus standard defines the form factors and physical requirements of modules that communicate on this bus. For a complete description of the Multibus architecture refer to Application Note 28A, "Intel Multibus Interfacing," in Volume 2 of this set, and Intel Multibus Specification (Document Number 9800603).

The 8289 Bus Arbiter

Multiprocessing systems require a means of coordinating the processor's use of the shared bus. The 8289 Bus Arbiter works in conjunction with the 8288 Bus Controller to provide this control. It is compatible with the Multibus architecture and can be used in other shared-bus designs as well.

The 8289 eliminates race conditions, resolves bus contention and matches processors operating asynchronously with respect to each other. Each processor on the bus is assigned a different priority. When simultaneous requests for the bus arrive, the 8289 resolves the contention and grants the bus to the processor with the highest priority; three different prioritizing techniques may be used. The 8289 Bus Arbiter is discussed in more detail in Volume 2 of this set.

4.3 INTERRUPT STRUCTURE

Interrupts play an important role in the control of the CPU. In 8086,88 based systems, each interrupt is assigned a type code that identifies it. Interrupts may be initiated by devices external to the CPU; in addition, they also may be triggered by software interrupt instructions and, under certain conditions, by the CPU itself (see Figure 4-7). Figure 4-8 illustrates the basic response of the 8086,88 to an interrupt. The next sections elaborate on the information presented in this drawing.

Interrupts 0-31 are reserved by Intel

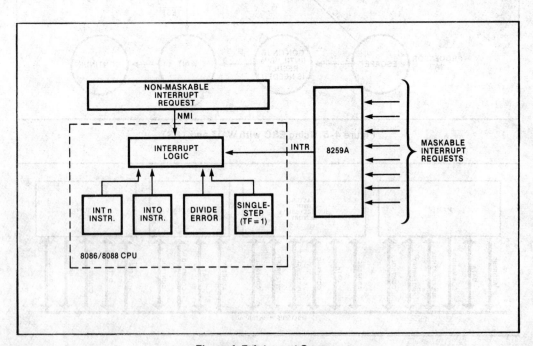

Figure 4-7 Interrupt Sources

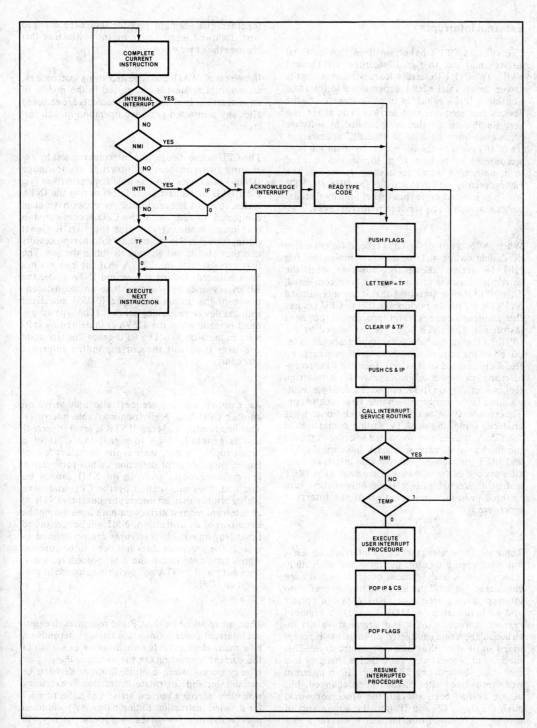

Figure 4-8 Interrupt Processing Sequence

External Interrupts

The 8086,88 CPUs have two lines that external devices may use to signal interrupts (INTR and NMI). The INTR (Interrupt Request) line is usually driven by an Intel 8259A Programmable Interrupt Controller (PIC), which in turn is connected to the devices that need interrupt services. The 8259A is a very flexible circuit that is controlled by software commands from the 8086,88 (the PIC appears as a set of I/O ports to the software). Its main job is to accept interrupt requests from the devices attached to it, determine which requesting device has the highest priority, and then activate the 8086,88 INTR line if the selected device has higher priority than the device currently being serviced (if there is one).

When INTR is active, the CPU takes different action depending on the state of the interrupt-enable flag (IF). No action takes place, however, until the currently-executing instruction has been completed. Then, if IF is clear (meaning that interrupts signaled on INTR are masked or disabled), the CPU ignores the interrupt request and processes the next instruction. The INTR signal is not latched by the CPU, so it must be held active until response is received or the request is withdrawn. If interrupts on INTR are enabled (if IF is set), then the CPU recognizes the interrupt request and processes it. Interrupt requests arriving on INTR can be enabled by executing an STI (set interrupt-enable flag) instruction. They also may be selectively masked (some types enabled, some disabled) by writing commands to the 8259A. It should be noted that in order to reduce the likelihood of excessive stack buildup, the STI and IRET instructions will reenable interrupts only after the end of the following instruction. (The IRET instruction reenables interrupts only if they were enabled prior to the execution of the interrupt procedure.)

There are a few cases in which an interrupt request is not recognized until after the following instruction. Repeat, LOCK and segment override prefixes are considered "part of" the instructions they prefix; no interrupt is recognized between execution of a prefix and an instruction. A MOV (move) to segment register instruction and a POP segment register instruction are treated similarly: no interrupt is recognized until after the following instruction. This mechanism protects a program that is changing to a new stack (by updating SS and SP). If an interrupt were recognized after SS had been changed, but before SP had been altered, the processor would push the flags, CS and IP into the wrong area of memory. It follows from this that whenever a segment register and another value must be updated together, the segment register should be changed first, followed immediately by the instruction that changes the other value.

In two cases, WAIT and repeated string instructions, an interrupt request is recognized in the middle of an instruction. In these cases, interrupts are accepted after any completed primitive operation or wait test cycle.

The CPU acknowledges the interrupt request by executing two consecutive interrupt acknowledge (INTA) bus cycles. If a bus hold request arrives (via the HOLD or request/grant lines) during the INTA cycles, it is not honored until the cycles have been completed. In addition, if the CPU is configured in maximum mode, it activates the $\overline{\text{LOCK}}$ signal during these cycles to indicate to other processors that they should not attempt to obtain the bus. The first cycle signals the 8259A that the request has been honored. During the second INTA cycle, the 8259A responds by placing a byte on the data bus that contains the interrupt type (0-255) associated with the device requesting service. (The type assignment is made when the 8259A is initialized by software in the 8086,88.) The CPU reads this type code and uses it to call the corresponding interrupt procedure.

An external interrupt request also may arrive on another CPU line, NMI (non-maskable interrupt). This line is edge-triggered (INTR is level triggered) and is generally used to signal the CPU of a "catastrophic" event, such as the imminent loss of power, memory error detection or bus parity error. Interrupt requests arriving on NMI cannot be disabled; they are latched by the CPU and have higher priority than an interrupt request on INTR. If an interrupt request arrives on both lines during the execution of an instruction, NMI will be recognized first. Non-maskable interrupts are predefined as type 2; the processor does not need to be supplied with a type code to call the NMI procedure, and it does not run the INTA bus cycles in response to a request on NMI.

The time required for the CPU to recognize an external interrupt request (interrupt latency) depends on how many clock periods remain in the execution of the current instruction. On the average, the longest latency occurs when a multiplication, division or variable-bit shift or rotate instruction is executing when the interrupt request arrives. (See Section 3.7 for detailed instruction timing data.) As mentioned previously, in a few cases, worst-case latency will span two instructions rather than one.

210911

Software Generated Interrupts

An INT (interrupt) instruction generates an interrupt immediately upon completion of its execution. The Interrupt type coded into the instruction supplies the CPU with the type code needed to call the procedure to process the interrupt. Since any type code may be specified, software interrupts may be used to test interrupt procedures written to service external devices.

The CPU generates a type 0 interrupt immediately following execution of a DIV or IDIV (divide, integer divide) instruction if the calculated quotient is larger than the specified destination.

If the trap flag (TF) is set, the CPU generates a type 1 interrupt following most instructions. This is called single-step execution and is a powerful debugging tool that is discussed in more detail later in this chapter.

If the overflow flag (OF) is set, an INTO (interrupt on overflow) instruction generates a type 4 interrupt upon completion of its execution.

All internal interrupts (INT, INTO, divide error, and single step) share these characteristics:

1) The interrupt type code is either contained in the instruction or is predefined.

2) No INTA bus cycles are run.

3) Internal interrupts cannot be disabled, except for single-step.

4) Any internal interrupt (except single-step) has higher priority than any external interrupt (see Table 4-1). If interrupt requests arrive on NMI and/or INTR during execution of an instruction that causes an internal interrupt (e.g., divide error), the internal interrupt is processed first.

Table 4-1 Interrupt Priorities

INTERRUPT	PRIORITY
Divide error, INT n, INTO NMI INTR Single-step	highest lowest

4.3.3 Interrupt Pointer Table

The interrupt pointer (or interrupt vector) table (Figure 4-9) is the link between an interrupt type code and the procedure that has been designated to service interrupts associated with that code. The interrupt pointer table occupies up to the first 1K bytes of low memory. There may be up to 256 entries in the table, one for each interrupt type that can occur in the system. Each entry in the table is a doubleword pointer containing the address of the procedure that is to service interrupts of that type. The higher-addressed word of the pointer contains the base address of the segment containing the procedure. The lower-addressed word contains the procedure's offset from the beginning of the segment. Since each entry is four bytes long, the CPU can calculate the location of the correct entry for a given interrupt type by simply multiplying (type*4).

Space at the high end of the table that would be occupied by entries for interrupt types that cannot occur in a given application may be used for other purposes. The dedicated and reserved portions of the interrupt pointer table (locations 0H through 7FH), however, should not be used for any other purpose to insure proper system operation and to preserve compatibility with future Intel hardware and software products.

After pushing the flags onto the stack, the 8086,88 CPUs activate an interrupt procedure by executing the equivalent of an intersegment indirect CALL instruction. The target of the "CALL" is the address contained in the interrupt pointer table element located at (type*4). The CPU saves the address of the next instruction by pushing CS and IP onto the stack. These are then replaced by the second and first words of the table element, thus transferring control to the procedure.

If multiple interrupt requests arrive simultaneously, the processor activates the interrupt procedures in priority order. Figure 4-10 shows how procedures would be activated in an extreme case. The processor is running in single-step mode with external interrupts enabled. During execution of a divide instruction, INTR is activated. Furthermore the instruction generates a divide error interrupt. Figure 4-10 shows that the interrupts are recognized in turn, in the order of their priorities except for INTR. INTR is not recognized until after the following instruction because recognition of the earlier interrupts cleared IF. Of course interrupts could be reenabled in any of the interrupt response routines if earlier response to INTR is desired.

As Figure 4-10 shows, all main-line code is executed in single-step mode. Also, because of the order of interrupt processing, the opportunity exists in each occurrence of the single-step routine to select whether pending interrupt routines (divide error and INTR routines in this example) are executed at full speed or in single-step mode.

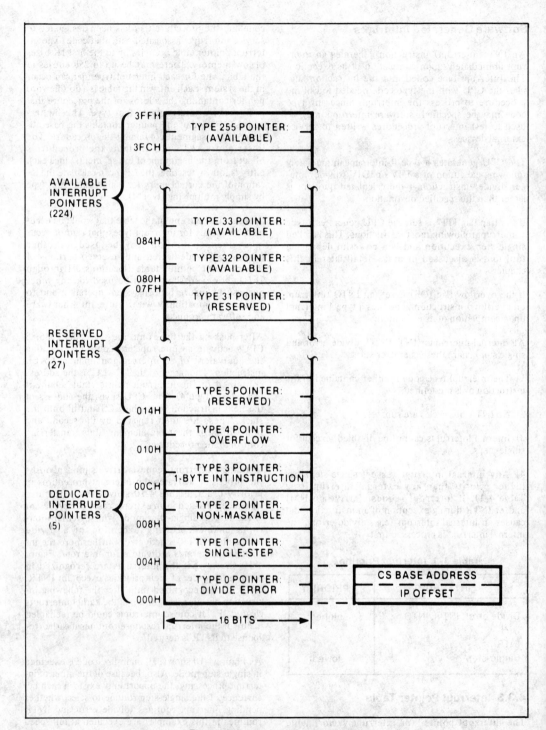

Figure 4-9 Interrupt Pointer Table

210911

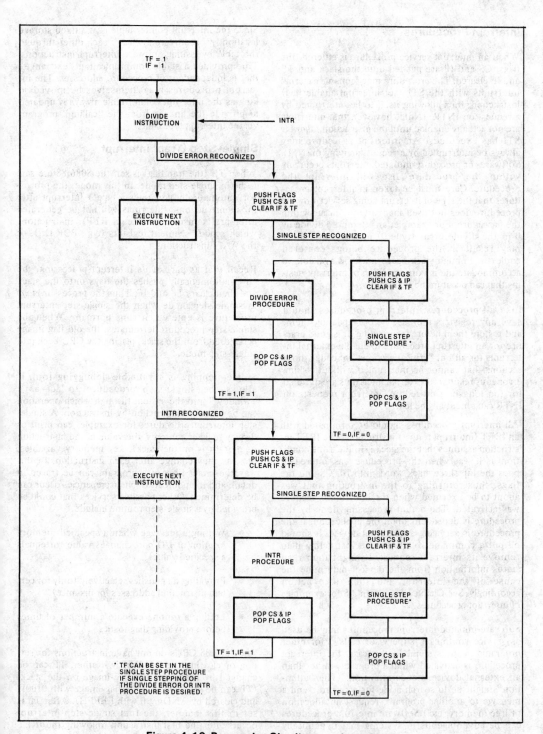

Figure 4-10 Processing Simultaneous Interrupts

Interrupt Procedures

When an interrupt service procedure is entered, the flags, CS and IP are pushed onto the stack and TF and IF cleared. The procedure may reenable external interrupts with the STI (set interrupt-enable flag) instruction, thus allowing itself to be interrupted by a request on INTR. (Note, however, that interrupts are not actually enabled until the instruction *following* STI has executed.) An interrupt procedure may always be interrupted by a request arriving on NMI. Software- or procedure-initiated interrupts occurring within the procedure also will interrupt the procedure. Care must be taken in interrupt procedures that the type of interrupt being serviced by the procedure does not itself inadvertently occur within the procedure. For example, an attempt to divide by 0 in the divide error (type 0) interrupt procedure may result in the procedure being reentered endlessly. Enough stack space must be available to accommodate the maximum depth of interrupt nesting that can occur in the system.

Like all procedures, interrupt procedures should save any registers they use before updating them, and restore them before terminating. It is good practice for an interrupt procedure to enable external interrupts for all but "critical sections" of code (those sections that cannot be interrupted without risking erroneous results). If external interrupts are disabled for too long in a procedure, interrupt requests on INTR can potentially be lost.

All interrupt procedures should be terminated with an IRET (interrupt return) instruction. The IRET instruction assumes that the stack is in the same condition as it was when the procedure was entered. It pops the top three stack words into IP, CS and the flags, thus returning to the instruction that was about to be executed when the interrupt procedure was activated. The actual processing done by the procedure is dependent upon the application. If the procedure is servicing an external device, it should output a command to the device instructing it to remove its interrupt request. It might then read status information from the device, determine the cause of the interrupt and then take action accordingly. See Chapter 3, Section 3.8 for examples of interrupt procedures.

Software-initiated interrupt procedures may be used as service routines ("supervisor calls") for other programs in the system. In this case. the interrupt procedure is activated when a program, rather than an external device, needs attention. (The "attention" might be to search a file for a record, send a message to another program, request an allocation of free memory, etc.) Software interrupt procedures can be advantageous in systems that dynamically relocate programs during execution.

Since the interrupt pointer table is at a fixed storage location, procedures may "call" each other through the table by issuing software interrupt instructions. This provides a stable communication "exchange" that is independent of procedure addresses. The interrupt procedures may themselves be moved so long as the interrupt pointer table always is updated to provide the linkage from the "calling" program via the interrupt type code.

Single-Step (Trap) Interrupt

When TF (the trap flag) is set, the 8086,88 are said to be in single-step mode. In this mode, the processor automatically generates a type 1 interrupt after most instructions. Interrupts will not be generated after prefix instructions (e.g., REP), instructions which modify segment registers (e.g., POP DS), or the WAIT instructions.

Recall that as part of its interrupt processing, the CPU automatically pushes the flags onto the stack and then clears TF and IF. Thus the processor is *not* in single-step mode when the single-step interrupt procedure is entered; it runs normally. When the single-step procedure terminates, the old flag image is restored from the stack, placing the CPU back into single-step mode.

Single-stepping is a valuable debugging tool. It allows the single-step procedure to act as a "window" into the system through which operation can be observed instruction-by-instruction. A single-step interrupt procedure, for example, can print or display register contents, the value of the instruction pointer (it is on the stack), key memory variables, etc., as they change after each instruction. In this way the exact flow of a program can be traced in detail, and the point at which discrepancies occur can be determined. Other possible services that could be provided by a single-step routine include:

- Writing a message when a specified memory location or I/O port changes value (or equals a specified value).

- Providing diagnostics selectively (only for certain instruction addresses for instance).

- Letting a routine execute a number of times before providing diagnostics.

The 8086,88 CPUs do not have instructions for setting or clearing the TF directly. Rather, TF can be changed by modifying the flag-image on the stack. (TF can be set by ORing the flag-image with 0100H and cleared by ANDing it with FEFFH). After TF is set in this manner, the first single-step interrupt occurs after the first instruction following the IRET from the single-step procedure.

If the processor is single-stepping, it processes an interrupt (either internal or external) as follows. Control is passed normally (flags, CS an IP are pushed) to the procedure designated to handle the type of interrupt that has occurred. However, before the first instruction of that procedure is executed, the single-step interrupt is "recognized" and control is passed normally (flags, CS and IP are pushed) to the type 1 interrupt procedure. When single-step procedure terminates, control returns to the previous interrupt procedure. Figure 4-10 illustrates this process in a case where two interrupts occur when the processor is in single-step mode.

Breakpoint Interrupt

A type 3 interrupt is dedicated to the breakpoint interrupt. A breakpoint is generally any place in a program where normal execution is arrested so that some sort of special processing may be performed. Breakpoints typically are inserted into programs during debugging as a way of displaying registers, memory locations, etc., at crucial points in the program.

The INT 3 (breakpoint) instruction is one byte long. This makes it easy to "plant" a breakpoint anywhere in a program. Chapter 3, Section 3.8, contains an example that shows how a breakpoint may be set, and how a breakpoint procedure may be used to place the processor into single-step mode.

The breakpoint instruction also may be used to "patch" a program (insert new instructions) without recompiling or reassembling it. This may be done by saving an instruction byte, and replacing it with an INT 3 (CCH) machine instruction. The breakpoint procedure would contain the new machine instructions, plus code to restore the saved instruction byte and decrement IP on the stack before returning, so that the displaced instruction would be executed after the patch instructions. The breakpoint example in Chapter 3, Section 3.8 illustrates these principles.

Note that patching a program requires machine-instruction programming and should be undertaken with considerable caution; it is easy to add new bugs to a program in an attempt to correct existing ones. Note also that a patch is only a temporary measure to be used in exceptional conditions. The affected code should be updated and retranslated as soon as possible.

System Reset

The 8086,88 RESET lines provide an orderly way to start or restart an executing system. When the processor detects the positive-going edge of a pulse on

RESET, it terminates all activities until the signal goes low, at which time it initializes the system as shown in Table 4-2.

Table 4-2 CPU State Following RESET

CPU COMPONENT	CONTENT
Flags	Clear
Instruction Pointer	0000H
CS Register	FFFFH
DS Register	0000H
SS Register	0000H
ES Register	0000H
Queue	Empty

Since the code segment register contains FFFFH and the instruction pointer contains 0H, the processor executes its first instruction following system reset from absolute memory location FFFF0H. This location normally contains an intersegment direct JMP instruction from information in the program that identifies its first instruction. As external (maskable) interrupts are disabled by system reset, the system software should reenable interrupts as soon as the system is initialized to the point where they can be processed.

Instruction Queue Status

When configured in maximum mode, the 8086,88 provide information about instruction queue operations on QS0 and QS1. Table 4-3 interprets the four states that these lines can represent.

Table 4-3 Queue Status Signals (Maximum Mode Only)

QS$_0$	QS$_1$	QUEUE OPERATION IN LAST CLK CYCLE
0	0	No operation; default value
0	1	First byte of an instruction was taken from the queue
1	0	Queue was reinitialized
1	1	Subsequent byte of an instruction was taken from the queue

The queue status lines are provided for external processors that receive instructions and/or operands via the ESC (escape) instruction (see Section 4.2). Such a processor may monitor the bus to see when an ESC instruction is fetched and then track the instruction through the queue to determine when (and if) the instruction is executed.

Processor Halt

When the HALT (halt) instruction is executed, the processor enters the halt state. This condition may be interpreted as "stop all operations until an external interrupt occurs or the system is reset." No signals are floated during the halt state, and the content of the address and data buses is undefined. A bus hold request arriving on the HOLD line (minimum mode) or either request/grant line (maximum mode) is acknowledged normally while the processor is halted.

The halt state can be used when an event prevents the system from functioning correctly. An example might be a power-fail interrupt. After recognizing that loss of power is imminent, the CPU could use the remaining time to move registers, flags and vital variables to (for example) a battery-powered CMOS RAM area - or EEPROM area and then halt until the return of power was signaled by an interrupt or system reset.

Status Lines

When configured in maximum mode, the 8086,88 CPUs emit eight status signals that can be used by external devices. Lines $\overline{S0}$, $\overline{S1}$ and $\overline{S2}$ identify the type of bus cycle that the CPU is starting to execute (Table 4-4). These lines are typically decoded by the

by the 8288 Bus Controller. S3 and S4 indicate which segment register was used to construct the physical address used in this bus cycle (see Table 4-5). Line S5 reflects the state of the interrupt-enable flag. S6 is always 0. S7 is a spare line whose content is undefined.

Table 4-4 Bus Cycle Status Signals

$\overline{S_2}$	$\overline{S_1}$	$\overline{S_0}$	TYPES OF BUS CYCLE
0	0	0	Interrupt Acknowledge
0	0	1	Read I/O
0	1	0	Write I/O
0	1	1	HALT
1	0	0	Instruction Fetch
1	0	1	Read Memory
1	1	0	Write Memory
1	1	1	Passive; no bus cycle

Table 4-5 Segment Register Status Lines

S_4	S_3	SEGMENT REGISTER
0	0	ES
0	1	SS
1	0	CS or none (I/O or Interrupt Vector)
1	1	DS

iAPX 186,188 Hardware Design Overview

5

CHAPTER 5
iAPX 186,188 HARDWARE DESIGN OVERVIEW

5.1 INTRODUCTION

This chapter is a discussion of the hardware design of the iAPX 186 (80186) and the iAPX 188 (80188) on a functional level. Electrical characteristics and other hardware references are found in Volume 2 of this set. Volume 2 also contains the Device Specifications for both processors.

This chapter will include the following topics:

- Enhancements to the 8086 CPU
- Bus Organization
- Interrupt Structure
- Clock Generator
- Internal Peripheral Interface
- Chip-Select/Ready Generation Logic

- DMA Controller
- Timers
- Interrupt Controller

5.2 80186 and 80188 CPU ENHANCEMENTS

The iAPX 186 and iAPX 188 are highly integrated microprocessors, effectively combining 15 to 20 of the most common iAPX 86 system components on a single chip. Block diagrams for both processors are shown in Figures 5-1 and 5-2. The iAPX 186,188 are designed to provide both higher performance and more highly integrated solutions to the total system problem of the microprocessor user. Higher performance results from enhancements to both general and specific areas of CPU operation, including faster effective address calculation, improvement in the

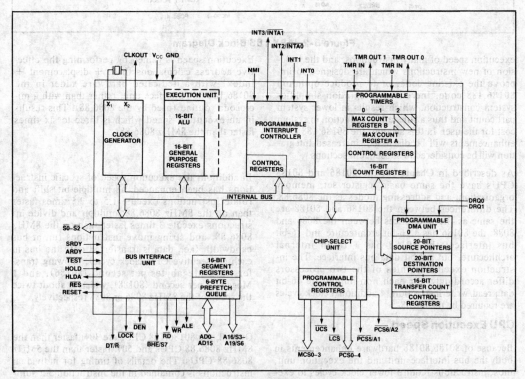

Figure 5-1 iAPX 186 Block Diagram

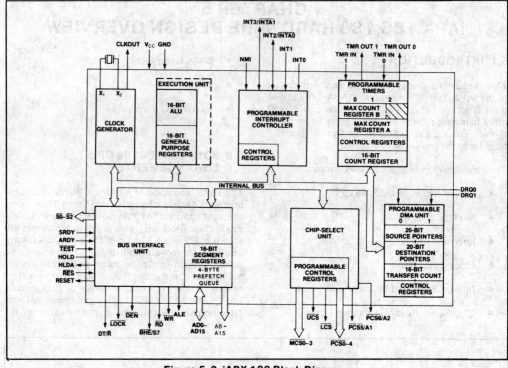

Figure 5-2 iAPX 188 Block Diagram

execution speed of many instructions, and the inclusion of new instructions which are designed to improve the existing code, or to produce optimum 80186,188 code. Increased integration simplifies system construction, which results in lower system part count and thus a substantial reduction in system cost for the user. In this section, the 80186,188 CPU enhancements will be discussed; increased integration will be considered in subsequent sections.

As described in Chapter 3, the 80186 and 80188 CPUs have the same basic register set, memory organization, and addressing modes as the 8086,88. The differences between the 80186 and 80188 are the same as the differences between the 8086 and 8088: the 80186 has a 16-bit architecture and 16-bit bus interface; the 80188 has a 16-bit internal architecture, but a 8-bit data bus interface. The instruction execution times of the two processors differ accordingly: for each non-immediate 16-bit data read/write instruction, 4 additional clock cycles are required by the 80188.

CPU Execution Speed

Because of 80186,80188 hardware enhancements in both the bus interface unit and the execution unit, most instructions require fewer clock cycles to execute than on the 8086,88.

Execution speed is gained by performing the effective address calculations (base + displacement + index) with a dedicated hardware adder in the 80186,188 bus-interface unit, rather than with a microcode routine (used by the 8086,88). This results in an execution speed which is three to six times faster than the 8MHz 8086,88.

In addition, the execution speed of specific instructions has been enhanced: all multiple-bit shift and rotate instructions execute 1.5 to 2.5 times faster than on the 8MHz 8086,88; multiply and divide instructions execute 3 times faster than on the 8MHz 8086,88; and string move instructions run at bus bandwidth (i.e., data is transferred onto the bus in each consecutive CPU clock cycle), allowing transfers in 2 Megabytes per second (80186), and 1 Megabyte per second (80188), which is about twice the speed of the 8MHz 8086 or 8088 respectively.

Overall, the 80186,188 CPUs are 30% faster than the 8MHz 8086,88 CPUs and 50% faster than the 5MHz 8086,88 CPUs. The details of timing for individual instructions is contained in the Instruction Set summary in Chapter 3.

210911

New Instructions

Ten new instructions have been added to the basic 8086,88 instruction set. These instructions are designed to simplify assembly language programming, enhance the performance of high-level language implementations, and the reduce the size of object code for the 80186,88. The new instructions are summarized below; for more detailed information, refer to the Instruction Set summary in Chapter 3.

INS/OUTS (Block I/O)

The INS (Input String), and OUTS (Output String) instructions move a string of bytes or words at bus bandwidth speed between memory and an I/O port. This is essentially a DMA transfer in one in-line instruction.

PUSHI (Push Immediate)

This instruction pushes an immediate 16-bit value or a sign extended 8-bit value onto the stack.

IMUL (Integer Immediate Multiply, signed)

This instruction performs a signed integer immediate multiplication with a 16-bit result.

PUSHA/POPA (Push All/Pop All)

These instructions push or pop all 8 general purpose registers onto or off the stack.

SHIFT/ROTATE IMMEDIATE

These logic instructions shift or rotate by an immediate value.

BOUND (Array Bounds)

This instruction detects a value out of range by checking an array index (contained in a register) against the array bounds in memory.

ENTER (Enter Procedure)

This instruction facilitates high-level language procedure calls. It copies the stack frame pointer from a calling procedure to the current stack frame.

LEAVE (Leave Procedure)

This instruction is also specifically designed for high-level languages. It deallocates the memory space of the the stack frame on procedure exit.

Additional Traps

The 80186,188 include two additional traps:

Unused Opcode. A trap type 6 is generated when opcodes 0FH, 63H-67H, F1H, FEH XX111XXXB and FFH XX111XXXB are executed. This trap is useful in detecting program errors (e.g., the execution of data), and provides a set of opcodes which the user may define for specific purposes, emulating the action of the instruction in software.

Escape Opcode. The 80186,188 CPUs may be programmed to cause a trap type 7 when an escape opcode (D8H-DFH) is encountered. This provides a straightforward method of giving instructions to coprocessors, e.g., the 8087. The programming is done by a bit in the relocation register. It is programmed not to cause a trap on reset.

5.3 BUS STRUCTURE

The 80186,188 bus structure is similar to that of the 8086,88. The 80186 has a multiplexed address/data bus, with 16-bit data and 20-bit address capability, as does the 8086. The 80188 differs by transferring 8-bits of data per bus cycle (taking two bus cycles to transfer a word).

For both processors, each bus cycle requires a minimum of 4 CPU clock cycles, in addition to any number of wait states which may be required to accommodate the speed access limitations of particular external memory or peripheral devices. The bus cycles initiated by the 80186,188 CPU are identical to those which are initiated by the 80186,188 integrated DMA controller.

The 80186,188 multiplexed address/data bus supports simultaneously the 8086,88 minimum mode local bus and the maximum mode system bus. It provides both local bus controller outputs ($\overline{RD}$, $\overline{WR}$, ALE, $\overline{DEN}$ and DT/$\overline{R}$), as well as system status outputs ($\overline{S0}$, $\overline{S1}$, $\overline{S2}$) for use with the 8288 bus controller. This differs from the 8086,88, where the local bus controller outputs (generated only in minimum mode) are unavailable if status outputs (generated only in maximum mode) are required.

Because the 80186,188 can simultaneously provide local bus control signals and status outputs, many systems supporting both a system bus (e.g., a Multibus) and a local bus will not require two separate external bus controllers. The bus control signals may be used to control the local bus, while the status signals are concurrently connected to the 8288 bus controller to drive the control signals of the system bus. To interface with the Multibus, the 80186,188 CPUs require an 8288 and 8289.

Local Bus Controller

The local bus signals are generated by the iAPX 186,88 integrated local bus controller. Control lines are also available that can be used to enable external buffers and to direct the flow of data on and off the local bus. These address/data, enable, and control signals eliminate the need for an external local bus controller in most systems.

Local Bus Arbitration

The 80186,188 employ a HOLD/HLDA system of local bus exchange (instead of a REQUEST/-GRANT protocol) in order to provide an asynchronous bus exchange mechanism. The HOLD/HLDA protocol allows multiple local bus masters, operating at separate clock frequencies, to gain control of the local bus. This protocol also allows compatibility with Intel's new generation of highly integrated bus master peripheral devices, for example, the 82586 Ethernet controller and the 82730 CRT controller/text co-processor.

In the HOLD/HLDA protocol, a device requiring bus control (for example, an external DMA device) raises the HOLD line. In response to this HOLD request, the 80186,188 raises its HLDA line after it has finished its current bus activity. When the external device is finished with the bus, it drops its bus HOLD request; the 80186 responds by dropping its HLDA line and resuming bus operation.

When there is more than one alternate local bus master, external circuitry is required to arbitrate which bus master will gain control of the bus.

Memory/Peripheral Control

Bus control signals are used to strobe data from memory to the CPU, or from the CPU to memory. The local bus controller does not provide a memory/$\overline{I/O}$ signal. If a memory/$\overline{I/O}$ signal is needed, the designer must use the $\overline{S2}$ signal (which requires external latching), make the memory and I/O space nonoverlapping, or use only the integrated chip-select circuitry.

Transceiver Control

The 80186,188 generates two control signals (DT/$\overline{R}$ and $\overline{DEN}$) to be connected to 8286/8287 transceiver chips. This allows the addition of transceivers for extra buffering without adding external logic. These control lines are generated to control the flow of data through the transceivers. The operation of these signals is shown in Table 5-1.

**Table 5-1 Transceiver Control
Signals Description**

Pin Name	Function
$\overline{DEN}$ (Data Enable)	Enables the output drivers of the transceivers. It is active LOW during memory, I/O, or INTA cycles.
DT/$\overline{R}$ (Data Transmit/Receive)	Determines the direction of travel through the transceivers. A HIGH level directs data away from the processor during write operations, while a LOW level directs data toward the processor during a read operation.

8086,88 and 80186,188 Bus Differences

The 80186,188 bus was designed to be upward compatible with the 8086,88 bus. As a result, the 8086,88 bus interface components (the 8288 bus controller and the 8289 bus arbiter) may be used directly with the 80186,188. However, there are a few significant differences which should be considered.

In the case of the 186,188:

- RESET OUT is synchronized with the processor clock, and indicates that the processor is being reset.

- The lines QS0 and QS1 come out one phase earlier (with $\overline{QSMD}$ option) than in the 8086,88.

- ALE comes active one phase earlier than in the 8086,88 but remains active throughout the 8288 ALE (the 80186,188 generate a longer pulse).

- On RESET the $\overline{RD}$/QSMD pin is sampled. If it is low, queue status mode is ientered, and ALE and $\overline{WR}$ become QS lines. If this mode is used, an 8288 is required ($\overline{RD}$ $\overline{WR}$ ALE pins are redefined).

- HOLD/HLDA lines take the place of $\overline{RQ}$/$\overline{GT}$.

- S3-S6 are defined differently: S3-S6 are always low, except during DMA, when S6 is high.

- There are no advanced write commands.

- There are no separate I/O-Memory $\overline{RD}/\overline{WR}$ lines.

For more detail on the hardware aspects of the 80186,188 bus see Chapter 2, Volume 2, and the iAPX 186 and iAPX 188 Device Specifications, Appendix B, Volume 2.

5.4 INTERRUPTS

The 80186,188 can service interrupts generated by software or hardware. Software interrupts are generated by specific instruction or the results of conditions specified by instructions. Hardware interrupts occur when any of the external interrupt lines (INT0-INT3) are activated. The vector types for all interrupts are given in Table 5-2.

Table 5-2 80186,188 Interrupt Vectors

Interrupt Name	Vector Type	Default Priority	Related Instructions
Divide Error Exception	0	*1	DIV, IDIV
Single Step Interrupt	1	12**2	All
NMI	2	1	All
Breakpoint Interrupt	3	*1	INT
INT0 Detected Overflow Exception	4	*1	INT0
Array Bounds Exception	5	*1	BOUND
Unused-Opcode Exception	6	*1	Undefined Opcodes
ESC Opcode Exception	7	*1***	ESC Opcodes
Timer 0 Interrupt	8	2A****	
Timer 1 Interrupt	18	2B****	
Timer 2 Interrupt	19	2C****	
Reserved	9	3	
DMA 0 Interrupt	10	4	
DMA 1 Interrupt	11	5	
INT0 Interrupt	12	6	
INT1 Interrupt	13	7	
INT2 Interrupt	14	8	
INT3 Interrupt	15	9	

NOTES:
*1. These are generated as the result of an instruction execution.
**2. This is handled as in the 8086.
****3. All three timers constitute one source of request to the interrupt controller. The Timer interrupts all have the same default priority level with respect to all other interrupt

NOTES: (continued)
sources. However, they have a defined priority ordering amongst themselves. (Priority 2A is higher priority than 2B.) Each Timer interrupt has a separate vector type number.
4. Default priorities for the interrupt sources are used only if the user does not program each source into a unique priority level.
***5. An escape opcode will cause a trap only if the proper bit is set in the peripheral control block relocation register.

Software-generated Interrupts

The 80186,188 software generated interrupts include those found on the 8086,88, namely:

- Divide error exception (type 0)

- Single-step interrupt (type 1)

- Breakpoint interrupt (type 3)

- INTO Detected overflow exception (type 4)

The divide error interrupt is generated by the CPU following execution of a DIV or IDIV instruction if the calculated quotient is larger than the specified destination.

The single-step interrupt is controlled by the trap flag (TF). If TF is set, the CPU generates a type 1 interrupt after every instruction.

The breakpoint interrupt is generated if the overflow flag (OF) is set.

The new interrupts available on the 80186,188 are:

- Array bounds exception (type 5)

- Unused opcode exception (type 6)

- Escape opcode exception (type 7)

The array bounds interrupt occurs during a BOUND instruction if the array index is outside the array bounds. The array bounds are located in memory at a location indicated by one of the instruction operands. The other operand indicates the value of the index to be checked. (Refer to the BOUND instruction in the Instruction Set Summary, Chapter 3 of this volume, for more details.)

The unused opcode interrupt is generated by the CPU if it is directed to execute any of the following unused opcodes: 0FH, 63H-67H, F1H, FEH XX111XXXB and FFH XX111XXXB.

An ESCape opcode interrupt is generated by the attempted execution of opcodes D8H-DFH. This interrupt is programmed by setting the ET bit in the relocation register. The return address of this interrupt will point to the ESC instruction causing the exception. If a segment override prefix preceded the ESC instruction, the return address will point to the segment override prefix.

Hardware-generated Interrupts

Hardware-generated interrupts are of two types: maskable and non-maskable types. For external maskable interrupts, the 80186,188 provide the INT0-INT3 interrupt request pins. Maskable interrupts may also be generated by the 80186,188 integrated DMA controller and the integrated timer unit. Software enables these inputs by setting the interrupt flag bit (IF) in the Status Word.

A non-maskable interrupt (NMI) is also provided. This interrupt is serviced regardless of the state of the IF bit, and is typically used to activate a power failure routine. The activation of this input causes an interrupt with an internally supplied vector value of 2. No external interrupt acknowledge sequence is performed. The IF bit is cleared at the beginning of an NMI interrupt to prevent maskable interrupts from being serviced.

5.5 CLOCK GENERATOR

The 80186,188 provides an integrated clock generator which generates the main clock signal for all 80186,188 integrated components, as well as all CPU synchronous devices in the system. The clock generator consists of a crystal-controlled oscillator, a divide-by-two counter, synchronous and asynchronous ready inputs, and reset circuitry.

The Oscillator

The oscillator circuit is designed to be used with a parallel resonant fundamental mode crystal at 2X the desired CPU clock speed (i.e., 16 MHz for an 8 MHz 80186,188), or with an external oscillator also at 2X the CPU clock. The crystal determines the CPU clock speed and is used for all instruction time calculations described in Chapter 3. The use of an LC or RC circuit with this oscillator is not advised. The recommended crystal configuration is shown in Figure 5-3.

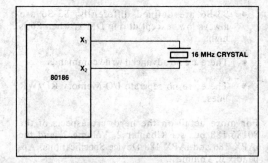

Figure 5-3 Recommended iAPX 186 Crystal Configuration

If an external oscillator is used, it can be connected directly to input pin X1 in lieu of a crystal (X2 should be left open). This oscillator input is used to drive an internal divide-by-two counter (see below) to generate the CPU clock signal; thus the external frequency input can be practically any duty cycle, so long as the minimum high and low times for the signal (as specified in the Device Specification) are met. The output of the oscillator is not directly available outside the iAPX 186,188.

Divide-by-two Counter

The clock generator provides the 50% duty cycle processor clock for the CPU. This is done by dividing the oscillator output by two, forming the symmetrical clock. If an external oscillator is used, the state of the clock generator will change on the falling edge of the oscillator signal. The CLKOUT pin provides the processor clock signal for use outside the 80186,188. This signal may be used to drive other system components. All timings are referenced to the output clock.

READY Synchronization

The clock generator also provides both synchronous and asynchronous ready inputs. Asynchronous ready synchronization is generated by circuitry which samples ARDY in the middle of T_2 and again in the middle of each T_W until ARDY is sampled HIGH. One-half CLKOUT cycle of resolution time is used.

A second ready input (SRDY) is provided to interface with externally synchronized ready signals. This input is sampled at the end of T_2 and again at the end of each T_W until it is sampled HIGH.

RESET Logic

The 80186,188 have both a $\overline{RES}$ input pin and a synchronized RESET pin for use with other system components. The $\overline{RES}$ input pin is provided with hysteresis in order to facilitate power-on Reset generation via an RC network. RESET is guaranteed to remain active for at least five clock cycles given a $\overline{RES}$ input of at least six clock cycles. RESET may be delayed up to two and one-half clock cycles behind $\overline{RES}$.

Multiple 80186,188 processors may be synchronized through the $\overline{RES}$ input pin, since this input resets both the processor and the divide-by-two internal counter in the clock generator. To insure that the divide-by-two counters all begin counting at the same time, the active going edge of $\overline{RES}$ must satisfy a 25 ns setup time before the falling edge of the 80186,188 clock input. In addition, in order to insure that all CPUs begin executing in the same clock cycle, the reset must satisfy a 25 ns setup time before the rising edge of the CLKOUT signal of all the processors.

5.6 INTERNAL PERIPHERAL INTERFACE

The iAPX 186 and iAPX 188 include six integrated peripheral devices along with the BIU and EU. These six are the chip select unit, the DMA controller, the timer unit, the interrupt controller, the local bus controller and the clock generator. The first four of these are programmable, and will be discussed in the remaining sections of this chapter. The clock generator and local bus controller, which have been discussed in previous sections, operate transparently to the programmer.

Peripheral Control Block

The four 80186,188 programmable integrated peripherals are controlled by 16-bit registers located in an internal 256-byte control block (see Figure 5-4). Control and status registers are provided for each of the programmable peripherals. The function of these registers will be discussed in subsequent sections under the appropriate peripheral device.

The control block may be mapped into memory or I/O space. Each of the integrated peripherals' control and status registers are located at a fixed location above the programmed base location of the peripheral control block. The base address must be on an even 256-byte boundary (i.e, the lower 8 bits of the base address are all zeros).

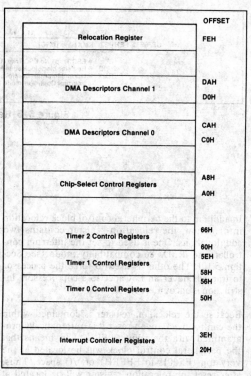

Figure 5-4 Internal Register Map

The integrated peripherals operate semi-autonomously from the CPU. Access to them is for the most part through read and write instructions to the control and data locations in the control block. Because the integrated peripherals are accessed exactly as if they were external devices, no new instruction types are required to access and control them.

Relocation Register

The control block base address is programmed via a 16-bit relocation register contained within the control block at offset FEH from the base address (see Figure 5-5). The relocation register provides the upper 12 bits of the base address of the control block. In addition, bit 12 of this register determines whether the control block will be mapped into I/O or memory space. If this bit is 1, the control block will be located in memory space; if the bit is 0, the control block will be located in I/O space. When the control register block is mapped into I/O space, the upper 4 bits of the base address must be programmed as 0, since I/O addresses are only 16 bits wide. The offset map of the 256-byte control register block is shown in Figure 5-4.

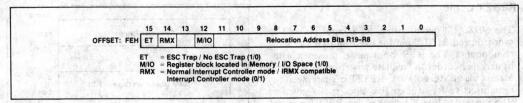

	15	14	13	12	11	10	9	8	7	6	5	4	3	2	1	0
OFFSET: FEH	ET	RMX		M/IO				Relocation Address Bits R19–R8								

ET = ESC Trap / No ESC Trap (1/0)
M/IO = Register block located in Memory / I/O Space (1/0)
RMX = Normal Interrupt Controller mode / iRMX compatible
Interrupt Controller mode (0/1)

Figure 5-5 Relocation Register

In addition to the peripheral control block relocation information, the relocation register contains two additional bits. One is used to set the interrupt controller into iRMX 86 compatibility mode (see Section 5.10). The other is used to force the processor to trap whenever an ESCape (to a coprocessor) instruction is encountered.

Because the relocation register is contained within the control block, upon reset it is automatically programmed with the value 20FFH. This means that the peripheral control block will be located at the very top (FF00H to FFFFH) of I/O space. Thus, after reset the relocation register will be located at word location FFFEH in I/O space.

If the user wished to locate the peripheral control block starting at memory location 10000H, he would program the peripheral control register with the value 1100H. In doing so, all registers within the integrated peripheral control block would be moved to memory locations 10000H to 100FFH. Note that since the relocation register is contained within the peripheral control block, it would also be moved to word location 100FEH in memory space.

5.7 CHIP SELECT UNIT

The iAPX 186,188 include an integrated chip select unit which provides programmable chip-select generation for both memory banks and peripherals. In addition, it can be programmed to provide READY (or WAIT state) generation, and can also provide latched address bits A1 and A2.

Six output lines are used for memory addressing and seven output lines are used for peripheral addressing. The chip-select lines are active for all memory and I/O cycles (in their programmed areas) generated by both the CPU and by the integrated DMA unit.

The chip select unit is programmable such that it can be used to fulfill the chip select requirements (in terms of memory device or bank size and speed) of most small and medium sized 80186,188 systems.

Memory Chip Selects

The memory chip select lines are divided into 3 groups which separately address the major areas of memory in a typical 8086/80186 system: upper memory for reset ROM, lower memory for interrupt vectors, and mid-range memory for program memory. One output each is provided for upper and lower memory; four outputs are provide for mid-range memory.

The size of each memory area is user programmable and can be set to 2K, 4K, 8K, 16K, 32K, 64K, 128K, plus 1K and 256K for upper and lower chip selects. In addition, the beginning or base address of the midrange memory chip select may be programmed to be active for any memory location at a time. Note that all chip select sizes are bytes, whereas the 80186 memory is arranged in words. This means that if, for example, 16 64K x 1 memories are used, the memory block size will be 128K bytes, not 64K bytes.

The starting location and ending location of both upper and lower memory areas are fixed at 00000H and FFFFFH respectively; the starting location of the mid-range memory is user programmable.

The memory chip selects are controlled by four registers located in the peripheral control block (see Figure 5-6). These include one register each for upper and lower memory, the values of which determine the size of the two memory blocks; the other two registers are used to set the size and base address of the mid-range block. These registers, and the areas of memory they select, are discussed in the following sections.

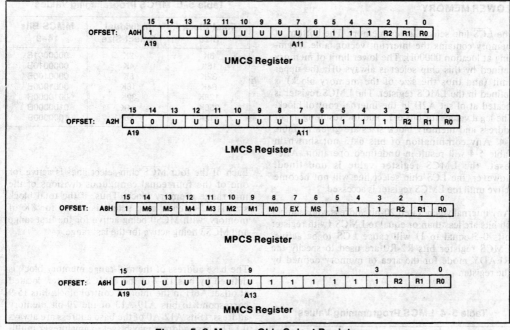

Figure 5-6 Memory Chip Select Registers

UPPER MEMORY

The $\overline{\text{UCS}}$ chip select line is used for the top of memory. This area is usually used as the system memory, because after reset the 80186,188 begin executing at memory location FFFF0H.

The upper limit of memory defined by this chip select is always FFFFFH; the lower limit (and thus the size of the memory block) is defined in the UMCS register. The UMCS register is located at offset A0H in the internal control block. The legal values for bits 6-13 and the resulting starting address and memory block sizes are given in Table 5-3. Any combgination of bits 6-13 not shown in Table 5-3 will result in undefined operation. After reset, the UMCS register is programmed for a 1K area. It must be reprogrammed if a larger upper memory area is desired.

Any internally generated 20-bit address whose upper 16 bits are greater than or equal to the UMCS register (with register bits 0-5 equal to 0) will cause $\overline{\text{UCS}}$

to be activated. UMCS bits R2-R0 are used to specify READY mode for the area of memory defined by the register (see below).

Table 5-3 UMCS Programming Values

Starting Address (Base Address)	Memory Block Size	UMCS Value (Assuming R0=R1=R2=0)
FFC00	1K	FFF8H
FF800	2K	FFB8H
FF000	4K	FF38H
FE000	8K	FE38H
FC000	16K	FC38H
F8000	32K	F838H
F0000	64K	F038H
E0000	128K	E038H
C0000	256K	C038H

210911

LOWER MEMORY

The $\overline{\text{LCS}}$ line selects lower memory. The bottom of memory contains the interrupt vector table, beginning at location 00000H. The lower limit of memory defined by this chip select is always 0H; the upper limit (and thus the size of the memory block) is defined in the LMCS register. The LMCS register is located at offset A2H in the internal control block. The legal values for bits 6-13 and the resulting upper address and memory block sizes are given in Table 5-4. Any combination of bits 6-13 not shown in Table 5-4 will result in undefined operation. After reset, the LMCS register value is undefined. However, the $\overline{\text{LCS}}$ chip select line will not become active until the LMCS register is accessed.

Any internally generated 20-bit address whose upper 16 bits are less than or equal to LMCS (with register bits 0-5 equal to 1) will cause $\overline{\text{LCS}}$ to be active. LMCS register bits R2-R0 are used to specify the READY mode for the area of memory defined by the register.

Table 5-4 LMCS Programming Values

Upper Address	Memory Block Size	LMCS Value (Assuming R0=R1=R2=0)
003FFH	1K	0038H
007FFH	2K	0078H
00FFFH	4K	00F8H
01FFFH	8K	01F8H
03FFFH	16K	03F8H
07FFFH	32K	07F8H
0FFFFH	64K	0FF8H
1FFFFH	128K	1FF8H
3FFFFH	256K	3FF8H

MID-RANGE MEMORY

The four $\overline{\text{MCS}}$ lines select locations within a user-locatable memory block, which can be located anywhere within the 1M byte memory address space exclusive of the areas defined by $\overline{\text{UCS}}$ and $\overline{\text{LCS}}$. Both the base address and size of this memory block are programmable.

The size of the memory block defined by the mid-range select lines, as shown in Table 5-5, is determined by bits 8-14 of the MPCS register. This register is located at offset A8H in the internal control block. Note that one, and only one, of bits 8-14 must be set at a time; unpredictable operation of the $\overline{\text{MCS}}$ lines will otherwise occur. The EX and MS bits in the MPCS register relate to peripheral functionality, and are described in Section 5.7.

Table 5-5 MPCS Programming Values

Total Block Size	Individual Select Size	MMCS Bits 14-8
8K	2K	0000001B
16K	4K	0000010B
32K	8K	0000100B
64K	16K	0001000B
128K	32K	0010000B
256K	64K	0100000B
512K	128K	1000000B

Each of the four $\overline{\text{MCS}}$ chip-select lines is active for one of the four equal contiguous divisions of the mid-range memory block. Thus, if the total block size is 32K, each chip select is active for 8K of memory, with $\overline{\text{MCS0}}$ being active for the first range and $\overline{\text{MCS3}}$ being active for the last range.

The base address of the mid-range memory block is defined by bits 15-9 of the MMCS register, located at offset A6H in the internal control block. Bits 15-9 correspond to bits A19-A13 of the 20-bit memory address. (Bits A12-A0 of the base address are always 0.) The base address may be set to any integer multiple of the size of the total memory block selected. For example, if the mid-range block size is 32K (or the size of the block for which each $\overline{\text{MCS}}$ line is active is 8K), the block could be located at 10000H or 18000H, but not at 14000H, since the first few integer multiples of a 32K memory block are 0H, 8000H, 10000H, 18000H, etc.

The 512K block size for the mid-range memory chip selects is a special case. When using 512K, the base address would have to be either 00000H or 80000H; if it were to be programmed at 00000H when the $\overline{\text{LCS}}$ line was programmed, there would be an internal conflict between the $\overline{\text{ICS}}$ ready generation logic and the $\overline{\text{MCS}}$ ready generation logic. Since the $\overline{\text{ICS}}$ chip-select line does not become active until programmed, while the $\overline{\text{UCS}}$ line is active at reset, the memory base can be set only at 00000H. If this base address is selected, however, the $\overline{\text{LS}}$ range must not be programmed.

MMCS bits R2-R0 specify the READY mode of operation for all mid-range chip selects. All devices in mid-range memory must use the same number of WAIT states.

After reset, the contents of the MPCS and MMCS registers are undefined. However, none of the $\overline{\text{MCS}}$ lines will be active until both registers are accessed.

Peripheral Chip Select

The iAPX 186,188 can generate chip selects for up to seven peripheral devices. The chip select lines $\overline{PCS0}$-$\overline{6}$ are active for seven contiguous blocks of 128 bytes. The base address of the memory block is user-programmable, and may be located in either I/O or memory space. Thus, peripheral devices may be I/O- or memory-mapped.

$\overline{PCS5}$ and $\overline{PCS6}$ can also be programmed to provide latched address bits A1, A2. (When so programmed, these lines cannot be used as peripheral selects.) The outputs can be connected directly to the A0, A1 pins used for selecting internal registers of 8-bit peripherals. This scheme simplifies the hardware interface because the 8-bit registers of peripherals are simply treated as 16-bit registers located on even boundaries in I/O space or memory space (only the lower 8-bits of the register are significant; the upper 8-bits are "don't cares").

The peripheral chip selects are controlled by the PACS and MPCS registers located in the internal peripheral control block (see Figure 5-7). These registers allow the base address of the peripherals to be set, and specify whether the peripherals are mapped into memory or I/O space. (The MPCS register is also used to set the size of the mid-range memory chip-select block, as described above.) Both registers must be accessed before any of the peripheral chip selects will become active.

The starting address of the peripheral chip-select block is defined by the PACS register, located at offset A4H in the internal control block. Bits 15-6 of this register correspond to bits 19-10 of the 20-bit programmable base address (PBA) of the peripheral chip-select block. Bits 9-0 of the PBA are all zeros. If the chip-select block is located in I/O space, bits 12-15 must be programmed zero, since the I/O address is only 16 bits wide. This address must be a multiple of 1K bytes, i.e., the least significant 10 bits of the starting address are always 0. Table 5-6 shows the address range of each peripheral chip select with respect to the PBA contained in the PACS register. PACS bits 0-2 are used to specify READY mode for $\overline{PCS0}$-$\overline{PCS3}$.

The mode of operation of the peripheral chip selects is defined by the MPCS register. Bit 7 (EX) of this register is used to select the function of $\overline{PCS5}$ and $\overline{PCS6}$; bit 6 (MS) is used to select whether the peripheral chip selects are mapped into memory or I/O space. The programming of these bits is described in Table 5-7. MPCS bits 0-2 are used to specify READY mode for $\overline{PCS4}$-$\overline{PCS6}$.

Table 5-6 PCS Address Ranges

PCS Line	Active between Locations
PCS0	PBA — PBA+127
PCS1	PBA+128 — PBA+255
PCS2	PBA+256 — PBA+383
PCS3	PBA+384 — PBA+511
PCS4	PBA+512 — PBA+639
PCS5	PBA+640 — PBA+767
PCS6	PBA+768 — PBA+895

Table 5-7 MS, EX Programming Values

Bit	Description
MS	1 = Peripherals mapped into memory space. 0 = Peripherals mapped into I/O space.
EX	0 = 5 $\overline{PCS}$ lines. A1, A2 provided. 1 = 7 $\overline{PCS}$ lines. A1, A2 are not provided.

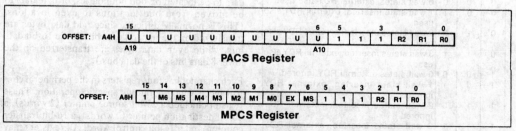

Figure 5-7 Peripheral Chip Select Registers

READY/WAIT Generation Logic

The 80186,188 can generate an internal READY signal for each of the memory or peripheral $\overline{CS}$ lines. In addition, 0-3 wait states may be inserted for all accesses to the area for which the chip select is active. Finally, each chip-select range may be individually programmed to either ignore external READY or to factor external READY with the integrated ready generator.

READY control consists of 3 bits for each $\overline{CS}$ line or group of lines generated by the 80186,188. The interpretation of the ready bits is shown in Table 5-8. This allows independent ready generation for each of upper memory, lower memory, mid-range memory, peripheral devices 0-3 and peripheral devices 4-6. The ready bits control an integrated wait state generator which allows a programmable number of wait states to be automatically inserted whenever an access is made to the area of memory I/O associated with the chip select area. Each set of ready bits includes a bit which determines whether the external ready signals (ARDY and SRDY) will be used, or whether they will be ignored (i.e., the bus cycle will terminate even though a ready has not been returned on the external pins).

If the external READY is used (R2=0), the internal ready generator operates in parallel with it, rather than in series. For example, if the internal generator is set to insert two wait states, but activity on the external READY lines inserts four wait states, the processor will insert four wait states, not six. This is because the two wait states generated by the internal generator overlapped the first two wait states generated by the external ready signal. Note that the external ARDY and SRDY lines are always ignored during cycles accessing internal peripherals.

R2-R0 of each control word specifies the READY mode for the corresponding block, with the exception of the peripheral chip selects: R2-R0 of PACS set the $\overline{PCS0\text{-}3}$ READY mode; R2-R0 of MPCS set the $\overline{PCS4\text{-}6}$ READY mode.

Chip Select/Ready Logic and Reset

Upon reset, the Chip-Select/Ready Logic will perform the following actions:

- All chip-select outputs will be driven HIGH

- Upon leaving RESET, the $\overline{UCS}$ line will be programmed to provide chip selects to a 1K block. The accompanying READY control bits will be set at 011 to allow the maximum number of internal wait states in conjunction with external Ready consideration (i.e., UMCS resets to FFFBH).

- No other chip select or READY control registers have any predefined values after RESET. They will not become active until the CPU accesses their control registers. Both the PACS and MPCS registers must be accessed before the $\overline{PCS}$ lines will become active.

5.8 DMA CONTROLLER

The iAPX 186,188 include two independent, high-speed DMA channels which operate independently of the CPU and drive all integrated bus interface components (bus controller, chip selects, etc.).

Data can be transferred over these channels at the rate of 2 MBytes/sec. The transfers can occur between memory and I/O, I/O and I/O, or memory and memory. Data may be transferred either in bytes or words, to or from even or odd addresses. Figure 5-8 shows the block diagram representation of the DMA unit.

Every DMA cycle requires two to four bus cycles — one or two to fetch the data to an internal register, and one or two to deposit the data. This allows word data to be located on odd boundaries, or byte data to be moved from odd locations to even locations. (This is normally difficult, since odd data bytes are transferred on the upper 8 data bits of the 16-bit data bus, while even data bytes are transferred on the lower 8 data bits of the data bus.)

Each channel has four registers in the peripheral control block which define its specific operation. These registers include a 20-bit source pointer (2 words), a 20-bit destination pointer (2 words), a 16-bit transfer counter, and a 16-bit control word. All registers may be modified or altered by the CPU during any DMA

Table 5-8 READY Bits Programming

R2	R1	R0	Number of WAIT States Generated
0	0	0	0 wait states, external RDY also used.
0	0	1	1 wait state inserted, external RDY also used.
0	1	0	2 wait states inserted, external RDY also used.
0	1	1	3 wait states inserted, external RDY also used.
1	0	0	0 wait states, external RDY ignored.
1	0	1	1 wait state inserted, external RDY ignored.
1	1	0	2 wait states inserted, external RDY ignored.
1	1	1	3 wait states inserted, external RDY ignored.

210911

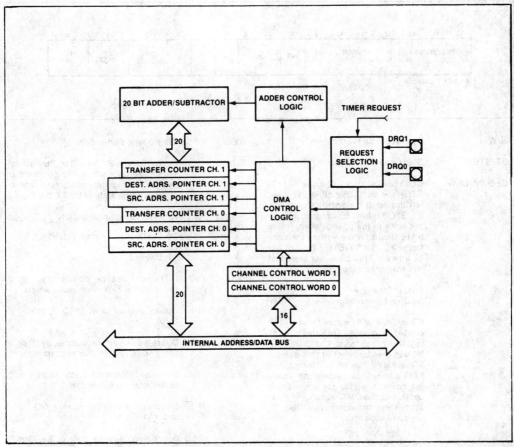

Figure 5-8 DMA Unit Block Diagram

activity. Changes made to these registers will be reflected immediately in DMA operation. Table 5-9 shows the format of these registers; the specific function of each register is discussed in the following sections.

Table 5-9 DMA Control Block Format

| Register Name | Register Address | |
	Ch. 0	Ch. 1
Control Word	CAH	DAH
Transfer Count	C8H	D8H
Destination Pointer (upper 4 bits)	C6H	D6H
Destination Pointer	C4H	D4H
Source Pointer (upper 4 bits)	C2H	D2H
Source Pointer	C0H	D0H

Channel Control Word Register

The DMA control word register (see Figure 5-9) contains bits which determine the precise mode of operation for each channel, including for both data source and destination whether the pointer points to memory or I/O space, and whether the pointer will be incremented, decremented or left alone after each DMA transfer. It also contains the ($\overline{\text{B}}$/W) bit which selects between byte or word transfers. Two synchronization bits are used to determine the source of the DMA requests: the TC bit determines whether DMA activity will cease after a programmed number of DMA transfers, and the INT bit is used to enable interrupts to the processor when this has occurred.

210911

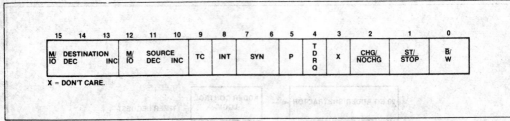

15	14	13	12	11	10	9	8	7	6	5	4	3	2	1	0
M/IO	DESTINATION DEC	INC	M/IO	SOURCE DEC	INC	TC	INT	SYN		P	TDRQ	X	CHG/NOCHG	ST/STOP	B/W

X = DON'T CARE.

B̄/W	Byte/Word (0/1) Transfers.	
ST/STOP:	Start/stop (1/0) Channel.	
CHG/NOCHG:	Change/Do not change (1/0) ST/STOP bit. If this bit is set when writing to the control word, the ST/STOP bit will be programmed by the write to the control word. If this bit is cleared when writing the control word, the ST/STOP bit will not be altered. This bit is not stored; it will always be a 0 on read.	
INT:	Enable interrupts to CPU on Transfer Count termination.	
TC:	If set, DMA will terminate when the contents of the Transfer Count register reach zero. The ST/STOP bit will also be reset at this point if TC is set. If this bit is cleared, the DMA unit will decrement the transfer count register for each DMA cycle, but the DMA transfer will not stop when the contents of the TC register reach zero.	

SYN: (2 bits)
00 No synchronization.

NOTE: the ST bit will be cleared automatically when the contents of the TC register reach zero regardless of the state of the TC bit.

01 Source synchronization.

10 Destination synchronization.

11 Unused.

SOURCE: INC Increment source pointer by 1 or 2 (depends on B̄/W after each transfer.

M/IO Source pointer is in M/IO space (1/0).

DEC Decrement source pointer by 1 or 2 (depends on B̄/W) after each transfer.

DEST: INC Increment destination pointer by 1 or 2 (B̄/W) after each transfer.

M/IO Destination pointer is in M/IO space (1/0).

DEC Decrement source pointer by 1 or 2 (depends on B̄/W) after each transfer.

P Channel priority - relative to other channel.

0 low priority.

1 high priority.

Channels will alternate cycles if both set at same priority level.

TDRQ 0: Disable DMA requests from timer 2.

1: Enable DMA requests from timer 2.

Bit 3 Bit 3 is not used.

If both INC and DEC are specified for the same pointer, the pointer will remain constant after each cycle.

Figure 5-9 DMA Control Word Register and Bit Descriptions

210911

The control word register also contains a start/stop bit which is used to enable DMA transfers. When this bit is set, a DMA transfer will occur whenever a DMA request is made to the channel; if this bit is cleared, no DMA transfers will be performed by the channel. A companion bit, the CHG/NOCHG bit, allows the contents of the DMA control register to be changed without modifying the state of the start/stop bit. The P bit is used to assign a priority to each channel. See Figure 5-9 for more information on each bit in the control word.

DMA Destination and Source Pointer Registers

Each DMA channel has a 20-bit source and a 20-bit destination pointer (see Figure 5-10). These pointers are used to access the I/O or memory location from which data will be fetched or to which data will be written. Each occupies two 16-bit registers in the peripheral control block, with the lower four bits of the upper register specifying the four high-order bits of the 20-bit physical address. Thus, these registers allow access to the entire 1 Mbyte address space of the 80186,188.

The source and destination pointers may be individually incremented or decremented after each transfer. If word transfers are performed, the pointer is incremented or decremented by two.

Since the DMA channels can perform transfers to or from odd addresses, there is no restriction on values for the pointer registers. However, higher transfer rates can be obtained if all word transfers are performed to even addresses, since this allows data to be accessed in a single memory access.

DMA Transfer Count Register

The transfer count register specifies the number of DMA transfers to be performed, up to a maximum of 64K bytes or words. This register is decremented after every DMA cycle (for both byte and word transfers), regardless of the state of the TC bit in the DMA control word register. If the TC bit in the DMA control word is set, however, DMA activity will terminate when the transfer count register reaches zero. A transfer count of zero allows 2^{16} transfers to be made.

DMA Requests

DMA transfers may be initiated by internally or externally generated requests. Internally generated requests are issued by timer 2 or by the DMA channel itself. Externally generated transfers are those requested by an external device. Each DMA channel has a single DMA request line by which an external device may request a DMA transfer. The synchronization bits in the DMA control register determine whether this line is interpreted to be connected to the source of the DMA data or the destination of the DMA data.

For internal interrupt requests, the DMA channel can be programmed such that whenever timer 2 reaches it maximum count, a DMA request is generated. This is accomplished by setting the TDRQ bit in the DMA channel control word register. The DMA channel can also be programmed to provide its own DMA requests. DMA transfer cycles will then run continuously at the maximum bus bandwidth until the programmed number of DMA transfers (specified in the transfer count register) have occurred. This is accomplished by programming the synchronization bits in the DMA control register for *unsynchronized* transfers. During unsynchronized transfers, the DMA controller monopolizes the bus, i.e., no cycle stealing by the CPU will occur.

Synchronized transfers are DMA transfers requested by an external device and are of two types: *source synchronized* or *destination synchronized*, that is, either the source of the data or the destination of the data may request the transfer. The only difference between the two is the time at which the DMA request pin is sampled to determine if another DMA transfer is required immediately after the currently executing transfer.

HIGHER REGISTER ADDRESS	XXX	XXX	XXX	A19–A16
LOWER REGISTER ADDRESS	A15–A12	A11–A8	A7–A4	A3–A0
	15			0

XXX = DON'T CARE

Figure 5-10 DMA Memory Pointer Register Format

When source synchronized (or unscynchronized) transfers are performed, the DMA channel may begin another transfer immediately after the end of a previous transfer. This allows a complete transfer to take place every two bus cycles or eight clock cycles, assuming there are no wait states (see Table 5-10).

When destination synchronization transfers are requested, the DMA controller relinquishes control of the bus after every transfer. If no other bus activity is initiated, another DMA cycle will begin after two processor clock cycles. This is done to allow the destination device time to remove its request if another transfer is not desired. Since the DMA controller relinquishes the bus, the CPU can initiate a bus cycle. As a result, a complete bus cycle will often be inserted between destination synchronized transfers. This results in the maximum DMA transfer rates shown in Table 5-10. Note that no DMA prefetching occurs when destination synchronization is performed. Data is not fetched from the source address until the destination device signals that it is ready to receive it.

Table 5-10 Maximum DMA Transfer Rates

Type of Synchronization Selected	CPU Running	CPU Halted
Unsynchronized	2MBytes/sec	2MBytes/sec
Source Synch	2MBytes/sec	2MBytes/sec
Destination Synch	1.3MBytes/sec	1.5MBytes/sec

DMA Acknowledge

The 80186,188 generate no explicit DMA acknowledge signal. Instead, the 80186,188 perform a read or write directly to the DMA requesting device. However, if required, a DMA acknowledge signal can be generated by a decode of an address. Also, since the chip-select lines can be programmed to be active for a given block of memory of I/O space, and the DMA pointers can be programmed to point to the same given block, a chip-select line could be used to indicate a DMA acknowledge.

DMA Priority

The channels may be programmed such that one channel is always given priority over the other, or they may be programmed to alternate cycles when both channels have DMA requests pending. DMA cycles always have priority over internal CPU cycles except between locked memory accesses or word accesses to odd memory locations. An external bus hold, however, takes priority over an internal DMA

cycle. Because an interrupt request cannot suspend a DMA operation and the CPU cannot access memory during a DMA cycle, interrupt latency time will suffer during sequences of continuous DMA cycles. An NMI request, however, will cause all internal DMA activity to halt. This allows the CPU to quickly respond to the NMI request.

DMA Programming

DMA cycles start whenever the ST/$\overline{\text{STOP}}$ bit of the Control Register is set. If synchronized transfers are programmed, a DRQ must also be generated. Therefore, the source and destination transfer pointers, and the transfer count register (if used) must be programmed before this bit is set.

Each DMA channel control register may be changed while the channel is operating. If the CHG/$\overline{\text{NOCHG}}$ bit is cleared when the control word register is written, the ST/$\overline{\text{STOP}}$ bit will not be modified by the write. If multiple channel registers are modified, it is recommended that a LOCKED string transfer be used to prevent a DMA transfer from occurring between updates to the channel registers.

DMA Channels and Reset

Upon RESET, the DMA channels will perform the following actions:

- The ST/$\overline{\text{STOP}}$ bit for each channel will be reset to STOP.

- Any transfer in progress will be aborted.

TIMER UNIT

The 80186,188 include an integrated timer unit which provides three 16-bit timer/counters (see Figure 5-11). These timers operate independently of the CPU. Two of the timers have input and output pins allowing counting of external events and generation of arbitrary waveforms. The third timer is not connected to any external pins and is useful for real-time coding and time delay applications. In addition, it can be used as a prescaler for the other two, or as a DMA request source.

The timers are controlled by eleven 16-bit registers located in the internal peripheral control block. Timers 0 and 1 are controlled by four registers each; timer 3 makes use of three registers. The configuration of these registers in the peripheral control block is shown in Table 5-11.

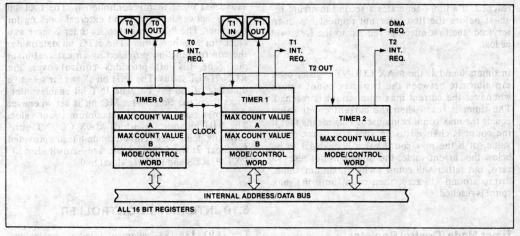

Figure 5-11 Timer Block Diagram

Table 5-11 Timer Control Block Format

Register Name	Register Offset		
	Tmr. 0	Tmr. 1	Tmr. 2
Mode/Control Word	56H	5EH	66H
Max Count B	54H	5CH	not present
Max Count A	52H	5AH	62H
Count Register	50H	58H	60H

The count register contains the current value of the timer and can be read or written whether the timer is running or not. The value of this register will be incremented for each timer event. The MAX COUNT register defines the maximum count the timer will reach. Timers 0 and 1 are equipped with a second MAX COUNT register, which enables them to alternate their count between two different MAX COUNT values programmed by the user. The mode/control register is used for programming the timer's specific mode of operation. These registers are discussed in detail in the following three sections.

Count Registers

Each of the three timers has a 16-bit count register. The current contents of this register may be read or written by the processor at any time. If the register is written into while the timer is counting, the new value will take effect in the current count cycle.

Because the count register is 16 bits wide, up to 2^{16} timer events can be counted by a single timer/counter. Every fourth CPU clock transition can act as a timer event. In addition, transitions on the external lines of timers 0 and 1 can act as timer events for these timers, and timer 2 can be set to produce interrupts that serve as timer events for timers 0 and 1.

Max Count Registers

Timers 0 and 1 have two MAX COUNT registers, while timer 2 has a single MAX COUNT register. These contain the number of events the timer will count.

After reaching the MAX COUNT register value, the timer count value will reset to zero during the same clock cycle, i.e., the maximum count value is never stored in the count register itself. Each timer can generate an interrupt whenever the timer count value reaches a maximum count value, that is, an interrupt can be generated whenever the value in maximum count register A is reached, and whenever the value in maximum count register B is reached. If a timer generates a second interrupt request before the first interrupt request has been serviced, the first interrupt request to the CPU will be lost.

In timers 0 and 1, the MAX COUNT register used can alternate between the two max count values whenever the current maximum count is reached. The timer is reset when the current count value equals the max count being used. This means that if the count is changed to be above the max count value, or if the max count value is changed to be below the current value, the timer will not reset to zero, but rather will count to its maximum value, "wrap around" to zero, then count until the max count is reached.

Timer Mode/Control Register

The mode/control register allows the user to program the specific mode of operation or check the current programmed status of any of the three integrated timers. Figure 5-12 shows the bits in this register and describes the function of each bit.

The ALT bit selects one of the two MAX COUNT registers for comparisons. The CONT bit causes the associated timer to run continuously. The EXT bit selects between internal and external clocking for the timer. The P bit is used to let timer 2 serve as a clock for another timer. The RTG bit determines the control function provided by an external input pin. The EN bit provides control over the RUN/HALT status. The $\overline{INH}$ bit allows for selective updating of the EN bit. The INT bit enables interrupts from the timer. The MC bit is set whenever the timer reaches its final maximum count value. The RIU bit indicates which MAX COUNT bit is currently being used. Not all mode bits are provided for timer 2; the following bits are hardwired: ALT, EXT, P, RTG and IRU are all set to 0.

5.10 INTERRUPT CONTROLLER

The iAPX 186,188 integrated interrupt controllers perform tasks of the interrupt controller in a typical system. These include synchronization of interrupt requests, prioritization of interrupt requests, and request type vectoring in response to a CPU interrupt acknowledge. Nesting is provided so interrupt service routines for lower priority interrupts may themselves be interrupt by higher priority interrupts. The integrated interrupt controller block diagram is shown in Figure 5-13.

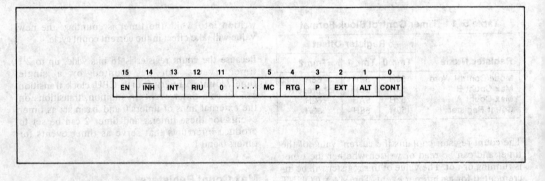

ALT:
The ALT bit determines which of two MAX COUNT registers is used for count comparison. If ALT = 0, register A for that timer is always used, while if ALT = 1, the comparison will alternate between register A and register B when each maximum count is reached. This alternation allows the user to change one MAX COUNT register while the other is being used, and thus provides a method of generating non-repetitive waveforms. Square waves and pulse outputs of any duty cycle are a subset of available signals obtained by not changing the final count registers. The ALT bit also determines the function of the timer output pin. If ALT is zero, the output pin will go LOW for one clock, the clock after the maximum count is reached. If ALT is one, the output pin will reflect the current MAX COUNT register being used (0/1 for B/A).

Figure 5-12 Timer Mode/Control Register

CONT:

Setting the CONT bit causes the associated timer to run continuously, while resetting it causes the timer to halt upon maximum count. If CONT = 0 and ALT = 1, the timer will count to the MAX COUNT register A value, reset, count to the register B value, reset, and halt.

EXT:

The external bit selects between internal and external clocking for the timer. The external signal may be asynchronous with respect to the 80186 clock. If this bit is set the timer will count LOW-to-HIGH transitions for the input pin. If cleared, it will count an internal clock while using the input pin for control. In this mode, the function of the external pin is defined by the RTF bit. The maximum input to output transition latency time may be as much as 6 clocks. However, clock inputs may be pipelined as closely together as every 4 clocks without losing clock pulses.

P:

The prescaler bit is ignored unless internal clocking has been selected (EXT = 0). If the P bit is a zero, the timer will count at one-fourth the internal CPU clock rate. If the P bit is a one, the output of timer 2 will be used as a clock for the timer. Note that the user must initialize and start timer 2 to obtain the prescaled clock.

RTG:

Retrigger bit is only active for internal clocking (EXT = 0). In this case it determines the control function provided by the input pin.

If RTG = 0, the input level gates the internal clock on and off. If the input pin is HIGH, the timer will count; if the input pin is LOW, the timer will hold its value. As indicated previously, the input signal may be asynchronous with respect to the 80186 clock.

When RTG = 1, the input pin detects LOW-to-HIGH transitions. The first such transition starts the timer running, clearing the timer value to zero on the first clock and then incrementing thereafter. Further transitions on the input pin will again reset the timer to zero, from which it will start counting up again. If CONT = 0 when the timer has reached maximum count, the EN bit will be cleared, inhibiting further timer activity.

EN:

The enable bit provides programmer control over the timer's RUN/HALT status. When set, the timer is enabled to increment subject to the input pin constraints in the internal clock mode (discussed previously). When cleared, the timer will be inhibited from counting. All input pin transitions during the time EN is zero will be ignored. If CONT as zero, the EN bit is automatically cleared upon maximum count.

INH:

The inhibit bit allows for selective updating of the enable (EN) bit. If $\overline{INH}$ is a one during the write to the mode/control word, then the state of the EN bit will be modified by the write. If $\overline{INH}$ is a zero diring the write, the EN bit will be unaffected by the operation. This bit is not stored; it will always be a 0 on a read.

INT:

When set, the INT bit enables interrupts from the timer, which will be generated on every terminal count. If the timer is configured in dual MAX COUNT register mode, an interrupt will be generated each time the value in MAX COUNT register A is reached, and each time the value in MAX COUNT register B is reached. If this enable bit is cleared after the interrupt request has been generated, but before a pending interrupt is serviced, the interrupt request will still be in force. (The request is latched in the interrupt Controller.)

MC:

The Maximum Count is set whenever the timer reaches its final maximum count value. If the timer is configured in dual MAX COUNT register mode, this bit will be set each time the value in MAX COUNT register A is reached, and each time the value in MAX COUNT register B is reached. This bit is set regardless of the timer's interrupt-enable bit. The MC bit gives the user the ability to monitor timer status through software instead of through interrupts. Programmer intervention is required to clear this bit.

RIU:

The Register in Use bit indicates which MAX COUNT register is currently being used for comparison to the timer count value. A zero value indicates register A. The RIU bit cannot be written, i.e., its value is not affected when the control register is written. It is always cleared when the ALT bit is zero.

Not all model bits are provided for timer 2. Certain bits are hardwired as indicated below:

$$ALT = 0, EXT = 0, P = 0, RTG = 0, RIU = 0$$

Figure 5-12 Timer Mode/Control Register (continued)

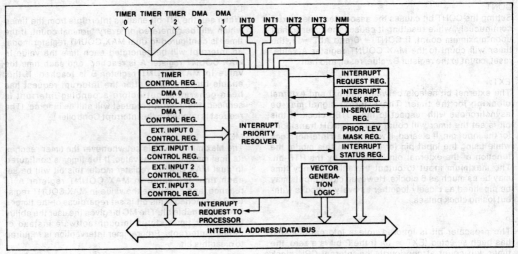

Figure 5-13 Interrupt Controller Block Diagram

The 80186,188 can receive interrupts from a number of sources, both internal and external. Internal interrupt sources (timers and DMA channels) can be disabled by their own control registers or by mask bits within the interrupt controller. The 80186,188 interrupt controller has its own control registers that set the mode of operation for the controller.

The interrupt controller operates in two major modes: non-iRMX 86 mode (also called master mode) and iRMX 86 mode. In master mode, the integrated controller acts as the master interrupt controller for the system; in iRMX 86 mode, the controller operates as a slave to an external interrupt controller which functions as the master interrupt controller for the system. Some of the interrupt controller registers and interrupt controller pins change definition between these two modes, but the basic function of the interrupt controller remains fundamentally the same.

Non-iRMX Mode

In non-iRMX (master) mode, the interrupt controller presents its interrupt input directly to the 80186,188 CPU. Five pins are provided for external interrupt sources. One of these pins is dedicated to NMI. The other four (INT0-INT3) may be configured in three ways: as four interrupt input lines with internally generated interrupt vectors; as an interrupt line and an interrupt acknowledge line (called the "cascade mode") along with two other input lines with internally generated interrupt

vectors; or as two interrupt input lines and two dedicated interrupt acknowledge output lines. These four interrupt inputs can be programmed in either edge- or level-trigger mode, as specified by the LTM bit in the source's control register.

The interrupt controller will generate interrupt vectors for the integrated DMA channels and the integrated timers. In addition, interrupt vectors for the external interrupt lines will be generated if they are not configured in cascade or special fully nested mode (see below).

Each interrupt source has a pre-assigned vector type (see Table 5-2). Vector types point to address information for interrupt service routines. The vectors generated are fixed and cannot be changed.

The user can program the interrupt sources into any of eight different priority levels. Programming is done by placing a 3-bit priority level (0-7) in the control register of each interrupt source. (A source with a priority level of 4 has higher priority over all priority levels from 5 to 7. Priority registers containing values lower than 4 have greater priority.) All interrupt sources have preprogrammed default priority levels.

If two requests with the same programmed priority level are pending at once, the priority ordering scheme shown in Table 5-2 is used. If the serviced interrupt routine reenables interrupts, it allows other requests to be serviced.

The interrupt controller has three basic modes of operation when it is configured in the non-iRMX mode: fully nested mode, cascade mode and special fully nested mode. The response to internal interrupts is identical in all three modes; the function of the four external interrupt pins differs in each mode. The interrupt controller is set into one of these modes by programming the correct bits in the INT0 and INT1 control registers (see below).

FULLY NESTED MODE

In the fully nested mode, INT0-INT3 are used as direct interrupt requests. The vectors for these four inputs are generated internally. An in-service (IS) bit is provided for every interrupt source. Setting this bit prevents the interrupt controller from generating interrupt requests from lower-priority devices, as well as from the interrupt source currently being serviced. This allows interrupt service routines to operate with interrupts enabled (thus insuring that higher-priority interrupts will be serviced) without being interrupted by lower-priority interrupts.

When a service routine has completed, the proper IS bit must be reset by writing the proper pattern to the EOI register. This is required to allow subsequent interrupts from this interrupt source, and to allow servicing of lower-priority interrupts. An EOI command is issued at the end of the service routine just before the execution of the return from interrupt instruction. If the fully nested structure has been upheld, the next highest-priority source with its IS bit set is then serviced.

CASCADE MODE

In the cascade mode, INT0-INT3 are configured into interrupt input-dedicated acknowledge signal pairs. The interconnection is shown in Figure 5-14. INT0 is an interrupt input interfaced to an 8259A; INT2/$\overline{\text{INTA0}}$ serves as the dedicated interrupt acknowledge signal to that peripheral. The same is true for INT1 and INT3/$\overline{\text{INTA1}}$. Each pair can selectively be placed in the cascade or non-cascade mode by programming the proper value in the INT0 and INT1 control registers. The use of the dedicated acknowledge signal eliminates the need for external logic to generate $\overline{\text{INTA}}$ and device select signals.

The primary cascade mode allows the capability to serve up to 128 external interrupt sources through the use of external master and slave 8259As. Three levels of priority are created, requiring priority resolution in the 80186,188 interrupt controller, the master 8259A, and the slave 8259As. If an external interrupt is serviced, one IS bit is set at each of these levels. When the interrupt service routine is completed, up to three end-of-interrupt commands must be issued by the programmer.

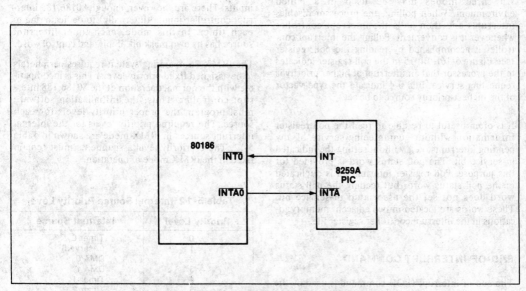

Figure 5-14 Cascade Mode Interrupt Connection

210911

SPECIAL FULLY NESTED MODE

The special fully nested mode is entered by setting the SFNM bit in the INT0 or INT1 control register. This mode enables complete nestability with external 8259A masters. Normally, an interrupt request from an interrupt source will not be recognized unless the in-service bit for that source is reset. If more than one interrupt source is connected to an external interrupt controller, all of the interrupts will be channelled through the same 80186,188 interrupt request pin. As a result, if the external interrupt controller receives a higher-priority interrupt, its interrupt will not be recognized by the 80186,188 controller until the 80186,188 in-service bit is reset. In special fully nested mode, the 80186,188 interrupt controller will allow interrupts from an external pin regardless of the state of the in-service bit for an interrupt source in order to allow multiple interrupts from a single pin. An in-service bit will continue to be set, however, to inhibit interrupts from other lower-priority 80186,188 interrupt sources.

Special procedures should be followed when resetting IS bits at the end of interrupt service routines. Software polling of the external master's IS register is required to determine if there is more than one bit set. If so, the IS bit in the 80186,188 remains active and the next interrupt service routine is entered.

OPERATION IN A POLLED ENVIRONMENT

All three modes may be used in a polled environment. When polling, the processor disables interrupts and then polls the interrupt controller whenever it is convenient. Polling the interrupt controller is accomplished by reading the poll register (see Figure 5-16). Bit 15 in the poll register indicates to the processor that an interrupt of higher priority is requesting service. Bits 0-4 indicate the type vector of the highest-priority source to be set.

It is often useful to be able to read the poll register information without guaranteeing service of any pending interrupts, i.e., without setting the indicated in-service bit. The poll status word is provided for this purpose. Poll register information is duplicated in the poll status word, but reading the poll status word does not set the associated in-service bit. These words are located in two adjacent memory locations in the interrupt controller register file.

END-OF-INTERRUPT COMMAND

The end-of-interrupt (EOI) command is used by the programmer to reset the In-Service (IS) bit when an interrupt service routine is completed. The EOI command is issued by writing the proper pattern to the EOI register. There are two types of EOI commands: specific and nonspecific. The nonspecific command does not specify which IS bit is reset. When issued, the interrupt controller automatically resets the IS bit of the highest priority source with an active service routine. A specific EOI command requires that the programmer send the interrupt vector type to the interrupt controller indicating which source's IS bit is to be reset. This command is used when the fully nested structure has been disturbed or the highest priority IS bit that was set does not belong to the service routine in progress.

iRMX 86 Compatability Mode

The iAPX 186,88 integrated interrupt controllers have a special iRMX 86 compatability mode that allows the use of the 80186,188 within the iRMX 86 operating system interrupt structure. The controller is set in this mode by setting bit 14 in the peripheral control block relocation register and providing special initialization software.

When iRMX mode is used, the internal 80186,188 interrupt controller will be used as a slave controller to an external master interrupt controller. The internal 80186,188 resources will be monitored through the internal interrupt controller, while the external controller functions as the system master interrupt controller.

Because of pin limitations caused by the need to interface to an external 8259A master, the internal interrupt controller will no longer accept external inputs. There are, however, enough 80186,188 interrupt controller inputs (internally) to dedicate one to each timer. In this mode, each timer interrupt source has its own mask bit, IS bit, and control word.

The iRMX 86 operating system requires peripherals to be assigned fixed priority levels. This is incompatible with the normal operation of the 80186,188 interrupt controller. Thus, the initialization software must program the proper priority levels for each source. The required priority levels for the internal interrupt sources in iRMX mode are shown in Table 5-12. These priority level assignments must remain fixed in the iRMX mode of operation.

Table 5-12 Internal Source Priority Level

Priority Level	Interrupt Source
0	Timer 0
1	(reserved)
2	DMA 0
3	DMA 1
4	Timer 1
5	Timer 2

The iRMX 86 mode of operation allows nesting of interrupt requests. When an interrupt is acknowledged, the priority logic masks off all priority levels except those with equal or higher priority.

The configuration of the 80186,188 with respect to an external 8259A master is shown in Figure 5-15. The INT0 input is used as the 80186 CPU interrupt input. INT3 functions as an output to send the 80186 slave-interrupt-requests to one of the 8 master-PIC-inputs.

For information on external interfacing in iRMX 86 mode, see Volume 2.

VECTOR GENERATION IN THE iRMX 86 MODE

Vector generation in iRMX 86 mode is exactly like that of an 8259A slave: the interrupt controller generates an 8-bit vector which the CPU multiplies by four and uses as an address into a vector table. The five most significant bits of the vector are programmed by writing to the Interrupt Vector register at offset 20H. The lower-order three bits are generated by the priority logic and represent the encoding of the priority level requesting service.

SPECIFIC END-OF-INTERRUPT

In iRMX 86 mode, the specific EOI command operates to reset an in-service bit of a specific priority. The user supplies a 3-bit priority level value that points to an in-service bit to be reset. The command is executed by writing the correct value in the specific EOI register at offset 22H.

Interrupt Controller Registers

The interrupt controller has a number of registers which are used to control its operation. These registers have been referred to in the preceding discussion of the interrupt controller's various operations; in the following sections they are individually discussed.

The interrupt controller register model is shown in Figure 5-16. It contains 15 registers, all of which can be read or written unless otherwise specified. Some of these registers have a different function depending on the processor's operating mode (master or iRMX 86). The interrupt controller registers for both modes will be discussed together; differences in function and implementation in the two modes will be indicated where appropriate.

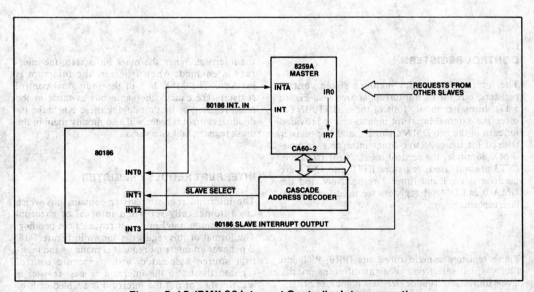

Figure 5-15 iRMX 86 Interrupt Controller Interconnection

	OFFSET
INT3 CONTROL REGISTER	3EH
INT2 CONTROL REGISTER	3CH
INT1 CONTROL REGISTER	3AH
INT0 CONTROL REGISTER	38H
DMA 1 CONTROL REGISTER	36H
DMA 0 CONTROL REGISTER	34H
TIMER CONTROL REGISTER	32H
INTERRUPT CONTROLLER STATUS REGISTER	30H
INTERRUPT REQUEST REGISTER	2EH
IN-SERVICE REGISTER	2CH
PRIORITY MASK REGISTER	2AH
MASK REGISTER	28H
POLL STATUS REGISTER	26H
POLL REGISTER	24H
EOI REGISTER	22H

Non-iRMX 86 Mode

	OFFSET
LEVEL 5 CONTROL REGISTER (TIMER 2)	3AH
LEVEL 4 CONTROL REGISTER (TIMER 1)	38H
LEVEL 3 CONTROL REGISTER (DMA 1)	36H
LEVEL 2 CONTROL REGISTER (DMA 0)	34H
LEVEL 0 CONTROL REGISTER (TIMER 0)	32H
INTERRUPT-REQUEST REGISTER	2EH
IN-SERVICE REGISTER	2CH
PRIORITY-LEVEL MASK REGISTER	2AH
MASK REGISTER	28H
SPECIFIC EOI REGISTER	22H
INTERRUPT VECTOR REGISTER	20H

iRMX 86 Mode

Figure 5-16 Interrupt Controller Registers

CONTROL REGISTERS

The interrupt controller includes seven control registers, one for each interrupt source (see Figure 5-17). In master mode, four of these (INT0-INT3) serve the external interrupt inputs, one is provided for each of the two DMA channels, and one register is used for the collective timer interrupts. In non-iRMX 86 mode, the control registers for INT2 and INT3 are not used, registers INT0 and INT1 are used for timer 1 and timer 2 respectively, and the DMA 0 and DMA 1 registers are used for internal interrupt sources.

These registers contain three bits (PR0, PR1 and PR2), which select one of eight different priority levels for the interrupt device (0 is highest priority, 7 is lowest priority), and a mask (MSK) bit to enable the interrupt. When the mask bit is zero, the interrupt is enabled; when it is set, the interrupt is masked. The MSK bits in the individual control registers are exactly the same bits as those in the mask register, so that modifying these bits in the individual control register will also modify them in the mask register, and vice versa.

INTERRUPT REQUEST REGISTER

The interrupt request register contains bits which are automatically set when internal or external (master mode only) interrupt requests are pending. The format of this register is shown in Figure 5-18. Whenever an interrupt request is made by the interrupt source associated with a specific control register, the bit in the interrupt request register is set, whether or not the interrupt is enabled or is of sufficient priority to cause an interrupt.

210911

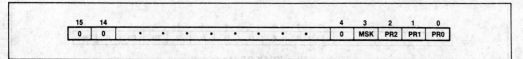

Timer/DMA Control Registers (Non-iRMX Mode)

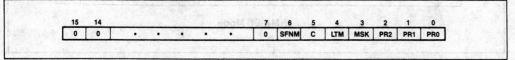

INT0/INT1 Control Registers (Non-iRMX Mode)

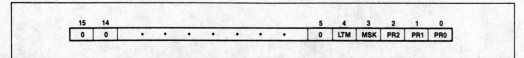

INT2/INT3 Control Registers (Non-iRMX Mode)

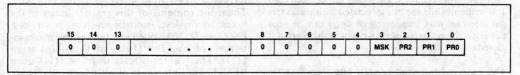

Control Word (iRMX 86 Mode)

PRO-2:	Priority programming information. Highest Priority = 000, Lowest Priority = 111
LTM:	Level-trigger mode bit. 1 = level triggered; 0 = edge-triggered. Interrupt input levels are active high. In level-triggered mode, an interrupt is generated whenever the external line is high. In edge-triggered mode, an interrupt will be generated only when this level is preceded by an inactive-to-active transition on the line. In both cases, the level must remain active until the interrupt is acknowledged.
MSK:	Mask bit, 1 = mask; 0 = nonmask.
C:	Cascade mode bit, 1 = cascade; 0 = direct
SFNM:	Special fully nested mode bit, 1 = SFNM

Figure 5-17 Control Register Format

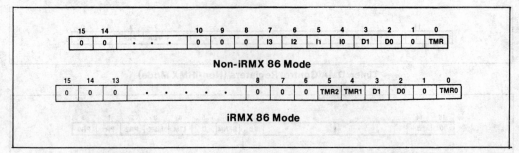

15	14		10	9	8	7	6	5	4	3	2	1	0
0	0	• • •	0	0	0	I3	I2	I1	I0	D1	D0	0	TMR

Non-iRMX 86 Mode

15	14	13		8	7	6	5	4	3	2	1	0
0	0	0	• • • • •	0	0	0	TMR2	TMR1	D1	D0	0	TMR0

iRMX 86 Mode

Figure 5-18 In-Service, Interrupt Request and Mask Register Format

D0 and D1 are the interrupt request bits for the DMA channels; the TMR bit is the logical OR of all timer interrupt requests. These bits can be both read and written, while the bits associated with the external interrupt pins (master mode only) can be read but not written (since values written to them are not stored).

The external interrupt request bits show exactly when an interrupt request is given to the interrupt controller, so that if edge-triggered mode is selected, the bit in the register will be HIGH only after an inactive-to-active transition. For internal interrupt sources, the register bits are set when a request arrives and are reset when the processor acknowledges the requests.

MASK REGISTER

The mask register contains a mask bit for each interrupt source. When the bit in this register corresponding to a particular interrupt source is set, all interrupts from that source will be masked. These mask bits are exactly the same bits which are used in the individual control registers; thus, changing the state of a mask bit in this register will also change the state of the mask bit in the individual interrupt control register corresponding to the bit, and vice versa. The format for this register is shown in Figure 5-18.

PRIORITY MASK REGISTER

This register allows masking of all interrupts below a particular interrupt priority level. The format of this register is shown in Figure 5-19. The register is set by user intervention only. The register is set by the processor only at reset. The value in the register pre-

vents any interrupts of lower priority (as set by the priority bits in the interrupt control registers for interrupt sources) from interrupting the processor. Thus, the contents of this register indicates the lowest priority-level interrupt which will be serviced. For example, 100 written into this register masks interrupts of level five (101), six (110), and seven (111). The register is reset to seven (111) upon RESET, i.e., interrupts of all priority levels are enabled.

IN-SERVICE REGISTER

This register contains In-Service (IS) bits for each interrupt source, indicating that its service routine is in progress (see Figure 5-18). When an IS bit is set, no interrupts will be generated from devices with a lower priority level.

In iRMX 86 mode, bit positions 0, 4, and 5 correspond to the integral timers. In master mode, a single TMR bit is the IS bit for all three timers, and I0-I3 are the IS bits for the external interrupt pins. D0 and D1 are the IS bits for the two DMA channels in both modes.

The IS bit is set when the processor acknowledges an interrupt request (either by an interrupt acknowledge or by reading the poll register). The IS bit is reset at the end of the interrupt service routine by an EOI command issued by the CPU. This register may be both read and written, i.e., the CPU may set in-service bits without an interrupt ever occurring, or may reset them without using the EOI function of the interrupt controller.

210911

POLL AND POLL STATUS REGISTERS (MASTER MODE ONLY)

The interrupt controller contains a poll register and a poll status register, both of which contain the same polling information. The format of this register is shown in Figure 5-20.

The INTREQ bit indicates an interrupt is pending and is set when an interrupt of sufficient priority has been received. It is automatically cleared when the interrupt is acknowledged. When an interrupt is pending, bits S0-S4 indicates the vector type of the highest priority interrupt pending.

Reading the poll register will acknowledge the pending interrupt to the interrupt controller, just as if the processor had acknowledged the interrupt through interrupt acknowledge cycles. The processor will not actually run any interrupt acknowledge cycles, and will not vector through a location in the interrupt vector table. Only the interrupt request, in-service and priority mask registers in the interrupt controller will be set appropriately.

Reading the poll status register, on the other hand, will merely transmit the status of the polling bits without modifying any of the other interrupt controller registers. Both registers are read only; data written to them is not stored.

Though these registers are not supported in iRMX 86 mode, accessing the poll register location when in iRMX 86 mode will cause the interrupt controller to "acknowledge" the interrupt (i.e., the in-service bit and priority level mask register bits will be set).

EOI REGISTER

The end of interrupt register is used by the programmer to issue an End Of Interrupt command to the controller. After receiving this command, the interrupt controller automatically resets the in-service bit for the interrupt (indicating its service routine has completed) and the priority mask register bits. Only the specific form of the EOI command is supported in iRMX 86 mode.

This register is write only; data written is not stored and cannot be read back. The format of this register is shown in Figure 5-21.

INTERRUPT STATUS REGISTER

This register contains general interrupt controller status information. All the significant bits in this register are read/write. The format of this register is shown in Figure 5-22.

Three bits (IRT0-IRT2) are used to differentiate among the three timer interrupts. This is required in master mode because the timers share a single interrupt control register. The bit associated with a timer is automatically cleared after the interrupt request for the timer is acknowledged. More than one of these bits may be set at a time.

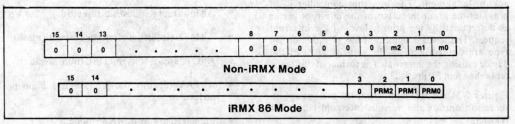

Figure 5-19 Priority Level Mask Register Format

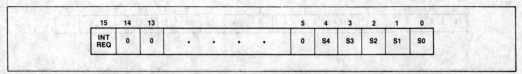

Figure 5-20 Poll Register Format

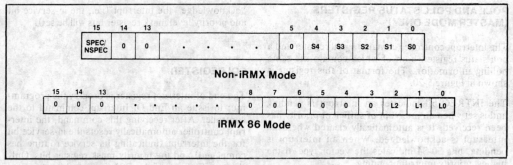

Non-iRMX Mode

iRMX 86 Mode

Figure 5-21 EOI Register Format

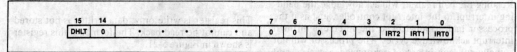

Figure 5-22 Interrupt Status Register Format

The DHLT (DMA Halt Transfer) bit insures prompt servicing of non-maskable interrupts by halting all DMA transfers. It is automatically set whenever a non-maskable interrupt occurs, and is reset when an IRET instruction is executed. This bit may also be set explicitly by the programmer. It is never automatically cleared (except by RESET), so that if DMA activity is desired, the programmer must clear this bit after each NMI is received.

INTERRUPT VECTOR REGISTER (iRMX 86 MODE ONLY)

The interrupt vector register is is used to specify the 5 most significant bits of the interrupt type vector placed on the CPU bus in response to an interrupt acknowledgement. The interrupt controller itself provides the lower three bits of the interrupt vector as determined by the priority level of the interrupt request. The lower 3 significant bits of the interrupt type are determined by the priority level of the device causing the interrupt. The format of this register is shown in Figure 5-23.

Figures 5-24 and 5-25 summarize the methods of interaction among the various interrupt controller registers.

Interrupt Controller and Reset

Upon RESET, the interrupt controller will perform the following actions:

- All SFNM bits reset to 0, implying fully nested mode.

- All PR bits in the various control registers set to 1. This places all sources at lowest priority (level 111).

- All LTM bits reset to 0, resulting in edge-sense mode.

- All Interrupt Service bits reset to 0.

- All Interrupt Request bits reset to 0.

- All MSK (Interrupt Mask) bits set to 1 (mask).

- All C (Cascade) bits reset to 0 (non-cascade).

- All PRM (Priority Mask) bits set to 1, implying no levels masked.

- Initialized to non-iRMX 86 mode.

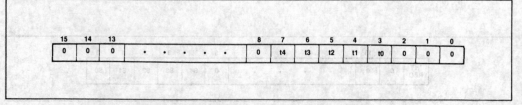

Figure 5-23 Interrupt Vector Register Format

210911

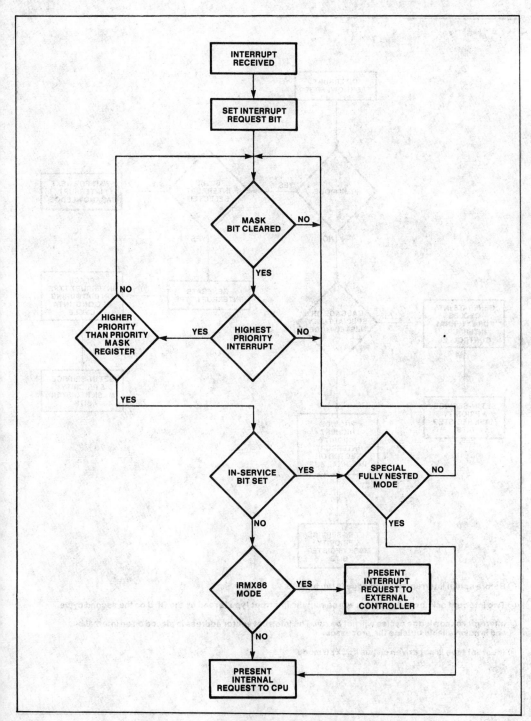

Figure 5-24 80186 Interrupt Request Sequencing

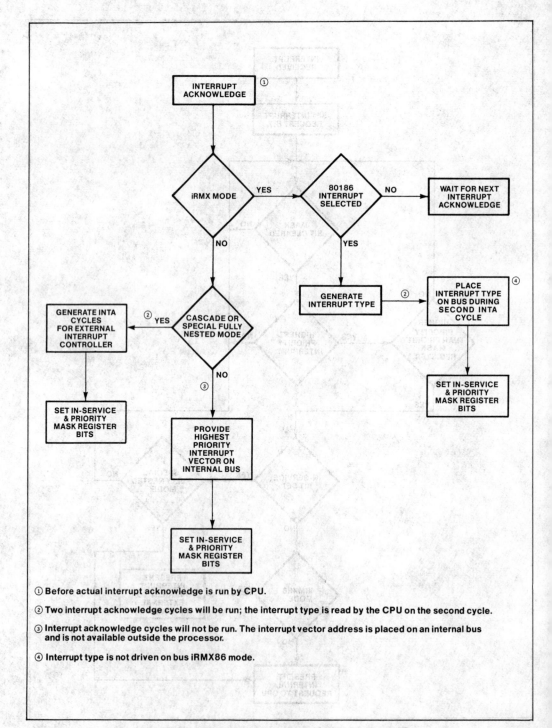

① Before actual interrupt acknowledge is run by CPU.

② Two interrupt acknowledge cycles will be run; the interrupt type is read by the CPU on the second cycle.

③ Interrupt acknowledge cycles will not be run. The interrupt vector address is placed on an internal bus and is not available outside the processor.

④ Interrupt type is not driven on bus iRMX86 mode.

Figure 5-25 80186 Interrupt Acknowledge Sequencing

210911

The 8087 Numeric Processor Extension

6

CHAPTER 6
THE 8087 NUMERIC PROCESSOR EXTENSION

6.1 INTRODUCTION

This chapter describes the 8087 Numeric Processor Extension (NPX). It is divided into the following sections:

- Processor Overview

- Processor Architecture

- Computation Fundamentals

- Instruction Set

- Programming Facilities

- Special Features

- Programming Examples

The processor overview section covers both hardware and software topics at a general level. Special Features describes those features of the NPX that will be of interest to specialized groups of users; it is not necessary to understand this section to successfully use the 8087 in most applications. Hardware coverage in this chapter is limited to discussing processor facilities in functional terms. Timing, electrical characteristics, and other physical interface data may be found in Volume 2 of this set.

Note that throughout this chapter the term "CPU" refers to either an 8086,88 configured in maximum mode, or an 80186,188. To make best use of the material in this chapter readers should have a good understanding of the operation of the 8086,88 and 80186,188 CPUs.

6.2 PROCESSOR OVERVIEW

The 8087 Numeric Processor Extension (NPX) performs arithmetic and comparison operations on a variety of numeric data types; it also executes numerous built-in transcendental functions (e.g., tangent and log functions). As a processor extension to a maximum mode 8086,88, or an 80186,188, the NPX effectively extends the register and instruction sets of the host CPU and adds several new data types as well. The programmer generally does not perceive the 8087 as a separate device; instead, the computational capabilities of the CPU appear greatly expanded.

The 8087 adds extensive high-speed numeric processing capabilities to an 8086,88- or 80186,188-based system. It is specifically designed to deliver stable, correct results when used in a straightforward fashion by programmers who are not expert in numerical analysis. Its applicability to accounting and financial environments, in addition to scientific and engineering settings, further distinguishes the 8087 from the "floating point accelerators" employed in many computer systems, including minicomputers and mainframes. The NPX is housed in a standard 40-pin dual in-line package (Figure 6-1) and requires a single +5V power source.

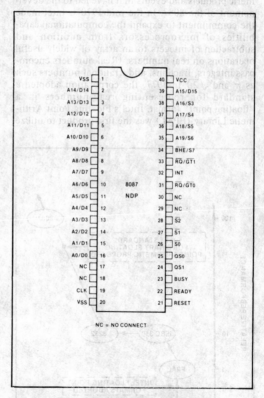

Figure 6-1 8087 Numeric Data Processor Pin Diagram

The description of the 8087 in this section deliberately omits some operating details in order to provide a coherent overall view of the processor's capabilities. Subsequent sections of the chapter will describe these capabilities, and others, in more detail.

Evolution

The performance of first- and second-generation microprocessor-based systems was limited in three principal areas: storage capacity, input/output speed, and numeric computation. The 8086,88 CPU broke the 64K memory barrier, allowing larger and more time-critical applications to be undertaken. The 8089 Input/Output Processor eliminated many of the I/O bottlenecks and permitted microprocessors to be employed effectively in I/O-intensive designs. The 8087 Numeric Processor Extension clears the third roadblock by enabling applications with significant computational requirements to be implemented with microprocessor technology.

Figure 6-2 illustrates the progression of Intel numeric products and events that have led to the development of the 8087. In the mid-1970's, Intel made the commitment to expand the computational capabilities of microprocessors from addition and subtraction of integers to an array of widely useful operations on real numbers. (Real numbers encompass integers, fractions, and irrational numbers such as π and $\sqrt{2}$.) In 1977, the corporation adopted a standard for representing real numbers in a "floating point" format. Intel's Floating Point Arithmetic Library (FPAL) was the first product to utilize this standard format. FPAL is a set of subroutines for the 8080/8085 microprocessors. These routines perform arithmetic and limited standard functions on single precision (32-bit) real numbers; an FPAL multiply executes in about 1.5 ms (1.6 MHz 8080A CPU). The next product, the iSBC™ 310 High Speed Math Unit, essentially implements FPAL in a single iSBC card, reducing a single-precision multiply to about 100μs. The Intel 8232 is a single-chip arithmetic processor for the 8080/8085 family. The 8232 accepts double precision (64-bit) operands as well as single precision numbers. It performs a single precision multiply in about 100μs and multiplies double precision numbers in about 875μs (2 MHz version).

In 1979, a working committee of the Institute for Electrical and Electronic Engineers (IEEE) proposed an industry standard for minicomputer and microcomputer floating point arithmetic (J. Coonen, W. Kahan, J. Palmer, T. Pittman, D. Stevenson, "A Proposed Standard for Binary Floating Point Arithmetic," *ACM SIGNUM Newsletter*, October 1979). The intent of the standard is to promote portability of numeric programs between computers and to provide a uniform programming environment that encourages the development of accurate, reliable software. The proposed standard specifies requirements and options for number formats as well as the results of computations on these numbers. The floating point number formats are identical to those previously adopted by Intel and used in the products described in this section.

The 8087 Numeric Processor Extension is the most advanced development in Intel's continuing effort to provide improved tools for numerically-oriented microprocessor applications. It is a single-chip hardware implementation of the proposed IEEE standard, including all its options for single and double precision numbers. As such, it is compatible with previous Intel numerics products; programs written for the 8087 will be transportable to future products that conform to the proposed IEEE standard. The NPX also provides many additional functions that are extensions to the proposed standard.

Performance

As Figure 6-2 indicates, the 8087 provides about 10 times the instruction speed of the 8232 and a 100-fold improvement over FPAL. The 8087 multiples 32-bit and 64-bit real numbers in about 19μs and 27μs respectively. Of course, the actual performance of the NPX in a given system depends on numerous application-specific factors.

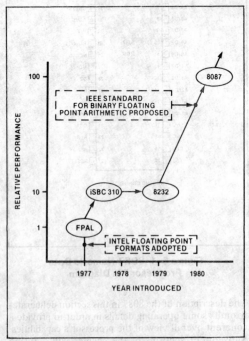

Figure 6-2 8087 Evolution and Relative Performance

Table 6-1 compares the execution times of several 8087 instructions with the equivalent operations executed in software on a 5 MHz 8086. The software equivalents are highly optimized assembly language procedures from the 8087 emulator, an NPX development tool discussed later in this section.

The performance figures quoted in this section are for operations on real (floating point) numbers. The 8087 also has instructions that enable it to utilize fixed point binary and decimal integers of up to 64 bits and 18 digits, respectively. Using an 8087, rather than multiple precision software algorithms for integer operations, can provide speed improvements of 10-100 times.

The 8087's unique processor extension interface to the CPU can yield an additional performance increment beyond that of simple instruction speed. No overhead is incurred in setting up the device for a computation; the 8087 decodes its own instructions automatically in parallel with the CPU. Moreover, built-in coordination facilities allow the CPU to proceed with other instructions while the 8087 is simultaneously executing its numeric instruction. Programs can exploit this processor parallelism to increase total system throughput.

Usability

Viewed strictly from the standpoint of raw speed, the 8087 enables serious computation-intensive tasks to be performed by microprocessors for the first time. The 8087 offers more than just high performance, however. By synthesizing advances made by numerical analysts in the past several years, the NPX provides a level of usability that surpasses existing minicomputer and mainframe arithmetic units. In fact, the charter of the 8087 design team was first to achieve exceptional functionality and then to obtain high performance.

The 8087 is explicitly designed to deliver stable, accurate results when programmed using straightforward "pencil and paper" algorithms. While this statement may seem trivial, experienced users of "floating point processors" will recognize its fundamental importance. For example, most computers can overflow when two single precision floating point numbers are multiplied together and then

Table 6-1 8087 Emulator Speed Comparison

Instruction	Approximate Execution Time (µs) (5 MHz Clock)	
	8087	8086 Emulation
Multiply (single precision)	19	1,600
Multiply (double precision)	27	2,100
Add	17	1,600
Divide (single precision)	39	3,200
Compare	9	1,300
Load (single precision)	9	1,700
Store (single precision)	18	1,200
Square root	36	19,600
Tangent	90	13,000
Exponentiation	100	17,100

divided by a third, even if the final result is a perfectly valid 32-bit number. The 8087 delivers the correctly rounded result. Other typical examples of undesirable machine behavior in straightforward calculations occur when solving for roots of a quadratic equation:

$$\frac{-b \pm \sqrt{b^2 - 4ac}}{2a}$$

or computing financial rate of return, which involves the expression: $(1+i)^n$. Straightforward algorithms will not deliver consistently correct results (and will not indicate when they are incorrect) on most machines. To obtain correct results on traditional machines under all conditions usually requires sophisticated numerical techniques that are foreign to most programmers. General application programmers using straightforward algorithms will produce much more reliable programs on the 8087. This simple fact greatly reduces the software investment required to develop safe, accurate computation-based products.

Beyond traditional numerics support for "scientific" applications, the 8087 has built-in facilities for "commercial" computing. It can process decimal numbers of up to 18 digits without rounding off errors, and it performs *exact arithmetic* on integers as large as 2^{64}. Exact arithmetic is vital in accounting applications where rounding errors may introduce money losses that cannot be reconciled.

The NPX contains a number of facilities that can optionally be invoked by sophisticated users. Examples of these advanced features include two models of infinity, directed rounding, gradual underflow, and traps to user-written exception handling software.

Applications

The NPX's versatility and performance make it appropriate for a broad array of numerically-oriented applications. In general, applications that exhibit any of the following characteristics can benefit by implementing numeric processing on the 8087:

- Numeric data vary over a wide range of values, or include non-integral values;

- Algorithms produce very large or very small intermediate results;

- Computations must be very precise, i.e., a large number of significant digits must be maintained;

- Performance requirements exceed the capacity of traditional microprocessors;

- Consistently safe, reliable results must be delivered using a programming staff that is not expert in numerical techniques.

Note also that the 8087 can reduce software development costs and improve the performance of systems that do not utilize real numbers but operate on multi-precision binary or decimal integer values.

A few examples, which show how the 8087 might be utilized in specific numerics applications, are described below. In many cases, these types of systems have been implemented in the past with minicomputers. The advent of the 8087 brings the size and cost savings of microprocessor technology to these applications for the first time.

- Business data processing — The NPX's ability to accept decimal operands and produce exact decimal results of up to 18 digits greatly simplifies accounting programming. Financial calculations which use power functions can take advantage of the 8087's exponentiation and logarithmic instructions.

- Process control — The 8087 solves dynamic range problems automatically, and its extended precision allows control functions to be fine-tuned for more accurate and efficient performance. Control algorithms implemented with the NPX also contribute to improved reliability and safety, while the 8087's speed can be exploited in real-time operations.

- Numerical control — The 8087 can move and position machine tool heads with extreme accuracy. Axis positioning also benefits from the hardware trigonometric support provided by the 8087.

- Robotics — Coupling small size and modest power requirements with powerful computational abilities, the NPX is ideal for on-board six-axis positioning.

- Navigation — Very small, light weight, and accurate inertial guidance systems can be implemented with the 8087. Its built-in trigonometric functions can speed and simplify the calculation of position from bearing data.

- Graphics terminals — The 8087 can be used in graphics terminals to locally perform many functions which normally demand the attention of a main computer; these include rotation, scaling, and interpolation. By also including an 8089 Input/Output Processor to perform high speed data transfers, very powerful and highly self-sufficient terminals can be built from a relatively small number of 8086,88 family parts.

- Data acquisition — The 8087 can be used to scan, scale, and reduce large quantities of data as it is collected, thereby lowering storage requirements as well as the time required to process the data for analysis.

The preceding examples are oriented toward "traditional" numerics applications. There are, in addition, many other types of systems that do not appear to the end user as "computational", but can employ the 8087 to advantage. Indeed, the 8087 presents the imaginative system designer with an opportunity similar to that created by the introduction of the microprocessor itself. Many applications can be viewed as numerically-based if sufficient computational power is available to support this view. This is analogous to the thousands of successful products that have been built around "buried" microprocessors, even though the products themselves bear little resemblance to computers.

Programming Interface

The combination of an 8086,88 or 80186,188 CPU and an 8087 generally appears to the programmer as a single machine. The 8087, in effect, adds new data types, registers, and instructions to the CPU. The programming languages and the coprocessor architecture take care of most interprocessor coordination automatically.

Table 6-2 lists the seven 8087 data types. Internally, the 8087 holds all numbers in the temporary real format; the extended range and precision of this format are key contributors to the NPX's ability to consistently deliver stable, expected results. The 8087's load and store instructions convert operands between the other formats and temporary real. The fact that these conversions are made, and that calculations may be performed on converted numbers, is transparent to the programmer. Integer operands, whether binary or decimal, yield correct integer results, just as real operands yield correct real results. Moreover, a rounding error does not occur when a number in an external format is converted to temporary real.

Computations in the 8087 center on the processor's register stack. These eight 80-bit registers provide the equivalent capacity of 40 of the 16-bit registers found in typical CPUs. This generous register space allows more constants and intermediate results to be held in registers during calculations, reducing memory access and consequently improving execution speed as well as bus availability. The 8087 register set is unique in that it can be accessed both as a stack, with instructions operating implicitly on the top one or two stack elements, and as a fixed register set, with instructions operating on explicitly designated registers.

Table 6-3 lists the 8087's major instructions by class. Assembly language programs are written in ASM-86, the 8086,88/80186,188/8087 common assembly language. ASM-86 provides directives for defining all 8087 data types and mnemonics for all

Table 6-2 Data Types

Data Type	Bits	Significant Digits (Decimal)	Approximate Range (Decimal)
Word integer	16	4	$-32,768 \leqslant X \leqslant +32,767$
Short integer	32	9	$-2 \times 10^9 \leqslant X \leqslant +2 \times 10^9$
Long integer	64	18	$-9 \times 10^{18} \leqslant X \leqslant +9 \times 10^{18}$
Packed decimal	80	18	$-99...99 \leqslant X \leqslant +99...99$ (18 digits)
Short real*	32	6-7	$8.43 \times 10^{-37} \leqslant |X| \leqslant 3.37 \times 10^{38}$
Long real*	64	15-16	$4.19 \times 10^{-307} \leqslant |X| \leqslant 1.67 \times 10^{308}$
Temporary real	80	19	$3.4 \times 10^{-4932} \leqslant |X| \leqslant 1.2 \times 10^{4932}$

*The short and long real data types correspond to the single and double precision data types defined in other Intel numerics products.

Table 6-3 Principal Instructions

Class	Instructions
Data Transfer	Load (all data types), Store (all data types), Exchange
Arithmetic	Add, Subtract, Multiply, Divide, Subtract Reversed, Divide Reversed, Square Root, Scale, Remainder, Integer Part, Change Sign, Absolute Value, Extract
Comparison	Compare, Examine, Test
Transcendental	Tangent, Arctangent, $2^X - 1$, $Y \bullet Log_2(X+1)$, $Y \bullet Log_2(X)$
Constants	0, 1, π, $Log_{10}2$, Log_e2, Log_210, Log_2e
Processor Control	Load Control Word, Store Control Word, Store Status Word, Load Environment, Store Environment, Save, Restore, Enable Interrupts, Disable Interrupts, Clear Exceptions, Initialize

instructions. The fact that some instructions in a program are executed by the 8087 and others by the CPU is usually of no concern to the programmer. All 8086,88 addressing modes may be used to access memory-based 8087 operands, enabling convenient processing of numeric arrays, structures, based variables, etc.

NPX routines may also be written in PL/M-86, Intel's high-level language for the 8086,88 and 80186,188 CPUs. PL/M-86 provides the programmer with access to many 8087 facilities while reducing the programmer's need to understand the architecture of the chip.

Two features of the 8087 hardware further simplify numeric application programming. First, the 8087 is invoked directly by the programmer's instructions. There is no need to write instructions that "address" the NPX as an "I/O device", or to incur the overhead of setting up a DMA operation to perform data transfers. Second, the NPX automatically detects exception conditions that can potentially damage a calculation at run-time. On-chip exception handlers are automatically invoked by default to field these exceptions, so that a reasonable result is produced and execution may proceed without program intervention. Alternatively, the 8087 can interrupt the CPU and thus trap to a user procedure when an exception is detected.

Besides the assembler and compiler, Intel provides a software emulator for the 8087. The 8087 emulator (E8087) is a software package that provides the functional equivalent of an 8087; it executes entirely on an 8086,88 or 80186,188 CPU. The emulator allows

8087 routines to be developed and checked out on an 8086,88 or 80186,188 execution vehicle before prototype 8087 hardware is operational.

At the source code level, there is no difference between a routine that will ultimately run on an 8087 or on a CPU emulation of an 8087. At link time, the decision is made whether to use the NPX or the software emulator; no recompilation or re-assembly is necessary. Source programs are independent of the numeric execution vehicle: except for timing, the operation of the emulated NPX is the same as for "real hardware". The emulator also makes it simple for a product to offer the NPX as a "plug-in" performance option without the necessity of maintaining two sets of source code. The 80186,188 provides a trap when an escape (to the 8087) opcode is encountered.

Hardware Interface

As a processor extension to an 8086,88 or 80186,188, the 8087 is wired directly to the CPU as shown in Figure 6-3. The CPU's queue status lines (QS0 and QS1) enable the NPX to obtain and decode instructions in synchronization with the CPU. The NPX's BUSY signal informs the CPU that the NPX is executing; the CPU WAIT instruction tests this signal to ensure that the NPX is ready to execute a subsequent instruction. The NPX can interrupt the CPU when it detects an exception. The NPX's interrupt request line is typically routed to the CPU through an 8259A Programmable Interrupt Controller or the 80186,18888 integrated controller.

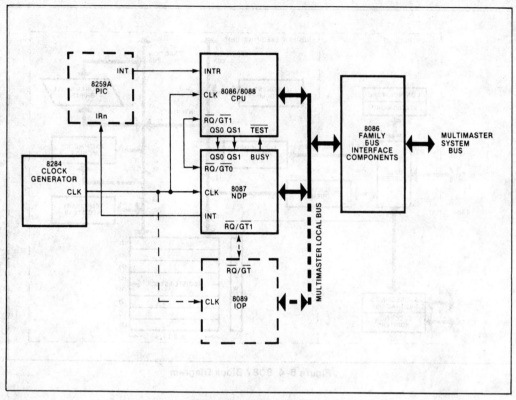

Figure 6-3 NDP Interconnect

The NPX uses one of its host CPU's request/grant lines to obtain control of the local bus for data transfers (loads and stores). The other CPU request/-grant line is available for general system use, for example, by a local 8089 Input/Output Processor. A local 8089 may also be connected to the 8087's RQ/GT1 line. In this configuration, the 8087 passes the request/grant handshake signals between the CPU and the IOP when the 8087 is not in control of the bus, the 8087 relinquishes the bus (at the end of the current bus cycle) upon a request from the connected IOP, giving the IOP higher priority than itself. In this way, two local 8089's can be configured in a module that also includes a CPU and an 8087.

The 8086, 8088 and 8087 all utilize the same clock generator and system bus interface components (bus controller, latches, transceivers, and bus arbiter). Thus, no additional hardware beyond the

8087 is required to add powerful computational capabilities to 8086, 88- based systems. For 80186, 188-based systems, some additional hardware is required to interface to the 8087. Refer to Volume 2 for more information.

6.3 PROCESSOR ARCHITECTURE

As shown in Figure 6-4, the NPX is internally divided into two processing elements, the control unit (CU) and the numeric execution unit (NEU). In essence, the NEU executes all numeric instructions, while the CU fetches instructions, reads and writes memory operands, and executes the processor control class of instructions. The two elements are able to operate independently of one another, allowing the CU to maintain synchronization with the CPU while the NEU executes numeric instructions.

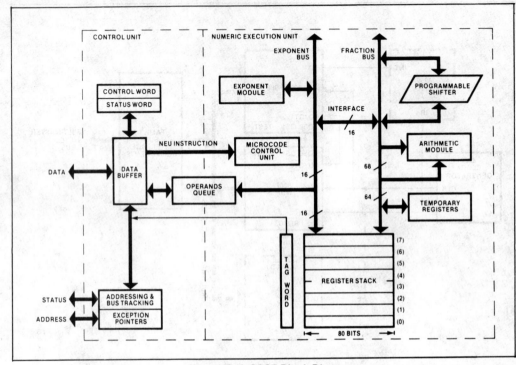

Figure 6-4 8087 Block Diagram

Control Unit

The CU keeps the 8087 operating in synchronization with its host CPU. 8087 instructions are intermixed with CPU instructions in a single instruction stream fetched by the CPU. By monitoring the status signals emitted by the CPU, the NPX control unit can determine when an instruction is being fetched. When the instruction byte or word becomes available on the local bus, the CU taps the bus in parallel with the CPU and obtains that portion of the instruction.

The CU maintains an instruction queue that is identical to the queue in the host CPU. By monitoring the CPU's queue status lines, the CU is able to obtain and decode instructions from the queue in synchronization with the CPU. In effect, both processors fetch and decode the instruction stream in parallel.

The two processors execute the instruction stream differently, however. The first five bits of all 8087 machine instructions are identical; these bits designate the coprocessor escape (ESC) class of instructions. The control unit ignores all instructions that do not match these bits, since these instructions are directed to the CPU only. When the CU decodes an instruction containing the escape code, it either executes the instruction itself, or passes it to the NEU, depending on the type of instruction.

The CPU distinguishes between ESC instructions that reference memory and those that do not. If the instruction refers to a memory operand, the CPU calculates the operand's address and then performs a "dummy read" of the word at that location. This is a normal read cycle, except that the CPU ignores the data it receives. If the ESC instruction does not contain a memory reference, the CPU simply proceeds to the next instruction.

A given 8087 instruction (an ESC to the CPU) will either require loading an operand from memory into the 8087, or will require storing an operand from the 8087 into memory, or will not reference memory at all. In the first two cases, the CU makes use of the "dummy read" cycle initiated by the CPU. The CU captures and saves the operand address that the CPU places on the bus early in the "dummy read". If the instruction is an 8087 load, the CU additionally captures the first (and possibly only) word of the operand when it becomes available on the bus. If the operand to be loaded is longer than one word, the CU immediately obtains the bus from the CPU and reads the rest of the operand in consecutive bus cycles. In a store operation, the CU captures and saves the operand address as in a load, and ignores the data word that follows in the "dummy read" cycle. When the 8087 is ready to perform the store, the CU obtains the bus from the CPU and writes the operand at the saved address using as many consecutive bus cycles as are necessary to store the operand.

Numeric Execution Unit

The NEU executes all instructions that involve the register stack; these include arithmetic, comparison, transcendental, constant, and data transfer instructions. The data path in the NEU is 68 bits wide and allows internal operand transfers to be performed at very high speeds.

Register Stack

Each of the eight registers in the 8087's register stack is 80 bits wide, and each is divided into the "fields" shown in Figure 6-5. This format corresponds to the NPX's temporary real data type that is used for all calculations. Section 6.6 describes in detail how numbers are represented in the temporary real format.

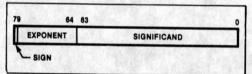

Figure 6-5 Register Structure

At a given point in time, the ST field in the status word (described shortly) identifies the current top-of-stack register. A load ("push") operation decrements ST by 1 and loads a value into the new top register. A store-and-pop operation stores the value from the current top register and then increments ST by 1. Thus, like 8086/80186 stacks in memory, the 8087 register stack grows "down" toward lower-addressed registers.

Instructions may address registers either implicitly or explicitly. Many instructions operate on the register at the top of the stack. These instructions implicitly address the register pointed to by ST. For example, the ASM-86 instruction FSQRT replaces the number at the top of the stack with its square root; this instruction takes no operands because the top-of-stack register is implied as the operand. Other instructions allow the programmer to explicitly specify the register that is to be used. Explicit register addressing is "top-relative" where the ASM-86 expression ST denotes the current stack top and ST(i)

refers to the ith register from ST in the stack (0 i 7). For example, if ST contains 011B (register 3 is the top of the stack), the following instruction would add registers 3 and 5:

    FADD ST,ST(2)

In typical use, the programmer may conceptually "divide" the registers into a fixed group and an adjustable group. The fixed registers are used like the conventional registers in a CPU, to hold constants, accumulations, etc. The adjustable group is used like a stack, with operands pushed on and results popped off. After loading, the registers in the fixed group are addressed explicitly, while those in the adjustable group are addressed implicitly. Of course, all registers may be addressed using either mode, and the "definition" of the fixed versus the adjustable areas may be altered at any time. Section 6.8 contains a programming example that illustrates typical register stack use.

The stack organization and top-relative addressing of the registers simplify subroutine programming. Passing subroutine parameters on the register stack eliminates the need for the subroutine to "know" which registers actually contain the parameters and allows different routines to call the same subroutine without having to observe a convention for passing parameters in dedicated registers. So long as the stack is not full, each routine simply loads the parameters on the stack and calls the subroutine. The subroutine addresses the parameters as ST, ST(1), etc., even though ST may, for example, refer to register 3 in one invocation and register 5 in another.

Status Word

The status word reflects the overall condition of the 8087; it may be examined by storing it into memory with an NPX instruction and then inspecting it with CPU code. The status word is divided into the fields shown in Figure 6-6. The busy field (bit 15) indicates whether the NPX is executing an instruction (B=1) or is idle (B=0).

Several 8087 instructions (for example, the comparison instructions) post their results to the condition code (bits 14 and 10-8 of the status word). The principal use of the condition code is for conditional branching. This may be accomplished by executing an instruction that sets the condition code, storing the status word in memory and then examining the condition code with CPU instructions.

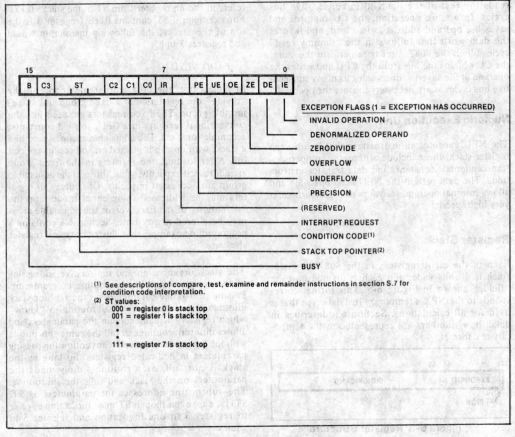

Figure 6-6 Status Word Format

Bits 13-11 of the status word point to the 8087 register that is the current stack top (ST). Note that if ST=000B, a "push" operation, which decrements ST, produces ST=111B; similarly, popping the stack with ST=111B yields ST=000B.

Bit 7 is the interrupt request field. The NPX sets this field to record a pending interrupt to the CPU.

Bits 5-0 are set to indicate that the NEU has detected an exception while executing an instruction. Section 6.4 explains these exceptions.

Control Word

To satisfy a broad range of application requirements, the NPX provides several processing options which are selected by loading a word from memory into the control word. Figure 6-7 shows the format and encoding of the fields in the control word; it is provided here for reference. Section 6.4 explains the use of each of these 8087 facilities except the interrupt-enable control field, which is covered in Volume 2 of this set.

Tag Word

The tag word marks the content of each register as shown in Figure 6-8. The principal function of the tag word is to optimize the NPX'S performance under certain circumstances, and programmers ordinarily need not be concerned with it.

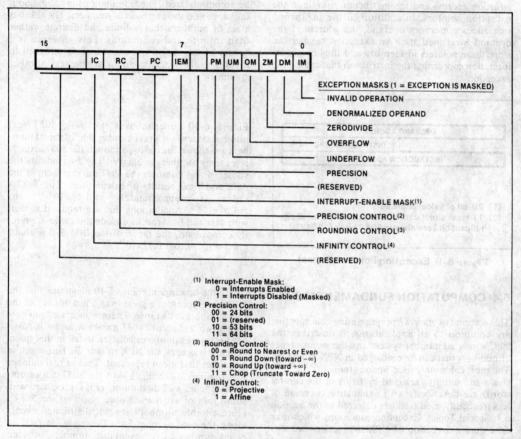

EXCEPTION MASKS (1 = EXCEPTION IS MASKED)
- INVALID OPERATION
- DENORMALIZED OPERAND
- ZERODIVIDE
- OVERFLOW
- UNDERFLOW
- PRECISION
- (RESERVED)
- INTERRUPT-ENABLE MASK[1]
- PRECISION CONTROL[2]
- ROUNDING CONTROL[3]
- INFINITY CONTROL[4]
- (RESERVED)

[1] **Interrupt-Enable Mask:**
  - 0 = Interrupts Enabled
  - 1 = Interrupts Disabled (Masked)

[2] **Precision Control:**
  - 00 = 24 bits
  - 01 = (reserved)
  - 10 = 53 bits
  - 11 = 64 bits

[3] **Rounding Control:**
  - 00 = Round to Nearest or Even
  - 01 = Round Down (toward $-\infty$)
  - 10 = Round Up (toward $+\infty$)
  - 11 = Chop (Truncate Toward Zero)

[4] **Infinity Control:**
  - 0 = Projective
  - 1 = Affine

Figure 6-7 Control Word Format

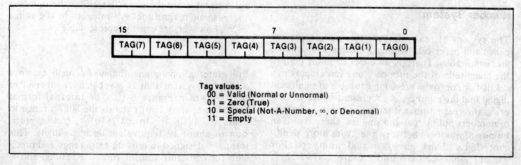

Tag values:
- 00 = Valid (Normal or Unnormal)
- 01 = Zero (True)
- 10 = Special (Not-A-Number, ∞, or Denormal)
- 11 = Empty

Figure 6-8 Tag Word Format

210911

Exception Pointers

The exception pointers (see Figure 6-9) are provided for user-written exception handlers. Whenever the 8087 executes an instruction, the CU saves the instruction address and the instruction opcode in the exception pointers. In addition, if the instruction references a memory operand, the address of the operand is retained also. An exception handler can store these pointers in memory and thus obtain information concerning the instruction that caused the exception.

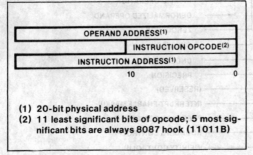

```
┌─────────────────────────────────────┐
│ OPERAND ADDRESS(1)                   │
│             INSTRUCTION OPCODE(2)    │
│ INSTRUCTION ADDRESS(1)               │
└─────────────────────────────────────┘
        10                    0
```

(1) 20-bit physical address
(2) 11 least significant bits of opcode; 5 most significant bits are always 8087 hook (11011B)

Figure 6-9 Exception Pointers Format

6.4 COMPUTATION FUNDAMENTALS

This section covers 8087 programming concepts that are common to all applications. It describes the 8087's internal number system and the various types of numbers that can be employed in NPX programs. The most commonly used options for rounding, precision and infinity (selected by fields in the control word) are described, with exhaustive coverage of less frequently used facilities deferred to the Section 6.7, Special Topics. Exception conditions which may arise during execution of NPX instructions are also described, along with the options that are available for responding to these exceptions.

Number System

The system of real numbers that people use for pencil and paper calculations is conceptually infinite and continuous. There is no upper or lower limit to the magnitude of the numbers one can employ in a calculation, or to the precision (number of significant digits) that the numbers can represent. When considering any real number, there are always an infinity of numbers both larger and smaller. There is also an infinity of numbers between (i.e., with more significant digits than) any two real numbers. For example, between 2.5 and 2.6 are 2.51, 2.5897, 2.500001, etc.

Ideally, it would be desirable for a computer to be able to operate on the entire real number system. In practice this is not possible. Computers, no matter how large, ultimately have fixed size registers and memories that limit the system of numbers that can be accommodated. These limitations proscribe both the range and the precision of numbers. The result is a set of numbers that is finite and discrete, rather than infinite and continuous. This sequence is a subset of the real numbers, which is designed to form a useful *approximation* of the real number system.

Figure 6-10 superimposes the basic 8087 real number system on a real number line (decimal numbers are shown for clarity, although the 8087 actually represents numbers in binary). The dots indicate the subset of real numbers the 8087 can represent as the data and final results of calculations. The 8087's range is approximately $\pm 4.19 \times 10^{-307}$ to $\pm 1.67 \times 10^{308}$. Applications that are required to deal with data and final results outside this range are rare. By comparison, the range of the IBM 370 is about $\pm 0.54 \times 10^{-78}$ to $\pm 0.72 \times 10^{76}$.

The finite spacing in Figure 6-10 illustrates that the NPX can represent a great many, but not all, of the real numbers in its range. There is always a "gap" between two "adjacent" 8087 numbers, and it is possible for the result of a calculation to fall in this space. When this occurs, the NPX rounds the true result to a number that it can represent. Thus, a real number that requires more digits than the 8087 can accommodate (e.g., a 20 digit number) is represented with some loss of accuracy. Notice also that the 8087's representable numbers are not distributed evenly along the real number line. There are, in fact, an equal number of representable numbers between successive powers of 2 (i.e., there are as many representable numbers between 2 and 4 as between 65,536 and 131,072). Therefore, the "gaps" between representable numbers are "larger" as the numbers increase in magnitude. All integers in the range $\pm 2^{64}$, however, are exactly representable.

In its internal operations, the 8087 actually employs a number system that is a substantial superset of that shown in Figure 6-10. The internal format (called temporary real) extends the 8087's range to about $\pm 3.4 \times 10^{-4932}$ to $\pm 1.2 \times 10^{4932}$, and its precision to about 19 (equivalent decimal) digits. This format is designed to provide extra range and precision for constants and intermediate results, and is not normally intended for data or final results.

From a practical standpoint, the 8087's set of real numbers is sufficiently "large" and "dense" so as not to limit the vast majority of microprocessor applications. Compared to most computers, including mainframes, the NPX provides a very good approximation of the real number system. It is important to remember, however, that it is not an exact representation, and that arithmetic on real numbers is inherently approximate.

Conversely, and equally important, the 8087 does perform exact arithmetic on its integer subset of the reals. That is, an operation on two integers returns an exact integral result, provided that the true result is an integer and is in range. For example, $4 \div 2$ yields an exact integer, $1 \div 3$ does not, and $2^{40} \times 2^{30} + 1$ does not, because the result requires greater than 64 bits of precision.

Data Types and Formats

The 8087 recognizes seven numeric data types, divided into three classes: binary integers, packed decimal integers, and binary reals. Figure 6-11 summarizes the format of each data type. In the figure, the most significant digits of all numbers (and fields within numbers) are the leftmost digits. Table 6-2 provides the range and number of significant (decimal) digits that each format can accommodate.

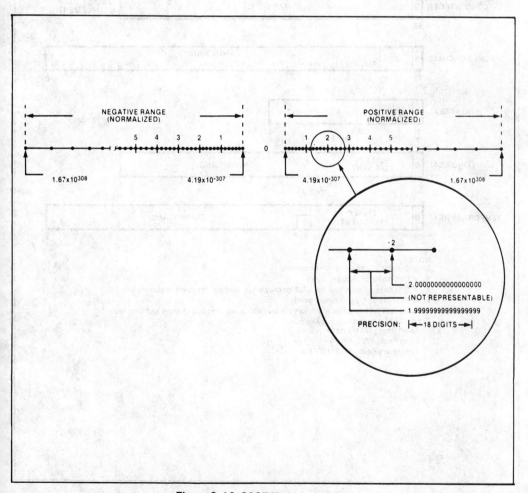

Figure 6-10 8087 Number System

210911

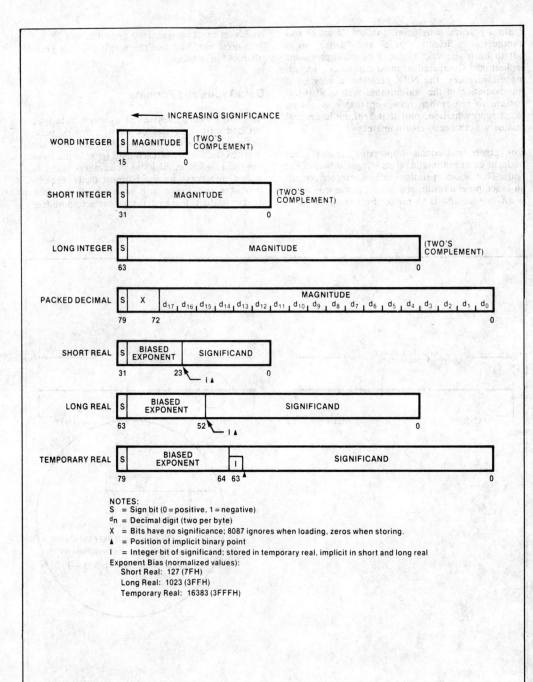

NOTES:
S   = Sign bit (0 = positive, 1 = negative)
d_n = Decimal digit (two per byte)
X   = Bits have no significance; 8087 ignores when loading, zeros when storing.
▲   = Position of implicit binary point
I   = Integer bit of significand; stored in temporary real, implicit in short and long real
Exponent Bias (normalized values):
   Short Real: 127 (7FH)
   Long Real: 1023 (3FFH)
   Temporary Real: 16383 (3FFFH)

Figure 6-11 Data Formats

BINARY INTEGERS

The three binary integer formats are identical except for length, which governs the range that can be accommodated in each format. The leftmost bit is interpreted as the number's sign: 0 = positive and 1 = negative. Negative numbers are represented in standard two's complement notation (the binary integers are the only 8087 format to use two's complement). The quantity zero is represented with a positive sign (all bits are 0). The 8087 word integer format is identical to the 16-bit signed integer data type of the 8086,88 and 80186,188.

DECIMAL INTEGERS

Decimal integers are stored in packed decimal notation, with two decimal digits "packed" into each byte, except the leftmost byte, which carries the sign bit (0 = positive, 1 = negative). Negative numbers are not stored in two's complement form and are distinguished from positive numbers only by the sign bit. The most significant digit of the number is the leftmost digit. All digits must be in the range 0H-9H.

REAL NUMBERS

The 8087 stores real numbers in a three-field binary format that resembles scientific, or exponential, notation. The number's significant digits are held in the *significand* field, the *exponent* field locates the binary point within the significant digits (and therefore determines the number's magnitude), and the *sign* field indicates whether the number is positive or negative. (The exponent and significand are analogous to the terms "characteristic" and "mantissa" used to describe floating point numbers on some computers.) Negative numbers differ from positive numbers only in their sign bits.

Table 6-4 shows how the real number 178.125 (decimal) is stored in the 8087 short real format. The table lists a progression of equivalent notations that express the same value to show how a number can be converted from one form to another. The ASM-86 and PL/M-86 language translators perform a similar process when they encounter programmer-defined real number constants. Note that not every decimal fraction has an exact binary equivalent. The decimal number 1/10, for example, cannot be expressed exactly in binary (just as the number 1/3 cannot be expressed in decimal). When a translator encounters such a value, it produces a rounded binary approximation of the decimal value.

The NPX usually carries the digits of the significand in normalized form. This means that, except for the value zero, the significand is an *integer* and a *fraction* as follows:

$$1_\triangle fff...ff$$

where $\triangle$ indicates an assumed binary point. The number of fraction bits varies according to the real format: 23 for short, 52 for long and 63 for temporary real. By normalizing real numbers so that their integer bit is always a 1, the 8087 eliminates leading zeros in small values ($|x| < 1$). This technique maximizes the number of significant digits that can be accommodated in a significand of a given width.

Table 6-4 Real Number Notation

Notation	Value		
Ordinary Decimal	178.125		
Scientific Decimal	$1_\triangle 78125E2$		
Scientific Binary	$1_\triangle 0110010001E111$		
Scientific Binary (Biased Exponent)	$1_\triangle 0110010001E10000110$		
8087 Short Real (Normalized)	Sign	Biased Exponent	Significand
	0	10000110	01100100010000000000000 $1_\triangle$ (implicit)

Note that in the short and long real formats the integer bit is *implicit* and is not actually stored; the integer bit is physically present in the temporary real format only.

If one were to examine only the significand with its assumed binary point, all normalized, real numbers would have values between 1 and 2. The exponent field locates the *actual* binary point in the significant digits. Just as in decimal scientific notation, a positive exponent has the effect of moving the binary point to the right, and a negative exponent effectively moves the binary point to the left, inserting leading zeros as necessary. An unbiased exponent of zero indicates that the position of the assumed binary point is also the position of the actual binary point. The exponent field, then, determines a real number's magnitude.

In order to simplify comparing real numbers (e.g., for sorting), the 8087 stores exponents in a biased form. This means that a constant is added to the *true exponent* described above. The value of this bias is different for each real format (see Figure 6-11). It has been chosen so as to force the *biased exponent* to be a positive value. This allows two real numbers (of the same format and sign) to be compared as if they are unsigned binary integers. that is, when comparing them bitwise from left to right (beginning with the left-most exponent bit), the first bit position that differs orders the numbers; there is no need to proceed further with the comparison. A number's true exponent can be determined simply by subtracting the bias value of its format.

The short and long real formats exist in memory only. If a number in one of these formats is loaded into a register, it is automatically converted to temporary real, the format used for all internal operations. Likewise, data in registers can be converted to short or long real for storage in memory. The temporary real format may be used in memory also, typically to store intermediate results that cannot be held in registers.

Most applications should use the long real form to store real number data and results; it provides sufficient range and precision to return correct results with a minimum of programmer attention. The short real format is appropriate for applications that are constrained by memory, but it should be recognized that this format provides a smaller margin of safety. It is also useful for debugging algorithms because roundoff problems will manifest themselves more quickly in this format. The temporary real format should normally be reserved for holding intermediate results, loop accumulations, and constants. Its extra length is designed to shield final results from the effects of rounding and overflow/underflow in intermediate calculations. When the

When the temporary real format is used to hold data or to deliver final results, the safety features built into the 8087 are compromised. Furthermore, the range and precision of the long real form are adequate for most microcomputer applications.

SPECIAL VALUES

Besides being able to represent positive and negative numbers, the 8087 data formats may be used to describe other entities. These special values provide extra flexibility but most users do not need to understand them in detail to use the 8087 successfully. Accordingly, they are discussed here only briefly; expanded coverage, including the bit encoding of each value, is provided in the Special Topics section.

The value zero may be signed positive or negative in the real and decimal integer formats; the sign of a binary integer zero is always positive. The fact that zero may be signed, however, is transparent to the programmer.

The real number formats allow for the representation of the special values $+\infty$ and $-\infty$. The 8087 may generate these values as its built-in response to exceptions such as division by zero, or the attempt to store a result that exceeds the upper range limit of the destination format. Infinities may participate in arithmetic and comparison operations, and in fact the processor provides two different conceptual models for handling these special values.

If a programmer attempts an operation for which the 8087 cannot deliver a reasonable result, it will, at the programmer's discretion, either request an interrupt, or return the special value *indefinite*. Taking the square root of a negative number is an example of this type of invalid operation. The recommended action in this situation is to stop the computation by trapping to a user-written exception handler. If, however, the programmer elects to continue the computation, the specially coded *indefinite* value will propagate through the calculation and thus flag the erroneous computation when it is eventually delivered as the result. Each format has an encoding that represents the special value *indefinite*.

In the real formats, a whole range of special values, both positive and negative, is designated to represent a class of values called NAN (Not-A-Number). The special value *indefinite* is a reserved NAN encoding, but all other encodings are made available to be defined in any way by application software. Using a NAN as an operand raises the invalid operation exception, and can trap to a user-written routine to process the NAN. Alternatively, the 8087's built-in exception handler will simply return the NAN itself as the result of the operation; in this way NANs, including *indefinite*, may be propagated through a calculation and delivered as a final, special-valued, result. One use for NANs is to detect uninitialized variables.

As mentioned earlier, the 8087 stores non-zero real numbers in "normalized floating point" form. It also provides for storing and operating on reals that are not normalized, i.e., whose significands contain one or more leading zeros. Nonnormals arise when the result of a calculation yields a value that is too small to be represented in normal form. The leading zeros of nonnormals permit smaller numbers to be represented, at the cost of some lost precision (the number of significant digits is reduced by the leading zeros). In typical algorithms, extremely small values are most likely to be generated as intermediate, rather than final results. By using the NPX's temporary real format for holding intermediates, values as small as $\pm 3.4 \times 10^{-4932}$ can be represented; this makes the occurrence of nonnormal numbers a rare phenomenon in 8087 applications. Nevertheless, the NPX can load, store and operate on nonnormalized real numbers.

Rounding Control

Internally, the 8087 employs three extra bits (guard, round and sticky bits) which enable it to represent the infinitely precise true result of a computation; these bits are not accessible to programmers. Whenever the destination can represent the infinitely precise true result, the 8087 delivers it. Rounding occurs in arithmetic and store operations when the format of the destination cannot exactly represent the infinitely precise true result. For example, a real

number may be rounded if it is stored in a shorter real format, or in an integer format. Or, the infinitely precise true result may be rounded when it is returned to a register.

The NPX has four rounding modes, selectable by the RC field in the control word (see Figure 6-7). Given a true result b that cannot be represented by the target data type, the 8087 determines the two representable numbers a and c that most closely bracket b in value ($a < b < c$). The processor then rounds (changes b to a or to c according to the mode selected by the RC field as shown in Table 6-5. Rounding introduces an error in a result that is less than one unit in the last place to which the result is rounded.

"Round to nearest or even" is the default mode and is suitable for most applications; it provides the most accurate and statistically unbiased estimate of the true result. The "chop" mode is provided for integer arithmetic applications.

"Round up" and "round down" are termed directed rounding and can be used to implement interval arithmetic. Interval arithmetic generates a certifiable result independent of the occurrence of rounding and other errors. The upper and lower bounds of an interval may be computed by executing an algorithm twice, rounding up in one pass and down in the other.

Precision Control

The 8087 allows results to be calculated with 64, 53, or 24 bits of precision as selected by the PC field of the control word. The default setting, and the one

Table 6-5 Rounding Modes

RC Field	Rounding Mode	Rounding Action
00	Round to nearest	Closer to b of a or c; if equally close, select even number (the one whose least significant bit is zero).
01	Round down (toward $-\infty$)	a
10	Round up (toward $+\infty$)	c
11	Chop (toward 0)	Smaller in magnitude of a or c

210911

that is best-suited for most applications, is the full 64 bits. The other settings are required by the proposed IEEE standard, and are provided to obtain compatibility with the specifications of certain existing programming languages. Specifying less precision nullifies the advantages of the temporary real format's extended fraction length, and does not improve execution speed. When reduced precision is specified, the rounding of the fraction zeros the unused bits on the right.

Infinity Control

The 8087's system of real numbers may be closed by either of two models of infinity. These two means of closing the number system, projective and affine closure, are illustrated schematically in Figure 6-12. The setting of the IC field in the control word selects one model or the other. The default means of closure is projective, and this is recommended for most computations. When projective closure is selected, the NPX treats the special values $+\infty$ and $-\infty$ as a single unsigned infinity (similar to its treatment of signed zeros). In the affine mode the NPX respects the signs of $+\infty$ and $-\infty$.

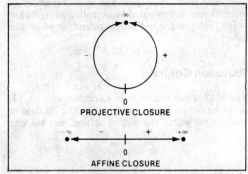

Figure 6-12 Projective Versus Affine Closure

While affine mode may provide more information than projective, there are occasions when the sign may in fact represent misinformation. For example, consider an algorithm that yields an intermediate result x of $+0$ and -0 the (the same numeric value) in different executions. If $1/x$ were then computed in affine mode, two entirely different values ($+\infty$ and $-\infty$) would result from numerically identical values of x. Projective mode on the other hand, provides less information but never returns misinformation. In general, then, projective mode should be used globally, with affine mode reserved for local computations where the programmer can take advantage of the sign and knows for certain that the nature of the computation will not produce misleading results.

Exceptions

During the execution of most instructions, the 8087 checks for six classes of exception conditions.

The 8087 reports *invalid operation* if any of the following occurs:

- An attempt to load a register that is not empty, (e.g., Stack overflow),

- An attempt to pop an operand from an empty register (e.g., stack underflow),

- An operand is a NAN,

- The operands cause the operation to be indeterminate (0/0, square root of a negative number, etc.).

An invalid operation generally indicates a program error.

If the exponent of the true result is too large for the destination real format, the 8087 signals *overflow*. Conversely, a true exponent that is too small to be represented results in the *underflow* exception. If either of these occur, the result of the operation is outside the range of the destination real format.

Typical algorithms are most likely to produce extremely large and small numbers in the calculation of intermediate, rather than final, results. Because of the great range of the temporary real format (recommended as the destination format for intermediates), overflow and underflow are relatively rare events in most 8087 applications.

If division of a finite non-zero operand by zero is attempted, the 8087 reports the *zerodivide* exception.

If an instruction attempts to operate on a denormal, the NPX reports the *denormalized* exception. This exception is provided for users who wish to implement, in software, an option of the proposed IEEE standard which specifies that operands must be prenormalized before they are used.

If the result of an operation is not exactly representable in the destination format, the 8087 rounds the number and reports the *precision* exception. This exception occurs frequently and indicates that some (generally acceptable) accuracy has been lost; it is provided for applications that need to perform exact arithmetic only.

Invalid operation, zerodivide, and denormalized exceptions are detected before an operation begins, while overflow, underflow, and precision exceptions are not raised until a true result has been computed.

When a "before" exception is detected, the register stack and memory have not yet been updated, and appear as if the offending instruction has not been executed. When an "after" exception is detected, the register stack and memory appear as if the instruction has run to completion, i.e., they may be updated. (However, in a store or store and pop operation, unmasked over/underflow is handled like a "before" exception; memory is not updated and the stack is not popped.) In cases where multiple exceptions arise simultaneously, one exception is signaled according to the following precedence sequence:

- Denormalized (if unmasked),

- Invalid operation,

- Zerodivide

- Denormalized (if masked),

- Over/underflow,

- Precision

(The terms "masked" and "unmasked" are explained shortly.) This means, for example, that zero divided by zero will result in an invalid operation and not a zerodivide exception.

The 8087 reports an exception by setting the corresponding flag in the status word to 1. It then checks the corresponding exception mask in the control word to determine if it should "field" the exception (mask=1), or if it should issue an interrupt request to invoke a user-written exception handler (mask=0). In the first case, the exception is said to be *masked* (from user software) and the NPX executes its on-chip *masked response* for that exception. In the second case, the exception is *unmasked*, and the processor performs its *unmasked response*. The masked response always produces a standard result and then proceeds with the instruction. The unmasked response always traps to user software by interrupting the CPU (assuming the interrupt path is clear). These responses are summarized in Table 6-6. Section 6.7 contains a complete description of all exception conditions and the NPX's masked responses. Note that when exceptions are masked, the NPX may detect multiple exceptions in a single

Table 6-6 Exception and Response Summary

Exception	Masked Response	Unmasked Response
Invalid Operation	If one operand is NAN, return it; if both are NANs, return NAN with larger absolute value; if neither is NAN, return *indefinite*.	Request interrupt.
Zerodivide	Return ∞ signed with "exclusive or" of operand signs.	Request interrupt.
Denormalized	Memory operand: proceed as usual. Register operand: convert to valid unnormal, then re-evaluate for exceptions.	Request interrupt.
Overflow	Return properly signed ∞.	Register destination: adjust exponent*, store result, request interrupt. Memory destination: request interrupt.
Underflow	Denormalize result.	Register destination: adjust exponent*, store result, request interrupt. Memory destination: request interrupt.
Precision	Return rounded result.	Return rounded result, request interrupt.

instruction, since it continues executing the instruction after performing its masked response. For example, the 8087 could detect a denormalized operand, perform its masked response to this exception, and then detect an underflow.

By writing different values into the exception masks of the control word, the user can accept responsibility for handling exceptions, or delegate this to the NPX. Exception handling software is often difficult to write, and the 8087's masked responses have been tailored to deliver the most "reasonable" result for each condition. The majority of applications will find that masking all exceptions other than invalid operation will yield satisfactory results with the least programming investment. An invalid operation exception normally indicates a fatal error in a program that must be corrected; this exception should not normally be masked.

The exception flags are "sticky" and can be cleared only by executing the FCLEX (clear exceptions) instruction, by reinitializing the processor, or by overwriting the flags with an FRSTOR or FLDENV instruction. This means that the flags can provide a cumulative record of the exceptions encountered in a long calculation. A program can therefore mask all exceptions (except, typically, invalid operation), run the calculation and then inspect the status word to see is any exceptions were detected at any point in the calculation.

Note that the 8087 has another set of internal exception flags that it clears before each instruction. It is these flags and not those in the status word that actually trigger the 8087's exception response. The flags in the status word provide a cumulative record of exceptions for the programmer only.

If the NPX executes an unmasked response to an exception, it is assumed that a user exception handler will be invoked via an interrupt from the 8087. The 8087 sets the IR (interrupt request) bit in the status word, but this, in itself, does not guarantee an immediate CPU interrupt. The interrupt request may be blocked by the IEM (interrupt-enable mask) in the 8087 control word, by the 8259A Programmable Interrupt Controller, or by the CPU itself. *If any exception flag is unmasked, it is imperative that the interrupt path to the CPU is eventually cleared so that the user's software can field the exception and the offending task can resume execution.* Note that the 8087 remains "busy" pending CPU intervention. Interrupts are covered in detail in Volume 2.

A user-written exception handler takes the form of an 8086,88/186,188 interrupt procedure. Although exception handlers will vary widely from one application to the next, most will include these basic steps:

- Store the 8087 environment (control, status and tag words, operand and instruction pointers) as it existed at the time of the exception;

- Clear the exception bits in the status word;

- Enable interrupts on the CPU;

- Identify the exception by examining the status and control words in the saved environment;

- Take application-dependent action;

- Return to the point of interruption, resuming normal execution.

Possible "application-dependent actions" include:

- Incrementing an exception counter for later display or printing;

- Printing or displaying diagnostic information (e.g., the 8087 environment and registers);

- Aborting further execution of the calculation causing the exception;

- Aborting all further execution;

- Using the exception pointers to build an instruction that will run without exception and executing it;

- Storing a diagnostic value (a NAN) in the result and continuing with the computation.

Notice that an exception may or may not constitute an error, depending on the application. For example, an invalid operation caused by a stack overflow could signal an ambitious exception handler to extend the register stack to memory and continue running.

6.5 INSTRUCTION SET

This section describes the operation of each of the 8087's 69 instructions. The first part of the section describes the function of each instruction in detail. For this discussion, the instructions are divided into six functional groups: data transfer, arithmetic, comparisons, transcendental, constant, and processor control. The second part provides instruction attributes such as execution speed, bus transfers, and exceptions, as well as a coding example for each combination of operands accepted by the instruction. This information is concentrated in a table, organized alphabetically by instruction mnemonic, for easy reference.

Throughout this section, the instruction set is described as it appears to the ASM-86 programmer who is coding a program. Appendix A, in Volume 2 of this set, covers the actual machine instruction encodings, which are principally of use to those reading unformatted memory dumps, monitoring instruction fetches on the bus, or writing exception handlers.

The instruction descriptions in this section concentrate on describing the normal function of each operation. Table 6-17 lists the exceptions that can occur for each instruction and Table 6-30 details the causes of exceptions as well as the 8087's masked responses.

The typical NPX instruction accepts one or two operands as "inputs", operates on these, and produces a result as an "output". Operands are most often (the contents of) register of memory locations. The operands of some instructions are predefined; for example, FSQRT always takes the square root of the number in the top stack element. Others allow, or require, the programmer to explicitly code the operand(s) along with the instruction mnemonic. Still others accept one explicit operand and one implicit operand, which is usually the top stack element.

Whether supplied by the programmer or utilized automatically, there are two basic types of operands, *sources* and *destinations*. A source operand simply supplies one of the "inputs" to an instruction; it is not altered by the instruction. Even when an instruction converts the source operand from one format to another (e.g., real to integer), the conversion is actually performed in an internal work area to avoid altering the source operand. A destination operand may also provide an "input" to an instruction. It is distinguished from a source operand, however, because its contents may be altered when it receives the result produced by the operation; that is, the destination is replaced by the result.

Many instructions allow their operands to be coded in more than one way. For example, FADD (add real) may be written without operands, with only a source or with a destination and a source. The instruction descriptions in this section employ the simple convention of separating alternative operand forms with slashes; the slashes, however, are not coded. Consecutive slashes indicate an option of no explicit operands. The operands for FADD are thus described as:

    //source/destination,source

This means that FADD may be written in any of three ways.

FADD
FADD *source*
FADD destination,source

When reading this section, it is important to bear in mind that memory operands may be coded with any of the CPU's memory addressing modes. Table 6-20 in this chapter also provides several addressing mode examples.

Data Transfer Instructions

These instructions (summarized in Table 6-7) move operands among elements of the register stack, and between the stack top and memory. Any of the seven data types can be converted to temporary real and loaded (pushed) onto the stack in a single operation; they can be stored to memory in the same manner. The data transfer instructions automatically update the 8087 tag word to reflect the register contents following the instruction.

Table 6-7 Data Transfer Instructions

Real Transfers	
FLD	Load real
FST	Store real
FSTP	Store real and pop
FXCH	Exchange registers

Integer Transfers	
FILD	Integer load
FIST	Integer store
FISTP	Integer store and pop

Packed Decimal Transfers	
FBLD	Packed decimal (BCD) load
FBSTP	Packed decimal (BCD) store and pop

FLD *source*

FLD (load real) loads (pushes) the source operand onto the top of the register stack. This is done by decrementing the stack pointer by one and then copying the contents of the source to the new stack top. The source may be a register on the stack (ST(i)) or any of the real data types in memory. Short and long real source operands are converted to temporary real automatically. Coding FLD ST(0) duplicates the stack top.

FST destination

FST (store real) transfers the stack top to the destination, which may be another register on the stack, or a short or long real memory operand. If the destination is short or long real, the significand is rounded to the width of the destination according to the RC field of the control word, and the exponent is converted to the width and bias of the destination format.

If, however, the stack top is tagged special (it contains, a NAN, or a denormal) then the stack top's significand is not rounded but is chopped (on the right) to fit the destination. Neither is the exponent converted, but it also is chopped on the right and transferred "as is". This preserves the value's identification as or a NAN (exponent all ones) or a denormal (exponent all zeros) so that it can be properly loaded and tagged later in the program if desired.

FSTP destination

FSTP (store real and pop) operates identically to FST except that the stack is popped following the transfer. This is done by tagging the top stack element empty and then incrementing ST. FSTP permits storing to a temporary real memory variable while FST does not. Coding FSTP ST(0) is equivalent to popping the stack with no data transfer.

FXCH//destination

FXCH (exchange registers) swaps the contents of the destination and the stack top registers. If the destination is not coded explicitly, ST(1) is used. Many 8087 instructions operate only on the stack top; FXCH provides a simple means of effectively using these instructions on lower stack elements. For example, the following sequence takes the square root of the third register from the top:

```
FXCH ST(3)
FSQRT
FXCH ST(3)
```

FILD source

FILD (integer load) converts the source memory operand from its binary integer format (word, short, or long,) to temporary real and loads (pushes) the result onto the stack. The (new) stack top is tagged zero of all bits in the source were zero, and is tagged valid otherwise.

FIST destination

FIST (integer store) rounds the contents of the stack top to an integer according to the RC field of the control word and transfers the result to the destination. The destination may define a word or short integer variable. Negative zero is stored in the same encoding as positive zero: 0000...00.

FISTP destination

FISTP (integer store and pop) operates like FIST and also pops the stack following the transfer. The destination may be any of the binary integer data types.

FBLD source

FBLD (packed decimal (BCD) load) converts the contents of the source operand from packed decimal to temporary real and loads (pushes) the result onto the stack. The sign of the source is preserved, including the case where the value is negative zero. FBLD is an exact operation; the source is loaded with no rounding error.

The packed decimal digits of the source are assumed to be in the range 0-9H. The instruction does not check for invalid digits (A-FH) and the result of attempting to load an invalid encoding is undefined.

FBSTP destination

FBSTP (packed decimal (BCD) store and pop) converts the contents of the stack top to a packed decimal integer, stores the result at the destination in memory, and pops the stack. FBSTP produces a rounded integer from a non-integral value by adding a value close to 0.5 to the value and chopping. Users who are concerned about rounding may precede FBSTP with FRNDINT.

Arithmetic Instructions

The 8087's arithmetic instruction set (Table 6-8) provides a wealth of variations on the basic add, subtract, multiply, and divide operations, and a number of other useful functions. These range from a simple absolute value to a square root instruction that executes faster than ordinary division; 8087 programmers no longer need to spend valuable time eliminating square roots from algorithms because they run too slowly. Other arithmetic instructions perform exact modulo division, round real numbers to integers, and scale values by powers of two.

The 8087's basic arithmetic instructions (addition, subtraction, multiplication, and division) are designed to encourage the development of very efficient algorithms. In particular, they allow the programmer to minimize memory references and to make optimum use of the NPX register stack.

Table 6-8 Arithmetic Instructions

Addition	
FADD	Add real
FADDP	Add real and pop
FIADD	Integer add

Subtraction	
FSUB	Subtract real
FSUBP	Subtract real and pop
FISUB	Integer subtract
FSUBR	Subtract real reversed
FSUBRP	Subtract real reversed and pop
FISUBR	Integer subtract reversed

Multiplication	
FMUL	Multiply real
FMULP	Multiply real and pop
FIMUL	Integer multiply

Division	
FDIV	Divide real
FDIVP	Divide real and pop
FIDIV	Integer divide
FDIVR	Divide real reversed
FDIVRP	Divide real reversed and pop
FIDIVR	Integer divide reversed

Other Operations	
FSQRT	Square root
FSCALE	Scale
FPREM	Partial remainder
FRNDINT	Round to integer
FXTRACT	Extract exponent and significand
FABS	Absolute value
FCHS	Change sign

Table 6-9 summarizes the available operation/operand forms that are provided for basic arithmetic. In addition to the four normal operations, two "reversed" instructions make subtraction and division "symmetrical" like addition and multiplication. The variety of instruction and operand forms give the programmer unusual flexibility:

- operands may be located in registers or memory;

- results may be deposited in a choice of registers;

- operands may be a variety of NPX data types: temporary real, long real, short real, short integer or word integer, with automatic conversion to temporary real performed by the 8087.

Five basic instruction forms may be used across all six operations, as shown in Table 6-9. The classical stack form may be used to make the 8087 operate like a classical stack machine. No operands are coded in this form, only the instruction mnemonic. The NDP picks the source operand from the stack top and the destination from the next stack element. It then pops the stack, performs the operation, and returns the result to the new stack top, effectively replacing the operands by the result. (Note that FADD, FSUB, FMUL and FDIV also pop if no operands are specified, in spite of the fact that the mnemonics do not have P as a last character.)

The register form is a generalization of the classical stack form; the programmer specifies the stack top as one operand and any register on the stack as the other operand. Coding the stack top as the destination provides a convenient way to access a constant, held elsewhere in the stack, from the stack top. The converse coding (ST is the source operand) allows, for example, adding the top into a register used as an accumulator.

Often the operand in the stack top is needed for one operation but then is of no further use in the computation. The register pop form can be used to pick up the stack top as the source operand, and then discard it by popping the stack. Coding operands of ST(1),ST with a register pop mnemonic is equivalent to a classical stack operation: the top is popped and the result is left at the new top.

Table 6-9 Basic Arithmetic Instructions and Operands

Instruction Form	Mnemonic Form	Operand Forms destination, source	ASM-86 Example	
Classical stack	F*op*	{ST(1),ST}	FADD	
Register	F*op*	ST(i),ST or ST,ST(i)	FSUB	ST,ST(3)
Register pop	F*op*P	ST(i),ST	FMULP	ST(2),ST
Real memory	F*op*	{ST,} short-real/long-real	FDIV	AZIMUTH
Integer memory	FI*op*	{ST,} word-integer/short-integer	FIDIV	N__PULSES

NOTES: Braces { } surround *implicit* operands; these are not coded, and are shown here for information only.

op = ADD destination ← destination + source
SUB destination ← destination − source
SUBR destination ← source − destination
MUL destination ← destination • source
DIV destination ← destination ÷ source
DIVR destination ← source ÷ destination

The two memory forms increase the flexibility of the 8087's arithmetic instructions. They permit a real number or a binary integer in memory to be used directly as a source operand. This is a very useful facility in situations where operands are not used frequently enough to justify holding them in registers. Note that any memory addressing mode may be used to define these operands, so they may be elements in arrays, structures or other data organizations, as well as simple scalars.

The six basic operations are discussed further in the next paragraphs, and descriptions of the remaining seven arithmetic operations follow.

Addition

FADD //source/destination, source
FADDP destination, source
FIADD source

The addition instructions (add real, add real and pop, integer add) add the source and destination operands and return the sum to the destination. The operand at the stack top may be doubled by coding:

FADD ST,ST(0)

Normal Subtraction

FSUB //source/destination, source
FSUBP destination, source
FISUB source

The normal subtraction instructions (subtract real, subtract real and pop, integer subtract) subtract the source operand from the destination and return the difference to the destination.

Reversed Subtraction

FSUBR //source/destination, source
FSUBRP //destination, source
FISUBR source

The reversed subtraction instruction (subtract real reversed, subtract real reversed and pop, integer subtract reversed) subtract the destination from the source and return the difference to the destination.

Multiplication

FMUL //source/destination, source
FMULP destination, source
FIMUL source

The mulitplication instructions (multiply real, multiply real and pop, integer multiply) multiply the source and destination operands and return the product to the destination. Coding FMUL ST,ST(0) squares the contents of the stack top.

210911

Normal Division

FDIV	//source/destination,source
FDIVP	destination,source
FIDIV	source

The normal division instructions (divide real, divide real and pop, integer divide) divide the destination by the source and return the quotient to the destination.

Reversed Division

FDIVR	//source/destination,source
FDIVRP	destination,source
FIDIVR	source

The reversed division instructions (divide real reversed, divide real reversed and pop, integer divide reversed) divide the source operand by the destination and return the quotient to the destination.

FSQRT

FSQRT (square root) replaces the contents of the top stack element with its square root. (Note: the square root of -0 is defined to be -0.)

FSCALE

FSCALE (scale) interprets the value contained in ST(1) as an integer, and adds this value to the exponent of the number in ST.

This is equivalent to:

$$ST < - ST \cdot 2^{ST(1)}$$

thus, FSCALE provides rapid multiplication or division by integral powers of 2. It is particularly useful for scaling the elements of a vector.

Note that FSCALE assumes the scale factor in ST(1) is an integral value in the range $-2^{15} \leq x < 2^{15}$. If the value is not integral, but is in-range and is greater in magnitude than 1, FSCALE uses the nearest integer smaller in magnitude, i.e., it chops the value toward 0. If the value is out of range, or $0 < |X| < 1$, the instruction will produce an undefined result and will not signal an exception. The recommended practice is to load the scale factor from a word integer to ensure correct operation.

FPREM

FPREM (partial remainder) performs modulo division of the top stack element by the next stack element, i.e., ST(1) is the modulus. FPREM produces an *exact* result; the precision exception does not occur. The sign of the remainder is the same as the sign of the original dividend.

FPREM operates by performing successive scaled subtractions; obtaining the exact remainder when the operands differ greatly in magnitude can consume large amounts of execution time. Since the 8087 can only be preempted between instructions, the remainder function could seriously increase interrupt latency in these cases. Accordingly, the instruction is designed to be executed iteratively in a software-controlled loop.

FPREM can reduce a magnitude difference of up to 2^{64} in one execution. If FPREM produces a remainder that is less than the modulus, the function is complete and bit C2 of the status word condition code is cleared. If the function is incomplete, C2 is set to 1; the result in ST is then called the partial remainder. Software can inspect C2 by storing the status word following execution of FPREM and re-execute the instruction (using the partial remainder in ST as the dividend), until "C" is cleared. Alternatively, a program can determine when the function is complete by comparing ST to ST(1). If $ST > ST(1)$ then FPREM must be executed again; if $ST = ST(1)$ then the remainder is 0; if $ST < ST(1)$ then the remainder is ST. A higher priority interrupting routine which needs the 8087 can force a context switch between the instructions in the remainder loop.

An important use for FPREM is to reduce arguments (operands) of periodic transcendental functions to the range permitted by these instructions. For example, the FPTAN (tangent) instruction requires its argument to be less than $\pi/4$. Using $\pi/4$ as a modulus, FPREM will reduce an argument so that it is in range of FPT. Because FPREM produces an exact result, the argument reduction does *not* introduce roundoff error into the calculation, even if several iterations are required to bring the argument into range. (The rounding of pi does not create the effect of a rounded argument, but of a rounded period.)

FPREM also provides the least-significant three bits of the quotient generated by FPREM (in C_0, C_3, C_1). This is also important for transcendental argument reduction since it locates the original angle in the correct one of eight $\pi 4$ segments of the unit circle.

The FPREM instruction also functions as a "universal normalizer". If the top stack element is unnormal and the modulus is greater than the top stack element, the top stack element will be normalized. In addition, if the number is normalized and the precision mode of the 8087 is set to less than 64 bits, the extra precision bits of the normalized element will be cleared.

210911

FRNDINT

FRNDINT (round to integer) rounds the top stack element to an integer. For example, assume that ST contains the 8087 real number encoding of the decimal value 155.625. FRNDINT will change the value to 155 if the RC field of the control word is set to down or chop, or to 156 if it is set up or nearest.

FXTRACT

FXTRACT (extract exponent and significand) "decomposes" the number in the stack top into two numbers that represent the actual value of the operand's exponent and significand fields. The "exponent" replaces the original operand on the stack and the significand is pushed onto the stack. Following execution of FXTRACT, ST (the new stack top) contains the value of the original significand expressed as a real number: its sign is the same as the operand's, its exponent is 0 true (16,383 or 3FFFH biased), and its significand is identical to the original operand's. ST(1) contains the value of the original operand's true (unbiased) exponent expressed as a real number. If the original operand is zero, FXTRACT produces zeros in ST and ST(1) and *both* are signed as the original operand.

To clarify the operation of FXTRACT, assume ST contains a number whose true exponent is $+4$ (i.e., its exponent field contains 4003H). After executing FXTRACT, ST(1) will contain the real number $+4.0$; its sign will be positive, its exponent field will contain 4001H ($+2$ true) and its significand field will contain $1 \triangle 00...00B$. In other words, the value in ST(1) will be $1.0 \times 2^2 = 4$. If ST contains an operand whose true exponent is -7 (i.e., its exponent field contains 3FF8H), then FXTRACT will return an "exponent" of -7.0; after the instruction executes, ST(1)'s sign and exponent fields will contain C001H (negative sign, true exponent of 2) and its significand will be $1 \triangle 1100...00B$. In other words, the value in ST(1) will be $-1.11 \times 2^2 = -7.0$. In both cases, following FXTRACT, ST's sign and significand fields will be the same as the original operand's, and its exponent field will contain 3FFFH, (0 true).

FXTRACT is useful in conjunction with FBSTP for converting numbers in 8087 temporary real format to decimal representations (e.g., for printing or displaying). It can also be useful for debugging, since it allows the exponent and significand parts of a real number to be examined separately.

FABS

FABS (absolute value) changes the top stack element to its absolute value by making its sign positive.

FCHS

FCHS (change sign) complements (reverses) the sign of the top stack element.

Comparison Instructions

Each of these instructions (Table 6-10) analyses the top stack element, often in relationship to another operand, and reports the result in the status word condition code. The basic operations are compare, test (compare with zero), and examine (report tag, sign, and normalization). Special forms of the compare operation are provided to optimize algorithms by allowing direct comparisons with binary integers and real numbers in memory, as well as popping the stack after a comparison.

Table 6-10 Comparison Instructions

FCOM	Compare real
FCOMP	Compare real and pop
FCOMPP	Compare real and pop twice
FICOM	Integer compare
FICOMP	Integer compare and pop
FTST	Test
FXAM	Examine

The FSTSW (store status word) instruction may be used following a comparison to transfer the condition code to memory for inspection.

Note that instructions other than those in the comparison group may update the condition code. To insure that the status word is not altered inadvertently, store it immediately following a comparison operation.

FCOM//source

FCOM (compare real) compares the stack top to the source operand. The source operand may be a register on the stack, or a short or long real memory operand. If an operand is not coded, ST is compared to ST(1). Positive and negative forms of zero compare identically as if they were unsigned. Following

210911

the instruction, the condition codes reflect the order of the operands as follows:

C3 C2 C0 Order

0	0	0	ST > source
0	0	1	ST < source
1	0	0	ST = source
1	1	1	ST ? source

NANs and ∞ (projective) cannot be compared and return C3 = C0 = 1 as shown above.

FCOMP//source

FCOMP (compare real and pop) operates like FCOM, and in addition pops the stack.

FCOMPP

FCOMPP (compare real and pop twice) operates like FCOM and additionally pops the stack twice, discarding both operands. The comparison is of the stack top to ST(1); no operands may be explicitly coded.

FICOMsource

FICOM (integer compare) converts the source operand, which may reference a word or short binary integer variable, to temporary real and compares the stack top to it.

FICOMPsource

FICOMP (integer compare and pop) operates identically to FICOM and additionally discards the value in ST by popping the stack.

FTST

FTST (test) tests the top stack element by comparing it to zero. The result is posted to the condition codes as follows:

C3 C2 C0 Result

0	0	0	ST is positive and nonzero
0	0	1	ST is negative and nonzero
1	0	0	ST is zero (+ or −)
1	1	1	ST is not comparable (i.e., it is a NAN or projective ∞)

FXAM

FXAM (examine) reports the contents of the top stack element as positive/negative and NAN/unnormal/denormal/normal/zero, or empty. Table 6-11 lists and interprets all the condition code values that FXAM generates. Although four different encodings may be returned for an empty register, bits C3 and C0 of the condition code are both 1 in all encodings. Bits C2 and C1 should be ignored.

Table 6-11 FXAM Condition Code Settings

Condition Code				Interpretation
C3	C2	C1	C0	
0	0	0	0	+ Unnormal
0	0	0	1	+ NAN
0	0	1	0	− Unnormal
0	0	1	1	− NAN
0	1	0	0	+ Normal
0	1	0	1	+ ∞
0	1	1	0	− Normal
0	1	1	1	− ∞
1	0	0	0	+ 0
1	0	0	1	Empty
1	0	1	0	− 0
1	0	1	1	Empty
1	1	0	0	+ Denormal
1	1	0	1	Empty
1	1	1	0	− Denormal
1	1	1	1	Empty

Transcendental Instructions

The instructions in this group (Table 6-12) perform the time-consuming *core calculations* for all common trigonometric, hyperbolic, inverse hyperbolic, logarithmic and exponential functions. Prologue and epilogue software may be used to reduce arguments to the range accepted by the instructions and to adjust the result to correspond to the original arguments if necessary. The transcendentals operate on the top one or two stack elements and they return their results to the stack also.

Table 6-12 Transcendental Instructions

FPTAN	Partial tangent
FPATAN	Partial arctangent
F2XM1	$2^X - 1$
FYL2X	$Y \cdot \log_2 X$
FYL2XP1	$Y \cdot \log_2(X + 1)$

The transcendental instructions assume that their operands are *valid and in-range*. The instruction descriptions in this section provide the range of each operation. To be considered valid, an operand to a transcendental must be normalized; denormals, unnormals, infinities and NANs are considered invalid. (Zero operands are accepted by some functions and are considered out-of-range by others.) If a transcendental operand is invalid or out of range, the instruction will produce an undefined result without signalling an exception. It is the programmer's responsibility to ensure that operands are valid and in-range before executing a transcendental. For periodic functions, FPREM may be used to bring a valid operand into range.

FPTAN

FPTAN (partial tangent) computes the function $Y/X = TAN (\Theta)$. Θ is taken from the top of the stack element; it must lie in the range $0 = or < \Theta = or < \pi 4$. The result of the operation is a ratio; Y replaces Θ in the stack and X is pushed, becoming the new stack top.

The ratio result of FPTAN and the ratio argument of FPATAN are designed to optimize the calculation of the other trigonometric functions, including SIN, COS, ARCSIN and ARCCOS. These can be derived from TAN and ARCTAN via standard trigonometric identities.

FPATAN

FPATAN (partial arctangent) computes the function $\Theta = ARCTAN (Y/X)$. X is taken from the top stack element and Y from $ST(1)$. Y and X must observe the inequality $0 < Y < X < \infty$. The instruction pops the stack and returns Θ to the (new) stack top, overwriting the Y operand; both original operands are destroyed.

F2XM1

F2XM1 (2 to the X minus 1) calculates the function $Y = 2^x - 1$. X is taken from the stack top and must be in the range $0 \leq X \leq 0.5$. The result Y replaces X at the stack top.

This instruction is designed to produce a very accurate result even when X is close to zero. To obtain $Y = 2^x$, add 1 to the result delivered by F2XM1.

The following formulas show how values other than 2 may be raised to a power of X:

$$10^x = 2^{x \cdot LOG\ 10}$$

$$e^x = 2^{x \cdot LOG\ e}$$

$$y^x = 2^{x \cdot LOG\ y}$$

As shown in the next section, the 8087 has built-in instructions for loading the constants $LOG_2 10$ and $LOG_2 e$, and the FYL2X instruction may be used to calculate $X \cdot LOG_2 Y$.

FYL2X

FYL2X (Y log base 2 of X) calculates the function $Z = Y \cdot LOG_2 X$. X is taken from the stack top and y from $ST(1)$. The operands must be in the ranges $0 < x < \infty$ and $-\infty < Y < +\infty$. The instruction pops the stack and returns Z at the (new) stack top, replacing the Y operand; both original operands are destroyed.

This function optimizes the calculation of log to any base other than two since a multiplication is always required:

$$LOG_n X = LOG_n 2 \cdot LOG_2 X$$

FYL2XP1

FYL2XP1 (Y log base 2 of (X + 1)) calculates the function $Z = Y \cdot LOG_2 (X = 1)$. X is taken from the stack top and must be in the range $0 < |X| < (1 - (\sqrt{2}/2))$. Y is taken from $ST(1)$ and must be in the range $-\infty < Y < \infty$. FYL2XP1 pops the stack and returns Z at the (new) stack top, replacing Y.

This instruction provides improved accuracy over FYL2X when computing the log of a number very close to 1, for example $1 + \epsilon$ where $\epsilon < < 1$. Providing ϵ rather than $1 + \epsilon$ as the input to the function allows more significant digits to be retained.

For example, this instruction is useful for any calculation (i.e., compounded interest rates) requiring a logarithm of $1.0 + N$ where $0 < /N < 0.29$. If only the

FYL2X instruction were available, the value 1.0
would have to be added to N, potentially losing
many significant bits in the result. By avoiding the
addition of 1.0 to N, the result of the FYL2XPI will
be as accurate (to within 3 units of temporary real
precision) as N.

Constant Instructions

Each of these instructions (Table 6-13) loads
(pushes) a commonly-used constant onto the stack.
The values have full temporary real precision (80
bits) and are accurate to approximately 19 decimal
digits. Since a temporary real constant occupies 10
memory bytes, the constant instructions, which are
only two bytes long, save storage and improve
execution speed, in addition to simplifying
programming.

Table 6-13 Constant Instructions

FLDZ	Load +0.0
FLD1	Load +1.0
FLDPI	Load π
FLDL2T	Load $\log_2 10$
FLDL2E	Load $\log_2 e$
FLDLG2	Load $\log_{10} 2$
FLDLN2	Load $\log_e 2$

FLDZ

FLDZ (load zero) loads (pushes) +0.0 onto the
stack.

FLD1

FLD1 (load one) loads (pushes) +1.0 onto the
stack.

FLDPI

FLDPI (load pi) loads (pushes) pi onto the stack.

FLDL2T

FLDL2T (load log base 2 of 10) loads (pushes)
value $\log_2 10$ onto the stack.

FLDL2E

FLDL2E (load log base 2 of e) loads (pushes) the
value $\log_{2e}$ onto the stack.

FLDLG2

FLDLG2 (load log base 10 of 2) loads (pushes) the
value $\log_{10} 2$ onto the stack.

FLDLN2

FLDLN2 (load log base e of 2) loads (pushes) the
value $\log_{e2}$ onto the stack.

Processor Control Instructions

Most of these instructions (Table 6-14) are not used
in computations; they are provided principally for
system-level activities. These include initialization,
exception handling and task switching.

As shown in Table 6-14, an alternate mnemonic is
available for many of the processor control

Table 6-14 Processor Control Instructions

FINIT/FNINIT	Initialize processor
FDISI/FNDISI	Disable interrupts
FENI/FNENI	Enable interrupts
FLDCW	Load control word
FSTCW/FNSTCW	Store control word
FSTSW/FNSTSW	Store status word
FCLEX/FNCLEX	Clear exceptions
FSTENV/FNSTENV	Store environment
FLDENV	Load environment
FSAVE/FNSAVE	Save state
FRSTOR	Restore state
FINCSTP	Increment stack pointer
FDECSTP	Decrement stack pointer
FFREE	Free register
FNOP	No operation
FWAIT	CPU wait

instructions. This mnemonic, distinguished by a second character of "N", instructs the assembler *not* to prefix the instruction with a CPU WAIT instruction (instead, a CPU NOP precedes the instruction). This "no-wait" form is intended for use in critical code regions where a WAIT instruction is not desired. When CPU interrupts are enabled, as will normally be the case when an application task is running, the "wait" forms of these instructions should be used.

Except for FNSTENV and FNSAVE, all instructions which provide a no-wait mnemonic are self-synchronizing and can be executed back-to-back in any combination without intervening FWAITs. These instructions can be executed by the 8087 CU while the NEU is busy with a previously decoded instruction. To insure that the processor control instruction executes after completion of any operation in progress in the NEU, the "wait" form of that instruction should be used.

FINIT/FNINIT

FINIT/FNINIT (initialize processor) performs the functional equivalent of a hardware RESET (see Volume 2, Processor Control and Monitoring), except that it does not affect the instruction fetch synchronization of the 8087 and its CPU.

For compatibility with the 8087 emulator, a system should call the INIT87 procedure in lieu of executing FINIT/FNINIT when the processor is first initialized (see Section 6.6 for details). Note that if FNINIT is executed while a previous 8087 memory referencing instruction is running, 8087 bus cycles in progress will be aborted.

FDISI/FNDISI

FDISI/FNDISI (disable interrupts) sets the interrupt enable mask in the control word and prevents the NPX from issuing an interrrupt request.

FENI/FNENI

FENI/FNENI (enable interrupts) clears the interrupt enable mask in the control word, allowing the 8087 to generate interrupt requests.

FLDCW *source*

FLDCW (load control word) replaces the current processor control word with the word defined by the source operand. This instruction is typically used to establish, or change, the 8087's mode of operation.

Note that if an exception bit in the status word is set, loading a new control word that unmasks that exception and clears the interrupt enable mask will generate an immediate interrupt request before the next instruction is executed. When changing modes, the recommended procedure is to first clear any exceptions and then load the new control word.

FSTCW/FNSTCW *destination*

FSTCW/FNSTCW (store control word) writes the current processor control word to the memory location defined by the destination.

FSTSW/FNSTSW *destination*

FSTSW/FNSTSW destination (store status word) writes the current value of the 8087 status word to the destination operand in memory. The instruction has many uses:

- to implement conditional branching following a comparison of FPREM instruction (FSTSW);

- to poll the 8087 to determine if it is busy (FNSTSW);

- to invoke exception handlers in environments that do not use interrupts (FSTSW).

If busy is set, the status bits are not valid.

FCLEX/FNCLEX

FCLEX/FNCLEX (clear exceptions) clears all exception flags, the interrupt request flag and the busy flag in the status word. As a consequence, the 8087's INT and BUSY lines go inactive. An exception handler must issue this instruction before returning to the interrupted computation, or another interrupt request will be generated immediately, and an endless loop may result.

FSAVE/FNSAVE *destination*

FSAVE/FNSAVE (save state) writes the full 8087 state — environment plus register stack — to the memory location defined by the destination operand. Figure 6-13 shows the layout of the 94-byte save area; typically the instruction will be coded to save this image on the CPU stack. If an instruction is executing in the 8087 NEU when FNSAVE is decoded, the CPU queues the FNSAVE and delays its execution until the running instruction completes normally encounters an unmasked exception. Thus, the save image reflects the state of the NPX FOLLOWING THE COMPLETION OF ANY running instruction. After writing the state image to memory, FSAVE/FNSAVE initializes the 8087 as if FINIT/FNINIT has been executed.

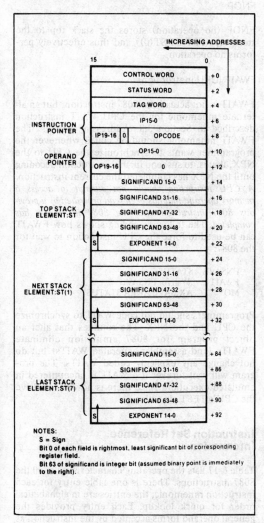

Figure 6-13 FSAVE/FRSTOR Memory Layout

FSAVE/FNSAVE is useful whenever a program wants to save the current state of the NPX and initialize it for a new routine. Three examples are:

- an operating system needs to perform a context switch (suspend the task that had been running and give control to a new task);

- an interrupt handler needs to use the 8087;

- an application task wants to pass a "clean" 8087 to a subroutine.

FNSAVE must be "protected" by executing it in a critical region, i.e., with CPU interrupts disabled. This prevents an interrupt handler from executing a second FNSAVE (or other "no-wait" processor control instruction that reference memory) which could destroy the first FNSAVE if is queued in the 8087. An FWAIT should be executed before CPU interrupts are enabled or any subsequent 8087 instruction is executed.

FRSTOR source

FRSTOR (restore state) reloads the 8087 from the 94-byte memory area defined by the source operand. This information should have been written by a previous FSAVE/FNSAVE instruction and not altered by any other instruction. CPU instructions (that do not reference the save image) may immediately follow FRSTOR, but no NPX instruction should be without an intervening FWAIT or an assembler-generated WAIT.

Note that the 8087 "reacts" to its new state at the conclusion of the FRSTOR; it will for example generate an immediate interrupt request if the exception and mask bits in the memory image so indicate.

FSTENV/FNSTENV destination

FSTENV/FNSTENV (store environment) writes the 8087's basic status — control, status and tag words, and exception pointers — to the memory location defined by the destination operand. Typically the environment is saved on the CPU stack. FSTENV/FNSTENV is often used by exception handlers because it provides access to the exception pointers which identify the offending instruction and operand. After saving the environment, FSTENV/-FNSTENV sets all exception masks (masking all exceptions) in the processor; it does not affect the interrupt-enable mask. Figure 6-14 shows the format of the environment data in memory. If FNSTENV is decoded while another instruction is executing concurrently in the NEU, the 8087 queues the FNSTENV and does not store the environment until the other instruction has completed. Thus, the data saved by the instruction reflects the 8087 after any previously decoded instruction has been executed.

210911

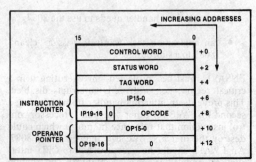

Figure 6-14 FSTENV/FLDENV Memory Layout

FSTENV/FNSTENV must be allowed to complete before any other 8087 instruction is decoded. When FSTENV is coded, an explicit FWAIT, or assembler-generated WAIT, should precede any subsequent 8087 instruction. An FNSTENV must be executed in a critical region that is protected from interruption, in the same manner as FNSAVE.

FLDENV source

FLDENV (load environment) reloads the 8087 environment from the memory area defined by the source operand. This data should have been written by a previous FSTENV/FNSTENV instruction. CPU instructions (that do not reference the environment image) may immediately follow FLDENV, but no subsequent NPX instruction should be executed without an intervening FWAIT or assembler-generated WAIT.

Note that loading an environment image that contains an unmasked exception will cause an immediate interrupt request from the 8087 (assuming IEM-0 in the environment image).

FINCSTP

FINCSTP (increment stack pointer) adds 1 to the stack top pointer (ST) in the status word. It does not alter tags or register contents, nor does it transfer data. It is not equivalent to popping the transfer data since it does not set the tag of the previous stack top to empty. Incrementing the stack pointer when ST=7 produces ST=0.

FDECSTP

FDECSTP (decrement stack pointer) subtracts 1 from ST, the stack top pointer in the status word. No tags or registers are altered, nor is any data transferred. Executing FDECSTP when ST=0 produces ST=7.

FFREE destination

FFREE (free register) changes the destination register's tag to empty; the contents of the register is unaffected.

FNOP

FNOP (no operation) stores the stack top to the stack top (FST ST,ST(0)) and thus effectively performs no operation.

FWAIT (CPU instruction)

FWAIT is not actually an 8087 instruction, but an alternate mnemonic for the CPU WAIT instruction described in Section 3.8, Addressing Modes. The FWAIT mnemonic should be coded whenever the programmer wants to synchronize the CPU to the NPX, that is, to suspend further instruction decoding until the NPX has completed the current instruction. *A CPU instruction should not attempt to access a memory operand that has been read or written by a previous 8087 instruction until the 8087 instruction has completed.* The following coding shows how FWAIT can be used to force the CPU instruction to wait for the 8087:

```
FNSAVE    STATUS
FWAIT     ;Wait for FNSAVE
MOV       AX,SAVE AREA STATUS
```

Programmers should not code WAIT to synchronize the CPU and the NPX. The routines that alter an object program for 8087 emulation eliminate FWAITs (and assembler-generated WAITs) but do not change any explicitly coded WAITs. The program will wait forever if a WAIT is encountered in emulated execution, since there is no 8087 to drive the CPU's TEST pin active.

Instruction Set Reference Information

Table 6-17 lists the operating characteristics of all the 8087 instructions. There is one table entry for each instruction mnemonic; the entries are in alphabetical order for quick lookup. Each entry provides the general operand forms accepted by the instruction as well as a list of all exceptions that may be detected during the operation.

There is one entry for each combination of operand types that can be coded with the mnemonic. Table 6-15 explains the operand identifiers allowed in Table 6-17. Following this entry are columns that provide execution time in clocks, the number of bus transfers run during the operation, the length of the instruction in bytes, and an ASM-86 coding sample.

Table 6-15 Key to Operand Types

Identifier	Explanation
ST	Stack top; the register currently at the top of the stack.
ST(1)	A register in the stack i (0≤i≤7) stack elements from the top. ST(1) is the next-on-stack register, ST(2) is below ST(1), etc.
Short-real	A short real (32 bits) number in memory.
Long-real	A long real (64 bits) number in memory.
Temp-real	A temporary real (80 bits) number in memory.
Packed-decimal	A packed decimal integer (18 digits, 10 bytes) in memory.
Word-integer	A word binary integer (16 bits) in memory.
Short-integer	A short binary integer (32 bits) in memory.
Long-integer	A long binary integer (64 bits) in memory.
nn-bytes	A memory area nn bytes long.

EXECUTION TIME

The execution of an 8087 instruction involves three principal activities, each of which may contribute to the total duration (execution time) of the operation:

- Instruction fetch

- Instruction execution

- Operand transfer

The CPU and NPX simutaneously prefetch and queue their common instruction stream from memory. This activity is performed during spare bus cycles and proceeds in parallel with the execution of instructions from the queue. Because of their complexity, 8087 instructions typically take much longer to execute than to fetch. This means that in a typical sequence of 8087 instructions the processors have a relatively large amount of time available to maintain full instruction queues. Instruction fetching is therefore fully overlapped with execution and does not contribute to the overall duration of a series of instructions.

Fetch time does become apparent when a CPU jump or call instruction alters the normal sequential execution. This empties the queues and delays execution of the target instruction until it is fetched from memory. The time required to fetch the instruction depends on its length, the type of CPU (8086/186 or 8088/188), and, if the CPU is an 8086, whether the instruction is located at an even or odd address. (Slow memories, which force the insertion of wait states in bus cycles, and the bus activities of other processors in the system, may also lengthen fetch time.) Section 4.4 covers this topic in more detail.

Table 6-17 quotes a typical execution time and a range for each instruction. Dividing the figures in the table by 5 (assuming a 5 MHz clock) produces execution time in microseconds. The typical case is an estimate for operand values that normally characterize most applications. The range encompasses best- and worst-case operand values that may be found in extreme circumstances. Where applicable, the figures *include* all overhead incurred by the CPU's execution of the ESC instruction, local bus arbitration (request/grant time), and the average overhead imposed by a preceding WAIT instruction (half of the 5-clock cycle that it uses to examine the TEST(pin).

The execution times assume that no exceptions are detected. Invalid operation, denormalized (unmasked), and zerodivide exceptions usually decrease execution time from the typical figure, but it will still fall within the quoted range. The precision exception has no effect on execution time. Unmasked overflow and underflow, and masked denormalized exceptions, impose the penalties shown in Table 6-16. Absolute worst-case execution time is therefore the high range figure plus the largest penalty that may be encountered.

For instructions that transfer operands to or from memory, the execution times in Table 6-17 show that the time required for the CPU to calculate the operand's effective address (EA) should be added. Effective address calculation time varies according to addressing mode and to the CPU processor (8086,88 or 80186,188) used; Table 2-18 supplies the figures.

Table 6-16 Execution Penalties

Exception	Additional Clocks
Overflow (unmasked)	14
Underflow (unmasked)	16
Denormalized (masked)	33

210911

BUS TRANSFERS

Instructions that reference memory execute bus cycles to transfer operands. Each transfer requires one bus cycle. The number of transfers depends on the length of the operand, the type of CPU, and the alignment of the operand if the CPU is an 8086. The figures in Table 6-17 *include* the "dummy read" transfer(s) performed by the CPU in its execution of the escape instruction. The first 8086 figure is for even-addressed operands, and the second is for odd-addressed operands.

A bus cycle (transfer) consumes four clocks if the bus is immediately available and if the memory is running at processor speed, without wait states. Additional time is required if slow memories are employed, because these insert wait states into the bus cycle. In multiprocessor environments, the bus may not be available immediately if a higher priority processor is using it; this also can increase effective transfer time.

INSTRUCTION LENGTH

Instructions that do not reference memory are two bytes long. Memory reference instructions vary between two and four bytes. The third and fourth bytes are used for 8- or 16-bit displacement values; the assembler generates the short displacement whenever possible. No displacements are required in memory references that use only CPU register contents to calculate an operand's effective address. Note that the lengths quoted in Table 6-17 do not include the one byte CPU WAIT instruction that the assembler automatically inserts in front of all NPX instructions (except those coded with a "no-wait" mnemonic).

Table 6-17 Instruction Set Reference Data

FABS	FABS (no operands) Absolute value				Exceptions: I	
Operands	**Execution Clocks**		**Transfers**		**Bytes**	**Coding Example**
	Typical	**Range**	**8086**	**8088**		
(no operands)	14	10-17	0	0	2	FABS

FADD	FADD //source/destination,source Add real				Exceptions: I, D, O, U, P	
Operands	**Execution Clocks**		**Transfers**		**Bytes**	**Coding Example**
	Typical	**Range**	**8086**	**8088**		
//ST,ST(i)/ST(i),ST	85	70-100	0	0	2	FADD ST,ST(4)
short-real	105+EA	90-120+EA	2/4	4	2-4	FADD AIR_TEMP [SI]
long-real	110+EA	95-125+EA	4/6	8	2-4	FADD [BX].MEAN

FADDP	FADDP destination,source Add real and pop				Exceptions: I, D, O, U, P	
Operands	**Execution Clocks**		**Transfers**		**Bytes**	**Coding Example**
	Typical	**Range**	**8086**	**8088**		
ST(i),ST	90	75-105	0	0	2	FADDP ST(2),ST

210911

Table 6-17 Instruction Set Reference Data (continued)

FBLD

FBLD source
Packed decimal (BCD) load

Exceptions: I

Operands	Execution Clocks		Transfers		Bytes	Coding Example
	Typical	Range	8086	8088		
packed-decimal	300+EA	290-310+EA	5/7	10	2-4	FBLD YTD_SALES

FBSTP

FBSTP destination
Packed decimal (BCD) store and pop

Exceptions: I

Operands	Execution Clocks		Transfers		Bytes	Coding Example
	Typical	Range	8086	8088		
packed-decimal	530+EA	520-540+EA	6/8	12	2-4	FBSTP [BX].FORECAST

FCHS

FCHS (no operands)
Change sign

Exceptions: I

Operands	Execution Clocks		Transfers		Bytes	Coding Example
	Typical	Range	8086	8088		
(no operands)	15	10-17	0	0	2	FCHS

FCLEX/FNCLEX

FCLEX (no operands)
Clear exceptions

Exceptions: None

Operands	Execution Clocks		Transfers		Bytes	Coding Example
	Typical	Range	8086	8088		
(no operands)	5	2-8	0	0	2	FNCLEX

FCOM

FCOM //source
Compare real

Exceptions: I, D

Operands	Execution Clocks		Transfers		Bytes	Coding Example
	Typical	Range	8086	8088		
//ST(i)	45	40-50	0	0	2	FCOM ST(1)
short-real	65+EA	60-70+EA	2/4	4	2-4	FCOM [BP].UPPER LIMIT
long-real	70+EA	65-75+EA	4/6	8	2-4	FCOM WAVELENGTH

210911

Table 6-17 Instruction Set Reference Data (continued)

FCOMP

FCOMP //source
Compare real and pop

Exceptions: I, D

Operands	Execution Clocks		Transfers		Bytes	Coding Example
	Typical	Range	8086	8088		
//ST(i)	47	42-52	0	0	2	FCOMP ST(2)
short-real	68+EA	63-73+EA	2/4	4	2-4	FCOMP BP+2 N READINGS
long-real	72+EA	67-77+EA	4/6	8	2-4	FCOMP DENSITY

FCOMPP

FCOMPP (no operands)
Compare real and pop twice

Exceptions: I, D

Operands	Execution Clocks		Transfers		Bytes	Coding Example
	Typical	Range	8086	8088		
(no operands)	50	45-55	0	0	2	FCOMPP

FDECSTP

FDECSTP (no operands)
Decrement stack pointer

Exceptions: None

Operands	Execution Clocks		Transfers		Bytes	Coding Example
	Typical	Range	8086	8088		
(no operands)	9	6-12	0	0	2	FDECSTP

FDISI/FNDISI

FDISI (no operands)
Disable interrupts

Exceptions: None

Operands	Execution Clocks		Transfers		Bytes	Coding Example
	Typical	Range	8086	8088		
(no operands)	5	2-8	0	0	2	FDISI

FDIV

FDIV //source/destination,source
Divide real

Exceptions: I, D, Z, O, U, P

Operands	Execution Clocks		Transfers		Bytes	Coding Example
	Typical	Range	8086	8088		
//ST(i),ST	198	193-203	0	0	2	FDIV
short-real	220+EA	215-225+EA	2/4	4	2-4	FDIV DISTANCE
long-real	225+EA	220-230+EA	4/6	8	2-4	FDIV ARC [DI]

210911

Table 6-17 Instruction Set Reference Data (continued)

FDIVP

FDIVP destination,source
Divide real and pop

Exceptions: I, D, Z, O, U, P

Operands	Execution Clocks		Transfers		Bytes	Coding Example
	Typical	Range	8086	8088		
ST(i),ST	202	197-207	0	0	2	FDIVP ST(4),ST

FDIVR

FDIVR //source/destination,source
Divide real reversed

Exceptions: I, D, Z, O, U, P

Operands	Execution Clocks		Transfers		Bytes	Coding Example
	Typical	Range	8086	8088		
//ST,ST(i)/ST(i),ST	199	194-204	0	0	2	FDIVR ST(2),ST
short-real	221+EA	216-226+EA	2/4	6	2-4	FDIVR [BX].PULSE__RATE
long-real	226+EA	221-231+EA	4/6	8	2-4	FDIVR RECORDER.FREQUENCY

FDIVRP

FDIVRP destination,source
Divide real reversed and pop

Exceptions: I, D, Z, O, U, P

Operands	Execution Clocks		Transfers		Bytes	Coding Example
	Typical	Range	8086	8088		
ST(i),ST	203	198-208	0	0	2	FDIVRP ST(1),ST

FENI/FNENI

FENI (no operands)
Enable interrupts

Exceptions: None

Operands	Execution Clocks		Transfers		Bytes	Coding Example
	Typical	Range	8086	8088		
(no operands)	5	2-8	0	0	2	FNENI

FFREE

FFREE destination
Free register

Exceptions: None

Operands	Execution Clocks		Transfers		Bytes	Coding Example
	Typical	Range	8086	8088		
ST(i)	11	9-16	0	0	2	FFREE ST(1)

210911

Table 6-17 Instruction Set Reference Data (continued)

FIADD

FIADD source
Integer add

Exceptions: I, D, O, P

Operands	Execution Clocks		Transfers		Bytes	Coding Example
	Typical	Range	8086	8088		
word-integer	120+EA	102-137·EA	1/2	2	2-4	FIADD DISTANCE TRAVELLED
short-integer	125+EA	108-143·EA	2/4	4	2-4	FIADD PULSE COUNT SI

FICOM

FICOM source
Integer compare

Exceptions: I, D

Operands	Execution Clocks		Transfers		Bytes	Coding Example
	Typical	Range	8086	8088		
word-integer	80+EA	72-86+EA	1/2	2	2-4	FICOM TOOL.N_PASSES
short-integer	85+EA	78-91+EA	2/4	4	2-4	FICOM [BP+4].PARM_COUNT

FICOMP

FICOMP source
Integer compare and pop

Exceptions: I, D

Operands	Execution Clocks		Transfers		Bytes	Coding Example
	Typical	Range	8086	8088		
word-integer	82+EA	74-88+EA	1/2	2	2-4	FICOMP [BP].LIMIT [SI]
short-integer	87+EA	80-93+EA	2/4	4	2-4	FICOMP N_SAMPLES

FIDIV

FIDIV source
Integer divide

Exceptions: I, D, Z, O, U, P

Operands	Execution Clocks		Transfers		Bytes	Coding Example
	Typical	Range	8086	8088		
word-integer	230+EA	224-238+EA	1/2	2	2-4	FIDIV SURVEY.OBSERVATIONS
short-integer	236+EA	230-243+EA	2/4	4	2-4	FIDIV RELATIVE_ANGLE [DI]

FIDIVR

FIDIVR source
Integer divide reversed

Exceptions: I, D, Z, O, U, P

Operands	Execution Clocks		Transfers		Bytes	Coding Example
	Typical	Range	8086	8088		
word-integer	230+EA	225-239+EA	1/2	2	2-4	FIDIVR [BP].X_COORD
short-integer	237+EA	231-245+EA	2/4	4	2-4	FIDIVR FREQUENCY

Table 6-17 Instruction Set Reference Data (continued)

FILD

FILD source
Integer load

Exception: I

Operands	Execution Clocks		Transfers		Bytes	Coding Example
	Typical	Range	8086	8088		
word-integer	50+EA	46-54+EA	1/2	2	2-4	FILD [BX].SEQUENCE
short-integer	56+EA	52-60+EA	2/4	4	2-4	FILD STANDOFF [DI]
long-integer	64+EA	60-68+EA	4/6	8	2-4	FILD RESPONSE.COUNT

FIMUL

FIMUL source
Integer multiply

Exceptions: I, D, O, P

Operands	Execution Clocks		Transfers		Bytes	Coding Example
	Typical	Range	8086	8088		
word-integer	130+EA	124-138+EA	1/2	2	2-4	FIMUL BEARING
short-integer	136+EA	130-144+EA	2/4	4	2-4	FIMUL POSITION.Z__AXIS

FINCSTP

FINCSTP (no operands)
Increment stack pointer

Exceptions: None

Operands	Execution Clocks		Transfers		Bytes	Coding Example
	Typical	Range	8086	8088		
(no operands)	9	6-12	0	0	2	FINCSTP

FINIT/FNINIT

FINIT (no operands)
Initialize processor

Exceptions: None

Operands	Execution Clocks		Transfers		Bytes	Coding Example
	Typical	Range	8086	8088		
(no operands)	5	2-8	0	0	2	FINIT

FIST

FIST destination
Integer store

Exceptions: I, P

Operands	Execution Clocks		Transfers		Bytes	Coding Example
	Typical	Range	8086	8088		
word-integer	86+EA	80-90+EA	2/4	4	2-4	FIST OBS COUNT [SI]
short-integer	88+EA	82-92+EA	3/5	6	2-4	FIST [BP] FACTORED PULSES

210911

Table 6-17 Instruction Set Reference Data (continued)

FISTP

FISTP destination
Integer store and pop

Exceptions: I, P

Operands	Execution Clocks		Transfers		Bytes	Coding Example
	Typical	Range	8086	8088		
word-integer	88+EA	82-92+EA	2/4	4	2-4	FISTP BX ALPHA COUNT SI
short-integer	90+EA	84-94+EA	3/5	6	2-4	FISTP CORRECTED TIME
long-integer	100+EA	94-105+EA	5/7	10	2-4	FISTP PANEL N READINGS

FISUB

FISUB source
Integer subtract

Exceptions: I, D, O, P

Operands	Execution Clocks		Transfers		Bytes	Coding Example
	Typical	Range	8086	8088		
word-integer	120+EA	102-137+EA	1/2	2	2-4	FISUB BASE_FREQUENCY
short-integer	125+EA	108-143+EA	2/4	4	2-4	FISUB TRAIN SIZE [DI]

FISUBR

FISUBR source
Integer subtract reversed

Exceptions: I, D, O, P

Operands	Execution Clocks		Transfers		Bytes	Coding Example
	Typical	Range	8086	8088		
word-integer	120+EA	103-139+EA	1/2	2	2-4	FISUBR FLOOR [BX] [SI]
short-integer	125+EA	109-144+EA	2/4	4	2-4	FISUBR BALANCE

FLD

FLD source
Load real

Exceptions: I, D

Operands	Execution Clocks		Transfers		Bytes	Coding Example
	Typical	Range	8086	8088		
ST(i)	20	17-22	0	0	2	FLD ST(0)
short-real	43+EA	38-56+EA	2/4	4	2-4	FLD READING [SI].PRESSURE
long-real	46+EA	40-60+EA	4/6	8	2-4	FLD [BP].TEMPERATURE
temp-real	57+EA	53-65+EA	5/7	10	2-4	FLD SAVEREADING

FLDCW

FLDCW source
Load control word

Exceptions: None

Operands	Execution Clocks		Transfers		Bytes	Coding Example
	Typical	Range	8086	8088		
2-bytes	10+EA	7-14+EA	1/2	2	2-4	FLDCW CONTROL_WORD

210911

Table 6-17 Instruction Set Reference Data (continued)

FLDENV

FLDENV source
Load environment

Exceptions: None

Operands	Execution Clocks		Transfers		Bytes	Coding Example
	Typical	Range	8086	8088		
14-bytes	40+EA	35-45+EA	7/9	14	2-4	FLDENV [BP+6]

FLDLG2

FLDLG2 (no operands)
Load log$_{10}$2

Exceptions: I

Operands	Execution Clocks		Transfers		Bytes	Coding Example
	Typical	Range	8086	8088		
(no operands)	21	18-24	0	0	2	FLDLG2

FLDLN2

FLDLN2 (no operands)
Load log$_e$2

Exceptions: I

Operands	Execution Clocks		Transfers		Bytes	Coding Example
	Typical	Range	8086	8088		
(no operands)	20	17-23	0	0	2	FLDLN2

FLDL2E

FLDL2E (no operands)
Load log$_2$e

Exceptions: I

Operands	Execution Clocks		Transfers		Bytes	Coding Example
	Typical	Range	8086	8088		
(no operands)	18	15-21	0	0	2	FLDL2E

FLDL2T

FLDL2T (no operands)
Load log$_2$10

Exceptions: I

Operands	Execution Clocks		Transfers		Bytes	Coding Example
	Typical	Range	8086	8088		
(no operands)	19	16-22	0	0	2	FLDL2T

210911

Table 6-17 Instruction Set Reference Data (continued)

FLDPI

FLDPI (no operands)
Load π

Exceptions: I

Operands	Execution Clocks		Transfers		Bytes	Coding Example
	Typical	Range	8086	8088		
(no operands)	19	16-22	0	0	2	FLDPI

FLDZ

FLDZ (no operands)
Load +0.0

Exceptions: I

Operands	Execution Clocks		Transfers		Bytes	Coding Example
	Typical	Range	8086	8088		
(no operands)	14	11-17	0	0	2	FLDZ

FLD1

FLD1 (no operands)
Load +1.0

Exceptions: I

Operands	Execution Clocks		Transfers		Bytes	Coding Example
	Typical	Range	8086	8088		
(no operands)	18	15-21	0	0	2	FLD1

FMUL

FMUL //source/destination,source
Multiply real

Exceptions: I, D, O, U, P

Operands	Execution Clocks		Transfers		Bytes	Coding Example
	Typical	Range	8086	8088		
//ST(i),ST/ST,ST(i)'	97	90-105	0	0	2	FMUL ST,ST(3)
//ST(i),ST/ST,ST(i)	138	130-145	0	0	2	FMUL ST,ST(3)
short-real	118+EA	110-125+EA	2/4	4	2-4	FMUL SPEED__FACTOR
long-real'	120+EA	112-126+EA	4/6	8	2-4	FMUL [BP].HEIGHT
long-real	161+EA	154-168+EA	4/6	8	2-4	FMUL [BP].HEIGHT

' occurs when one or both operands is "short"—it has 40 trailing zeros in its fraction (e.g., it was loaded from a short-real memory operand).

FMULP

FMULP destination,source
Multiply real and pop

Exceptions: I, D, O, U, P

Operands	Execution Clocks		Transfers		Bytes	Coding Example
	Typical	Range	8086	8088		
ST(i),ST'	100	94-108	0	0	2	FMULP ST(1),ST
ST(i),ST	142	134-148	0	0	2	FMULP ST(1),ST

' occurs when one or both operands is "short"—it has 40 trailing zeros in its fraction (e.g., it was loaded from a short-real memory operand).

210911

Table 6-17 Instruction Set Reference Data (continued)

FNOP

FNOP (no operands)
No operation

Exceptions: None

Operands	Execution Clocks		Transfers		Bytes	Coding Example
	Typical	Range	8086	8088		
(no operands)	13	10-16	0	0	2	FNOP

FPATAN

FPATAN (no operands)
Partial arctangent

Exceptions: U, P (operands not checked)

Operands	Execution Clocks		Transfers		Bytes	Coding Example
	Typical	Range	8086	8088		
(no operands)	650	250-800	0	0	2	FPATAN

FPREM

FPREM (no operands)
Partial remainder

Exceptions: I, D, U

Operands	Execution Clocks		Transfers		Bytes	Coding Example
	Typical	Range	8086	8088		
(no operands)	125	15-190	0	0	2	FPREM

FPTAN

FPTAN (no operands)
Partial tangent

Exceptions: I, P (operands not checked)

Operands	Execution Clocks		Transfers		Bytes	Coding Example
	Typical	Range	8086	8088		
(no operands)	450	30-540	0	0	2	FPTAN

FRNDINT

FRNDINT (no operands)
Round to integer

Exceptions: I, P

Operands	Execution Clocks		Transfers		Bytes	Coding Example
	Typical	Range	8086	8088		
(no operands)	45	16-50	0	0	2	FRNDINT

Table 6-17 Instruction Set Reference Data (continued)

FRSTOR

FRSTOR source
Restore saved state

Exceptions: None

| Operands | Execution Clocks | | Transfers | | Bytes | Coding Example |
	Typical	Range	8086	8088		
94-bytes	208+EA	197-207+EA	47/49	96	2-4	FRSTOR [BP]

FSAVE/FNSAVE

FSAVE destination
Save state

Exceptions: None

| Operands | Execution Clocks | | Transfers | | Bytes | Coding Example |
	Typical	Range	8086	8088		
94-bytes	208+EA	197-207+EA	48/50	94	2-4	FSAVE [BP]

FSCALE

FSCALE (no operands)
Scale

Exceptions: I, O, U

| Operands | Execution Clocks | | Transfers | | Bytes | Coding Example |
	Typical	Range	8086	8088		
(no operands)	35	32-38	0	0	2	FSCALE

FSQRT

FSQRT (no operands)
Square root

Exceptions: I, D, P

| Operands | Execution Clocks | | Transfers | | Bytes | Coding Example |
	Typical	Range	8086	8088		
(no operands)	183	180-186	0	0	2	FSQRT

FST

FST destination
Store real

Exceptions: I, O, U, P

| Operands | Execution Clocks | | Transfers | | Bytes | Coding Example |
	Typical	Range	8086	8088		
ST(i)	18	15-22	0	0	2	FST ST(3)
short-real	87+EA	84-90+EA	3/5	6	2-4	FST CORRELATION [DI]
long-real	100+EA	96-104+EA	5/7	10	2-4	FST MEAN__READING

Table 6-17 Instruction Set Reference Data (continued)

FSTCW/FNSTCW

FSTCW destination
Store control word

Exceptions: None

Operands	Execution Clocks		Transfers		Bytes	Coding Example
	Typical	Range	8086	8088		
2-bytes	15+EA	12-18+EA	2/4	4	2-4	FSTCW SAVE_CONTROL

FSTENV/FNSTENV

FSTENV destination
Store environment

Exceptions: None

Operands	Execution Clocks		Transfers		Bytes	Coding Example
	Typical	Range	8086	8088		
14-bytes	45+EA	40-50+EA	8/10	16	2-4	FSTENV [BP]

FSTP

FSTP destination
Store real and pop

Exceptions: I, O, U, P

Operands	Execution Clocks		Transfers		Bytes	Coding Example
	Typical	Range	8086	8088		
ST(i)	20	17-24	0	0	2	FSTP ST(2)
short-real	89+EA	86-92+EA	3/5	6	2-4	FSTP [BX].ADJUSTED_RPM
long-real	102+EA	98-106+EA	5/7	10	2-4	FSTP TOTAL_DOSAGE
temp-real	55+EA	52-58+EA	6/8	12	2-4	FSTP REG_SAVE [SI]

FSTSW/FNSTSW

FSTSW destination
Store status word

Exceptions: None

Operands	Execution Clocks		Transfers		Bytes	Coding Example
	Typical	Range	8086	8088		
2-bytes	15+EA	12-18+EA	2/4	4	2-4	FSTSW SAVE_STATUS

FSUB

FSUB //source/destination,source
Subtract real

Exceptions: I,D,O,U,P

Operands	Execution Clocks		Transfers		Bytes	Coding Example
	Typical	Range	8086	8088		
//ST,ST(i)/ST(i),ST	85	70-100	0	0	2	FSUB ST,ST(2)
short-real	105+EA	90-120+EA	2/4	4	2-4	FSUB BASE_VALUE
long-real	110+EA	95-125+EA	4/6	8	2-4	FSUB COORDINATE_X

210911

Table 6-17 Instruction Set Reference Data (continued)

FSUBP

FSUBP destination,source
Subtract real and pop   Exceptions: I,D,O,U,P

| Operands | Execution Clocks | | Transfers | | Bytes | Coding Example |
	Typical	Range	8086	8088		
ST(i),ST	90	75-105	0	0	2	FSUBP ST(2),ST

FSUBR

FSUBR //source/destination,source
Subtract real reversed   Exceptions: I,D,O,U,P

| Operands | Execution Clocks | | Transfers | | Bytes | Coding Example |
	Typical	Range	8086	8088		
//ST,ST(i)/ST(i),ST	87	70-100	0	0	2	FSUBR ST,ST(1)
short-real	105+EA	90-120+EA	2/4	4	2-4	FSUBR VECTOR[SI]
long-real	110+EA	95-125+EA	4/6	8	2-4	FSUBR [BX].INDEX

FSUBRP

FSUBRP destination,source
Subtract real reversed and pop   Exceptions: I,D,O,U,P

| Operands | Executon Clocks | | Transfers | | Bytes | Coding Example |
	Typical	Range	8086	8088		
ST(i),ST	90	75-105	0	0	2	FSUBRP ST(1),ST

FTST

FTST (no operands)
Test stack top against +0.0   Exceptions: I, D

| Operands | Execution Clocks | | Transfers | | Bytes | Coding Example |
	Typical	Range	8086	8088		
(no operands)	42	38-48	0	0	2	FTST

FWAIT

FWAIT (no operands)
(CPU) Wait while 8087 is busy   Exceptions: None (CPU instruction)

| Operands | Execution Clocks | | Transfers | | Bytes | Coding Example |
	Typical	Range	8086	8088		
(no operands)	3+5n*	3+5n*	0	0	1	FWAIT

*n = number of times CPU examines $\overline{\text{TEST}}$ line before 8087 lowers BUSY.

Table 6-17 Instruction Set Reference Data (continued)

FXAM

FXAM (no operands)
Examine stack top

Exceptions : None

Operands	Execution Clocks		Transfers		Bytes	Coding Example
	Typical	Range	8086	8088		
(no operands)	17	12-23	0	0	2	FXAM

FXCH

FXCH //destination
Exchange registers

Exceptions: I

Operands	Execution Clocks		Transfers		Bytes	Coding Example
	Typical	Range	8086	8088		
//ST(i)	12	10-15	0	0	2	FXCH ST(2)

FXTRACT

FXTRACT (no operands)
Extract exponent and significand

Exceptions: I

Operands	Execution Clocks		Transfers		Bytes	Coding Example
	Typical	Range	8086	8088		
(no operands)	50	27-55	0	0	2	FXTRACT

FYL2X

FYL2X (no operands)
Y • Log$_2$ X

Exceptions: P (operands not checked)

Operands	Execution Clocks		Transfers		Bytes	Coding Example
	Typical	Range	8086	8088		
(no operands)	950	900-1100	0	0	2	FYL2X

FYL2XP1

FYL2XP1 (no operands)
Y • log$_2$(X + 1)

Exceptions: P (operands not checked)

Operands	Execution Clocks		Transfers		Bytes	Coding Example
	Typical	Range	8086	8088		
(no operands)	850	700-1000	0	0	2	FYL2XP1

210911

Table 6-17 Instruction Set Reference Data (continued)

F2XM1	F2XM1 (no operands) 2^X-1				Exceptions: U, P (operands not checked)	
Operands	**Execution Clocks**		**Transfers**		**Bytes**	**Coding Example**
	Typical	Range	8086	8088		
(no operands)	500	310-630	0	0	2	F2XM1

6.6 PROGRAMMING FACILITIES

Writing programs for the 8087 is a natural extension of the process described in Section 2.9, just as the NPX itself is an extension to the CPU. This section describes how PL/M-86 and ASM-86 programmers work with the 8087 in these languages. It also covers the 8087 software emulators provided for both translators.

The level of detail in this section is intended to give programmers a basic understanding of the software tools that can be used with the 8087, but this information is not sufficient to document the full capabilities of these facilities. The definitive description of ASM-86 and the full 8087 emulator is provided in *MCS^{TM}-86 Assembly Language Reference Manual,* Order No. 9800640, and *MCS^{TM}-86 Assembler Operating Instructions for ISIS-II Users,* Order No. 9800641. PL/M-86 and the partial emulator are documented in *PL/M-86 Programming Manual,* Order No. 9800466 and *ISIS-II PL/M-86 Compiler Operator's Manual,* Order No. 9800478. These publications may be ordered from Intel's Literature Department.

Readers should be familiar with Section 2.9 of the 8086 Family User's Manual in order to benefit from the material in this section.

PL/M-86

High level language programmers can access a useful subset of the 8087's (real or emulated) capabilities. The PL/M-86 REAL data type corresponds to the NPX's short real (32-bit) format. This data type provides a range of about $8.43*10^{-37} \leq |X| \leq 3.38*10^{38}$, with about seven significant decimal digits. This representation is adequate for the data manipulated by many microcomputer applications.

The utility of the REAL data type is extended by the PL/M-86 compiler's practice of holding intermediate results in the 8087's temporary real format. This means that the full range and precision of the processor may be utilized for intermediate results. Underflow, overflow, and rounding errors are most likely to occur during intermediate computations rather than during calculation of an expression's final result. Holding intermediate results in temporary real format greatly reduces the likelihood of overflow and underflow and eliminates roundoff as a serious source of error until the final assignment of the result is performed.

The compiler generates 8087 code to evaluate expressions that contain REAL data types, whether variables or constants or both. This means that addition, subtraction, multiplication, division, comparison, and assignment of REALs will be performed by the NPX. INTEGER expressions, on the other hand, are evaluated on the CPU.

Five built-in procedures (Table 6-18) give the PL/M-86 programmer access to 8087 functions manipulated by the processor control instructions. Prior to any arithmetic operations, a typical PL/M-86 program will setup the NPX after power up using the INIT$REAL$MATH$UNIT procedure and then issue SET$REAL$MODE to configure the NPX. SET$REAL$MODE loads the 8087 control word, and its 16-bit parameter has the format shown in Figure 6-7. The recommended value of this parameter is 033EH (projective closure, round to nearest, 64-bit precision, interrupts enabled, all exceptions masked except invalid operation). Other settings may be used at the programmer's discretion.

If any exceptions are unmasked, an exception handler must be provided in the form of an interrupt procedure that is designated to be invoked by CPU interrupt pointer (vector) number 16. The exception handler can use the GET$REAL$ERROR procedure to obtain the low-order byte of the 8087 status word and to then clear the exception flags. The byte returned by GET$REAL$ERROR contains the exception flags; these can be examined to determine the source of the exception.

The SAVE$REAL$STATUS and RESTORE$REAL$STATUS procedures are provided for multitasking environments where a running task that uses the 8087 may be preempted by another task that also uses the 8087. It is the responsibility of the preempting task to issue SAVE$REAL$STATUS before it executes any statements that affect the 8087; these include the INIT$REAL$MATH$UNIT and SET$REAL$MODE procedures as well as arithmetic expressions. SAVE$REAL$STATUS saves the 8087 state (registers, status, and control words,

etc.) on the CPU's stack. RESTORE$REAL$STATUS reloads the state information; the preempting task must invoke this procedure before terminating in order to restore the 8087 to its state at the time the running task was preempted. This enables the preempted task to resume execution from the point of its preemption.

Note that the PL/M-86 compiler prefixes every 8087 instruction with a CPU WAIT. Therefore, programmers should not code PL/M-86 statements that generate 8087 instructions if the NPX can request an interrupt and that interrupt is blocked (this may result in the endless wait condition described in Volume 2).

ASM-86

The ASM-86 assembly language provides a single uniform set of facilities for all combinations of the 8086,88/80186,188/8087 processors. Assembly language programs can be written to be completely independent of the processor set on which they are destined to execute.

This means that a program written originally for an 8088 alone will execute on an 8086/8087 or 80186,88/8087 combination without re-assembling. The programmer's view of the hardware is a single machine with these resources:

- 160 instructions
- 12 data types
- 8 general registers

Table 6-18 PL/M-86 Built-In Procedures

Procedure	8087 Instruction	Description
INIT$REAL$MATH$UNIT[1]	FINIT	Initialize processor.
SET$REAL$MODE	FLDCW	Set exception masks, rounding precision, and infinity controls.
GET$REAL$ERROR[2]	FNSTSW & FNCLEX	Store, then clear, exception flags.
SAVE$REAL$STATUS	FNSAVE	Save processor state.
RESTORE$REAL$STATUS	FRSTOR	Restore processor state.

[1]Also initializes interrupt pointers for emulation.

[2]Returns low-order byte of status word.

- 4 segment registers

- 8 floating-point registers, organized as a stack

The combination of the assembly language and the 8087 emulator decouples the source code from the execution vehicle. For example, the assembler automatically inserts CPU WAIT instructions in front of those 8087 instructions that require them. If the program actually runs with the emulator rather than the 8087, the WAITs are automatically removed at link time (since there is no NPX for which to wait).

DEFINING DATA

The ASM-86 directives shown in Table 6-19 allocate storage for 8087 variables and constants. As with other storage allocation directives, the assembler associates a type with any variable defined with these directives. The type value is equal to the length of the storage unit in bytes (10 for DT, 8 for DQ, etc.). The assembler checks the type of any variable coded in an instruction to be certain that it is compatible with the instruction. For example, the coding FIADD ALPHA will be flagged as an error if ALPHA's type is not 2 or 4, because integer addition is only available for word and short integer data types. The operand's type also tells the assembler which machine instruction to produce; although to the programmer there is only an FIADD instruction, a different machine instruction is required for each operand type.

On occasion it is desirable to use an instruction with an operand that has no declared type. For example, if register BX points to a short integer variable, a programmer may want to code FIADD [BX]. This can be done by informing the assembler of the operand's type in the instruction, coding FIADD DWORD

PTR [BX]. The corresponding overrides for the other storage allocations are WORD PTR, QWORD PTR, and TBYTE PTR.

The assembler does not, however, check the types of operands used in processor control instructions. Coding FRSTOR [BP] implies that the programmer has set up register BP to point to the stack location where the processor's 94-byte state record has been previously saved.

The initial values for 8087 constants may be coded in several different ways. Binary integer constants may be specified as bit strings, decimal integers, octal integers, or hexadecimal strings. Packed decimal values are normally written as decimal integers, although the assembler will accept and convert other representations of integers. Real values may be written as ordinary decimal real numbers (decimal point required), as decimal numbers in scientific notation, or as hexadecimal strings. Using hexadecimal strings is primarily intended for defining special values such as infinities, NANs, and nonnormalized numbers. Most programmers will find that ordinary decimal and scientific decimal provide the simplest way to initialize 8087 constants. Figure 6-15 compares several ways of setting the various 8087 data types to the same initial value.

Note that preceding 8087 variables and constants with the ASM-86 EVEN directive ensures that the operands will be word-aligned in memory. This will produce the best performance in 8086/80186-based systems, and is good practice even for 8088/80188 software, in the event that the programs are transferred to an 8086/80186. All 8087 data types occupy integral numbers of words so that no storage is "wasted" if blocks of variables are defined together and preceded by a single EVEN declarative.

```
; THE FOLLOWING ALL ALLOCATE THE CONSTANT: -126
; NOTE TWO'S COMPLEMENT STORAGE OF NEGATIVE BINARY INTEGERS.
;
; EVEN                               ; FORCE WORD ALIGNMENT
WORD_INTEGER    DW   1111111110000010B ; BIT STRING
SHORT_INTEGER   DD   0FFFFFF82H       ; HEX STRING MUST START WITH DIGIT
LONG_INTEGER    DQ   -126             ; ORDINARY DECIMAL
SHORT_REAL      DD   -126.0           ; NOTE PRESENCE OF '.'
LONG_REAL       DD   -1.26E2          ; ''SCIENTIFIC''
PACKED_DECIMAL  DT   -126             ; ORDINARY DECIMAL INTEGER
; IN THE FOLLOWING, SIGN AND EXPONENT IS 'C005',
;    SIGNIFICAND IS '7E00...00', 'R' INFORMS ASSEMBLER THAT
;    THE STRING REPRESENTS A REAL DATA TYPE.
;
TEMP_REAL       DT   0C0057E00000000000000R  ; HEX STRING
```

Figure 6-15 Sample 8087 Constants

Table 6-19 8087 Storage Allocation Directives

Directive	Interpretation	8087 Data Types
DW	Define Word	Word integer
DD	Define Doubleword	Short integer, short real
DQ	Define Quadword	Long integer, long real
DT	Define Tenbyte	Packed decimal, temporary real

RECORDS AND STRUCTURES

The ASM-86 RECORD and STRUC (structure de-claratives can be very useful in NPX programming. The record facility can be used to define the bit fields of the control, status, and tag words.

Figure 6-16 shows one definition of the status words and how it might be used in a routine that polls the 8087 until it has completed an instruction.

```
; RESERVE SPACE FOR STATUS WORD
STATUS_WORD              DW ?
; LAY OUT STATUS WORD FIELDS
STATUS RECORD
&       BUSY:               1,
&       COND_CODE3:         1,
&       STACK_TOP:          3,
&       COND_CODE2:         1,
&       COND_CODE1:         1,
&       COND_CODE0:         1,
&       INT_REQ:            1,
&       RESERVED:           1,
&       P_FLAG:             1,
&       U_FLAG:             1,
&       O_FLAG:             1,
&       Z_FLAG:             1,
&       D_FLAG:             1,
&       I_FLAG:             1
; POLL STATUS WORD UNTIL 8087 IS NOT BUSY
POLL:       FNSTSW   STATUS_WORD
            TEST     STATUS_WORD, MASK BUSY
            JNZ      POLL
```

Figure 6-16 Status Word RECORD Definition

Because structures allow different but related data types to be grouped together, they often provide a natural way to represent "real world" data organizations. The fact that the structure template may be "moved" about in memory adds to its flexibility. Figure 6-17 shows a simple structure that might be used to represent data consisting of a series of test score samples. A structure could also be used to define the organization of the information stored and loaded by the FSTENV and FLDENV instructions.

```
SAMPLE      STRUC

  N_OBS             DD    ?    ;SHORT INTEGER
  MEAN              DQ    ?    ;LONG REAL
  MODE              DW    ?    ;WORD INTEGER
  STD_DEV           DQ    ?    ;LONG REAL
  ;ARRAY OF OBSERVATIONS -- WORD INTEGER
  TEST_SCORES       DW    1000 DUP (?)
SAMPLE ENDS
```

Figure 6-17 Structure Definition

ADDRESSING MODES

8087 memory data can be accessed with any of the CPU's twenty-two memory addressing modes. This means that 8087 data types can be incorporated in data aggregates ranging from simple to complex according to the needs of the application. The address-ing modes, and the ASM-86 notation used to specify them in instructions, make the accessing of structures, arrays, arrays of structures, and other or-ganizations direct and straightforward.

Table 6-20 gives several examples of 8087 instruc-tions coded with operands that illustrate different ad-dressing modes.

8087 EMULATORS

Intel offers two software products that provide the functional equivalent of an 8087, implemented in 8086,88/80186,88 software. The full emulator (E8087) emulates all 8087 instructions. The partial emulator (PE8087) is a smaller version that imple-ments only the instructions needed to support PL/M-86 programs. The full emulator adds about 16K bytes to a program, while the partial emulator executes in about 8K. Any emulated program will deliver the same results (except for timing) if it is ex-ecuted on 8087 hardware. (The partial emulator does not support transcendental functions.)

Table 6-20 Addressing Mode Examples

Coding		Interpretation
FIADD	ALPHA	ALPHA is a simple scalar (mode is direct).
FDIVR	ALPHA.BETA	BETA is a field in a structure that is "overlaid" on ALPHA (mode is direct).
FMUL	QWORD PTR [BX]	BX contains the address of a long real variable (mode is register indirect).
FSUB	ALPHA [SI]	ALPHA is an array and SI contains the offset of an array element from the start of the array (mode is indexed).
FILD	[BP].BETA	BP contains the address of a structure on the CPU stack and BETA is a field in the structure (mode is based).
FBLD	TBYTE PTR [BX] [DI]	BX contains the address of a packed decimal array and DI contains the offset of an array element (mode is based indexed).

The emulators may be viewed as consisting of emulated hardware and emulated instructions. The emulators establish in CPU memory the equivalent of the 8087 register stack, control, and status words and all other programmer-accessible elements of the NPX architecture. The emulator instructions utilize the same algorithms as their hardware counterparts. Emulator instructions are actually implemented as CPU interrupt procedures. During relocation and linkage, the 8087 machine instructions generated by the ASM-86 and PL/M-86 translators are changed to software interrupt (INT) instructions which invoke these procedures as the CPU processes its instruction stream.

Since the decision to produce real or emulated 8087 instructions is made at link time, a program may be switched from one mode to the other without retranslating the source code. When the PL/M-86 compiler or ASM-86 assembler places an 8087 machine instruction into an object module, it also inserts a special external reference. This reference is satisfied by linking the object module to one of two Intel-supplied libraries: the real library, or the emula-

tor library. If the real library is specified, LINK-86 simply deletes the external references, leaving the original 8087 machine instructions.

To run on an emulated 8087, the object program is linked to the emulator library and to a file containing the code of either the full or the partial emulator. LINK-86 then adds the emulator code to the program and changes the 8087 machine instructions (and their preceding WAITs) to CPU software interrupt instructions. Any FWAIT instructions are also changed to CPU NOPs.

Note that an explicitly-coded CPU WAIT instruction will *not* be changed; if it is executed under emulation, the CPU will wait forever. This is why the FWAIT mnemonic should always be used when the external processor that the CPU is to wait for is an 8087.

In order to be compatible with E8087, ASM-86 programs should observe the following conventions:

- Their stack segment and class should be named STACK.

- Interrupt pointer (vector) 16 should be designated for the user's exception handler interrupt procedure. Interrupt pointer 16 only needs designating if any exceptions are unmasked.

- The external procedure INIT87 should be called in the program's initialization (power-up) sequence. If the emulator is being used, this procedure will initialize CPU interrupt pointers 20-31 to the addresses of emulator procedures and will execute an (emulated) FINIT instruction. If the program is not being emulated, INIT87 simply executes the FINIT instruction.

PL/M-86 automatically observes corresponding conventions.

Programming Example

Figures 6-18 and 6-19 show the PL/M-86 and ASM-86 code for a simple 8087 program, called ARRSUM. The program references an array (X$ARRAY), which contains 0-100 short real values; the integer variable NOFX indicates the number of array elements the program is to consider. ARRSUM steps through X$ARRAY accumulating three sums:

- SUM$X, the sum of the array values;

- SUM$INDEXES, the sum of each array value times its index, where the index of the first element is 1, the second is 2, etc.;

- SUM$SQUARES, the sum of each array element squared.

```
PL/M-86 COMPILER    DICE

ISIS-II PL/M-86 V1.2 COMPILATION OF MODULE DICE
OBJECT MODULE PLACED IN :F1:DICE.OBJ
COMPILER INVOKED BY:  PLM86 :F1:DICE.P86 XREF

     1          DICE: DO;
                 /* THIS PROGRAM SIMULATES THE ROLL OF A PAIR OF DICE */

                 /* GIVE NAMES TO CONSTANTS */
     2     1     DECLARE CLEAR$CRT1    LITERALLY '01BH';  /* INTELLEC  */
     3     1     DECLARE CLEAR$CRT2    LITERALLY '045H';  /*  CRT      */
     4     1     DECLARE HOME$CURSOR1  LITERALLY '01BH';  /* CONTROL   */
     5     1     DECLARE HOME$CURSOR2  LITERALLY '048H';  /*  CODES    */
     6     1     DECLARE SPACE         LITERALLY '020H';  /*ASCII BLANK*/

                 /* PROGRAM VARIABLES */
     7     1     DECLARE (RANDOM$NUMBER,SAVE)  WORD;

                 /* CONSOLE OUTPUT PROCEDURE */
     8     1     CO: PROCEDURE(X) EXTERNAL;
     9     2        DECLARE X    BYTE;
    10     2        END CO;

                 /* RANDOM NUMBER GENERATOR PROCEDURE         */
                 /* ALGORITHM FOR 16-BIT RANDOM NUMBER FROM:  */
                 /* "A GUIDE TO PL/M PROGRAMMING FOR          */
                 /*    MICROCOMPUTER APPLICATIONS,"           */
                 /*     DANIEL D. MCCRACKEN,                  */
                 /*     ADDISON-WESLEY, 1978                  */
    11     1     RANDOM: PROCEDURE WORD;
    12     2        RANDOM$NUMBER = SAVE;          /*START WITH OLD NUMBER*/
    13     2        RANDOM$NUMBER = 2053 * RANDOM$NUMBER + 13849;
    14     2        SAVE = RANDOM$NUMBER;          /*SAVE FOR NEXT TIME*/
                    /*FORCE 16-BIT NUMBER INTO RANGE 1-6*/
    15     2        RANDOM$NUMBER = RANDOM$NUMBER MOD 6  + 1;
    16     2        RETURN RANDOM$NUMBER;
    17     2        END RANDOM;

                 /* MAIN ROUTINE */
                 /* CLEAR THE SCREEN*/
    18     1     CALL CO(CLEAR$CRT1);
    19     1     CALL CO(CLEAR$CRT2);

                 /* ROLL THE DICE UNTIL INTERRUPTED */
    20     1     DO WHILE 1;  /*"DO FOREVER"*/
                    /*NOTE THAT ADDING 30 TO THE DIE VALUE */
                    /*  CONVERTS IT TO ASCII.              */
    21     2        CALL CO(RANDOM + 030H);        /*1ST DIE*/
    22     2        CALL CO(SPACE);                /*BLANK*/
    23     2        CALL CO(RANDOM + 030H);        /*2ND DIE*/
                    /* HOME THE CURSOR */
```

Figure 6-18 Sample PL/M-86 Program

```
24  2          CALL CO(HOME$CURSOR1);
25  2          CALL CO(HOME$CURSOR2);
26  2          END;

27  1    END DICE;
```

CROSS-REFERENCE LISTING

```
    DEFN  ADDR   SIZE  NAME, ATTRIBUTES, AND REFERENCES
    ----  ------ ----- -------------------------------------------

      2                CLEARCRT1               LITERALLY
                                                 18

      3                CLEARCRT2               LITERALLY
                                                 19

      8  0000H         CO                      PROCEDURE EXTERNAL(0) STACK=0000H
                                                 18   19   21   22   23   24   25

      1  0002H   71    DICE                    PROCEDURE STACK=0004H

      4                HOMECURSOR1             LITERALLY
                                                 24

      5                HOMECURSOR2             LITERALLY
                                                 25

     11  0049H   44    RANDOM                  PROCEDURE WORD STACK=0002H
                                                 21   23

      7  0000H    2    RANDOMNUMBER            WORD
                                                 12   13   14   15   16

      7  0002H    2    SAVE                    WORD
                                                 12   14

      6                SPACE                   LITERALLY
                                                 22

      8  0000H    1    X                       BYTE PARAMETER
                                                  9
```

MODULE INFORMATION:

```
    CODE AREA SIZE     = 0075H    117D
    CONSTANT AREA SIZE = 0000H      0D
    VARIABLE AREA SIZE = 0004H      4D
    MAXIMUM STACK SIZE = 0004H      4D
    51 LINES READ
    0 PROGRAM ERROR(S)
```

END OF PL/M-86 COMPILATION

Figure 6-18 Sample PL/M-86 Program (continued)

```
MCS-86 MACRO ASSEMBLER    DICE

ISIS-II MCS-86 MACRO ASSEMBLER V2.0 ASSEMBLY OF MODULE DICE
OBJECT MODULE PLACED IN :F1:DICE.OBJ
ASSEMBLER INVOKED BY: ASM86 :F1:DICE.A86 XREF

LOC  OBJ                LINE    SOURCE

                          1     ; THIS PROGRAM SIMULATES THE ROLL OF A PAIR OF DICE
                          2
                          3     ; CONSOLE OUTPUT PROCEDURE
                          4            EXTRN   CO:NEAR
                          5
                          6     ; SEGMENT GROUP DEFINITIONS NEEDED FOR PL/M-86 COMPATIBILITY
                          7     CGROUP  GROUP   CODE
                          8     DGROUP  GROUP   DATA,STACK
                          9
                         10     ; INFORM ASSEMBLER OF SEGMENT REGISTER CONTENTS.
                         11            ASSUME  CS:CGROUP,DS:DGROUP,SS:DGROUP,ES:NOTHING
                         12
                         13     ; ALLOCATE DATA
----                     14     DATA    SEGMENT PUBLIC  'DATA'
                         15     ; NOTE THAT THE FOLLOWING ARE PASSED ON THE STACK TO THE PL/M-86
                         16     ; PROCEDURE 'CO'.  BY CONVENTION, A BYTE PARAMETER IS PASSED IN
                         17     ; THE LOW-ORDER 8-BITS OF A WORD ON THE STACK.  HENCE, THESE ARE
                         18     ; DEFINED AS WORD VALUES, THOUGH THEY OCCUPY 1 BYTE ONLY.
```

Figure 6-19 Sample ASM-86 Program

```
0000 1B00        19    CLEAR_CRT1     DW     01BH    ; INTELLEC
0002 4500        20    CLEAR_CRT2     DW     045H    ; CRT
0004 1B00        21    HOME_CURSOR1   DW     01BH    ; CONTROL
0006 4800        22    HOME_CURSOR2   DW     048H    ; CODES
0008 2000        23    SPACE          DW     020H    ; ASCII BLANK
000A ????        24    SAVE           DW     ?       ; HOLDS LAST 16-BIT RANDOM NUMBER
----             25    DATA    ENDS
                 26
                 27
                 28    ; ALLOCATE STACK SPACE
0000 (20         29    STACK    SEGMENT STACK   'STACK'
     ????        30             DW      20 DUP (?)
     )
                 31    ; LABEL INITIAL TOS: FOR LATER USE.
0028             32    STACK_TOP       LABEL   WORD
----             33    STACK    ENDS
                 34
                 35
                 36    ; PROGRAM CODE
----             37    CODE     SEGMENT PUBLIC  'CODE'
                 38
                 39
                 40    ; RANDOM NUMBER GENERATOR PROCEDURE
                 41    ; ALGORITHM FOR 16-BIT RANDOM NUMBER FROM:
                 42    ;    "A GUIDE TO PL/M PROGRAMMING FOR
                 43    ;    MICROCOMPUTER APPLICATIONS,"
                 44    ;     DANIEL D. MCCRACKEN
                 45    ;     ADDISON-WESLEY, 1978
0000             46    RANDOM   PROC
0000 A10A00      R    47             MOV     AX,SAVE    ; NEW NUMBER =
```

```
MCS-86 MACRO ASSEMBLER     DICE


LOC  OBJ              LINE    SOURCE

0003 B90508          48             MOV     CX,2053      ;   OLD NUMBER * 2053
0006 F7E1            49             MUL     CX           ;      + 13849
0008 051936          50             ADD     AX,13849
000B A30A00      R   51             MOV     SAVE,AX      ; SAVE FOR NEXT TIME
                    52             ; FORCE 16-BIT NUMBER INTO RANGE 1 - 6
                    53             ;   BY MODULO 6 DIVISION + 1
000E 2BD2           54             SUB     DX,DX        ; CLEAR UPPER DIVIDEND
0010 B90600         55             MOV     CX,6         ; SET DIVISOR
0013 F7F1           56             DIV     CX           ; DIVIDE BY 6
0015 8BC2           57             MOV     AX,DX        ; REMAINDER TO AX
0017 40             58             INC     AX           ; ADD 1
0018 C3             59             RET                  ; RESULT IN AX
                    60    RANDOM   ENDP
                    61
                    62    ; MAIN PROGRAM
                    63
                    64
                    65    ; LOAD SEGMENT REGISTERS
                    66    ; NOTE PROGRAM DOES NOT USE ES; CS IS INITIALIZED BY HARDWARE RESET;
                    67    ; DATA & STACK ARE MEMBERS OF SAME GROUP, SO ARE TREATED AS A SINGLE
                    68    ; MEMORY SEGMENT POINTED TO BY BOTH DS & SS.
0019 B8----     R   69    START:   MOV     AX,DGROUP
001C 8ED8           70             MOV     DS,AX
001E 8ED0           71             MOV     SS,AX
                    72
                    73    ; INITIALIZE STACK POINTER
0020 BC2800         74             MOV     SP,OFFSET DGROUP:STACK_TOP
                    75
                    76    ; CLEAR THE SCREEN
0023 FF360000   R   77             PUSH    CLEAR_CRT1
0027 E80000     E   78             CALL    CO
002A FF360200   R   79             PUSH    CLEAR_CRT2
002E E80000     E   80             CALL    CO
                    81
                    82    ; ROLL THE DICE UNTIL INTERRUPTED
0031 E8CCFF         83    ROLL:    CALL    RANDOM       ; GET 1ST DIE IN AL
0034 0430           84             ADD     AL,030H      ; CONVERT TO ASCII
0036 50             85             PUSH    AX           ; PASS IT TO
0037 E80000     E   86             CALL    CO           ;   CONSOLE OUTPUT
003A FF360800   R   87             PUSH    SPACE        ; OUTPUT
003E E80000     E   88             CALL    CO           ;   A BLANK
0041 E8BCFF         89             CALL    RANDOM       ; GET 2ND DIE IN AL
0044 0430           90             ADD     AL,030H      ; CONVERT TO ASCII
0046 50             91             PUSH    AX           ; PASS IT TO
0047 E80000     E   92             CALL    CO           ;   CONSOLE OUTPUT
```

Figure 6-19 Sample ASM-86 Program (continued)

```
                                    93    ; HOME THE CURSOR
     004A FF360400      R           94          PUSH    HOME_CURSOR1
     004E E80000        E           95          CALL    CO
     0051 FF360600      R           96          PUSH    HOME_CURSOR2
     0055 E80000        E           97          CALL    CO
                                    98    ; CONTINUE FOREVER
     0058 EBD7                      99          JMP     ROLL
     ----                         100    CODE    ENDS
                                  101

     XREF SYMBOL TABLE LISTING
     ---- ------ ----- -------

     NAME              TYPE    VALUE   ATTRIBUTES, XREFS

     ??SEG . . . .     SEGMENT         SIZE=0000H PARA PUBLIC
     CGROUP. . . .     GROUP           CODE    7# 11
     CLEAR_CRT1. .     V WORD  0000H   DATA   19# 77
     CLEAR_CRT2. .     V WORD  0002H   DATA   20# 79
     CO. . . . . .     L NEAR  0000H   EXTRN   4# 78 80 86 88 92 95 97
     CODE. . . . .     SEGMENT         SIZE=005AH PARA PUBLIC 'CODE'   7# 37 100
     DATA. . . . .     SEGMENT         SIZE=000CH PARA PUBLIC 'DATA'   8# 14 25
     DGROUP. . . .     GROUP           DATA STACK    8# 11 11 69 74
     HOME_CURSOR1.     V WORD  0004H   DATA   21# 94
     HOME_CURSOR2.     V WORD  0006H   DATA   22# 96
     RANDOM. . . .     L NEAR  0000H   CODE   46# 60 83 89
     ROLL. . . . .     L NEAR  0031H   CODE   83# 99
     SAVE. . . . .     V WORD  000AH   DATA   24# 47 51
     SPACE . . . .     V WORD  0008H   DATA   23# 87
     STACK . . . .     SEGMENT         SIZE=0028H PARA STACK 'STACK'
     STACK_TOP . .     V WORD  0028H   STACK  32# 74
     START . . . .     L NEAR  0019H   CODE   69# 104


     ASSEMBLY COMPLETE, NO ERRORS FOUND
```

Figure 6-19 Sample ASM-86 Program (continued)

(A true program, of course, would go beyond these steps to store and use the results of these calculations.) The control word is set with the recommended values: projective closure, round to nearest, 64-bit precision, interrupts enabled, and all exceptions masked except invalid operation. It is assumed that an exception handler has been written to field the invalid operation, if it occurs, and that it is invoked by interrupt pointer 16. Either version of the program will run on an actual or an emulated 8087 without altering the code shown.

The PL/M-86 version of ARRSUM (Figure 6-18) is very straight forward and illustrates how easily the 8087 can be used in this language. After declaring variables, the program calls built-in procedures to initialize the processor (or its emulator) and to load the control word. The program clears the sum variables and then steps through X$ARRAY with a DO-loop. The loop control takes into account PL/M-86's practice of considering the index of the first element of an array to be 0. In the computation of SUM$INDEXES, the built-in procedure FLOAT converts I+1 from integer to real because the language does not support "mixed mode" arithmetic. One of the strengths of the NPX, of course, is that it *does* support arithmetic on mixed data types, and assembly language programmers can take advantage of this facility.

The ASM-86 version (Figure 6-19) defines the external procedure INIT87, which makes the different initialization requirements of the processor and its emulator transparent to the source code. After defining the data, and setting up the segment registers and stack pointer, the program calls INIT87 and loads the control word. The computation begins with the next three instructions, which clear three registers by loading (pushing) zeros onto the stack. As shown in Figure 6-20, these registers remain at the bottom of the stack throughout the computation while temporary values are pushed on and popped off the stack above them.

The program uses the CPU LOOP instruction to control its iteration through X__ARRAY; register CX, which LOOP automatically decrements, is loaded with N__OF__X, the number of array elements to be summed. Register S1 is used to select (index) the array elements. The program steps through X__ARRAY from "back to front", so SI is initialized to point at the element just beyond the first element to be processed. The ASM-86 TYPE operator is used to determine the number of bytes in each array element. This permits changing X__ARRAY to a long real array by simply changing its definition (DD to DQ) and re-assembling.

Figure 6-20 shows the effect of the instructions in the program loop on the NPX register stack. The figure assumes that the program is in its first iteration, that N__OF__X is 20, and that X__ARRAY(19) (the 20th element) contains the value 2.5. When the loop terminates, the three sums are left as the top stack elements so that the program ends by simply popping them into memory variables.

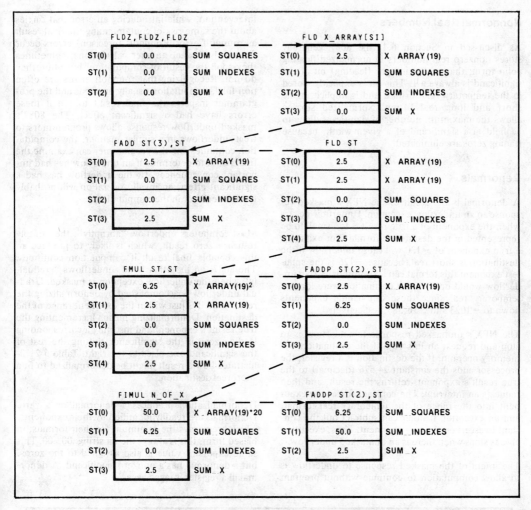

Figure 6-20 Instructions and Register Stack

6.7 SPECIAL TOPICS

This section describes features of the 8087 which will be of interest to groups of users who have special requirements. Most users will not need to understand this material in detail in order to utilize the NPX successfully. Most readers, then, can either browse this section, or skip it altogether in favor of the programming examples in Section 6.8.

The first four topics in this section cover the 8087's generation and handling of nonnormalized real values, zeros, infinities, and NANs. In the great majority of applications, these special values will either not appear at all, or in the case of zeros, will function according to the normal rules of arithmetic. Next the bit encodings of each data type are summarized in table form, including special values. This information may be of use to programmers who are sorting these data types or are decoding unformatted memory dumps or data monitored from the bus. At the end of the section is a table that lists all 8087 exception conditions by class, and the processor's masked response to each exception. This information will principally be of use to writers of exception handlers and to anyone else interested in ascertaining the exact conditions under which the NPX signals a given type of exception.

Nonnormal Real Numbers

As discussed in Section 6.4, the 8087 generally stores nonzero real numbers in normalized floating point form; that is, the integer (leading) bit of the significand is always a 1. This bit is explicitly stored in the temporary real format, and is implicit in the short and long real forms. Normalized storage allows the maximum number of significant digits to be held in a significand of a given width, because leading zeros are eliminated.

Denormals

A denormal is the result of the NPX's masked response to an underflow exception. Underflow occurs when the exponent of a true result is too small to be represented in the destination format. For example, a true exponent of -130 will cause underflow if the destination is short real, because -126 is the smallest exponent this format can accommodate. (No underflow would occur if the destination were long or temporary real since these can handle exponents down to -1023 and $-16,383$, respectively.)

The NPX's unmasked response to underflow is to stop and request an interrupt if the destination is a memory operand. If the destination is a register, the processor adds the constant 24,576 (decimal) to the true result's exponent, returns the result, and then requests an interrupt. The constant forces the exponent into the range of the temporary real format, and an exception handler can subtract out the constant to ascertain the true exponent. Thus, execution always stops when there is an unmasked underflow.

The intent of the masked response to underflow is to allow computation to continue without program intervention, while introducing an error that carries about the same risk of contaminating the final result as roundoff error. Roundoff (precison) errors occur frequently in real number calculations; sometimes they spoil the result of computation, but often they do not. Recognizing that roundoff errors are often non-fatal, computation usually proceeds and the programmer inspects the final result to see if these errors have had a significant effect. The 8087's masked underflow response allows programmers to treat underflows in a similar manner; the computation continues and the programmer can examine the final result to determine if an underflow has had important consequences. (If the underflow has had a significant effect, an invalid operation will probably be signaled later in the computation.)

Most computers underflow "abruptly"; they simply return a zero result, which is likely to produce an unacceptable final result if computation continues. The 8087, on the other hand, underflows "gradually" when the underflow exception is masked. Gradual underflow is accomplished by denormalizing the result until it is just within the exponent range of the destination. Denormalizing means incrementing the true result's exponent and inserting a corresponding leading zero in the significand, shifting the rest of the significand one place to the right. Table 6-21 illustrates how a result might be denormalized to fit a short real destination.

Denormalization produces a denormal or a zero. Denormals are readily identified by their exponents, which are always the minimum for their formats; in biased form, this is always the bit string: 00...00. This same exponent value is also assigned to the zeros, but a denormal has a nonzero significand. A denormal in a register is tagged special.

Operation	Sign	Exponent[1]	Significand
True Result	0	-129	1△01011100...00
Denormalize	0	-128	0△101011100...00
Denormalize	0	-127	0△0101011100...00
Denormalize	0	-126	0△00101011100...00
Denormal Result[2]	0	-126	0△00101011100...00

Notes:

[1]expressed as unbiased, decimal number

[2]Before storing, significand is rounded to 24 bits, integer bit is dropped, and exponent is biased by adding 126.

The denormalization process may cause the loss of the low-order significand bits as they are shifted off the right. In a severe case, *all* the significand bits of the true result are shifted out and replaced by the leading zeros. In this case, the result of denormalization is a true zero, and if the value is in a register, it is tagged as such. However, this is a comparatively rare occurrence, and, in any case, is no worse than "abrupt" underflow.

Denormals are rarely encountered in most applications. Typical debugged algorithms generate extremely small results during the evaluation of intermediate subexpressions; the final result is usually of an appropriate magnitude for its short or long real destination. If intermediate results are held in temporary real, as is recommended, the great range of this format makes underflow very unlikely. Denormals are likely to arise only when an application generates a great many intermediates, so many that they cannot be held on the register stack or in temporary real memory variables. If storage limitations force the use of short or long reals for intermediates, and small values are produced, underflow may occur, and if masked, may generate denormals.

Accessing a denormal may produce an exception as shown in Table 6-22. (The denormalized exception signals that a denormal has been fetched.) Denormals may have reduced significance due to lost low-order bits, and an option of the proposed IEEE standard precludes operations on non-normalized operands. This option may be implemented in the form of an exception handler that responds to unmasked denormalized exceptions. Most users will mask this exception so that computation may proceed; any loss of accuracy will be analyzed by the user when the final result is delivered.

As Table 6-22 shows, the division and remainder operations do not accept denormal divisors and raise the invalid operation exception. Recall, also, that the transcendental instructions require normalized operands and do *not* check for exceptions. In all other cases, the NPX converts denormals to unnormals, and the unnormal arithmetic rules then apply.

Unnormals

An unnormal is the "descendent" of a denormal and therefore of a masked underflow response. An unnormal may exist only in the temporary real format; it may have any exponent that a normal may have, but it is distinguished from a normal by the integer bit of its significand, which is always 0. An unnormal in a register is tagged valid.

Unnormals allow arithmetic to continue following an underflow while still retaining their identity as numbers which may have reduced significance. That is, unnormal operands generate unnormal results, so long as their unnormality has a significant effect on the result. Unnormals are thus prevented from "masquerading" as normals, numbers which have full significance. On the other hand, if an unnormal has an insignificant effect on a calculation with a normal, the result will be normal. For example, adding a small unnormal to a large normal yields a normal result. The converse situation yields an unnormal.

Table 6-23 shows how the instruction set deals with unnormal operands. Note that the unnormal may be the original operand or a temporary created by the 8087 from a denormal. Unnormals can be converted to normals using the FPREM instruction (refer to this instruction in Section 6.5)

Table 6-22 Exceptions Due to Denormal Operands

Operation	Exception	Masked Response
FLD (short/long real)	D	Load as equivalent unnormal
arithmetic (except following)	D	Convert (in a work area) denormal to equivalent unnormal and proceed
Compare and test	D	Convert (in a work area) denormal to equivalent unnormal and proceed
Division or FPREM with denormal divisor	I	Return real *indefinite*

Table 6-23 Unnormal Operands and Results

Operation	Result
Addition/subtraction	Normalization of operand with larger absolute value determines normalization of result.
Multiplication	If either operand is unnormal, result is unnormal.
Division (unnormal dividend only)	Result is unnormal.
FPREM (unnormal dividend only)	Result is normalized.
Division/FPREM (unnormal divisor)	Signal invalid operation.
Compare/FTST	Normalize as much as possible before making comparison.
FRNDINT	Normalize as much as possible before rounding.
FSQRT	Signal invalid operation.
FST, FSTP (short/long real destination)	If value is above destination's underflow boundary, then signal invalid operation; else signal underflow.
FSTP (temporary real destination)	Store as usual.
FIST, FISTP, FBSTP	Signal invalid operation.
FLD	Load as usual.
FXCH	Exchange as usual.
Transcendental instructions	Undefined; operands must be normal and are not checked.

Zeros and Pseudo-Zeros

As discussed in Section 6.4, the real and packed decimal data types support signed zeros, while the binary integers represent a single zero, signed positive. The signed zeros behave, however, as though they are a single unsigned quantity. If necessary, the FXAM instruction may be used to determine a zero's sign.

The zeros discussed are called true zeros; if one of them is loaded or generated in a register, the register is tagged zero. Table 6-24 lists the result of instructions executed with zero operands and also shows how a true zero may be created from nonzero operands. (Nonzero operands are denoted "X" or "Y" in the table.)

Only the temporary real format may contain a special class of values called pseudo-zeros. A pseudo-zero is an unnormal whose significand is all zeros, but whose (biased) exponent is nonzero (true zeros have a zero exponent). Neither is a pseudo-zero's exponent all ones, since this encoding is reserved for infinities and NANs. A pseudo-zero result will be produced if two unnormals, containing a total of more than 64 leading zero bits in their significands, are multiplied together. This is a remote possibility in most applications, but it can happen.

Pseudo-zero operands behave like unnormals, except in the following cases where they produce the same results as true zeros:

- compare and test instructions

- FRNDINT (round to integer 9)

- division, where the dividend is either a true zero or a pseudo-zero (the divisor is a pseudo-zero).

In addition and subtraction of a pseudo-zero and a true zero or another pseudo-zero, the pseudo-zero(s) behave like unnormals, except for the determination of the result's sign. The sign is determined as shown in Table 6-24 for two true zero operands.

Table 6-24 Zero Operands and Results

Operation/Operands	Result	Operation/Operands	Result
FLD, FBLD [1]		**Division**	
+0	+0	±0 ÷ ±0	Invalid operation
−0	−0	±X ÷ ±0	Zerodivide
FILD [2]		+0 ÷ +X, −0 ÷ −X	+0
+0	+0	+0 ÷ −X, −0 ÷ +X	−0
FST, FSTP		−X ÷ −Y, +X ÷ +Y	+0, underflow [8]
+0	+0	−X ÷ +Y, +X ÷ −Y	−0, underflow [8]
−0	−0		
+X [3]	+0	**FPREM**	
−X [3]	−0	±0 rem ±0	Invalid operation
FBSTP		±X rem ±0	Invalid operation
+0	+0	+0 rem +X, +0 rem −X	+0
−0	−0	−0 rem +X, −0 rem −X	−0
FIST, FISTP		+X rem +Y, +X rem −Y	+0 [9]
+0	+0	−X rem −Y, −X rem +Y	−0 [9]
−0	+0		
+X [4]	+0	**FSQRT**	
−X [4]	+0	−0	−0
		+0	+0
Addition			
+0 plus +0	+0	**Compare**	
−0 plus −0	−0	±0 : +X	A < B
+0 plus −0, −0 plus +0	*0 [5]	±0 : ±0	A = B
−X plus +X, +X plus −X	*0 [5]	±0 : −X	A > B
±0 plus ±X, ±X plus ±0	†X [6]		
		FTST	
Subtraction		±0	Zero
+0 minus −0	+0	**FCHS**	
−0 minus +0	−0	+0	−0
+0 minus +0, −0 minus −0	*0 [5]	−0	+0
+X minus +X, −X minus −X	*0 [5]	**FABS**	
±0 minus ±X, ±X minus ±0	†X [6]	±0	+0
		F2XM1	
Multiplication		+0	+0
+0 • +0, −0 • −0	+0	−0	−0
+0 • −0, −0 • +0	−0	**FRNDINT**	
+0 • +X, +X • +0	+0	+0	+0
+0 • −X, −X • +0	−0	−0	−0
−0 • +X, +X • −0	−0	**FXTRACT**	
−0 • −X, −X • −0	+0	+0	Both +0
+X • +Y, −X • −Y	+0, underflow [7]	−0	Both −0
+X • −Y, −X • +Y	−0, underflow [7]		

Notes:

[1] Arithmetic and compare operations with real memory operands interpret the memory operand signs in the same way.

[2] Arithmetic and compare operations with binary integers interpret the integer sign in the same manner.

[3] Severe underflows in storing to short or long real may generate zeros.

[4] Small values ($|X| < 1$) stored into integers may round to zero.

[5] Sign is determined by rounding mode:
   * = + for nearest, up or chop
   * = − for down

[6] † = sign of X.

210911

Infinities

The real formats support signed representations of infinities. These values are encoded with a biased exponent of all ones and a significand of $1 \triangle 00...00$; if the infinity is in a register, it is tagged special. The significand distinguishes infinities from NANs, including real indefinite.

A programmer may code an infinity, or it may be created by the NPX as its masked response to an overflow or a zerodivide exception. Note that when rounding is up or down, the masked response may create the largest valid value representable in the destination rather than infinity. See Table 6-31 for details. As operands, infinities behave somewhat differently depending on how the infinity control field in the control word is set (see Table 6-25). When the projective model of infinity is selected, the infinities behave as a single unsigned representation; because of this, infinity cannot be compared with any value except infinity. In affine mode, the signs of the infinities are observed, and comparisons are possible.

NANs

A NAN (Not-A-Number) is a member of a class of special values that exist in the real formats only. A NAN has an exponent of 11...11B, may have either sign, and may have any significand except $1 \triangle 00...00B$, which is assigned to the infinities. A NAN in a register is tagged special.

The 8087 will generate the special NAN, real *indefinite,* as its masked response to an invalid operation exception. This NAN is signed negative; its significand is encoded $1 \triangle 100...00$. All other NANs represent programmer-created values.

Whenever the NPX uses an operand that is a NAN, it signals invalid operation. Its masked response to this exception is to return the NAN as the operation's result. If both operands of an instruction are NANs, the result is the NAN with the larger absolute value. In this way, a NAN that enters a computation propagates through the computation and will eventually be delivered as the final result. Note, however, that the transcendental instructions do not check their operands, and a NAN will produce an undefined result.

Table 6-25 Infinity Operands and Results

Operation	Projective Result	Affine Result
Division		
$\pm\infty \div \pm\infty$	Invalid operation	Invalid operation
$\pm\infty \div \pm X$	$\oplus\infty$	$\oplus\infty$
$\pm X \div \pm\infty$	$\oplus 0$	$\oplus 0$
FSQRT		
$-\infty$	Invalid operation	Invalid operation
$+\infty$	Invalid operaton	$+\infty$
FPREM		
$\pm\infty$ rem $\pm\infty$	Invalid operation	Invalid operation
$\pm\infty$ rem $\pm X$	Invalid operation	Invalid operation
$\pm Y$ rem $\pm\infty$	*Y	*Y
± 0 rem $\pm\infty$	*0	*0
FRNDINT		
$\pm\infty$	*∞	*∞
FSCALE		
$\pm\infty$ scaled by $\pm\infty$	Invalid operation	Invalid operation
$\pm\infty$ scaled by $\pm X$	*∞	*∞
± 0 scaled by $\pm\infty$	*0	*0
$\pm Y$ scaled by $\pm\infty$	Invalid operation	Invalid operation

210911

Table 6-25 Infinity Operands and Results (continued)

Operation	Projective Result	Affine Result
FXTRACT		
±∞	Invalid operation	Invalid operation
Compare		
±∞ : ±∞	A = B	−∞ < +∞
±∞ : ±Y	A ? B (and) invalid operation	−∞ < Y < +∞
±∞ : ±0	A ? B (and) invalid operation	−∞ < 0 < +∞
FTST		
±∞	A ? B (and) invalid operation	* ∞
Addition		
+∞ plus +∞	Invalid operation	+∞
−∞ plus −∞	Invalid operation	−∞
+∞ plus −∞	Invalid operation	Invalid operation
−∞ plus +∞	Invalid operation	Invalid operation
±∞ plus ±X	* ∞	* ∞
±X plus ±∞	* ∞	* ∞
Subtraction		
+∞ minus −∞	Invalid operation	+∞
−∞ minus +∞	Invalid operation	−∞
+∞ minus +∞	Invalid operation	Invalid operation
−∞ minus −∞	Invalid operation	Invalid operation
±∞ minus ±X	* ∞	* ∞
±X minus ±∞	† ∞	† ∞
Multiplication		
±∞ • ±∞	⊕ ∞	⊕ ∞
±∞ • ±Y	⊕ ∞	⊕ ∞
±0 • ±∞, ±∞ * ±0	Invalid operation	Invalid operation

Notes: X = zero or nonzero operand

Y = nonzero operand

* = sign of original operand

† = sign is complement of original operand's sign

⊕= sign is "exclusive or" original operand signs (+ if operands had same sign, − if operands had different signs)

By unmasking the invalid operation exception, the programmer can use NANs to trap to the exception handler. The generality of this approach and the large number of NAN values that are available, provide the sophisticated programmer with a tool that can be applied to a variety of special situations.

For example, a compiler could use NANs to reference uninitialized (real) array elements. The compiler could pre-initialize each array element with a NAN whose significand contained the index (relative position) of the element. If an application program attempted to access an element that it had not initialized, it would use the NAN placed there by the compiler. If the invalid operation exception where unmasked, an interrupt would occur, and the exception handler would be invoked. The exception handler could determine which element had been accessed, since the operand address field of the exception pointers would point to the NAN, and the NAN would contain the index number of the array element.

NANs could also be used to speed up debugging. In its early testing phase, a program often contains multiple errors. An exception handler could be written to save diagnostic information in memory whenever it was invoked. After storing the diagnostic data, it could supply a NAN as the result of the erroneous instruction, and that NAN could point to its associated diagnostic area in memory. The program would then continue, creating a different NAN for each error. When the program ended, the NAN results could be used to access the diagnostic data saved at the time the errors occurred. Many errors could thus be diagnosed and corrected in one test run.

Data Type Encoding

Tables 6-26 through 6-29 summarize how various types of values are encoded in the seven NPX data types. In all tables, the less significant bits are to the

right and are stored in the lowest memory addresses. The sign bit is always the left-most bit of the highest-addressed byte.

Notice that in every format, one encoding is interpreted as representing the special value *indefinite*. The 8087 produces this encoding as its response to a masked invalid operation exception. In the case of the reals, *indefinite* can be loaded and stored like any NAN and it always retains its special identity; programmers are advised not to use this encoding for

Table 6-26 Binary Integer Encodings

	Class	Sign	Magnitude
Positives	(Largest)	0	11...11
	•	•	•
	•	•	•
	•	•	•
	(Smallest)	0	00...01
	Zero	0	00...00
Negatives	(Smallest)	1	11...11
	•	•	•
	•	•	•
	•	•	•
	(Largest/*Indefinite**)	1	00...00

Word: |← 15 bits →|
Short: |← 31 bits →|
Long: |← 63 bits →|

Table 6-27 Packed Decimal Encodings

	Class	Sign		Magnitude					
				digit	digit	digit	digit	. . .	digit
Positives	(Largest)	0	0000000	1 0 0 1	1 0 0 1	1 0 0 1	1 0 0 1	. . .	1 0 0 1
	•	•	•				•		
	•	•	•						
	•	•	•				•		
	(Smallest)	0	0000000	0 0 0 0	0 0 0 0	0 0 0 0	0 0 0 0	. . .	0 0 0 1
	Zero	0	0000000	0 0 0 0	0 0 0 0	0 0 0 0	0 0 0 0	. . .	0 0 0 0
Negatives	Zero	1	0000000	0 0 0 0	0 0 0 0	0 0 0 0	0 0 0 0	. . .	0 0 0 0
	(Smallest)	1	0000000	0 0 0 0	0 0 0 0	0 0 0 0	0 0 0 0	. . .	0 0 0 1
	•	•	•				•		
	•	•	•				•		
	(Largest)	1	0000000	1 0 0 1	1 0 0 1	1 0 0 1	1 0 0 1	. . .	1 0 0 1
	Indefinite*	1	1111111	1 1 1 1	1 1 1 1	U U U U	U U U U	. . .	U U U U

|← 1 byte →|← 9 bytes →|

* The *packed decimal indefinite* encoding is stored by FBSTP in response to a masked invalid operation exception. Attempting to load this value via FBLD produces an undefined result. Note: "UUUU" means bit values are undefined and may contain any value.

210911

Table 6-28 Real and Long Real Encodings

	Class		Sign	Biased Exponent	Significand* $_\Delta ff...ff$
Positives	NANs		0 • • • 0	11...11 • • • 11...11	11...11 • • • 00...01
	∞		0	11...11	00...00
	Reals	Normals	0 • • • 0	11...10 • • • 00...01	11...11 • • • 00...00
		Denormals	0 • • • 0	00...00 • • • 00...00	11...11 • • • 00...01
		Zero	0	00...00	00...00

	Class		Sign	Biased Exponent	Significand* $_\Delta ff...ff$
Negatives	**Reals**	Zero	1	00...00	00...00
		Denormals	1 • • • 1	00...00 • • • 00...00	00...01 • • • 11...11
		Normals	1 • • • 1	00...01 • • • 11...10	00...00 • • • 11...11
	∞		1	11...11	00...00
	NANs		1 •	11...11 •	00...01 •
		Indefinite	1 • • • 1	11...11 • • • 11...11	10...00 • • • 11...11

Short: ◄— 8 bits —►◄— 23 bits —►
Long: ◄—11 bits—►◄—52 bits—►

* Integer bit is implied and not stored.

Table 6-29 Temporary Real Encodings

	Class		Sign	Biased Exponent	Significand $_{\Delta}ff...ff$
Positives	NANs		0 • • • 0	11...11 • • • 11...11	111...11 • • • 100...01
	∞		0	11...11	100...00
	Reals	Normals	0 • • • 0	11...10 • • • 00...01	111...11 • • • 100...00
		Unnormals			011...11 • • • 000...00
		Denormals	0 • • • 0	00...00 • • • 00...00	011...11 • • • 000...01
		Zero	0	00...00	000...00
Negatives	**Reals**	Zero	1	00...00	000...00
		Denormals	1 • • • 1	00...00 • • • 00...00	000...01 • • • 011...11
		Unnormals	1 • • • 1	00...01 • • • 00...01	000...00 • • • 011...11
		Normals	1 • • • 1	00...00 • • • 11...10	100...00 • • • 111...11
	∞		1	11...11	100...00
	NANs	Indefinite	1 • • • 1	11...11 • • • 11...11	100...00 • • • 110...00 • • • 111...11

◄—15 bits—►◄—64 bits—►

any other purpose. Packed decimal *indefinite* may be stored by the NPX in a FBSTP instruction; attempting to use this encoding in a FBLD instruction, however, will have an undefined result. In the binary integers, the same encoding may represent either *indefinite* or the largest negative number supported by the format (-2^{15}, -2^{31} or -2^{63}). The 8087 will store this encoding as its masked response to an invalid operation, or when the value in a source register represents, or rounds to, the largest negative integer representable by the destination. In situations where its origin may be ambiguous, the invalid operation exception flag can be examined to see if the value was produced by an exception response. When this encoding is loaded, or used by an integer arithmetic or compare operation, it is always interpreted as a negative number; thus *indefinite* cannot be loaded from a packed decimal or binary integer.

Exception Handling Details

Table 6-30 lists every exception condition that the NPX detects and describes the processor's response when the relevant exception mask is set. The unmasked responses are described in Table 6-6. Note that if an unmasked overflow or underflow occurs in an FST or FSTP instruction, no result is stored, and the stack and memory are left as they existed *before* the instruction was executed. This gives an exception handler the opportunity to examine the offending operand on the stack top.

Table 6-30 Exception Conditions and Masked Responses

Condition	Masked Response
Invalid Operation	
Source register is tagged empty (usually due to stack underflow).	Return real *indefinite*.
Destination register is not tagged empty (usually due to stack overflow).	Return real *indefinite* (overwrite destination value).
One or both operands is a NAN.	Return NAN with larger absolute value (ignore signs).
(Compare and test operations only): one or both operands is a NAN.	Set condition codes "not comparable".
(Addition operations only): closure is affine and operands are opposite-signed infinities; or closure is projective and both operands are ∞ (signs immaterial).	Return real *indefinite*
(Subtraction operations only): closure is affine and operands are like-signed infinities; or closure is projective and both operands are ∞ (signs immaterial).	Return real *indefinite*.
(Multiplication operations only): ∞ * 0; or 0 * ∞.	Return real *indefinite*.
(Division operations only): ∞ ÷ ∞; or 0 ÷ 0; or 0 ÷ pseudo-zero; or divisor is denormal or unnormal.	Return real *indefinite*.
(FPREM instruction only): modulus (divisor) is unnormal or denormal; or dividend is ∞.	Return real *indefinite*, set condition code = "complete remainder".
(FSQRT instruction only): operand is nonzero and negative; or operand is denormal or unnormal; or closure is affine and operand is -∞; or closure is projective and operand is ∞.	Return real *indefinite*.

210911

Table 6-30 Exception Conditions and Masked Responses (continued)

Invalid Operation	
(Compare operations only): closure is projective and ∞ is being compared with 0 or a normal, or ∞.	Set condition code = "not comparable"
(FTST instruction only): closure is projective and operand is ∞.	Set condition code = "not comparable".
(FIST, FISTP instructions only): source register is empty, or a NAN, or denormal, or unnormal, or ∞, or exceeds representable range of destination.	Store integer *indefinite*.
(FBSTP instruction only): source register is empty, or a NAN, or denormal, or unnormal, or ∞, or exceeds 18 decimal digits.	Store packed decimal *indefinite*.
(FST, FSTP instructions only): destination is short or long real and source register is an unnormal with exponent in range.	Store real *indefinite*.
(FXCH instruction only): one or both registers is tagged empty.	Change empty register(s) to real *indefinite* and then perform exchange.

Denormalized Operand	
(FLD instruction only): source operand is denormal.	No special action; load as usual.
(Arithmetic operations only): one or both operands is denormal.	Convert (in a work area) the operand to the equivalent unnormal and proceed.
(Compare and test operations only): one or both operands is denormal *or unnormal* (other than pseudo-zero).	Convert (in a work area) any denormal to the equivalent unnormal; normalize as much as possible, and proceed with operation.

Zerodivide	
(Division operations only): divisor = 0.	Return ∞ signed with "exclusive or" of operand signs.

Overflow	
(Arithmetic operations only): rounding is nearest or chop, and exponent of true result > 16,383.	Return properly signed ∞and signal precision exception.
(FST, FSTP instructions only): rounding is nearest or chop, and exponent of true result > +127 (short real destination) or > +1023 (long real destination).	Return properly signed ∞ and signal precision exception.

210911

Table 6-30 Exception Conditions and Masked Responses (continued)

Underflow	
(Arithmetic operations only): exponent of true result <−16,382 (true).	Denormalize until exponent rises to −16,382 (true), round significand to 64 bits. If denormalized rounded significand = 0, then return true 0; else, return denormal (tag = special, biased exponent =0).
(FST, FSTP instructions only): destination is short real and exponent of true result <−126 (true).	Denormalize until exponent rises to −126 (true), round significand to 24 bits, store true 0 if denormalized rounded significand = 0; else, store denormal (biased exponent = 0).
(FST, FSTP instructions only): destination is long real and exponent of true result <−1022 (true).	Denormalize until exponent rises to −1022 (true), round significand to 53 bits, store true 0 if rounded denormalized significand = 0; else, store denormal (biased exponent = 0).

Precision	
True rounding error occurs.	No special action.
Masked response to overflow exception earlier in instruction.	No special action.

When rounding is directed (the RC field of the control word is set to "up" or "down"), the 8087 handles a masked overflow differently than it does for the "nearest" or "chop" rounding modes. Table 6-31 shows the NPX's masked response when the true result is too large to be represented in it's destination real format. For a normalized result, the essence of this response is to deliver ∞ or the largest valid number representable in the destination format, as dictated by the rounding mode and the

Table 6-31 Masked Overflow Response for Directed Rounding

True Result		Rounding Mode	Result Delivered
Normalization	Sign		
Normal	+	Up	+∞
Normal	+	Down	Largest finite positive number[1]
Normal	−	Up	Largest finite negative number[1]
Normal	−	Down	−∞
Unnormal	+	Up	+∞
Unnormal	−	Down	Largest exponent, result's significand[2]
Unnormal	+	Up	Largest exponent, result's significand[2]
Unnormal	−	Down	−∞

(1) The largest valid representable reals are encoded:
   exponent: 11...10B
   significand: (1)$_\Delta$11...10B

(2) The significand retains its identity as an unnormal; the true result is rounded as usual (effectively chopped toward 0 in this case). The exponent is encoded 11...10B.

210911

sign of the true result. Thus, when RC=down, a positive overflow is rounded down to the largest positive number. Conversely, when RC=up, a negative overflow is rounded up to the largest negative number. A properly signed ∞ is returned for a positive overflow with RC=up, or a negative overflow with RC=down. For an unnormalized result, the action is similar except that the unnormal character of the result is preserved if the sign and rounding mode do not indicate that ∞ should be delivered.

In all masked overflow responses for directed rounding, the overflow flag is *not* set, but the precision exception *is* raised to signal that the exact true result has not been returned.

6.8 PROGRAMMING EXAMPLES

Conditional Branching

As discussed in Section 6.5, the comparison instructions post their results to the condition code bits of the 8087 status word. Although there are many ways

to implement conditional branching following a comparison, the basic approach is as follows:

- execute the comparison,

- store the status word,

- inspect the condition code bits,

- jump on the result.

Figure 6-21 is a code fragment that illustrates how two memory-resident long real numbers might be compared (similar code could be used with the FTST instruction). The numbers are called A and B, and the comparison is A to B. The comparison itself simply requires loading A onto the top of the 8087 register stack and then comparing it to B and popping the stack in the same instruction. The status word is written to memory and the code waits for completion of the store before attempting to use the result.

```
A       DQ   ?
B       DQ   ?
STAT_87 DW   ?


        FLD   A          ;LOAD A ONTO TOP OF 87 STACK
        FCOMP B          ;COMPARE A:B, POP A
        FSTSW STAT_87    ;STORE RESULT
        FWAIT            ;WAIT FOR STORE

        ;LOAD CPU REGISTER AH WITH BYTE OF
        ;    STATUS WORD CONTAINING CONDITION CODE
        MOV   AH, BYTE PTR STAT_87+1
        ;
        ;LOAD CONDITION CODES INTO CPU FLAGS
        SAHF

        ;USE CONDITIONAL JUMPS TO DETERMINE
        ;    ORDERING OF A AND B
        JB    A_LESS_OR_UNORDERED
        ;CF (C0) = 0
        JNE   A_GREATER
A_EQUAL:
        ;CF (C0) = 0, ZF (C3) = 1
        .
        .
        .
A_GREATER:
        ;CF (C0) = 0, ZF (C3) = 0
```

Figure 6-21 Conditional Branching for Compares

210911

```
        .
        .
        .
    A_LESS_OR_UNORDERED:
        ;CF (C0) = 1, TEST ZF (C3)
        JNE     A_LESS
    A_B_UNORDERED:
        ;CF (C0) = 1, ZF (C3) = 1
        .
        .
        .
    A_LESS:
        ;CF (C0) = 1, ZF (C3) = 0
```

Figure 6-21 Conditional Branching for Compares (continued)

There are four possible orderings of A and B, and bits C3 and C0 of the condition code indicate which ordering holds. These bits are positioned in the upper byte of the status word so as to correspond to the CPU's zero and carry flags (ZF and CF), if the byte is written into the flags (see Figures 3-28 and 6-6). The code fragment, then, sets ZF and CF to the values of C3 and C0 and then uses the CPU conditional jumps to test the flags. Table 3-12 shows how each conditional jump instruction tests the CPU flags.

The FXAM instruction updates all four condition code bits. Figure 6-22 shows how a jump table can be used to determine the characteristics of the value examined. The jump table (FXAM_TBL) is initialized to contain the 16-bit displacement of 16 labels, one for each possible condition code setting. Note that four of the table entries contain the same value,

since there are four condition code settings that correspond to "empty."

The program fragment performs the FXAM and stores the status word. It then manipulates the condition code bits to finally produce a number in register BX that equals the condition code times 2. This involves zeroing the unused bits in the byte that contains the code, shifting C3 to the right so that it is adjacent to C2, and then shifting the code to multiply it by 2. The resulting value is used as an index which selects one of the displacements from FXAM_TBL (the multiplication of the condition code is required because of the 2-byte length of each value in FXAM_TBL). The unconditional JMP instruction effectively vectors through the jump table to the labeled routine that contains code (not shown in the example) to process each possible result of the FXAM instruction.

```
        .
        .
        .
    FXAM_TBL            DW POS_UNNORM, POS_NAN, NEG_UNNORM,
    &                      NEG_NAN, POS_NORM, POS_INFINITY,
    &                      NEG_NORM, NEG_INFINITY, POS_ZERO,
    &                      EMPTY, NEG_ZERO, EMPTY, POS_DENORM,
    &                      EMPTY, NEG_DENORM, EMPTY
    STAT_87            DW ?
```

Figure 6-22 Conditional Branching for FXAM

```
      ;EXAMINE ST, STORE RESULT, WAIT FOR COMPLETION
          FXAM
          FSTSW         STAT_87
          FWAIT
      ;CLEAR UPPER HALF OF BX, LOAD CONDITION CODE
      ;    IN LOWER HALF
          MOV           BH,0
          MOV           BL, BYTE PTR STAT_87+1
      ;COPY ORIGINAL IMAGE
          MOV           AL,BL
      ;CLEAR ALL BITS EXCEPT C2-C0
          AND           BL,00000111B
      ;CLEAR ALL BITS EXCEPT C3
          AND           AL,01000000B
      ;SHIFT C3 TWO PLACES RIGHT
          SHR           AL,1
          SHR           AL,1
      ;SHIFT C2-C0 ONE PLACE LEFT (MULTIPLY BY 2)
          SAL           BX,1
      ;DROP C3 BACK IN ADJACENT TO C2 (000XXXX0)
          OR            BL,AL
      ;JUMP TO THE ROUTINE ''ADDRESSED'' BY CONDITION CODE
          JMP           FXAM_TBL[BX]
      ;
      ;HERE ARE THE JUMP TARGETS, ONE TO HANDLE
      ;    EACH POSSIBLE RESULT OF FXAM
POS_UNNORM:
          .
          .
POS_NAN:
          .
          .
NEG_UNNORM:
          .
          .
NEG_NAN:
          .
          .
POS_NORM:
          .
          .
POS_INFINITY:
          .
          .
NEG_NORM:
          .
          .
NEG_INFINITY:
          .
          .
POS_ZERO:
```

Figure 6-22 Conditional Branching for FXAM (continued)

```
EMPTY:
                .
                .
                .
NEG_ZERO:
                .
                .
                .
POS_DENORM:
                .
                .
                .
NEG_DENORM:
                .
                .
                .
```

Figure 6-22 Conditional Branching for FXAM (continued)

Exception Handlers

There are many approaches to writing exception handlers. One useful technique is to consider the exception handler interrupt procedure as consisting of "prologue," "body" and "epilogue" sections of code. (For compatibility with the 8087 emulators, this procedure should be invoked by interrupt pointer (vector) number 16.)

At the beginning of the prologue, CPU interrupts have been disabled by the CPU's normal interrupt response mechanism. The prologue performs all functions that must be protected from possible interruption by higher-priority sources. Typically this will involve saving CPU registers and transferring diagnostic information from the 8087 to memory. When the critical processing has been completed, the prologue may enable CPU interrupts to allow higher-priority interrupt handlers to preempt the exception handler.

The exception handler body examines the diagnostic information and makes a response that is necessarily application-dependent. This response may range from halting execution, to displaying a message, to attempting to repair the problem and proceed with normal execution.

The epilogue essentially reverses the actions of the prologue, restoring the CPU and the NPX so that normal execution can be resumed. The epilogue must *not* load an unmasked exception flag into the 8087 or another interrupt will be requested immediately (assuming 8087 interrupts are also loaded as unmasked).

Figures 6-23 through 6-25 show the ASM-86 coding of three skeleton exception handlers. They show how prologues and epilogues can be written for various situations, but only provide comments indicating

where the application-dependent exception handling body should be placed.

Figures 6-23 and 6-24 are very similar; their only substantial difference is their choice of instructions to save and restore the 8087. The tradeoff here is between the increased diagnostic information provided by FNSAVE and the faster execution of FNSTENV. For applications that are sensitive to interrupt latency, or do not need to examine register contents, FNSTENV reduces the duration of the "critical region," during which the CPU will not recognize another interrupt request (unless it is a non-maskable interrupt).

After the exception handler body, the epilogues prepare the CPU and the NPX to resume execution from the point of interruption (i.e., the instruction following the one that generated the unmasked exception). Notice that the exception flags in the memory image that is loaded into the 8087 are cleared to zero prior to reloading (in fact, in these examples, the entire status word image is cleared). The prologue also provides for indicating to the interrupt controller hardware (e.g., an 8259A) that the interrupt has been processed. The actual processing done here is application-dependent, but might typically involve writing an "end of interrupt" command to the interrupt controller.

The examples in Figures 6-23 and 6-24 assume that the exception handler itself will not cause an unmasked exception. Where this is a possibility, the general approach shown in Figure 6-25 can be employed. The basic technique is to save the full 8087 state and then to load a new control word in the prologue. Note that considerable care should be taken when designing an exception handler of this type to prevent the handler from being reentered endlessly.

```
SAVE_ALL              PROC
;
; SAVE CPU REGISTERS, ALLOCATE STACK SPACER
; FOR 8087 STATE IMAGE
; NOTE! INTERRUPTS MUST BE DISABLED.
    PUSH        BP
      .
      .
      .
    MOV         BP,SP
    SUB         SP,94
;SAVE FULL 8087 STATE, WAIT FOR COMPLETION,
;ENABLE CPU INTERRUPTS
    FNSAVE      [BP-94]
    FWAIT
    STI
;
;APPLICATION-DEPENDENT EXCEPTION HANDLING
;CODE GOES HERE
;
;CLEAR EXCEPTION FLAGS IN STATUS WORD
;RESTORE MODIFIED STATE
;IMAGE
    MOV         BYTE PTR [BP-92], 0H
    FRSTOR      [BP-94]
;WAIT FOR RESTORE TO FINISH BEFORE RELEASING MEMORY
    FWAIT
;DE-ALLOCATE STACK SPACE, RESTORE CPU REGISTERS
    MOV         SP,BP
      .
      .
      .
    POP         BP
;
;CODE TO SEND ''END OF INTERRUPT'' COMMAND TO
;8259A GOES HERE
;
;RETURN TO INTERRUPTED CALCULATION
    IRET
SAVE_ALL              ENDP
```

Figure 6-23 Full State Exception Handler

```
SAVE_ENVIRONMENT PROC
;
; SAVE CPU REGISTERS, ALLOCATE STACK SPACE
; FOR 8087 ENVIRONMENT
; NOTE! INTERRUPTS MUST BE DISABLED.
      PUSH       BP
         .
         .
         .
      MOV        BP,SP
      SUB        SP,14
;SAVE ENVIRONMENT, WAIT FOR COMPLETION,
;ENABLE CPU INTERRUPTS
      FNSTENV    [BP-14]
      FWAIT
      STI
;
;APPLICATION EXCEPTION-HANDLING CODE GOES HERE
;
;CLEAR EXCEPTION FLAGS IN STATUS WORD
;RESTORE MODIFIED
;ENVIRONMENT IMAGE
      MOV        BYTE PTR [BP-12], 0H
      FLDENV     [BP-14]
;WAIT FOR LOAD TO FINISH BEFORE RELEASING MEMORY
      FWAIT
;DE-ALLOCATE STACK SPACE, RESTORE CPU REGISTERS
      MOV        SP,BP
         .
         .
         .
      POP        BP
;
;CODE TO SEND ''END OF INTERRUPT'' COMMAND TO
;8259A GOES HERE
;
;RETURN TO INTERRUPTED CALCULATION
      IRET
SAVE_ENVIRONMENT ENDP
```

Figure 6-24 Reduced Latency Exception Handler

210911

```
            .
            .
            .
        LOCAL_CONTROL   DW  ?   ;ASSUME INITIALIZED
            .
            .
            .
REENTRANT              PROC
;
;SAVE CPU REGISTERS, ALLOCATE STACK SPACE FOR
;8087 STATE IMAGE
    PUSH     BP
            .
            .
            .
    MOV      BP,SP
    SUB      SP,94
;SAVE STATE, LOAD NEW CONTROL WORD, WAIT
;FOR COMPLETION, ENABLE CPU INTERRUPTS
    FNSAVE   [BP-94]
    FLDCW    LOCAL_CONTROL
    FWAIT
    STI
;CODE TO SEND ''END OF INTERRUPT'' COMMAND TO
;8259A GOES HERE
            .
            .
            .
;APPLICATION EXCEPTION HANDLING CODE GOES HERE.
;AN UNMASKED EXCEPTION GENERATED HERE WILL
;CAUSE THE EXCEPTION HANDLER TO BE REENTERED.
;IF LOCAL STORAGE IS NEEDED, IT MUST BE
;ALLOCATED ON THE CPU STACK.
            .
            .
            .
;CLEAR EXCEPTION FLAGS IN STATUS WORD
;RESTORE MODIFIED STATE IMAGE
    MOV      BYTE PTR [BP-92], 0H
    FRSTOR   [BP-94]
;WAIT FOR RESTORE TO FINISH BEFORE RELEASING MEMORY
    FWAIT
;DE-ALLOCATE STACK SPACE, RESTORE CPU REGISTERS
    MOV      SP,BP
            .
            .
            .
    POP      BP
;RETURN TO POINT OF INTERRUPTION
    IRET
REENTRANT              ENDP
```

Figure 6-25 Reentrant Exception Handler

The 8089 Input/Output Processor

7

CHAPTER 7
THE 8089 INPUT/OUTPUT PROCESSOR

7.1 INTRODUCTION

This chapter describes the 8089 Input/Output Processor (IOP). The following topics are discussed:

- Processor Overview

- Processor Architecture

- Input/Output

- Instruction Set

- Addressing Modes

- Programming Facilities

- Programming Guidelines and Examples

The discussion is confined to covering the hardware in functional terms; timing, electrical characteristics and other physical interfacing data are in Volume 2, Chapter 4.

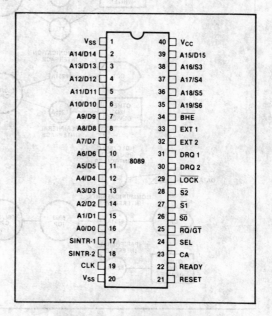

Vss	1	40	Vcc
A14/D14	2	39	A15/D15
A13/D13	3	38	A16/S3
A12/D12	4	37	A17/S4
A11/D11	5	36	A18/S5
A10/D10	6	35	A19/S6
A9/D9	7	34	BHE
A8/D8	8	33	EXT 1
A7/D7	9	32	EXT 2
A6/D6	10	31	DRQ 1
A5/D5	11	30	DRQ 2
A4/D4	12	29	LOCK
A3/D3	13	28	S̄2
A2/D2	14	27	S̄1
A1/D1	15	26	S̄0
A0/D0	16	25	RQ/GT
SINTR-1	17	24	SEL
SINTR-2	18	23	CA
CLK	19	22	READY
Vss	20	21	RESET

Figure 7-1 8089 Input/Output Processor Pin Diagram

7.2 PROCESSOR OVERVIEW

The 8089 Input/Output Processor is a high-performance, general purpose I/O system implemented on a single chip. Within the 8089 are two independent channels, each of which combines attributes of a CPU with those of a very flexible DMA (direct memory access) controller. For example, channels can execute programs like CPUs; the IOP instruction set has about 50 different types of instructions specifically designed for efficient input/output processing. Each channel also can perform high-speed DMA transfers; a variety of optional operations allow the data to be manipulated (e.g., translated or compared) as it is transferred. The 8089 is contained in a 40-pin dual in-line package (Figure 7-1) and operates from a single +5V power source. An integral member of the iAPX 86,88 family, the IOP is directly compatible with both the 8086 and 8088 when these processors are configured in maximum mode. The IOP also may be used in any system that incorporates Intel's Multibus™ shared bus architecture, or a superset of the Multibus™ design.

Evolution

Figure 7-2 depicts the general trend in CPU and I/O device relationships in the first three generations of microprocessors. First generation CPUs were forced to deal directly with substantial numbers of TTL components, often performing transfers at the bit level. Only a very limited number of relatively slow devices could be supported.

Single-chip interface controllers were introduced in the second generation. These devices removed the lowest level of device control from the CPU and let the CPU transfer whole bytes at once. With the introduction of DMA controllers, high-speed devices could be added to a system, and whole blocks of data could be transferred without CPU intervention. Compared to the previous generation, I/O device and DMA controllers allowed microprocessors to be applied to problems that required moderate levels of I/O, both in terms of the numbers of devices that could be supported and the transfer speeds of those devices.

210911

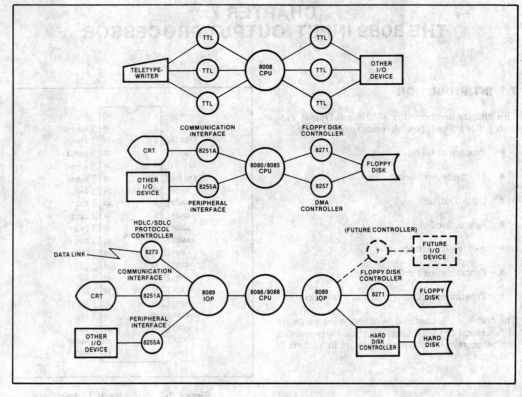

Figure 7-2 IOP Evolution

The controllers themselves, however, still required a considerable amount of attention from the CPU, and in many cases the CPU had to respond to an interrupt with every byte read or written. The CPU also had to stop while DMA transfers were performed.

The 8089 introduces the third generation of input/output processing. It continues the trend of simplifying the CPU'S "view" of I/O devices by removing another level of control from the CPU. The CPU performs an I/O operation by building a message in memory that describes the function to be performed; the IOP reads the message, carries out the operation and notifies the CPU when it has finished. All I/O devices appear to the CPU as transmitting and receiving whole blocks of data; the IOP can make both byte- and word-level transfers invisible to the CPU. The IOP assumes all device controller overhead, performs both programmed and DMA transfers, and can recover from "soft" I/O errors without CPU intervention; all of these activities may be performed while the CPU is attending to other tasks.

Principles of Operation

Since the 8089 is a new concept in microprocessor components, this section surveys the basic operation of the IOP as background to the detailed descriptions provided in the rest of the chapter. This summary deliberately omits some operating details in order to provide an integrated overview of basic concepts.

CPU/IOP Communications

A CPU communicates with an IOP in two distinct modes: initialization and command. The initialization sequence is typically performed when the system is powered-up or reset. The CPU initializes the IOP by preparing a series of linked message blocks in memory. On a signal from the CPU, the IOP reads these blocks and determines from them how the data buses are configured and how access to the buses is to be controlled.

Following initialization, the CPU directs all communications to either of the IOP's two channels; during normal operation the IOP appears to be two separate devices - channel 1 and channel 2. All CPU-to-channel communications center on the channel control block (CB) illustrated in Figure 7-3. The CB is located in the CPU's memory space, and its address is passed to the IOP during initialization. Half of the block is dedicated to each channel. The channel maintains the BUSY flag that indicates whether it is in the midst of an operation or is available for a new command. The CPU sets the CCW (channel command word) to indicate what kind of operation the IOP is to perform. Six different commands allow the CPU to start and stop programs, remove interrupt requests, etc.

If the CPU is dispatching a channel to run a program, it directs the channel to a parameter block (PB) and a task block (TB); these are also shown in Figure 7-3. The parameter block is analogous to a parameter list passed by a program to a subroutine; it contains variable data that the channel program is to use in carrying out its assignment. The parameter block also may contain space for variables (results)

that the channel is to return to the CPU. Except for the first two words, the format and the size of a parameter block are completely open; based on the specific I/O task, the PB may be set up to exchange any kind of information between the CPU and the channel program.

A task block is a channel program - a sequence of 8089 instructions that will perform an operation. A typical channel program might use parameter block data to set up the IOP and a device controller for a transfer, perform the transfer, return the results, and then halt. However, there are no restrictions on what a channel program can do; its function may be simple or elaborate to suit the needs of the application.

Before the CPU starts a channel program, it links the program (TB) to the parameter block and the parameter block to the CB as shown in Figure 7-3. The links are standard 8086/8088 doubleword pointer variables; the lower-addressed word contains an offset, and the higher-addressed word contains a segment base value. A system may have many different parameter and task blocks; however, only one of each is ever linked to a channel at any given time.

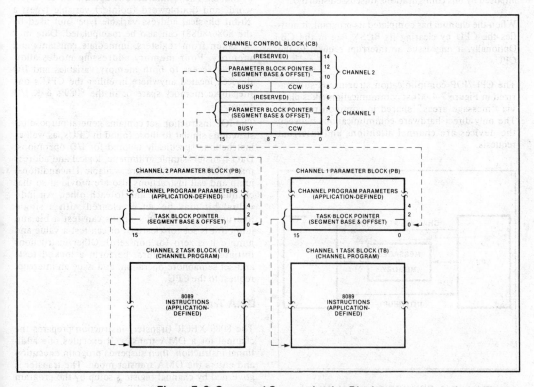

Figure 7-3 Command Communication Blocks

After the CPU has filled in the CCW and has linked the CB to a parameter block and a task block, if appropriate, it issues a channel attention (CA). This is done by activating the IOP's CA (channel attention) and SEL (channel select) pins. The state of SEL at the falling edge of CA directs the channel attention to channel 1 or channel 2. If the IOP is located in the CPU's I/O space, it appears to the CPU as two consecutive I/O ports (one for each channel), and an OUT instruction to the port functions as a CA. If the IOP is memory-mapped, the channels appear as two consecutive memory locations, and any memory reference instruction (e.g., MOV) to these locations causes a channel attention.

An IOP channel attention is functionally similar to a CPU interrupt. When the channel recognizes the CA, it stops what it is doing (it will typically be idle) and examines the command in the CCW. If it is to start a program, the channel loads the addresses of the parameter and task blocks into internal registers, sets its BUSY flag and starts executing the channel program. After it has issued the CA, the CPU is free to perform other processing; the channel can perform its function in parallel, subject to limitations imposed by bus configurations (discussed shortly).

When the channel has completed its program, it notifies the CPU by clearing its BUSY flag in the CB. Optionally, it may issue an interrupt request to the CPU.

The CPU/IOP communication structure is summarized in Figure 7-4. Most communication takes place via "message areas" shared in common memory. The only direct hardware communications between the devices are channel attentions and interrupt requests.

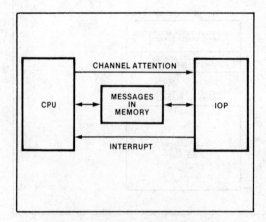

CHANNEL ATTENTION

CPU

MESSAGES
IN
MEMORY

IOP

INTERRUPT

Figure 7-4 CPU/IOP Communication

Channels

Each of the two IOP channels operates independently, and each has its own register set, channel attention, interrupt request and DMA control signals. At a given point in time, a channel may be idle, executing a program, performing a DMA transfer, or responding to a channel attention. Although only one channel actually runs at a time, the channels can be active concurrently, alternating their operations (e.g., channel 1 may execute instructions in the periods between successive DMA transfer cycles run by channel 2). A built-in priority system allows high-priority activities on one channel to preempt less critical operations on the other channel. The CPU is able to further adjust priorities to handle special cases. The CPU starts the channel and can halt it, suspend it, or cause it to resume a suspended operation by placing different values in the CCW.

Channel Programs (Task Blocks)

Channel programs are written in ASM-89, the 8089 assembly language. About 50 basic instructions are available. These instructions operate on bit, byte, word, and doubleword (pointer) variable types; a 20-bit physical address variable type (not used by the 8086/8088) can also be manipulated. Data may be taken from registers, immediate constants and memory. Four memory addressing modes allow flexible access to both memory variables and I/O devices located anywhere in either the CPU's one megabyte memory space or in the 8089's 64K I/O space.

The IOP instruction set contains general purpose instructions similar to those found in CPUs, as well as instructions specifically tailored for I/O operations. Data transfer, simple arithmetic, logical and address manipulation operations are available. Unconditional jump and call instructions also are provided so that channel programs can link to each other. An individual bit may be set or cleared with a single instruction. Conditional jumps can test a bit and jump if it is set (or cleared), or can test a value and jump if it is zero (or non-zero). Other instructions initiate DMA transfers, perform a locked test-and-set semaphore operation, and issue an interrupt request to the CPU.

DMA Transfers

The 8089 XFER (transfer) instruction prepares the channel for a DMA transfer. It executes one additional instruction, then suspends program execution and enters the DMA transfer mode. The transfer is governed by channel registers setup by the program prior to executing the XFER instruction.

Data is transferred from a source to a destination. The source and destination may be any locations in the CPU's memory space or in the IOP's I/O space; the IOP makes no distinction between memory components and I/O devices. Thus transfers may be made from I/O device to memory, memory to I/O device, memory to memory and I/O device to I/O device. The IOP automatically matches 8- and 16-bit components to each other.

Individual transfer cycles (i.e., the movement of a byte or a word) may be synchronized by a signal (DMA request) from the source or from the destination. In the synchronized mode, the channel waits for the synchronizing signal before starting the next transfer cycle. The transfer also may be unsynchronized, in which case the channel begins the next transfer cycle immediately upon completion of the previous cycle.

A transfer cycle is performed in two steps: fetching a byte or word from the source into the IOP and then storing it from the IOP into the destination. The IOP automatically optimizes the transfer to make best use of the available data bus widths. For example, if data is being transferred from an 8-bit device to memory that resides on a 16-bit bus (e.g., 8086 memory), the IOP will normally run two one-byte fetch cycles and then store the full word in a single cycle.

Between the fetch and store cycles, the IOP can operate on the data. A byte may be translated to another code (e.g., EBCDIC to ASCII), or compared to a search value, or both, if desired.

A transfer can be terminated by several programmer-specified conditions. The channel can stop the transfer when a specified number (up to 64K) of bytes has been transferred. An external device may stop a transfer by signaling on the channel's external terminate pin. The channel can stop the transfer when a byte (possibly translated) compares equal, or unequal, to a search value. Single-cycle termination, which stops unconditionally after one byte or word has been stored, is also available.

When the transfer terminates, the channel automatically resumes program execution. The channel program can determine the cause of the termination in situations where multiple terminations are possible (e.g., terminating when 80 bytes are transferred or a carriage return character is encountered, whichever occurs first). As an example of post-transfer processing, the channel program could read a result register from the I/O device controller to determine if the transfer was performed successfully. If not (e.g., a CRC error was detected by the controller), the channel program could retry the operation without CPU intervention.

A channel program typically ends by posting the result of the operation to a field supplied in the parameter block, optionally interrupting the CPU, and then halting. When the channel halts, its BUSY flag in the channel control block is cleared to indicate its availability for another operation. As an alternative to being interrupted by the channel, the CPU can poll this flag to determine when the operation has been completed.

Bus Configuration

As shown in Figure 7-5, the IOP can access memory or ports (I/O devices) located in a 1-megabyte system space and memory or ports located in a 64-kilobyte I/O space. Although the IOP only has one physical data bus, it is useful to think of the IOP as accessing the system space via a system data bus and the I/O space over an I/O data bus. The distinction between the "two" buses is based on the type-of-cycle signals output by the 8288 Bus Controller. Components in the system space respond to the memory read and memory write signals, whether they are memory or I/O devices. Components in the I/O space respond to the I/O read and I/O write signals. Thus I/O devices located in the system space are memory-mapped, and memory in the I/O space is I/O-mapped. The two basic configuration operations differ in the degree to which the IOP shares these buses with the CPU.

Both configurations require an 8086/8088 CPU to be strapped in maximum mode.

In the local configuration, shown in Figure 7-6, the IOP (or IOPs if two are used) shares both buses with the CPU. The system bus and the I/O bus are the

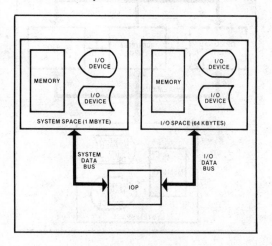

Figure 7-5 IOP Data Buses

same width (8 bits if the CPU is an 8088 or 16 bits if the CPU is an 8086). The IOP system space corresponds to the CPU memory space, and the IOP I/O space corresponds to the CPU I/O space. Channel programs are typically located in the system space; I/O devices may be located in either space. The IOP requests use of the bus for channel program instruction fetches as well as for DMA and programmed transfers. In the local configuration, either the IOP or the CPU may use the buses, but not both simultaneously. The advantage of the local configuration is that intelligent DMA may be added to a system with minimal additional components beyond the IOP. The disadvantage is that parallel operation of the processors is limited to cases in which the CPU has instruction in its queue that can be executed without using the bus.

In the remote configuration (Figure 7-7), the IOP (or IOPs) shares a common system bus with the CPU. Access to this bus is controlled by 8289 Bus Arbiters. The IOP's I/O bus, however, is physically separated from the CPU in the remote configuration. Two IOPs can share the local I/O bus. Any number of remote IOPs may be contained in a system, configured in remote clusters of one or two. The local I/O bus need not be the same physical width as the shared system bus, allowing an IOP, for example, to interface 8-bit peripherals to an 8086. In the remote configuration, the IOP can access local

I/O devices and memory without using the shared system bus, thereby reducing bus contention with the CPU. Contention can further be reduced by locating the IOP's channel programs in the local I/O space. The IOP can then also fetch instructions without accessing the system bus. Parameter, channel control and other CPU/IOP communication blocks must be located in system memory, however, so that both processors can access them. The remote configuration thus increases the degree to which an IOP and a CPU can operate in parallel and thereby increases a system's throughput potential. The price paid for this is that additional hardware must be added to arbitrate use of the shared bus, and to separate the shared and local buses (see Chapter 4 for details).

It is also possible to configure an IOP remote to one CPU, and local to another CPU (see Figure 7-8). The local CPU could be used to perform computational-intensive routines for the IOP.

A Sample Transaction

Figure 7-9 shows how a CPU and an IOP might work together to read a record (sector) from a floppy disk. This example is not illustrative of the IOP's full capabilities, but it does review its basic operation and its interaction with a CPU.

The CPU must first obtain exclusive use of a channel. This can be done by performing a "test and set lock" operation on the selected channel's BUSY flag. Assuming the CPU wants to use channel 1, this could be accomplished in PL/M-86 by coding similar to the following:

        DO WHILE LOCKSET (@CH1,BUSY,0FFH);
        END

In ASM-86 a loop containing the XCHG instruction prefixed by LOCK would accomplish the same thing, namely testing the BUSY flag until it is clear (OH), and immediately setting it to FFH (busy) to prevent another task or processor from obtaining use of the channel.

Having obtained the channel, the CPU fills in a parameter block (see Figure 7-10). In this case, the CPU passes the following parameters to the channel: the address of the floppy disk controller, the address of the buffer where the data is to be placed, and the drive, track and sector to be read. It also supplies space for the IOP to return the result of the operation. Note that this is quite a "low-level" parameter block in that it implies that the CPU has detailed knowledge of the I/O system. For a "real" system, a higher-level parameter block would isolate the CPU from I/O device characteristics. Such a block might contain more general parameters such as file name and record key.

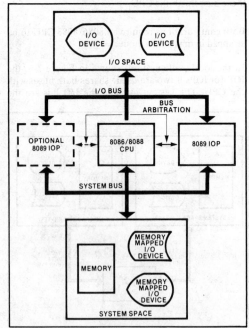

Figure 7-6 Local Configuration

THE 8089 INPUT/OUTPUT PROCESSOR

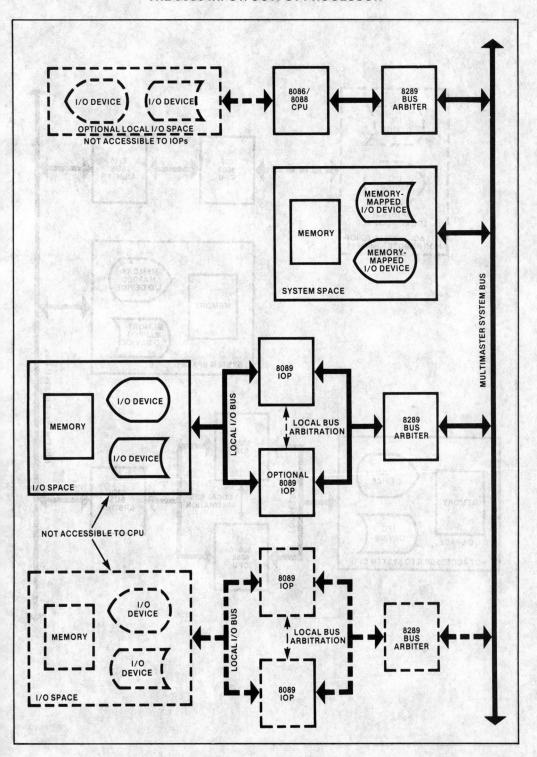

Figure 7-7 Remote Configuration

210911

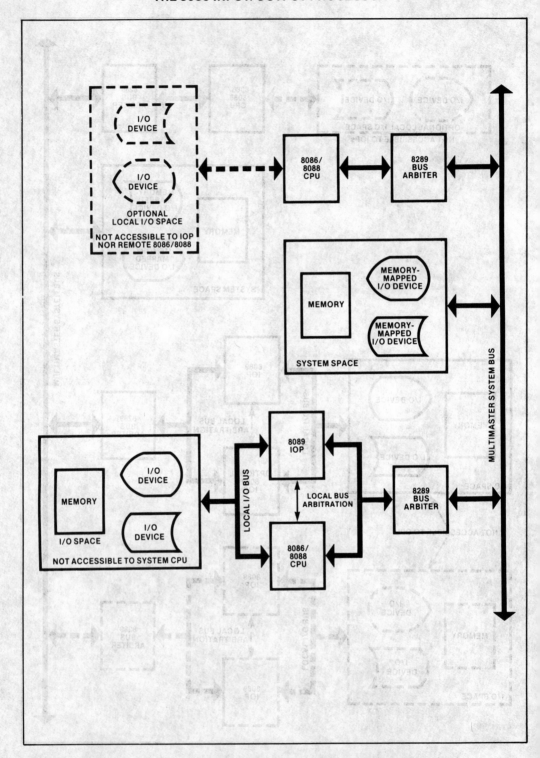

Figure 7-8 Remote IOP Configured With Local 8086/8088

210911

THE 8089 INPUT/OUTPUT PROCESSOR

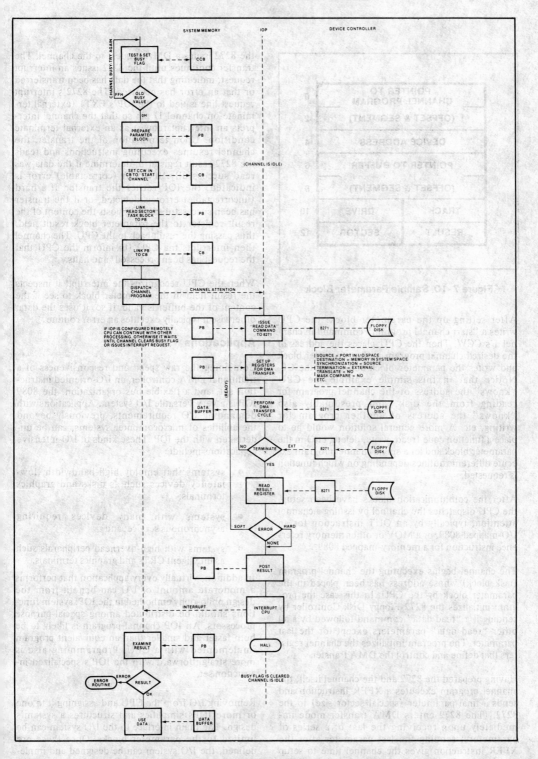

Figure 7-9 Sample CPU/IOP Transaction

210911

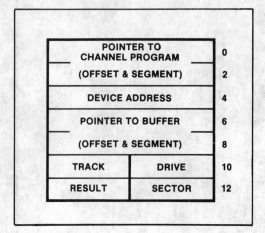

POINTER TO CHANNEL PROGRAM		0
(OFFSET & SEGMENT)		2
DEVICE ADDRESS		4
POINTER TO BUFFER		6
(OFFSET & SEGMENT)		8
TRACK	DRIVE	10
RESULT	SECTOR	12

Figure 7-10 Sample Parameter Block

After setting up the parameter block, the CPU writes a "start channel program" command in channel 1's CCW. Then the CPU places the address of the desired channel program in the parameter block and writes the parameter block address in the CB. Notice that in this simple example the CPU "knows" the address of the channel program for reading from the disk, and presumably also "knows" the address of another program for writing, etc. A more general solution would be to place a function code (read, write, delete, etc.) in the parameter block and let a single channel program execute different routines depending on which function is requested.

After the communication blocks have been setup, the CPU dispatches the channel by issuing a channel attention, typically by an OUT instruction for an I/O-mapped 8089, or a MOV or other memory reference instruction for a memory-mapped 8089.

The channel begins executing the channel program (task block) whose address has been placed in the parameter block by the CPU. In this case the program initializes the 8272 Floppy Disk Controller by sending it a "read data" command followed by a all other "read data" parameters except for the last parameter. The program initializes the channel registers that define and control the DMA transfer.

Having prepared the 8272 and the channel itself, the channel program executes a XFER instruction and sends a final parameter (special sector size) to the 8272. (The 8272 enters DMA transfer mode immediately upon receiving the last of a series of parameters; sending the last parameter after the XFER instruction gives the channel time to setup for the transfer.) The DMA transfer begins when the 8272 issues a DMA request to the channel. The transfer continues until the 8272 issues an interrupt request, indicating that the data has been transferred or that an error has occurred. The 8272's interrupt request line is tied to the IOP's EXT1 (external terminate on channel 1) pin so that the channel interprets an interrupt request as an external terminate condition. Upon termination of the transfer, the channel resumes executing instructions and reads the 8272 result register to determine if the data was read successfully. If a soft (correctable) error is indicated, the IOP retries the transfer. If a hard (uncorrectable) error is detected, or if the transfer has been successful, the IOP posts the content of the result register to the parameter block result field, thus passing the result back to the CPU. The channel then interrupts the CPU (to inform the CPU that the request has been processed) and halts.

When the CPU recognizes the interrupt, it inspects the result field in the parameter block to see if the content of the buffer is valid. If so, it uses the data; otherwise it typically executes an error routine.

Applications

Combining the raw speed and responsiveness of a traditional DMA controller, an I/O-oriented instruction set, and a flexible bus organization, the 8089 IOP is a very versatile I/O system. Applications with demanding I/O requirements, previously beyond the abilities of microcomputer systems, can be undertaken with the IOP. These kinds of I/O-intensive applications include:

- systems that employ high-bandwidth, low-latency devices such as disks and graphics terminals;

- systems with many devices requiring asynchronous service; and

- systems with high-overhead peripherals such as intelligent CRTs and graphics terminals.

In addition, virtually every application that performs a moderate amount of I/O can benefit from the design philosophy embodied in the IOP: system functions should be distributed among special-purpose processors. An IOP channel program is likely to be both faster and smaller than an equivalent program implemented with a CPU. Programming also is more straightforward with the IOP's specialized instruction set.

Removing I/O from the CPU and assigning it to one or more IOPs simplifies and structures a system's design. The main interface to the I/O system can be limited to the parameter blocks. Once these are defined, the I/O system can be designed and implemented in parallel with the rest of the system. I/O specialists can work on the I/O system without detailed knowledge of the application; conversely, the operating system and application teams do not need to be expert in the operation of I/O devices. Standard high-level I/O systems can be used in multiple application systems. Because the application and I/O systems are almost independent, application system changes can be introduced without affecting the I/O system. New peripherals can similarly be incorporated into a system without impacting applications or operating system software. The IOP's simple CPU interface also is designed to be compatible with future Intel CPUs.

Keeping in mind the true general-purpose nature of the IOP, some of the situations where it can be used to advantage are:

- Bus matching—The IOP can transfer data between virtually any combination of 8- and 16-bit memory and I/O components. For example, it can interface a 16-bit peripheral to an 8-bit CPU bus, such as the 8088 bus. The IOP also provides a straightforward means of performing DMA between an 8-bit peripheral and 8086 memory that is split into odd- and even-addressed banks. The 8089 can access both 8- and 16-bit peripherals connected to a 16-bit bus.

- String processing—The 8089 can perform a memory move, translate, scan-for-match or scan-for-nonmatch operation much faster than the equivalent instructions in an 8086 or 8088. Translate and scan operations can be setup so that the source and destination refer to the same addresses to permit the string to be operated on in place.

- Spooling—Data from low-speed devices such as terminals and paper tape readers can be read by the 8089 and placed into memory or on disk until the transmission is complete. The IOP can then transfer the data at high speed when it is needed by an application program. Conversely, output data ultimately destined for a low-speed device such as a printer, can be temporarily spooled to disk and then printed later. This permits batches of data to be gathered or distributed by low-priority programs that run in the background, essentially using up "spare" CPU and IOP cycles. Application programs that use or produce the data can execute faster because they are not bound by the low-speed devices.

- Multitasking operating systems—A multitasking operating system can dispatch I/O tasks to channels with an absolute minimum of overhead. Because a remote channel can run

in parallel with the CPU, the operating system's capacity for servicing application tasks can increase dramatically, as can its ability to handle more, and faster, I/O devices. If both channels of an IOP are active concurrently, the IOP automatically gives preference to the higher-priority activity (e.g., DMA normally preempts channel program execution). The operating system can adjust the priority mechanism and also can halt or suspend a channel to take care of a critical asynchronous event.

- Disk systems—The IOP can meet the speed and latency requirements of hard disks. It can be used implement high-level, file-oriented systems that appear to application programs as simple commands: OPEN, READ, WRITE, etc. The IOP can search and update disk directories and maintain free space maps. "Hierarchical memory" systems that automatically transfer data among memory, high-speed disks and low-speed disks, based on frequency of use, can be built around IOPs. Complex database searches (reading data directly or following pointer chains) can appear to programs as simple commands and can execute in parallel with application programs if an IOP is configured remotely.

- Display terminals—The 8089 is well suited to handling the DMA requirements of CRT controllers. The IOP's transfer bandwidth is high enough to support both alphanumeric and graphic displays. The 8089 can assume responsibility for refreshing the display from memory data; in the remote configuration, the refresh overhead display algorithms may be programmed to perform sophisticated modes of display.

Each time it performs a refresh operation, the IOP can scan a keyboard for input and translate the key's row-and-column format into an ASCII or EBCDIC character. The 8089 can buffer the characters, scanning the stream until an end-of-message character (e.g., carriage return) is detected, and then interrupt the CPU.

A single IOP can concurrently support an alphanumeric CRT and keyboard on one channel and a floppy disk on the other channel. This configuration makes use of approximately 30 percent of the available bus bandwidth. Performance can be increased within the available bus bandwidth by adding an 8086 or 8088 CPU to a remote IOP configuration. This configuration can provide scaling, rotation or other sophisticated display transformations.

7.3 PROCESSOR ARCHITECTURE

The 8089 is internally divided into the functional units depicted schematically in Figure 7-11. The units are connected by a 20-bit data path to obtain maximum internal transfer rates.

Common Control Unit (CCU)

All IOP operations (instructions, DMA transfer cycles, channel attention responses, etc.) are composed of sequences of more basic processes called internal cycles. A bus cycle takes one internal cycle; the execution of an instruction may require several internal cycles. There are 23 different types of internal cycles, each of which takes from two to eight clocks to execute, not including possible wait states and bus arbitration times.

The common control unit (CCU) coordinates the activities of the IOP primarily by allocating internal cycles to the various processor units; i.e., it determines which unit will execute the next internal cycle. For example, when both channels are active, the CCU determines which channel has priority and lets that channel run; if the channels have equal priority, the CCU "interleaves" their execution

(this is discussed more fully later in this section). The CCU also initializes the processor.

Arithmetic/Logic Unit (ALU)

The ALU can perform unsigned binary arithmetic on 8- and 16-bit binary numbers. Arithmetic results may be up to 20 bits in length. Available arithmetic instructions include addition, increment and decrement. Logical operations ("and," "or" and "not") may be performed on either 8- or 16-bit quantities.

Assembly/Disassembly Registers

All data entering the chip flows through these registers. When data is being transferred between different width buses, the 8089 uses the assembly/disassembly registers to effect the transfer in the fewest possible bus cycles. In a DMA transfer from an 8-bit peripheral to 16-bit memory, for example, the IOP runs two bus cycles, picking up eight bits in each cycle, assembles a 16-bit word, and then transfers the word to memory in a single bus cycles. (The first and last cycles of a transfer may be performed differently to accommodate odd-addressed words; the IOP automatically adjusts for this condition.)

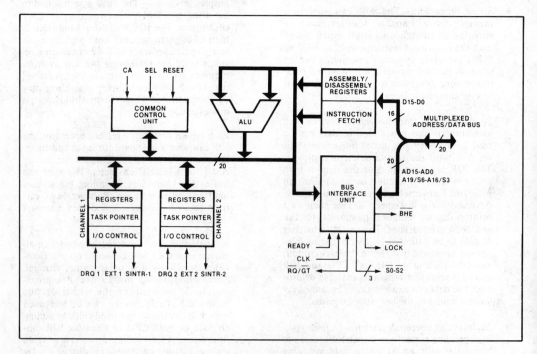

Figure 7-11 8089 Block Diagram

210911

Instruction Fetch Unit

The unit controls instruction fetching for the executing channel (one channel actually runs at a time). If the bus over which the instructions are being fetched is eight bits wide, then the instructions are obtained one byte at a time, and each fetch requires one bus cycle. If the instructions are being fetched over a 16-bit bus, then the instruction fetch unit automatically employs a 1-byte queue to reduce the number of bus cycles. Each channel has its own queue, and the activity of one channel does not affect the other's queue.

During sequential execution, instructions are fetched one word at a time from even addresses; each fetch requires one bus cycle. This process is shown graphically in Figure 7-12. When the last byte of an instruction falls on an even address, the odd-addressed byte (the first byte of the following instruction) of the fetched word is saved in the queue. When the channel begins execution of the next instruction, it fetches the first byte from the queue rather than from memory. The queue, then, keeps the processor fetching words, rather than bytes, thereby reducing its use of the bus and increasing throughput.

The processor fetches bytes rather than words in two cases. If a program transfer instruction (e.g., JMP or CALL) directs the processor to an instruction located at an odd address, the first byte of the instruction is fetched by itself as shown in Figure 7-13. This is because the program transfer invalidates the content of the queue by changing the serial flow of execution.

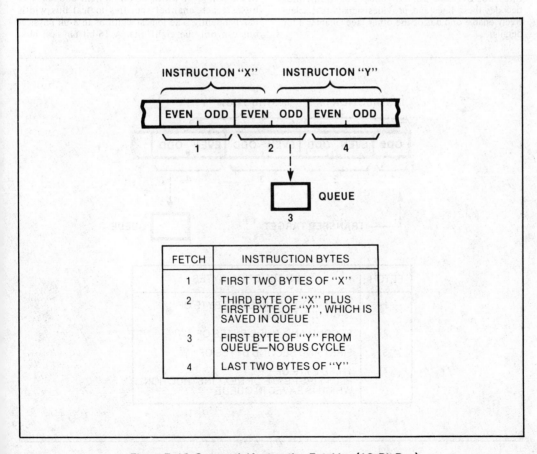

INSTRUCTION "X"   INSTRUCTION "Y"

| EVEN | ODD | EVEN | ODD | EVEN | ODD |

1   2   4

QUEUE
3

FETCH	INSTRUCTION BYTES
1	FIRST TWO BYTES OF "X"
2	THIRD BYTE OF "X" PLUS FIRST BYTE OF "Y", WHICH IS SAVED IN QUEUE
3	FIRST BYTE OF "Y" FROM QUEUE—NO BUS CYCLE
4	LAST TWO BYTES OF "Y"

Figure 7-12 Sequential Instruction Fetching (16-Bit Bus)

210911

The second case arises when an LPDI instruction is located at an odd address. In this situation, the six-byte LPDI instruction is fetched: byte, word, byte, byte, byte, and the queue is not used. The first byte of the following instruction is fetched in one bus cycle as if it had been the target of a program transfer. Word fetching resumes with this instruction's second byte.

Bus Interface Unit (BIU)

The BIU runs all bus cycles, transferring instructions and data between the IOP and external memory or peripherals. Every bus access is associated with a register tag bit that indicates to the BIU whether the system or I/O space is to be addressed. The BIU outputs the type of bus cycle (instruction fetch from I/O space, data store into system space, etc.) on status lines S0, S1, and S2. An 8288 Bus Controller decodes these lines and provides signals that selectively enable one bus or the other (see Chapter 4 for details).

The BIU further distinguishes between the physical and logical widths of the system and I/O buses. The physical widths of the buses are fixed and are communicated to the BIU during initialization. In the local configuration, both buses must be the same width, either 8 or 16 bits (matching the width of the host CPU bus). In the remote configuration, the IOP system bus must be the same physical width as the bus it shares with the CPU. The width of the IOP's I/O bus, which is local to the 8089, may be selected independently. If any 16-bit peripherals are located in the I/O space, then a 16-bit I/O bus must be used. If only 8-bit devices reside on the I/O bus, then either an 8-bit or a 16-bit I/O bus may be selected. A 16-bit I/O bus has the advantage of easy accommodation of future 16-bit devices and fewer instruction fetches if channel programs are placed in the I/O space.

For a given DMA transfer, a channel program specifies the logical width of the system and the I/O buses; each channel specifies logical bus width independently. The logical width of an 8-bit physical bus can only be eight bits. A 16-bit physical bus,

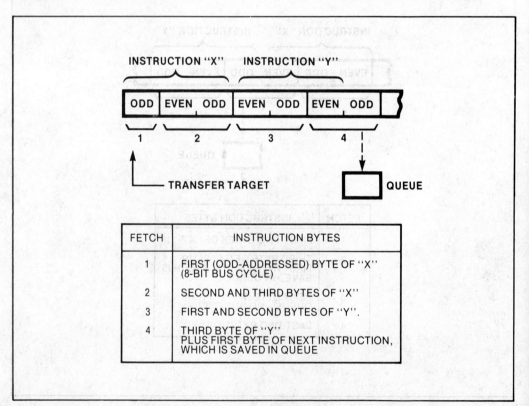

FETCH	INSTRUCTION BYTES
1	FIRST (ODD-ADDRESSED) BYTE OF "X" (8-BIT BUS CYCLE)
2	SECOND AND THIRD BYTES OF "X"
3	FIRST AND SECOND BYTES OF "Y".
4	THIRD BYTE OF "Y" PLUS FIRST BYTE OF NEXT INSTRUCTION, WHICH IS SAVED IN QUEUE

Figure 7-13 Instruction Fetching Following a Program Transfer to an Odd Address (16-Bit Bus)

however, can be used as either an 8- or 16-bit logical bus. This allows both 8- and 16-bit devices to be accessed over a single 16-bit physical bus. Table 7-1 lists the permissible physical and logical bus widths for both locally and remotely configured IOPs. Logical bus width pertains to DMA transfers only. Instructions are fetched and operands are read and written in bytes or words depending on physical bus width.

Table 7-1 Physical/Logical Bus Combinations

Configuration	System Bus Physical:Logical	I/O Bus Physical:Logical
Local	8:8 16:8/16	8:8 16:8/16
Remote	8:8 16:8/16 16:8/16 8:8	8:8 16:8/16 8:8 16:8/16

In addition to performing transfers, the BIU is responsible for local bus arbitration. In the local configuration, the BIU uses the $\overline{RQ/GT}$ (request/grant) line to obtain the bus from the CPU and to return it after a transfer has been performed. In the remote configuration, the BIU uses $\overline{RQ/GT}$ to coordinate use of the local I/O bus with another IOP or a local CPU, if present. System bus arbitration in the remote configuration is performed by an 8289 Bus Arbiter that operates invisibly to the IOP. The BIU automatically asserts the $\overline{LOCK}$ (bus lock) signal during execution of a TSL (test and set lock) instruction and, if specified by the channel program, can assert the $\overline{LOCK}$ signal for the duration of a DMA transfer. Volume 2 contains a complete discussion of bus arbitration.

Channels

Although the 8089 is a single processor, under most circumstances it is useful to think of it as two independent channels. A channel may perform DMA transfers and may execute channel programs; it also may be idle. This section describes the hardware features that support these operations.

I/O Control

Each channel contains its own I/O control section that governs the operation of the channel during DMA transfers. If the transfer is synchronized, the channel waits for a signal on its DRQ (DMA

request) line before performing the next fetch-store sequence in the transfer. If the transfer is to be terminated by an external signal, the channel monitors its EXT (external terminate) line and stops the transfer when this line goes active. Between the fetch and store cycles (when the data is in the IOP) the channel optionally counts, translates, and scans the data, and may terminate the transfer based on the results of these operations. Each channel also has a SINTR (system interrupt) line that can be activated by software to issue an interrupt request to the CPU.

Registers

Figure 7-14 illustrates the channel register set, and Table 7-2 summarizes the uses of each register. Each channel has an independent set of registers; they are not accessible to the other channel. Most of the registers play different roles during channel program execution than in DMA transfers. Channel programs must be careful to save these registers in memory prior to a DMA transfer if their values are needed following the transfer.

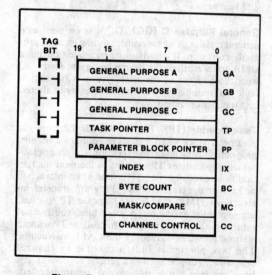

Figure 7-14 Channel Register Set

General Purpose A (GA). A channel program may use GA for a general register or a base register. A general register can be an operand of most IOP instructions; a base register is used to address memory operands (see Section 7.6). Before initiating a DMA transfer, the channel program points GA to either the source or destination address of the transfer.

210911

Table 7-2 Channel Register Summary

Register	Size	Program Access	System or I/O Pointer	Use by Channel Programs	Use in DMA Transfers
GA	20	Update	Either	General, base	Source/destination pointer
GB	20	Update	Either	General, base	Source/destination pointer
GC	20	Update	Either	General, base	Translate table pointer
TP	20	Update	Either	Procedure return, instruction pointer	Adjusted to reflect cause of termination
PP	20	Reference	System	Base	N/A
IX	16	Update	N/A	General, auto-increment	N/A
BC	16	Update	N/A	General	Byte counter
MC	16	Update	N/A	General, masked compare	Masked compare
CC	16	Update	N/A	Restricted use recommended	Defines transfer options

General Purpose B (GB). GB is functionally interchangeable with GA. If GA points to the source of a DMA transfer, then GB points to the destination, and vice versa.

General Purpose C (GC). GC may be used as a general register or a base register during channel program execution. If data is to be translated during a DMA transfer, then the channel program loads GC with the address of the first byte of a translation table before initiating the transfer. GC is not altered by a transfer operation.

Task Pointer (TP). The CCU loads TP from the parameter block when it starts or resumes a channel program. During program execution, the channel automatically updates TP to point to the next instruction to be executed; i.e., TP is used as an instruction pointer or program counter. Program transfer instructions (JMP, CALL, etc.) update TP to cause nonsequential execution. A procedure (subroutine) returns to the calling program by loading TP with an address previously saved by the CALL instruction. The task pointer is fully accessible to channel programs; it can be used as a general register or as a base register. Such use is not recommended, however, as it can make programs very difficult to understand.

Parameter Block Pointer (PP). The CCU loads this register with the address of the parameter block before it starts a channel program. The register cannot be altered by a channel program, but is very useful as a base register for accessing data in the parameter block. PP is not used during DMA transfers.

Index (IX). IX may be used as a general register during channel program execution. It also may be used as an index register to address memory operands (the address of the operand is computed by adding the content of IX to the content of a base register). When specified as an index register, IX may be optionally auto-incremented as the last step in the instruction to provide a convenient means of "stepping" through arrays or strings. IX is not used in DMA transfers.

Byte Count (BC). BC may be used as a general register during channel program execution. If DMA is to be terminated when a specific number of bytes has been transferred, BC should be loaded with the desired byte count before initiating the transfer. During DMA, BC is decremented for each byte transferred, whether byte count termination has been specified. If byte count termination has not been selected, BC "wraps around" from 0H to FFFFH and continues to be decremented.

Mask/Compare (MC). A channel program may use MC for a general register. This register also may be used either in a channel program or in a DMA transfer to perform a masked compare of a byte value. To use MC in this way, the program loads a compare value in the low-order eight bits of the register and a mask value in the upper eight bits (see Figure 7-15). A "1" in a mask bit *selects* the bit in the corresponding position in the compare value; a "0" in a mask bit *masks* the corresponding bit in the compare value. In Figure 7-15, a value compared with MC will be considered equal if its low-order five bits contain the value 00100; the upper three bits may contain any value since they are masked out of the comparison.

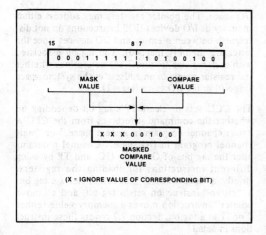

Figure 7-15 Mask/Compare Register

Channel Control (CC). The content of the channel control register governs a DMA transfer (see Figure 7-16). A channel program loads this register with appropriate values before beginning the transfer operation; Section 7.4 covers the encoding of each field in detail. Bit 8 (the chain bit) of CC pertains to channel program execution rather than to a DMA

transfer. When this bit is zero, the channel program runs at a normal priority; when it is one, the priority of the program is raised to the same level as DMA (priorities are covered later in this section). Although a channel program may use CC as a general register, such use is not recommended because of the side effects on the chain bit and thus on the priority of the channel program. Channel programs should restrict their use of CC to loading control values in preparation for a DMA transfer, setting and clearing the chain bit, and storing the register. When initializing or updating the CC register, the MOV or MOVI instruction must be used.

Program Status Word (PSW)

Each channel maintains its own program status word (PSW) as shown in Figure 7-17. Channel programs do not have access to the PSW. The PSW records the state of the channel so that channel operation may be suspended and then resumed later. When the CPU issues a "suspend" command, the channel saves the PSW, task pointer, and task pointer tag bit in the first four bytes of the channel's parameter block as shown in Figure 7-18. Upon receipt of a subsequent "resume" command, the PSW, TP, and TP tag bit are restored from the parameter block save area and execution resumes.

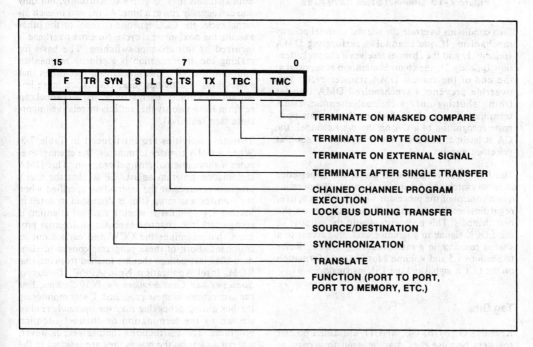

Figure 7-16 Channel Control Register

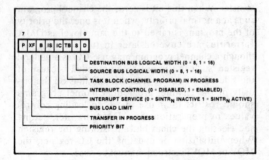

Figure 7-17 Program Status Word

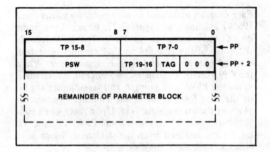

Figure 7-18 Channel State Save Area

Two conditions override the normal channel priority mechanism. If one channel is performing DMA (priority 1) and the channel receives a channel attention (priority 2), the channel attention is serviced at the end of the current DMA transfer cycle. This override prevents a synchronized DMA transfer from "shutting out" a channel attention. DMA terminations and chained channel programs postpone recognition of a CA on the *other* channel; the CA is latched, however, and is serviced as soon as priorities permit.

The IOP's $\overline{LOCK}$ (bus lock) signal also supersedes channel switching . A running channel will not relinquish control of the processor while $\overline{LOCK}$ is active, regardless of the priorities of the activities on the two channels. This is consistent with the purpose of the $\overline{LOCK}$ signal: to guarantee exclusive access to a shared resource in a multiprocessing system. Refer to Sections 7.5 and Volume 2 for further information on the $\overline{LOCK}$ signal and the TSL instruction.

Tag Bits

Registers GA, GB, GC, and TP are called pointer registers because they may be used to access, or point to, addresses in either the system space or the

I/O space. The pointer registers may address either memory or I/O devices (IOP instructions do not distinguish between memory and I/O devices since the latter are memory-mapped). The tag bit associated with each register (Figure 7-14) determines whether the register points to an address in the system space (tag=0) or the I/O space (tag=1).

The CCU sets or clears TP's tag bit depending on whether the command it receives from the CPU is "start channel program in system space," or "start channel program in I/O space." Channel programs alter the tag bits of GA, GB, GC, and TP by using different instructions for loading the registers. Briefly, a "load pointer" instruction clears a tag bit, a "move" instruction sets a tag bit, and a "move pointer" instruction moves a memory value (either 0 or 1) to a tag bit. Section 7.7 covers these instructions in detail.

If a register points to the system space, all 20 bits are placed on the address lines to allow the full megabyte to be directly addressed. If a register points to the I/O space, the upper four bits of the address lines are undefined; the lower 16 bits are sufficient to access any location in the 64K byte I/O space.

Concurrent Channel Operation

Both channels may be active concurrently, but only one can actually run at a time. At the end of each internal cycle, the CCU lets one channel or the other execute the next internal cycle. No extra overhead is incurred by this channel switching. The basis for making the determination is a priority mechanism built into the IOP. This mechanism recognizes that some kinds of activities (e.g., DMA) are more important than others. Each activity that a channel can perform has a priority that reflects its relative importance (see Table 7-3).

Two new activities are introduced in Table 7-3. When a DMA transfer terminates, the channel executes a short internal channel program. This DMA termination program adjusts TP so that the user's program resumes at the instruction specified when the transfer was setup (this is discussed in detail in Section 7.4). Similarly, when a channel attention is recognized, the channel executes an internal program that examines the CCW and carries out its command. Both of these programs consist of standard 8089 instructions that are fetched from internal ROM. Intel Application Note AP-50, *Debugging Strategies and Considerations for 8089 Systems*, lists the instructions in these programs. Users monitoring the bus during debugging may see operands read or written by the termination or channel attention programs. The instructions themselves, however, will not appear on the bus as they are resident in the chip.

Table 7-3 Channel Priorities and Interleave Boundaries

Channel Activity	Priority (1 = highest)	Interleave Boundary	
		By DMA	By Instruction
DMA transfer	1	Bus cycle[1]	Bus cycle[1]
DMA termination sequence	1	Internal cycle	None
Channel program (chained)	1	Internal cycle[2]	Instruction
Channel attention sequence	2	Internal cycle	None
Channel program (not chained)	3	Internal cycle[2]	Instruction
Idle	4	Two clocks	Two clocks

[1]DMA is not interleaved while $\overline{\text{LOCK}}$ is active.
[2]Except TSL instruction; see section 3.7.

Notice also that, according to Table 7-3, a channel program may run at priority 3 or at priority 1. Channel program priority is determined by the chain bit in the channel control register. If this bit is cleared, the program runs at normal priority (3); if it is set, the program is said to be chained, and it runs at the same priority as DMA. Thus, the chain bit provides a way to raise the priority of a critical channel program.

The CCU lets the channel with the highest priority run. If both channels are running activities with the same priority, the CCU examines the priority bits in the PSWs. If the priority bits are unequal, the channel with the higher value (1) runs. Thus, the priority bits serves as a "tie breaker" when the channels are otherwise at the same priority level. The value of the priority bit in the PSW is loaded from a corresponding bit in the CCW; therefore, the CPU can control which channel will run when the channels are at the same priority level. The priority bit has no effect when the channel priorities are different. If both channels are at the same priority level and if both priority bits are equal, the channels run alternately without any additional overhead.

The CCU switches channels only at certain points called interleave boundaries; these vary according to the type of activity running in each channel and are shown in Table 7-3. In Table 7-3 and in the following discussion, the terms "channel A" and "channel B" are used to identify two active channels that are bidding for control of an IOP. "Channel A" is the channel that last ran and will run again unless the CCU switches to "channel B." Where the CCU switches from one channel (channel A) to another (channel B) depends on whether channel B is performing DMA or is executing instructions. For this determination, instructions in the internal ROM are considered the same as instructions executed in user-written channel programs (chained or not chained). Table 7-3 shows that a switch from channel A to channel B will occur sooner if channel B is running DMA. DMA, then, interleaves instruction execution at internal cycle boundaries. Since instructions are often composed of several internal cycles, instruction execution on channel A can be suspended by DMA on channel B (when channel A next runs, the instruction is resumed from the point of suspension). DMA on channel A is interleaved by DMA on channel B after any bus cycle (when channel A runs again, the DMA transfer sequence is resumed from the point of suspension). If both channels are executing programs, the interleaved boundaries are extended to instruction boundaries: a program on channel B will not run until channel A reaches the end of an instruction. Note that a DMA termination sequence or channel attention sequence on channel A cannot be interleaved by instructions on channel B, regardless of channel B's priority. These internal programs are short, however, and will not delay channel B for long (see Chapter 4 for timing information).

Table 7-4 summarizes the channel switching mechanism with several examples. It is important to remember that channel switching occurs only when both channels are ready to run. In typical applications, one of the channels will be idle much of the time, either because it is waiting to be dispatched by the CPU, or because it is waiting for a DMA request in a synchronized transfer. (During a synchronized transfer, the channel is idle between DMA requests; for many peripherals, the channel will spend much more time idling than executing DMA cycles.) The real potential for one channel "shutting out" a priority 1 activity on the other channel is largely limited to unsynchronized DMA transfers and locked transfers (synchronized or unsynchro-

unsynchronized). Long, chained channel programs and high-speed synchronized DMA will slow a priority 1 activity on the other channel, but will not shut it out because the channels will alternate (assuming their priority bits are equal). A chained channel program will shut out any lower priority activity on the other channel, including a channel attention. (The channel attention is latched by the IOP, however, so it will execute when the other channel drops to a lower priority.) Chained channel programs should therefore be used with discretion and should be made as short as possible.

7.4 INPUT/OUTPUT

The 8089 combines the programmed I/O capabilities of a CPU with the high-speed block transfer facility of a DMA controller. It also provides additional features (e.g., compare and translate during DMA) and is more flexible than a typical CPU or DMA controller. The 8089 transfers data from a source address to a destination address. Whether the component mapped into a given address is actually memory or I/O is immaterial. All addresses in both the system and I/O spaces are equally accessible, and transfers may be made between the two spaces as well as within either address space.

Programmed I/O

A channel program performs I/O similar to the way a CPU communicates with memory-mapped I/O devices. Memory reference instructions perform the transfer rather than "dedicated" I/O instructions, such as the 8086, 8088 IN and OUT instructions. Programmed I/O is typically used to prepare a device controller for a DMA transfer and to obtain status/result information from the controller following termination of the transfer. It may, however, be used with any device whose transfer rate does not require DMA.

I/O Instructions

Since the 8089 does not distinguish between memory components and I/O devices, any instruction that accepts a byte or word memory operand can be used to access an I/O device. Most memory reference instructions take a source operand or a destination operand, or both. The instructions generally obtain data from the source operand, operate on the data, and then place the result of the operation in the destination operand. Therefore, when a source operand refers to an address where an I/O device is located, data is input from the device. Similarly, when a destination operand refers to an I/O device address, data is output to the device.

Table 7-4 Channel Switching Examples

Channel A (Ran Last)				Channel B			Result
Activity	Chain Bit	Priority Bit	LOCK	Activity	Chain Bit	Priority Bit	
DMA transfer	X	X	Inactive	Idle	X	X	A runs.
DMA transfer	X	X	Inactive	Channel attention	X	X	A runs until end of current transfer cycle; then B runs.
Channel program	X	0	Inactive	Channel program	X	1	B runs.
Channel program	X	0	Inactive	Channel program	X	0	A and B alternate by instruction.
Channel program	1	X	Inactive	Channel program	0	X	A runs.
DMA transfer	X	1	Inactive	Channel program	1	1	B runs one bus or internal cycle following each bus cycle run by A.*
Channel attention	X	X	Inactive	Channel program	1	X	A runs if it has started the sequence; otherwise B runs.
DMA transfer	X	X	Active	Channel attention	X	X	A runs until DMA terminates.
Channel program (TSL instruction)	0	X	Active	DMA transfer	X	X	A completes TSL instruction, LOCK goes inactive and B runs.

*If transfer is synchronized, B also runs when A goes idle between transfer cycles.

Most I/O device controllers have one or more internal registers that accept commands and supply status or result information. Working with these registers typically involves:

- reading or writing the entire register;

- setting or clearing some bits in a register while leaving others alone; or

- testing a single bit in a register.

Table 7-5 shows some of the 8089 instructions that are useful for performing these kinds of operations. Section 7.5 covers the 8089 instruction set in detail.

Table 7-5 Memory Reference Instructions Used for I/O

Instruction	Effect on I/O Device
MOV/MOVB	Read or write word/byte
AND/ANDB	Clear multiple bits in word/byte
OR/ORB	Set multiple bits in word/byte
CLR	Clear single bit (in byte)
SET	Set single bit (in byte)
JBT	Read (byte) and jump if single bit =1
JNBT	Read (byte) and jump if single bit =0

Device Addressing

Since memory reference instructions are used to perform programmed I/O, device addressing is very similar to memory addressing. An operand that refers to an I/O device always specifies one of the pointer registers GA, GB, or GC (PP is legal, but an I/O device would not normally be mapped into a parameter block). The base address of the device is taken from the specified pointer register. Any of the memory addressing modes (see Section 7.6) may be used to modify the base address to produce the effective (actual) address of the device. The pointer register's tag bit locates the device in the system space (tag=0) or in the I/O space (tag=1). If the device is in the I/O space, only the low-order 16 bits of the pointer register are used for the base address; all 20 bits are used for a system space address. The IOP's system and I/O spaces are fully compatible with the corresponding address spaces of the other iAPX 86,186 family processors.

I/O Bus Transfers

Table 7-6 shows the number of bus cycles the IOP runs for all combinations of bus size, transfer size (byte or word), and transfer address (even or odd). Bus width refers to the physical bus implementation; the instruction mnemonic determines whether a byte or a word is transferred.

Both 8- and 16-bit devices may reside on a 16-bit bus. All 16-bit devices should be located at even addresses so that transfers will be performed in one bus cycle. The 8-bit devices on a 16-bit bus may be located at odd or even addresses. The internal registers in an 8-bit device on a 16-bit bus must be assigned all-odd or all-even addresses that are two bytes apart (e.g., 1H, 3H, 5H, or 2H, 4H, 6H). All 8-bit peripherals should be referenced with byte instructions, and 16-bit devices should be referenced with word instructions. Odd-addressed 8-bit devices must be able to transfer data on the upper eight bits of the 16-bit physical data bus.

Only 8-bit devices should be connected to an 8-bit bus, and these should only be referenced with byte instructions. An 8-bit device on an 8-bit bus may be located at an odd or even address, and its internal

Table 7-6 Programmed I/O Bus Transfers

Bus Width:	8				16			
Instruction:	byte		word*		byte		word	
Device Address:	even	odd	even	odd	even	odd	even	odd*
Bus Cycles:	1	1	2	2	1	1	1	2

* not normally used

210911

registers may be assigned consecutive addresses (e.g., 1H, 2H, 3H). Assigning all-odd or all-even addresses, however, will simplify conversion to a 16-bit bus at a later date.

DMA Transfers

In addition to byte- and word-oriented programmed I/O, the 8089 can transfer blocks of data by direct memory access. A block may be transferred between any two addresses; memory-to-memory transfers are performed as easily as memory-to-port, port-to-memory or port-to-port exchanges. There is no limitation on the size of the block that can be transferred except that the block cannot exceed 64K bytes if byte count termination is used. A channel program typically prepares for a DMA transfer by writing commands to a device controller and initializing channel registers that are used during the transfer. No instructions are executed during the transfer, however, and very high throughput speeds can be achieved.

Preparing the Device Controller

Most controllers that can perform DMA transfers are quite flexible in that they can perform several different types of operations. For example, an 8272 Floppy Disk Controller can read a sector, write a sector, seek to track 0, etc. The controller typically has one or more internal registers that are "programmed" to perform a given operation. Often, certain registers will contain status information that can be read to determine if the controller is busy, if it has detected an error, etc.

An 8089 channel program views these device registers as a series of memory locations. The channel program typically places the device's base address in a pointer register and uses programmed I/O to communicate with the registers.

Some controllers start a DMA transfer immediately upon receiving the last of a series of parameters. If this type of controller is being used, the channel program instruction that sends the last parameter should *follow* the 8089 XFER instruction. (The XFER instruction places the channel in DMA mode after the next instruction; this is explained in more detail later in this section).

Preparing the Channel

For a channel to perform a DMA transfer, it must be provided with information that describes the operation. The channel program provides this information by loading values into channel registers and, in one case, by executing a special instruction (see Table 7-7).

Source and destination pointers. One register is loaded to point to the transfer source; the other points to the destination. A bit in the channel control register is set to indicate which register is the source pointer. If a register is pointed at a memory location, it should contain the address where the transfer is to begin — i.e., the lowest address in the buffer. The channel automatically increments a memory pointer as the transfer proceeds. If the tag bit selects the I/O space, the upper four bits of the register are ignored; if the tag selects the system space, all 20 bits are used. The source and destination may be located in the same or in different address spaces.

Translate Table Pointer. If the data is to be translated as it is transferred, GC should be pointed at the first (lowest-addressed) byte in a 256-byte translation table. The table may be located in either the system or I/O space, and GC should be loaded by an instruction that sets or clears its tag bit as appropriate. The translate operation is only defined for byte data; source and destination logical bus width must both be set to eight bits.

Table 7-7 DMA Transfer Control Information

Information	Register or Instruction	Required or Optional
Source Pointer	GA or GB	Required
Destination Pointer	GA or GB	Required
Translate Table Pointer	GC	Optional
Byte Count	BC	Optional
Mask/Compare Values	MC	Optional
Logical Bus Width	WID	Optional*
Channel Control	CC	Required

*Must be executed once following processor RESET.

The channel translates a byte by treating it as an unsigned 8-bit binary number. This number is added to the contents of register GC to form a memory address; GC is not altered by the operation. If GC points to the I/O space, its upper four bits are ignored in the operation. The byte at this address (which is in the translate table) is then fetched from memory, replacing the source byte. Figure 7-19 illustrates the translate process.

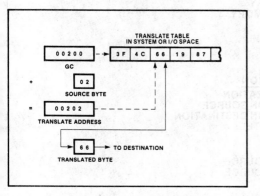

Figure 7-19 Translate Operation

Byte Count. If the transfer is to be terminated on byte count—i.e., after a specific number of bytes have been transferred—the desired count should be loaded into register BC as an unsigned 16-bit number. The channel decrements BC as the transfer proceeds, whether or not byte count termination has been specified. There are cases (discussed later in this section) where the difference between BC's value before and after the transfer does not accurately reflect the number of bytes transferred to the destination.

Mask/Compare Values. If the transfer is to be terminated when a byte (possibly translated) is found equal or unequal to a search value, MC should be loaded as described in Section 7.3. MC is not altered during the transfer. Normally, the logical destination bus width is set to eight bits when transferred data is being compared. If the logical destination width is 16 bits, only the low-order byte of each word is compared.

Logical Bus Width. The 8089 WID (logical bus width) instruction is used to set the logical width of the source and destination buses for a DMA transfer. Any bus whose physical width is eight bits can only have a logical width of eight bits. A 16-bit physical bus, however, can have a logical width of 8 or 16 bits; i.e., it can be used as either an 8-bit or 16-bit bus in any given transfer. Logical bus widths are set independently for each channel.

For a transfer to or from an I/O device on a 16-bit physical bus, the logical bus width should be set equal to the peripheral's width; i.e., 8 or 16 bits. Transfers to or from 16-bit memory will run at maximum speed if the logical bus width is set to 16, since the channel will fetch/store words. In the following cases, however, the logical width should be set to 8:

- the data is being translated,

- the data is being compared under mask, and the 16-bit memory is the destination of the transfer.

The WID instruction sets both logical widths and remains in effect until another WID instruction is executed. Following processor reset, the settings of the logical bus widths are unpredictable. Therefore, the WID instruction must be executed before the first DMA transfer.

Channel Control. The 16 bits of the CC register are divided into 10 fields that specify how the DMA transfer is to be executed (see Figure 7-20). A channel program typically sets these fields by loading a word into the register. When initializing or updating the CC register, the MOV or MOVI instruction must be used.

The *function field* (bits 15-14) identifies the source and destination as memory or ports (I/O devices). During the transfer, the channel increments source/destination pointer registers that refer to memory, so that the data will be placed in successive locations. Pointers that refer to I/O devices remain constant throughout the transfer.

The *translate field* (bit 13) controls data translation. If it is set, each incoming byte is translated using the table pointed to by register GC. Translate is defined only for byte transfers; the destination bus must have a logical width of eight.

The *synchronization field* (bits 12-11) specifies how the transfer is to be synchronized. Unsynchronized ("free running") transfers are typically used in memory-to memory moves. The channel begins the next transfer cycle immediately upon completion of the current cycle (assuming it has the bus). Slow memories, which cannot run as fast as the channel, can extend bus cycles by signaling "not ready" to the 8284A Clock Generator, which will insert wait states into the bus cycle. A similar technique may be used with peripherals whose speed exceeds the channel's ability to execute a synchronized transfer: in effect, the peripheral synchronizes the transfer through the use of wait states. Chapter 4 discusses synchronization in more detail.

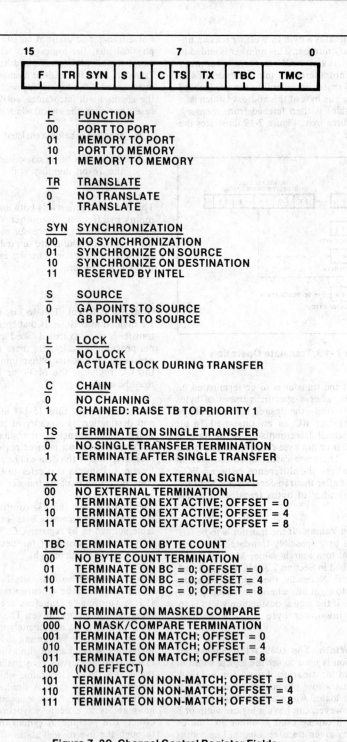

15						7				0
F	TR	SYN	S	L	C	TS	TX	TBC	TMC	

F	**FUNCTION**	
00	PORT TO PORT	
01	MEMORY TO PORT	
10	PORT TO MEMORY	
11	MEMORY TO MEMORY	
TR	**TRANSLATE**	
0	NO TRANSLATE	
1	TRANSLATE	
SYN	**SYNCHRONIZATION**	
00	NO SYNCHRONIZATION	
01	SYNCHRONIZE ON SOURCE	
10	SYNCHRONIZE ON DESTINATION	
11	RESERVED BY INTEL	
S	**SOURCE**	
0	GA POINTS TO SOURCE	
1	GB POINTS TO SOURCE	
L	**LOCK**	
0	NO LOCK	
1	ACTUATE LOCK DURING TRANSFER	
C	**CHAIN**	
0	NO CHAINING	
1	CHAINED: RAISE TB TO PRIORITY 1	
TS	**TERMINATE ON SINGLE TRANSFER**	
0	NO SINGLE TRANSFER TERMINATION	
1	TERMINATE AFTER SINGLE TRANSFER	
TX	**TERMINATE ON EXTERNAL SIGNAL**	
00	NO EXTERNAL TERMINATION	
01	TERMINATE ON EXT ACTIVE; OFFSET = 0	
10	TERMINATE ON EXT ACTIVE; OFFSET = 4	
11	TERMINATE ON EXT ACTIVE; OFFSET = 8	
TBC	**TERMINATE ON BYTE COUNT**	
00	NO BYTE COUNT TERMINATION	
01	TERMINATE ON BC = 0; OFFSET = 0	
10	TERMINATE ON BC = 0; OFFSET = 4	
11	TERMINATE ON BC = 0; OFFSET = 8	
TMC	**TERMINATE ON MASKED COMPARE**	
000	NO MASK/COMPARE TERMINATION	
001	TERMINATE ON MATCH; OFFSET = 0	
010	TERMINATE ON MATCH; OFFSET = 4	
011	TERMINATE ON MATCH; OFFSET = 8	
100	(NO EFFECT)	
101	TERMINATE ON NON-MATCH; OFFSET = 0	
110	TERMINATE ON NON-MATCH; OFFSET = 4	
111	TERMINATE ON NON-MATCH; OFFSET = 8	

Figure 7-20 Channel Control Register Fields

Source synchronization is typically selected when the source is an I/O device and the destination is memory. The I/O device starts the next transfer cycle by activating the channel's DRQ (DMA request) line. The channel then runs one transfer cycle and waits for the next DRQ.

Destination synchronization is most often used when the source is memory and the destination is an I/O device. Again, the I/O device controls the transfer frequency by signaling on DRQ when it is ready to receive the next byte or word.

The *source field* (bit 10) identifies register GA or GB as the source pointer (and the other as the destination pointer).

The *lock field* (bit 9) may be used to instruct the channel to assert the processor's bus lock (LOCK) signal during the transfer. In a source-synchronized transfer, $\overline{LOCK}$ is active from the time the first DMA request is received until the channel enters the termination sequence. In a destination synchronized transfer, $\overline{LOCK}$ is active from the first fetch (which precedes the first DMA request) until the channel enters the termination sequence.

The *chain field* (bit 8) is not used during the transfer. As discussed previously, setting this bit raises channel program execution to priority level 1.

The *terminate on single transfer field* (bit 7) can be used to cause the channel to run one complete transfer cycle only — i.e., to transfer one byte or word and immediately resume channel program execution. When single transfer is specified, any other termination conditions are ignored. Single transfer termination can be used with low-speed devices, such as keyboards and communication lines, to translate and/or compare one byte as it is transferred.

The *three low-order fields* in register CC instruct the channel when to terminate the transfer, assuming that single transfer has not been selected. Three termination conditions may be specified singly or in combination.

External termination allows an I/O device (typically, the one that is synchronizing the transfer) to stop the transfer by activating the channel's EXT (external terminate) line. If byte count termination is selected, the channel will stop when BC=0. If masked compare termination is specified, the channel will stop the transfer when a byte is found that is equal or unequal (two options are available) to the low-order byte in MC as masked by MC's high-order byte. The byte that stops the termination is transferred. If translate has been specified, the translated byte is compared.

When a DMA transfer ends, the channel adds a value called the termination offset to the task pointer and resumes channel program execution at that point in the program. The termination offset may assume a value of 0, 4, or 8. Single transfer termination always results in a termination offset of 0. Figure 7-21 shows how the termination offsets can be used as indices into a three-element "jump table" that identifies the condition that caused the termination.

As an example of using the jump table, consider a case in which a transfer is to terminate when 80 bytes have been transferred or a linefeed character is detected, whichever occurs first. The program would load 50H into BC and 000AH into MC (ASCII line feed, no bits masked). The channel program could assign byte count termination an offset of 0 and masked compare termination an offset of 4. If the transfer is terminated by byte count (no linefeed is found), the instruction at location TP + 0 will be executed first after the termination. If the linefeed is found before the byte count expires, the instruction at TP + 4 will be executed first. The LJMP (long unconditional jump, see Section 7.5) instruction is four bytes long and can be placed at TP + 0 and TP + 4 to cause the channel program to jump to a different routine, depending on how the transfer terminates.

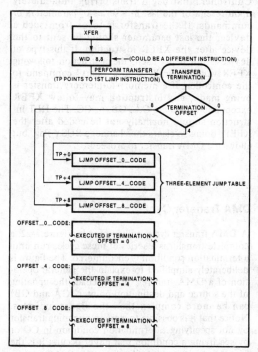

Figure 7-21 Termination Jump Table

210911

If the transfer can only terminate in one way and that condition is assigned an offset of 0, there is no need for the jump table. Code which is to be unconditionally executed when the transfer ends can immediately follow the instruction after XFER. This is also the case when single transfer is specified (execution always resumes at TP + 0).

It is possible, however, for two, or even three, termination conditions to arise at the same time. In the preceding example, this would occur if the 80th character were a linefeed. When multiple terminations occur simultaneously, the channel indicates that termination resulted from the condition with the largest offset value. In the preceding example, if byte count and search termination occur at the same time, the channel program resumes at TP + 4.

Beginning the Transfer

The 8089 XFER (transfer) instruction puts the channel into DMA transfer mode after the *following instruction* has been executed. This technique allows the channel time to set itself up when it is used with device controllers, such as the 8272 Floppy Disk Controller, that begin transferring immediately upon receipt of the last in a series of parameters or commands. If the transfer is to or from such a device, the last parameter should be sent to the device after the XFER instruction. If this type of device is not being used, the instruction following XFER would typically send a "start" command to the controller. If a memory-to-memory transfer is being made, any instruction may follow XFER except one that alters GA, GB, or CC. The HLT instruction should normally not be coded after the XFER; doing so clears the channel's BUSY flag, but allows the DMA transfer to proceed.

DMA Transfer Cycle

A DMA transfer cycle is illustrated in Figure 7-22; a complete transfer is a series of these cycles run until a termination condition is encountered. The figure is deliberately simplified to explain the general operation of a DMA transfer; in particular, the updating of the source and destination pointer (GA and GB) can be more complex than the figure indicates. Notice that it is possible to start an unending transfer by not specifying a termination condition in CC or by specifying a condition that never occurs; it is the programmer's responsibility to ensure that the transfer eventually stops.

If the transfer is source-synchronized, the channel waits until the synchronizing device activates the channel's DRQ line. The other channel is free to run during this idle period. The channel fetches a byte or a word, depending on the source address (contained in GA or GB) and the logical bus width. Table 7-8 shows how a channel performs the fetch/store sequence for all combinations of addresses and bus widths. If the destination is on a 16-bit logical bus and the source in on an 8-bit logical bus, and the transfer is to an even address, the channel fetches a second byte and assembles a word internally. During each fetch, the channel decrements BC according to whether a byte or word is obtained. Thus BC always indicates the number of bytes fetched.

The channel samples its EXT line after every bus cycle in the transfer. If EXT is recognized after the first of two scheduled fetches, the second fetch is not run. After the fetch sequence has been completed, the channel translates the data if this option is specified in CC.

If a word has been fetched or assembled, and bytes are to be stored (destination bus is eight bits or transfer is to an odd address), the channel disassembles the word into two bytes. If the transfer is destination-synchronized (only one type of synchronization may be specified for a given transfer), the channel waits for DRQ before running a store cycle. It stores a word or the lower-addressed byte (which may be the only byte or the first of two bytes). Table 7-8 shows the possible combinations of even/odd addresses and logical bus widths that define the store cycle. Whenever stores are to memory on a 16-bit logical bus, the channel stores words, except that bytes may be stored on the first and last cycles.

Table 7-8 DMA Transfer Assembly/Disassembly

Address (Source→ Destination)	Logical Bus Width (Source→Destination)			
	8→8	8→16	16→8	16→16
EVEN→EVEN	B→B	B/B→W	W→B/B	W→W
EVEN→ODD	B→B	B→B	W→B/B	W→B/B
ODD→EVEN	B→B	B/B→W	B→B	B/B→W
ODD→ODD	B→B	B→B	B→B	B→B

B= Byte Fetched or Stored in 1 Bus Cycle
W= Word Fetched or Stored in 1 Bus Cycle

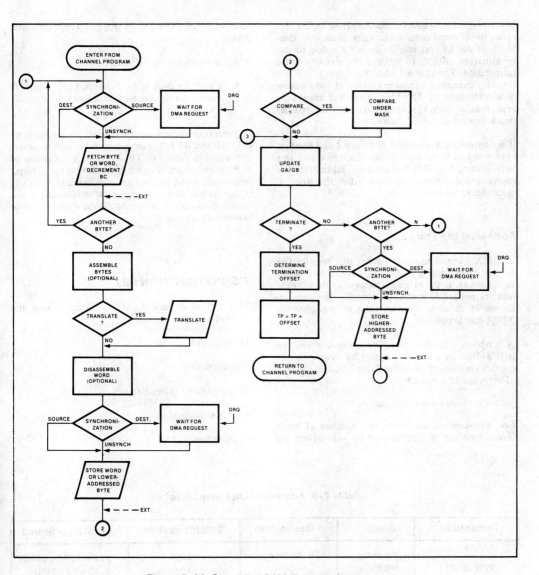

Figure 7-22 Simplified DMA Transfer Flowchart

The channel samples EXT again after the first store cycle and, if it is active, the channel prevents the second store cycle from running. If specified in the CC register, the low-order byte is compared to the value in MC. A "hit" on the comparison (equal or unequal, as indicated in CC) also prevents the second of two scheduled store cycles from running. In both of these cases, one byte has been "overfetched," and this is reflected in BC's value. It

would be unusual, however, for a synchronizing device to issue EXT in the midst of a DMA cycle. Note also that EXT is valid only when DRQ is inactive. Chapter 4 covers the timing requirements for these two signals in detail.

GA and GB are updated next. Only memory pointers are incremented; pointers to I/O devices remain constant throughout the transfer.

If a termination condition has occurred during this cycle, the channel stops the transfer. It uses the contents of the CC register to assign a value to the termination offset, to reflect the cause of the termination. The channel adds this offset to TP and resumes channel program execution at the location now addressed by TP. This offset will always be zero, four, or eight bytes past the end of the instruction following the XFER instruction.

If no termination condition is detected and another byte remains to be stored, the channel stores this byte, waiting for DRQ if necessary, and updates the source and destination pointers. After the store, it again checks for termination.

Following the Transfer

A DMA transfer updates register BC, register GA (if it points to memory), and register GB (if it points to memory). If the original contents of these registers are needed following the transfer, the contents should be saved in memory prior to executing the XFER instruction.

A program may determine the address of the last byte stored by a DMA transfer by inspecting the pointer registers as shown in Table 7-9. The number of bytes stored is equal to:

last_byte_address-first_byte_address + 1.

For port-to-port transfers, the number of bytes transferred can be determined by subtracting the final value of BC from its original value provided that:

- the original BC > final BC,

- a transfer cycle is not "chopped off" before it completes by a masked compare or external termination.

In general, programs should not use the contents of GA, GB and BC following a transfer except as noted above and in Table 7-9. This is because the contents of the registers are affected by numerous conditions, particularly when the transfer is terminated by EXT. In particular, when a program is performing a sequence of transfers, it should reload these registers before each transfer.

7.5 INSTRUCTION SET

This section divides the IOP's 53 instruction into five functional categories:

1) data transfer,

2) arithmetic,

3) logic and bit manipulation,

4) program transfer,

5) processor control.

Table 7-9 Address of Last Byte Store

Termination	Source	Destination	Synchronization	Last Byte Stored
byte count	memory	memory	any	destination pointer[1]
	memory	port	any	source pointer
	port	memory	any	destination pointer
masked compare	memory	memory	any	destination pointer
	memory	port	any	source pointer
	port	memory	any	destination pointer
external	memory	memory	unsynchronized	destination pointer
	memory	port	destination	source pointer[2]
	port	memory	source	destination pointer

[1]Source pointer may also be used.
[2]If transfer is B/B→W, source pointer must be decremented by 1 to point to last byte transferred.

210911

The description of each instruction in these categories explains how the instruction operates, and how it may be used in channel programs. Instructions that perform essentially the same operation (e.g., ADD and ADDB, which add words and bytes respectively), are described together. A reference table at the end of the section lists every instruction alphabetically and provides execution time, encoded length, and sample ASM-89 coding for each permissible operand combination.

In reading this section, it is important to recall that the instruction set does not differentiate between memory addresses and I/O device addresses. Instructions that are described as accepting byte and word memory operands may also be used to read and write I/O devices.

Data Transfer Instructions

These instructions move data between memory and channel registers. Traditional byte and word moves (including memory-to-memory) are available, as are special instructions that load addresses into pointer registers and update tag bits in the process.

MOV *destination, source*

MOV transfers a byte or word from the source to the destination. Four instructions are provided:

MOV	Move Word Variable,
MOVB	Move Byte Variable,
MOVI	Move Word Immediate,
MOVBI	Move Byte Immediate.

Figure 7-23 shows how these instructions affect register operands. Notice that when a pointer register is specified as the destination of a MOV, its tag bit is unconditionally set to 1. MOV instructions are therefore used to load I/O space addresses into pointer registers.

MOVP *destination, source*

MOVP (move pointer) transfers a physical address variable between a pointer register and memory. If the source is a pointer register, the contents of the 20-bit pointer register and its tag bit are stored in three consecutive memory bytes beginning at the destination (memory location). If the source is a memory location, the three consecutive bytes beginning at the source (memory location) are loaded into the 20-bit pointer register and its tag bit. MOVP is typically used to save and restore pointer registers. If the destination is a memory location, this memory location must be at an even address.

LPD *destination, source*

LPD (load pointer with doubleword) converts a doubleword pointer to a 20-bit physical address and loads it into the destination, which must be a pointer register. The pointer register's tag bit is unconditionally cleared to 0, indicating a system address. Two instructions are provided:

LPD	Load Pointer With Doubleword Variable
LPDI	Load Pointer With Doubleword Immediate

An 8086 or 80186 can pass any address in its megabyte memory space to a channel program in the form of a doubleword pointer. The channel program can access the location by using LPD to load the location address into a pointer register.

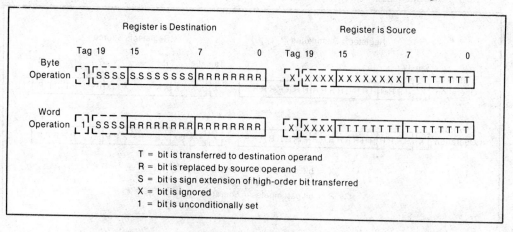

Figure 7-23 Register Operands in MOV Instructions

210911

Arithmetic Instructions

The arithmetic instructions interpret all operands as unsigned binary numbers of 8, 16 or 20 bits. Signed values may be represented in standard two's complement notation with the high-order bit representing the sign (0=positive, 1=negative). The processor, however, has no way of detecting an overflow into a sign bit, so this possibility must be provided for in the user's software.

The 8089 performs arithmetic operations to 20 significant bits as follows. Byte and word operands are sign-extended to 20 bits (e.g., bit 7 of a byte operand is propagated through bits 8-19 of an internal register). Sign extension does not affect the magnitude of the operand. The operation is then performed, and the 20-bit result is returned to the destination operand. High-order bits are truncated as necessary to fit the result in the available space. A carry out of, or borrow into, the high-order bit of the result is not detected. However, if the destination is a register that is larger than the source operand, carries will be reflected in the upper register bits, up to the size of the register.

Figure 7-24 shows how the arithmetic instructions treat registers when they are specified as source and destination operands.

ADD destination, source

The sum of the two operands replaces the destination operand. Four addition instructions are provided.

ADD	Add Word Variable
ADDB	Add Byte Variable

ADDI	Add Word Immediate
ADDBI	Add Byte Immediate

INC destination

The destination is incremented by 1. Two instructions are available:

INC	Increment Word
INCB	Increment Byte

DEC destination

The destination is decremented by 1. Word and byte instructions are provided:

DEC	Decrement Word
DECB	Decrement Byte

Logical and Bit Manipulation Instructions

The logical instructions include the boolean operators AND, OR, and NOT. Two bit manipulation instructions are provided for setting or clearing a single bit in memory or in an I/O device register. As shown in Figure 7-25, the logical operations always leave the upper four bits of 20-bit destination registers undefined. These bits should not be assumed to contain reliable values or the same values from one operation to the the next. Notice also that when a register is specified as the destination of a byte operation, bits 8-15 are overwritten by bit 7 of the result. Bits 8-15 can be preserved in AND and OR instructions by using word operations in which the upper byte of the source operand is FFH or 00H, respectively.

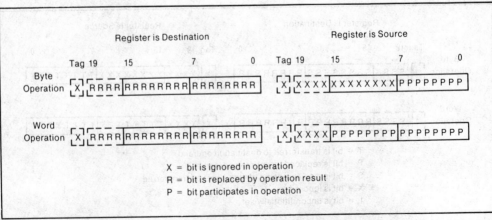

Figure 7-24 Register Operands in Arithmetic Instructions

210911

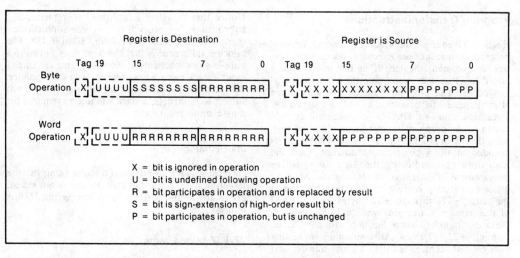

Figure 7-25 Register Operands in Logical Instructions

AND destination, source

The two operands are logically ANDed and the result replaces the destination operand. A bit in the result is set if the bits in the corresponding positions of the operands are both set; otherwise the result bit is cleared. The following AND instructions are available:

AND	Logical AND Word Variable
ANDB	Logical AND Byte Variable
ANDI	Logical AND Word Immediate
ANDBI	Logical AND Byte Immediate

AND is useful when more than one bit of a device register must be cleared while leaving the remaining bits intact. For example, ANDing an 8-bit register with EEH only clears bits 0 and 4.

OR destination, source

The two operands are logically ORed, and the result replaces the destination operand. A bit in the result is set if either or both of the corresponding bits of the operands are set; if both operand bits are cleared, the result bit is cleared. Four types of OR instructions are provided:

OR	Logical OR Word Variable
ORB	Logical OR Byte Variable
ORI	Logical OR Word Immediate
ORBI	Logical OR Byte Immediate

OR can be used to selectively set multiple bits in a device register. For example, ORing an 8-bit register with 30H sets bits 4 and 5, but does not affect the other bits.

NOT destination/destination,source

NOT inverts the bits of an operand. If a single operand is coded, the inverted result replaces the original value. If two operands are coded, the inverted bits of the source replace the destination value (which must be a register), but the source retains its original value. In addition to these two operand forms, separate mnemonics are provided for word and byte values:

NOT	Logical NOT Word
NOTB	Logical NOT Byte

NOT followed by INC will negate (create the two's complement of) a positive number.

SETB destination, bit-select

The bit-select operand specifies one bit in the destination, which must be a memory byte, that is unconditionally set to 1. A bit-select value of 0 specifies the low-order bit of the destination while the high-order bit is set if bit-select is 7. SETB is handy for setting a single bit in an 8-bit device register.

CLR destination, bit-select

CLR operates exactly like SETB except that the selected bit is unconditionally cleared to 0.

210911

Program Transfer Instructions

Register TP controls the sequence in which channel program instructions are executed. As each instruction is executed, the length of the instruction is added to TP so that it points to the next sequential instruction. The program transfer instructions can alter this sequential execution by adding a signed displacement value to TP. The displacement is contained in the program transfer instruction and may be either 8 or 16 bits long. The displacement is encoded in two's complement notation, and the high-order bit indicates the sign (0 = positive displacement, 1 = negative displacement). An 8-bit displacement may cause a transfer to a location in the range −128 through +127 bytes from the end of the transfer instruction, while a 16-bit displacement can transfer to any location within −32,768 through +32,767 bytes. An instruction containing an 8-bit displacement is called a short transfer and an instruction containing a 16-bit displacement is called a long transfer.

The program transfer instructions have alternate mnemonics. If the mnemonic begins with the letter "L," the transfer is long, and the distance to the transfer target is expressed as a 16-bit displacement regardless of how far away the target is located. If the mnemonic does not begin with "L," the ASM-89 assembler may build a short or long displacement according to rules discussed in Section 7.7.

The "self-relative" addressing technique used by program transfer instructions has two important consequences. First, it promotes position-independent code, i.e., code that can be moved in memory and still execute correctly. The only restriction here is that the entire program must be moved as a unit so that the distance between the transfer instruction and its target does not change. Second, the limited addressing range of the instructions must be kept in mind when designing large (over 32K bytes of code) channel programs.

CALL/LCALL TPsave, target

CALL invokes an out-of-line routine, saving the value of TP so that the subroutine can transfer back to the instruction following the CALL. The instruction stores TP and its tag bit in the TPsave operand, which must be a physical address variable at an even address, and then transfers to the target address formed by adding the target operand's displacement to TP. The subroutine can return to the instruction following the CALL by using a MOVP instruction to load TPsave back into TP.

Notice that the 8089's facilities for implementing subroutines, or procedures, is less sophisticated than its counterparts in the 8086,88/80186,188. The principal difference is that the 8089 does not have a built-in stack mechanism. 8089 programs can implement a stack using a base register as a stack pointer. On the other hand, since channel programs are not subject to interrupts, a stack will not be required for most channel programs.

JMP/LJMP target

JMP causes an unconditional transfer (jump) to the target location. Since the task pointer is not saved, no return to the instruction following the JMP is implied.

JZ/LJZ source, target

JZ (jump if zero) effects a transfer to the target location if the source operand is zero; otherwise the instruction following JZ is executed. Word and byte values may be tested by alternate instructions:

JZ/LJZ   Jump/Long Jump if Word Zero
JZB/LJZB   Jump/Long Jump if Byte Zero

If the source operand is a register, only the low-order 16 bits are tested; any additional high-order bits in the register are ignored. To test the low-order byte of a register, clear bits 8-15 and then use the word form of the instruction.

JNZ/LJNZ source, target

JNZ operates exactly like JZ except that control is transferred to the target if the source operand does not contain all 0-bits. Word and byte sources may be tested using these mnemonics:

JNZ/LJNZ   Jump/Long Jump if Word Not Zero
JNZB/LJNZB   Jump/Long Jump if Byte Not Zero

JMCE/LJMCE source, target

This instruction (jump if masked compare equal) effects a transfer to the target location if the source (a memory byte) is equal to the lower byte in register MC as masked by the upper byte in register MC. Figure 7-15 illustrates how 0-bits in the upper half of MC cause the corresponding bits in the lower half of MC and the source operand to compare equal, regardless of their actual values. For example, if bits 8-15 of MC contain the value 01H, then the transfer will occur if bit 0 of the source and register MC are equal. This instruction is useful for testing multiple bits in 8-bit device registers.

JMCNE/LJMCNE *source, target*

This instruction causes a jump to the target location if the source is not equal to the mask/compare value in MC. It otherwise operates identically to JMCE.

JBT/LBJT *source, bit-select, target*

JBT (jump if bit true) tests a single bit in the source operand and jumps to the target if the bit is a 1. The source must be a byte in memory or in an I/O device register. The bit-select value may range from 0 - 7, with 0 specifying the low-order bit. This instruction may be used to test a bit in an 8-bit device register. If the target is the JBT instruction itself, the operation effectively becomes "wait until bit is 0."

JNBT/LJNBT *source, bit-select, target*

This instruction operates exactly like JBT, except that the transfer is made if the bit is not true, i.e., if the bit is 0.

Processor Control Instructions

These instructions enable channel programs to control IOP hardware facilities such as the LOCK and SINTR1-2 pins, logical bus width selection and the initiation of a DMA transfer.

TSL *destination, set-value, target*

Figure 7-26 illustrates the operation of the TSL (test and set while locked) instruction. TSL can be used to implement a semaphore variable that controls access to a shared resource in a multiprocessor system (see Volume 2). If the target operand specifies the address of the TSL instruction, the instruction is repetitively executed until the semaphore (destination) is found to contain zero. Thus the channel program does not proceed until the resource is free.

WID *source-width, dest-width*

WID (set logical bus widths) alters bits 0 and 1 of the PSW, thus specifying logical bus widths for a DMA transfer. The operands may be specified as 8 or 16 (bits), with the restriction that the logical width of a bus cannot exceed its physical width. The logical bus widths are undefined following a processor RESET; therefore the WID instruction must be executed before the first transfer. Thereafter the logical widths retain their values until the next WID instruction or processor RESET.

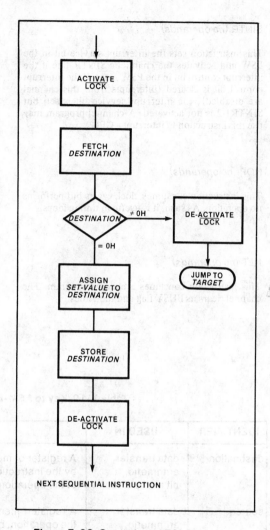

Figure 7-26 Operation of TSL Instruction

XFER *(no operands)*

XFER (enter DMA transfer mode after following instruction) prepares the channel for a DMA transfer operation. In a synchronized transfer, the instruction following XFER may ready the synchronizing device (e.g., send a "start" command or the last of a series of parameters). Any instruction, including NOP and WID, may follow XFER, except an instruction that alters GA, GB or CC.

SINTR *(no operands)*

This instruction sets the interrupt service bit in the PSW and activates the channel's SINTR line if the interrupt control bit in the PSW is set. If the interrupt control bit is cleared (interrupts from this channel are disabled), the interrupt service bit is set, but SINTR1-2 is not activated. A channel program may use this instruction to interrupt a CPU.

NOP *(no operands)*

This instruction consumes clock cycles but performs no operation. As such, it is useful in timing loops.

HLT *(no operands)*

This instruction concludes a channel program. The channel clears its BUSY flag and then idles.

Instruction Set Reference Information

Table 7-12 lists every 8089 instruction alphabetically by its ASM-89 mnemonic. The ASM-89 coding format is shown (see Table 7-10 for an explanation of operand identifiers) along with the instruction name. For every combination of operand types (see Table 7-11 for key), the instruction's execution time, its length in bytes, and a coding example are provided.

The instruction timing figures are the number of clock periods required to execute the instruction with the given combination of operands. At 5 MHz, one clock period is 200 ns; at 8 MHz a clock period is 125 ns. Two timings are provided when an instruction operates on a memory word. The first (lower) figure indicates execution time when the word is aligned on an even address and is accessed over a 16-bit bus. The second figure is for odd-addressed words on 16-bit buses and any word accessed via an 8-bit bus.

Table 7-10 Key to ASM-89 Operand Identifiers

IDENTIFIER	USED IN	EXPLANATION
destination	data transfer, arithmetic, bit manipulation	A register or memory location that may contain data operated on by the instruction, and which receives (is replaced by) the result of the operation.
source	data transfer, arithmetic, bit manipulation	A register, memory location, or immediate value that is used in the operation, but is not altered by the instruction.
target	program transfer	Location to which control is to be transferred.
TPsave	program transfer	A 24-bit memory location where the address of the next sequential instruction is to be saved.
bit-select	bit manipulation	Specification of a bit location within a byte; 0=least-significant (rightmost) bit, 7=most-significant (leftmost) bit.
set-value	TSL	Value to which destination is set if it is found 0.
source-width	WID	Logical width of source bus.
dest-width	WID	Logical width of destination bus.

Instruction fetch time is shown in Table 7-13 and should be added to the execution times shown in Table 7-12 to determine how long a sequence of instructions will take to run. (Section 7.3 explains the effect of the instruction queue on 16-bit instruction fetches.) External delays such as bus arbitration, wait states and activity on the other channel will increase the elapsed time over the figures shown in Tables 7-12 and 7-13. These delays are application dependent.

7.6 ADDRESSING MODES

8089 instruction operands may reside in registers, in the instruction itself, or in the system or I/O address spaces. Operands in the system and I/O spaces may be either memory locations or I/O device registers and may be addressed in four different ways. This section describes how the channel processes different types of operands and how it calculates addresses using its addressing modes. Section 7.7 describes the ASM-89 conventions that programmers use to specify these operands and addressing modes.

Table 7-11 Key to Operand Types

IDENTIFIER	EXPLANATION
(no operands)	No operands are written
register	Any general register
ptr-reg	A pointer register
immed8	A constant in the range 0-FFH
immed16	A constant in the range 0-FFFFH
mem8	An 8-bit memory location (byte)
mem16	A 16-bit memory location (word)
mem24	A 24-bit memory location (physical address pointer)
mem32	A 32-bit memory location (doubleword pointer)
label	A label within −32,768 to +32,767 bytes of the end of the instruction
short-label	A label within −128 to +127 bytes of the end of the instruction
0-7	A constant in the range: 0-7
8/16	The constant 8 or the constant 16

Table 7-12 Instruction Set Reference Data

ADD destination, source		Add Word Variable		
Operands	**Clocks**	**Bytes**	**Coding Example**	
register, mem16	11/15	2-3	ADD BC, [GA].LENGTH	
mem16, register	16/26	2-3	ADD [GB], GC	

210911

Table 7-12 Instruction Set Reference Data (continued)

ADDB	destination, source	Add Byte Variable	
Operands	**Clocks**	**Bytes**	**Coding Example**
register, mem8	11	2-3	ADDB GC, [GA].N__CHARS
mem8, register	16	2-3	ADDB [PP].ERRORS, MC

ADDBI	destination, source	Add Byte Immediate	
Operands	**Clocks**	**Bytes**	**Coding Example**
register, immed8	3	3	ADDBI MC,10
mem8, immed8	16	3-4	ADDBI [PP+IX+], 2CH

ADDI	destination, source	Add Word Immediate	
Operands	**Clocks**	**Bytes**	**Coding Example**
register, immed16	3	4	ADDI GB, 0C25BH
mem16, immed16	16/26	4-5	ADDI [GB].POINTER, 5899

AND	destination, source	Logical AND Word Variable	
Operands	**Clocks**	**Bytes**	**Coding Example**
register, mem16	11/15	2-3	AND MC, [GA].FLAG__WORD
mem16, register	16/26	2-3	AND [GC].STATUS, BC

ANDB	destination, source	Logical AND Byte Variable	
Operands	**Clocks**	**Bytes**	**Coding Example**
register, mem8	11	2-3	AND BC, [GC]
mem8, register	16	2-3	AND [GA+IX], GA

ANDBI	destination, source	Logical AND Byte Immediate	
Operands	**Clocks**	**Bytes**	**Coding Example**
register, immed8	3	3	GA, 01100000B
mem8, immed8	16	3-4	[GC+IX], 2CH

ANDI	destination, source	Logical AND Word Immediate	
Operands	**Clocks**	**Bytes**	**Coding Example**
register, immed16	3	4	IX, 0H
mem16, immed16	16/26	4-5	[GB+IX] , 40H

210911

Table 7-12 Instruction Set Reference Data (continued)

CALL TPsave, target		Call	
Operands	Clocks	Bytes	Coding Example
mem24, label	17/23	3-5	CALL [GC+IX] , GET__NEXT

CLR destination, bit select		Clear Bit To Zero	
Operands	Clocks	Bytes	Coding Example
mem8, 0-7	16	2-3	CLR [GA], 3

DEC destination		Decrement Word By 1	
Operands	Clocks	Bytes	Coding Example
register	3	2	
mem16	16/26	2-3	DEC [PP].RETRY

DECB destination		Decrement Byte By 1	
Operands	Clocks	Bytes	Coding Example
mem8	16	2-3	DECB [GA+IX+]

HLT (no operands)		Halt Channel Program	
Operands	Clocks	Bytes	Coding Example
(no operands)	11	2	HLT

INC destination		Increment Word by 1	
Operands	Clocks	Bytes	Coding Example
register	3	2	INC GA
mem16	16/26	2-3	INC [GA].COUNT

INCB destination		Increment Byte by 1	
Operands	Clocks	Bytes	Coding Example
mem8	16	2-3	INCB [GB].POINTER

210911

Table 7-12 Instruction Set Reference Data (continued)

JBT	source, bit-select, target		Jump if Bit True (1)	
Operands	**Clocks**	**Bytes**	**Coding Example**	
mem8, 0-7, label	14	3-5	JBT [GA].RESULT__REG, 3, DATA__VALID	

JMCE	source, target		Jump if Masked Compare Equal	
Operands	**Clocks**	**Bytes**	**Coding Example**	
mem8, label	14	3-5	JMCE [GB].FLAG, STOP__SEARCH	

JMCNE	source, target		Jump if Masked Compare Not Equal	
Operands	**Clocks**	**Bytes**	**Coding Example**	
mem8, label	14	3-5	JMCNE [GB+IX], NEXT__ITEM	

JMP	target		Jump Unconditionally	
Operands	**Clocks**	**Bytes**	**Coding Example**	
label	3	3-4	JMP READ__SECTOR	

JNBT	source, bit-select, target		Jump if Bit Not True (0)	
Operands	**Clocks**	**Bytes**	**Coding Example**	
mem8, 0-7, label	14	3-5	JNBT [GC], 3, RE__READ	

JNZ	source, target		Jump if Word Not Zero	
Operands	**Clocks**	**Bytes**	**Coding Example**	
register, label	5	3-4	JNZ BC, WRITE__LINE	
mem16, label	12/16	3-5	JNZ [PP].NUM__CHARS, PUT__BYTE	

JNZB	source, target		Jump if Byte Not Zero	
Operands	**Clocks**	**Bytes**	**Coding Example**	
mem8, label	12	3-5	JNZB [GA], MORE__DATA	

JZ	source, target		Jump if Word is Zero	
Operands	**Clocks**	**Bytes**	**Coding Example**	
register, label	5	3-4	JZ BC, NEXT__LINE	
mem16, label	12/16	3-5	JZ [GC+IX] BUF__EMPTY	

Table 7-12 Instruction Set Reference Data (continued)

JZB   source, target — Jump if Byte Zero

Operands	Clocks	Bytes	Coding Example
mem8, label	12	3-5	JZB [PP].LINES__LEFT, RETURN

LCALL   TPsave, target — Long Call

Operands	Clocks	Bytes	Coding Example
mem24, label	17/23	4-5	LCALL [GC].RETURN__SAVE, INIT__8279

LJBT   source, bit-select, target — Long Jump if Bit True (1)

Operands	Clocks	Bytes	Coding Example
mem8, 0-7, label	14	4-5	LJBT [GA].RESULT, 1, DATA__OK

LJMCE   source, target — Long jump if Masked Compare Equal

Operands	Clocks	Bytes	Coding Example
mem8, label	14	4-5	LJMCE [GB], BYTE__FOUND

LJMCNE   source, target — Long jump if Masked Compare Not Equal

Operands	Clocks	Bytes	Coding Example
mem8, label	14	4-5	LJMCNE [GC+IX+], SCAN__NEXT

LJMP   target — Long Jump Unconditional

Operands	Clocks	Bytes	Coding Example
label	3	4	LJMP GET__CURSOR

LJNBT   source, bit-select, target — Long Jump if Bit Not True (0)

Operands	Clocks	Bytes	Coding Example
mem8, 0-7, label	14	4-5	LJNBT [GC], 6, CRCC__ERROR

LJNZ   source, target — Long Jump if Word Not Zero

Operands	Clocks	Bytes	Coding Example
register, label	5	4	LJNZ BC, PARTIAL__XMIT
mem16, label	12/16	4-5	LJNZ [GA+IX], PUT__DATA

210911

Table 7-12 Instruction Set Reference Data (continued)

LJNZB source, target			Long Jump if Byte Not Zero
Operands	**Clocks**	**Bytes**	**Coding Example**
mem8, label	12	4-5	LJNZB [GB+IX+]., BUMP__COUNT

LJZ source, target			Long Jump if Word Zero
Operands	**Clocks**	**Bytes**	**Coding Example**
register, label	5	4	LJZ IX, FIRST__ELEMENT
mem16, label	12/16	4-5	LJZ [GB].XMIT__COUNT, NO__DATA

LJZB source, target			Long Jump if Byte Zero
Operands	**Clocks**	**Bytes**	**Coding Example**
mem8, label	12	4-5	LJZB [GA], RETURN__LINE

LPD destination, source			Load Pointer With Doubleword Variable
Operands	**Clocks**	**Bytes**	**Coding Example**
ptr-reg, mem32	20/28*	2-3	LPD GA, [PP].BUF__START

*20 clocks if operand is on even address; 28 if on odd address

LPDI destination, source			Load Pointer With Doubleword Immediate
Operands	**Clocks**	**Bytes**	**Coding Example**
ptr-reg, immed32	12/16*	6	LPDI GB, DISK__ADDRESS

*12 clocks if instruction is on even address; 16 if on odd address

MOV destination, source			Move Word
Operands	**Clocks**	**Bytes**	**Coding Example**
register, mem16	8/12	2-3	MOV IX, [GC]
mem16, register	10/16	2-3	MOV [GA].COUNT, BC
mem16, mem16	18/28	4-6	MOV [GA].READING, [GB]

MOVB destination, source			Move Byte
Operands	**Clocks**	**Bytes**	**Coding Example**
register, mem8	8	2-3	MOVB BC, [PP].TRAN__COUNT
mem8, register	10	2-3	MOVB [PP].RETURN__CODE, GC
mem8, mem8	18	4-6	MOVB [GB+IX+], [GA+IX+]

Table 7-12 Instruction Set Reference Data (continued)

MOVBI destination, source			Move Byte Immediate
Operands	**Clocks**	**Bytes**	**Coding Example**
register, immed8	3	3	MOVBI MC, 'A'
mem8, immed8	12	3-4	MOVBI [PP].RESULT, 0

MOVI destination, source			Move Word Immediate
Operands	**Clocks**	**Bytes**	**Coding Example**
register, immed16	3	4	MOVI BC, 0
mem16, immed16	12/18	4-5	MOVI [GB], 0FFFFH

MOVP destination, source			Move Pointer
Operands	**Clocks**	**Bytes**	**Coding Example**
ptr-reg, mem24	19/27*	2-3	MOVP TP, [GC+IX]
mem24, ptr-reg	16/22*	2-3	MOVP [GB].SAVE__ADDR, GC

*First figure is for operand on even address; second is for odd-addressed operand.

NOP (no operands)			No Operation
Operands	**Clocks**	**Bytes**	**Coding Example**
(no operands)	4	2	NOP

NOT destination/destination, source			Logical NOT Word
Operands	**Clocks**	**Bytes**	**Coding Example**
register	3	2	NOT MC
mem16	16/26	2-3	NOT [GA].PARM
register, mem16	11/15	2-3	NOT BC, [GA+IX]

NOTB destination/destination, source			Logical NOT Byte
Operands	**Clocks**	**Bytes**	**Coding Example**
mem8	16	2-3	NOTB [GA].PARM__REG
register, mem8	11	2-3	NOTB IX, [GB].STATUS

OR destination, source			Logical OR Word
Operands	**Clocks**	**Bytes**	**Coding Example**
register, mem16	11/15	2-3	OR MC, [GC].MASK
mem16, register	16/26	2-3	OR [GC], BC

Table 7-12 Instruction Set Reference Data (continued)

ORB destination, source			Logical OR Byte
Operands	**Clocks**	**Bytes**	**Coding Example**
register, mem8	11	2-3	ORB IX, [PP].POINTER
mem8, register	16	2-3	ORB [GA+IX+], GB

ORBI destination, source			Logical OR Byte Immediate
Operands	**Clocks**	**Bytes**	**Coding Example**
register, immed8	3	3	ORBI IX, 00010001B
mem8, immed8	16	3-4	ORBI [GB].COMMAND, 0CH

ORI destination, source			Logical OR Word Immediate
Operands	**Clocks**	**Bytes**	**Coding Example**
register, immed16	3	4	ORI MC, 0FF0DH
mem16, immed16	16/26	4-5	ORI [GA], 1000H

SETB destination, bit-select			Set Bit to 1
Operands	**Clocks**	**Bytes**	**Coding Example**
mem8, 0-7	16	2-3	SETB [GA].PARM__REG, 2

SINTR (no operands)			Set Interrupt Service Bit
Operands	**Clocks**	**Bytes**	**Coding Example**
(no operands)	4	2	SINTR

TSL destination, set-value, target			Test and Set While Locked
Operands	**Clocks**	**Bytes**	**Coding Example**
mem8, immed8, short-label	14/16*	4-5	TSL [GA].FLAG, 0FFH, NOT__READY

*14 clocks if destination ≠ 0; 16 clocks if destination = 0

WID source-width, dest-width			Set Logical Bus Widths
Operands	**Clocks**	**Bytes**	**Coding Example**
8/16, 8/16	4	2	WID 8, 8

XFER (no operands)			Enter DMA Transfer Mode After Next Instruction
Operands	**Clocks**	**Bytes**	**Coding Example**
(no operands)	4	2	XFER

210911

**Table 7-13 Instruction Fetch Timings
(Clock Periods)**

INSTRUCTION LENGTH (BYTES)	BUS WIDTH		
	8	16	
		(1)	(2)
2	14	7	11
3	18	14	11
4	22	14	15
5	26	18	15

Register and Immediate Operands

Registers may be specified as source or destination operands in many instructions. Instructions that operate on registers are generally both shorter and faster than instructions that specify immediate or memory operands.

Immediate operands are data contained in instructions rather than in registers or in memory. The data may be either 8 or 16 bits in length. The limitations of immediate operands are that they may only serve as source operands and that they are constant values.

Memory Addressing Modes

Whereas the channel has direct access to register and immediate operands, operands in the system and I/O space must be transferred to or from the IOP over the bus. To do this, the IOP must calculate the address of the operand, called its effective address (EA). The programmer may specify that an operand's address be calculated in any of four different ways; these are the 8089's memory addressing modes.

Effective Address

An operand in the system space has 20-bit effective address, and an operand in the I/O space has a 16-bit effective address. These addresses are unsigned numbers that represent the distance (in bytes) of the low-order byte of the operand from the beginning of the address space. Since the 8089 does not "see" the segmented structure of the system space that it may share with an 8086,88 or an 80186,188, the 8089 effective addresses are equivalent to 8086,88/80186,-188 physical addresses.

All memory addressing modes use the content of one of the pointer registers, and the state of that register's tag bit determines whether the operand lies in the system or the I/O space. If the operand is in the I/O space (tag = 1), bits 16-19 of the pointer register are ignored in the effective address calculation. Volume 2 describes the two fields (AA and MM) in the encoded machine instruction that specify the addressing mode and base (pointer) register.

Base Addressing

In based addressing (Figure 7-27), the effective address is taken directly from the contents of GA, GB, GC or PP. Using this addressing mode, one instruction may access different locations if the register is updated before the instruction executes. LPD, MOV, MOVP or arithmetic instructions might be used to change the value of the base register.

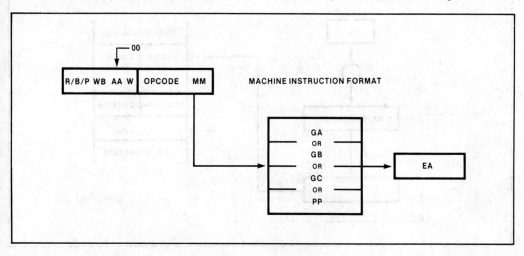

Figure 7-27 Based Addressing

210911

Offset Addressing

In this mode (Figure 7-28), an 8-bit unsigned value contained in the instruction is added to the contents of a base register to form the effective address. The offset mode provides a convenient way to address elements in structures (a parameter block is a typical example of a structure). As shown in Figure 7-29, a base register can be pointed at the base (first element) in the structure, and then different offsets can be used to access the elements within the structure. By changing the base address, the same structure can be relocated elsewhere in memory.

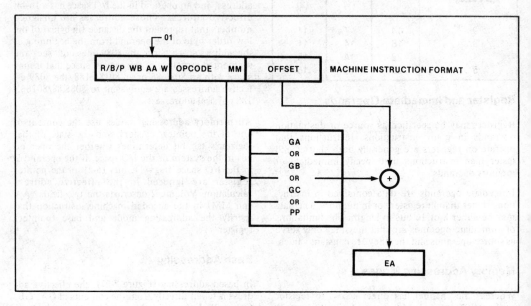

Figure 7-28 Offset Addressing

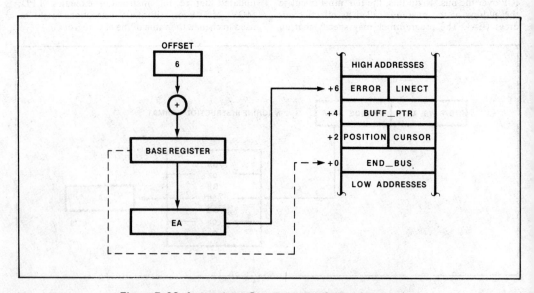

Figure 7-29 Accessing a Structure with Offset Addressing

210911

Indexed Addressing

An indexed address is formed by adding the contents of register IX (interpreted as an unsigned quantity) to a base register as shown in Figure 7-30. Indexed addressing is often used to access array elements (see Figure 7-31). A base register locates the beginning of the array and the value in IX selects one element, i.e., it acts as the array subscript. The ith element of a byte array is selected when IX contains $(i - 1)$. To access the ith element of a word array. IX should contain $((i\text{th} - 1)*2)$.

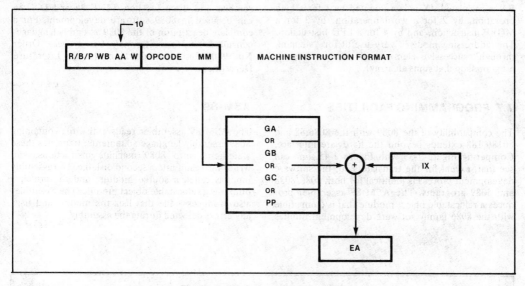

Figure 7-30 Indexed Addressing

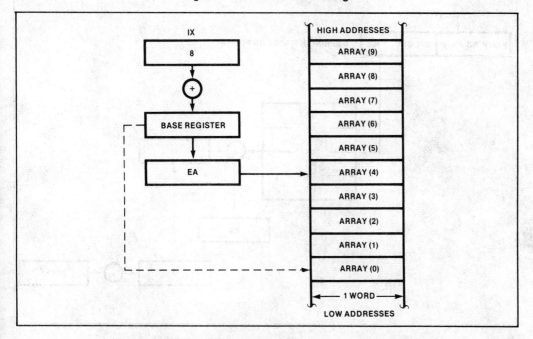

Figure 7-31 Accessing a Word Array with Indexed Addressing

210911

Indexed Auto-Increment Addressing

In this variation of indexed addressing, the effective address is formed by summing IX and a base register; IX is then incremented automatically. (See Figure 7-32.) The incrementing takes place after the EA is calculated. IX is incremented by 1 for a byte operation, by 2 for a word operation, by 3 for a MOVP instruction, and by 4 for a LPD instruction. This addressing mode is very useful for "stepping through" successive elements of an array (e.g., a program loop that sums an array).

7.7 PROGRAMMING FACILITIES

The compatibility of the 8089 with the 8086,88 and 80186,188 extends beyond the hardware interface. Comparing Figure 7-33 with Figure 2-45, one can see that, except for the translate step, the software development process is identical for both 8086/8088 and 8089 programs. The ASM-89 assembler produces a relocatable object module that is compatible with the 8086 family software development utilities

LIB-86, LINK-86, LOC-86 and OH-86, described in Section 2-9. All of these development tools run on an INTELLEC R 800 or Series II and III microcomputer development system.

This section surveys the facilities of the ASM-89 assembler and discusses how LINK-86 and LOC-86 can be used in 8089 software development. For a complete description of the 8089 assembly language, consult *8089 Macro Assembly User's Guide*, Order No. 9800938, available from Intel's Literature Department.

ASM-89

The ASM-89 assembler reads a disk file containing 8089 assembly language statements, translates these statements into 8089 machine instructions, and writes the result into a second disk file. The assembly input is called a source module, and the principal output is a relocatable object module. The assembler also produces a file that lists the module and flags any errors detected during the assembly.

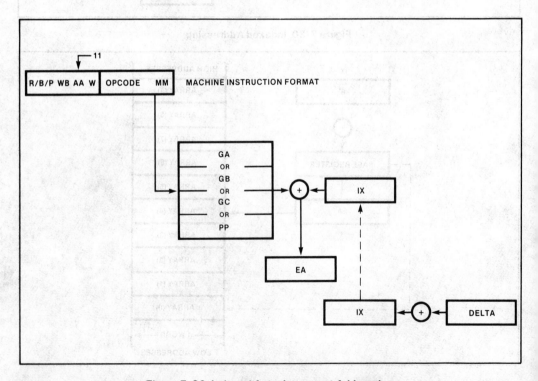

Figure 7-32 Indexed Auto-Increment Addressing

210911

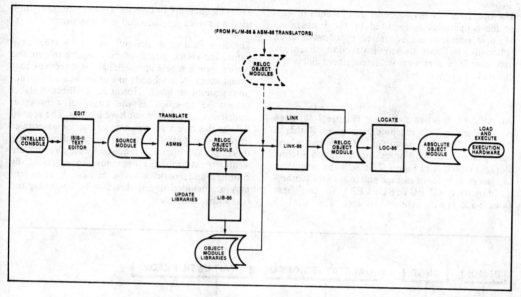

Figure 7-33 8089 Software Development Process

Statements

Statements are the building blocks of ASM-89 programs. Figure 7-34 shows several examples of ASM-89 statements. The ASM-89 assembler gives programmers considerable flexibility in formatting program statements. Variable names and labels (identifiers) may be up to 31 characters long, and the underscore (_) character may be used to improve the readability of longer names (e.g., WAIT_UNTIL_READY). The component parts of statements (fields) need not be located at particular "columns" of the statement. Any number of blank characters may separate fields and multiple identifiers within the operand field. Long statements may be continued onto the next link by coding an ampersand (&) as the first character of the continued line.

A statement whose first non-blank character is a semicolon is a comment statement. Comments have no affect on program execution and, in fact, are ignored by the ASM-89 assembler. Nevertheless, carefully selected comments are included in all well written ASM-89 programs. They summarize, annotate and clarify the logic of the program where the instructions are too "microscopic" to make the operation of the program self-evident.

An ASM-89 instruction statement (Figure 7-35) directs the assembler to build an 8089 machine instruction. The optional label field assigns a symbolic identifier to the address where the instruction will be stored in memory. A labeled instruction can be the target of a program transfer; the transferring instruction specifies the label for its target operand. In Figure 3-35, the labeled instruction conditionally transfers to itself; the program will loop on this one instruction as long as bit 3 of the byte addressed by [GA].STATUS is not true. The mnemonic field of an instruction statement specifies the type of 8089 machine instruction that the assembler is to build.

```
; THIS STATEMENT CONTAINS A COMMENT FIELD ONLY
ADDI    BC,5                    ; TYPICAL ASM89 INSTRUCTION
    ADDI    BC,    5            ; NO "COLUMN" REQUIREMENTS
MOV    [GA].STATUS,
&    6                          ; A CONTINUED STATEMENT
SOURCE    EQU GA                ; A SIMPLE ASM89 DIRECTIVE
LINE_BUFFER_ADDRESS DD         ; A LONG IDENTIFIER
```

Figure 7-34 ASM-89 Statements

The operand field may contain no operands or one or more operands as required by the instruction. Multiple operands are separated by commas and, optionally, by blanks. Any instruction statement may contain a comment field (comment fields are initiated by a semicolon).

An ASM-89 directive statement (Figure 7-36) does not produce an 8089 machine instruction. Rather, a directive gives the assembler information to use during the assembly. For example, the DS (define storage) directive in Figure 7-36 tells the assembler to reserve 80 bytes of storage and to assign a symbolic identifier (INPUT_BUFFER) to the first (lowest-addressed) byte of this area. The ASM-89

assembler accepts 14 directives; the more commonly used directives are discussed in this section.

The first field in a directive may be a label or a name; individual directives may require or prohibit names, while labels are optional for directives that accept them. A label ends in a colon like an instruction statement label. However, a directive label cannot be specified as the target of a program transfer. A name does not have a colon. The second field is the directive mnemonic, and the assembler distinguishes between instructions and directives by this field. Any operands required by the directive are written next; multiple operands are separated by commas and, optionally, by blanks. A comment may be included in any directive by beginning the text with a semicolon.

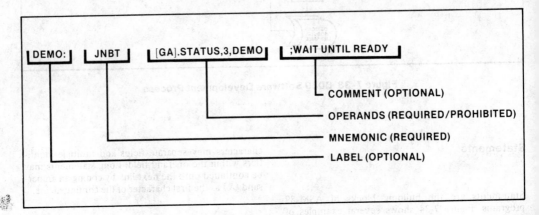

Figure 7-35 ASM-89 Instruction Format

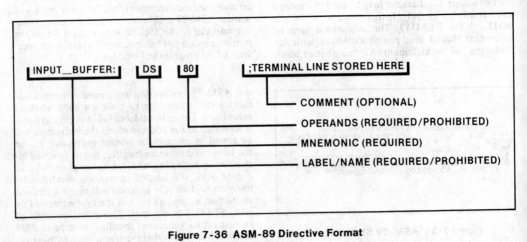

Figure 7-36 ASM-89 Directive Format

Constants

Binary, decimal, octal and hexadecimal numeric constants (Figure 7-37) may be written in ASM-89 instructions and directives. The assembler can add and subtract constants at assembly time. Numeric constants, including the results of arithmetic operations, must be representable in 16 bits. Positive numbers cannot exceed 65,535 (decimal); negative numbers, which the assembler represents in two's complement notation, cannot be "more negative" than −32,768 (decimal).

Character constants are enclosed in single quote marks as shown in Figure 7-37. Strings of characters up to 255 bytes long may be written when initializing storage. Instruction operands, however, can only be one or two characters long (for byte and word instructions respectively).

As an aid to program clarity, the EQU (equate) directive may be used to give names to constants (e.g., DISK_STATUS EQU 0FF20H).

Defining Data

Four ASM-89 directives reserve space for memory variables in the ASM-89 program (see Figure 7-38). The DB, DW and DD directives allocate units of bytes, words and doublewords, respectively, initialize the locations, and optionally label them so that they may be referred to by name in instruction statements. The label of a storage directive always refers to the first (lowest-addressed) byte of the area reserved by the directive.

The DB and DW directives may be used to define byte- and word-constant scalars (individual data items) and arrays (sequences of the same type of item). For example, a character string constant could be defined as a byte array:

    SIGN_ON_MSG: DB 'PLEASE ENTER PASSWORD'

The DD directive is typically used to define the address of a location in the system space, i.e., a doubleword pointer variable. The address may be loaded into a pointer register with the LPD instruction.

The DS directive reserves, and optionally names, storage in units of bytes, but does not initialize any of the reserved bytes. DS is typically used for RAM-based variables such as buffers. As there is no special directive for defining a physical address pointer, DS is typically used to reserve the three bytes used by the MOVP instruction.

Structures

An ASM-89 structure is a map or template that gives names and relative locations to a collection of related variables that are called structure elements or members. Defining a structure, however, does not allocate storage. The structure is, in effect, overlaid on a particular area of memory when one of its elements is used as an instruction operand. Figure 7-39 shows how a structure representing a parameter block could be defined and then used in a channel program. The assembler uses the structure element name to produce an offset value (structures are used with the offset addressing mode). Compared to "hard coded" offsets, structures improve program clarity and simplify maintenance. If the layout of a memory block changes, only the structure definition must be modified. When the program is reassembled, all symbolic references to the structure are automatically adjusted. When multiple areas of memory are laid out identically, a single structure can be used to address any area by changing the contents of the pointer (base) register that specifies the structure's "starting address."

```
MOVBI    GA, 'A'          ; CHARACTER
MOVBI    GA, 41H          ; HEXADECIMAL
MOVBI    GA, 65           ; DECIMAL
MOVBI    GA, 65D          ; DECIMAL ALTERNATIVE
MOVBI    GA, 101Q         ; OCTAL
MOVBI    GA, 101O         ; OCTAL ALTERNATIVE
MOVBI    GA, 01000001B    ; BINARY
; NEXT TWO STATEMENTS ARE EQUIVALENT AND
;    ILLUSTRATE TWO'S COMPLEMENT REPRESENTATION
;       OF NEGATIVE NUMBERS
MOVBI    GA, −5
MOVBI    GA, 11111011B
```

Figure 7-37 ASM-89 Constants

```
; ASM89 DIRECTIVE                    ; MEMORY CONTENT (HEX)
ALPHA:  DB    1                      ; 01
        DB    -2                     ; FE (TWO'S COMPLEMENT)
        DB    'A', 'B'               ; 4142
BETA:   DW    1                      ; 0100
        DW    -5                     ; FAFF
        DW    'AB'                   ; 4241
        DW    400, 500              |; 2410F401
        DW    400H, 500H             ; 0004 0005
gamma:  DW    BETA                   ; OFFSET OF BETA ABOVE,
                                     ; FROM BEGINNING OF PROGRAM
DELTA   DD    GAMMA                  ; ADDRESS (SEGMENT & OFFSET)
                                     ; OF GAMMA
ZETA:   DS    80                     ; 80 BYTES, UNINITIALIZED
```

Figure 7-38 ASM-89 Storage Directives

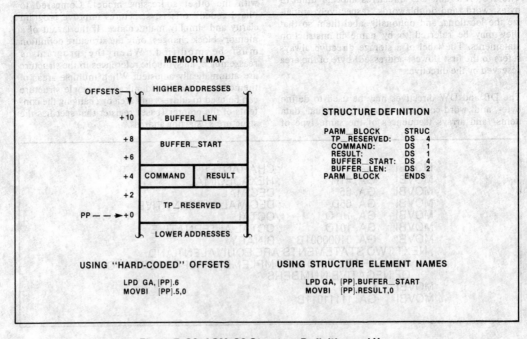

MEMORY MAP

USING "HARD-CODED" OFFSETS

```
LPD GA, [PP].6
MOVBI   [PP].5,0
```

STRUCTURE DEFINITION

```
PARM_BLOCK        STRUC
TP_RESERVED:      DS    4
COMMAND:          DS    1
RESULT:           DS    1
BUFFER_START:     DS    4
BUFFER_LEN:       DS    2
PARM_BLOCK        ENDS
```

USING STRUCTURE ELEMENT NAMES

```
LPD GA, [PP].BUFFER_START
MOVBI   [PP].RESULT,0
```

Figure 7-39 ASM-89 Structure Definition and Use

7-50

210911

Addressing Modes

Table 7-14 summarizes the notation a programmer uses to specify how the effective address of a memory operand is to be computed. Examples of typical ASM-89 coding for each addressing mode, as well as register and immediate operands, are provided in Figure 7-40. Notice that a bracketed reference to a register indicates that the contents of the register is to be used to form the effective address of a memory operand, while an unbracketed register reference specifies that the register itself is the operand.

Table 7-14 ASM-89 Memory Addressing Mode Notation

Notation	Addressing Mode
[ptr-reg]	Based
[ptr-reg].offset	Offset
[ptr-reg + IX]	Indexed
[ptr-reg + IX +]	Indexed Post Auto-increment

ptr-reg = GA, GB, GC or PP
offset = 8-bit signed value; may be structure element

The following examples summarize how the memory addressing modes can be used to access simple variables, structures and arrays.

- If GA contains the address of a memory operand, then [GA] refers to that operand.

- If GA contains the base address of a structure, then [GA].DATA refers to the DATA element (field) in that structure. If DATA is six bytes from the beginning of the structure, then [GA].6 refers to the same location.

- If GA contains the starting address of an array, then [GA + IX] addresses the array element indexed by IX. For example, if IX contains the value 4H, the effective address refers to the fifth element of a byte array, or the third element of a word array. [GA + IX +] selects the same elements and additionally auto-increments IX by 1 (byte operation), 2 (word operation), 3 (MOVP instruction), or 4 (LPD instruction) in anticipation of accessing the next array element.

Note that any pointer register could have been substituted for GA in the previous examples.

Program Transfer Targets

As discussed in Section 7.5, program transfer instructions operate by adding a signed byte or word displacement to the task pointer. Table 7-15 shows how the ASM-89 assembler determines the sign and size of the displacement value it places in a program transfer machine instruction. In the table, the terms "backward" and "forward" refer to the location of a label specified as a transfer target relative to the transfer instruction. "Backward" means the label physically precedes the instruction in the source module, and "forward" means the label follows the instruction in the source text. The distances are from the end of the transfer instruction; the distance to the instruction immediately following the transfer is 0 bytes.

```
ADDI    GA, 5           ; REGISTER, IMMEDIATE
ADD     GC, [GB]        ; REGISTER, MEMORY (BASED)
ADDBI   [PP],10         ; MEMORY (BASED), IMMEDIATE
ADDB    IX, [GB].5      ; REGISTER, MEMORY (OFFSET)
ADDB    BC, [GC].COUNT  ; REGISTER, MEMORY (OFFSET)
ADD     [GC + IX], BC   ; MEMORY (INDEXED), REGISTER
ADDI    [GA + IX +],5   ; MEMORY (INDEXED AUTO-INCREMENT), IMMED
ADDB    [PP].ERROR, [GA] ; MEMORY (OFFSET), MEMORY (BASED)
```

Figure 7-40 ASM-89 Operand Coding Examples

Table 7-15 Program Transfer Displacement

Mnemonic Form	Target Location		Displacement Sign Bytes
	Direction	Distance	
Short (e.g., JMP)	Backward	≤128	− 1
	Forward	≤127	+ 1
	Backward	≤32,768	− 2
	Forward	≤32,767	Error
	Backward	>32,768	Error
	Forward	>32,767	Error
Long (e.g., LJMP)	Backward	≤128	− 2
	Forward	≤127	+ 2
	Backward	≤32,768	− 2
	Forward	≤32,767	+ 2
	Backward	>32,768	Error
	Forward	>32,767	Error

Two important points can be drawn from Table 7-15. First, a target must lie within 32K bytes of a transfer instruction; this should not prove restrictive except in very large programs. Second, one byte can be saved in the assembled instruction by writing the short mnemonic when the target is known to be within −128 through +127 assembled bytes of the transfer.

It is also important to note that a program transfer target must reside in the same module as the transferring instruction, i.e., the target address must be known at assembly time.

Procedures

An ASM-89 program may invoke an out-of-line procedure (subroutine) with the CALL/LCALL instruction. The first instruction operand specifies a memory location where the contents of TP will be stored as a physical address pointer before control is transferred to the procedure. The procedure may return to the instruction following the CALL/LCALL by using the MOVP instruction to restore TP from the save area. Figure 7-41 illustrates one approach to procedure linkage.

A channel program may use the first two words of its parameter block (pointed to by PP) as a task pointer save area. However, this is not recommended if there is any chance that the CPU will issue a "suspend" command to the channel; this command stores the current value of TP in the same location, possibly overwriting a return address.

As in any program transfer, the target of a CALL/LCALL instruction must be contained in the same module and within 32K bytes of the instruction.

Segment Control

The relocatable object module produced by the ASM-89 assembler consists of a single logical segment. (A segment is a storage unit up to 64K bytes long; for a more complete description, refer to Sections 3.4 and 3.7). The ASM-89 SEGMENT and ENDS directives name the segment as shown in Figure 7-42. Typically, all instructions and most directives are coded in between these directives. The END directive, which terminates the assembly, is an exception.

The LOC-86 utility can assign this logical segment to any memory address that is a physical segment boundary (i.e., whose low-order four bits are 0000). In a ROM-based system, variable data (which must be in RAM) can be "clustered" together at one "end" of the program as shown in Figure 7-43. The ORG directive can then be used to force assembly of the variables to start at a given offset from the beginning of the segment (2,000 hexadecimal bytes in Figure 7-43). As the figure shows, the segment can then be located so that instructions and constants fall into the ROM portion of memory, while the variable part of the segment is located in RAM. The entire segment, including any "unused" portions, of course, cannot exceed 64K bytes.

```
        .
        .
        .
CALL SAVE:   DS   3   ; TP SAVE AREA
        .
        .
        .
; SET UP TP SAVE AREA
;    NOTE: EXAMPLE ASSUMES PROGRAM
;          IS IN I/O SPACE. USE LPDI
;          IF IN SYSTEM SPACE.
         MOVI   GC, CALLSAVE      ; LOAD ADDRESS TO GC
; CALL IT.
         LCALL   [GC],DEMO
        .
        .
        .
         HLT   ; LOGICAL END OF PROGRAM

; DEFINE THE PROCEDURE.
DEMO:
; PROCEDURE INSTRUCTIONS GO HERE.
; NOTE: PROCEDURE MUST NOT UPDATE GC
;       AS IT POINTS TO THE RETURN ADDRESS.



; RETURN TO CALLER.
         MOVP   TP, [GC]
```

Figure 7-41 ASM-89 Procedure Example

```
CHANNEL1     SEGMENT     ; START OF SEGMENT
             .
             .
ASM89 SOURCE STATEMENTS
             .
             .
CHANNEL1     ENDS        ; END OF SEGMENT
             END         ; END OF ASSEMBLY
```

Figure 7-42 ASM-89 SEGMENT and ENDS Directives

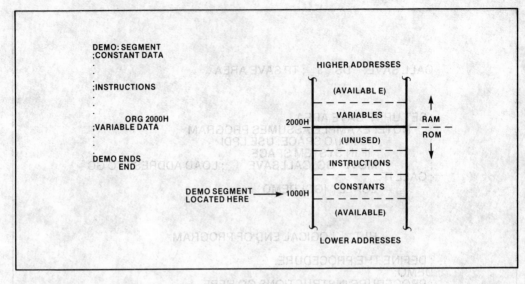

Figure 7-43 Using the ASM-89 ORG Directive

Intermodule Communication

An ASM-89 module can make some of its addresses available to other modules by defining symbols with the PUBLIC directive. At a minimum, a channel program must make the address of its first instruction available to the CPU module that starts the channel program. Figure 7-44 shows an ASM-89 module that contains three channel programs labeled READ, WRITE and DELETE. The example shows how a PL/M-86 program and an ASM-86 program could define these "entry points" as EXTERNAL and EXTRN symbols respectively. When the modules are linked together, LINK-86 will match the externals with the publics, thus providing the CPU programs with the addresses they need.

Conversely, an ASM-89 module can obtain the address of a public symbol in another module by defining it with the EXTRN directive. An external symbol, however, can only appear as the initial value operand of a DD directive (see Figure 7-45). This effectively means that an ASM-89 program's use of external symbols is limited to obtaining the addresses of data located in the system space. Another way of doing this, which may be preferable in many cases, is to have the CPU program system space addresses in the parameter block.

Sample Program

Figure 7-46 diagrams the logic of a sample ASM-89 program; the code is shown in Figure 7-47. The program reads one physical record (sector) from a diskette drive controlled by an 8272 Floppy Disk Controller. No particular system configuration is implied by the program, except that the 8272 resides in the IOP's I/O space.

Hardware address decoding logic is assumed to be set up as follows:

- reading location FF00H selects the 8272 status register,

- writing location FF00H selects the 8272 command register,

- reading location FF01H selects the 8272 result register,

- writing location FF01H selects the 8272 parameter register,

- decoding the address FF04H provides the 8272 DACK (DMA acknowledge) signal.

The program uses structures to address the parameter block and the 8272 registers. Register PP contains the address of the parameter block, and the program loads GC with FF00H to point to the 8272 registers. The program's entry point (the label START) is defined as a PUBLIC symbol so that the CPU program can place its address in the parameter block when it starts the program.

210911

Register IX is used as a retry counter. If the transfer is not completed successfully (bit 3 of the 8272 result register ≠ 0), the program retries the transfer up to 10 times.

Since the 8272 automatically requests a DMA transfer upon receipt of the last parameter, this parameter is sent immediately following the XFER command.

Linking and Locating ASM-89 Modules

The LINK-86 utility program combines multiple relocatable object modules into a single relocatable module. The input modules may consist of modules produced by any of the iAPX 86,88/186,188 family language translators; ASM-89, ASM-86, PL/M-86, PASCAL-86 or FORTRAN-86. LINK-86's principal function is to satisfy external references made in the modules. Any symbol that is defined with the EXTRN directive in ASM-89 or ASM-86 or is declared EXTERNAL in PL/M-86 is an external reference, i.e., a reference to an address contained

in another module. Whenever LINK-86 encounters an external reference, it searches the other modules for a PUBLIC symbol of the same name. If it finds the matching symbol, it replaces the external reference with the address of the object.

The most common occurrence of an external reference in a system that employs one or more 8089s is the channel program address. In order for a CPU program to start a channel program, it must ensure that the address of the first channel program instruction is contained in the first two words of the parameter block. Since the channel program is assembled separately, the translator that processes the CPU program will not typically know its address. If this address is defined as an external (see Figure 7-44), LINK-86 will obtain the address from the ASM-89 channel program when the two are linked together. (The ASM-89 program must, of course, define the symbol in a PUBLIC directive.)

Other external references may arise when one module uses data (e.g., a buffer) that is contained in another module, and (in PL/M-86 and ASM-86 modules) when one module executes another module, typically by a CALL statement or instruction.

```
           ASM-89 MODULE DEFINES THREE PUBLIC SYMBOLS

   .

   .
PUBLIC     READ, WRITE, DELETE
   .
   .

READ:      ; ASM89 INSTRUCTIONS FOR "READ" OPERATION
   .
   .
           HLT
WRITE:     ; ASM89 INSTRUCTIONS FOR "WRITE" OPERATION
   .
           HLT
DELETE:    ; ASM89 INSTRUCTIONS FOR "DELETE" OPERATION
   .

           HLT
```

Figure 7-44 ASM-89 PUBLIC Directive

210911

```
                    PL/M-86 MODULE USES "WRITE" SYMBOL

DECLARE     (READ,WRITE,DELETE) POINTER EXTERNAL;
DECLARE     PARM$BLOCK   STRUCTURE
            (TP$START              POINTER,
             BUFFER$ADDR           POINTER,
             BUFFER$LEN            WORD);



/*SET UP "WRITE" CHANNEL OPERATION*/
PARM$BLOCK. TP$START = WRITE;



                    ASM-86     MODULE USES "READ" SYMBOL



EXTRN          READ,WRITE,DELETE
.
.
.
READ__PTR     DD    READ
WRITE__PTR    DD    WRITE
DELETE__PTR   DD    DELETE
.
.
.
; PARM__BLOCK
              EVEN        ; FORCE TO EVEN ADDRESS
TP__START     DD ?
BUFFER__ADDRDD ?
BUFFER__LEN   DW ?
.
.
.
; SET UP "READ" CHANNEL OPERATION
    MOV   AX, WORD PTR READ__PTR        ; 1ST WORD
    MOV   WORD PTR TP__START, AX
    MOV   AX, WORD PTR READ__PTR        ; 2ND WORD
    MOV   WORD PTR TP__START + 2, AX
.
.
.
```

Figure 7-44 ASM-89 PUBLIC Directive (continued)

210911

When an 8089 module (or modules) is to be located in the system space, it may be linked together with PL/M-86 or ASM-86 modules as described above and shown in Figure 7-48. LINK-86 resolves external references and combines the input modules into a single relocatable object module. This module can be input to LOC-86 (LOC-86 assigns final absolute memory addresses to all of the instructions and data). This absolute object module may, in turn, be processed by the OH-86 utility to translate the module into the hexadecimal format. This format makes the module readable (the records are written in ASCII characters) and is required by some PROM programmers and RAM loaders. Intel's Universal PROM Programmer (UPP) and iSBC 957TM Execution Package (loader) use the hexadecimal format.

If the 8089 code is to reside in its I/O space, a different technique is required since separate absolute object modules must be produced for the system and I/O spaces. Figure 7-49 shows how to link and locate when there are external references between I/O space modules and system space modules.

The normal link and locate sequence is followed and culminates in the production of an absolute module in hexadecimal format. Since the records in this file are human-readable, the file can be edited using the ISIS-II text editor. The editing task involves finding the 8089 I/O space records in the file, writing them to one file, and then writing the 8086,88/80186,188 records (destined for the system space) to another file. *MCS-86 ABSOLUTE OBJECT FILE FORMATS*, Order No. 9800921, available from Intel's Literature Department, describes the records in absolute (including hexadecimal) object modules.

When using the previous method, it is likely that LOC-86 will issue messages warning that segments overlap. For example, the 8089 code would typically be located starting at absolute location 0H of the I/O space. However, the 8086,88/186,188 interrupt pointer table occupies these low memory addresses in the system space. Since LOC-86 has no way to know that the segment will ultimately be located in different address spaces, it will warn of the conflict; the warning may be ignored.

PL/M-86 PROGRAM DECLARES PUBLIC SYMBOL "BUFFER"

.
.

DECLARE BUFFER (80) BYTE PUBLIC;

.
.

- - - - - - - - - - - - - - - - -

ASM-89 PROGRAM OBTAINS ADDRESS OF PUBLIC SYMBOL "BUFFER"

.
.

EXTRN BUFFER

.
.

BUF__ADDRESS   DD   BUFFER

.
.

LPD   GA, BUF__ADDRESS   ; POINT TO SYSTEM BUFFER

Figure 7-45 ASM-89 EXTRN Directive

210911

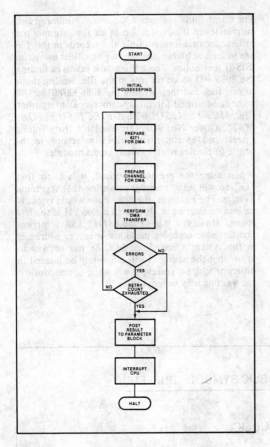

Figure 7-46 ASM-89 Sample Program Flow

An alternative to linking the modules together and then separating them is to link system space modules separately from I/O space modules as shown in Figure 7-50. This approach avoids the manual edit of the absolute object module and the segment conflict messages from LOC-86. It requires, however, that modules in the two spaces not use the EXTRN/PUBLIC mechanism to refer to each other. Modules in the same space can define external and public symbols, however.

External references from I/O space modules to system space modules can be eliminated if the CPU programs pass all system space addresses in parameter blocks. In other words, a channel program can obtain any address in the system space if the address is in the parameter block. Using this approach allows the system space addresses to be changed during execution. If the addresses are constant values, they

may also be altered as system development proceeds without relinking the channel programs.

External references from system space modules to addresses in the I/O space may be eliminated by assigning the addresses values that are known at assembly or compilation time. Figure 7-51 illustrates how the ASM-89 ORG directive can be used to force the first instruction (entry point) of a channel program to an absolute address. In the case of the example, one module contains two entry points labeled "READ" and "WRITE." Assuming the module is located at absolute address 0H in the I/O space, the channel programs will begin at 200H and 600H respectively. In the example, these values have been chosen arbitrarily; in a typical application they would be based on the length of the programs and the location of RAM and ROM areas. By starting the programs at fixed addresses that are known to the CPU programs that activate them, the channel programs can be reassembled without needing to relink the CPU programs.

7.8 PROGRAMMING CONSIDERATIONS

This section provides two types of 8089 programming information. A series of general guidelines, which apply to system and program design, is presented first. These guidelines are followed by specific coding examples that illustrate programming techniques that may be applied to many different types of applications.

Programming Guidelines

The practices in this section are recommended to simplify system development and, particularly, for system maintenance and enhancement. Software that is designed in accordance with these guidelines will be adaptable to the changing environment in which most systems operate, and will be in the best position to take advantage of new Intel hardware and software products.

Segments

Although the IOP does not "see" the segmented organization of system memory, it should respect this logical structure. The IOP should only address the system space through pointers passed by the CPU in the parameter block. It should not perform arithmetic on these addresses or otherwise manipulate them except for the automatic incrementing that occurs during DMA transfers. It is the responsibility of the CPU to pass addresses such that transfer operations do not cross segment boundaries.

```
8089 ASSEMBLER


ISIS-II 8089 ASSEMBLER V1.0 ASSEMBLY OF MODULE FLOPPY
OBJECT MODULE PLACED IN :F0:FLOPPY.OBJ
ASSEMBLER INVOKED BY ASM89 FLOPPY.A89


                           1
0000                       2 FLOPPY          SEGMENT
                           3 ;***
                           4 ;*** 8089 PROGRAM TO READ SECTOR FROM FLOPPY DISK
                           5 ;***
                           6
                           7 ;*** LAY OUT PARAMETER BLOCK.
                           8 PARM BLOCK        STRUC
0000                       9    RESERVED TP:   DS     4
0004                      10    BUFF PTR:      DS     4
0008                      11    TRACK:         DS     1
0009                      12    SECTOR:        DS     1
000A                      13    RETURN CODE:   DS     1
000B                      14    PARM BLOCK     ENDS
                          15
                          16 ;***LAY OUT 8271 DEVICE REGISTERS.
                          17 FLOPPY REGS        STRUC
0000                      18    COMMAND STAT:  DS     1
0001                      19    PARM RESULT:   DS     1
0002                      20    FLOPPY REGS    ENDS
                          21
                          22 ;***8271 ADDRESSES.
    FF00                  23 FLOPPY REG ADDR  EQU   OFF00H       ;LOW-ADDRESSED REGISTER
    FF04                  24 DACK 8271        EQU   OFF04H       ;DMA ACKNOWLEDGE
                          25
                          26 ;***MAKE PROGRAM ENTRY POINT ADDRESS
                          27 ;     AVAILABLE TO OTHER MODULES.
                          28 PUBLIC            START
                          29
                          30 ;***CLEAR RETURN CODE IN PARAMETER BLOCK.
0000   0A4F 0A 00         31 START:          MOVBI   [PP].RETURN CODE,0
                          32
                          33 ;***INITIALIZE RETRY COUNT.
0004   B130 0A00          34                 MOVI    IX,10
                          35
                          36 ;***POINT GC AT LOW-ORDER 8271 REGISTER.
0008   5130 00FF          37                 MOVI    GC,FLOPPY REG ADDR
                          38
                          39 ;***SEND COMMAND SEQUENCE TO 8271, HOLDING FINAL PARM.
                          40 ;***WAIT UNTIL 8271 IS NOT BUSY.
000C   EABA 00 FC         41 RETRY:          JNBT    [GC].COMMAND STAT,7,RETRY
                          42 ;***SEND "READ SECTOR, DRIVE 0" COMMAND.
0010   0A4E 00 12         43                 MOVBI   [GC].COMMAND STAT,012H
                          44 ;***SEND TRACK ADDRESS PARAMETER.
0014   0293 08 02CE 01    45                 MOVB    [GC].PARM RESULT,[PP].TRACK
                          46
                          47 ;***LOAD CHANNEL CONTROL REGISTER SPECIFYING:
                          48 ;    FROM PORT TO MEMORY,
                          49 ;    SYNCHRONIZE ON SOURCE,
                          50 ;    GA POINTS TO SOURCE,
                          51 ;    TERMINATE ON EXT,
                          52 ;    TERMINATION OFFSET = 0.
001A   L130 2088          53                 MOVI    CC,08820H
                          54
                          55 ;***SET SOURCE BUS = 8, DEST BUS = 16.
001E   A000               56                 WID     8,16
                          57
                          58 ;***POINT GB AT DESTINATION, GA AT SOURCE.
0020   238B 04            59                 LPD     GB,[PP].BUFF PTR
```

Figure 7-47 ASM-89 Sample Program

```
0023    1130 04FF        60                      MOVI    GA,DACK_8271
                         61
                         62 ;***INSURE THAT 8271 IS READY FOR LAST PARAMETER.
0027    AABA 00 FC       63 WAIT1:               JNBT    [GCJ.COMMAND_STAT,5,WAIT1
                         64
                         65 ;***PREPARE FOR DMA.
002B    6000            66                      XFER
                         67
                         68 ;***START DMA BY SENDING FINAL PARAMETER TO 8271.
002D    0293 09 02CE 01  69                      MOVB    [GCJ.PARM_RESULT,[PP].SECTOR
                         70
                         71 ;***PROGRAM RESUMES HERE FOLLOWING EXT.
                         72
                         73 ;***IF TRANSFER IS OK THEN EXIT, ELSE TRY AGAIN.
0033    6ABE 01 05       74                      JBT     [GCJ.PARM_RESULT,3,EXIT
                         75
                         76 ;***DECREMENT RETRY COUNT.
0037    A03C            77                      DEC     IX
                         78
                         79 ;***TRY AGAIN IF COUNT NOT EXHAUSTED.
0039    A840 D0          80                      JNZ     IX,RETRY
                         81
                         82 ;***WAIT UNTIL 8271 IS NOT BUSY.
003C    EABA 00 FC       83 EXIT:                JNBT    [GCJ.COMMAND_STAT,7,EXIT
                         84
                         85 ;***SEND "READ RESULT" COMMAND TO 8271.
0040    0A4E 00 2C       86                      MOVBI   [GCJ.COMMAND_STAT,02CH
                         87
                         88 ;***WAIT FOR RESULT.
0044    8ABA 00 FC       89 WAIT2:               JNBT    [GCJ.COMMAND_STAT,4,WAIT2
                         90
                         91 ;***POST RESULT IN PARAMETER BLOCK FOR CPU.
0048    0292 01 02CF 0A  92                      MOVB    [PP].RETURN_CODE,[GCJ.PARM_RESULT
                         93
                         94 ;***INTERRUPT CPU.
004E    4000            95                      SINTR
                         96
                         97 ;***STOP EXECUTION.
0050    2048            98                      HLT
                         99
0052                    100 FLOPPY               ENDS
                        101                      END


SYMBOL TABLE
------------

DEFN VALUE TYPE  NAME
---- ----- ----  ----

  10  0004  SYM   BUFF_PTR
  18  0000  SYM   COMMAND_STAT
  24  FF04  SYM   DACK_8271
  83  003C  SYM   EXIT
   2  0000  SYM   FLOPPY
  17  0000  STR   FLOPPY_REGS
  23  FF00  SYM   FLOPPY_REG_ADDR
   8  0000  STR   PARM_BLOCK
  19  0001  SYM   PARM_RESULT
   9  0000  SYM   RESERVED_TP
  41  000C  SYM   RETRY
  13  000A  SYM   RETURN_CODE
  12  0009  SYM   SECTOR
  31  0000  PUB   START
  11  0008  SYM   TRACK
  63  0027  SYM   WAIT1
  89  0044  SYM   WAIT2


ASSEMBLY COMPLETE; NO ERRORS FOUND
```

Figure 7-47 ASM-89 Sample Program (continued)

210911

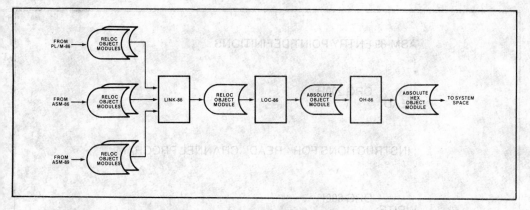

Figure 7-48 Creating a Single Absolute Object Module

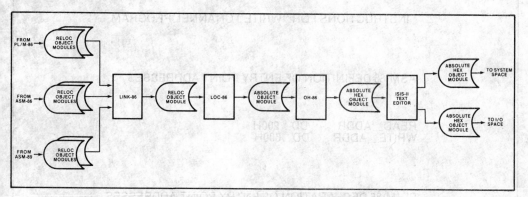

**Figure 7-49 Creating Separate Absolute Object Modules
— External References in Relocatable Modules**

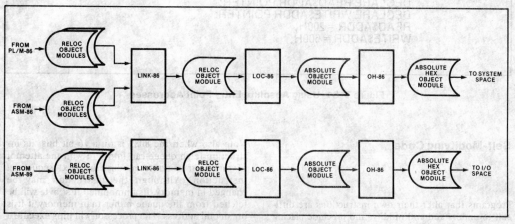

**Figure 7-50 Creating Separate Absolute Object Modules
— No External References in Relocatable Modules**

```
            ASM-89 ENTRY POINT DEFINITIONS
            .
            .
            .
                    ORG 200H
            READ:
            .
            .
            .
            ; INSTRUCTIONS FOR "READ" CHANNEL PROGRAM
            .
            .
            .
                    ORG 600H
            WRITE:
            .
            .
            .
            ; INSTRUCTIONS FOR "WRITE" CHANNEL PROGRAM
            .
            .
            .
            ASM-86 DEFINITION OF ENTRY POINT ADDRESSES
            .
            .
            .
            READ__ADDR       DD   200H
            WRITE__ADDR      DD   600H
            .
            .
            .
            PL/M-86 DECLARATION OF ENTRY POINT ADDRESSES
            .
            .
            DECLARE READ$ADDR POINTER;
            DECLARE WRITE$ADDR POINTER;
            READ$ADDR = 200H;
            WRITE$ADDR = 600H;
```

Figure 7-51 Using Absolute Entry Point Addresses

Self-Modifying Code

Programs that alter their own instructions are difficult to understand and modify, and preclude placing
the code in ROM. They may also inhibit compatibility with future Intel hardware and software products.

Note also when the 8089 is on a 16-bit bus, its instruction fetch queue can interfere with the attempt
of one instruction to modify the next sequential
instruction. Although the instruction may be
changed in memory, its unmodified first byte will be
fetched from the queue rather than memory if it is
on an odd address. The processor will thus execute a
partially-modified instruction with unpredictable
results.

I/O System Design

Section 2.10 notes that I/O systems should be designed hierarchically. Application programs "see" only the topmost level of the structure; all details pertaining to the physical characteristics and operation of I/O devices are relegated to lower levels. Figure 7-52 shows how this design approach might be employed in a system that uses an 8089 to perform I/O. The same concept can be expanded to larger systems with multiple IOPs.

The application system is clearly separated from the I/O system. No application programs perform I/O; instead they send an I/O request to the I/O supervisor. (In systems with file-oriented I/O, the request might be sent to a file system that would then invoke the I/O supervisor.) The I/O request should be expressed in terms of a logical block of data—a record, a line, a message, etc. It should also be devoid of any device-dependent information such as device address, sector size, etc.

The I/O supervisor transforms the application program's request for service into a parameter block and dispatches a channel program to carry out the operation. The I/O supervisor controls the channels; therefore, it knows the correspondence between channels and I/O devices, the locations of CBs and channel programs, and the format of all of the parameter blocks. The I/O supervisor also coordinates channel "events," monitoring BUSY flags and responding to channel-generated interrupt requests. The I/O supervisor does not, however, communicate with I/O devices that are controlled by the channels. If the CPU performs some I/O itself (this should be restricted to devices other than those run by the channels), the I/O supervisor invokes the equivalent of a channel program in the CPU to do the physical I/O. Note that although the I/O supervisor is drawn as a single box in Figure 7-52, it is likely to be structured as a hierarchy itself, with separate modules performing its many functions.

The software interface between the CPU's I/O supervisor and an IOP channel program should be completely and explicitly defined in the parameter block. For example, the I/O supervisor should pass the addresses of all system memory areas that the channel program will use. The channel program should not be written so that it "knows" any of these addresses, even if they are constants. Concentrating the interface into one place like this makes the system easier to understand and reduces the likelihood of an undesirable side effect if it is modified. It also generalizes the design so that it may be used in other application systems.

Figure 7-52 shows a simple channel program running on channel 1 and a more complex program running on channel 2. Channel 1's program performs a single function and is therefore designed as a simple program. The program on channel 2 performs three functions (e.g., "read," "write," "delete") and is structured to separate its functions. The functions might be implemented as procedures called by the "channel supervisor" depending on the content of the parameter block. Notice that to the I/O supervisor, both programs appear alike; in particular, both have a single entry point.

In some channel programs, different functions will need different information passed to them in the parameter block. Figure 7-53 shows one technique that accommodates different formats while still allowing the channel supervisor to determine which procedure to call from the PB. The parameter block is divided into fixed and variable portions, and a function code in the fixed area indicates the type of operation that is to be performed. Part of the fixed area has been set asede so that additional parameters can be added in the future.

Programming Examples

The first example in this section illustrates how a CPU can initialize a group of IOPs and then dispatch channel programs. The code is written in PL/M-86.

The remaining examples, written in ASM-89, demonstrate the 8089 instruction set and addressing modes in various commonly encountered programming situations. These include:

- memory-to-memory transfers

- saving and restoring registers

Initialization and Dispatch

The PL/M-86 code in Figure 7-54 initializes two IOPs and dispatches two channel programs on one of the IOPs. The same general technique can be used to initialize any number of IOPs. The hypothetical system that this code runs on is configured as follows:

- 8086 CPU (16-bit system bus);

- two remote IOPs share an 8-bit local I/O bus via the request/grant lines operating in mode 1;

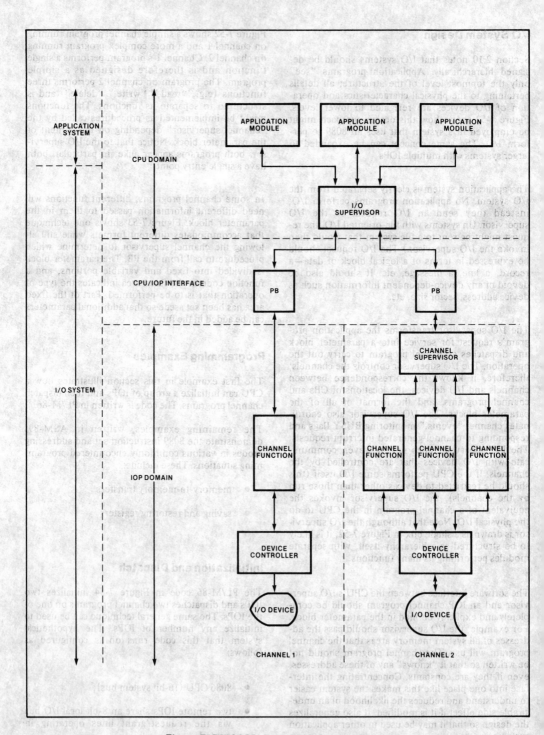

Figure 7-52 8089-Based I/O System Design

- 8089 channel attentions are mapped into four port addresses in the CPU's I/O space;

- channel programs reside in the 8089 I/O space;

- one 8089 controls a CRT terminal, one channel running the display, the other scanning the keyboard and building input messages;

- the function of the second 8089 is not defined in the example.

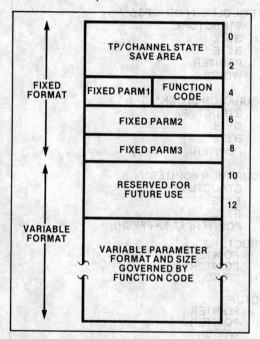

FIXED FORMAT

TP/CHANNEL STATE SAVE AREA		0
		2
FIXED PARM1	FUNCTION CODE	4
FIXED PARM2		6
FIXED PARM3		8

VARIABLE FORMAT

RESERVED FOR FUTURE USE	10
	12
VARIABLE PARAMETER FORMAT AND SIZE GOVERNED BY FUNCTION CODE	

Figure 7-53 Variable Format Parameter Block

The code declares one CB (channel control block) for each 8089. The CBs are declared as two-element arrays, each element defining the structure of one channel's portion of the CB. The SCB (system configuration block) and SCP (system configuration pointer) are also declared as structures. The SCP is located at its dedicated system space address of FFFF6H. The other structures are not located at specific addresses since they are all linked together by a chain of pointers "anchored" at the SCP.

Two simple parameter blocks define messages to be transmitted between the PL/M-86 program and the CRT. Each PB contains a pointer to the beginning of the message area and the length of the message. In the case of the keyboard (input) message, the channel program builds the message in the buffer pointed to by the pointer in the PB and returns the length of the message in the PB.

The code initializes one IOP at a time since the chain of control blocks read by the IOP during initialization must remain static until the process is complete. To initialize the first IOP, the code fills in the SYSBUS and SOC fields and links the blocks to each other using the PL/M-86 @ (address) operator. It sets channel 1's BUSY flag to FFH so that it can monitor the flag to determine when the initialization has been completed (the IOP clears the flag to 0H when it has finished). Channel 2's BUSY flag is cleared, although this could just as well have been done after the initialization (the IOP does not alter channel 2's BUSY flag during initialization). The code starts the IOP by issuing a channel attention to channel 1 to indicate that the IOP is a bus master. PL/M-86's OUT function is used to select the port address to which the IOP's CA and SEL lines have been mapped. The data placed on the bus (0H) is ignored by the IOP. It then waits until the IOP clears the channel 1 BUSY flag.

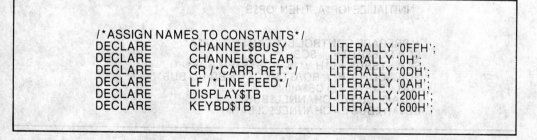

```
                /*ASSIGN NAMES TO CONSTANTS*/
        DECLARE          CHANNEL$BUSY          LITERALLY '0FFH';
        DECLARE          CHANNEL$CLEAR         LITERALLY '0H';
        DECLARE          CR /*CARR. RET.*/     LITERALLY '0DH';
        DECLARE          LF /*LINE FEED*/      LITERALLY '0AH';
        DECLARE          DISPLAY$TB            LITERALLY '200H';
        DECLARE          KEYBD$TB              LITERALLY '600H';
```

Figure 7-54 Initialization and Dispatch Example

210911

```
DECLARE    /*IOP CHANNEL ATTENTION ADDRESSES*/
IOP$A$CH1    LITERALLY              '0FFE0H',
IOP$A$CH2    LITERALLY              '0FFE1H',
IOP$B$CH1    LITERALLY              '0FFE2H',
IOP$B$CH2    LITERALLY              '0FFE3H';
DECLARE    /*CHANNEL CONTROL BLOCK FOR IOP$A)
             CB$A(2)        STRUCTURE
             (CCW           BYTE
             BUSY           BYTE
             PB$PTR         POINTER
             RESERVED       WORD);

DECLARE    /*CHANNEL CONTROL BLOCK FOR IOP$B*/
             CB$B(2)        STRUCTURE
             (CCW           BYTE
             BUSY           BYTE
             PB$PTR         POINTER
             RESERVED       WORD);

DECLARE    /*SYSTEM CONFIGURATION BLOCK*/
             SCB            STRUCTURE
             (SOC           BYTE
             RESERVED       BYTE
             CB$PTR         POINTER);

DECLARE    /*SYSTEM CONFIGURATION POINTER*/
             SCP            STRUCTURE
             (SYSBUS        BYTE
             RESERVED       BYTE,
             SCB$PTR        POINTER) AT (0FFFF6H);

DECLARE    MESSAGE$PB STRUCTURE
             (TB$PTR        POINTER,
             MSG$PTR        POINTER,
             MSG$LENGTH     WORD);

DECLARE    KEYBD$PB STRUCTUE
             (TP$PTR        POINTER,
             BUFF__PTR      POINTER,
             MSG$SIZE       WORD);

DECLARE    SIGN$ON BYTE (*) DATA
             (CR, LF, 'PLEASE ENTER USER ID');

DECLARE    KEYBD$BUFF BYTE (256);

/*
 *INITIALIZE IOP$A, THEN IOP$B
 */

/*PREPARE CONTROL BLOCKS FOR IOP$A*/
SCP.SCB$PTR = @ SCB;
SCP.SYSBUS = 01H; /*16-BIT SYSTEM BUS*/
SCB.SOC = 02H; /*RQ/GT MODE1, 8-BIT I/O BUS*/
SCB.CB$PTR = @ CB$A(0);
CB$A(0).BUSY = CHANNEL$BUSY
CB$A(1).BUSY = CHANNEL$CLEAR;
```

Figure 7-54 Initialization and Dispatch Example (continued)

```
/*ISSUE CA FOR CHANNEL1, INDICATING IOP IS MASTER*/
OUT (IOP$A$CH1) = 0H;

/*WAIT UNTIL FINISHED*/
DO WHILE CB$A(0).BUSY = CHANNEL$BUSY;
    END;

/*PREPARE CONTROL BLOCKS FOR IOP$B*/
SCB.CB$PTR = @CB$B(0);
CB$B(0).BUSY = CHANNEL$BUSY;
CB$B(1).BUSY = CHANNEL$CLEAR;

/*ISSUE CA FOR CHANNEL2, INDICATING SLAVE STATUS*/
OUT (IOP$B$CH2) = 0H;

/*WAIT UNTIL IOP IS READY*/
DO WHILE CB$B(0).BUSY = CHANNEL$BUSY;
    END;

/*
*SEND SIGN ON MESSAGE TO CRT CONTROLLED
*BY CHANNEL 1 OF IOP$A
*/
/*WAIT UNTIL CHANNEL IS CLEAR, THEN SET TO BUSY*/
DO WHILE LOCKSET (@CB$A(0).BUSY, CHANNEL$BUSY);
    END;

/*SET CCW AS FOLLOWS:
*      PRIORITY = 1,
*      NO BUS LOAD LIMIT,
*      DISABLE INTERRUPTS,
*      START CHANNEL PROGRAM IN I/O SPACE*/
CB$A(0).CCW = 10011001B;

/*LINK MESSAGE PARAMETER BLOCK TO CB*/
CB$A(0).PB$PTR = @ MESSAGE$PB;

/*FILL IN PARAMETER BLOCK*/
MESSAGE$PB.TB$PTR = DISPLAY$TB;
MESSAGE$PB.MSG$PTR = @SIGN$ON;
MESSAGE$PB. MSB$LENGTH = LENGTH (SIGN$ON);

/*DISPATCH THE CHANNEL*/
OUT (IOP$A$CH1) = 0H;

/*
*DISPATCH CHANNEL 2 OF IOP$A TO
*CONTINUOUSLY SCAN KEYBOARD, INTERRUPTING
*WHEN A COMPLETE MESSAGE IS READY
*/
/*WAIT UNTIL CHANNEL IS CLEAR, THEN SET TO BUSY*/
DO WHILE LOCKSET (@ CB$A(1).BUSY, CHANNEL$BUSY);
    END;
```

Figure 7-54 Initialization and Dispatch Example (continued)

```
/*SET CCW AS FOLLOWS:
*      PRIORITY = 0
*      BUS LOAD LIMIT,
*      ENABLE INTERRUPTS,
*      START CHANNEL PROGRAM IN I/O SPACE*/
CB$A(1).CCW = 00110001B;
/*LINK KEYBOARD PARAMETER BLOCK TO CB*/
CB$A(1).PB$PTR = @ KEYBD$PB;
/*FILL IN PARAMETER BLOCK*/
KEYBD$PB.TB$PTR = KEYBD$TB;
KEYBD$PB.BUFF$PTR = @ KEYBD$BUFF;
KEYBD$PB.MSG$SIZE = 0H;
/*DISPATCH THE CHANNEL*/
OUT (IOP$A$CH2) = 0H;
```

Figure 7-54 Initialization and Dispatch Example (continued)

The second IOP is initialized in the same manner, first changing the pointer in the SCB to point to the second IOP's channel control block. If this IOP were on a different I/O bus, the SOC field would have been altered if a different request/grant mode were being used or if the IOP had a 16-bit I/O bus. The second IOP is a slave so its initialization is started by issuing a CA to channel 2 rather than channel 1.

After both IOPs are ready, the code dispatches two channel programs (not coded in the example); one program is dispatched to each channel of one of the IOPs. To avoid external references, the system has been set up so that the PL/M-86 code "knows" the starting addresses of these channel programs (200H and 600H). The code uses the PL/M-86 LOCKSET function to:

- lock the system bus;

- read the BUSY flag;

- set the BUSY flag to FFH if it is clear;

- unlock the system bus.

This operation continues until the BUSY flag is found to be clear (indicating that the channel is available). Setting the flag immediately to FFH prevents another processor (or another task in this program activated as a result of an interrupt) from using the channel. The code fills in the parameter block with the address and length of the message to be displayed, sets the CCW and then links the channel program (task block) start address to the parameter block and links the parameter block to the CB. The channel is dispatched with the OUT function that effects a channel attention for channel 1.

A similar procedure is followed to start channel 2 scanning the terminal keyboard. In this case, the code allows channel 2 to generate an interrupt request (which it might do to signal that a message has been assembled). An interrupt procedure would then handle the interrupt request.

Memory-to-Memory Transfer

Figure 7-55 shows a channel program that performs a memory-to-memory block transfer in seven instructions. The program moves up to 64K bytes between any two locations in the system space. A 16-bit system bus is assumed, and the CPU is assumed to be monitoring the channel's BUSY flag to determine when the program has finished.

To attain maximum transfer speed, the program locks the bus during each transfer cycle. This ensures that another processor does not acquire the bus in the interval between the DMA fetch and store operations. By setting this channel's priority bit in the CCW to 1 and the other channel's to 0, the CPU could effectively prevent the other channel from running during the transfer. Byte count termination is selected so that the transfer will stop when the number of bytes specified by the CPU has been moved. Since there is only a single termination condition, a termination offset of 0 is specified. The transfer begins after the WID instruction, and the HLT instruction is executed immediately upon termination.

210911

Saving and Restoring Registers

A CPU program can "interrupt" a channel program by issuing a "suspend" channel command. The channel responds to this command by saving the task pointer and PSW in the first two words of the parameter block. The suspended program can be restarted by issuing a "resume" command that loads TP and the PSW from the save area.

If the CPU wants to execute another channel program between the suspend and resume operations, the suspended program's registers will usually have to be saved first. If the "interrupting" program "knows" that the registers must be saved, it can perform the operation and also restore the registers before it halts.

A more general solution is shown in Figure 7-56. This is a program that does nothing but save the contents of the channel registers. The registers are saved in the parameter block because PP is the only register that is known to point to an available area of memory. A similar program could be written to restore registers from the same parameter block.

Using this approach, the CPU would "interrupt" a running program as follows:

- suspend the running program,
- run the register save program,
- run the "interrupting" program,
- run the register restore program,
- resume the suspended program.

```
MEMEXAMP            SEGMENT
;**MEMORY-TO-MEMORY TRANSFER PROGRAM**
PB                 STRUC
TP_RESERVED:       DS    4
FROM_ADDR:         DS    4
TO_ADDR:           DS    4
SIZE:              DS    2
PB                 ENDS

;POINT GA AT SOURCE, GB AT DESTINATION.
                   LPD           GA, [PP].FROM_ADDR
                   LPD           GB, [PP].TO_ADDR
;LOAD BYTE COUNT INTO BC.
                   MOV           BC, [PP].SIZE
;LOAD CC SPECIFYING:
;      MEMORY TO MEMORY,
;      NO TRANSLATE,
;      UNSYNCHRONIZED,
;      GA POINTS TO SOURCE,
;      LOCK BUS DURING TRANSFER,
;      NO CHAINING,
;      TERMINATING ON BYTE COUNT,OFFSET = 0.
                   MOV           CC, 0C208H
;PREPARE CHANNEL FOR TRANSFER.
                   XFER

;SET LOGICAL BUS WIDTH.
                   WID           16,16

;STOP EXECUTION AFTER DMA.
                   HLT
MEMEXAMP           ENDS
                   END
```

Figure 7-55 Memory-to-Memory Transfer Example

```
SAVEREGS             SEGMENT
;SAVE ANOTHER CHANNEL'S REGISTERS IN PB
PB                   STRUC
TP__RESERVED:        DS        4
GA__SAVE:            DS        3
GB__SAVE:            DS        3
GC__SAVE:            DS        3
IX__SAVE:            DS        2
BC__SAVE:            DS        2
MC__SAVE:            DS        2
CC__SAVE:            DS        2
PB                   ENDS

                     MOVP      [PP].GA__SAVE, GA
                     MOVP      [PP].GB__SAVE, GB
                     MOVP      [PP].GC__SAVE, GC
                     MOV       [PP].IX__SAVE, IX
                     MOV       [PP].BC__SAVE, BC
                     MOV       [PP].MC__SAVE, MC
                     MOV       [PP].CC__SAVE, CC
                     HLT
SAVEREGS             ENDS
                     END
```

Figure 7-56 Register Save Example

210911

The 80130 Operating System Firmware Component

8

CHAPTER 8
THE 80130 OPERATING SYSTEM
FIRMWARE COMPONENT

8.1 INTRODUCTION

This chapter describes the 80130 Operating System Firmware (OSF) component. The 80130 OSF component (software in silicon) is a processor extension in the form of of an extremely sophisticated integrated circuit. In conjunction with the 8086,88 or the 80186,188 CPU, it forms the nucleus of a high-performance, real-time multitasking operating system. The 80130 adds task management, interrupt management, message passing, synchronization and memory allocation capabilities to the CPU, and extends the basic data types of the CPU by adding new, system data types (JOB'S, TASK'S, MAILBOX's, SEGMENT's, and REGION's). To create, manipulate and delete these new data types, the 80130 uses 35 operating-system instructions or "primitives." Programs using the 80130 primitives may be written in ASM-86, PL/M-86, Fortran-86, or Pascal-86.

In addition, the 80130 OSF contains a programmable interrupt controller, 16-bit operating-system and delay timers, and a variable baud-rate generator. It is connected directly to the multiplexed address/data bus of the CPU. The 80130 is compatible with the MULTIBUS system as well as the iRMX 86 operating system.

For additional information about the 80130 OSF component, the reader is referred to the iOSP 86 Support Package Reference Manual, Order Number: 14443, which has been used as the reference document for this chapter.

This chapter contains a discussion of the software aspects of the OSF. Hardware considerations are discussed in Chapter 5, Volume 2 of this set.

The OSF provides the foundation of an operating system. To do so, it provides a collection of features that can serve as the heart of any operating system. Specifically, the OSP processor (see below) provides:

- Object-Oriented Architecture
- Multitasking
- Multiprogramming
- Intertask Coordination
- Dynamic Memory Allocation

- Management of Objects
- Management of Exceptions
- Management of Interrupts
- Extendability
- Primitives
- Programming Considerations
- iRMX 86 Features

The following sections describe all of these features in detail.

8.2 80130 OSF OVERVIEW

The 80130 is a component that is designed to work in conjunction with either the 8086,88 or the 80186,188 microprocessor. When the 80130 is combined with the iAPX 86/10 (8086) microprocessor, the pair of components is called the iAPX 86/30 Operating System Processor (OSP). When the 80130 is combined with the iAPX 186/10 (80186) microprocessor, the pair of components is called the iAPX 186/30 Operating System Processor. Figure 8-1 shows the names of these combinations of components. In order to simplify nomenclature, this manual uses the term OSP to refer to either pair of components.

The 8087 Numeric Processor Extension (NPX) can be added to either pair of components. Figure 8-2 shows the notation used to refer to these combinations.

The 80130 component expands the capabilities of the microprocessor to provide a new set of functions called primitives. These primitives are designed specifically to serve as the foundation for a real-time, multitasking operating system.

In other words, the OSP provides an expanded instruction set. In addition to the instructions provided by the microprocessor alone, the OSP provides more sophisticated instructions that can be used to build a real-time operating system.

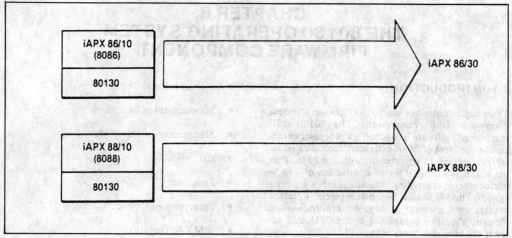

Figure 8-1 Combining the 80130 and a Microprocessor

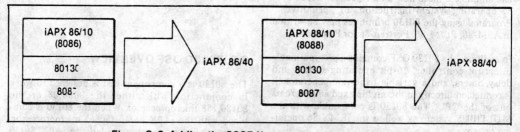

Figure 8-2 Adding the 8087 Numeric Processor Extension

In the same way that high-level programming languages reduce the manpower needed to write a program, the more powerful instructions of the OSP reduce the manpower needed to write an operating system. This results in less development time and expense.

8.3 ARCHITECTURE

The OSP uses an object-oriented architecture in order to make operating systems easy to learn about and to use.

An operating system is a collection of functions meant to be used by software engineers. Many operating systems are so complex that the majority of the engineers using them are unable to fully grasp their organization. In contrast, systems having object-oriented architectures are easier to understand. Their mechanisms are well defined, and they demonstrate a consistency that makes the operating system seem less awesome.

Explanation of Object-Oriented Architecture

An Object-Oriented Architecture is a means of humanizing an operating system. It uses a collection of building blocks that are manipulated by operators. For purposes of illustration, the architecture of FORTRAN will be used as an example.

FORTRAN has a typed architecture. Its building blocks are variables of several types. For instance, it has integers, real numbers, double-precision real numbers, etc. It also has operators (+, −, *, /, **, and others) that act on variables to produce understandable results.

The OSP provides building blocks called objects. As with FORTRAN variables, OSP objects are of several types. The types are tasks, jobs, mailboxes, regions, and segments.

210911

Just as the variables in a FORTRAN program are acted upon by operators, the objects in an OSP-based system are acted upon by primitives. "Primitives" are procedures that the OSP provides to allow you to manipulate objects. For instance, the CREATE$TASK primitive does precisely what its name suggests as shown in Figure 8-3.

In the text portions of this manual, the primitives are consistently referred to by their informal names, such as CREATE$TASK. In the example in Figure 8-3 and throughout most of Chapter 8, the primitives are referred to by their formal names. A formal name is derived from an informal name by adding "RQ$" or "RQ" at the beginning. Consequently, the formal counterpart of CREATE$TASK is RQ$CREATE$TASK.

The purpose of this example is to show that primitives are invoked as PL/M-86 procedures. Figure 8-3 shows how to create a task using the CREATE$TASK primitive. The parameters of the primitive vary according to the type of task you are creating.

An object-oriented architecture makes a system easier to learn and to use. It does this by taking advantage of classification of objects. In the case of FORTRAN, the variables are classified into types, because each type exhibits certain characteristics. For instance, all integer variables are similar, though they can take on different values. This similarity makes FORTRAN easy to master. For the same reasons, the OSP objects are classified into types. Each object type (such as a mailbox) has a specific set of attributes. Once the programmer has become familiar with the attributes of a mailbox, he is familiar with all mailboxes. There are no special cases.

Classification by type also applies to OSP primitives. Each type of OSP object has an associated set of primitives. These primitives cannot be used to manipulate objects of another type without causing an error. (The analogy breaks down at this point. FORTRAN operators almost always work on several types of variables.)

The beauty of the object-oriented architecture of the OSP can be summed up in one statement: Once the programmer learns the attributes and the primitives associated with a type of object, he has complete knowledge of the behavior of the object type.

Means of Referring to an Object

One of the by-products of an object-oriented architecture is that the programmer must have a means of referring to a particular object. For this purpose,

the OSP provides TOKENs. A *TOKEN* is a 16-bit value that the OSP gives to you whenever you create an object. This value is unique in that no two objects can have the same TOKEN at the same time. In order to manipulate a particular object, the appropriate primitive is invoked using the object's TOKEN as one of the parameters.

8.4 MULTITASKING

The OSP provides multitasking to simplify the development of systems that process real-time events.

The essence of real-time operating systems is the ability to process numerous events occurring at seemingly random times. These events are asynchronous because they can occur at any time, and they are potentially concurrent because one event might occur while another is being processed.

Any single program that attempts to process multiple, concurrent, asynchronous events is bound to be complex. The program must perform several functions. It must process the events. It must remember which events have occurred and the order in which they occurred. It must remember which events have occurred but have not been processed. The complexity obviously grows greater as the system monitors more events.

Multitasking is a technique that dissipates unwinds this confusion. Rather than writing a single program to process N events, N programs can be written, each of which processes a single event. This technique eliminates the need to monitor the order in which events occur.

Each of these N programs forms an OSP task, one of the types of objects in the object-oriented architecture. Tasks are the only active objects provided by the OSP, as only tasks can invoke primitives.

Multitasking simplifies the process of building a system. This allows systems to be built faster and with less expense. Furthermore, because of the one-to-one relationship between events and tasks, the system's code is less complex and is easier to maintain.

Tasks

Tasks are the active objects provided by the OSP. For each task in a running operating system, the OSP keeps track of a code segment, a task priority, a task state, and other attributes that are described below.

```
/****************************************************************
 * This example illustrates how the CREATE$TASK primitive can be used.*
 ****************************************************************/


        $INCLUDE(:F1:OSXPRM.EXT);   /* Declares all primitive calls */

    TASK_CODE: PROCEDURE EXTERNAL;
    END TASK_CODE;

    DECLARE TOKEN                 LITERALLY 'SELECTOR';
                                  /* if your PL/M compiler does not
                                     support this variable type,
                                     declare TOKEN a WORD */
    DECLARE task$token            TOKEN;
    DECLARE priority$level$66     LITERALLY '66';
    DECLARE start$address         POINTER;
    DECLARE data$seg              WORD;
    DECLARE stack$pointer         POINTER;
    DECLARE stack$size$512        LITERALLY '512';
                                  /* new task's stack
                                     size is 512 bytes */
    DECLARE task$flags            WORD;
    DECLARE status                WORD;

SAMPLE_PROCEDURE:
    PROCEDURE;
    start$address = @TASK_CODE; /* first instruction of the new task */
    data$seg = 0;               /* task sets up own data segment */
    stack$pointer = 0;          /* automatic stack allocation   */
    task$flags = 0;             /* designates no floating-point
                                   instructions */
    •
    •  }   Typical PL/M-86 Statements
    •


/****************************************************************
 * The task TASK_CODE is created when the calling task invokes the  *
 * CREATE$TASK primitive.                                           *
 ****************************************************************/
    task$token = RQ$CREATE$TASK   (priority$level$66,
                                   start$address,
                                   data$seg,
                                   stack$pointer,
                                   stack$size$512,
                                   task$flags,
                                   @status);

    •
    •  }   Typical PL/M-86 Statements
    •
END SAMPLE_PROCEDURE;
```

Figure 8-3 Example Showing How to Use a Primitive

CODE SEGMENTS FOR TASKS

A code segment is simply an iAPX 86/186 segment that contains code. Each task has an associated code segment that contains instructions for the task to execute. When writing code for a task, whether the code is in assembly language or a high-level language, procedures rather than main modules, must be used.

TASK PRIORITY

A task's priority is an integer value between 0 and 255 (decimal). The lower the priority number, the higher the priority of the task. A high priority task has favored status as it competes with other tasks for the microprocessor.

Unless a task is involved in processing interrupts (described later in this chapter), its priority should be between 129 and 255. When a task having a priority in the range 0 to 128 is running, certain external interrupt lines are disabled, depending on the priority.

Also, if a task's code uses instructions that execute on the 8087 NPX (Numeric Processor Extension), that task should not have a priority high enough to disable the interrupt line of the 8087 NPX, or a deadlock situation could result. The interrupt line of the 8087 is configurable. Refer to Section 8.8 of this chapter for a correlation between priorities and interrupt lines.

TASK STATES

A task is always in one of five execution states. The states are asleep, suspended, asleep-suspended, ready, and running.

● The Asleep State

A task is in the asleep state when it is waiting for a request to be granted. Also, a task can put itself to sleep for a specified amount of time by using the SLEEP primitive.

● The Suspended State

A task enters the suspended state when it is placed there by another task, when it is waiting for a interrupt, or when it suspends itself. Associated with each task is a suspension depth, which reflects the number of "suspends" outstanding against it. Each suspend operation must be countered with a

resume operation before the task can leave the suspended state.

● The Asleep-Suspended State

When a sleeping task is suspended, it enters the asleep-suspended state. In effect, it is then in both the asleep and suspended states. While asleep-suspended, the task's sleeping time might expire, putting the task in the suspended state. Also, if another task resumes an asleep-suspended task, the latter task will enter the asleep state.

● The Ready State

A task is ready if it is not asleep, suspended, or asleep-suspended.

● The Running State

For a task to become the running (executing) task, it must be the highest priority task in the ready state. A system built upon the OSP can have only one running task at any given instant.

Task State Transitions

The OSP does not use a time-slicing algorithm to allocate the processor to tasks. Instead, it uses a priority-based, event-driven algorithm. As the operating system executes, events occur which cause tasks to pass from state to state. Figure 8-4 shows the paths of transition between states.

The following list describes, by number, the events that cause the transitions in Figure 8-4. In the list, the migrating task is called "the task."

1) When the task is created, it is placed in the ready state.

2) The task goes from the ready state to the running state when one of the following occurs:

   ● The task has just become ready and has higher priority than does any other ready task.

   ● The task is ready, no other ready task has higher priority, no other task of equal priority has been ready for a longer time, and the previously running task has just left the running state by transitions (4), (6), or (10).

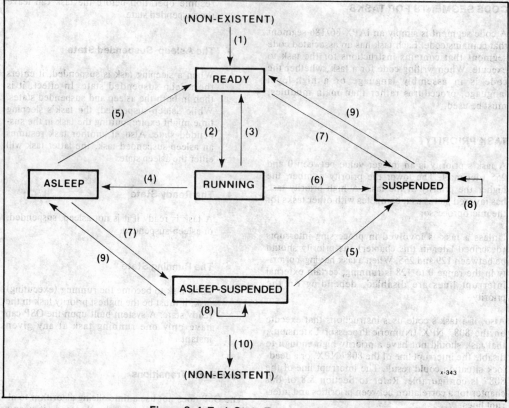

Figure 8-4 Task State Transition Diagram

3) The task goes from the running state to the ready state when the task is preempted by a higher priority task that has just become ready.

4) The task goes from the running state to the asleep state when one of the following occurs:

- The task puts itself to sleep (by the SLEEP primitive).

- The task makes a request (by the LOOK-UP$OBJECT, RECEIVE$MESSAGE, or RECEIVE$CONTROL primitive) that cannot be granted immediately and expresses, in the request, its willingness to wait.

5) The task goes from the asleep state to the ready state or from the asleep-suspended state to the suspended state when one of the following occurs:

- The time period specified in the invocation of the SLEEP primitive expires.

- The task's designated waiting period expires without its request being granted.

- The task's request is granted (because another task called the CATALOG$OB-JECT, SEND$MESSAGE, or the SEND$CONTROL primitive. These calls correspond to those mentioned earlier in (4).)

6) The task goes from the running state to the suspended state when the task suspends itself (by the SUSPEND$TASK or WAIT$INTERRUPT primitive.)

7) The task goes from the ready state to the suspended state or from the asleep state to the asleep-suspended when the task is suspended by another task (by the SUSPEND$TASK primitive.)

210911

8) The task remains in the suspended state or the asleep-suspended state when one of the following occurs:

- The task is, once again, suspended by another task using the SUSPEND$TASK primitive.

- The task has a suspension depth greater than one and the task is resumed by another task (by the RESUME$TASK primitive.)

9) The task goes from the suspended state to the ready state or from the asleep-suspended state to the asleep state when the task has a suspension depth of one and the task is resumed by another task (by the RESUME$TASK or SIGNAL$INTERRUPT primitive) or when a task awaiting an interrupt receives the interrupt.

10) The task goes from any state to non-existence when it is deleted (by the DELETE$TASK, or RESET$INTERRUPT primitives.)

ADDITIONAL TASK ATTRIBUTES

In addition to priority, execution state, and suspension depth, the OSP maintains the following attributes for each task: containing job, contents of registers, starting address of its exception handler, the task's exception mode, whether the task is an interrupt task, and whether the task uses the 8087 NPX. Jobs, interrupts, exception handlers, and exception modes are discussed later in this chapter.

Task Resources

When a task is created, the OSP takes any resources that it needs at that time (such as memory) from the task's job. If the task is subsequently deleted, the OSP returns those resources to the task's job. (Jobs are discussed in detail in the section of this chapter entitled "Multiprogramming.")

The task's code, however, is not a resource in this sense. It does not come from nor does it return to the task's job, because it is static during system operation.

Primitives for Tasks

The OSP provides the following primitives to manipulate tasks:

- CREATE$TASK
  The CREATE$TASK primitive creates a task and returns a token for it.

- DELETE$TASK
  The DELETE$TASK primitive deletes a task from the system.

- SUSPEND$TASK
  The SUSPEND$TASK primitive increases a task's suspension depth by one, and suspends the task if it is not already suspended.

- RESUME$TASK
  The RESUME$TASK primitive decreases a task's suspension depth by one. If the depth becomes zero and the task was suspended, this primitive makes the task ready. If the depth becomes zero and the task was asleep-suspended, this primitive puts the task into the asleep state.

- SLEEP
  The SLEEP primitive places the calling task in the asleep state for a specified amount of time.

- GET$TASK$TOKENS
  The GET$TASK$TOKENS primitive allows a task to obtain a token for any of the following objects:

  — the job containing the task

  — the parameter object for the job containing the task

  — the system's root job

  — the task itself

- SET$PRIORITY
  The SET$PRIORITY primitive allows a task to change its own priority or that of another task.

8.5 MULTIPROGRAMMING

Multiprogramming is a technique used to run several applications on a single hardware system. In order to take full advantage of multiprogramming, the OSP provides each application with a separate environment; that is, separate memory and objects. The reason for this isolation is to prevent independently-developed applications from causing problems for each other.

The OSP provides a type of object that can be used to obtain this kind of isolation. The object is called a job, and it has the following characteristics:

- Unlike tasks, jobs are passive. They cannot invoke primitives.

- Each job includes a collection of tasks and those resources needed by those tasks.

- Jobs serve as useful boundaries for dynamically allocating memory. When two tasks of one job request memory, they share the memory associated with their job. Two tasks in different jobs do not directly compete for memory.

- An application consists of one or more jobs.

Multiprogramming provides application systems with two benefits:

- Multiprogramming increases the amount of work a system can do. By running several applications rather than one, hardware is being utilized a greater percentage of the time, thus reducing hardware implementation costs.

- Because of the correspondence between jobs and applications, new jobs can be added to a system without affecting other jobs. This makes system modifications easier and faster.

Definition of JOB

A JOB is an OSP object that serves as an environment in which other OSP objects such as tasks, mailboxes, regions, segments, and (offspring) jobs reside. In addition, each job has a pool of memory. The job's memory pool provides the raw material from which objects can be created by the tasks in the job.

Applications consist of one or more jobs. Although the jobs within an application can be independent of one another, they can share resources. Objects may be shared between jobs, although each object is owned by only one job.

The programmer must decide which tasks belong in the same job. In general, tasks should be placed in the same job if:

- They have similar or related purposes

- They share many resources

Job Tree and Resource Sharing

The jobs in a system are arranged in the form of a tree. The root job is a job provided by the OSP. The remaining jobs, including jobs that are created dynamically while the system runs, are descendants of the root job. A job containing tasks that create other jobs is a parent job. A newly created job is a child of the job whose task created it.

Associated with each job is a set of limits. The limits of a job are as follows:

- Maximum and minimum allowable sizes of the job's memory pool.

- Maximum allowable number of simultaneously existing objects that the job can contain.

- Maximum allowable number of simultaneously existing tasks that the job can contain.

- Highest allowable priority of any task contained in the job.

These limits must be specified whenever a job is created. These limits apply collectively to the job and all of its descendant jobs.

For example, suppose Job A creates Job B. When this happens:

- The memory for Job B's memory pool is taken from Job A's memory pool.

- The numbers of tasks and total objects that Job A can contain are reduced by the corresponding values specified for Job B.

- The specified maximum priority for tasks in Job B cannot exceed the maximum priority for tasks in Job A.

Job Creation

When a job is created it has one task. The functions of this task include doing some initializing for the new job. Initializing activities can include housekeeping and creating other objects in the new job.

When a task creates a job, it has the option of passing a token for a parameter object to the newly created job. The parameter object can be an OSP object of any type and it can be used for any purpose. For example, the parameter object might be a segment containing data, arranged in a predefined format, needed by tasks in the new job. Tasks in the new job can obtain a token for the job's parameter object by means of the GET$TASK$TOKENS primitive, described in Chapter 3.

Jobs differ from other OSP objects in duration. Once a job is created, it exists as long as the system exists.

Primitives for Jobs

The OSP provides one primitive that relates to jobs. The CREATE$JOB primitive creates a job containing one task. During the creation, the primitive draws resources for the new job from the resources of the parent job (the job containing the calling task). After the job has been created, the primitive returns a token for the job to the calling task.

8.6 INTERTASK COORDINATION

The OSP provides simple techniques for tasks to coordinate their activities. These techniques allow tasks in a multitasking system to mutually exclude, synchronize, and communicate with each other.

Multitasking is a technique used to simplify the design of real-time application systems that monitor multiple, concurrent, asynchronous events. Multitasking allows engineers to focus their attention on the processing of a single event rather than having to contend with numerous other events occurring in an unpredictable order.

However, the processing of several events may be related. For instance, the task processing Event A may need to know how many times Event B has occurred since Event A last occurred. This kind of processing requires that tasks be able to coordinate with each other. The OSP provides for this coordination.

Tasks can interract with each other in three ways. They can exchange information, mutually exclude each other, and synchronize with each other. Each of these will be examined in the following sections.

EXCHANGING INFORMATION

Tasks exchange information for two purposes. One purpose is to pass data from one task to another. For instance, suppose that one task accumulates key-

strokes from a terminal until a carriage return is encountered. It then passes the entire line of text to another task, which is responsible for decoding commands.

The second reason for passing data is to draw attention to a specific object in the application system. In effect, one task says to another, "I am talking about *that* object."

The OSP facilitates intertask communication by supplying objects called mailboxes along with primitives to manipulate mailboxes. The primitives associated with mailboxes are CREATE$MAILBOX, DELETE$MAILBOX, SEND$MESSAGE, and RECEIVE$MESSAGE. Tasks use the first two primitives to build and eradicate a particular mailbox. They use the second two to communicate with each other. If Task A wants Task B to become aware of a particular object, Task A uses the SEND$MESSAGE primitive to mail a token for the object to the mailbox. Task B uses the RECEIVE$MESSAGE primitive to get the token from the mailbox.

NOTE: The foregoing example, along with all of the examples in this section, is somewhat simplified in order to serve as an introduction. For detailed information, refer to Section 8.10, in which each OSP primitive is individually described.

As mentioned previously, tasks can use mailboxes to send information to each other. This is accomplished by putting the information into a *segment* (an OSP object consisting of a contiguous block of memory) and using the SEND$MESSAGE primitive to mail a token for the segment. The other task invokes the RECEIVE$MESSAGE primitive to get the token for the segment containing the message.

Why don't tasks just send tokens for messages directly between each other, rather than through mailboxes? Because tasks are asynchronous—they run in unpredictable order. If two tasks want to communicate with each other, they need a place to store messages and to wait for messages. If the receiver uses the RECEIVE$MESSAGE primitive before the message has been sent, the receiver can wait at the mailbox until a message arrives. Similarly, if the sender uses the SEND$MESSAGE primitive before the receiver is ready to receive, the message is held at the mailbox until a task requests a message from the mailbox. In other words, mailboxes allow tasks to communicate with each other even though tasks are asynchronous.

MUTUAL EXCLUSION

Occasionally, when tasks are running concurrently, the following kind of situation arises:

- Task A is in the process of reading information from a segment.

- An interrupt occurs and Task B, which has higher priority than Task A, preempts Task A.

- Task B modifies the contents of the segment that Task A was in the midst of reading.

- Task B finishes processing its event and surrenders the processor.

- Task A resumes reading the segment.

The problem is that Task A might obtain information that is completely invalid. For instance, suppose the application is air traffic control. Task A is responsible for detecting potential collisions, and Task B is responsible for updating the Plane Location Table with the new X- and Y-coordinates of each plane's location. Unless Task A can obtain exclusive use of the Plane Location Table, Task B can make Task A fail to spot a collision.

Here's how it could happen. Task A reads the X-coordinate of the plane's location and is preempted by Task B. Task B updates the entry that Task A was reading, changing both the X- and Y-coordinates of the plane's location. Task B finishes its function and surrenders the processor. Task A resumes execution and reads the new Y-coordinate of the plane's location. As a direct result of Task B changing the Plane Location Table while Task A was reading it, Task A thinks the plane is at old X and new Y.

This problem can be avoided by mutual exclusion. If Task A can prevent Task B from modifying the table until after A has finished using it, A can be assured of valid information. Somehow, Task A must obtain exclusive use of the table.

Corruption of data can occur in this manner whenever the following three conditions are met:

- The data is shared between two or more tasks.

- The tasks sharing the data run concurrently. (In other words, one of the tasks could possibly preempt another.)

- At least one of the tasks changes the data.

Whenever all three of these conditions can exist, special precautions must be taken to protect the validity of the shared data. The programmer must ensure that only one task has access to the shared data at any instant, and that the task having access cannot be preempted by other tasks desiring access. This protocol for sharing data is called *mutual exclusion*, and providing mutual exclusion is the function of regions, which are described later in this chapter.

SYNCHRONIZATION

As mentioned earlier, tasks are asynchronous. Nonetheless, occasionally a task must know that a certain event has occurred before the task starts running. For instance, suppose that a particular application system requires that Task A cannot run until after Task B has run. This kind of requirement calls for *synchronizing* Task A with Task B.

Application systems can achieve synchronization by using mailboxes. Before executing either Task A or Task B, a mailbox must be created. Then Task A invokes the RECEIVE$MESSAGE primitive for that mailbox. Task A is forced to wait at the mailbox until Task B sends a message. This achieves the desired synchronization.

The intertask coordination supplied by the OSP is flexible and simple to use. Mailboxes and regions can accommodate a wide variety of situations. A particular application system is not limited to some arbitrary number of mailboxes or regions; it can create as many as it needs.

Mailboxes

The principal function of mailboxes is to support intertask communication and synchronization. A sending task uses a mailbox to pass a token for an object to another task. For example, the object might be a segment containing data needed by the receiving task.

NOTE: Throughout the remainder of this chapter we refer to the passing of objects between jobs or between tasks. Be aware that this does not actually occur, that tokens, not objects, are passed, and that this means of description is adopted for convenience only.

MAILBOX QUEUES

Each mailbox has two queues, one for tasks that are waiting to receive objects, the other for objects that have been sent by tasks but have not yet been received. The OSP ensures that waiting tasks receive objects as soon as they are available. So, at any given time, at least one of the mailbox's queues is empty.

MAILBOX MECHANICS

When a task sends a token to a mailbox, using the SEND$MESSAGE primitive, one of two things happens. If no tasks are waiting at the mailbox, the object is placed at the rear of the object queue (which might be empty). Object queues are processed in a first-in/first-out (FIFO) manner, so the object remains in the queue until it makes its way to the front and is given to a task.

On the other hand, if there are tasks waiting, the task at the front of the task queue receives the object and goes either from the asleep state to the ready state or from the asleep-suspended state to the suspended state.

NOTE: If the receiving task has a higher priority than the sending task and is not suspended, then the receiving task preempts the sender and becomes the running task.

When a task attempts to receive an object from a mailbox via the RECEIVE$MESSAGE primitive, and the object queue at the mailbox is not empty, the task receives the object immediately and remains ready. However, if there are no objects at the mailbox two things can happen:

If the task, in its request, elects to wait, it is placed in the mailbox's task queue and is put to sleep. If the designated waiting period elapses before the task gets an object, the task is made ready and receives an E$TIME exception code.

If the task is not willing to wait, it remains ready and immediately receives an E$TIME exception code.

When using the SEND$MESSAGE primitive, a task has the option of specifying that it wants acknowledgment from the receiving task. Thus, any task using the RECEIVE$MESSAGE primitive should check to see if an acknowledgment has been requested. For details, see the description of the RECEIVE$-MESSAGE primitive in Section 8.11.

As stated earlier, the object queue for a mailbox is processed in a first-in/first-out manner. However, the task queue of a mailbox can be either first-in/first-out or priority-based, with higher-priority tasks toward the front of the queue. When a task creates a mailbox, the task specifies which kind of task queue the mailbox is to have.

HIGH-PERFORMANCE OBJECT QUEUE

Directly associated with each mailbox is a high-performance object queue. A task, when creating a mailbox with the CREATE$MAILBOX primitive, can specify the number of objects this queue can hold, from 4 to 60. By using this high-performance object queue, the task can greatly improve the performance of SEND$MESSAGE and RECEIVE$-MESSAGE when these primitives actually get or place objects on the queue. (It has no effect when tasks are already waiting at the task queue). When more objects than the high-performance queue can hold are queued at a mailbox, the objects overflow into a slower queue whose size is limited only by the amount of memory in the job containing the mailbox.

The high-performance queue obtains its high speed because the OSP allocates memory space for it when the mailbox is created. This memory space is permanently allocated to the mailbox, even if no objects are queued there. No space is allocated for the overflow portion of the queue until the space is needed to contain objects. Thus the overflow portion of the queue is slower.

The user must weigh performance against size when deciding how large to make the high performance queue. Specifying a high performance queue that is too large wastes memory. Conversely, a smaller queue that is constantly overflowing slows down the system.

PRIMITIVES FOR MAILBOXES

The following primitives manipulate mailboxes:

- CREATE$MAILBOX—creates a mailbox and returns a token for it.

- DELETE$MAILBOX—deletes a mailbox from the system.

- SEND$MESSAGE—sends an object to a mailbox.

- RECEIVE$MESSAGE—sends the calling task to a mailbox for an object; the task has the option of waiting if no objects are present.

Regions

A region is an OSP object that tasks can use to guard a specific collection of shared data such as a table of data. Each task desiring access to shared data can wait its turn at the region associated with that data. When the task currently using the shared data no longer needs access, it notifies the Operating System Processor, which then allows the next task to access the shared data.

The following facts regarding regions are noteworthy:

The priority of the task that currently has access to the shared data may temporarily be raised. This happens automatically whenever the region has a priority queue and the task at the head of the region's queue has a priority higher than that of the task that has access. Under such circumstances, the priority of the task having access is raised to match that of the task at the head of the queue. When the task having access surrenders access, its priority automatically reverts to its original value.

Once a task gains access to shared data through a region, the task cannot be suspended or deleted until it surrenders access. This characteristic prevents tasks from tying up shared data.

When a task gains access through a region, it must not attempt to suspend or delete itself. Any attempt to do so will lock up the region, preventing other tasks from accessing the data guarded by the region. In addition, the task will never run again and its memory will not be returned to the memory pool. Also, if the task in the region attempts to delete itself, all other tasks that later attempt to delete themselves will be unable to do so.

When a region is created, one of two rules must be specified to determine which waiting task next gains access to the shared data. One rule is first-in/first-out (FIFO), and the other is priority.

REGIONS AND DEADLOCK

A major concern in any multitasking system is avoiding deadlock. Deadlock occurs when one or more tasks permanently lock each other out of required resources. The following hypothetical situation illustrates a method for quickly causing deadlock by using nested regions. An explanation of how to avoid the illustrated deadlock situation follows the example.

NOTE: In the following example, the only primitive used to gain access is the RECEIVE$CONTROL primitive. Tasks using the ACCEPT$CONTROL primitive cannot deadlock at a region unless they keep trying endlessly to accept control.

Suppose that two tasks, A (high priority) and B (low priority), both need access to two collections of shared data. Call the two collections of data Set 1 and Set 2. Access to each set is governed by a region (Region 1 and Region 2).

Now suppose that the following events take place in the order listed:

1) Task B requests access to Set 1 via Region 1. Access is granted.

2) Before Task B can request access to Set 2, an interrupt occurs and Task A preempts Task B.

3) Task A requests access to Set 2 via Region 2. Access is granted.

4) Task A requests access to Set 1 via Region 1. Task A must wait because Task B already has access.

5) Task B resumes running and requests access to Set 2 via Region 2. Task B must wait because Task A already has access.

At this point Task A is waiting for Task B and vice versa. Tasks A and B are hopelessly deadlocked, and any other tasks that request access to either set of data will also become deadlocked.

This type of deadlock situation applies only to systems in which regions are nested. For systems which must use nested regions, team deadlock can be prevented by adhering to the following rule:

A strict ordering must be applied to all the regions in a system, and tasks must be written so that they gain access to these regions according to the specified order. The precise order is unimportant as long as all tasks obey it. If this rule is followed consistently, regions can be nested to any depth.

PRIMITIVES FOR REGIONS

The following primitives manipulate regions:

*   ACCEPT$CONTROL
    This primitive allows a task to gain access to shared data only when access is immediately available. If a different task already has access, the requesting task remains ready but receives an exception code.

- CREATE$REGION
  This primitive creates a region and returns a token for it. One of the parameters passed during this call specifies the queuing rule (FIFO or priority.)

- DELETE$REGION
  This primitive deletes a region.

- RECEIVE$CONTROL
  This primitive causes a task to wait at the region until the task gains access to the shared data.

- SEND$CONTROL
  This primitive, when issued by a task, frees the OSP to grant a different task access to the shared data.

8.7 DYNAMIC MEMORY ALLOCATION

Occasionally a task needs more memory than was initially allocated to its job. By using OSP primitives for allocating and deallocating memory, tasks can usually satisfy their memory needs.

Segments

Allocated memory is treated as a collection of segments. A segment is a contiguous collection of 16-byte paragraphs, with its starting address evenly divisible by 16. In addition to serving as an address, the base address functions as a token for the segment. For each segment, the OSP maintains, as attributes, the base address, the length in bytes, and the containing job.

When a task needs a segment, it can request one of the desired length by calling the CREATE$SEGMENT primitive. If enough memory is available, the OSP returns a token for the segment.

NOTE: The token of a segment can be used as the base portion of a pointer to the segment. Thus, the token can be used as a base address (as when writing a message in the segment) or as an object reference (as when sending the segment-with-message to a mailbox). The PL/M-86 SELECTOR data type is especially useful when used to refer to the segment.

Memory Pools

A memory pool is the memory available to a job and its descendants. Each job has a memory pool. When a job is created, the memory for its pool is allocated from the pool of its parent job. Thus, there is effectively a tree-structured hierarchy of memory pools, identical in structure to the hierarchy of jobs. Memory that a job borrows from its parent remains in the pool of the parent as well as being in the pool of the child. Such memory, however, is available for use only by tasks in the child job, and not by tasks in the parent job. Figure 8-5 illustrates the relationship between the job and memory hierarchies. In the figure, the pool sizes shown are actually the maximum sizes of those pools.

Two parameters, pool$min and pool$max, of the CREATE$JOB primitive, dictate the range of sizes (in 16-byte paragraphs) of a new job's memory pool. Initially, the pool size is equal to pool$min, the pool minimum. Memory allocated to tasks in the job is still considered to be in the job's pool.

Movement of Memory Between Jobs

When a task tries to create a segment (or an object of any other type), and the unallocated part of its job's pool is not sufficient to satisfy the request, the OSP tries to borrow more memory from the job's parent (and then, if necessary, from its parent's parent, and so on). Such borrowing increases the pool size of the borrowing job and is thus restricted by the pool maximum attribute of the borrowing job. The smallest contiguous piece of memory that a job may borrow from its parent is a configuration parameter.

Observe that, if a job has equal pool minimum and pool maximum attributes, then its pool is fixed at that common value. This means that the job may not borrow memory from its parent.

Memory Allocation

The memory pool of a job consists of two classes of memory: allocated and unallocated. Memory in a job is unallocated unless it has been requested, either explicitly or implicitly, by tasks in the job or if it is on loan to a child job. A task's request for memory is explicit when it calls the CREATE$SEGMENT primitive. A request is implicit when the task attempts to create any type of object other than a segment.

The OSP borrows small amounts of memory from a job's pool each time a task in that job creates an object. This memory is needed for bookkeeping purposes. When the object is deleted, the borrowed memory is returned to the pool.

When a task no longer needs a segment, it can return the segment to the unallocated part of the job's pool by using the DELETE$SEGMENT primitive. Figure 8-6 shows how memory "moves."

210911

Deadlocks

Under certain circumstances, memory allocation and the use of some primitives can cause deadlock. For a description of the deadlock concept and preventive measures, as well as techniques for eliminating deadlocks, see the iOSP Support Package Reference Manual.

Primitives for Segments

The OSP provides the following primitives for manipulating segments:

- CREATE$SEGMENT—creates a segment and returns a token for it.

- DELETE$SEGMENT—returns a segment to the pool from which it was allocated.

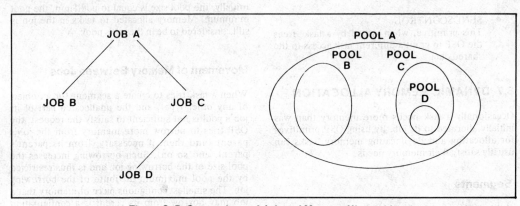

Figure 8-5 Comparison of Job and Memory Hierarchies

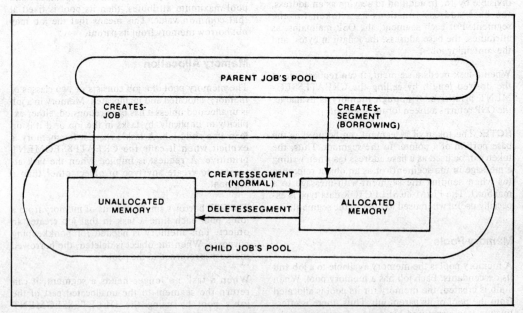

Figure 8-6 Memory Allocation and Deallocation

8.8 MANAGEMENT OF OBJECTS

Three OSP primitives apply to all objects. These primitives allow tasks to inquire about an object's type and to use object directories.

OBJECT TYPES

The GET$TYPE primitive enables a task to present a token to the OSP and get an object's type code in return. (Type codes for OSP objects are listed in Section 8.10, description of the GET$TYPE primitive.)

This primitive is useful, for example, when a task is expecting to receive objects of several different types. By invoking the GET$TYPE primitive, the task can ascertain the type of object it received.

USING OBJECT DIRECTORIES

Each job has its own object directory. An entry in an object directory consists of a token for an object and the object name. The name contains from one to twelve characters, where a character is a one-byte value (from 0 to 0FFH). Such a feature is often needed because some tasks might only know some objects by their associated names.

By using the LOOKUP$OBJECT primitive, a task can present the name of an object to the OSP. The OSP consults the object directory corresponding to the specified job and, if the object has been cataloged there, returns the token.

NOTE: In object directories, upper and lower case alphabetic characters are treated as being different. The OSP sees the name as just a string of bytes. It does not interpret these bytes as ASCII characters.

If the object has not yet been cataloged, and the task is not willing to wait, the task remains ready and receives an E$TIME exceptional condition. However, if the task is willing to wait, it is put to sleep; then there are two possibilities:

If the designated waiting period elapses before the task gets its requested token, the task is made ready and receives an E$TIME exceptional condition.

If the task gets its requested token within the designated waiting period, it is made ready with no exceptional condition. This case is possible because another task can, while the requesting task is waiting, catalog the appropriate entry in the specified object directory.

When a task wants to share an object with the other tasks in a job (not necessarily its own job), its can use the CATALOG$OBJECT primitive to put the object in that job's object directory. Typically, the task that created the object does this.

When using an object directory, a task must present a token for the job directory. The root job's object directory, called the root object directory, is special in that its token is easily accessible. Any task can call the GET$TASK$TOKENS primitive to obtain a token for the root job.

PRIMITIVES FOR ANY OBJECTS

The following primitives apply to all objects:

- CATALOG$OBJECT — places a name and an associated token in an object directory.

- LOOKUP$OBJECT — accepts a name and returns a token if the OSP can find an entry with the name in the specified time.

- GET$TYPE — accepts a token for an object and returns the object's type code.

Management of Exceptions

The OSP allows operating systems to specify an error handling procedure for each task. This procedure is called an exception handler.

EXCEPTION HANDLING

The OSP does provides protection from some types of errors. The concepts involved in the OSP exception handling scheme are condition codes, exception handlers, and exception modes:

- **Condition Codes**

  Whenever a task invokes a primitive, the OSP attempts to perform the requested function. Whether or not the attempt is successful, the OSP generates a *condition code*. This code indicates two things. First, it shows whether the primitive succeeded or failed. Second, in the case of failure, the code, which is then called an *exception code* shows which exception prevented successful completion.

  For the sake of flexibility in processing exception codes, they are divided into two categories. The first category, environmental

210911

exception codes, consists of errors that a task cannot anticipate. An example of such an error is insufficient memory. The second category, programming exception codes, consists of two subcategories:

— Errors Detected by the Processor
The 8086 or 8088 microprocessor detects several kinds of errors. One of these, for instance, is an attempted division by zero. Such errors can be avoided by using good programming techniques.

— Incorrect Invocation of a Primitive
If a task makes an impossible request, such as trying to SLEEP forever, the problem is considered a programming error. This kind of error can usually be avoided by good programming techniques.

Table 8-1 lists the condition codes, with their associated mnemonics and numeric values. Values not listed are reserved.

• **Exception Handlers**
An exception handler is a procedure that the OSP can invoke when a task receives an exception code. The alternative to using exception handlers is to explicitly incorporate in each task any code needed to process exception codes.

• **Exception Modes**
An *exception mode* is an attribute of a task. Once a task is running, it can invoke the SET$EXCEPTION$HANDLER primitive to set its exception mode to any of four values. This value governs the processing of exception codes received by the task. The exception mode indicates one of the following:

— No exception handling. This means that the code segment of the task must explicitly provide code to process any exceptions.

— The task's exception handler processes only environmental exception codes. This means that the code segment of the task must explicitly provide code to process any exceptions caused by programming errors.

— The task's exception handler processes only programming error exception

codes. This means that the code segment of the task must explicitly provide code to process any exceptions caused by environmental conditions.

— The task's exception handler processes both environmental exception codes and programming error exception codes.

When control passes to an exception handler, the errant task is still the running task.

NOTE: The E$INTERRUPT$SATURATION and the E$INTERRUPT$OVERFLOW condition codes never cause control to be passed to an exception handler. These exceptional conditions must be handled in-line or not at all.

In summary, exception handling works as follows. The OSP generates a condition code for each invocation of each primitive. If the code indicates successful completion, the OSP detected no problems. If the code indicates an error, the problem can be processed in either of two ways:

• Within the code segment of the task that invoked the primitive.

• By the task's exception handler, which is invoked by the OSP.

The decision as to which way the error is to be dealt with is a function of the task's exception mode and the category of the exception code (programming error or environmental condition).

The actions of a task's error handler can be controlled because the programmer writes the handler. Consequently, the handler can recover from the error, merely log the error, delete the task containing the error, warn the operator of the error, or ignore the error altogether.

ADVANTAGE OF EXCEPTION HANDLING

Exception handling provides an operating system with several methods of reacting to unusual conditions. One of these methods, having the OSP automatically invoke a task's exception handler, greatly simplifies error processing. The other method, dealing with some or all unusual conditions within a task's code segment, allows the user to provide special processing for very unusual circumstances. The OSP allows an operating system to use both methods.

Table 8-1 Conditions and Their Codes

CATEGORY MNEMONIC	MEANING	NUMERIC CODE	
		HEX	DECIMAL
E$OK	The most recent primitive ran successfully.	0H	0
Environmental Exceptions			
E$TIME	A time limit (possibly a limit of zero time) expired without a task's request being satisfied.	1H	1
E$MEM	There is not sufficient memory available to satisfy a task's request.	2H	2
E$BUSY	Another task currently has access to data protected by the specified region.	3H	3
E$LIMIT	A task attempted on operation which, if it had been successful, would have violated an iOSP processor-enforced limit.	4H	4
E$CONTEXT	A primitive was issued out of context or the iOSP processor was asked to perform an impossible operation	5H	5
E$EXIST	A token parameter has a value which is not a token for an existing object.	6H	6
E$STATE	A task attempted an operation which would have caused an impossible transition of a task's state.	7H	7
ENOTCONFIGURED	The most recently called primitive is not in the preset configuraton.	8H	8
E$INTERRUPT$SATURATION	An interrupt task has accumulated the maximum allowable number of SIGNAL$INTERRUPT requests.	9H	9
E$INTERRUPT$OVERFLOW	An interrupt task has accumulated more than the maximum allowable number of SIGNAL$INTERRUPT requests.	0AH	10
Programmer Errors			
E$ZERO$DIVIDE	A task attempted to divide by zero.	8000H	32768

Table 8-1 Conditions and Their Codes (continued)

CATEGORY MNEMONIC	MEANING	NUMERIC CODE	
		HEX	DECIMAL
E$OVERFLOW	An overflow interrupt occurred.	8001H	32769
E$TYPE	A token parameter referred to an existing object that is not of the required type.	8002H	32770
E$BOUNDS	An offset parameter is out of a segment's boundaries.	8003H	32771
E$PARAM	A parameter which is neither a token nor an offset has invalid value.	8004H	32772
EBADCALL	When you configured your operating system, you used an OSP diskette that was designed for a different version of the 80130 component.	8005H	32773
E$ARRAY$BOUNDS	Hardware or Language has detected an array overflow.	8006H	32774
ENDPERROR	An 8087 (Numeric Processor Extension) error has been detected; the 8087 status information is contained in a parameter to the exception handler.	8007H	32775

CREATING EXCEPTION HANDLERS

For a complete description of exception handler creation and assignment, as well as in-line exception handling and primitives for exception handlers see the iOSP Support Package Reference Manual.

Management of Interrupts

The OSP manages interrupts. When an interrupt occurs, the iOSP processor can schedule a task to process the interrupt. This method of event detection improves the system performance.

INTERRUPT PROCESSING

There are two ways that computer systems can schedule processing associated with detecting and controlling events in the real world—polling and interrupt processing. Polling is implemented by having the software periodically check to see if certain events have occurred. Its major shortcoming is that

a significant amount of the processor's time is spent in such checking, and, if events have not occurred, the processor's time has been wasted.

The second method of controlling processing is interrupt processing. In this method, when an event occurs the processor is literally interrupted. Rather than executing the next sequential instruction, the processor executes an interrupt handler, which may then invoke a task associated specifically with the detected event.

ADVANTAGES OF INTERRUPT PROCESSING

Interrupt processing of external events provides three benefits for an operating system:

- Better Performance
  Interrupt processing allows the system to spend all of its time running the tasks that process events, rather than executing a polling loop to see if events have occurred.

- **More Flexibility**
  Because of the direct correlation between interrupts and tasks, the system can easily be modified to process different events. The user simply writes the tasks to process the new (or old) types of interrupts.

- **Economic Benefits**
  Because interrupt processing allows the system to respond to events by means of modularly coded tasks, a system's code is more structured and easier to understand. Modular code is less costly to develop and maintain, and it can be developed more quickly than unstructured code.

INTERRUPT MANAGEMENT IN THE OSP

An interrupt, signalling the occurrence of an external event, triggers an implicit "call" to a location specified in a section of memory known as the Interrupt Vector Table. From there, control is redirected to an interrupt procedure called an interrupt handler. At this point, one of two things happens. If handling the interrupt takes little time and requires no primitives, other than certain interrupt-related primitives, the interrupt handler processes the interrupt. Otherwise, the interrupt handler signals an interrupt task which deals with the interrupt. After the interrupt has been serviced, control returns to the ready application task with highest priority.

OSP INTERRUPT MECHANISMS

Three major concepts in OSP interrupt processing are the Interrupt Vector Table, interrupt lines, and the ability to enable and disable interrupts.

THE INTERRUPT VECTOR TABLE

The Interrupt Vector Table is composed of 256 entries. The entries are numbered 0 to 255, and the purpose of each entry is to contain the address of the first instruction to be executed when the corresponding interrupt occurs.

Some of the entries in the Interrupt Vector Table are reserved and therefore are not available to be defined by user tasks. The entries are allocated as follows:

0	divide by zero
1	single step (used by the iSBC 957B package)
2	non-maskable interrupt (used by the iSBC 957B package)
3	one byte interrupt instruction (used by the iSBC 957B package)
4	interrupt on overflow (used by the hardware)
5	runtime array bounds error (used by compilers and assembler)

6-55	reserved for Intel
56-63	external interrupts (PIC master lines)
64-127	external interrupts (PIC slave lines)
128-183	unused (available to users for software interrupts)
184-223	reserved for Intel
224-255	unused (available to users for operating system extensions)

The interrupt lines, programmable interrupt controller and other hardware related topics are discussed in Chapter 5, Volume 2 of this set.

INTERRUPT LINES

In the discussion that follows, the word "line" refers directly to a pin on a component. This is synonomous with the word "level".

External interrupts are funneled through one or more hardware programmable interrupt controllers (PICs). The master controller is part of the 80130 component, but additional PICs (such as the Intel 8259A PIC) can be used to obtain additional interrupt lines.

The on-chip PIC that is part of the OSP can manage interrupts from as many as eight external sources. However, the OSP also supports an expended (or cascaded) environment in which up to seven input lines of the on-chip PIC (the master interrupt controller) are each connected to a 8259A PIC (called a slave interrupt controller). One input line from the master PIC cannot be attached to a slave because it must be connected directly to the system clock.

Since each of the slaves can manage eight interrupts, and as many as seven slaves can be attached to the master PIC, the OSP can support as many as 56 interrupt lines from external sources. These 56 lines are in addition to the one master line required for the system clock.

The interrupt lines of the master PIC and the interrupt lines of the slave 8259A PICs are each assigned entries to the Interrupt Vector Table, as shown in Figure 8-7. The master interrupt lines, numbered M0 through M7, correspond to entries 56 through 63 (decimal) in the Interrupt Vector Table. The slave interrupt lines, numbered x0 to x7 (where x ranges from 0 to 7 and identifies the master line to which the slave PIC is attached) correspond to entries 64 through 127 (decimal) of the Interrupt Vector Table. Table 8-2 shows the numbered interrupt lines and their corresponding entries in the Interrupt Vector Table.

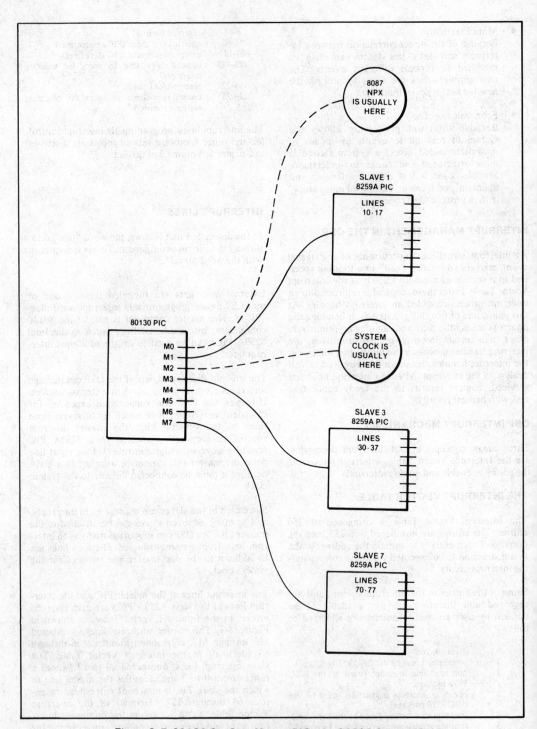

Figure 8-7 80130 On-Chip Master PIC with 8259A Slave PICs

**Table 8-2 Interrupt Line Numbers
and Interrupt Vector Numbers**

Line Numbers	Vector Table Entry
M0-M7	53-63
00-07	64-71
10-17	72-79
20-27	80-87
30-37	88-95
40-47	96-103
50-57	104-111
60-67	112-119
70-77	120-127

DISABLING AND ENABLING INTERRUPT LINES

Occasionally the user may want to prevent signals from causing an immediate interrupt. For example, it is desirable to prevent low priority interrupts from interfering with the servicing of a high priority interrupt. The OSP provides mechanisms for disabling and enabling interrupts.

If a signal is received on a line that is enabled, the 8086 and 8088 microprocessor transfers control to the address contained in the Interrupt Vector Table entry that corresponds to the line on which the interrupt occurred.

On the other hand, if a signal is received on a line that is disabled, the processor will continue running, uninterrupted, until the interrupt line is again enabled. Once re-enabled, the interrupt will occur if the interrupt signal is still active. For more information on interrupt enabling and disabling, see the iOSP 86 Support Package Reference Manual.

INTERRUPT HANDLERS AND INTERRUPT TASKS

Whether an interrupt handler services an interrupt line by itself or invokes an interrupt task to service the interrupt depends on two factors:

- the kinds of primitives needed

- the amount of time required

Regarding the first factor, interrupt handlers can invoke only the ENTER$INTERRUPT, EXIT$INTERRUPT, GET$LEVEL, DISABLE and SIGNAL$INTERRUPT primitives. If it is necessary to use other primitives to service the interrupt, an interrupt task can be used in conjunction with the interrupt handler.

Regarding the second factor, an interrupt handler should always invoke an interrupt task unless the handler can service interrupts quickly. This is because an interrupt signal disables all interrupts, and they remain disabled until the interrupt handler either services the interrupt or invokes an interrupt task. Invoking an interrupt task allows higher priority interrupts (and in some cases, the same priority interrupts) to be accepted.

For more information about interrupt handlers and interrupt tasks, consult the iOSP 86 Support Package Reference Manual.

PRIMITIVES FOR INTERRUPTS

The following primitives manipulate interrupts:

- SET$INTERRUPT—Assigns an interrupt handler and, if desired, an interrupt task to an interrupt line.

- RESET$$INTERRUPT—Cancels the assignment made to a line by SET$INTERRUPT and, if applicable, deletes the interrupt task for that line.

- EXIT$INTERRUPT—Used by interrupt handlers to send an end-of-interrupt signal to hardware.

- SIGNAL$INTERRUPT—Used by interrupt handlers to invoke interrupt tasks.

- WAIT$INTERRUPT—Suspends the calling interrupt task until it is called into service by an interrupt handler.

- ENABLE—Enables an external interrupt line.

- DISABLE—Disables an external interrupt line.

- GET$LEVEL—Returns the highest priority interrupt line for which an interrupt handler has started but has not yet finished processing.

- ENTER$INTERRUPT—Sets up a previously designated data segment base address for the calling interrupt handler.

210911

8.9 EXTENDABILITY

The services provided by the OSP are extendable. The user can create his own primitives and add them to the operating system without having to modify any OSP codes. From the standpoint of an application programmer, these customized primitives are just as much a part of the operating system as are the primitives provided by the OSP.

NOTE: Another way of extending the OSP is to add features and/or subsystems of the iRMX 86 Operating System. This is the subject of Section 8.11 of this chapter.

Three Ways of Adding Functionality

Whenever more than one job in an application system requires a function not supplied by the OSP, the following three methods of adding the needed function may be used:

1) The function can be written as a procedure and placed it in a library by using LIB86. After each job that requires the function has been compiled, LINK86 can be used to link the library to the object module for the job.

2) The function can be written as a task, and application tasks can invoke the function through a mailbox-segment interface.

3) The function can be written as a procedure and added to the operating system. Application programs then invoke the function by means of a primitive.

The relative advantages and disadvantages of the three alternatives are summarized in Table 8-3.

Alternative 3 involves extending the operating system. The procedures that must be added in order to support the added function are called an Operating System Extension or OS extension. From the application programmer's standpoint, an OS extension appears to be a collection of one or more customized primitives, no different in style than, say, the primitives for manipulating mailboxes.

Creating an Operating System Extension

Creating an OS extension involves both writing several procedures and initializing the Interrupt Vector Table of the iAPX 86/186 microprocessor. For detailed treatment of procedures used in operating system extensions see the iOSP 86 Support Package Reference Manual.

Primitives Used in Extending the Operating System

The following primitives are used exclusively by OS extensions:

- **DISABLE$DELETION**
  This primitive increases the deletion disabling depth of an object by one.

- **ENABLE$DELETION**
  This primitive removes one level of deletion disabling from an object, reversing the effect of one DISABLE$DELETION call.

- **SET$EXTENSION**
  This primitive can be used either to place an address in a specific entry of the Interrupt Vector Table or to remove such an entry.

- **SIGNAL$EXCEPTION**
  This primitive advises a task that an exception has occurred in an OS extension that the task has called.

The use of these primitives is covered in detail in the following section 8.10.

Table 8-3 Comparison of Techniques for Creating Command Functions

	PROCEDURE LIBRARY	TASK	OS EXTENSION
APPLICATION PROGRAMMER'S INTERFACE	SIMPLE	COMPLEX	SIMPLE
RELATIVE PERFORMANCE	GOOD (for all functions)	POOR (for quick functions) MODERATE (for slower functions)	MODERATE (for quick functions) GOOD (for slower functions)
SYNCHRONOUS or ASYNCHRONOUS CALLS	BOTH	ASYNCHRONOUS ONLY	BOTH
SYSTEM PROGRAMMER	NOT REQUIRED	NOT REQUIRED	REQUIRED
DUPLICATE CODE	Difficult to avoid	Easy to avoid	Automatically avoided
POTENTIAL FOR COSTLY MAINTENANCE	YES	NO	NO
SUPPORTS NEW OBJECT TYPES	NO	NO	YES

8.10 OSP PRIMITIVES

This section contains the calling sequences and other information about the OSP primitives. The descriptions of the primitives are in alphabetical order. Information for each primitive is organized into the following categories:

- A brief sketch of the effects of the primitive.

- The PL/M-86 calling sequence for the primitive.

- Definitions of the output parameters, if any.

- A detailed description of the effects of the primitive.

- An example of how the primitive can be used.

- The condition codes that can result from using the primitive, with a description of the possible causes of each exception.

The examples used in this section assume that the reader is familiar with PL/M-86. In these examples, the appropriate DECLARE statements are made first. Before the first of these DECLARE statements is an INCLUDE statement that declares all of the primitive calls included in the OSF firmware. For the sake of simplicity, the examples assume that an established exception handler is to deal with exceptional conditions. Consequently, they do not illustrate in-line exception processing.

Additional condition codes can be returned if the OSF firmware is extended to include parameter validation (see Section 8.9).

Following the individual descriptions of the primitives is a command dictionary, in which the calls are grouped according to type. The dictionary includes a short description and the page number of the primitive's complete description in this section.

210911

ACCEPT$CONTROL

The ACCEPT$CONTROL primitive requests immediate access to data protected by a region.

```
CALL RQ$ACCEPT$CONTROL (region, except$ptr);
```

INPUT PARAMETER

region   A WORD containing a TOKEN for the target region.

OUTPUT PARAMETER

except$ptr   A POINTER to a WORD to which the OSP will return the condition code generated by this primitive.

DESCRIPTION

The ACCEPT$CONTROL primitive provides access to data protected by a region if access is immediately available. If access is not immediately available, the primitive generates the E$BUSY condition code and the calling task remains ready.

EXAMPLE

```
/* *************************************************************************
 *     This example illustrates how the ACCEPT$CONTROL primitive can be used to access data protected   *
 *     by a region.                                                                                      *
 ************************************************************************* */
```

```
$INCLUDE(:F1:OSXPRM.EXT);              /* declares all primitive calls */

DECLARE TOKEN                          LITERALLY 'SELECTOR';
                                       /* if your PL/M compiler does not support this variable
                                       type, declare TOKEN a WORD */
DECLARE region$token                   TOKEN;
DECLARE priority$queue                 literally '1'; /* tasks wait in priority order */
DECLARE status                         WORD;

SAMPLE_PROCEDURE:
    PROCEDURE;
         •
         •  }  Typical PL/M-86 Statements
         •
```

```
/* *************************************************************************
 *     In order to access the data within a region, a task must know the TOKEN for that region. In this example,   *
 *     the needed TOKEN is known because the calling task creates the region.                                       *
 ************************************************************************* */
```

```
region$token = RQ$CREATE$REGION        (priority$queue,
                                       @status);
         •
         •  }  Typical PL/M-86 Statements
         •
```

/•••
*   At some point in the task, access is needed to the data protected by the region. The calling task then in-
*   vokes the ACCEPT$CONTROL primitive and obtains access to the data if access is immediately
*   available.
•••/

```
CALL RQ$ACCEPT$CONTROL          (region$token,
                                 @status);

    :
    :}       Typical PL/M-86 Statements
```

/•••
*   When the task is ready to relinquish access to the data protected by the region, it invokes the SEND$-
*   CONTROL primitive.
•••/

```
CALL RQ$SEND$CONTROL            (@status);

    :
    :}       Typical PL/M-86 Statements
```

END SAMPLE_PROCEDURE;

CONDITION CODES

E$OK	No exceptional conditions.
E$BUSY	Another task currently has access to the data.
E$EXIST	The region parameter does not refer to an existing object.
E$TYPE	The region parameter is a TOKEN for an object that is not a region.

210911

CATALOG$OBJECT

The CATALOG$OBJECT primitive places an entry for an object in an object directory.

CALL RQ$CATALOG$OBJECT (job, object, name, except$ptr);

INPUT PARAMETERS

job
: A WORD that indicates where the object is to be cataloged.

- If zero, the WORD indicates that the object is to be cataloged in the object directory of the job to which the calling task belongs.

- If not zero, the WORD contains the TOKEN for the job in whose object directory the object is to be cataloged.

object
: A WORD containing a TOKEN for the object to be cataloged.

name
: A POINTER to a STRING containing the name under which the object is to be cataloged. The name itself must not exceed 12 characters in length. Each character can be a byte consisting of any value from 0 to 0FFH.

OUTPUT PARAMETER

except$ptr
: A POINTER to a WORD to which the OSP will return the condition code generated by this primitive.

DESCRIPTION

The CATALOG$OBJECT primitive places an entry for an object in the object directory of a specific job. The entry consists of both a name and a TOKEN for the object. There may be several such entries for a single object in a directory, because the object may have several names. (However, in a given object directory, only one object may be cataloged under a given name.) If another task is waiting, via the LOOKUP$OBJECT primitive, for the object to be cataloged, that task is awakened when the entry is cataloged.

EXAMPLE

```
/***********************************************************************
*                                                                     *
*     This example illustrates how the CATALOG$OBJECT primitive can be used to place an entry in an     *
*     object directory.                                                *
*                                                                     *
***********************************************************************/

        $INCLUDE(:F1:OSXPRM.EXT);              /* Declares all primitive calls */

        DECLARE TOKEN                          LITERALLY 'SELECTOR';
                                               /* if your PL/M compiler does not support this variable
                                               type, declare TOKEN a WORD */

        DECLARE mbx$token                      TOKEN;
        DECLARE mbx$flags                      WORD;
        DECLARE job                            TOKEN;
        DECLARE status                         WORD;
```

SAMPLE_PROCEDURE:
    PROCEDURE;

        mbx$flags = 0;   /* designates four objects to be queued on the high performance object queue; designates a first-in/first-out task queue. */

        job = 0;   /* indicates objects to be cataloged into the object directory of the calling task's job */

        •
        • } Typical PL/M-86 Statements
        •

/* **
*   The calling task creates an object, in this example a mailbox, before cataloging the object's TOKEN.   *
** */

        mbx$token = RQ$CREATE$MAILBOX   (mbx$flags,
                                                       @status);

        •
        • } Typical PL/M-86 Statements
        •

/* **
*   After creating the mailbox, the calling task catalogs the mailbox TOKEN in the object directory of its   *
*   own job.   *
** */

        CALL RQ$CATALOG$OBJECT   (job,
                                                  mbx$token,
                                                  @(3, 'MBX'),
                                                  @status);

        •
        • } Typical PL/M-86 Statements
        •

END SAMPLE_PROCEDURE;

CONDITION CODES

    E$OK   No exceptional conditions.

    E$CONTEXT   At least one of the following is true:

            • The name being cataloged is already in the designated object directory.

            • The directory's maximum allowable size is 0.

    E$LIMIT   The designated object directory is full.

    E$PARAM   The first BYTE of the STRING pointed to by the name parameter contains a zero or a value greater than 12.

CREATE$JOB

The CREATE$JOB primitive creates a job containing a single task.

---

job = RQ$CREATE$JOB (directory$size, param$obj, pool$min, pool$max, max$objects, max$tasks,
    max$priority, except$handler, job$flags, task$priority, start$address, data$seg, stack$ptr,
    stack$size, task$flags, except$ptr);

INPUT PARAMETERS

directory$size	A WORD specifying the maximum allowable number of entries a job can have in its object directory. The value zero is permitted, for the case where no object directory is desired. The maximum value for this parameter is OFFOH.
param$obj	A WORD indicating the presence or absence of a parameter object. See Chapter 2 for an explanation of parameter objects.

- If zero, it indicates that the new job has no parameter object.

- If not zero, it contains a valid TOKEN for the new job's parameter object.

pool$min	A WORD which contains the minimum allowable size of the new job's pool, in 16-byte paragraphs. The pool$min parameter is also the initial size of the new job's pool. Pool$min should be at least 32 (decimal.) If the stack$ptr parameter has a base value of 0, pool$min should be at least 32 (decimal) plus the value of stack$size in 16-byte paragraphs.
pool$max	A WORD which contains the maximum allowable size of the new job's memory in 16-byte paragraphs.
max$objects	A WORD that specifies the maximum number of objects that the created job can own.

- If not OFFFFH, it contains the maximum number of objects, created by tasks in the new job, that can exist at one time.

- If OFFFFH, it indicates that there is no limit to the number of objects.

max$tasks	A WORD that specifies the maximum number of tasks that can exist simultaneously in the new job.

- If not OFFFFH, it contains the maximum number of tasks that can exist simultaneously in the new job.

- If OFFFFH, it indicates that there is no limit to the number of tasks that tasks in the new job can create.

max$priority	A BYTE that sets an upper limit on the priority of the tasks created in the new job.

- If not zero, it contains the maximum allowable priority of tasks in the new job.

- If zero, it indicates that the new job is to inherit the maximum priority attribute of its parent job.

except$handler	A POINTER to a structure of the following form:

```
STRUCTURE(
    EXCEPTION$HANDLER$PTR    POINTER,
    EXCEPTION$MODE           BYTE);
```

If exception$handler$ptr is not zero, then it is a POINTER to the first instruction of the new job's own exception handler. If exception$handler$ptr is zero, the new job's exception handler is the system default exception handler. In both cases, the exception handler for the new task becomes the default exception handler for the job. The exception$mode indicates when control is to be passed to the exception handler. It is encoded as follows:

Value	When Control Passes To Exception Handler
0	Never
1	On programmer errors only
2	On environmental conditions only
3	On all exceptional conditions

job$flags — A reserved WORD which should be set to 2 (decimal.)

task$priority — A BYTE that controls the priority of the new job's initial task.

- If not zero, it contains the priority of the new job's initial task.

- If zero, it indicates that the new job's initial task is to have a priority equal to the new job's maximum priority attribute.

start$address — A POINTER to the first instruction of the new job's initial task.

data$seg — A WORD that specifies which data segment the new job is to use.

- If not zero, it contains the base address of the data segment of the new job's initial task.

- If zero, it indicates that the new job's initial task assigns its own data segment. Refer to Chapter 5 for more information about data segment allocation.

stack$ptr — A POINTER that specifies the location of the stack for the new job's initial task.

- If the base portion is not zero, the pointer points to the base of the user-provided stack of the new job's initial task.

- If the base portion is zero, it indicates that the OSP Processor is to allocate a stack for the new job's initial task. The length of the allocated stack will be equal to the value of the stack$size parameter.

stack$size — A WORD containing the size, in bytes, of the stack of the new job's initial task. This size must be at least 16 (decimal) bytes. The OSP Processor increases specified values that are not multiples of 16 up to the next (higher) multiple of 16.

The stack size should be at least 300 (decimal) bytes if the new task is going to invoke primitives. See Chapter 4 for more information about stack space required by primitives.

task$flags — A WORD containing information that the OSP Processor needs in order to create and maintain the job's initial task. The bits (where bit 15 is the high order bit) have the following meanings:

Bit	Meaning
15-1	Reserved bits which should be set to zero.
0	If one, the initial task contains floating-point instructions. These instructions require the 8087 Numeric Processor Extension for execution.

If zero, the initial task does not contain floating-point instructions.

OUTPUT PARAMETERS

job   A WORD containing a TOKEN for the new job.

except$ptr   A POINTER to a WORD to to which the OSP will return the condition code generated
                       by the primitive.

DESCRIPTION

The CREATE$JOB primitive creates a job with an initial task and returns a TOKEN for the job. The new job's parent is
the calling task's job. The new job counts as one against the parent job's object limit. The new task counts as one
against the new job's object and task limits. The new job's resources come from the parent job, as described in Chapter 2. In particular, the max$task and max$objects values are deducted from the creating job's maximum task and
maximum objects attributes, respectively.

EXAMPLE

```
/**************************************************************************************
*                                                                                    *
*      This example illustrates how the CREATE$JOB primitive can be used.            *
*                                                                                    *
**************************************************************************************/

      $INCLUDE(:F1:OSXPRM.EXT);                    /* Declares all primitive calls */

      INITIAL_TASK: PROCEDURE EXTERNAL;
      END INITIAL_TASK;

      DECLARE TOKEN                                LITERALLY 'SELECTOR';
                                                   /* if your PL/M compiler does not support this variable
                                                   type, declare TOKEN a WORD */
      DECLARE job$token                            TOKEN;
      DECLARE directory$size                       WORD;
      DECLARE param$obj                            WORD;
      DECLARE pool$min                             WORD;
      DECLARE pool$max                             WORD;
      DECLARE max$objects                          WORD;
      DECLARE max$tasks                            WORD;
      DECLARE max$priority                         BYTE;
      DECLARE except$handler                       POINTER;
      DECLARE job$flags                            WORD;
      DECLARE task$priority                        BYTE;
      DECLARE start$address                        POINTER;
      DECLARE data$seg                             WORD;
      DECLARE stack$pointer                        POINTER;
      DECLARE stack$size                           WORD;
      DECLARE task$flags                           WORD;
      DECLARE status                               WORD;

SAMPLE_PROCEDURE:
      PROCEDURE;

      directory$size = 10;                         /* max 10 entries in object directory */
      param$obj = 0;                               /* new job has no parameter object */
      pool$min = 1FFH;                             /* min 1FFH/ max 0FFFFH 16-byte */
      pool$max = 0FFFFH;                           /*paragraphs in job pool */
      max$objects = 0FFFFH;                        /* no limit to number of objects */
      max$tasks = 0AH;                             /* 0AH tasks can exist simultaneously */
      max$priority = 0;                            /* inherit max priority of parent */
      except$handler = 0;                          /* use system default except handler */
      job$flags = 0;                               /* no flags set */
      task$priority = 0;                           /* set initial task to max priority */
      start$address = @INITIAL_TASK;

                                                   /* points to first instruction of initial task */
```

```
data$seg = 0;                              /* initial task sets up own data segment */
stack$pointer = 0;                         /* allocate a stack for initial task */
stack$size = 512;                          /* 512 bytes in stack of initial task */
task$flags = 0;                            /* no floating-point instructions */
```

 Typical PL/M-86 Statements

```
/* ••••••••••••••••••••••••••••••••••••••••••••••••••••••••••••••••••••••••••••••••••••••••••••••••••
*    The calling task creates a job with an initial task labeled INITIAL_TASK.                    *
••••••••••••••••••••••••••••••••••••••••••••••••••••••••••••••••••••••••••••••••••••••••••••••••••• */
```

```
job$token = RQ$CREATE$JOB                  (directory$size,
                                            param$obj,
                                            pool$min,
                                            pool$max,
                                            max$objects,
                                            max$tasks,
                                            max$priority,
                                            except$handler,
                                            job$flags,
                                            task$priority,
                                            start$address,
                                            data$seg,
                                            stack$pointer,
                                            stack$size,
                                            task$flags,
                                            @status);
```

 Typical PL/M-86 Statements

END SAMPLE_PROCEDURE;

CONDITION CODES

E$OK   No exceptional conditions.

E$LIMIT   At least one of the following is true:

              • max$objects is larger than the unused portion of the object allotment in the calling task's
                job.

              • max$tasks is larger than the unused portion of the task allotment in the calling task's job.

E$MEM   At least one of the following is true:

              • The memory available to the new job is not sufficient to create the job.

              • The memory available to the new job is not sufficient to satisfy the pool$min parameter.

              • The memory available to the new job is not sufficient to create the initial task as specified.

210911

CREATE$MAILBOX

The CREATE$MAILBOX primitive creates a mailbox.

---

    mailbox = RQ$CREATE$MAILBOX (mailbox$flags, except$ptr);

INPUT PARAMETER

mailbox$flags   A WORD containing information about the new mailbox. The bits (where bit 15 is the high-order bit) have the following meanings:

Bit	Meaning
15-5	Reserved bits, which should be set to zero.
4-1	A value that, when multiplied by four, specifies the number of objects that can be queued on the high-performance object queue. Additional objects are queued on the slower, overflow queue. Four is the minimum size for the high performance queue; that is, specifying zero or one in these bits results in a high performance queue that holds four objects.
0	A bit that determines the queuing scheme for the task queue of the new mailbox, as follows:

Value	Queueing Scheme
0	First-in/first-out
1	Priority based

OUTPUT PARAMETERS

mailbox   A WORD containing a TOKEN for the new mailbox.

except$ptr   A POINTER to a WORD to which the OSP will return the condition code generated by the primitive.

DESCRIPTION

The CREATE$MAILBOX primitive creates a mailbox and returns a TOKEN for it. The new mailbox counts as one against the object limit of the calling task's job.

EXAMPLE

```
/* ******************************************************************************
 *    This example illustrates how the CREATE$MAILBOX primitive can be used.    *
 * ****************************************************************************** /
```

$INCLUDE(:F1:OSXPRM.EXT);	/* Declares all primitive calls */
DECLARE TOKEN	LITERALLY 'SELECTOR'; /* if your PL/M compiler does not support this variable type, declare TOKEN a WORD */
DECLARE mbx$token	TOKEN;
DECLARE mbx$flags	WORD;
DECLARE status	WORD;

SAMPLE_PROCEDURE:
    PROCEDURE;

    mbx$flags = 0;   /* designates four objects to be queued on the high performance object queue; designates a first-in/first-out task queue. */

    :
    } Typical PL/M-86 Statements

/***
   The TOKEN mbx$token is returned when the calling task invokes the CREATE$MAILBOX primitive.
***/

    mbx$token = RQ$CREATE$MAILBOX   (mbx$flags,
                                        @status);

    :
    } Typical PL/M-86 Statements

END SAMPLE_PROCEDURE;

CONDITION CODES

E$OK	No exceptional conditions.
E$LIMIT	The requested mailbox would exceed the object limit of the calling task's job.
E$MEM	The memory available to the calling task's job is

CREATE$REGION

The CREATE$REGION primitive creates a region.

region = RQ$CREATE$REGION (region$flags, except$ptr);

INPUT PARAMETER

region$flags   A WORD that specifies the queueing protocol of the new region. If the low order bit equals zero, tasks await access in FIFO order. If the low order bit equals one, tasks await access in priority order. The other bits in the WORD are reserved and should be set to zero.

OUTPUT PARAMETERS

region   A WORD to which the OSP will return a TOKEN for the new region.

except$ptr   A POINTER to a WORD to which the OSP will return the condition code generated by the primitive.

DESCRIPTION

The CREATE$REGION primitive creates a region and returns a TOKEN for the region.

EXAMPLE

```
/*****************************************************************************
*      This example illustrates how the CREATE$REGION primitive can be used.        *
******************************************************************************/

        $INCLUDE(:F1:OSXPRM.EXT);              /* Declares all primitive calls */

        DECLARE TOKEN                          LITERALLY 'SELECTOR';
                                               /* if your PL/M compiler does not support this variable
                                               type, declare TOKEN a WORD */
        DECLARE region$token                   TOKEN;
        DECLARE priority$queue                 LITERALLY '1'; /* tasks wait in priority order */
        DECLARE status                         WORD;

SAMPLE_PROCEDURE:
        PROCEDURE;

            •
            •  }  Typical PL/M-86 Statements
            •

/*****************************************************************************
*      The TOKEN region$token is return when the calling task invokes the CREATE$REGION primitive.    *
******************************************************************************/

        region$token = RQ$CREATE$REGION        (priority$queue,
                                               @status);
```

210911

Typical PL/M-86 Statements

END SAMPLE_PROCEDURE;

CONDITION CODES

E$OK	No exceptional conditions.
E$LIMIT	The calling task's job has reached its object limit.
E$MEM	The memory pool of the calling task's job does not contain a sufficiently large block to satisfy the request.

CREATE$SEGMENT

CREATE$SEGMENT

The CREATE$SEGMENT primitive creates a segment.

```
segment = RQ$CREATE$SEGMENT (size, except$ptr);
```

INPUT PARAMETER

size   A WORD that specifies the size of the new segment.

- If not zero, the WORD contains the size, in bytes, of the requested segment. If the size parameter is not a multiple of 16, it will be rounded up to the nearest higher multiple of 16 before the OSP Processor creates the segment.

- If zero, the WORD indicates that the size of the request is 65536 (64K) bytes.

OUTPUT PARAMETERS

segment   A WORD to which the OSP will return a TOKEN for the new segment.

except$ptr   A POINTER to a WORD to which the OSP will return the condition code generated by the primitive.

DESCRIPTION

The CREATE$SEGMENT primitive creates a segment and returns the TOKEN for it. The memory for the segment is taken from the free portion of the memory pool of the calling task's job, unless borrowing from the parent job is both necessary and possible. The new segment counts as one against the object limit of the calling task's job.

To gain access to the segment, you should base an array or structure on a pointer by setting the base portion equal to the segment TOKEN and the offset portion equal to zero. Or, if you have a PL/M-86 compiler that supports the SELECTOR data type, you can accomplish the same thing by setting a variable of type SELECTOR equal to the TOKEN value.

EXAMPLE

```
/*******************************************************************************
*     This example illustrates how the CREATE$SEGMENT primitive can be used.     *
*******************************************************************************/

    $INCLUDE(:F1:OSXPRM.EXT);                /* Declares all primitive calls */

    DECLARE TOKEN                            LITERALLY 'SELECTOR';
                                             /* if your PL/M compiler does not support this variable
                                             type, declare TOKEN a WORD */
    DECLARE seg$token                        TOKEN;
    DECLARE size                             WORD;
    DECLARE status                           WORD;

SAMPLE_PROCEDURE:
    PROCEDURE;

    size = 64;                               /* designates new segment to contain 64 bytes */

    •
    •    Typical PL/M-86 Statements
    •
```

210911

```
/**********************************************************************************
 *    The TOKEN seg$token is returned when the calling task invokes the CREATE$SEGMENT primitive.    *
 **********************************************************************************/

        set$token = RQ$CREATE$SEGMENT              (size,
                                                    @ status);

        •
        •   }   Typical PL/M-86 Statements
        •
```

END SAMPLE_PROCEDURE;

CONDITION CODES

E$OK	No exceptional conditions.
E$LIMIT	The requested segment would exceed the object limit of the calling task's job.
E$MEM	The memory available to the calling task's job is not sufficient to create the specified segment.

CREATE$TASK

The CREATE$TASK primitive creates a task.

---

    task = RQ$CREATE$TASK (priority, start$address, data$seg, stack$ptr, stack$size, task$flags,
                           except$ptr);

INPUT PARAMETERS

priority
:   A BYTE that specifies the priority of the new task.

    - If not zero, the BYTE contains the priority of the new task. The priority parameter must not exceed the maximum allowable priority of the calling task's job.

    - If zero, the BYTE indicates that the new task's priority is to equal the maximum allowable priority of the calling task's job.

start$address
:   A POINTER to the first instruction of the new task.

data$seg
:   A WORD that specifies the new task's data segment.

    - If not zero, the WORD contains the base address of the new task's data segment.

    - If zero, the WORD indicates that the new task assigns its own data segment. Refer to Chapter 5 for further information on data segment allocation.

stack$ptr
:   A POINTER that specifies the location of the stack for the new task.

    - If the base portion is not zero, the POINTER points to the base of the new task's stack.

    - If the base portion is zero, the OSP Processor will allocate a stack to the new task. The length of the stack will be equal to the value of the stack$size parameter.

stack$size
:   A WORD containing the size, in bytes, of the new task's stack segment. The stack size must be at least 16 bytes. The OSP Processor increases values that are not multiples of 16 up to the next higher multiple of 16.

    The stack size should be at least 300 (decimal) bytes if the new task is going to invoke OSP primitives. See Chapter 4 for more information about stack size required by primitives.

task$flags
:   A WORD containing information that the OSP Processor uses to create and maintain the task. The bits (where bit 15 is the high-order bit) have the following meanings:

Bit	Meaning
15-1	Reserved bits which should be set to zero.
0	If one, the task contains floating-point instructions. These instructions require the 8087 Numeric Processor Extension for execution.
	If zero, the task does not contain floating-point instructions.

OUTPUT PARAMETERS

task
:   A WORD in which the OSP will return a TOKEN for the new task.

except$ptr
:   A POINTER to a WORD to which the OSP will return the condition code generated by this primitive.

210911

DESCRIPTION

The CREATE$TASK primitive creates a task and returns a TOKEN for it. The new task counts as one against the object and task limits of the calling task's job. Attributes of the new task are initialized upon creation as follows:

- priority: as specified in the invocation.

- execution state: ready.

- suspension depth: 0.

- containing job: the job that contains the calling task.

- exception handler: the exception handler of the containing job.

- exception mode: the exception mode of the containing job.

EXAMPLE

```
/*********************************************************************************************
*    This example illustrates how the CREATE$TASK primitive can be used.                     *
*********************************************************************************************/

     $INCLUDE(:F1:OSXPRM.EXT);                   /* Declares all primitive calls */

     TASK_CODE: PROCEDURE EXTERNAL;
     END TASK_CODE;

     DECLARE TOKEN                               LITERALLY 'SELECTOR';
                                                 /* if your PL/M compiler does not support this variable
                                                 type, declare TOKEN a WORD */
     DECLARE task$token                          TOKEN;
     DECLARE priority$level$66                    LITERALLY '66';
     DECLARE start$address                       POINTER;
     DECLARE data$seg                            WORD;
     DECLARE stack$pointer                       POINTER;
     DECLARE stack$size$512                      LITERALLY '512'; /* new task's stack size is 512 bytes
                                                 */
     DECLARE task$flags                          WORD;
     DECLARE status                              WORD;

SAMPLE_PROCEDURE:
     PROCEDURE;

     start$address = @TASK_CODE;                 /* first instruction of the new task */
     data$seg = 0;                               /* task sets up own data segment */
     stack$pointer = 0;                          /* automatic stack allocation */
     task$flags = 0;                             /* designates no floating-point instructions */

          :
          :  }    Typical PL/M-86 Statements

/*********************************************************************************************
*    The task TASK_CODE is created when the calling task invokes the CREATE$TASK primitive.  *
*********************************************************************************************/
```

CREATE$TASK

task$token = RQ$CREATE$TASK

(priority$level$66,
start$address,
data$seg,
stack$pointer,
stack$size$512,
task$flags,
@status);

 } Typical PL/M-86 Statements

END SAMPLE_PROCEDURE;

CONDITION CODES

E$OK	No exceptional conditions.
E$LIMIT	The new task would exceed the object limit or the task limit of the calling task's job.
E$MEM	The memory available to the calling task's job is not sufficient to create a task as specified.

210911

DELETE$MAILBOX

The DELETE$MAILBOX primitive deletes a mailbox.

```
CALL RQ$DELETE$MAILBOX (mailbox, except$ptr);
```

INPUT PARAMETER

mailbox   A WORD containing a TOKEN for the mailbox to be deleted.

OUTPUT PARAMETER

except$ptr   A POINTER to a WORD to which the OSP will return the condition code generated by this primitive.

DESCRIPTION

The DELETE$MAILBOX primitive deletes the specified mailbox. If any tasks are queued at the mailbox at the moment of deletion, they are awakened with an E$EXIST exceptional condition. If there is a queue of object TOKENs at the moment of deletion, the queue is discarded. Deleting the mailbox counts as a credit of one toward the object total of the containing job.

EXAMPLE

```
/************************************************************************
*                                                                      *
*   This example illustrates how the DELETE$MAILBOX primitive can be used.   *
*                                                                      *
************************************************************************/

   DECLARE TOKEN                          LITERALLY 'SELECTOR';
                                          /* if your PL/M compiler does not support this variable
                                          type, declare TOKEN a WORD */
   DECLARE mbx$token                      TOKEN;
   DECLARE mbx$flags                      WORD;
   DECLARE status                         WORD;

SAMPLE_PROCEDURE:
   PROCEDURE;

   mbx$flags = 0;                         /* designates four objects to be queued on the high
                                          performance object queue; designates a first-
                                          in/first-out task queue. */


      •
      •   } Typical PL/M-86 Statements
      •

/************************************************************************
*                                                                      *
*   In order to delete a mailbox, a task must know the name of the TOKEN for that mailbox. In this example,   *
*   the needed TOKEN is known because the calling task creates the mailbox.   *
*                                                                      *
************************************************************************/

   mbx$token = RQ$CREATE$MAILBOX          (mbx$flags,
                                          @status);
```

DELETE$MAILBOX

```
:
} Typical PL/M-86 Statements
:
```

/•••
* When the mailbox is no longer needed, it may be deleted by any task that knows the TOKEN for the
* mailbox.
•••/

```
CALL RQ$DELETE$MAILBOX                (mbx$token,
                                       @status);
```

```
:
} Typical PL/M-86 Statements
:
```

END SAMPLE_PROCEDURE;

CONDITION CODES

E$OK	No exceptional conditions.
E$EXIST	Either the mailbox parameter is not a TOKEN for an existing object.
E$TYPE	The mailbox parameter is a TOKEN for an object that is not a mailbox.

DELETE$REGION

The DELETE$REGION primitive deletes a region.

```
CALL RQ$DELETE$REGION (region, except$ptr);
```

INPUT PARAMETER

region   A WORD containing a TOKEN for the region to be deleted.

OUTPUT PARAMETER

except$ptr   A POINTER to a WORD to which the OSP will return the condition code generated by this primitive.

DESCRIPTION

The DELETE$REGION primitive deletes a region. If a task that has access to data protected by the region requests that the region be deleted, the task receives an E$CONTEXT exceptional condition. If a task requests deletion while another task has access, deletion is delayed until access is surrendered. When the region is deleted, any waiting tasks awaken with an E$EXIST exceptional condition.

EXAMPLE

```
/*************************************************************************
*       This example illustrates how the DELETE$REGION primitive can be used.         *
**************************************************************************/

        $INCLUDE(:F1:OSXPRM.EXT);               /* Declares all primitive calls */

        DECLARE TOKEN                           LITERALLY 'SELECTOR';
                                                /* if your PL/M compiler does not support this variable
                                                type, declare TOKEN a WORD */
        DECLARE region$token                    TOKEN;

        DECLARE priority$queue                  LITERALLY '1'; /* tasks wait in priority order */
        DECLARE status                          WORD;

SAMPLE_PROCEDURE:
    PROCEDURE;
```

    Typical PL/M-86 Statements

```
/*************************************************************************
*       In order to delete a region, a task must know the name of the TOKEN for that region. In this example, the   *
*       needed TOKEN is known because the calling task creates the region.                                          *
**************************************************************************/

        region$token = RQ$CREATE$REGION         (priority$queue,
                                                @status);
```

210911

DELETE$REGION

```
:
}   Typical PL/M-86 Statements
```

/**
*   When the region is no longer needed, it may be deleted by any task that knows the TOKEN for the   *
*   region.   *
***/

     CALL RQ$DELETE$REGION   (region$token,
                                                 @status);

```
:
}   Typical PL/M-86 Statements
```

END SAMPLE_PROCEDURE;

CONDITION CODES

E$OK	No exceptional conditions.
E$CONTEXT	The deletion is being requested by a task that currently holds access to data protected by the region.
E$EXIST	The region parameter does not contain a TOKEN for an existing object.
E$TYPE	The region parameter is a TOKEN for an object that is not a region.

210911

DELETE$SEGMENT

The DELETE$SEGMENT primitive deletes a segment.

    CALL RQ$DELETE$SEGMENT (segment, except$ptr);

INPUT PARAMETER

segment
: A WORD containing a TOKEN for the segment that is to be deleted.

OUTPUT PARAMETER

except$ptr
: A POINTER to a WORD to which the OSP will return the condition code generated by this primitive.

DESCRIPTION

The DELETE$SEGMENT primitive returns the specified segment to the memory pool from which it was allocated. The deleted segment counts as a credit of one toward the object total of the containing job.

EXAMPLE

```
/********************************************************************************
 *                                                                              *
 *      This example illustrates how the DELETE$SEGMENT primitive can be used.  *
 *                                                                              *
 ********************************************************************************/

    $INCLUDE(:F1:OSXPRM.EXT);                /* Declares all primitive calls */

    DECLARE TOKEN                            LITERALLY 'SELECTOR';
                                             /* if your PL/M compiler does not support this variable
                                             type, declare TOKEN a WORD */
    DECLARE seg$token                        TOKEN;
    DECLARE size                             WORD;
    DECLARE status                           WORD;

SAMPLE_PROCEDURE:
    PROCEDURE;

    size = 64;                               /* designates new segment to contain 64 bytes */

        •
        •  }  Typical PL/M-86 Statements
        •

/********************************************************************************
 *                                                                              *
 *      In order to delete a segment, a task must know the name of the TOKEN for that segment. In this  *
 *      example, the needed TOKEN is known because the calling task creates the segment.  *
 *                                                                              *
 ********************************************************************************/

    seg$token = RQ$CREATE$SEGMENT            (size,
                                             @status);

        •
        •  }  Typical PL/M-86 Statements
        •
```

210911

DELETE$SEGMENT

/••
• When the segment is no longer needed, it may be deleted by any task that knows the TOKEN for the •
• segment. •
••/

CALL RQ$DELETE$SEGMENT   (seg$token,
                                      @status);

} Typical PL/M-86 Statements

END SAMPLE_PROCEDURE;

CONDITION CODES

E$OK   No exceptional conditions.

E$EXIST   The segment parameter is not a TOKEN for an existing object.

E$TYPE   The segment parameter is a TOKEN for an object that is not a segment.

210911

DELETE$TASK

The DELETE$TASK primitive deletes a task.

```
CALL RQ$DELETE$TASK (task, except$ptr);
```

INPUT PARAMETER

task   A WORD that identifies the task to be deleted.

- If not zero, the WORD contains a TOKEN for the task that is to be deleted.

- If zero, the OSP Processor will delete the calling task.

OUTPUT PARAMETER

except$ptr   A POINTER to a WORD to which the OSP will return the condition code generated by this primitive.

DESCRIPTION

The DELETE$TASK primitive deletes the specified task from the system and from any queues in which the task was waiting. Deleting the task counts as a credit of one toward the object count of the containing job. It also counts as a credit of one toward the containing job's task count.

You cannot successfully delete an interrupt task by invoking this primitve. Any attempt to do so will result in an E$CONTEXT exceptional condition. To delete an interrupt task, invoke the RESET$INTERRUPT primitive.

EXAMPLE

```
/* *************************************************************************************
*    This example illustrates how the DELETE$TASK primitive can be used.              *
***************************************************************************************/

$INCLUDE(:F1:OSXPRM.EXT);                        /* Declares all primitive calls */

TASK_CODE: PROCEDURE EXTERNAL;
END TASK_CODE;

DECLARE TOKEN                                    LITERALLY 'SELECTOR';
                                                 /* if your PL/M compiler does not support this variable
                                                 type, declare TOKEN a WORD */
DECLARE task$token                               TOKEN;
DECLARE priority$level$66                        LITERALLY '66';
DECLARE start$address                            POINTER;
DECLARE data$seg                                 WORD;
DECLARE stack$pointer                            POINTER;
DECLARE stack$size$512                           LITERALLY '512'; /* new task's stack size is 512 bytes
                                                 */
DECLARE task$flags                               WORD;
DECLARE status                                   WORD;
```

DELETE$TASK

SAMPLE_PROCEDURE:
    PROCEDURE;

```
        start$address = @TASK_CODE;              /* points to first instruction of the new task */
        data$seg = 0;                            /* task sets up own data segment */
        stack$pointer = 0;                       /* automatic stack allocation */
        task$flags = 0;                          /* indicates no floating-point instructions */
```

•   In order to delete a task, a task must know the name of the TOKEN for that task. In this example, the
•   needed TOKEN is known because the calling task creates the new task (labeled TASK_CODE).

```
        task$token = RQ$CREATE$TASK              (priority$level$66,
        start$address,
        data$seg,
        stack$pointer,
        stack$size$512,
        task$flags,
        @status);
```

       :}   Typical PL/M-86 Statements

•   The calling task has created TASK_CODE which is not an interrupt task. When TASK_CODE is no
•   longer needed, it may be deleted by any task that knows its TOKEN.

```
        CALL RQ$DELETE$TASK                      (task$token,
                                                 @status);
```

       :}   Typical PL/M-86 Statements

END SAMPLE_PROCEDURE;

CONDITION CODES

E$OK	No exceptional conditions.
E$CONTEXT	The task parameter is a TOKEN for an interrupt task.
E$EXIST	The task parameter is not a TOKEN for an existing object.
E$TYPE	The task parameter is a TOKEN for an object which is not a task.

DISABLE

The DISABLE primitive disables an interrupt line.

CALL RQ$DISABLE (line, except$ptr);

INPUT PARAMETER

line
A WORD that specifies an interrupt line encoded as follows (bit 15 is the high-order bit):

Bits	Value
15-7	0
6-4	first digit of the interrupt line (0-7)
3	if one, the line is a master line and bits 6-4 specify the entire line number
	if zero, the line is on a slave interrupt controller and bits 2-0 specify the second digit of the line
2-0	second digit of the interrupt line (0-7), if bit 3 is zero

OUTPUT PARAMETER

except$ptr
A POINTER to a WORD to which the OSP will return the condition code generated by this primitive. The calling task must process all exceptional conditions in-line, as control does not pass to an exception handler.

DESCRIPTION

The DISABLE primitive disables the specified interrupt line. It has no effect on other lines. The line must have an interrupt handler assigned to it.

The line reserved for the system clock should not be disabled. This line is specified during system configuration. Refer to Chapter 5 for configuration information.

EXAMPLE

```
/************************************************************************
*                                                                      *
*    This example illustrates how the DISABLE primitive can be used to disable an interrupt line.    *
*                                                                      *
************************************************************************/

$INCLUDE(:F1:OSXPRM.EXT);                  /* Declares all primitive calls */

INTERRUPT_HANDLER: PROCEDURE EXTERNAL;
END INTERRUPT_HANDLER;

DECLARE interrupt$line$7                    LITERALLY '0000 0000 0111 1000B';
                                            /* specifies master interrupt line 7 */
DECLARE interrupt$task$flag                 BYTE;
DECLARE interrupt$handler                   POINTER;
DECLARE data$segment                        WORD;
DECLARE status                              WORD;
```

DISABLE

PROCEDURE;

```
interrupt$task$flag = 0;                        /* indicates no interrupt task on line 7 */
data$segment = 0;                               /* indicates that interrupt handler will load its own data
                                                   segment */
interrupt$handler = INTERRUPT$PTR (@INTERRUPT_HANDLER);
                                                /* points to first instruction of interrupt handler */
```

```
: }  Typical PL/M-86 Statements
```

/**
* An interrupt line must have an interrupt handler or an interrupt task assigned to it. Invoking the SET$IN- *
* TERRUPT primitive, the calling task assigns INTERRUPT_HANDLER to interrupt line 7. *
**/

```
CALL RQ$SET$INTERRUPT                            (interrupt$line$7,
                                                 interrupt$task$flag,
                                                 interrupt$handler,
                                                 data$segment,
                                                 @status);
```

```
: }  Typical PL/M-86 Statements
```

/**
* The SET$INTERRUPT primitive enabled interrupt line 7. In order to disable line 7, the calling task in- *
* vokes the DISABLE primitive. *
**/

```
CALL RQ$DISABLE                                  (interrupt$line$7,
                                                 @status);
```

```
: }  Typical PL/M-86 Statements
```

END SAMPLE_PROCEDURE;

CONDITION CODES

E$OK	No exceptional conditions.
E$CONTEXT	The line indicated by the line parameter is already disabled.
E$PARAM	The line parameter is invalid.

DISABLE$DELETION

The DISABLE$DELETION primitive makes an object immune to ordinary deletion.

```
CALL RQ$DISABLE$DELETION (object, except$ptr);
```

INPUT PARAMETER

object A WORD containing a TOKEN for the object whose deletion is to be disabled.

OUTPUT PARAMETER

except$ptr A POINTER to a WORD to which the OSP will return the condition code generated by this primitive.

DESCRIPTION

The DISABLE$DELETION primitive increases by one the disabling depth of an object, making it immune to deletion. If a task attempts to delete the object while it is immune, the task sleeps until the immunity is removed. At that time, the object is deleted and the task is awakened.

NOTE

An attempt to raise an object's disabling depth above 255 causes an E$LIMIT exceptional condition.

EXAMPLE

```
/*****************************************************************
*    This example illustrates how the DISABLE$DELETION primitive can be used to make an object immune   *
*    to ordinary deletion.                                                                              *
*****************************************************************/

        $INCLUDE(:F1:OSXPRM.EXT);          /* Declares all primitive calls */

        DECLARE TOKEN                       LITERALLY 'SELECTOR';
                                            /* if your PL/M compiler does not support this variable
                                               type, declare TOKEN a WORD */
        DECLARE task$token                  TOKEN;
        DECLARE calling$task                LITERALLY '0';
        DECLARE status                      WORD;

SAMPLE_PROCEDURE:
    PROCEDURE;

        :}  Typical PL/M-86 Statements

/*****************************************************************
*    In this example the calling task will be the object to become immune to ordinary deletion. The GET$-  *
*    TASK$TOKEN is invoked by the calling task to obtain its own TOKEN.                                     *
*****************************************************************/
```

DISABLE$DELETION

```
task$token = RQ$GET$TASK$TOKENS          (calling$task,
                                          @status);

        •}
        •        Typical PL/M-86 Statements
        •
```

/••
*   Using its own TOKEN, the calling task invokes the DISABLE$DELETION primitive to increase its own   *
*   disabling depth by one. This makes the calling task immune to deletion.   *
••/

```
CALL RQ$DISABLE$DELETION                 (task$token,
                                          @status);

        •}
        •        Typical PL/M-86 Statements
        •
```

END SAMPLE_PROCEDURE;

CONDITION CODES

E$OK   No exceptional conditions.

E$LIMIT   The object's disabling depth is already 255.

210911

ENABLE

The ENABLE primitive enables an interrupt line.

CALL RQ$ENABLE (line, except$ptr);

INPUT PARAMETER

line
A WORD that specifies the an interrupt line encoded as follows (bit 15 is the high-order bit):

Bits	Value
15-7	0
6-4	first digit of the interrupt line (0-7)
3	if one, the line is a master line and bits 6-4 specify the entire line number
	if zero, the line is on a slave interrupt controller and bits 2-0 specify the second digit of the line
2-0	second digit of the interrupt line (0-7), if bit 3 is zero

OUTPUT PARAMETER

except$ptr
A POINTER to a WORD to which the OSP will return the condition code generated by this primitive.

DESCRIPTION

The ENABLE primitive enables the specified interrupt line. The line must have an interrupt handler assigned to it. A task must not enable the line associated with the system clock.

EXAMPLE

```
/*********************************************************************************
*                                                                               *
*    This example illustrates how the ENABLE primitive can be used to enable an interrupt line.  *
*                                                                               *
*********************************************************************************/

$INCLUDE(:F1:OSXPRM.EXT);                           /* Declares all primitive calls */

INTERRUPT_HANDLER: PROCEDURE EXTERNAL;
END INTERRUPT_HANDLER;

DECLARE interrupt$line$7                             LITERALLY '0000 0000 0111 1000B';
                                                    /* specifies master interrupt line 7 */
DECLARE interrupt$task$flag                          BYTE;
DECLARE interrupt$handler                            POINTER;
DECLARE data$segment                                WORD;
DECLARE status                                      WORD;
```

SAMPLE_PROCEDURE:
    PROCEDURE;

```
interrupt$task$flag = 0;                          /* indicates no interrupt task on line 7 */
data$segment = 0;                                 /* indicates that interrupt handler will load its own data
                                                     segment */
interrupt$handler = INTERRUPT$PTR (@INTERRUPT_HANDLER);
/* points to first instruction of interrupt handler */
```

    :}   Typical PL/M-86 Statements

/***
* An interrupt line must have an interrupt handler or an interrupt task assigned to it. Invoking the SET$IN-
* TERRUPT primitive, the calling task assigns INTERRUPT_HANDLER to interrupt line 7.
***/

```
CALL RQ$SET$INTERRUPT                    (interrupt$line$7,
                                          interrupt$task$flag,
                                          interrupt$handler,
                                          data$segment,
                                          @status);
```

    :}   Typical PL/M-86 Statements

/***
* The SET$INTERRUPT primitive enabled interrupt line 7. In order to illustrate the use of the ENABLE
* primitive, interrupt line 7 must first be disabled. The calling task invokes the DISABLE primitive to dis-
* able interrupt line 7.
***/

```
CALL RQ$DISABLE                          (interrupt$line$7,
                                          @status);
```

    :}   Typical PL/M-86 Statements

/***
* When an interrupt line needs to be enabled, a task must invoke the ENABLE primitive.
***/

```
CALL RQ$ENABLE                           (interrupt$line$7,
                                          @status);
```

    :}   Typical PL/M-86 Statements

END SAMPLE_PROCEDURE;

CONDITION CODES

E$OK	No exceptional conditions.
E$CONTEXT	At least one of the following is true:

        • A non-interrupt task tried to enable a line that was already enabled.

        • There is not an interrupt handler assigned to the specified interrupt line.

        • There has been an interrupt overflow on the specified interrupt line.

E$PARAM	The line parameter is invalid.

210911

ENABLE$DELETION

The ENABLE$DELETION primitive enables the deletion of objects that have had deletion disabled.

    CALL RQ$ENABLE$DELETION (object, except$ptr);

INPUT PARAMETER

object   A WORD containing a TOKEN for the object whose deletion is to be enabled.

OUTPUT PARAMETER

except$ptr   A POINTER to a WORD to which the OSP will return the condition code generated by this primitive.

DESCRIPTION

The ENABLE$DELETION primitive decreases by one the disabling depth of an object. If there is a pending deletion request against the object, and the ENABLE$DELETION primitive makes the object eligible for deletion, the object is deleted and the task which made the deletion request is awakened.

EXAMPLE

```
/*****************************************************************************
*                                                                           *
*    This example illustrates how the ENABLE$DELETION primitive can be used to enable the deletion of a  *
*    task that had been deletion disabled.                                   *
*                                                                           *
*****************************************************************************/

    $INCLUDE(:F1:OSXPRM.EXT);            /* Declares all primitive calls */

    DECLARE TOKEN                        LITERALLY 'SELECTOR';
    DECLARE task$token                   TOKEN;
    DECLARE calling$task                 LITERALLY '0';
    DECLARE status                       WORD;

SAMPLE_PROCEDURE:
    PROCEDURE;
```

  Typical PL/M-86 Statements

```
/*****************************************************************************
*                                                                           *
*    In this example the calling task will be the object to become immune to deletion. The GET$TASK$TO-  *
*    KEN is invoked by the calling task to obtain its own TOKEN.             *
*                                                                           *
*****************************************************************************/

    task$token = RQ$GET$TASK$TOKENS      (calling$task,
                                          @status);
```

  Typical PL/M-86 Statements

210911

ENABLE$DELETION

```
/*************************************************************************************
*   Using its own TOKEN, the calling task invokes the DISABLE$DELETION primitive to increase its own   *
*   disabling depth by one. This makes the calling task immune to deletion.                             *
**************************************************************************************/
```

CALL RQ$DISABLE$DELETION   (task$token,
                  @status);

> •   Typical PL/M-86 Statements

```
/*************************************************************************************
*   In order to allow itself to be deleted, the calling task invokes the ENABLE$DELETION primitive. This   *
*   primitive decreases by one the disabling depth of an object. In this example, the object is the calling   *
*   task.                                                                                                   *
**************************************************************************************/
```

CALL RQ$ENABLE$DELETION   (task$token,
                @status);

> •   Typical PL/M-86 Statements

END SAMPLE_PROCEDURE;

CONDITION CODES

E$OK   No exceptional conditions.

E$CONTEXT   The object's deletion is not disabled.

210911

ENTER$INTERRUPT

ENTER$INTERRUPT is used by interrupt handlers to load a previously specified segment base address into the DS register.

CALL RQ$ENTER$INTERRUPT (line, except$ptr);

INPUT PARAMETER

line   A WORD specifying an interrupt line that is encoded as follows (bit 15 is the high-order bit):

Bits	Value
15-7	0
6-4	first digit of the interrupt line (0-7)
3	if one, the line is a master line and bits 6-4 specify the entire line number
	if zero, the line is on a slave device and bits 2-0 specify the second digit of the interrupt line
2-0	second digit of the interrupt line (0-7), if bit 3 is zero

OUTPUT PARAMETER

except$ptr   A POINTER to a WORD to which the OSP will return the condition code generated by this primitive. The calling interrupt handler must process all exceptional conditions in-line, as control does not pass to an exception handler.

DESCRIPTION

ENTER$INTERRUPT, on behalf of the calling interrupt handler, loads a base address value into the DS register. The value is what was specified when the interrupt handler was set up by an earlier call to SET$INTERRUPT.

If the handler is going to call an interrupt task, ENTER$INTERRUPT allows the handler to place data in the 8086 data segment that will be used by the interrupt task. This provides a mechanism for the interrupt handler to pass data to the interrupt task.

EXAMPLE

```
/*********************************************************************************
*                                                                               *
*   This example illustrates how the ENTER$INTERRUPT primitive can be used to load a segment base ad-  *
*   dress into the data segment register.                                       *
*                                                                               *
*********************************************************************************/

$INCLUDE(:F1:OSXPRM.EXT);                    /* Declares all primitive calls */

DECLARE the$first$word                       WORD;
DECLARE interrupt$line$7                      LITERALLY '0000 0000 0111 1000B';
                                             /* specifies master interrupt line 7 */
DECLARE interrupt$task$flag                   BYTE;
DECLARE intrpt$handlr$addrs                   POINTER;
DECLARE data$segment                          WORD;
```

ENTER$INTERRUPT

```
            DECLARE status                            WORD;
            DECLARE interrupt$status                  WORD;
            DECLARE ds$pointer                        POINTER;
            DECLARE PTR$OVERLAY                       LITERALLY 'STRUCTURE (offset WORD, base
                                                      WORD)';
                                                      /* establishes a structure for overlays */
            DECLARE ds$pointer$ovly                   PTR$OVERLAY AT (@ds$pointer);
                                                      /* using the overlay structure, the base address of the
                                                      interrupt handler's data segment is identified */

    INTERRUPT_HANDLER: PROCEDURE INTERRUPT 59 PUBLIC;

            •
            •  }   Typical PL/M-86 Statements
            •
    /***********************************************************************************************
    *
    *      The calling interrupt handler invokes the ENTER$INTERRUPT primitive which loads a base address      •
    *      value (defined by ds$pointer$ovly.base) into the data segment register.                             •
    ***********************************************************************************************/

            CALL RQ$ENTER$INTERRUPT                   (interrupt$line$7,
                                                      @interrupt$status);
            CALL INLINE_ERROR_PROCESS                 (interrupt$status);

            •
            •  }   Typical PL/M-86 Statements
            •


    /***********************************************************************************************
    *
    *      Interrupt handlers that do not invoke interrupt tasks need to invoke the EXIT$INTERRUPT primitive to      •
    *      send an end-of-interrupt signal to the hardware.                                                          •
    ***********************************************************************************************/

            CALL RQ$EXIT$INTERRUPT                    (interrupt$line$7,
                                                      @interrupt$status);
            CALL INLINE_ERROR_PROCESS                 (interrupt$status);
    END INTERRUPT_HANDLER;

    INLINE_ERROR_PROCESS: PROCEDURE(interrupt$status);
        IF interrupt$status < > E$OK THEN
            DO;
                                            •
                                            •  }   In-line Error Processing PL/M-86 Statements
                                            •
            END;
    END INLINE_ERROR_PROCESS;


    SAMPLE_PROCEDURE:
        PROCEDURE;

        ds$pointer = @the$first$word;                /* a dummy identifier used to point to interrupt han-
                                                      dler's data segment */
        data$segment = ds$pointer$ovly.base;         /* identifies the base address of the interrupt handler's
                                                      data segment */
        intrpt$handlr$addrs = INTERRUPT$PTR (@INTERRUPT_HANDLER);
                                                      /* points to the first instruction of the interrupt handler
                                                      */
        interrupt$task$flag = 0;                     /* indicates no interrupt task on line 7 */

            •
            •  }   Typical PL/M-86 Statements
            •
```

/••
* By first invoking the SET$INTERRUPT primitive, the calling task sets up an interrupt line. *
••/

```
CALL RQ$SET$INTERRUPT                    (interrupt$line$7,
                                          interrupt$task$flag,
                                          interrupt$handler,
                                          data$segment,
                                          @status);
```

   } Typical PL/M-86 Statements

END SAMPLE_PROCEDURE;

NOTE

Because the OSP initializes the Interrupt Vector Table, you should use the NOINTVECTOR control when you compile your interrupt handlers.

CONDITION CODES

E$OK	No exceptional conditions.
E$CONTEXT	No data segment base address had previously been specified in the call to SET$INTERRUPT.
E$PARAM	The line parameter is invalid.

EXIT$INTERRUPT

The EXIT$INTERRUPT primitive is used by interrupt handlers when they don't invoke interrupt tasks. This primitive sends an end-of-interrupt signal to the hardware.

```
        CALL RQ$EXIT$INTERRUPT (line, except$ptr);
```

INPUT PARAMETER

line   A WORD specifying an interrupt line that is encoded as follows (bit 15 is the high-order bit):

Bits	Value
15-7	0
6-4	first digit of the interrupt line (0-7)
3	if one, the line is a master line and bits 6-4 specify the entire line number
	if zero, the line is on a slave device and bits 2-0 specify the second digit of the interrupt line
2-0	second digit of the interrupt line (0-7), if bit 3 is zero

OUTPUT PARAMETER

except$ptr   A POINTER to a WORD to which the OSP will return the condition code generated by this primitive. The calling interrupt handler must process all exceptional conditions in-line, as control does not pass to an exception handler.

DESCRIPTION

The EXIT$INTERRUPT primitive sends an end-of-interrupt signal to the hardware. This sets the stage for re-enabling interrupts. The re-enabling actually occurs when control passes from the interrupt handler to an application task.

EXAMPLE

```
/*************************************************************************************
 *     This example illustrates how the EXIT$INTERRUPT primitive can be used to send an end-of-interrupt     *
 *     signal to the hardware.                                                                                *
 *************************************************************************************/

    $INCLUDE(:F1:OSXPRM.EXT);              /* Declares all primitive calls */

    DECLARE interrupt$line$7               LITERALLY '0000 0000 0111 1000B';
                                           /* specifies master interrupt line 7 */
    DECLARE interrupt$task$flag            BYTE;
    DECLARE interrupt$handler             POINTER;
    DECLARE data$segment                   WORD;
    DECLARE status                         WORD;
    DECLARE interrupt$status               WORD;

INTERRUPT_HANDLER: PROCEDURE INTERRUPT 59 PUBLIC;
```

```
    :
    :  } Typical PL/M-86 Statements
```

/***
*   *
*   Interrupt handlers that do not invoke interrupt tasks need to invoke the EXIT$INTERRUPT primitive to   *
*   send an end-of-interrupt signal to the hardware.   *
*   *
***/

```
    CALL RQ$EXIT$INTERRUPT              (interrupt$line$7,
                                        @interrupt$status);

    IF interrupt$status < > E$OK THEN
        DO;
               :
               :  } In-line Error Processing PL/M-86 Statements
               :
        END;
END INLINE_ERROR_PROCESS;
```

SAMPLE_PROCEDURE:
    PROCEDURE;

```
    interrupt$task$flag = 0;                  /* indicates no intrpt task on line 7 */
    data$segment = 0;                         /* indicates that the interrupt handler will load its own
                                                 data segment */
    interrupt$handler = INTERRUPT$PTR (@INTERRUPT_HANDLER);
                                              /* points to the first instruction of the interrupt handler
                                                 */
```

```
       :
       :  } Typical PL/M-86 Statements
       :
```

/***
*   *
*   By first invoking the SET$INTERRUPT primitive, the calling task sets up an interrupt line.   *
*   *
***/

```
    CALL RQ$SET$INTERRUPT              (interrupt$line$7,
    interrupt$task$flag,
    interrupt$handler,
    data$segment,
    @status);
```

```
       :
       :  } Typical PL/M-86 Statements
       :
```

END SAMPLE_PROCEDURE;

NOTE

Because the OSP initializes the Interrupt Vector Table, you should use the NOINTVECTOR control when you compile your interrupt handlers.

CONDITION CODES

E$OK	No exceptional conditions.
E$CONTEXT	The SET$INTERRUPT primitive has not been invoked for the specified line.
E$PARAM	The line parameter is invalid.

GET$EXCEPTION$HANDLER

The GET$EXCEPTION$HANDLER primitive returns information about the calling task's exception handler.

CALL RQGETEXCEPTION$HANDLER (exception$info$ptr, except$ptr);

OUTPUT PARAMETERS

exception$info$ptr   A POINTER to a structure of the following form:

```
STRUCTURE (
    EXCEPTION$HANDLER$OFFSET    WORD,
    EXCEPTION$HANDLER$BASE      WORD,
    EXCEPTION$MODE             BYTE);
```

Where, after the call,

- exception$handler$offset contains the offset of the first instruction of the exception handler.

- exception$handler$base contains a base for the segment containing the first instruction of the exception handler.

- exception$mode contains an encoded indication of the calling task's current exception mode. The value is interpreted as follows:

Value	When to Pass Control to Exception Handler
0	Never
1	On programmer errors only
2	On environmental conditions only
3	On all exceptional conditons

except$ptr   A POINTER to a WORD to which the OSP will return the condition code generated by this primitive.

DESCRIPTION

The GET$EXCEPTION$HANDLER primitive returns both the address of the calling task's exception handler and the current value of the task's exception mode.

EXAMPLE

```
/*********************************************************************
 *     This example illustrates how the GET$EXCEPTION$HANDLER primitive can be used to return informa-   *
 *     tion about the calling task's exception handler.                                                   *
 *********************************************************************/

$INCLUDE(:F1:OSXPRM.EXT);                    /* Declares all primitive calls */

DECLARE x$handler STRUCTURE          (x$handler$offset  WORD,

                                      x$handler$base    WORD,

                                      x$mode            BYTE);
DECLARE status                        WORD;
```

210911

SAMPLE_PROCEDURE:
    PROCEDURE;

        •
        •   Typical PL/M-86 Statements
        •

/•••
*   The address of the calling task's exception handler and the value of the task's exception mode (which   *
*   specifies when to pass control to the exception handler) are both returned when the calling task invokes   *
*   the GET$EXCEPTION$HANDLER primitive.   *
•••/

    CALL RQGETEXCEPTION$HANDLER   (@x$handler,
                                        @status);

        •
        •   Typical PL/M-86 Statements
        •

END SAMPLE_PROCEDURE;

CONDITION CODES

    E$OK   No exceptional conditions.

GET$LEVEL

The GET$LEVEL primitive returns the number of the highest priority interrupt line being serviced.

```
line = RQ$GET$LEVEL (except$ptr);
```

OUTPUT PARAMETERS

line   A WORD whose value is interpreted as follows (bit 15 is the high-order bit):

Bits	Value
15-8	ignore
7	if zero, some line is being serviced and bits 6-0 are significant
	if one, no line is being serviced and bits 6-0 are not significant
6-4	first digit of the interrupt line (0-7)
3	if one, the line is a master line and bits 6-4 specify the entire line number
	if zero, the line is on a slave device and bits 2-0 specify the second digit
2-0	second digit of the interrupt line (0-7), if bit 3 is zero

except$ptr   A POINTER to a WORD to which the OSP will return the condition code generated by this primitive. The calling task must process all exceptional conditions in-line, as control does not pass to an exception handler.

DESCRIPTION

The GET$LEVEL primitive returns to the calling task the highest priority (numerically lowest) line which an interrupt handler has started servicing but has not yet finished. To interpret the returned line number with more ease, strip away unwanted one bits by logically ANDing the returned value with 00FFH.

EXAMPLE

```
/*************************************************************************
 *                                                                      *
 *   This example illustrates how the GET$LEVEL primitive can be used.  *
 *                                                                      *
 *************************************************************************/

        $INCLUDE(:F1:OSXPRM.EXT);              /* Declares all primitive calls */

        DECLARE interrupt$line                 WORD;
        DECLARE status                         WORD;


SAMPLE_PROCEDURE:
        PROCEDURE;

                    :
                    } Typical PL/M-86 Statements
```

```
/*••••••••••••••••••••••••••••••••••••••••••••••••••••••••••••••••••••••••••••••••
 *    The GET$LEVEL primitive returns to the calling task the number of the highest interrupt line being   •
 *    serviced.                                                                                            •
 ••••••••••••••••••••••••••••••••••••••••••••••••••••••••••••••••••••••••••••••••••/
```

interrupt$line = RQ$GET$LEVEL   (@status);

```
}
}   Typical PL/M-86 Statements
}
```

END SAMPLE_PROCEDURE;

CONDITION CODES

E$OK   No exceptional conditions.

210911

GET$TASK$TOKENS

The GET$TASK$TOKENS primitive returns the TOKEN requested by the calling task.

---

token = RQGETTASK$TOKENS (selection, except$ptr);

INPUT PARAMETER

selection   A BYTE that tells the OSP Processor what information is desired. Encoded as follows:

Value	Object for which a Token is Requested
0	The calling task.
1	The calling task's job.
2	The parameter object of the calling task's job.
3	The root job.

OUTPUT PARAMETERS

token   A WORD to which the OSP will return the requested TOKEN.

except$ptr   A POINTER to a WORD to which the OSP will return the condition code generated by this primitive.

DESCRIPTION

The GET$TASK$TOKENS primitive returns a TOKEN for either the calling task, the calling task's job, the parameter object of the calling task's job, or the root job, depending on the encoded request.

EXAMPLE

```
/************************************************************************
*     This example illustrates how the GET$TASK$TOKENS primitive can be used to return the TOKEN     *
*     requested by the calling task.                                                                 *
************************************************************************/
```

```
        $INCLUDE(:F1:OSXPRM.EXT);              /* Declares all primitive calls */

        DECLARE TOKEN                          LITERALLY 'SELECTOR';
                                               /* if your PL/M compiler does not support this variable
                                                  type, declare TOKEN a WORD */
        DECLARE task$token                     TOKEN;
        DECLARE calling$task                   LITERALLY '0';
        DECLARE status                         WORD;

SAMPLE_PROCEDURE:
        PROCEDURE;
```

 Typical PL/M-86 Statements

```
/*****************************************************************************
 *   By setting the selection parameter to zero, the GET$TASK$TOKENS primitive will return a TOKEN for   *
 *   the calling task.                                                                                   *
 *****************************************************************************/
```

    task$token = RQ$GET$TASK$TOKENS   (calling$task,
                                             @status);

    :
    }   Typical PL/M-86 Statements

END SAMPLE_PROCEDURE;

CONDITION CODES

    E$OK   No exceptional conditions.

    E$PARAM   The selection parameter is greater than 3.

210911

GET$TYPE

The GET$TYPE primitive returns the encoded type of an object.

```
type$code = RQ$GET$TYPE (object, except$ptr);
```

INPUT PARAMETER

object   A WORD containing the TOKEN for an object.

OUTPUT PARAMETERS

type$code   A WORD to which the OSP will return the encoded type of the specified object. The types for OSP objects are encoded as follows:

Value	Type
1	job
2	task
3	mailbox
4	not used by the OSP
5	region
6	segment

except$ptr   A POINTER to a WORD to which the OSP will return the condition code generated by this primitive.

DESCRIPTION

The GET$TYPE primitive returns the type code for an object.

EXAMPLE

```
/***********************************************************************************
*    This example illustrates how the GET$TYPE primitive can be used to return the encoded type of an    *
*    object.                                                                                              *
***********************************************************************************/
```

$INCLUDE(:F1:OSXPRM.EXT);	/* Declares all primitive calls */
DECLARE TOKEN	LITERALLY 'SELECTOR';
DECLARE type$code	WORD;
DECLARE mbx$token	TOKEN;
DECLARE calling$tasks$job	LITERALLY '0';
DECLARE wait$forever	LITERALLY '0FFFFH';
DECLARE object$token	TOKEN;
DECLARE response	TOKEN;
DECLARE status	WORD;

```
SAMPLE_PROCEDURE:
PROCEDURE;
```

```
:
:
:
} Typical PL/M-86 Statements
```

* In order to invoke the GET$TYPE primitive, the calling task must have the TOKEN for an object. In this
* example, the calling task invokes the LOOKUP$OBJECT primitive and then the RECEIVE$MESSAGE
* primitive to receive the TOKEN for an object of unknown type (object$token).

```
mbx$token = RQ$LOOKUP$OBJECT          (calling$tasks$job,
                                      @(3,'MBX'),
                                      wait$forever,
                                      @status);
```

:
: } Typical PL/M-86 Statements

* The RECEIVE$MESSAGE primitive returns object$token to the calling task after the calling task in-
* voked LOOKUP$OBJECT to receive the TOKEN for the mailbox named 'MBX'. 'MBX' had been prede-
* signated as the mailbox another task would use to send an object.

```
object$token = RQ$RECEIVE$MESSAGE     (mbx$token,
                                      wait$forever,
                                      @response,
                                      @status);
```

:
: } Typical PL/M-86 Statements

* Using the type code returned by the GET$TYPE primitive, the calling task can determine if the object is
* a job, a task, a mailbox, a region, or a segment.

```
type$code = RQ$GET$TYPE               (object$token,
                                      @status);
```

END SAMPLE_PROCEDURE;

CONDITION CODES

E$OK	No exceptional conditions.
E$EXIST	The object parameter is not a TOKEN for an existing object.

LOOKUP$OBJECT

The LOOKUP$OBJECT primitive returns a TOKEN for a cataloged object.

---

object = RQ$LOOKUP$OBJECT (job, name, time$limit, except$ptr);

INPUT PARAMETERS

job
A WORD indicating the object directory to be searched.

- If not zero, the WORD contains a TOKEN for the job whose object directory is to be searched.

- If zero, the object directory to be searched is that of the calling task's job.

name
A POINTER to a STRING containing the name under which the object is cataloged. During the lookup operation, upper and lower case letters are treated as being different.

time$limit
A WORD indicating the task's willingness to wait.

- If zero, the WORD indicates that the calling task is not willing to wait.

- If 0FFFFH, the WORD indicates that the task will wait as long as is necessary.

- If between 0 and 0FFFFH, the WORD indicates the number of clock intervals that the task is willing to wait. The length of a clock interval is a configuration option. Refer to Chapter 5 for further information.

OUTPUT PARAMETERS

object
A WORD containing the requested TOKEN.

except$ptr
A POINTER to a WORD to which the OSP will return the condition code for this primitive.

DESCRIPTION

The LOOKUP$OBJECT primitive returns the TOKEN for the specified object after searching for its name in the specified object directory. Because it is possible that the object is not cataloged at the time of the call, the calling task has the option of waiting, either indefinitely or for a specific period of time, for another task to catalog the object.

EXAMPLE

```
/* **********************************************************************
 *    This example illustrates how the LOOKUP$OBJECT primitive can be used to return a TOKEN for a cata-     *
 *    loged object.                                                                                           *
 ********************************************************************** */

    $INCLUDE(:F1:OSXPRM.EXT);                  /* Declares all primitive calls */

    DECLARE TOKEN                              LITERALLY 'SELECTOR';
    DECLARE mbx$token                          TOKEN;
    DECLARE calling$tasks$job                  LITERALLY '0';
    DECLARE wait$forever                       LITERALLY '0FFFFH';
    DECLARE status                             WORD;
```

210911

SAMPLE_PROCEDURE:
PROCEDURE;

 Typical PL/M-86 Statements

```
/*••••••••••••••••••••••••••••••••••••••••••••••••••••••••••••••••••••••••••••••••••
*    In this example, the calling task invokes LOOKUP$OBJECT in order to search the object directory of    *
*    the calling task's job for an object with the name 'MBX'.                                              *
••••••••••••••••••••••••••••••••••••••••••••••••••••••••••••••••••••••••••••••••••*/
```

    mbx$token = RQ$LOOKUP$OBJECT   (calling$tasks$job,
                                           @ (3,'MBX'),
                                           wait$forever,
                                           @status);

 Typical PL/M-86 Statements

END SAMPLE_PROCEDURE;

CONDITION CODES

E$OK	No exceptional conditions.
E$CONTEXT	The specified job has an object directory of size 0.
E$EXIST	The name was found, but the cataloged object has a null (zero) TOKEN.
E$LIMIT	The specified object directory is full and the object being looked-up has not yet been cataloged.
E$PARAM	The first BYTE of the STRING pointed to by the name parameter contains a zero or a value greater than 12.
E$TIME	One of the following is true:

- The calling task indicated its willingness to wait a certain amount of time, then waited without satisfaction.

- The task was not willing to wait, and the entry indicated by the name parameter is not in the specified object directory.

210911

RECEIVE$CONTROL

The RECEIVE$CONTROL primitive allows the calling task to gain access to data protected by a region.

CALL RQ$RECEIVE$CONTROL (region, except$ptr);

INPUT PARAMETER

region
A WORD containing a TOKEN for the region protecting the data to which the calling task wants access.

OUTPUT PARAMETER

except$ptr
A POINTER to a WORD to which the OSP will return the condition code generated by this primitive.

DESCRIPTION

The RECEIVE$CONTROL primitive requests access to data protected by a region. If no task currently has access, entry is immediate. If another task currently has access, the calling task is placed in the region's task queue and goes to sleep. The task remains asleep until it gains access to the data.

If the region has a priority-based task queue, the OSP boosts the priority of the task currently having access, if necessary, to match that of the task at the head of the queue. See Chapter 2 for a discussion of how regions affect task priority.

EXAMPLE

```
/**********************************************************************************
 *    This example illustrates how the RECEIVE$CONTROL primitive can be used to gain access to data pro-   *
 *    tected by a region.                                                                                   *
 **********************************************************************************/

    $INCLUDE(:F1:OSXPRM.EXT);              /* Declares all primitive calls */

    DECLARE TOKEN                          LITERALLY 'SELECTOR';
    DECLARE region$token                   TOKEN;
    DECLARE priority$queue                 LITERALLY '1'; /* tasks wait in priority order */
    DECLARE status                         WORD;


SAMPLE_PROCEDURE:
    PROCEDURE;
```

 Typical PL/M-86 Statements

```
/**********************************************************************************
 *    In order to access the data within a region, a task must know the name of the TOKEN for that region. In  *
 *    this example, the needed TOKEN is known because the calling task creates the region.                      *
 **********************************************************************************/

    region$token = RQ$CREATE$REGION        (priority$queue,
                                            @status);
```

Typical PL/M-86 Statements

/•••
* When access to the data protected by a region is needed, the calling task may invoke the RECEIVE$- *
* CONTROL primitive. *
•••/

CALL RQ$RECEIVE$CONTROL (region$token, @status);

 Typical PL/M-86 Statements

END SAMPLE_PROCEDURE;

CONDITION CODES

E$OK   No exceptional conditions.

E$CONTEXT   The region parameter refers to a region already accessed by the calling task.

E$EXIST   The region parameter does not contain a TOKEN for an existing object.

E$TYPE   The region parameter is a TOKEN for an object that is not a region.

RECEIVE$MESSAGE

The RECEIVE$MESSAGE primitive queues the calling task at a mailbox, where it can wait for an object TOKEN to be returned.

---

object = RQ$RECEIVE$MESSAGE (mailbox, time$limit, response$ptr, except$ptr);

INPUT PARAMETERS

mailbox
    A WORD containing a TOKEN for the mailbox at which the calling task expects to receive an object TOKEN.

time$limit
    A WORD which,

- if zero, indicates that the calling task is not willing to wait.

- if 0FFFFH, indicates that the task will wait as long as is necessary.

- if between 0 and 0FFFFH, indicates the number of clock intervals that the task is willing to wait. The length of a clock interval is configurable. Refer to Chapter 5 for further information.

OUTPUT PARAMETERS

object
    A WORD containing the TOKEN for the object being received.

response$ptr
    A POINTER to a WORD to which the OSP returns a value. The returned word,

- if not zero, contains a TOKEN for the mailbox to which the receiving task is to send a response.

- if zero, indicates that no response is expected by the sending task.

CAUTION

The response$ptr points to a location for the sending task to use. If you specify a constant value for response$ptr, be careful to ensure that the value does not conflict with system requirements.

except$ptr
    A POINTER to a WORD to which the OSP will return the condition code generated by this primitive.

DESCRIPTION

The RECEIVE$MESSAGE primitive causes the calling task either to get the TOKEN for an object or to wait for the TOKEN in the task queue of the specified mailbox. If the object queue at the mailbox is not empty, then the calling task immediately gets the TOKEN at the head of the queue and remains ready. Otherwise, the calling task goes into the task queue of the mailbox and goes to sleep, unless the task is not willing to wait. In the latter case, or if the task's waiting period elapses without a TOKEN arriving, the task is awakened with an E$TIME exceptional condition.

It is possible that the TOKEN returned by RECEIVE$MESSAGE is a TOKEN for an object that has already been deleted. To verify that the TOKEN is valid, the receiving task can invoke the GET$TYPE primitive. However, you can avoid receiving an invalid TOKEN by adhering to proper programming practices.

One such practice is for the sending task to request a response from the receiving task and not delete the object until it gets a response. When the receiving task finishes with the object, it sends a response, the nature of which must be determined by the writers of the two tasks, to the response mailbox. When the sending task gets this response, it can then delete the original object if it so desires.

210911

EXAMPLE

```
/************************************************************************
 *    This example illustrates how the RECEIVE$MESSAGE primitive can be used to receive a message    *
 *    segment.                                                                                        *
 ************************************************************************/

        $INCLUDE(:F1:OSXPRM.EXT);                    /* Declares all primitive calls */

        DECLARE TOKEN                                LITERALLY 'SELECTOR';
        DECLARE mbx$token                            TOKEN;
        DECLARE calling$tasks$job                    LITERALLY '0';
        DECLARE wait$forever                         LITERALLY 'OFFFFH';
        DECLARE seg$token                            WORD;
        DECLARE response                             WORD;
        DECLARE status                               WORD;

SAMPLE_PROCEDURE:
        PROCEDURE;

            •
            •  } Typical PL/M-86 Statements
            •

/************************************************************************
 *    In this example the calling task looks up the TOKEN for the mailbox prior to invoking the RECEIVE$-   *
 *    MESSAGE primitive.                                                                             *
 ************************************************************************/

        mbx$token = RQ$LOOKUP$OBJECT                 (calling$tasks$job,
        @(3,'MBX'),
        wait$forever,
        @status);

            •
            •  } Typical PL/M-86 Statements
            •

/************************************************************************
 *    Knowing the TOKEN for the mailbox, the calling task can wait for a message from this mailbox by invok-   *
 *    ing the RECEIVE$MESSAGE primitive.                                                             *
 ************************************************************************/

        seg$token = RQ$RECEIVE$MESSAGE              (mbx$token,
        wait$forever,
        @response,
        @status);

            •
            •  } Typical PL/M-86 Statements
            •

END SAMPLE_PROCEDURE;
```

CONDITION CODES

E$OK   No exceptional conditions.

E$EXIST   The mailbox was deleted while the task was waiting.

E$TIME   One of the following is true:

              ● The calling task was not willing to wait and there was not a TOKEN available.

              ● The task waited in the task queue, and its designated waiting period elapsed before the
                task got the desired TOKEN.

210911

RESET$INTERRUPT

The RESET$INTERRUPT primitive cancels the assignment of an interrupt handler to an interrupt line.

```
CALL RQ$RESET$INTERRUPT (line, except$ptr);
```

INPUT PARAMETER

line   A WORD specifying an interrupt line that is encoded as follows (bit 15 is the high-order bit):

Bits	Value
15-7	0
6-4	first digit of the interrupt line (0-7)
3	if one, the line is a master line and bits 6-4 specify the entire line number
	if zero, the line is on a slave device and bits 2-0 specify the second digit of the interrupt line
2-0	second digit of the interrupt line (0-7), if bit 3 is zero

OUTPUT PARAMETER

except$ptr   A POINTER to a WORD to which the OSP will return the condition code generated by this primitive.

DESCRIPTION

The RESET$INTERRUPT primitive cancels the assignment of the current interrupt handler to the specified interrupt line. If an interrupt task had also been assigned to the line, the interrupt task is deleted. RESET$INTERRUPT also disables the line.

The line reserved for the system clock should not be reset and is a configuration option. Refer to the Chapter 5 for further information.

EXAMPLE

```
/**********************************************************************************
*                                                                                *
*    This example illustrates how the RESET$INTERRUPT primitive can be used to cancel the assignment  *
*    of an interrupt handler to an interrupt line.                               *
*                                                                                *
**********************************************************************************/

$INCLUDE(:F1:OSXPRM.EXT);              /* Declares all primitive calls */

DECLARE TOKEN                          LITERALLY 'SELECTOR';
DECLARE task$token                     TOKEN;
DECLARE priority$level$66              LITERALLY '66';
DECLARE start$address                  POINTER;
DECLARE data$segment                   WORD;
DECLARE stack$pointer                  POINTER;
DECLARE stack$size$512                 LITERALLY '512'; /* new task's stack size is 512 bytes
                                       */
```

210911

```
        DECLARE task$flags                          WORD;
        DECLARE interrupt$line$7                     LITERALLY '0000 0000 0111 1000B';
                                                     /* specifies master interrupt line 7 */
        DECLARE interrupt$task$flag                  BYTE;
        DECLARE intrpt$handlr$addrs                  POINTER;
        DECLARE interrupt$status                     WORD;
        DECLARE status                               WORD;

INTERRUPT_TASK: PROCEDURE PUBLIC;

        interrupt$task$flag = 001H;                  /* indicates that calling task is to be interrupt task */
        data$segment = 0;                            /* use own data segment */
        intrpt$handlr$addrs = INTERRUPT$PTR (@INTERRUPT_HANDLER);
                                                     /* points to the first instruction of the interrupt handler
```

```
/**************************************************************************************
*       The first primitive in this example, SET$INTERRUPT, makes the calling task (INTERRUPT_TASK) the    *
*       interrupt task for the interrupt line.                                                              *
**************************************************************************************/
```

```
        CALL RQ$SET$INTERRUPT                        (interrupt$line$7,
                                                     interrupt$task$flag,
                                                     intrpt$handlr$addrs,
                                                     data$segment,
                                                     @interrupt$status);
```

```
/**************************************************************************************
*       The second primitive, WAIT$INTERRUPT, is used by the interrupt task to signal its readiness to service   *
*       an interrupt.                                                                                             *
**************************************************************************************/
```

```
        CALL RQ$WAIT$INTERRUPT                       (interrupt$line$7,
                                                     @interrupt$status);
```

```
        :
        :  } Typical PL/M-86 Statements
```

```
/**************************************************************************************
*       When the interrupt task invokes the RESET$INTERRUPT primitive, the assignment of the current inter-    *
*       rupt handler to interrupt line 7 is canceled and, because an interrupt task has also been assigned to the  *
*       line, the interrupt task is deleted.                                                                       *
**************************************************************************************/
```

```
        CALL RQ$RESET$INTERRUPT                      (interrupt$line$7,
                                                     @interrupt$status);

END INTERRUPT_TASK;
```

```
SAMPLE_PROCEDURE:
        PROCEDURE;

        start$address = @INTERRUPT_TASK;             /* 1st instruction of interrupt task */
        stack$pointer = 0;                           /* automatic stack allocation */
        task$flags = 0;                              /* indicates no floating-point instructions */
        data$segment = 0;                            /* use own data segment */
```

```
        :
        :  } Typical PL/M-86 Statements
```

210911

RESET$INTERRUPT

task$token = RQ$CREATE$TASK   (priority$level$66,
start$address,
data$segment,
stack$pointer,
stack$size$512,
task$flags,
@status);

```
:
:
}  Typical PL/M-86 Statements
```

END SAMPLE_PROCEDURE;

CONDITION CODES

E$OK   No exceptional conditions.

E$CONTEXT   There is not an interrupt handler assigned to the specified interrupt line.

E$PARAM   The line parameter is invalid.

RESUME$TASK

The RESUME$TASK primitive decreases by one the suspension depth of a task.

```
        CALL RQ$RESUME$TASK (task, except$ptr);
```

INPUT PARAMETER

task
A WORD containing a TOKEN for the task whose suspension depth is to be decremented.

OUTPUT PARAMETER

except$ptr
A POINTER to a WORD to which the OSP will return the condition code generated by this primitive.

DESCRIPTION

The RESUME$TASK primitive decreases by one the suspension depth of the specified non-interrupt task. The task should be in either the suspended or asleep-suspended state, so its suspension depth should be at least one. If the suspension depth is still positive after being decremented, the state of the task is not changed. If the depth becomes zero, and the task is in the suspended state, then it is placed in the ready state. If the depth becomes zero, and the task is in the asleep-suspended state, then it is placed in the asleep state.

EXAMPLE

```
/*******************************************************************************************
 *   This example illustrates how the RESUME$TASK primitive can be used to decrease by one the suspen-    *
 *   sion depth of a task.                                                                                 *
 *******************************************************************************************/

        $INCLUDE(:F1:OSXPRM.EXT);                       /* Declares all primitive calls */

        TASK_CODE: PROCEDURE EXTERNAL;
        END TASK_CODE;

        DECLARE TOKEN                           LITERALLY 'SELECTOR';
        DECLARE task$token                      TOKEN;

        DECLARE priority$level$200              LITERALLY '200';
        DECLARE start$address                   POINTER;
        DECLARE data$seg                        WORD;
        DECLARE stack$pointer                   POINTER;
        DECLARE stack$size$512                  LITERALLY '512'; /* new task's stack size is 512 bytes
                                                */
        DECLARE task$flags                      WORD;
        DECLARE status                          WORD;

SAMPLE_PROCEDURE:
        PROCEDURE;

        start$address = @TASK_CODE;             /* first instruction of the new task */
        data$seg = 0;                           /* task sets up own data seg */
        stack$pointer = 0;                      /* automatic stack allocation */
        task$flags = 0;                         /* indicates no floating-point instructions */
```

RESUME$TASK

$\left.\begin{array}{c} \bullet \\ \bullet \\ \bullet \end{array}\right\}$ Typical PL/M-86 Statements

```
/*******************************************************************
*   In this example the calling task creates a non-interrupt task and suspends that task before invoking the   *
*   RESUME$TASK primitive.                                                                                      *
*******************************************************************/
```

```
task$token = RQ$CREATE$TASK        (priority$level$200,
                                    start$address
                                    data$seg
                                    stack$pointer,
                                    stack$size$512,
                                    task$flags,
                                    @status);
```

$\left.\begin{array}{c} \bullet \\ \bullet \\ \bullet \end{array}\right\}$ Typical PL/M-86 Statements

```
/*******************************************************************
*   After creating the task, the calling task invokes SUSPEND$TASK. This primitive increases by one the        *
*   suspension depth of the new task (TASK_CODE).                                                               *
*******************************************************************/
```

```
CALL RQ$SUSPEND$TASK               (task$token,
                                    @status);
```

$\left.\begin{array}{c} \bullet \\ \bullet \\ \bullet \end{array}\right\}$ Typical PL/M-86 Statements

```
/*******************************************************************
*   Using the TOKEN for the suspended the task (TASK_CODE), the calling task invokes RESUME$TASK               *
*   to decrease by the one the suspension depth of TASK_CODE.                                                   *
*******************************************************************/
```

```
CALL RQ$RESUME$TASK                (task$token,
                                    @status);
```

END SAMPLE_PROCEDURE;

CONDITION CODES

E$OK   No exceptional conditions.

E$STATE   The task indicated by the task parameter was not suspended when the call was made.

SEND$CONTROL

The SEND$CONTROL primitive allows a task to surrender access to data protected by a region.

```
CALL RQ$SEND$CONTROL (except$ptr);
```

OUTPUT PARAMETER

except$ptr   A POINTER to a WORD to which the OSP will return the condition code generated by this primitive.

DESCRIPTION

When a task finishes using data protected by a region, the task invokes the SEND$CONTROL primitive to surrender access. If the task is using more than one set of data, each of which is protected by a region, the SEND$CONTROL primitive surrenders the most recently obtained access. When access is surrendered, the OSP Processor allows the next task in line to gain access.

If a task invoking SEND$CONTROL has had its priority boosted while it had access through a region, its priority is restored when it relinquishes the access.

EXAMPLE

```
/*********************************************************************************
 *     This example illustrates how the SEND$CONTROL primitive can be used to surrender access to data     *
 *     protected by a region.                                                                               *
 *********************************************************************************/

     $INCLUDE(:F1:OSXPRM.EXT);              /* Declares all primitive calls */

     DECLARE TOKEN                          LITERALLY 'SELECTOR';
     DECLARE region$token                   WORD;
     DECLARE priority$queue                 LITERALLY '1'; /* tasks wait in priority order */
     DECLARE status                         WORD;

        •
        •  }  Typical PL/M-86 Statements
        •


SAMPLE_PROCEDURE:
     PROCEDURE;


/*********************************************************************************
 *     In order to access the data within a region, a task must know the TOKEN for that region. In this example,  *
 *     the needed TOKEN is known because the calling task creates the region.                                     *
 *********************************************************************************/

     region$token = RQ$CREATE$REGION          (priority$queue,
                                               @status);

        •
        •  }  Typical PL/M-86 Statements
        •
```

SEND$CONTROL

```
/*********************************************************************************
*      When access to the data protected by a region is needed, the calling task may invoke the RECEIVE$-   *
*      CONTROL primitive.                                                                                    *
*********************************************************************************/

        CALL RQ$RECEIVE$CONTROL                    (region$token,
                                                    @status);

        •
        •}     Typical PL/M-86 Statements
        •


/*********************************************************************************
*      When a task finishes using data protected by a region, the task invokes the SEND$CONTROL primitive   *
*      to surrender access.                                                                                  *
*********************************************************************************/

        CALL RQ$SEND$CONTROL                       (@status);

        •
        •}     Typical PL/M-86 Statements
        •

END SAMPLE_PROCEDURE;
```

CONDITION CODES

E$OK   No exceptional conditions.

E$CONTEXT   A task invoking the SEND$CONTROL primitive did not have access to data protected by any
              region.

SEND$MESSAGE

The SEND$MESSAGE primitive sends an object TOKEN to a mailbox.

```
CALL RQ$SEND$MESSAGE (mailbox, object, response, except$ptr);
```

INPUT PARAMETERS

mailbox   A WORD containing a TOKEN for the mailbox to which an object TOKEN is to be sent.

object   A WORD containing an object TOKEN that is to be sent.

response   A WORD that,

- if not zero, contains a TOKEN for the desired response mailbox.

- if zero, indicates that no response is requested.

OUTPUT PARAMETER

except$ptr   A POINTER to a WORD to which the OSP will return the condition code generated by this primitive.

DESCRIPTION

The SEND$MESSAGE primitive sends the specified object TOKEN to the specified mailbox. If there are tasks in the task queue at that mailbox, the task at the head of the queue is awakened and is given the TOKEN. Otherwise, the object TOKEN is placed at the tail of the object queue of the mailbox. The sending task has the option of specifying a mailbox at which it will wait for a response from the task that receives the object. The nature of the response must be agreed upon by the writers of the two tasks.

EXAMPLE

```
/****************************************************************************
*                                                                          *
*   This example illustrates how the SEND$MESSAGE primitive can be used to send a segment TOKEN to  *
*   a mailbox.                                                              *
*                                                                          *
****************************************************************************/

    $INCLUDE(:F1:OSXPRM.EXT);                /* Declares all primitive calls */

    DECLARE TOKEN                            LITERALLY 'SELECTOR';
    DECLARE seg$token                        TOKEN;
    DECLARE size                             WORD;
    DECLARE mbx$token                        TOKEN;
    DECLARE mbx$flags                        WORD;
    DECLARE no$response                      LITERALLY '0';
    DECLARE status                           WORD;
    DECLARE job                              WORD;

SAMPLE_PROCEDURE:
    PROCEDURE;

    size = 64;                               /* designates new segment to contain 64 bytes */
    mbx$flags = 0;                           /* designates four objects to be queued on the high
                                             performance object queue; designates a first-
                                             in/first-out task queue. */
    job = 0;                                 /* indicates objects to be cataloged into the object
                                             directory of the calling task's job */
```

SEND$MESSAGE

```
:}   Typical PL/M-86 Statements
```

/***
*   The calling task creates a segment and a mailbox and catalogs the mailbox TOKEN. The calling task   *
*   then uses the TOKENs for both objects to send a message.   *
**/

```
seg$token = RQ$CREATE$SEGMENT          (size,
                                        @status);
mbx$token = RQ$CREATE$MAILBOX          (mbx$flags,
                                        @status);
```

/***
*   It is not mandatory for the calling task to catalog the mailbox TOKEN in order to send a message. It is   *
*   necessary, however, to catalog the mailbox TOKEN if another task is to receive the message.   *
**/

```
CALL RQ$CATALOG$OBJECT                 (job,
                                        mbx$token,
                                        @(3, 'MBX'),
                                        @status);
```

```
:}   Typical PL/M-86 Statements
```

/***
*   The calling task invokes the SEND$MESSAGE primitive to send the TOKEN for the segment to the   *
*   specified mailbox.   *
**/

```
CALL RQ$SEND$MESSAGE                   (mbx$token,
                                        seg$token,
                                        no$response,
                                        @status);
```

```
:}   Typical PL/M-86 Statements
```

END SAMPLE_PROCEDURE;

CONDITION CODES

E$OK   No exceptional conditions.

E$MEM   The high performance queue is full and there is not sufficient memory in the job containing
              the mailbox for the OSP Processor to do the housekeeping that supports a send message
              operation.

210911

SET$EXCEPTION$HANDLER

The SET$EXCEPTION$HANDLER primitive assigns an exception handler to the calling task.

CALL RQSETEXCEPTION$HANDLER (exception$info$ptr, except$ptr);

INPUT PARAMETER

exception$info$ptr   A POINTER to a structure of the following form:

```
STRUCTURE(
    EXCEPTION$HANDLER$OFFSET    WORD,
    EXCEPTION$HANDLER$BASE      WORD,
    EXCEPTION$MODE              BYTE);
```

Where:

- exception$handler$offset contains the offset of the first instruction of the exception handler.

- exception$handler$base contains the base of the 8086 segment containing the first instruction of the exception handler.

- exception$mode specifies the calling task's exception mode. The value is encoded as follows:

Value	When to Pass Control To Exception Handler
0	Never
1	On programmer errors only
2	On environmental conditions only
3	On all exceptional conditions

If exception$handler$offset and exception$handler$base both contain zeros, the exception handler of the calling task's parent job is assigned.

OUTPUT PARAMETER

except$ptr   A POINTER to a WORD to which the OSP will return the condition code generated by this primitive.

DESCRIPTION

The SET$EXCEPTION$HANDLER primitive enables a task to set its exception handler and exception mode attributes.

EXAMPLE

```
/********************************************************************
*    This example illustrates how the SET$EXCEPTION$HANDLER primitive can be used to assign an ex-   *
*    ception handler to the calling task.                                                            *
********************************************************************/
```

210911

SET$EXCEPTION$HANDLER

```
$INCLUDE(:F1:OSXPRM.EXT);                    /* Declares all primitive calls */

EXCEPTION_HANDLER: PROCEDURE EXTERNAL;
END EXCEPTION_HANDLER;

DECLARE X$HANDLER$STRUCTURE         LITERALLY 'STRUCTURE offset WORD,
                                                       base  WORD,
                                                       mode BYTE)';
                                    /* establishes a structure for exception handlers */

DECLARE x$handler                   X$HANDLER$STRUCTURE;
                                    /* using the exception handler structure, the pointer to
                                    the old exception handler is defined */
DECLARE new$x$handler               X$HANDLER$STRUCTURE;
                                    /* using the exception handler structure, the new ex-
                                    ception handler is defined */
DECLARE all$exceptions              LITERALLY '3';
                                    /* control is passed to the exception handler on all ex-
                                    ceptional conditions */
DECLARE PTR$OVERLAY                 LITERALLY 'STRUCTURE offset WORD,
                                                       base  WORD)';
                                    /* establishes a structure for overlays */
DECLARE seg$pointer                 POINTER;
DECLARE seg$pointer$ovly            PTR$OVERLAY AT (@seg$pointer);
                                    /* using the overlay structure, the first instruction of
                                    the exception handler is identified */
DECLARE status                      WORD;



SAMPLE_PROCEDURE:
    PROCEDURE;

seg$pointer = @EXCEPTION_HANDLER;            /* pointer to exception handler */
new$x$handler.offset = seg$pointer$ovly.offset;

                                    /* offset of the first instruction of the exception handler
                                    */

new$x$handler.base = seg$pointer$ovly.base;

                                    /* base address of the exception handler 8086 segment
                                    containing the first instruction of the exception handler
                                    */

new$x$handler.mode = all$exceptions;

                                    /* pass control on all conditions */


        •}  Typical PL/M-86 Statements
        •
```

/***
*   The address of the calling task's exception handler and the value of the task's exception mode (when to   *
*   pass control to the exception handler) are both returned when the calling task invokes the GET$EX-   *
*   CEPTION$HANDLER primitive.   *
**/

```
CALL RQ$GET$EXCEPTION$HANDLER        (@x$handler,
                                     @status);


        •}  Typical PL/M-86 Statements
        •
```

/***
*   The calling task may invoke the SET$EXCEPTION$HANDLER primitive to first set a new exception han-   *
*   dler and then to later reset the old old exception handler.   *
**/

```
CALL RQ$SET$EXCEPTION$HANDLER              (@new$x$handler,
                                            @status);
```

•
• } Typical PL/M-86 Statements
•

/•••
•   No longer needing the new exception handler, the calling task uses the address and mode of the old ex-   •
•   ception handler to return exception handling to its original exception handler.   •
•••/

```
CALL RQ$SET$EXCEPTION$HANDLER              (@x$handler,
                                            @status);
```

•
• } Typical PL/M-86 Statements
•

END SAMPLE_PROCEDURE;

CONDITION CODES

E$OK   No exceptional conditions.

E$PARAM   The exception$mode parameter is greater than 3.

SET$INTERRUPT

The SET$INTERRUPT primitive assigns an interrupt handler to an interrupt line and, optionally, makes the calling task the interrupt task for the line.

CALL RQSETINTERRUPT (line, interrupt$task$flag, interrupt$handler, interrupt$handler$ds, except$ptr);

INPUT PARAMETERS

line — A WORD containing an interrupt line that is encoded as follows (bit 15 is the high-order bit):

Bits	Value
15-7	0
6-4	first digit of the interrupt line (0-7)
3	if one, the line is a master line and bits 6-4 specify the entire line number
	if zero, the line is on a slave interrupt controller and bits 2-0 specify the second digit of the interrupt line
2-0	second digit of the interrupt line (0-7), if bit 3 is zero

interrupt$task $flag — A BYTE which,

- if zero, indicates that no interrupt task is to be associated with the specified interrupt line and that the new interrupt handler will not invoke the SIGNAL$INTERRUPT primitive.

- if not equal to zero, indicates that the calling task is to be the interrupt task that will be invoked by the interrupt handler being set. The priority of the calling task is adjusted by the OSP Processor according to the interrupt line being serviced. Table 2-4 lists the interrupts lines and the corresponding interrupt task priorities. Be certain that priorities set in this manner do not violate the max$priority attribute of the containing job.

  The value of this parameter indicates the number of outstanding SIGNAL$INTERRUPT requests that can exist for this line. When this limit is reached, the associated interrupt line is disabled. The maximum value for this parameter is 255 decimal. Chapter 2 describes this feature in more detail.

interrupt$handler — A POINTER to the first instruction of the interrupt handler. To obtain the proper start address for interrupt handlers written in PL/M-86, place the following instruction before the call to SET$INTERRUPT:

interrupt$handler
= interrupt$ptr (inter);

where interrupt$ptr is a PL/M-86 built-in procedure and inter is the name of your interrupt handling procedure.

interrupt$handler$ds — A WORD which,

- if not zero, contains the base address of the interrupt handler's data segment. See the description of ENTER$INTERRUPT in this chapter for information concerning the significance of this parameter.

It is often desirable for an interrupt handler to pass information to the interrupt task that it calls. The following PL/M-86 statements, when included in the interrupt task's code (with the first statement listed here being the first statement in the task's code), will extract the DS register value used by the interrupt task and make it available to the interrupt handler, which in turn can access it by calling ENTER$INTERRUPT:

DECLARE BEGIN WORD; /* A DUMMY VARIABLE */

DECLARE DATA$PTR POINTER;

DECLARE DATA$ADDRESS STRUCTURE (

    OFFSET WORD,

    BASE WORD) AT (@DATA$PTR); /* THIS MAKES ACCESSIBLE THE TWO
                HALVES OF THE POINTER DATA$PTR */

DATA$PTR = @BEGIN; /* PUTS THE WHOLE ADDRESS OF THE DATA
             SEGMENT INTO DATA$PTR AND DATA$ADDRESS */

DS$BASE = DATA$ADDRESS.BASE;

CALL RQSETINTERRUPT (...,DS$BASE,...);

- if zero, indicates that the interrupt handler will load its own data segment and may not invoke ENTER$INTERRUPT.

OUTPUT PARAMETER

except$ptr   A POINTER to a WORD to which the OSP will return the condition code generated by this primitive.

DESCRIPTION

The SET$INTERRUPT primitive informs the OSP Processor that the specified interrupt handler is to service interrupts which come in on the specified line. In a call to SET$INTERRUPT, a task must indicate whether the interrupt handler will invoke an interrupt task and whether the interrupt handler has its own data segment. If the handler is to invoke an interrupt task, the call to SET$INTERRUPT also specifies the number of outstanding SIGNAL$INTERRUPT requests that the handler can make before the associated interrupt line is disabled. This number generally corresponds to the number of buffers used by the handler and interrupt task. Refer to Chapter 2 for further information.

If there is to be an interrupt task, the calling task becomes that interrupt task. If there is no interrupt task, SET$INTERRUPT also enables the specified line, which must be disabled at the time of the call.

EXAMPLE

```
/*****************************************************************************
*                                                                           *
*    This example illustrates how the SET$INTERRUPT primitive can be used.  *
*                                                                           *
*****************************************************************************/

$INCLUDE(:F1:OSXPRM.EXT);                /* Declares all primitive calls */

INTERRUPT_HANDLER: PROCEDURE EXTERNAL;
END INTERRUPT_HANDLER;

DECLARE interrupt$line$7                 LITERALLY '0000 0000 0111 1000B';
                                         /* specifies master interrupt line 7 */
DECLARE interrupt$task$flag              BYTE;
DECLARE interrupt$handler                POINTER;
DECLARE data$segment                     WORD;
DECLARE status                           WORD;
```

SET$INTERRUPT

SAMPLE_PROCEDURE:
    PROCEDURE;

    interrupt$task$flag = 0;   /* indicates no interrupt task on line 7 */
    data$segment = 0;   /* indicates that the interrupt handler will load its own
                                                             data segment */
    interrupt$handler = INTERRUPT$PTR (@INTERRUPT_HANDLER);
                                                             /* points to the first instruction of the interrupt handler
                                                             */

 Typical PL/M-86 Statements

/* •

  •   An interrupt line must have an interrupt handler and may have an interrupt task assigned to it. If there is
  •   no interrupt task assigned to the line, the level is enabled by this primitive invocation. Otherwise, the
  •   line is enabled by a call to WAIT$INTERRUPT. By invoking the SET$INTERRUPT primitive, the calling
  •   task assigns INTERRUPT_HANDLER to interrupt line 7.

• */

    CALL RQSETINTERRUPT   (interrupt$line$7,
                                                     interrupt$task$flag,
                                                    interrupt$handler,
                                                    data$segment,
                                                      @status);

    ⋮} Typical PL/M-86 Statements

END SAMPLE_PROCEDURE;

CONDITION CODES

    E$OK   No exceptional conditions.

SETOSEXTENSION

The SETOSEXTENSION primitive either enters the address of an entry (or function) procedure in the Interrupt Vector Table or it deletes such an entry.

```
CALL RQ$SET$OS$EXTENSION (os$extension, start$address, except$ptr);
```

INPUT PARAMETERS

os$extension A BYTE designating the entry of the Interrupt Vector Table to be set or reset. This value must be between 224 and 255 (decimal), inclusive. The values in the range 192 to 223 will not cause exceptions, but are reserved for Intel use.

start$address A POINTER to the first instruction of an entry (or function) procedure. If start$address contains a zero value, the specified entry of the Interrupt Vector Table is being reset (deallocated.)

OUTPUT PARAMETER

except$ptr A POINTER to a WORD to which the OSP will return the condition code generated by this primitive.

DESCRIPTION

The SETOSEXTENSION primitive sets or resets any one of the 32 operating system extension entries in the Interrupt Vector Table. An entry must be reset before its contents can be changed. An attempt to set an already set entry causes an E$CONTEXT exceptional condition.

EXAMPLE

```
/************************************************************************
 *   This example illustrates how the SET$OS$EXTENSION primitive can be used to reset an entry in the In-   *
 *   terrupt Vector Table. The example assumes that the entry for the level (number 250) was set earlier by   *
 *   another procedure.                                                                                       *
 ************************************************************************/

        $INCLUDE(:F1:OSXPRM.EXT);              /* Declares all primitive calls */

        DECLARE vector$entry$250               LITERALLY '250';
        DECLARE reset                          LITERALLY '0';
        DECLARE status                         WORD;

SAMPLE_PROCEDURE:
     PROCEDURE;

          •
          •  }   Typical PL/M-86 Statements
          •

/************************************************************************
 *   The calling task invokes the SET$OS$EXTENSION primitive to reset entry 250 (decimal) of the Interrupt   *
 *   Vector Table.                                                                                            *
 ************************************************************************/
```

SETOSEXTENSION

CALL RQSETOS$EXTENSION   (vector$entry$250,
                                            reset,
                                            @status);

        •
        • } Typical PL/M-86 Statements
        •

END SAMPLE_PROCEDURE;

CONDITION CODES

E$OK	No exceptional conditions.
E$CONTEXT	An attempt is being made to set an entry that already is set.
E$PARAM	The os$extension byte value is less than 192.

SET$PRIORITY

The SET$PRIORITY primitive changes the priority of a task.

```
CALL RQ$SET$PRIORITY (task, priority, except$ptr);
```

INPUT PARAMETERS

task
A WORD containing a TOKEN for the task whose priority is to be changed. A zero value specifies the invoking task.

priority
A BYTE containing the task's new priority. A zero value specifies the maximum priority of the specified task's containing job.

OUTPUT PARAMETER

except$ptr
A POINTER to a WORD to which the OSP will return the condition code generated by this primitive.

DESCRIPTION

The SET$PRIORITY primitive allows the priority of a noninterrupt task to be altered dynamically.

If the priority parameter is set to the zero, the task's new priority is its containing job's maximum priority. Otherwise, the priority parameter contains the new priority of the specified task. The new priority, if explicitly specified, must not exceed the containing job's maximum priority.

EXAMPLE

```
/***************************************************************************************************
*    This example illustrates how the SET$PRIORITY primitive can be used to change the priority of a task.    *
***************************************************************************************************/

        $INCLUDE(:F1:OSXPRM.EXT);                    /* Declares all primitive calls */

        TASK_CODE: PROCEDURE EXTERNAL;
        END TASK_CODE;

        DECLARE TOKEN                                LITERALLY 'SELECTOR';
        DECLARE task$token                           TOKEN;
        DECLARE priority$level$66                     LITERALLY '66';
        DECLARE priority$level$0                      LITERALLY '0';
        DECLARE start$address                        POINTER;
        DECLARE data$seg                             WORD;
        DECLARE stack$pointer                        POINTER;
        declare stack$size$512                       LITERALLY '512'; /* new task's stack size is 512 bytes
                                                     */
        DECLARE task$flags                           WORD;
        DECLARE status                               WORD;
        DECLARE job                                  WORD;

SAMPLE_PROCEDURE:
        PROCEDURE;

        start$address = @TASK_CODE;                  /* pointer to first instruction of interrupt task */
        data$seg = 0                                 /* task sets up own data seg */
        stack$pointer = 0;                           /* automatic stack allocation
        tsk$flags = 0;                               /* designates no floating-point instructions */
```

SET$PRIORITY

```
        •
        •  }  Typical PL/M-86 Statements
        •
```

/••
* In this example, the calling task creates a task whose priority is to be changed. The new task initially
* has a priority level 66.
•••/

```
        task$token = RQ$CREATE$TASK           (priority$level$66,
                                              start$address,
                                              data$seg,
                                              stack$pointer,
                                              stack$size$512,
                                              task$flags,
                                              @status);
```

/••
* The calling task in this example does not need to invoke the CATALOG$OBJECT primitive to ensure the
* successful use of the SET$PRIORITY primitive. To allow other tasks access to the new task, however,
* requires that the task's object TOKEN be cataloged.
•••/

```
        CALL RQ$CATALOG$OBJECT                (job,
                                              task$token,
                                              @(12, 'TASK_CODE'),
                                              @status);
```

```
        •
        •  }  Typical PL/M-86 Statements
        •
```

/••
* The new task, TASK_CODE, is not an interrupt task, so its priority may be changed dynamically by
* invoking the SET$PRIORITY primitive.
•••/

```
        CALL RQ$SET$PRIORITY                  (task$token,
                                              priority$level$0,
                                              @status);
```

```
        •
        •  }  Typical PL/M-86 Statements
        •
```

/••
* Once the need for the higher priority is no longer present, the priority of TASK_CODE can be changed
* back to its original priority by invoking SET$PRIORITY a second time.
•••/

```
        CALL RQ$SET$PRIORITY                  (task$token,
                                              priority$level$66,
                                              @status);
```

```
        •
        •  }  Typical PL/M-86 Statements
        •
```

END SAMPLE_PROCEDURE;

CONDITION CODES

        E$OK   No exceptional conditions.

SIGNAL$EXCEPTION

The SIGNAL$EXCEPTION primitive is invoked by extensions of the OS Processor to signal the occurrence of an exceptional condition.

```
CALL RQ$SIGNAL$EXCEPTION(exception$code, param$num, stack$pointer, reserved$param,
                          NPX$status$word, except$ptr);
```

INPUT PARAMETERS

exception$code	A WORD containing the code (see list in Appendix B) for the exceptional condition detected.
param$num	A BYTE containing the number of the parameter which caused the exceptional condition. If param$num equals zero, then no parameter is at fault.
stack$pointer	A WORD which, if not zero, must contain the value of the stack pointer saved on entry to the operating system extension (see the entry procedure in Chapter 2 for an example). The top five words in the stack (where BP is at the top of the stack) must be as follows:

> FLAGS Saved by software interrupt to OS Processor extension
> CS
> IP
>
> DS Saved by OS Processor extension on entry
> BP

Upon completion of SIGNAL$EXCEPTION, control is returned to either of two instructions. If the stack$pointer contains a zero, control returns to the instruction following the call to SIGNAL$EXCEPTION. Otherwise, control returns to the instruction identified in CS and IP.

reserved$param	A WORD reserved for Intel use. Set this word to zero.
NPX$status$word	A WORD containing the status of the 8087 NPX.

OUTPUT PARAMETER

except$ptr	A POINTER to a WORD to which the OSP will return the condition code for this parameter.

DESCRIPTION

OSP extensions use the SIGNAL$EXCEPTION primitive to signal the occurrence of exceptional conditions. Depending on the exceptional condition and the calling task's exception mode, control may or may not pass directly to the task's exception handler.

If the exception handler does not get control, the exceptional condition code is returned to the calling task. The task can then access the code by checking the contents of the word pointed to by the except$ptr parameter *for its call* (not for the call to SIGNAL$EXCEPTION).

EXAMPLE

```
/*************************************************************************
 *
 *    This example illustrates how the SIGNAL$EXCEPTION primitive can be used to signal the occurrence    *
 *    of the exceptional condition E$CONTEXT.                                                              *
 *
 *************************************************************************/
```

SIGNAL$EXCEPTION

```
$INCLUDE(:F1:OSXPRM.EXT);                    /* Declares all primitive calls */

DECLARE e$context          LITERALLY '5H';
DECLARE param$num          BYTE;
DECLARE stack$pointer      WORD;
DECLARE reserved$word      LITERALLY '0';
DECLARE status             WORD;

SAMPLE_PROCEDURE:
    PROCEDURE;

    param$num = 0;                           /* no parameter at fault */
    stack$pointer = 0;                       /* return control to instruction following call */
```

  Typical PL/M-86 Statements

---
* In this example the SIGNAL$EXCEPTION primitive is invoked by extensions of the OSP to signal the oc-
* currence of an E$CONTEXT exceptional condition.

```
CALL RQ$SIGNAL$EXCEPTION                     (e$context,
                                             param$num,
                                             stack$pointer,
                                             reserved$word,
                                             reserved$word,
                                             @status);
```

  Typical PL/M-86 Statements

END SAMPLE_PROCEDURE;

CONDITION CODES

E$OK   No exceptional conditions.

SIGNAL$INTERRUPT

The SIGNAL$INTERRUPT primitive is used by an interrupt handler to activate an interrupt task.

```
CALL RQ$SIGNAL$INTERRUPT (line, except$ptr);
```

INPUT PARAMETER

line
A WORD specifying an interrupt line which is encoded as follows (bit 15 is the high-order bit):

Bits	Value
15-7	0
6-4	first digit of the interrupt line (0-7)
3	if one, the line is a master line and bits 6-4 specify the entire line number
	if zero, the line is on a slave interrupt controller, and bits 2-0 specify the second digit
2-0	second digit of the interrupt line (0-7), if bit 3 is zero

OUTPUT PARAMETER

except$ptr
A POINTER to a WORD to which the OSP will return the condition code generated by this primitive. The calling interrupt handler must process all exceptional conditions in-line, as control does not pass to an exception handler.

DESCRIPTION

An interrupt handler uses SIGNAL$INTERRUPT to start up its associated interrupt task. The interrupt task runs in its own environment with higher (and possibly the same) interrupt lines enabled, whereas the interrupt handler runs in the environment of the interrupted task with all interrupts disabled. The interrupt task can also make use of exception handlers, whereas the interrupt handler always handles exceptions in-line.

EXAMPLE

```
/*************************************************************************
 *  This example illustrates how the SIGNAL$INTERRUPT primitive can be used to activate an interrupt   *
 *  task.                                                                                               *
 *************************************************************************/

$INCLUDE(:F1:OSXPRM.EXT);                    /* Declares all primitive calls */

DECLARE the$first$word                       WORD;
DECLARE interrupt$line$7                      LITERALLY '0000 0000 0111 1000B';
                                             /* specifies master interrupt line 7 */
DECLARE interrupt$task$flag                   BYTE;
DECLARE interrupt$handler                     POINTER;
DECLARE data$segment                          WORD;
DECLARE status                                WORD;
DECLARE interrupt$status                      WORD;
DECLARE ds$pointer                            POINTER;
```

SIGNAL$INTERRUPT

```
    DECLARE PTR$OVERLAY                          LITERALLY 'STRUCTURE (offset WORD,
                                                                      base  WORD)';
                                                 /* establishes a structure for overlays */
    DECLARE ds$pointer$ovly                      PTR$OVERLAY AT (@ds$pointer);
                                                 /* using the overlay structure, the base address of the
                                                    interrupt handler's data segment is identified */

INTERRUPT_HANDLER: PROCEDURE INTERRUPT 59 PUBLIC;

           •
           •  }   Typical PL/M-86 Statements
           •
```

/•••
*   The calling interrupt handler invokes the ENTER$INTERRUPT primitive which loads a base address   *
*   value (defined by ds$pointer$ovly.base) into the data segment register. This register provides a mecha-   *
*   nism for the interrupt handler to pass data to the interrupt task to be started up by the SIGNAL$INTER-   *
*   RUPT primitive.   *
•••/

```
    CALL RQ$ENTER$INTERRUPT                       (interrupt$line$7,
                                                  @interrupt$status);
    CALL INLINE_ERROR_PROCESS                     (interrupt$status);

           •
           •  }   Typical PL/M-86 Statements
           •
```

/•••
*   The interrupt handler uses SIGNAL$INTERRUPT to start up its associated interrupt task.   *
•••/

```
    CALL RQ$SIGNAL$INTERRUPT                      (interrupt$line$7,
                                                  @interrupt$status);
    CALL INLINE_ERROR_PROCESS                     (interrupt$status);

END INTERRUPT_HANDLER;

INLINE_ERROR_PROCESS: PROCEDURE(interrupt$status);
    IF interrupt$status < > E$OK THEN
        DO;
           •
           •  }   In-line Error Processing PL/M-86 Statements
           •
        END;
END INLINE_ERROR_PROCESS;


SAMPLE_PROCEDURE:
    PROCEDURE;

    ds$pointer = @the$first$word;                /* a dummy identifier used to point to interrupt han-
                                                    dler's data segment */
    data$segment = ds$pointer$ovly.base;         /* identifies the base address of the interrupt handler's
                                                    data segment */
    intrpt$handlr$addrs = INTERRUPT$PTR (@INTERRUPT_HANDLER);
                                                 /* points to the first instruction of the interrupt handler
                                                    */
    interrupt$task$flag = 01H;                    /* indicates that calling task is to be interrupt task */

           •
           •  }   Typical PL/M-86 Statements
           •
```

/**
* By first invoking the SET$INTERRUPT primitive, the calling task enables an interrupt line and becomes *
* the interrupt task for line 7. *
**/

CALL RQSETINTERRUPT   (interrupt$line$7,
                                          interrupt$task$flag,
                                          interrupt$handler,
                                          data$segment,
                                          @status);

  Typical PL/M-86 Statements

END SAMPLE_PROCEDURE;

NOTE

Because the OSP initializes the Interrupt Vector Table, you should use the NOINTVECTOR control when you compile your interrupt handlers.

CONDITION CODES

E$OK	No exceptional conditions.
E$CONTEXT	There is not an interrupt task assigned to the specified interrupt line.
E$INTERRUPT$ SATURATION	The interrupt task has accumulated the maximum allowable number of SIGNAL$INTERRUPT requests. This is an informative message only. It does not indicate an error.
E$INTERRUPT$ OVERFLOW	The interrupt task has accumulated more than the maximum allowable number of SIGNAL$INTERRUPT requests. It had reached its saturation point and then called ENABLE to allow the handler to receive further interrupt signals. It subsequently received an additional SIGNAL$INTERRUPT request before calling WAIT$INTERRUPT.
E$LIMIT	An overflow has occurred because the interrupt task has received more than 255 SIGNAL$INTERRUPT requests.
E$PARAM	The line parameter is invalid.

SLEEP

The SLEEP primitive puts the calling task to sleep.

CALL RQ$SLEEP (time$limit, except$ptr);

INPUT PARAMETER

time$limit   A WORD which,

- if not zero and not 0FFFFH, causes the calling task to go to sleep for that many clock intervals, after which it will be awakened. The length of a clock interval is configurable. Refer to Chapter 5 for further information.

- if zero, causes the calling task to be placed on the list of ready tasks, immediately behind all tasks of the same priority. If there are no such tasks, there is no effect and the calling task continues to run.

- if 0FFFFH, is invalid.

OUTPUT PARAMETER

except$ptr   A POINTER to a WORD to which the OSP will return the condition code generated by this primitive.

DESCRIPTION

The SLEEP primitive has two uses. One use places the calling task in the asleep state for a specific amount of time. The other use allows the calling task to defer to the other ready tasks with the same priority. When a task defers in this way it is placed on the list of ready tasks, immediately behind all other tasks of equal priority.

EXAMPLE

```
/*********************************************************************************
*      This example illustrates how the SLEEP primitive can be used.            *
*********************************************************************************/

    $INCLUDE(:F1:OSXPRM.EXT);                    /* Declares all primitive calls */

    DECLARE time$limit                           WORD;
    DECLARE status                               WORD;

SAMPLE_PROCEDURE:
    PROCEDURE;

    time$limit = 100;                            /* sleep for 100 clock ticks */

    •
    •  }  Typical PL/M-86 Statements
    •

/*********************************************************************************
*      The calling task puts itself in the asleep state for one second by invoking the SLEEP primitive.   *
*********************************************************************************/
```

CALL RQ$SLEEP   (time$limit,
                                                       @status);

    Typical PL/M-86 Statements

END SAMPLE_PROCEDURE;

CONDITION CODES

E$OK   No exceptional conditions.

E$PARAM   The time$limit parameter contains the invalid value 0FFFFH.

SUSPEND$TASK

SUSPEND$TASK

The SUSPEND$TASK primitive increases by one the suspension depth of a task.

    CALL RQ$SUSPEND$TASK (task, except$ptr);

INPUT PARAMETER

task A WORD which,

- if not zero, contains a TOKEN for the task whose suspension depth is to be incremented.

- if zero, indicates that the calling task is suspending itself.

OUTPUT PARAMETER

except$ptr A POINTER to a WORD to which the OSP will return the condition code generated by this primitive.

DESCRIPTIONS

The SUSPEND$TASK primitive increases by one the suspension depth of the specified task. If the task is already in either the suspended or asleep-suspended state, its state is not changed. If the task is in the ready or running state, it enters the suspended state. If the task is in the asleep state, it enters the asleep-suspended state.

The SUSPEND$TASK primitive should not be used to suspend interrupt tasks.

EXAMPLE

```
/**********************************************************************************************
 *    This example illustrates how the SUSPEND$TASK primitive can be used to increase the suspension    *
 *    depth of a non-interrupt task.                                                          *
 **********************************************************************************************/

        $INCLUDE(:F1:OSXPRM.EXT);                    /* Declares all primitive calls */

        TASK_CODE: PROCEDURE EXTERNAL;
        END TASK_CODE;

        DECLARE TOKEN                                LITERALLY 'SELECTOR';
        DECLARE task$token                           TOKEN;
        DECLARE priority$level$200                   LITERALLY '200';
        DECLARE start$address                        POINTER;
        DECLARE data$seg                             WORD;
        DECLARE stack$pointer                        POINTER;
        DECLARE stack$size$512                       LITERALLY '512'; /* new task's stack size is 512 bytes
                                                     */
        DECLARE task$flags                           WORD;
        DECLARE status                               WORD;

SAMPLE_PROCEDURE:
        PROCEDURE;
```

21091

```
start$address = @TASK_CODE;        /* first instruction of the new task */
data$seg = 0;                      /* task sets up own data seg */
stack$pointer = 0;                 /* automatic stack allocation */
task$flags = 0;                    /* designates no floating-point instructions */
```

•
•
•⎬   Typical PL/M-86 Statements

/•••
•
•   In order to suspend a task, a task must know the TOKEN for that task. In this example, the needed   •
•   TOKEN is known because the calling task creates the new task (labeled TASK_CODE).   •
•
•••/

```
task$token = RQ$CREATE$TASK        (priority$level$200,
                                   start$address,
                                   data$seg,
                                   stack$pointer,
                                   stack$size$512,
                                   task$flags,
                                   @status);
```

•
•
•⎬   Typical PL/M-86 Statements

/•••
•
•   After creating the task, the calling task invokes SUSPEND$TASK. This primitive increases by one the   •
•   suspension depth of the new task (TASK_CODE).   •
•
•••/

```
CALL RQ$SUSPEND$TASK               (task$token,
                                   @status);
```

•
•
•⎬   Typical PL/M-86 Statements

END SAMPLE_PROCEDURE;

CONDITION CODES

E$OK	No exceptional conditions.
E$CONTEXT	The task indicated by the task parameter is an interrupt task.
E$EXIST	The task parameter is not a TOKEN for an existing object.

210911

WAIT$INTERRUPT

The WAIT$INTERRUPT primitive is used by an interrupt task to signal its readiness to service an interrupt.

CALL RQ$WAIT$INTERRUPT (line, except$ptr);

INPUT PARAMETER

line
A WORD specifying an interrupt line which is encoded as follows (bit 15 is the high-order bit):

Bits	Value
15-7	0
6-4	first digit of the interrupt line (0-7)
3	if one, the line is a master line and bits 6-4 specify the entire line number
	if zero, the line is on a slave interrupt controller and bits 2-0 specify the second digit of the interrupt line
2-0	second digit of the interrupt line (0-7), if bit 3 is zero

OUTPUT PARAMETER

except$ptr
A POINTER to a WORD to which the OSP will return the condition code generated by this primitive.

DESCRIPTION

The WAIT$INTERRUPT primitive is used by interrupt tasks immediately after initializing and immediately after servicing interrupts. Such a call suspends an interrupt task until the interrupt handler for the same line resumes the task by invoking the SIGNAL$INTERRUPT primitive.

While the interrupt task is running, all lower-priority interrupt lines are disabled. The associated interrupt line is either disabled or enabled, depending on the option originally specified with the SET$INTERRUPT primitive. If the associated interrupt line is enabled, all SIGNAL$INTERRUPT calls that the handler makes (up to the limit specified with SET$INTERRUPT) are logged. If this count of SIGNAL$INTERRUPT calls is greater than zero when the interrupt task invokes WAIT$INTERRUPT, the task is not suspended. Instead it continues processing the next SIGNAL$INTERRUPT request.

If the associated interrupt line is disabled while the interrupt task is running and the number of outstanding SIGNAL$INTERRUPT requests is less than the user-specified limit, the call to WAIT$INTERRUPT enables that line.

EXAMPLE

```
/• ••••••••••••••••••••••••••••••••••••••••••••••••••••••••••••••••••••••••••••••••
•    This example illustrates how the WAIT$INTERRUPT primitive can be used to signal a task's readiness   •
•    to service an interrupt.                                                                               •
••••••••••••••••••••••••••••••••••••••••••••••••••••••••••••••••••••••••••••••••••
```

```
        $INCLUDE(:F1:OSXPRM.EXT);                    /* Declares all primitive calls */

        DECLARE TOKEN                                LITERALLY 'SELECTOR';
        DECLARE task$token                           TOKEN;
        DECLARE priority$level$66                     LITERALLY '66';
        DECLARE start$address                        POINTER;
        DECLARE data$segment                         WORD;
        DECLARE stack$pointer                        POINTER;
        DECLARE stack$size$512                        LITERALLY '512'; /* new task's stack size is 512 bytes
                                                     */
        DECLARE task$flags                           WORD;
        DECLARE interrupt$line$7                      LITERALLY '0000 0000 0111 1000B';
                                                     /* specifies master interrupt line 7 */
        DECLARE interrupt$task$flag                   BYTE;
        DECLARE interrupt$handler                     POINTER;
        DECLARE interrupt$status                      WORD;
        DECLARE status                               WORD;

INTERRUPT_TASK: PROCEDURE PUBLIC;

        interrupt$task$flag = 01H;                    /* indicates that calling task is to be interrupt task */
        data$segment = 0;                            /* use own data segment */
        intrpt$handlr$addrs = INTERRUPT$PTR (@INTERRUPT_HANDLER);
                                                     /* points to the first instruction of the interrupt handler
                                                     */
```

/***
*   The first primitive in this example, SET$INTERRUPT, makes the calling task (INTERRUPT_TASK) the   *
*   interrupt task for interrupt line seven.   *
**/

```
        CALL RQ$SET$INTERRUPT                         (interrupt$line$7,
                                                     interrupt$task$flag,
                                                     interrupt$handler,
                                                     data$segment,
                                                     @interrupt$status);

            :}   Typical PL/M-86 Statements
            :
```

/***
*   The calling interrupt task invokes WAIT$INTERRUPT to suspend itself until the interrupt handler for   *
*   the same line resumes the task by invoking the SIGNAL$INTERRUPT primitive.   *
**/

```
        CALL RQ$WAIT$INTERRUPT                        (interrupt$line$7,
                                                     @interrupt$status);

            :}   Typical PL/M-86 Statements
            :
```

/***
*   When the interrupt task invokes the RESET$INTERRUPT primitive, the assignment of the current inter-   *
*   rupt handler to interrupt line 7 is canceled and, because an interrupt task has also been assigned to the   *
*   line, the interrupt task is deleted.   *
**/

```
        CALL RQ$RESET$INTERRUPT                       (interrupt$line$7,
                                                     @interrupt$status);
END INTERRUPT_TASK;
```

210911

WAIT$INTERRUPT

```
SAMPLE_PROCEDURE:
    PROCEDURE;

    start$address = @INTERRUPT_TASK;        /* 1st instruction of interrupt task */
    stack$pointer = 0;                      /* automatic stack allocation*/
    task$flags = 0;                         /* designates no floating-point instructions */
    data$segment = 0;                       /* use own data segment */
```

 } Typical PL/M-86 Statements

/* ••
*   In this example the calling task invokes the primitive CREATE$TASK to create a task labeled   *
*   INTERRUPT_TASK.   *
•• */

```
    task$token = RQ$CREATE$TASK             (priority$level$66,
                                             interrupt$task,
                                             data$segment,
                                             stack$pointer,
                                             stack$size$512,
                                             task$flags,
                                             @status);
```

. } Typical PL/M-86 Statements

END SAMPLE_PROCEDURE;

CONDITION CODES

E$OK   No exceptional conditions.

E$CONTEXT   The calling task is not the interrupt task for the given interrupt line.

E$PARAM   The line parameter is invalid.

COMMAND DICTIONARY

Command	Page	Command	Page

PRIMITIVES FOR ALL OBJECTS

CATALOG$OBJECT 8-26
Places an entry for an object in an object directory.

DISABLE$DELETION 8-51
Makes an object immune to ordinary deletion.

ENABLE$DELETION 8-55
Makes an object susceptible to ordinary deletion. Required only if the object has had its deletion diabled.

GET$TYPE 8-68
Accepts a TOKEN for an object and returns the object's type code.

LOOK$UP 8-70
Returns a TOKEN for a cataloged object.

PRIMITIVES FOR EXCEPTION HANDLERS

SET$EXCEPTION$HANDLER 8-85
Sets the exception handler and exception mode attributes of the calling task.

GET$EXCEPTION$HANDLER 8-62
Returns the current values of the exception handler and exception mode attributes for the calling task.

PRIMITIVES FOR INTERRUPT HANDLERS, TASKS, AND LINES

(An asterisk (*) marks primitives that an interrupt handler can invoke.)

SET$INTERRUPT 8-88
Assigns an interrupt handler and, if desired, an interrupt task to an interrupt line.

RESET$INTERRUPT 8-76
Cancels the assignment of an interrupt handler to an interrupt line and, if applicable, deletes the interrupt task for that line.

*ENTER$INTERRUPT 8-57
Sets up a previously designated data segment base address for the calling interrupt handler.

*EXIT$INTERRUPT 8-60
Used by interrupt handlers to send an end-of-interrupt signal to hardware.

*SIGNAL$INTERRUPT 8-97
Used by interrupt handlers to invoke interrupt tasks.

WAIT$INTERRUPT 8-104
Puts the calling interrupt task to sleep until it is called into service by an interrupt handler.

ENABLE 8-53
Enables an external interrupt line.

*DISABLE 8-49
Disables an external interrupt line.

*GET$LEVEL 8-64
Returns the interrupt line number of the highest priority for which an interrupt handler has started by has not yet finished processing.

PRIMITIVES FOR EXTENDING THE OPERATING SYSTEM PROCESSOR

SETOSEXTENSION 8-91
Either enters the address of an entry (or function) procedure in the Interrupt Vector Table or it deletes such an entry.

SIGNAL$EXCEPTION 8-95
Used by extensions of the OS Processor to signal the occurrence of an exception.

8.11 ADDING iRMX 86 FEATURES TO THE OSP

There are two ways to add functionality to the OSP. One way, discussed in Section 8.9, is to create OS extensions. The other way is adding iRMX 86 system calls (and possibly object types as well) to the OSP.

The iRMX 86 Operating System is a functional superset of the OSP and consists of the following parts:

Nucleus: The Nucleus is the core of the iRMX 86 Operating System and includes all of the features and primitives of the OSP, among other things. Every application system built upon the iRMX 86 Operating System includes the Nucleus.

Basic I/O System: The Basic I/O System provides file management and a device-independent interface to input and output devices. It supplies all file drivers and a number of device drivers. It offers an asynchronous interface for I/O operations, allowing I/O functions to run concurrently with other operations.

Extended I/O System: The Extended I/O System provides higher-level management of files than does the Basic I/O System. It offers a simple synchronous interface for I/O operations and automatically performs read-ahead and write-behind buffering.

Application Loader: The Application Loader provides a mechanism for loading application code and data files from I/O devices into system memory. It can load absolute code into fixed locations and relocatable code into dynamically-allocated locations, and it can load files containing overlays.

Bootstrap Loader: The Bootstrap Loader provides a means of loading the entire application system into system memory from an I/O device. It can be configured to load from a specific device or to use the first device that becomes ready once the system has been started. It can also be configured to load a file specified by an operator at a terminal.

Human Interface: The Human Interface is an interactive interface and an application system. It gives the operator the ability to invoke an application program from a terminal.

Supplied with the Human Interface are commands that perform the following operations:

- Creating, copying, renaming, and deleting files

- Loading and starting application programs

- Formatting and verifying device volumes

- Backing up and restoring files on devices

- Reading commands from a file, rather than from a terminal

- Communicating with the iSBC 957B package to debug programs and to copy files to and from an Intel development system

The Human Interface also provides a number of system calls that applications programs can invoke to utilize Human Interface services.

Terminal Handler: The Terminal Handler provides a real-time interface between a terminal and an application system. It is useful for users who require the ability to communicate with their systems but who do not need the full services of an I/O System.

Debugger: The debugger provides the facilities for debugging tasks interactively. It allows several tasks to be debugged while the remainder of the system continues to run.

For readers who want to know more about the iRMX 86 Operating System, its documentation package consists of the following:

TITLE	NUMBER
Introduction to the iRMX 86 Operating System	9803124
iRMX 86 Nucleus Reference Manual	9803122
iRMX 86 Basic I/O System Reference Manual	9803123
iRMX 86 Extended I/O System Reference Manual	143308
iRMX 86 Loader Reference Manual	143318
iRMX 86 Human Interface Reference Manual	9803202
iRMX 86 Terminal Handler Reference Manual	143324
iRMX 86 Debugger Reference Manual	143323
iRMX 86 Programming Techniques	142982
iRMX 86 System Programmer's Reference Manual	142721
Guide to Writing Device Drivers for the iRMX 86 and iRMX 88 I/O Systems	142926
iRMX 86 Installation Guide	9803125
iRMX 86 Configuration Guide	9803126
Guide to Using the iRMX 86 Languages	143907
iRMX 86 Disk Verification Utility Reference Manual	144133
iRMX 86 System Debug Monitor Reference Manual	143908
iRMX 86 Pocket Reference	142861
Run-Time Support Manual for iAPX 86,88 Applications	121776
Getting Started with the iRMX 86 System	144340

DOMESTIC SALES OFFICES

ALABAMA

Intel Corp.
5015 Bradford Drive
Suite 2
Huntsville 35805
Tel: (205) 830-4010

ARIZONA

Intel Corp.
11225 N. 28th Drive
Suite 214D
Phoenix 85029
Tel: (602) 869-4980

Intel Corp.
1161 N. El Dorado Place
Suite 301
Tucson 85715
Tel: (602) 299-6815

CALIFORNIA

Intel Corp.
21515 Vanowen Street
Suite 116
Canoga Park 91303
Tel: (818) 708-0333

Intel Corp.
2250 E. Imperial Highway
Suite 218
El Segundo 90245
Tel: (213) 640-6040

Intel Corp.
1010 Hurley Way
Suite 300
Sacramento 95825
Tel: (916) 929-4078

Intel Corp.
4350 Executive Drive
Suite 150
San Diego 92111
(619) 452-5880

Intel Corp.*
2000 East 4th Street
Suite 100
Santa Ana 92705
Tel: (714) 835-9642
TWX: 910-595-1114

Intel Corp.*
1350 Shorebird Way
Mt. View 94043
Tel: (415) 968-8086
TWX: 910-339-9279
910-338-0255

Intel Corp.*
5530 Corbin Avenue
Suite 120
Tarzana 91356
Tel: (818) 708-0333
TWX: 910-495-2045

COLORADO

Intel Corp.
4445 Northpark Drive
Suite 100
Colorado Springs 80907
Tel: (303) 594-6622

Intel Corp.*
650 S. Cherry Street
Suite 720
Denver 80222
Tel: (303) 321-8086
TWX: 910-931-2289

CONNECTICUT

Intel Corp.
26 Mill Plain Road
Danbury 06810
Tel: (203) 748-3130
TWX: 710-456-1199

EMC Corp.
222 Summer Street
Stamford 06901
Tel: (203) 327-2934

FLORIDA

Intel Corp.
242 N. Westmonte Drive
Suite 105
Altamonte Springs 32714
Tel: (305) 869-5588

FLORIDA (Cont'd)

Intel Corp.
1500 N.W. 62nd Street
Suite 104
Ft. Lauderdale 33309
Tel: (305) 771-0600
TWX: 510-956-9407

Intel Corp.
11300 4th Street South
Suite 170
St. Petersburg 33702
Tel: (813) 577-2413

GEORGIA

Intel Corp.
3280 Pointe Parkway
Suite 200
Norcross 30092
Tel: (404) 449-0541

ILLINOIS

Intel Corp.*
2550 Golf Road
Suite 815
Rolling Meadows 60008
Tel: (312) 981-7200
TWX: 910-651-5881

INDIANA

Intel Corp.
9100 Purdue Road
Suite 400
Indianapolis 46268
Tel: (317) 875-0623

IOWA

Intel Corp.
St. Andrews Building
1930 St. Andrews Drive N.E.
Cedar Rapids 52402
Tel: (319) 393-5510

KANSAS

Intel Corp.
8400 W. 110th Street
Suite 170
Overland Park 66210
Tel: (913) 642-8080

LOUISIANA

Industrial Digital Systems Corp.
Tel: (504) 899-1654

MARYLAND

Intel Corp.*
7321 Parkway Drive South
Suite C
Hanover 21076
Tel: (301) 796-7500
TWX: 710-862-1944

Intel Corp.
7833 Walker Drive
Greenbelt 20770
Tel: (301) 441-1020

MASSACHUSETTS

Intel Corp.*
27 Industrial Avenue
Chelmsford 01824
Tel: (617) 256-1800
TWX: 710-343-6333

MICHIGAN

Intel Corp.
7071 Orchard Lake Road
Suite 100
West Bloomfield 48033
Tel: (313) 851-8096

MINNESOTA

Intel Corp.
3500 W. 80th Street
Suite 360
Bloomington 55431
Tel: (612) 835-6722
TWX: 910-576-2867

MISSOURI

Intel Corp.
4203 Earth City Expressway
Suite 131
Earth City 63045
Tel: (314) 291-1990

NEW JERSEY

Intel Corp.*
Raritan Plaza III
Raritan Center
Edison 08837
Tel: (201) 225-3000
TWX: 710-480-6238

NEW MEXICO

Intel Corp.
8500 Menual Boulevard N.E.
Suite B 295
Albuquerque 87112
Tel: (505) 292-8086

NEW YORK

Intel Corp.*
300 Vanderbilt Motor Parkway
Hauppauge 11788
Tel: (516) 231-3300
TWX: 510-227-6236

Intel Corp.*
80 Washington Street
Poughkeepsie 12601
Tel: (914) 473-2303
TWX: 510-248-0060

Intel Corp.*
211 White Spruce Boulevard
Rochester 14623
Tel: (716) 424-1050
TWX: 510-253-7391

T-Squared
6443 Ridings Road
Syracuse 13206
Tel: (315) 463-8592
TWX: 710-541-0554

T-Squared
7353 Pittsford
Victor Road
Victor 14564
Tel: (716) 924-9101
TWX: 510-254-8542

NORTH CAROLINA

Intel Corp.
2700 Wycliff Road
Suite 102
Raleigh 27607
Tel: (919) 781-8022

OHIO

Intel Corp.*
6500 Poe Avenue
Dayton 45414
Tel: (513) 890-5350
TWX: 810-450-2528

Intel Corp.*
Chagrin-Brainard Bldg., No. 300
28001 Chagrin Boulevard
Cleveland 44122
Tel: (216) 464-2736
TWX: 810-427-9298

OKLAHOMA

Intel Corp.
4157 S. Harvard Avenue
Suite 123
Tulsa 74135
Tel: (918) 749-8688

OREGON

Intel Corp.
10700 S.W. Beaverton
Hillsdale Highway
Suite 22
Beaverton 97005
Tel: (503) 641-8086
TWX: 910-467-8741

PENNSYLVANIA

Intel Corp.*
455 Pennsylvania Avenue
Fort Washington 19034
Tel: (215) 641-1000
TWX: 510-661-2077

Intel Corp.*
400 Penn Center Boulevard
Suite 610
Pittsburgh 15235
Tel: (412) 823-4970

Q.E.D. Electronics
139 Terwood Road
Willow Grove 19090
Tel: (215) 657-5600

TEXAS

Intel Corp.*
12300 Ford Road
Suite 380
Dallas 75234
Tel: (214) 241-8087
TWX: 910-860-5617

Intel Corp.*
7322 S.W. Freeway
Suite 1490
Houston 77074
Tel: (713) 988-8086
TWX: 910-881-2490

Industrial Digital Systems Corp.
5925 Sovereign
Suite 120
Houston 77036
Tel: (713)988-9421

Intel Corp.
313 E. Anderson Lane
Suite 314
Austin 78752
Tel: (512) 454-3628

UTAH

Intel Corp.
5201 Green Street
Suite 290
Salt Lake City 84123
Tel: (801) 263-8051

VIRGINIA

Intel Corp.
1603 Santa Rosa Road
Suite 109
Richmond 23288
Tel: (804) 282-5668

WASHINGTON

Intel Corp.
110 110th Avenue N.E.
Suite 510
Bellevue 98004
Tel: (206) 453-8086
TWX: 910-443-3002

Intel Corp.
408 N. Mullan Road
Suite 102
Spokane 99206
Tel: (509) 928-8086

WISCONSIN

Intel Corp.
450 N. Sunnyslope Road
Chancellory Park I
Brookfield 53005
Tel: (414) 784-9060

CANADA

ONTARIO

Intel Semiconductor of Canada, Ltd.
Suite 202, Bell Mews
39 Highway 7
Nepean K2H 8R2
Tel: (613) 829-9714
TELEX: 053-4115

Intel Semiconductor of Canada, Ltd.
190 Attwell Drive
Suite 500
Rexdale M9W 6H8
Tel: (416) 675-2105
TELEX: 06983574

QUEBEC

Intel Semiconductor of Canada, Ltd.
3860 Cote Vertu Rd.
Suite 210
St. Laurent H4R 1V4
Tel: (514) 334-0560
TELEX: 05-824172

*Field Application Location

DOMESTIC DISTRIBUTORS

ALABAMA

†Arrow Electronics, Inc.
3611 Memorial Parkway So.
Huntsville 35801
Tel: (205) 882-2730

†Hamilton/Avnet Electronics
4940 Research Drive
Huntsville 35805
Tel: (205) 837-7210
TWX: 810-726-2162

†Pioneer Electronics
1207 Putnam Drive N.W.
Huntsville 35805
Tel: (205) 837-9300
TWX: 810-726-2197

ARIZONA

†Hamilton/Avnet Electronics
505 S. Madison Drive
Tempe 85281
Tel: (602) 231-5140
TWX: 910-950-0077

†Wyle Distribution Group
8155 N. 24th Avenue
Phoenix 85021
Tel: (602) 249-2232
TWX: 910-951-4282

CALIFORNIA

†Arrow Electronics, Inc.
521 Weddell Drive
Sunnyvale 94086
Tel: (408) 745-6600
TWX: 910-339-9371

†Arrow Electronics, Inc.
19748 Dearborn Street
Chatsworth 91311
Tel: (213) 701-7500
TWX: 910-493-2086

Arrow Electronics, Inc.
2961 Dow Avenue
Tustin 92680
Tel: (714) 838-5422
TWX: 910-595-2860

†Avnet Electronics
350 McCormick Avenue
Costa Mesa 92626
Tel: (714) 754-6051
TWX: 910-595-1928

†Hamilton/Avnet Electronics
1175 Bordeaux Drive
Sunnyvale 94086
Tel: (408) 743-3300
TWX: 910-339-9332

†Hamilton/Avnet Electronics
4545 Viewridge Avenue
San Diego 92123
Tel: (619) 571-7500
TWX: 910-595-2638

†Hamilton/Avnet Electronics
20501 Plummer Street
Chatsworth 91311
Tel: (213) 700-6271
TWX: 910-494-2207

†Hamilton/Avnet Electronics
4103 Northgate Boulevard
Sacramento 95834
Tel: (916) 920-3150

Hamilton/Avnet Electronics
3002 G Street
Ontario 91311
Tel: (714) 989-9411

Hamilton/Avnet Electronics
19515 So. Vermont Avenue
Torrance 90502
Tel: (213) 615-3913
TWX: 910-349-6263

†Hamilton Electro Sales
10912 W. Washington Boulevard
Culver City 20230
Tel: (213) 558-2458
TWX: 910-340-6364

†Hamilton Electro Sales
3170 Pullman Street
Costa Mesa 92626
Tel: (714) 641-4150
TWX: 910-595-2638

Hamilton Electro Sales
9650 De Soto Avenue
Chatsworth 91311
Tel: (818) 700-6500

Kierulff Electronics, Inc.
1180 Murphy Avenue
San Jose 95131
Tel: (408) 971-2600
TWX: 910-379-6430

CALIFORNIA (Cont'd)

Kierulff Electronics, Inc.
14101 Franklin Avenue
Tustin 92680
Tel: (714) 731-5711
TWX: 910-595-2599

Kierulff Electronics, Inc.
2585 Commerce Way
Los Angeles 90040
Tel: (213) 725-0325
TWX: 910-580-3106

†Wyle Distribution Group
124 Maryland Street
El Segundo 90245
Tel: (213) 322-8100
TWX: 910-348-7140 or 7111

†Wyle Distribution Group
17872 Cowan Avenue
Irvine 92714
Tel: (714) 843-9953
TWX: 910-595-1572

†Wyle Distribution Group
11151 Sun Center Drive
Rancho Cordova 95670
Tel: (916) 638-5282

†Wyle Distribution Group
9525 Chesapeake Drive
San Diego 92123
Tel: (619) 565-9171
TWX: 910-335-1590

†Wyle Distribution Group
3000 Bowers Avenue
Santa Clara 95051
Tel: (408) 727-2500
TWX: 910-338-0296

Wyle Military
17810 Teller Avenue
Irvine 92750
Tel: (714) 851-9958
TWX: 310-371-9127

Wyle Systems
15292 Bolsa Chica
Huntington Beach 92649
Tel: (714) 851-9953
TWX: 910-595-2642

COLORADO

†Wyle Distribution Group
451 E. 124th Avenue
Thornton 80241
Tel: (303) 457-9953
TWX: 910-936-0770

†Hamilton/Avnet Electronics
8765 E. Orchard Road
Suite 708
Englewood 80111
Tel: (303) 740-1017
TWX: 910-935-0787

CONNECTICUT

†Arrow Electronics, Inc.
12 Beaumont Road
Wallingford 06492
Tel: (203) 265-7741
TWX: 710-476-0162

†Hamilton/Avnet Electronics
Commerce Industrial Park
Commerce Drive
Danbury 06810
Tel: (203) 797-2800
TWX: 710-456-9974

†Pioneer Northeast Electronics
112 Main Street
Norwalk 06851
Tel: (203) 853-1515
TWX: 710-468-3373

FLORIDA

†Arrow Electronics, Inc.
1001 N.W. 62nd Street
Suite 108
Ft. Lauderdale 33309
Tel: (305) 776-7790
TWX: 910-599-9456

†Arrow Electronics, Inc.
50 Woodlake Drive W.
Bldg. B
Palm Bay 32905
Tel: (305) 725-1480
TWX: 510-959-6337

†Hamilton/Avnet Electronics
6801 N.W. 15th Way
Ft. Lauderdale 33309
Tel: (305) 971-2900
TWX: 510-956-3097

†Hamilton/Avnet Electronics
3197 Tech. Drive North
St. Petersburg 33702
Tel: (813) 576-3930
TWX: 810-863-0374

FLORIDA (Cont'd)

Hamilton/Avnet Electronics
6947 University Boulevard
Winterpark 32792
Tel: (305) 628-3888
TWX: 810-853-0322

†Pioneer Electronics
221 N. Lake Boulevard
Suite 412
Alta Monte Springs 32701
Tel: (305) 834-9090
TWX: 810-853-0284

†Pioneer Electronics
1500 62nd Street N.W.
Suite 506
Ft. Lauderdale 33309
Tel: (305) 771-7520
TWX: 510-955-9653

GEORGIA

†Arrow Electronics, Inc
2979 Pacific Drive
Norcross 30071
Tel: (404) 449-8252
TWX: 810-766-0439

†Hamilton/Avnet Electronics
5825 D. Peachtree Corners
Norcross 30092
Tel: (404) 447-7500
TWX: 810-766-0432

†Pioneer Electronics
5835B Peachtree Corners E
Norcross 30092
Norcross 30092
Tel: (404) 448-1711
TWX: 810-766-4515

ILLINOIS

†Arrow Electronics, Inc.
2000 E. Alonquin Street
Schaumberg 60195
Tel: (312) 397-3440
TWX: 910-291-3544

†Hamilton/Avnet Electronics
1130 Thorndale Avenue
Bensenville 60106
Tel: (312) 860-7780
TWX: 910-227-0060

†Pioneer Electronics
1551 Carmen Drive
Elk Grove Village 60007
Tel: (312) 437-9680
TWX: 910-222-1834

INDIANA

†Arrow Electronics, Inc.
2718 Rand Road
Indianapolis 46241
(317) 243-9353
TWX: 810-341-3119

†Hamilton/Avnet Electronics
485 Gradle Drive
Carmel 46032
Tel: (317) 844-9333
TWX: 810-260-3966

†Pioneer Electronics
6408 Castleplace Drive
Indianapolis 46250
Tel: (317) 849-7300
TWX: 810-260-1794

KANSAS

†Hamilton/Avnet Electronics
9219 Quivera Road
Overland Park 66215
Tel: (913) 888-8900
TWX: 910-743-0005

MARYLAND

Arrow Electronics, Inc.
4801 Benson Avenue
Baltimore 21227
Tel: (301) 247-5200
TWX: 710-236-9005

†Hamilton/Avnet Electronics
6822 Oak Hall Lane
Columbia 21045
Tel: (301) 995-3500
TWX: 710-862-1861

†Mesa Technology Corporation
16021 Industrial Drive
Gaithersburg 20877
Tel: (301) 948-4350
TWX: 710-828-9702

†Pioneer Electronics
9100 Gaither Road
Gaithersburg 20877
Tel: (301) 948-0710
TWX: 710-828-0545

MASSACHUSETTS

†Arrow Electronics, Inc.
1 Arrow Drive
Woburn 01801
Tel: (617) 933-8130
TWX: 710-393-6770

†Hamilton/Avnet Electronics
50 Tower Office Park
Woburn 01801
Tel: (617) 935-9700
TWX: 710-393-0382

†Pioneer Northeast Electronics
44 Hartwell Avenue
Lexington 02173
Tel: (617) 863-1200
TWX: 710-326-6617

MICHIGAN

†Arrow Electronics, Inc.
3810 Varsity Drive
Ann Arbor 48104
Tel: (313) 971-8220
TWX: 810-223-6020

†Pioneer Electronics
13485 Stamford
Livonia 48150
Tel: (313) 525-1800
TWX: 810-242-3271

†Hamilton/Avnet Electronics
32487 Schoolcraft Road
Livonia 48150
Tel: (313) 522-4700
TWX: 810-242-8775

†Hamilton/Avnet Electronics
2215 29th Street S.E.
Space A5
Grand Rapids 49508
Tel: (616) 243-8805
TWX: 810-273-6921

MINNESOTA

†Arrow Electronics, Inc.
5230 W. 73rd Street
Edina 55435
Tel: (612) 830-1800
TWX: 910-576-3125

†Hamilton/Avnet Electronics
10300 Bren Road East
Minnetonka 55343
Tel: (612) 932-0600
TWX: (910) 576-2720

†Pioneer Electronics
10203 Bren Road East
Minnetonka 55343
Tel: (612) 935-5444
TWX: 910-576-2738

MISSOURI

†Arrow Electronics, Inc.
2380 Schuetz
St. Louis 63141
Tel: (314) 567-6888
TWX: 910-764-0882

†Hamilton/Avnet Electronics
13743 Shoreline Court
Earth City 63045
Tel: (314) 344-1200
TWX: 910-762-0684

NEW HAMPSHIRE

†Arrow Electronics, Inc.
1 Perimeter Road
Manchester 03103
Tel: (603) 668-6968
TWX: 710-220-1684

NEW JERSEY

†Arrow Electronics, Inc.
6000 Lincoln East
Marlton 08053
Tel: (215) 928-1800
TWX: 710-897-0829

†Arrow Electronics, Inc.
2 Industrial Road
Fairfield 07006
Tel: (201) 575-5300
TWX: 710-998-2206

†Hamilton/Avnet Electronics
1 Keystone Avenue
Bldg. 36
Cherry Hill 08003
Tel: (609) 424-0110
TWX: 710-940-0262

†Hamilton/Avnet Electronics
10 Industrial
Fairfield 07006
Tel: (201) 575-3390
TWX: 710-734-4388

†Microcomputer System Technical Demonstrator Center

DOMESTIC DISTRIBUTORS

NEW JERSEY (Cont'd)

†Pioneer Northeast Electronics
45 Route 46
Pinebrook 07058
Tel: (201) 575-3510
TWX: 710-734-4382

†MTI Systems Sales
383 Route 46 W
Fairfield 07006
Tel: (201) 227-5552

NEW MEXICO

†Alliance Electronics Inc.
11030 Cochiti S.E.
Albuquerque 87123
Tel: (505) 292-3360
TWX: 910-989-1151

†Hamilton/Avnet Electronics
2524 Baylor Drive S.E.
Albuquerque 87106
Tel: (505) 765-1500
TWX: 910-989-0614

NEW YORK

†Arrow Electronics, Inc.
25 Hub Drive
Melville 11735
Tel: (516) 694-6800
TWX: 510-224-6126

†Arrow Electronics, Inc.
3000 South Winton Road
Rochester 14623
Tel: (716) 275-0300
TWX: 510-253-4766

†Arrow Electronics, Inc.
7705 Maltage Drive
Liverpool 13088
Tel: (315) 652-1000
TWX: 710-545-0230

†Arrow Electronics, Inc.
20 Oser Avenue
Hauppauge 11788
Tel: (516) 231-1000
TWX: 510-227-6623

†Hamilton/Avnet Electronics
333 Metro Park
Rochester 14623
Tel: (716) 475-9130
TWX: 510-253-5470

†Hamilton/Avnet Electronics
16 Corporate Circle
E. Syracuse 13057
Tel: (315) 437-2641
TWX: 710-541-1560

†Hamilton/Avnet Electronics
5 Hub Drive
Melville, Long Island 11747
Tel: (516) 454-6000
TWX: 510-224-6166

†Pioneer Northeast Electronics
1806 Vestal Parkway East
Vestal 13850
Tel: (607) 748-8211
TWX: 510-252-0893

†Pioneer Northeast Electronics
60 Crossway Park West
Woodbury, Long Island 11797
Tel: (516) 921-8700
TWX: 510-221-2184

†Pioneer Northeast Electronics
840 Fairport Park 14450
Tel: (716) 381-7070
TWX: 510-253-7001

†MTI Systems Sales
38 Harbor Park Drive
P.O. Box 271
Port Washington 11050
Tel: (516) 621-6200
TWX: 510-223-0846

NORTH CAROLINA

†Arrow Electronics, Inc.
5240 Greendairy Road
Raleigh 27604
Tel: (919) 876-3132
TWX: 510-928-1856

†Hamilton/Avnet Electronics
3510 Spring Forest Drive
Raleigh 27604
Tel: (919) 878-0819
TWX: 510-928-1836

†Pioneer Electronics
9801 A-Southern Pine Boulevard
Charlotte 28210
Tel: (704) 524-8188
TWX: 810-621-0366

OHIO

†Arrow Electronics, Inc.
7620 McEwen Road
Centerville 45459
Tel: (513) 435-5563
TWX: 810-459-1611

†Arrow Electronics, Inc.
6238 Cochran Road
Solon 44139
Tel: (216) 248-3990
TWX: 810-427-9409

†Hamilton/Avnet Electronics
954 Senate Drive
Dayton 45424
Tel: (513) 433-0610
TWX: 810-450-2531

†Hamilton/Avnet Electronics
4588 Emery Industrial Parkway
Warrensville Heights 44128
Tel: (216) 831-3500
TWX: 810-427-9452

†Pioneer Electronics
4433 Interpoint Boulevard
Dayton 45424
Tel: (513) 236-9900
TWX: 810-459-1622

†Pioneer Electronics
4800 E. 131st Street
Cleveland 44105
Tel: (216) 587-3600
TWX: 810-422-2211

OKLAHOMA

†Arrow Electronics, Inc.
4719 S. Memorial Drive
Tulsa 74145
Tel: (918) 665-7700

OREGON

†Almac Electronics Corporation
8022 S.W. Nimbus, Bldg. 7
Beaverton 97005
Tel: (503) 641-9070
TWX: 910-467-8743

†Hamilton/Avnet Electronics
6024 S.W. Jean Road
Bldg. C, Suite 10
Lake Oswego 97034
Tel: (503) 635-7848
TWX: 910-455-8179

PENNSYLVANIA

†Arrow Electronics, Inc.
650 Seco Road
Monroeville 15146
Tel: (412) 856-7000

†Pioneer Electronics
259 Kappa Drive
Pittsburgh 15238
Tel: (412) 782-2300
TWX: 710-795-3122

PENNSYLVANIA (Cont'd)

†Pioneer Electronics
261 Gibralter Road
Horsham 19044
Tel: (215) 674-4000
TWX: 510-665-6778

TEXAS

†Arrow Electronics, Inc.
3220 Commander Drive
Carrollton 75006
Tel: (214) 380-6464
TWX: 910-860-5377

†Arrow Electronics, Inc.
10899 Kinghurst
Suite 100
Houston 77099
Tel: (713) 530-4700
TWX: 910-880-4439

†Arrow Electronics, Inc.
10125 Metropolitan
Austin 78758
Tel: (512) 835-4180
TWX: 910-874-1348

†Hamilton/Avnet Electronics
2401 Rutland
Austin 78757
Tel: (512) 837-8911
TWX: 910-874-1319

†Hamilton/Avnet Electronics
2111 W. Walnut Hill Lane
Irving 75062
Tel: (214) 659-4100
TWX: 910-860-5929

†Hamilton/Avnet Electronics
8750 West Park
Hosuton 77063
Tel: (713) 780-1771
TWX: 910-881-5523

†Pioneer Electronics
9901 Burnet Road
Austin 78758
Tel: (512) 835-4000
TWX: 910-874-1323

†Pioneer Electronics
13710 Omega Road
Dallas 75234
Tel: (214) 386-7300
TWX: 910-850-5563

†Pioneer Electronics
5853 Point West Drive
Houston 77036
Tel: (713) 988-5555
TWX: 910-881-1606

UTAH

†Hamilton/Avnet Electronics
1585 West 2100 South
Salt Lake City 84119
Tel: (801) 972-2800
TWX: 910-925-4018

Wyle Distribution Group
1959 South 4130 West, Unit B
Salt Lake City 84104
Tel: (801) 974-9953

WASHINGTON

†Almac Electronics Corporation
14360 S.E. Eastgate Way
Bellevue 98007
Tel: (206) 643-9992
TWX: 910-444-2067

†Arrow Electronics, Inc.
14320 N.E. 21st Street
Bellevue 98007
Tel: (206) 643-4800
TWX: 910-444-2017

†Hamilton/Avnet Electronics
14212 N.E. 21st Street
Bellevue 98005
Tel: (206) 453-5874
TWX: 910-443-2469

WISCONSIN

†Arrow Electronics, Inc.
430 W. Rausson Avenue
Oakcreek 53154
Tel: (414) 764-6600
TWX: 910-262-1193

†Hamilton/Avnet Electronics
2975 Moorland Road
New Berlin 53151
Tel: (414) 784-4510
TWX: 910-262-1182

CANADA

ALBERTA

†Hamilton/Avnet Electronics
2816 21st Street N.E.
Calgary T2E 6Z2
Tel: (403) 230-3586
TWX: 03-827-642

Zentronics
Bay No. 1
3300 14th Avenue N.E.
Calgary T2A 6J4
Tel: (403) 272-1021

BRITISH COLUMBIA

Zentronics
108-11400 Bridgeport Road
Richmond V6X 1T2
Tel: (604) 273-5575
TWX: 04-5077-89

MANITOBA

Zentronics
590 Berry Street
Winnipeg R3H OS1
Tel: (204) 775-8661

ONTARIO

Hamilton/Avnet Electronics
6845 Rexwood Road
Units G & H
Mississauga L4V 1R2
Tel: (416) 677-7432
TWX: 610-492-8867

Hamilton/Avnet Electronics
210 Colonnade Road South
Nepean K2E 7L5
Tel: (613) 226-1700
TWX: 05-349-71

Zentronics
8 Tilbury Court
Brampton L6T 3T4
Tel: (416) 451-9600
TWX: 06-976-78

Zentronics
564/10 Weber Street North
Waterloo N2L 5C6
Tel: (519) 884-5700

Zentronics
155 Colonnade Road
Unit 17
Nepean K2E 7K1
Tel: (613) 225-8840
TWX: 06-976-78

QUEBEC

Hamilton/Avnet Electronics
2670 Sabourin Street
St. Laurent H4S 1M2
Tel: (514) 331-6443
TWX: 610-421-3731

Zentronics
505 Locke Street
St. Laurent H4T 1X7
Tel: (514) 735-5361
TWX: 05-827-535

†Microcomputer System Technical Demonstrator Centers

EUROPEAN SALES OFFICES

BELGIUM

Intel Corporation S.A.
Parc Seny
Rue du Moulin a Papier 51
Boite 1
B-1160 Brussels
Tel: (02)661 07 11
TELEX: 24814

DENMARK

Intel Denmark A/S*
Glentevej 61 - 3rd Floor
DK-2400 Copenhagen
Tel: (01) 19 80 33
TELEX: 19567

FINLAND

Intel Finland OY
Hameentie 103
SF - 00550 Helsinki 55
Tel: 0/716 955
TELEX: 123 332

FRANCE

Intel Corporation, S.A.R.L.*
5 Place de la Balance
Silic 223
94528 Rungis Cedex
Tel: (01) 687 22 21
TELEX: 270475

FRANCE (Cont'd)

Intel Corporation, S.A.R.L.
Immeuble BBC
4 Quai des Etroits
69005 Lyon
Tel: (7) 842 40 89
TELEX: 305153

WEST GERMANY

Intel Semiconductor GmbH*
Seidlstrasse 27
D-8000 Munchen 2
Tel: (89) 53891
TELEX: 05-23177 INTL D

Intel Semiconductor GmbH*
Mainzer Strasse 75
D-6200 Wiesbaden 1
Tel: (6121) 70 08 74
TELEX: 04186183 INTW D

Intel Semiconductor GmbH
Brueckstrasse 61
7012 Fellbach
Stuttgart
Tel: (711) 58 00 82
TELEX: 7254826 INTS D

Intel Semiconductor GmbH*
Hohenzollern Strasse 5*
3000 Hannover 1
Tel: (511) 34 40 81
TELEX: 923625 INTH D

ISRAEL

Intel Semiconductor Ltd.*
P.O. Box 1659
Haifa
Tel: 4/524 261
TELEX: 46511

ITALY

Intel Corporation Italia Spa*
Milanofiori, Palazzo E
20094 Assago (Milano)
Tel: (02) 824 00 06
TELEX: 315183 INTMIL

NETHERLANDS

Intel Semiconductor Nederland B.V.*
Alexanderpoort Building
Marten Meesweg 93
3068 Rotterdam
Tel: (10) 21 23 77
TELEX: 22283

NORWAY

Intel Norway A/S
P.O. Box 92
Hvamveien 4
N-2013
Skjetten
Tel: (2) 742 420
TELEX: 18018

SPAIN

Intel Iberia
Calle Zurbaran 28
Madrid 04
Tel: (34) 1410 40 04
TELEX: 46880

SWEDEN

Intel Sweden A.B.*
Dalvagen 24
S-17136 Solna
Tel: (08) 734 01 00
TELEX: 12261

SWITZERLAND

Intel Semiconductor A.G.*
Talackerstrasse 17
8152 Glattbrugg postfach
CH-8065 Zurich
Tel: (01) 829 29 77
TELEX: 57989 ICH CH

UNITED KINGDOM

Intel Corporation (U.K.) Ltd.*
5 Hospital Street
Nantwich, Cheshire CW5 5RE
Tel: (0270) 626 560
TELEX: 36620

Intel Corporation (U.K.) Ltd.*
Pipers Way
Swindon, Wiltshire SN3 1RJ
Tel: (0793) 488 388
TELEX: 444447 INT SWN

*Field Application Location

EUROPEAN DISTRIBUTORS/REPRESENTATIVES

AUSTRIA

Bacher Elektronische Geraete GmbH
Rotenmuehlgasse 26
A-1120 Vienna
Tel: (222) 83 56 46
TELEX: 11532 BASAT A

BELGIUM

Inelco Belgium S.A.
Ave. des Croix de Guerre 94
B1120 Brussels
Tel: (02) 216 01 60
TELEX: 25441

DENMARK

ITT MultiKomponent A/S
Naverland 29
DK-2600 Gloskrup
Tel: (02) 45 66 45
TX: 33355

FINLAND

Oy Fintronic AB
Melkonkatu 24 A
SF-00210
Helsinki 21
Tel: (0) 692 60 22
TELEX: 124 224 Ftron SF

FRANCE

Generim
Z.I. de Courtaboeuf
Avenue de la Baltique
91943 Les Ulis Cedex-B.P.88
Tel: (1) 907 78 78
TELEX: F691700

Jermyn S.A.
16, Avenue Jean-Jaures
94600 Choisy-Le-Roi
Tel: (1) 853 12 00
TELEX: 260967

Metrologie
La Tour d' Asnieres
4, Avenue Laurent Cely
92606-Asnieres
Tel: (1) 790 62 40
TELEX: 611-448

Tekelec Airtronic
Cite des Bruyeres
Rue Carle Vernet B.P. 2
92310 Sevres
Tel: (1) 534 75 35
TELEX: 204552

WEST GERMANY

Electronic 2000 Vertriebs A.G.
Stahlgruberring 12
D-8000 Munich 82
Tel: (89) 42 00 10
TELEX: 522561 EIEC D

Jermyn GmbH
Postfach 1180
Schulstrasse 84
D-6277 Bad Camberg
Tel: (06434) 231
TELEX: 484426 JERM D

CES Computer Electronics Systems
GmbH
Gutenbergstrasse 4
2359 Henstedt-Ulzburg
Tel: (04193) 4026
TELEX: 2180260

Metrologie GmbH
Hansastrasse 15
8000 Munich 21
Tel: (89) 57 30 84
TELEX: D 5213189

Proelectron Vertriebs GmbH
Max Planck Strasse 1-3
6072 Dreieich bei Frankfurt
Tel: (6103) 33564
TELEX: 417983

IRELAND

Micro Marketing
Glenageary Office Park
Glenageary
Co. Dublin
Tel: (1) 85 62 88
TELEX: 31584

ISRAEL

Eastronics Ltd.
11 Rozanis Street
P.O. Box 39300
Tel Aviv 61390
Tel: (3) 47 51 51
TELEX: 33638

ITALY

Eledra 3S S.P.A.
Viale Elvezia, 18
I 20154 Milano
Tel: (2) 34 97 51
TELEX: 332332

ITALY (Cont'd)

Intesi
Milanofiori Pal. E/5
20090 Assago
Milano
Tel: (02) 82470
TELEX: 311351

NETHERLANDS

Koning & Hartman
Koperwerf 30
P.O. Box 43220
2544 EN's Gravenhage
Tel: 31 (70) 210.101
TELEX: 31528

NORWAY

Nordisk Elektronic (Norge) A/S
Postoffice Box 122
Smedsvingen 4
1364 Hvalstad
Tel: (2) 846 210
TELEX: 17546

PORTUGAL

Ditram
Componentes E Electronica LDA
Av. Miguel Bombarda, 133
P1000 Lisboa
Tel: (19) 545 313
TELEX: 14182 Brieks-P

SPAIN

Interface S.A.
Av. Pompeu Fabra 12
08024 Barcelona
Tel: (3) 219 80 11
TELEX: 51508

ITT SESA
Miguel Angel 21, 6 Piso
Madrid 10
Tel: (34) 14 1954 00
TELEX: 27461

SWEDEN

AB Gosta Backstrom
Box 12009
Alstroemergatan 22
S-10221 Stockholm 12
Tel: (8) 541 080
TELEX: 10135

Nordisk Electronik AB
Box 27301
Sandhamnsgatan 71
S-10254 Stockholm
Tel: (8) 635 040
TELEX: 10547

SWEDEN (Cont'd)

Telko AB
Gardsfogdevagen 1
Box 186
S-161 26 Bromma
Tel: (8) 98 08 20
TELEX: 11941

SWITZERLAND

Industrade AG
Herlistrasse 31
CH-8304 Wallisellen
Tel: (01) 830 50 40
TELEX: 56788 INDEL CH

UNITED KINGDOM

Bytech Ltd.
Unit 57
London Road
Earley, Reading
Berkshire
Tel: (0734) 61031
TELEX: 848215

Comway Microsystems Ltd.
Market Street
UK-Bracknell, Berkshire
Tel: 44 (344) 55333
TELEX: 847201

Jermyn Industries
Vestry Estate
Sevenoaks, Kent
Tel: (0732) 450144
TELEX: 95142

M.E.D.L.
East Lane Road
North Wembley
Middlesex HA9 7PP
Tel: (190) 49307
TELEX: 28817

Rapid Recall, Ltd.
Rapid House/Denmark St
High Wycombe
Berks, England HP11 2ER
Tel: (0494) 26 271
TELEX: 837931

YUGOSLAVIA

H. R. Microelectronics Enterprises
P.O. Box 5604
San Jose, California 95150
Tel: 408/978-8000
TELEX: 278-559

INTERNATIONAL SALES OFFICES

AUSTRALIA
Intel Australia Pty. Ltd.*
(Mailing Address)
P.O. Box 571
North Sydney NSW, 2060

(Shipping Address)
Spectrum Building
200 Pacific Highway
Level 6
Crows Nest, NSW, 2089
Tel: 011-61-2-957-2744
TELEX: 790-20097
FAX: 011-61-2-923-2632

HONG KONG
Intel Semiconductor Ltd.*
1701-3/1720 Connaught Centre
1 Connaught Road
Tel: 011-852-5-215311
TWX: 60410 ITLHK

JAPAN
Intel Japan K.K.
5-6 Tokodai, Toyosato-machi
Tsukuba-gun, Ibaraki-ken 300-26
Tel: 029747-8511
TELEX: 03656-160

Intel Japan K.K.*
2-1-15 Naka-machi
Atsugi, Kanagawa 243
Tel: 0462-23-3511

Intel Japan K.K.*
2-51-2 Kojima-cho
Chofu, Tokyo 182
Tel: 0424-88-3151

Intel Japan K.K.*
2-69 Hon-cho
Kumagaya, Saitama 360
Tel: 0485-24-6871

JAPAN (Cont'd)
Intel Japan K.K.*
2-4-1 Terauchi
Toyonaka, Osaka 560
Tel: 06-863-1091

Intel Japan K.K.
1-5-1 Marunouchi
Chiyoda-ku, Tokyo 100
Tel: 03-201-3621

Intel Japan K.K.*
1-23-9 Shinmachi
Setagaya-ku, Tokyo 154
Tel: 03-426-2231

Intel Japan K.K.*
Mitsui-Seimei Musashi-Kasugi Bldg.
915 Shinmaruko, Nakahara-ku
Kawasaki-Shi, Kanagawa 211
Tel: 044-733-7011

JAPAN (Cont'd)
Intel Japan K.K.
1-1 Shibahon-cho
Mishima-shi
Shizuoka-Ken 411
Tel: 0559-72-4121

SINGAPORE
Intel Semiconductor Ltd.
101 Thomson Road
21-06 Goldhill Square
Singapore 1130
Tel: 011-65-2507811
TWX: RS 39921
CABLE: INTELSGP

*Field Application Location

INTERNATIONAL DISTRIBUTORS/REPRESENTATIVES

ARGENTINA
VLC S.R.L.
Sarmiento 1630, 1 Piso
1042 Buenos Aires
Tel: 011-54-1-35-1201/9242
TELEX: 17575 EDARG

Agent:
Soimex International Corporation
15 Park Row, Room #1730
New York, New York 10038
Tel: (212) 406-3052
Attn: Gaston Briones

AUSTRALIA
Total Electronics
(Mailing Address)
Private Bag 250
Burwood, Victoria 3125

(Shipping Address)
9 Harker Street
Burwood
Victoria 3125
Tel: 011-61-3-288-4044
TELEX: AA 31261

Total Electronics
P.O. Box 139
Artarmon, N.S.W. 2064
Tel: 011-61-02-438-1855
TELEX: 26297

BRAZIL
Icotron S.A.
05110 Av. Mutinga 3650-6 Andar
Pirituba Sao Paulo
Tel: 011-55-11-833-2572
TELEX: 1122274 ICOTBR

CHILE
DIN
(Mailing Address)
Av. VIC, MacKenna 204
Casilla 6055
Santiago
Tel: 011-56-2-277-564
TELEX: 352-0003

(Shipping Address)
A102 Greenville Center
3801 Kennett Pike
Wilmington, Delaware 19807

HONG KONG
Novel Precision Machinery Co., Ltd.
Flat D 20 Kingsford Ind. Bldg.
Phase 1 26 Kwai Hei Street NT
Tel: 011-852-5-0-223222
TWX: 39114 JINMI HX

Schmidt & Co. Ltd.
18/F. Great Eagle Centre
Wanchai
Tel: 011-852-5-833-0222
TWX: 74766 SCHMC HK

INDIA
Micronic Devices
65 ARUN Complex
D V G Road
Basavan Gudi
Bangalore 560004
Tel: 011-91-812-600-631
TELEX: 011-5947 MDEV

Micronic Devices
104/109C Nirmal Industrial Estate
Sion (E)
Bombay 400022
Tel: 011-91-22-48-61-70
TELEX: 011-71447 MDEV IN

Micronic Devices
R-694 New Rajinder Nager
New Delhi 110060

Ramlak International, Inc. (Agent)
465 S. Mathilda Avenue
Suite 302
Sunnyvale, CA 94086
Tel: (408) 733-8767

S & S Corporation
(Mailing Address)
P.O. Box 1185
Mauldin, South Carolina 29657

(Shipping Address)
308 Green Drive
Liberty, South Carolina 29657

JAPAN
Asahi Electronics Co. Ltd.
KMM Bldg. Room 407
2-14-1 Asano, Kokurakita-Ku
Kitakyushu City 802
Tel: (093) 511-6471
TELEX: AECKY 7126-16

JAPAN (Cont'd)
Hamilton-Avnet Electronics Japan Ltd.
YU and YOU Bldg. 1-5-7 Horidome-
Cho
Nihonbashi Chuo-Ku, Tokyo 103
Tel: (03) 662-9911
TELEX: 2523774

Ryoyo Electric Corporation
Konwa Bldg.
1-12-22, Tsukiji
Chuo-Ku, Tokyo 104
Tel: (03) 5443-7711/541-7311

Tokyo Electron Ltd.
Shinjuku Nomura Bldg.
26-2 Nishi-Shinjuku 1-Chome
Shinjuku-Ku, Tokyo 160
Tel. (03) 343-4411
TELEX: 232-2220 LABTEL J

KOREA
J-TEK Corporation
2nd Floor, Government Pension Bldg.
24-3, Yoido-Dong
Youngdungpo-Ku
Seoul 150
Tel: 011-82-2-782-8039
TELEX: KODIGIT K25299

Koram Digital USA (Agent)
14066 East Firestone Boulevard
Sante Fe Springs, CA 90670
Tel: (714) 739-2204
TWX: 194715 KORAM DIGIT LSA

NEW ZEALAND
McLean Information Technology Ltd.
459 Kyber Pass Road, Newmarket,
P.O. Box 9464, Newmarket
Auckland 1, New Zealand
Tel: 011-64-9-501-219, 501-801, 587-
037
TELEX: NZ21570 THERMAL

PAKISTAN
Computer Applications Ltd.
7D Gizri Boulevard
Defense
Karachi-46
Tel: 011-92-21-530-306/7
TELEX: 24434 GAFAR PK

PAKISTAN (Cont'd)
Horizon Training Co., Inc. (Agent)
1 Lafayette Center
1120 20th Street N.W.
Suite 530
Washington, D.C. 20036
Tel: (202) 887-1900
TWX: 248890 HORN

SINGAPORE
General Engineers Corporation Pty.
Ltd.
Units 1003-1008 Block 3
10th Floor PSA Multi Storey Complex
Telok Blangahl Pasir
Pan Jang
Singapore 5
Tel: 011-65-271-3163
TELEX: RS23987 GENERCO
CABLE: GENERRCORP

SOUTH AFRICA
Electronic Building Elements, Pty. Ltd.
P.O. Box 4609
Pretoria 0001
Tel: 011-27-12-46-9221
TELEX: 3-0181 SA
TELEGRAM: ELBILEM

TAIWAN
Mitac Corporation
3rd Floor #75, Section 4
Nanking East Road
Taipei
Tel: 011-886-2-771-0940, 0941
TELEX: 11942 TAIAUTO

Mectel International, Inc. (Agent)
3385 Viso Court
Santa Clara, CA 95050
Tel: (408) 988-4513
TWX: 910-338-2201
FAX: 408-980-9742

YUGOSLAVIA
H. R. Microelectronics Enterprises
P.O. Box 5604
San Jose, California 95150
Tel: (408) 978-8000
TELEX: 278-559

*Field Application Location

U.S. SERVICE OFFICES

CALIFORNIA

Intel Corp.
1350 Shorebird Way
Mt. View 94043
Tel: (415) 968-8211
TWX: 910-339-9279
910-338-0255

Intel Corp.
2000 E. 4th Street
Suite 110
Santa Ana 92705
Tel: (714) 835-5577
TWX: 910-595-2475

Intel Corp.
7670 Opportunity Road
San Diego 92111
Tel: (619) 268-3563

Intel Corp.
5530 N. Corbin Avenue
Suite 120
Tarzana 91356
Tel: (213) 708-0333

COLORADO

Intel Corp.
650 South Cherry
Suite 720
Denver 80222
Tel: (303) 321-8086
TWX: 910-931-2289

CONNECTICUT

Intel Corp.
36 Padanaram Road
Danbury 06810
Tel: (203) 792-8366

FLORIDA

Intel Corp.
1500 N.W. 62nd Street
Suite 104
Ft. Lauderdale 33309
Tel: (305) 771-0600
TWX: 510-956-9407

Intel Corp.
500 N. Maitland Avenue
Suite 205
Maitland 32751
Tel: (305) 628-2393
TWX: 810-853-9219

GEORGIA

Intel Corp.
3300 Holcombe Bridge Road
Suite 225
Norcross 30092
Tel: (404) 441-1171

ILLINOIS

Intel Corp.
2550 Golf Road
Suite 815
Rolling Meadows 60008
Tel: (312) 981-7270
TWX: 910-253-1825

KANSAS

Intel Corp.
8400 W. 110th Street
Suite 170
Overland Park 66210
Tel: (913) 642-8080

MARYLAND

Intel Corp.
5th Floor Product Service
7833 Walker Drive
Greenbelt 20770
Tel: (301) 441-1020

Intel Corp.
7257 Parkway Drive
Hanover 21076
Tel: (301) 796-7500
TWX: 710-862-1944

MASSACHUSETTS

Intel Corp.
27 Industrial Avenue
Chelmsford 01824
Tel: (617) 256-1800
TWX: 710-343-6333

MICHIGAN

Intel Corp.
26500 Northwestern Highway
Suite 401
Southfield 48075
Tel: (313) 354-1540
TWX: 810-244-4915

MINNESOTA

Intel Corp.
7401 Metro Boulevard
Suite 355
Edina 55435
Tel: (612) 835-6722
TWX: 910-567-2867

MISSOURI

Intel Corp.
4203 Earth City Expressway
Suite 143
Earth City 63045
Tel: (314) 291-2015

NEW JERSEY

Intel Corp.
385 Sylvan Avenue
Englewood Cliffs 07632
Tel: (201) 567-0820
TWX: 710-991-8593

NEW YORK

Intel Corp.
2255 Lyell Avenue
Rochester 14606
Tel: (716) 254-6120

NORTH CAROLINA

Intel Corp.
5600 Executive Drive
Suite 113
Charlotte 28212
Tel: (704) 568-8966

Intel Corp.
2306 W. Meadowview Road
Suite 206
Greensboro 27407
Tel: (919) 294-1541

OHIO

Intel Corp.
Chagrin-Brainard Bldg.
Suite 305
28001 Chagrin Boulevard
Cleveland 44122
Tel: (216) 464-6915
TWX: 810-427-9298

Intel Corp.
6500 Poe Avenue
Dayton 45414
Tel: (800) 325-4415
TWX: 810-450-2528

OREGON

Intel Corp.
10700 S.W. Beaverton-Hillsdale
Highway
Suite 22
Beaverton 97005
Tel: (503) 641-8086
TWX: 910-467-8741

PENNSYLVANIA

Intel Corp.
500 Pennsylvania Avenue
Fort Washington 19034
Tel: (215) 641-1000
TWX: 510-661-2077

Intel Corp.
201 Penn Center Boulevard
Suite 301 W
Pittsburgh 15235
Tel: (313) 354-1540

TEXAS

Intel Corp.
313 E. Anderson Lane
Suite 314
Austin 78752
Tel: (512)454-3628
TWX: 910-874-1347

Intel Corp.
12300 Ford Road
Suite 380
Dallas 75234
Tel: (214) 241-8087
TWX: 910-860-5617

Intel Corp.
7322 S.W. Freeway
Suite 1490
Houston 77074
Tel: (713) 988-8088
TWX: 910-881-2490

VIRGINIA

Intel Corp.
7700 Leesburg Pike
Suite 412
Falls Church 22043
Tel: (703) 734-9707
TWX: 710-931-0625

WASHINGTON

Intel Corp.
110 110th Avenue N.E.
Suite 510
Bellevue 98004
Tel: 1-800-538-0662
TWX: 910-443-3002

WISCONSIN

Intel Corp.
150 S. Sunnyslope Road
Suite 148
Brookfield 53005
Tel: (414) 784-9060